548-6977

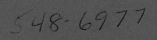 W9-CEA-489

CONSUMER BEHAVIOR

Consumer Behavior

John C. Mowen
Oklahoma State University

MACMILLAN PUBLISHING COMPANY
New York
COLLIER MACMILLAN PUBLISHERS
London

Copyright © 1987, Macmillan Publishing Company, a division of Macmillan, Inc.

Printed in the United States of America

All rights reserved.
No part of this book may be reproduced or
transmitted in any form or by any means, electronic or mechanical,
including photocopying, recording, or any information storage and
retrieval system, without permission in writing from the Publisher.

MACMILLAN PUBLISHING COMPANY
866 Third Avenue, New York, New York 10022

Collier Macmillan Canada, Inc.

Library of Congress Cataloging-in-Publication Data

Mowen, John C.
  Consumer behavior.

  Includes index.
  1. Consumers.   2. Consumers—United States.
I. Title.
HF5415.3.M68   1987   658.8'342   86-5375
ISBN 0-02-384590-2

Printing: 3 4 5 6 7   Year: 7 8 9 0 1 2 3

ISBN 0-02-384590-2

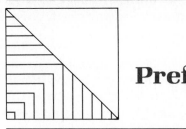

Preface

When I was a child, my mother read to me *The Friendly Book*, which my children now enjoy. The book begins:

I LIKE CARS
Red cars   Green cars
Sport limousine cars . . .[1]

Well, I still like cars, especially sports cars. Indeed, I like consuming much more than my pocketbook allows. I also like to study, do research on, and write about the consumption process. Writing this textbook was a logical extension of these interests, and I have enjoyed it.

Because all of us are consumers, students bring to class an intrinsic interest in the study of consumer behavior. Targeted to the introductory student, a major goal of the text is to retain this enthusiasm by presenting concepts and theories within the context of interesting managerial and experiential examples. This approach has resulted in a comprehensive and accurate text that avoids the jargon and dryness of the journal articles on which it is based.

A second goal involves integrating the theoretical and conceptual material with its managerial, public policy, and personal implications. I chose a route of first presenting the conceptual and theoretical material in each chapter. Wherever possible managerial and experiential examples are provided with this information. However, the heavy discussion of managerial implications is saved for a section that is near the end of each chapter. In addition, the last two chapters consist of a final detailed analysis of the applications of consumer behavior principles to public policy and marketing management decision making.

A third goal was to capture the movement of the research literature away

---

[1] Margaret Wise Brown, *The Friendly Book*, Racine, Wisconsin: Western Publishing Company, 1982.

from the narrow decision-making perspective of consumer buying and its emphasis on the consumer decision stages. The current literature clearly shows that some consumer actions occur without a decision process. This text is written from a wholistic perspective and specifically focuses on two other approaches from which consumer action may be analyzed, in addition to the decision-making perspective. The *experiential perspective* centers on identifying the affective and motivational processes that influence consumers. The *behavioral influence perspective* focuses on identifying how environmental forces can influence consumer action.

THE EXPANDED COVERAGE OF THE TEXTBOOK

The view that consumer actions are influenced by three sets of factors (i.e., decision making, experiential, and behavioral influence) results in the addition of a number of topics new to contemporary texts. To give the experiential perspective adequate coverage, information on motivational and affective processes is needed; thus, a separate chapter on motivation is included to cover such topics as opponent-process theory, maintaining optimum stimulation levels, the motivation for hedonic experiences, and the motivation to maintain behavioral freedom.

The development of the behavioral influence perspective requires extra attention to the environmental factors that influence consumer action. Thus, separate chapters on the "Economics of Consumption" and "Situational Influences" are included. In addition, two chapters are devoted to the discussion of subcultural influences on consumption.

Other topics new to consumer behavior texts are covered, such as social traps and fences, ingratiation techniques, and negligent consumer behaviors.

THE TEXTBOOK'S ORGANIZATION: FROM INDIVIDUAL TO ENVIRONMENTAL INFLUENCES

The text's organization evolved from a field theory based model, which states that individuals live within a lifespace and are buffeted by a series of environmental forces. Within the individual, various psychological factors may influence how that person responds to these environmental forces. Based on the simple model, I chose to discuss the individual consumer in Part I of the text. In addition to discussing consumer buying processes, these chapters analyze the areas of motivation, personality and psychographics, information processing, learning, attitudes, persuasion, and postpurchase processes. Part II of the text focuses on the environmental forces that influence individuals in the marketplace. Thus, the chapters analyze situational factors, personal influence, group influence, families and households, consumer subcultures, social class, culture and cross-cultural factors, and the economics of consumption. Finally, Part III presents the public policy and managerial implications of consumer behavior principles.

Some instructors prefer to discuss the environmental consumer processes prior to the presentation of the material on the individual consumer. The text is modular in organization, and Parts I and II of the text may be rearranged to accommodate such a preference.

Three important topics have been integrated into the text rather than treated as separate chapters—organizational buying, consumer research, and store choice. The literature indicates that the same behavioral principles and theories that apply to consumer buying also influence industrial buying. Thus, many of the examples throughout the text relate to organizational buying. Chapter 20 discusses the various areas in which organizational buying may differ from consumer buying. Similarly, discussions of consumer research techniques are found throughout the text. For example, the chapter on "Attitudes, Beliefs, and Behaviors" contains material on how to measure attitudes. A variety of sections of the text apply to store choice. For example, a section in the chapter on consumer situations discusses the effects of the physical environment of stores on consumers.

Some instructors like to organize the field around the comprehensive models of consumer behavior. For this reason the Teacher's Manual describes two of the models and provides transparency masters of each.

SOME NOTABLE FEATURES OF THE TEXT

Several features of the text help to differentiate it from those currently on the market:

- □ *Approach.* While it discusses the decision process approach, as well as high and low involvement buying, the text moves ahead to discuss the experiential and behavioral influence perspectives on consumption. The result is a comprehensive book that introduces a number of topics new to consumer behavior texts.
- □ *Vignettes.* The text explicitly shows how consumer behavior principles may be used by managers in designing strategy. Frequent use has been made of vignettes and managerial examples to illustrate consumer behavior principles.
- □ *Writing style.* Students like the text. It is written in an understandable and interesting manner yet covers the material comprehensively.
- □ *Pedagogy.* The text and much of the teacher's manual are student tested. The teacher's manual includes a test bank, answers to the discussion questions, alternative ways of handling topics, as well as cases that can be handed out.
- □ *Illustrations.* Particular care was taken in selecting print advertisements to illustrate concepts. How each ad demonstrates a consumer behavior idea is specifically discussed.

ACKNOWLEDGMENTS

A number of individuals were instrumental in the completion of the text. Most importantly I wish to thank my wife, Maryanne Myers Mowen, for her painstaking help in the production of the text and encouragement throughout the project. I also wish to acknowledge the fine people at Macmillan Publishing Company for their excellent support of the text. Ron Stefanski and Bill Oldsey, as marketing editors, kept the project on track and did an outstanding job obtaining reviewers. Wendy Polhemus, production editor, performed wonderfully seeing the book through the production process. Similarly, thanks go to David Horvath who directed the marketing effort of the text. A number of colleagues at Oklahoma State University assisted with various aspects of the project. Mariea Hoy in particular was helpful in writing Chapter 19. I would also like to thank my research assistant, Amy Fong, for her assistance in obtaining permissions and in working on the glossary. Appreciation is also expressed to Josh Weiner, Roxanne Stell, and Joby John for helping to student test the draft of the text in their classes. Finally, I would like to express my gratitude to the reviewers who evaluated the text. In particular Russ Belk and Hal Kassarjian are acknowledged for their many insights and willingness to assist a colleague. I am also grateful to the other reviewers of the text for their assistance, including:

Barbara D. Bart, Savannah State College
Gordon C. Bruner II, Southern Illinois University at Carbondale
Dennis E. Clayson, University of Northern Iowa
Kathleen Debevec, University of Massachusetts-Amherst
Rohit Deshpande, University of Texas-Austin
Joel Evans, Hofstra University
Thomas W. Falcone, Indiana University of Pennsylvania
G. Ray Funkhouser, Graduate School of Management, Rutgers University
Pradeep K. Korgaonkar, Florida Atlantic University
Mary C. LaForge, Clemson University
Jim McCullough, Washington State University
M. Alan Miller, Tennessee State University
Robert D. O'Keefe, DePaul University
Teresa A. Swartz, Arizona State University
Hale N. Tongren, George Mason University
Joshua Wiener, Oklahoma State University
John Wong, Iowa State University

J. C. M.

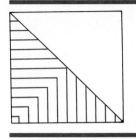

Contents

Part I
Individual
Consumer
Processes

1

An Introduction to Consumer Behavior

Have a Taste of Consumer Behavior

Perhaps the product that best exemplifies the importance of consumer behavior to marketing and business is *food*. Centered around the consumption of nourishment are myriad examples of consumer behavior concepts and principles.

What color would you use for the background hue of the packaging of Barrelhead Sugar-Free Root Beer? When the colors were changed from blue to beige, consumers swore that the root beer tasted more like the old-fashioned kind. Of course, the beverage remained the same. When the color of Canada Dry Sugar-Free Ginger-Ale containers was changed from red to green and white, the company reported the sales increased 25 percent. Taste perception results in part from expectancies of how things should taste based on their color.

When Coca-Cola used blind taste tests to compare "New Coke" with "Old Coke," they revealed that most consumers preferred the new formulation. Why then was there such a furor over the new beverage when it appeared in April 1985? The answer may exist in reactance theory. Consumers have a need to maintain their behavioral freedom. When Coca-Cola suddenly changed the product, the behavioral freedom to purchase the original was threatened, and consumers reacted by demonstrating, filing lawsuits, and generally becoming angry. Within six weeks the public outcry was so great that Coca-Cola brought back the original formulation in Coke Classic. The entire affair shows the importance of not forgetting brand loyalty and the idea that consumers value their behavioral freedom.

The Coke affair also illustrates the concept of regional consumer preferences. Nine months after the brand's introduction it was outsold by Classic Coke by 9 to 1 in Minneapolis and by 8 to 1 in Dallas. However, in Detroit

New Coke outsold Classic. Because of such differences, many companies segment markets by regions.

Cross-cultural differences in food preferences also exist. For example, in Canada New Coke outsold Classic Coke by a wide margin. Some cross-cultural food preferences may be explained by economic factors. For example, one reason why pork is forbidden among many Middle Eastern originated cultures may be because swine are ill adapted to nomadic life. They prefer cool, muddy places that are highly scarce and expensive to provide in the Middle East. Investigating the economic factors that influence consumption is an important subarea of consumer behavior.

Even within one culture major changes can result in food preferences over time because of new lifestyle patterns. For example, over the past 15 years lifestyle trends emphasizing fitness and nutrition have influenced consumer eating habits. Thus, the per capita consumption of broccoli has doubled while beef and pork sales have decreased.

The study of perception, reactance, brand loyalty, lifestyle trends, and the economics of consumption are all part of a wide ranging consumer behavior menu. I hope you enjoy the bill-of-fare.

Based in part on Ronald Alsop, "Color Grows More Important in Catching Consumer's Eyes," *The Wall Street Journal,* Thursday, November 25, 1984, 35; *Advertising Age;* "Coke 'Family' Sales Fly as New Coke Stumbles," Monday, January 27, 1986, 1, 91; Marvin Harris, *Good to Eat: Riddles of Food and Culture,* Simon and Schuster, 1986; Peter Francese, "Eating Habits Changing with Life Styles," *Advertising Age,* December 6, 1984, 38.

INTRODUCTION

As noted in the introductory vignette, the acquisition and consumption of food illustrate many of the concepts investigated by consumer behaviorists. For example, the consumption of certain types of food products is strongly influenced by the culture in which a person lives. Thus, foods that are commonly accepted as good and nutritious in one culture may be perceived as revolting in another. In certain Far Eastern cultures, monkey brains and bird nests are gustatory delicacies. For most Americans the thought of eating such things is perfectly awful. However, whereas many Americans enjoy eating beef, people in India who practice the Hindu religion think munching on a steak is repugnant.

One of the primary goals of many product managers is to have their brand distinguished from other competing brands by consumers. The process is called **product differentiation** and involves using the marketing mix to create a clear impression among consumers that the brand is special or different. Heinz Company avidly pursues such a strategy of product differentiation. The goal of the company for its brands, such as Star-Kist Tuna, Ore-Ida Potatoes, and Heinz Ketchup, is to differentiate them sufficiently from competing brands so that a premium price can be charged. Between 1980 and 1984 the company massively advertised these and other brands to cause consumers to perceive them as different from the competition. The strategy worked, and profits and market share increased substantially.[1]

In 1963 the largest-selling beverage in the United States was coffee. By 1983 the amount of coffee sold per year had fallen by 50 percent. The cause of the decrease in consumption is complex, but it probably involved the major changes in lifestyle that occurred over the twenty years. In the mid-1980s coffee manufacturers recognized that their advertising had to be changed. The use of middle-aged endorsers, such as Mrs. Olsen (Folger's), Cora (Maxwell House), and Robert Young (Sanka) was not reaching a highly important segment of consumers—the baby boomers born between 1946 and 1964. With the baby boomers beginning to mature and focus on their careers, the coffee manufacturers began an advertising campaign using the theme, "Join the Coffee Achievers."[2] The trade association was targeting the twenty- to thirty-five-year-old success-oriented group, who represent about 29 percent of all consumers in the United States.[3] Changing the tastes and preferences of consumers is extremely difficult, but the coffee manufacturers were probably on the right track. Cross-sectional evidence indicates that people tend to drink more coffee as they grow older, and a carefully conceived advertising campaign could help push the process along among the soft-drink-loving baby-boom group.

The consumption of food products also vividly illustrates a major thrust of the textbook. The text takes what is called a wholistic approach to the study of consumer behavior. From a wholistic approach consumption should be viewed from all sides, and the factors that influence consumption should be analyzed to see how they fit together. Thus, to understand the purchase and use of some type of good, such as food, one must pull together knowledge from a diverse group of fields. At the environmental level one must look at the effects of such factors as culture, subculture, group influence, personal influence, and situations. At the individual level, one should investigate such processes as perception, motivation, attitudes, personality, and decision making. The consumption process is complex, and its understanding requires a well-rounded view of consumer behavior, which this text hopes to provide.

This introductory chapter seeks to familiarize the student with the field of consumer behavior. In the following sections the field of consumer behavior is defined, and the reasons for its study are delineated. In addition, the various foundation areas from which many of the consumer behavior ideas and theories emerge are discussed. A brief history of the field is also presented in order to familiarize the reader with the youth and vitality of consumer behavior. Finally, the chapter presents a simple model of consumer behavior in order to help organize the diversity of factors influencing the acquisition, consumption, and disposition of goods, services, and ideas.

WHAT IS CONSUMER BEHAVIOR?

Consumer behavior is the study of the decision-making units and the processes involved in acquiring, consuming, and disposing of goods, services, experiences, and ideas. The term *decision-making unit* rather than consumer, is used because in many cases consumer decisions are made by groups of people. For example, a couple may select an engagement ring, a family of five may vote on where to vacation, or a company could have several individuals jointly make a decision concerning the purchase of an industrial item. (Although the textbook focuses on consumer buying behavior, the principles discussed apply to industrial buying as well.)

The definition of consumer behavior also recognizes that consumption is a process. A series of steps are involved, beginning with **product acquisition,** moving to consumption, and ending with **product disposition.** Much of the research in consumer behavior has focused on the acquisition of goods and services. For example, a manager might be interested in knowing why consumers are having difficulty remembering an advertisement for a product. Information on learning and memory would be central to knowing how to approach the problem. The study of the factors that influence the recall of advertisements deals with one part of the acquisition process. That is, if an advertisement is to influence the buying process, it must have some impact on the consumer. Oftentimes, companies assess the effectiveness of an advertisement by determining the extent to which consumers can recall the message.

Consumer researchers have also recognized the potential importance of the consumption and disposition phases. On a national level the difficulties of nuclear-waste disposal have created major problems for an entire industry. In this case, all Americans may be viewed as consumers of electricity. As such, many have become concerned with disposal of the product used to make the electricity—i.e., uranium. Such concern has dramatically influenced the behavior of these consumers, leading to such actions as demonstrations and political maneuvering. Similarly, disposition problems have influenced the bottling industry. Consumer concerns over litter and the energy used to produce metal containers have led to legislative actions concerning the types of containers used by soft-drink and beer manufacturers. In addition, small local industries develop around product disposition in most cities. Thus, one of the purposes of auction companies, flea markets, garage sales, and used-goods retailers is to dispose of products.

One problem with a focus on the study of the acquisition, consumption, and disposition of goods and services is that it tends to omit the emotional component of consumer behavior. People buy many products (e.g., an automobile), go to scary movies, and attend cultural events for the feelings and experiences that result.[4] Many consumers buy a car not only for its utilitarian aspects but also for the feelings and experiences that it will generate. The study of experiential consumer behavior is a new area that is growing in importance.

A final point concerning the scope of consumer behavior is that the field's ideas and concepts may be applied to nontraditional business areas. Much of the average marketing curriculum focuses on the marketing of tangible

HIGHLIGHT 1–1

Marketing Textbooks Is Like Selling Disposable Diapers

What do the following products have in common: disposable diapers, textbooks, and men's underwear? In each case the decision maker is not the user of the product. Although mothers, professors, and wives tend to decide which diapers, books, and shorts to buy, babies, students, and "hubbies" actually use the product. The buying process has three aspects: acquisition, consumption, and disposition. Marketing becomes more complex when different people are involved in the steps. For example, the users of college textbooks are students, but professors select the texts. Unfortunately, the tastes and preferences of the two groups can be quite different.

The pet-food industry is another area in which the user of the product is not the buyer. The $5 billion-a-year industry thrives by making food that appeals to humans but is eaten by animals. The industry is segmented. For example, the dog food manufacturers segment the market on the age of the dog, the size of the dog, the price of the product, and the moistness of the product (dry, semimoist, and canned). There are also specialty items—gourmet, frozen, and nutri-

tion dog foods. A segment of dog snacks also exists— Milk Bones, Bonz, Jerky Treats, and People Crackers are examples. Do dogs care about this stuff? Not really, but humans do. Of course, packaging and advertising are geared to people, not dogs. Thus, the names of the foods sound delicious—like Home Style Blend, Ground Round, and Butcher's Blend.

A surprising number of other products are bought by one individual and used by a second person. Some examples are: children's toys, clothing, and food; diamond rings; the wife's auto; and men's underwear. Women buy 70 percent of men's underwear. Perhaps that's why Jockey was so successful with their fashion shorts. Jim Palmer, the sexy baseball-star–pitcher, who endorsed the underwear clad only in his shorts, didn't necessarily appeal to the men; he appealed to the real buyers—wives.

A final point. Although buyers and users may be different, if the user is unhappy with the product, the buyer usually hears about it. Brand loyalty must be built among both buyers and users of the product.

products, such as autos, toothpaste, and televisions. More recently, marketers have recognized that service marketing is taking on increased importance. Thus, one finds banks, accounting firms, real estate brokers, restaurants, attorneys, and hospitals engaging heavily in marketing. The study of consumer behavior is as important for marketing such service industries as for marketing tangible goods. In either case marketers must recognize that the decision maker, who selects a product or service, and the user may not be one and the same. Some considerations marketers face are described in Highlight 1–1. Similarly, nonbusiness entities have a need to study the behavior of their consumers. Political parties, religious organizations, and charitable groups all engage in consumer research. However, rather than marketing tangible products, these organizations tend to market intangible ideas.

WHY STUDY CONSUMER BEHAVIOR?

An understanding of consumers and the consumption process provides a number of benefits in that it assists managers in their decision making, provides marketing researchers with the theory and questions to investigate, helps legislators and regulators create laws and regulations, and assists the average consumer in making better purchase decisions. In addition, the study of consumers can help us to understand more about the psychological, sociological, and economic factors that influence human behavior.

Consumer Behavior as a Foundation of Marketing Management

Marketing strategy and planning should be built around an understanding of the consumers who make up a firm's target market. In developing new product opportunities, identifying target markets through segmentation analysis, and fine tuning the marketing mix, marketers find knowledge of consumer behavior valuable.

The importance of understanding the consumer is found in the definition of **marketing.** Although many scholars and practitioners have developed definitions of marketing, in the last decade consensus has formed that the field can be defined as follows. Marketing is a

> human activity directed at satisfying needs and wants through human exchange processes.[5]*

From this definition emerge two key components of what marketers do. First, marketers attempt to satisfy needs and wants of others. Second, marketers study the **exchange process,** in which two parties transfer something of value between each other. Indeed, some argue that the central point on which marketing is based as an applied discipline is that of **consumer primacy.**[6] The consumer is, therefore, at the center of the marketing effort. As Peter Drucker, the well-known management scholar, stated, "Marketing . . . is the whole business seen from the point of view of its final result, that is, from the customer's point of view."[7]

As noted earlier in the chapter, consumer behavior principles are used in four specific managerial areas: environmental analysis, product positioning, segmentation, and marketing-mix development. The marketing environment is defined as the "totality of forces and institutions that are external and potentially relevant to the firm."[8] Thus, **environmental analysis** refers to the assessment of the forces and institutions external to the firm and to the identification of how these may impact upon the marketing effort. A number of these forces involve consumers and their activities. In particular, the demographic and lifestyle trends of consumers may create either major opportunities or liabilities for corporations. For example, the trend toward promoting good health in the 1980s has increased sales of lower-calorie food products, such as chicken and fish, while harming sales of products per-

---

*In 1985 the American Marketing Association developed the following definition of marketing: "Marketing is the process of planning and executing the conception, pricing, promotion, and distribution of ideas, goods, and services to create exchanges that satisfy individual and organizational objectives." This definition does emphasize the importance of the idea of exchange. However, it seems to move away from a consumer focus. In the author's view, such a move is a setback for marketing.

ceived to have higher fat content, such as beef. Other environmental factors having an impact on consumers and corporations include the economic, natural, technological, political, and cultural environments. The diagnostic and research activity of anticipating environmental change is called **marketing opportunity analysis.**

Consumer behavior is also important for purposes of **product positioning.** When attempting to position a product, a company tries to develop a product image that differentiates the product from the competitors'. A classic example is the use of the "uncola" theme by Seven-Up. To engage in product-positioning activities, a company should have a good understanding of the information-processing characteristics of consumers and of attitude formation and change processes.

The third managerial use of consumer behavior ideas is for the segmentation of the marketplace. **Segmentation** refers to the subdivision of the marketplace into relatively homogeneous subsets of consumers who can be reached with a distinct **marketing mix.** Consumer behavior provides a number of bases for segmenting the marketplace, including demographic factors such as age, sex, and income. The consumption behavior of consumers can also be used. For example, consumers may be divided into **target markets** based upon their usage rates (e.g., heavy versus moderate users of a product), the demand elasticity, brand loyalty, and the benefits sought. Consumers can also be segmented upon their personality or psychographic categories. Finally, the situations in which consumers use products are useful segmentation variables. For example, products can be designed either for occasions defined as formal (a Thanksgiving dinner) or informal (eating while watching football on New Year's Day).

Consumer behavior principles are also used in the development of the marketing mix. In developing a new product, designing advertising campaigns, and setting prices, the marketing manager should utilize consumer behavior concepts.

Consumer Behavior and Marketing Research

The realms of consumer behavior and marketing research are closely related. Within a firm major functions of the marketing researchers are to identify the characteristics of the target market of the firm, to gather information on consumer reactions to the firm's offerings, and to identify potential new market opportunities. The performance of these functions requires the market research department to engage heavily in consumer research. Indeed, market research is in part "applied consumer research," and many individuals trained in consumer behavior end up in a marketing research department.

Consumer behavior also contributes to marketing research through its **theory.** Without consumer behavior theory, market researchers would have little guidance on how to approach the questions they are supposed to answer. For example, suppose that a marketing manager realizes that a product is receiving negative publicity. He is concerned about how consumers are reacting, so he asks the marketing research department to do a study. How should the researchers proceed? What they should do is consider the various theories that relate to consumer attitudes and impression formation. Using these theories, they should then formulate a research methodology and set of questions and issues to address.

Johnson & Johnson in reacting to the Tylenol tragedy in 1982 used just such a procedure. After discovering that people were dying after taking Tylenol capsules, the company recalled the product. Then, they began doing surveys to track consumer impressions of the product and the firm. Their approach to the problem and the questions asked were based in part on theories of attitude and of how consumers determine the cause of an event. That is, was Johnson & Johnson responsible for the deaths, or was it simply an unavoidable accident? Their surveys revealed that the public viewed the problem an an unfortunate accident, and they retained their confidence in the product and the company. As a result, the company repackaged the product and within a year had nearly regained their market share in the over-the-counter pain-reliever market. Unfortunately, tragedy again struck Johnson & Johnson in March 1986 when capsule tampering was again discovered. The company concluded that the repeated tamperings had doomed the product and withdrew it completely from the market.

Other Reasons for Studying Consumer Behavior

In addition to assisting marketing managers, a knowledge of consumer behavior has other benefits. The federal government in its legislative, regulatory, and judicial roles often deals with issues involving consumers. Increasingly, theories and research related to consumer behavior are being used as a foundation for making laws and regulations. For example, proposals have periodically surfaced to limit or even cut off entirely commercials accompanying television programming aimed at young children. Research done by consumer behaviorists concerning the impact of advertising on children has figured prominently in the formulation of the regulations. The area dealing with the impact of government laws and regulations on consumers is called **public policy.** Chapter 19 discusses the relationship between consumer behavior and public policy in some detail.

A general knowledge of consumer behavior also has personal value. It can help people become better consumers by informing them of the way in which they and others go about their consumption activities. In addition, it can assist consumers in the buying process by informing them of some of the strategies used by companies to market their products.

Finally, knowledge of the factors influencing consumption has intrinsic value for many people. It is simply fun to know, for example, why rumors start, why Joe Namath was so popular as an endorser and then faded, and why more beer will be sold in 1990 than ever before. Understanding one's own consumption motivations as well as those of others is satisfying and is one part of being a well-rounded, educated person.

From a broader perspective, consumer behavior provides consumers, managers, and government officials with three types of information. First, it provides an orientation. By studying the consumer and the factors that influence his or her actions, one gains an appreciation for the importance of a consumer focus, rather than a sales or product approach. Put simply, knowledge of consumer behavior is the underpinning of the successful implementation of the marketing concept.

Facts are the second type of information supplied by consumer behavior. In the planning function, facts are required to assess marketing opportunities and to plan the marketing mix. Consumer research supplies many of these facts. Demographic data, cultural trends, economic relationships, and basic knowledge of consumer perceptual processes are examples of the types of factual information supplied by consumer researchers and used by managers and planners.

Finally, consumer behavior provides theories. The term *theory* tends to be ridiculed with statements like "That's only theory; it has nothing to do with what really happens." In fact, nothing is more practical than a theory. Detectives develop theories for why a crime was committed. Medical doctors develop theories for why a person gets sick. Managers develop theories for why a product does not sell.

A theory is a set of interrelated statements defining the causal relationships among a group of ideas. Whether large- or small-scale, theories should always have research support. Planners and practitioners of consumer behavior benefit from having a variety of theories with research support, which they can use to understand and solve managerial and public policy problems.

WHAT DO CONSUMER RESEARCHERS STUDY?

One difficulty of the field of consumer behavior is its diversity. It incorporates theories and concepts from all of the behavioral sciences. When one studies the consumer, one studies economics, psychology, social psychology, sociology, anthropology, and demography.

Economics and Consumer Behavior

Just as the earliest marketers were trained in economics, so too were the first consumer researchers. In particular, beginning in the 1940s, George Katona's work on how economic factors influence the buying behavior and buying confidence of consumers provided the first systematic work focusing on individual consumer behavior. Much earlier, however, the economist Thorstein Veblen, in 1899 talked about the idea of conspicuous consumption.[9]

Because of the importance of economics to consumer behavior, Chapter 18 is devoted to the topic. Economic principles are particularly important in assisting managers in the setting of prices and the assessment of factors that influence the supply and demand of particular products. Furthermore, knowledge of economic principles can assist in developing promotional messages. For example, if the supply of a product is perceived to have changed so that it is extremely low, consumers will respond by paying more for the available units. Companies will seek to take advantage of this economic principle by creating special editions of their products. The advertisement shown in Figure 1–1 illustrates such an approach for the Impulse, made by Isuzu. In the ad the car is described as "Rarer Than a Ferrari."

The Psychology of Consumption

Psychologists study the individual and how he or she behaves, and their field is divided into a number of subdivisions. The physiological psychologists are similar to biologists or medical researchers and attempt to explain behavior through basic biological and physiological processes. For example, how do hormones influence anger and aggression? Other psychologists investigate how our memories function and how we process information. Others study how we learn. Additional areas focus on the behavior of children or old people and on how various elements of the physical environment (e.g., buildings or the arrangement of aisles in a grocery store) influence our actions and feelings. The field is broad and plays a major role in helping us understand the consumer.

A major portion of this text deals with the psychological basis of consumer behavior. Some areas about which psychology contributes insights on consumer behavior are: how advertisements can be made to gain the consumer's attention, how manufacturers can help consumers remember their product's name, what impact television has on children, what factors motivate consumers to buy products and seek creative activities, and what factors cause different consumers to make divergent purchase decisions. The example described in Highlight 1–2 illustrates the dramatic effect a product name change can have on sales.

Social Psychology

Social psychology stands midway between sociology and psychology. Hence, social psychologists investigate the interactions among small groups of people as well as how one person influences another. Problem areas related to consumer behavior that social psychologists deal with include: how attitudes form and change, how one person influences the actions of another, what the various ways to communicate messages are, what factors influence how consumers perceive products and companies, and how reference groups influence consumers.

The Sociology of Consumption

Whereas psychologists study the individual and social psychologists investigate small groups, sociologists deal with large masses of people who make up societies. Areas of interest to sociologists that apply to consumer behavior include the impact of culture and subcultures on consumption, the influence of the family on consumption, how social classes affect the buying preferences, and how group norms are formed and influence consumption. In addition, sociologists would ask how the various roles we might enter, such as housekeeper or provider, influence the behavior of consumers. Sociological areas of study form a portion of the environment in which the consumer

Figure 1–1   Isuzu attempts to raise the perceived value of its product by creating a limited edition. *(Courtesy of American Isuzu Motors, Inc.)*

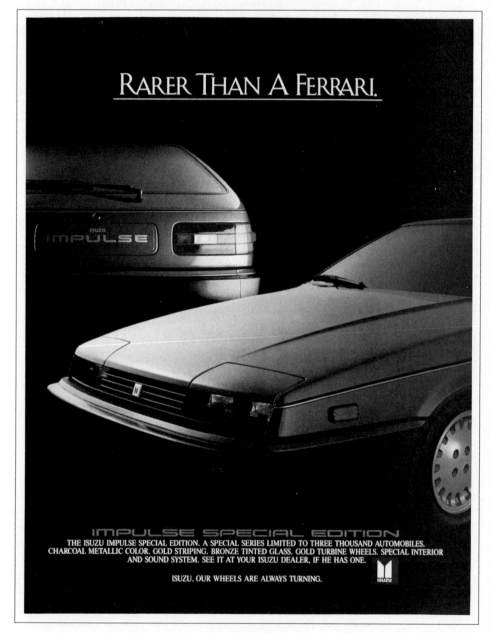

Could You Remember the Name "Body by Thixo-Tex?"

Later in the text you will learn about various learning theories and about how memory works. Memory processes are crucial to manufacturers and advertisers. If consumers cannot remember the name of a product, they hardly can be expected to buy it in the marketplace.

In some instances it is better to change a name than to retain one that cannot be remembered. Such was the case with a product called "Body by Thixo-Tex." The product is a rustproofing compound which chemically binds to metal. In the early 1970s it was found to be good for rustproofing cars against water and salt damage. Produced by Matex Corporation, the product was excellent, but no one could remember its name. In 1976 sales were around $2 million, but management felt that they should be much better. An advertising agency was hired. One of their first actions was to suggest a name change. The advertising executives correctly recognized that "Body by Thixo-Tex" simply was too unfamiliar to consumers for them to be able to remember it. After some searching, they arrived at the name "Rusty Jones." Furthermore, they developed an animated character with rust-colored hair, who wore overalls and a work shirt, to be "Rusty Jones"—the trade character for the rustproofing product.

The roll-out of the campaign was done slowly, with the first ads appearing in Buffalo—thought to be a location where rusting autos could be a problem. Through only radio and newspaper ads, sales increased by 258 percent. The company then went to television, using a seven-foot animated character. Sales increased an additional 300 percent.

By 1980 the product became the leading rustproofing chemical in the Midwest. Sales went from $2 million in 1976 to over $70 million in 1979. The development of a memorable name for the product and a trade character that could tie the entire advertising campaign together was largely responsible for the incredible increase in sales.

Based on Hooper White, "Name Change to Rusty Jones Helps Polish Product's Identity," *Advertising Age*, February 18, 1980, 45, 50.

lives and functions. The consumer's social class, what subcultures he is a part of, his particular family situation, and the various roles he must enter all influence preferences and the way the consumer approaches buying decisions.

Anthropology

Anthropology, although closely related to sociology, has a distinct value for consumer behaviorists. Anthropologists are involved in cross-cultural analysis, which has application to consumer behavior in international settings. In addition, anthropologists study folklore, cultural myths, and the overall organization of a society.

The research methods used by anthropologists are currently having an important impact on the study of consumer behavior. Within the past ten years consumer behaviorists have become much more interested in studying the factors that influence consumers to seek playful experiences, such as going to amusement parks, and aesthetic experiences, such as going to the theater. Research methods that involve the investigator in directly observing

HIGHLIGHT 1–3

Some Anthropological Problems

"Peruvian Indians carry around small, rectangular rocks painted to look like transistor radios. San Blas Cuna hoard boxes of dolls, safety pins, children's hats and shoes, marbles, enamelware kettles, and bedsheets and pillowcases in their original wrappings. Kekchi Maya Swidden farmers relax in the evenings to the sounds of Freddie Fender on portable cassette players. When a Swazi princess weds a Zulu king, she wears red touraco wing feathers around her forehead and a cape of windowbird feathers and oxtails. He wears a leopard skin cloak. Yet all is recorded with a Kodak movie camera, and the band plays the "Sound of Music." In Niger, pastoral Bororo nomads race to market on camelback carrying beach umbrellas. Veiled noble Tuareg men carry swords modelled after the Crusaders' weapons and sport mirrored sunglasses with tiny hearts etched into the lenses."

These sometimes bizarre images illustrate the uneven diffusion of Western products into Third World cultures. Even though anthropologists can devise logical explanations for why certain groups adopt certain products, the results are certainly odd.

Extracted from Eric Arnould and Richard Wilk, "Why Do the Natives Wear Adidas?" *Advances in Consumer Research, XI,* Thomas Kinnear, (ed.), Association for Consumer Research, Ann Arbor, Michigan, 1984, 748-752.

and recording the activities of interest, or even actively participating in the activities, are increasingly being borrowed from anthropologists to study such consumer activities. Other anthropological research methods include sifting through garbage cans to identify the types of products that people consume and recording the folklore and traditions of societies.[10] An interesting example of the types of issues that anthropologists investigate is found in Highlight 1–3.

Demography

Demographers study the numbers and distribution of various segments of people. The field is increasingly of importance to consumer behaviorists, in part because demographic characteristics are used to delineate the nature of market segments. In addition, demographic trends can raise or lower the number of people in a company's target market, substantially altering the demand for a product. Tracking the changing demographic makeup of potential target groups is an important market research activity.

A BRIEF HISTORY OF CONSUMER BEHAVIOR

The history of consumer behavior as a discipline is short—less than twenty-five years. Although researchers were investigating consumer processes long before the 1960s, it was not until this time period that a separate field emerged. The history of consumer behavior can be divided into four phases: the **predisciplinary phase,** the **developmental phase,** the **cognitive era,** and the **current phase.**

The Predisciplinary Phase

Prior to the 1960s a separate field of consumer behavior did not exist, so the pre-1960s era constitutes the predisciplinary phase. As noted earlier, the first individuals to make the consumer a focus of study were economists attempting to explain factors influencing the demand for a product. In addition, one occasionally found researchers with a psychological or sociological orientation studying consumers. For example, in 1903 a professor wrote an advertising text which included material on how knowledge of psychological principles could improve advertising effectiveness.[11]

Freudian theory also received a great deal of attention in the 1940s and 1950s in the field of **motivation research.** The idea was to find the "real" reasons why people buy products. Using long, probing interviews and projective tests, researchers sought to identify the basic motivations behind buying behavior. In addition, motivations could be interpreted within a Freudian framework. For example, marketing researchers found that women preferred to add an egg to a cake mix rather than purchase a mix that contained the egg. Some Freudian-oriented marketers speculated that this motivation to add an egg to a prepared cake mix symbolizes the urge to give birth to a child.

A number of factors evolved to create an environment for emergence in the 1960s of consumer behavior as a discipline. The work in the 1950s by George Katona and his colleagues on the economics of consumption was certainly one factor. Katona revealed that knowledge of consumer attitudes and expectations influences consumers' purchase patterns. Paul Lazersfeld and his colleagues in sociology began doing longitudinal research on voting trends. This research led to the establishment of consumer panels through which buyer preferences could be studied.[12] Finally, the 1950s witnessed an explosion of growth in psychology and sociology, and the theories and concepts developed in these fields were borrowed and used as the basis of the new field of consumer behavior.

Although the research done by such people as Katona and Lazersfeld was important, a philosophical groundwork had to be laid. This was accomplished in the 1950s with the enunciation of the marketing concept. The idea that marketers function to fulfill consumer needs and wants made the study of the consumer necessary.

The Developmental Phase— 1960–1974

The developmental phase actually consisted of two separate stages. In the borrowing stage, consumer behaviorists utilized theories and concepts originating in the behavioral sciences. Thus, early consumer researchers used concepts borrowed from psychology involving learning and perception. From social psychology they borrowed theories relating to personality and attitude formation and change. From sociology ideas were taken involving the diffusion of innovations and the adoption processes.

Beginning about 1965, consumer behaviorists began to turn from the rather narrow theories borrowed from other fields and develop their own comprehensive models of behavior. No less than five such models were developed. These complex models had a major impact on the field. They clearly revealed the complexity of the discipline, thereby emphasizing the limitations of the narrow behavioral theories. They also marked the coming of age of the new field because consumer behaviorists had gained the confidence to strike out on their own to develop new theories and models.

A logical ending point of the development phase of consumer behavior was the launching of the field's first academic journal in 1974—the *Journal of Consumer Research*. The respected multidisciplinary journal is now the major outlet for articles by researchers on topics related to consumer behavior. Its founding marked the end of the field's infancy and its graduation to the status of a separate discipline.

The Cognitive Era— 1975–1981

The seven-year period after the initiation of the *Journal of Consumer Research* was marked by a number of trends, the most significant of which was a focus on the cognitive elements of consumer behavior. The term *cognitive* refers to the mental functions involved in the consumption process. During the cognitive era three areas received major attention. One involved the study of attitudes and the relation of attitudes to buying behavior. A second area focused on consumer information processing. Here researchers investigated such areas as perception, memory, and product choice processes. The third aspect of the cognitive approach was a focus on decision making. That is, what are the steps that consumers go through in buying a product? Importantly, researchers recognized that the study of attitudes, information processing, and decision making are not mutually exclusive. In each case the consumer is viewed as a rational being who attempts to solve problems in a logical way.

Another trend emerging between 1975 and 1981 involved public-policy research. Academicians began to apply buyer behavior theories and research for the purpose of developing improved regulation of the marketplace. The research was problem oriented and dealt with questions such as, "How can you encourage consumers to use less energy or water?" "Why don't consumers use seat belts?" and "What is the impact of television on children?" Despite periodic ebbs of interest, public-policy research is likely to continue to have importance for consumer researchers for the foreseeable future.

The Current Status of Consumer Behavior

The cognitive approach to consumer behavior still has much to offer, and this book discusses in some depth this approach. For example, from this perspective one would ask such questions as, "How do consumer memory processes influence advertisers?" "Do consumers have rules that they follow in making choices among products?" and "How do consumers form attitudes about products and companies?" Because the cognitive era still exerts a strong influence on consumer behaviorists today, to state that 1981 marked the beginning of its retreat may prove overly hasty. However, one could begin to see the first signs of its retreat at the national conference of the Association of Consumer Research in 1981. At this conference, where the leading consumer behavior researchers congregate to present their latest research, a new set of ideas and thoughts emerged. Researchers began to talk about the role of emotion in buying behavior. They began to question whether the cognitive paradigm—and particularly the information processing approach—was adequate to explain the complexity of the consumption process.

That advertisers attempt to utilize emotion to spur consumers is without doubt. The advertisement by the AT&T System in Figure 1–2 exemplifies its use. The ad appeared as a part of the "Reach Out and Touch Someone" campaign. Using the highly effective motivational themes of affiliation and belongingness (plus a cute kid), the campaign increased sales in the highly competitive long-distance market.

At the 1981 Association of Consumer Research conference other new consumer topics were discussed. For example, researchers analyzed the impact of the economy on consumption. Consumer behaviorists also began to speculate on the physiological basis of consumption. For example, could the presence of two brain hemispheres in humans explain some of the differences in the impact of television versus print media? Others noted that insufficient attention had been paid to such areas as fads and fashions, the sociology of consumption, and hedonistic behavior. In general, a willingness to move beyond the cognitive approach to explore a wider body of thought prevailed. Now in addition to the study of cognition, the areas of emotion, physiology, anthropology, and sociology shape the new trends in consumer behavior that are most likely to influence the field through the rest of the 1980s.

A CONSUMER BEHAVIOR MODEL

As noted earlier in the chapter, consumer behavior is a broad field that utilizes concepts and theories from a variety of disciplines. Because of this diversity, an overall model that links the various consumer behavior concepts together is extremely useful. Such a model can help the student understand the interrelationships among the areas of study that make up consumer behavior. In addition, a model can assist the student in organizing the major components of consumer behavior into a meaningful and memorable whole.

The model of consumer behavior used in the text is based on two sets of ideas. The first is that consumer behavior must be viewed wholistically. That is, consumers are influenced by a variety of forces rather than by isolated factors. In general, the actions of consumers are complex and will not be explained by any single concept or theory. The framework for the model is borrowed from a loose set of concepts labeled "field theory." The second idea on which the model is based is that consumer purchases and actions may be analyzed from three broad perspectives: the decision making, the experiential, and the behavioral influence perspectives. Different types of products tend to be purchased and different environmental and individual forces come into play for each type of process. The next two sections discuss field theory and the model.

Figure 1–2   AT&T creates good feelings and emotions through its "Uncle Bill" ad. *(Courtesy of AT&T.)*

Field Theory

The model of consumer behavior proposed in this text borrows from the work on **field theory** done by the psychologist Kurt Lewin. As a field theorist, Lewin was influenced by certain ideas prevalent in Germany in the early twentieth century that also affected such great physicists as Albert Einstein.[13] A number of Lewin's ideas are particularly relevant to the understanding of consumer behavior. One is that "analysis must begin with the situation as a whole."[14] In order to understand why a consumer buys a car, purchases a Colgate pump rather than a Crest tube, or goes to a Bruce Springsteen concert, the researcher must have an understanding of the diversity of factors influencing that person.

Figure 1–3 depicts the model of consumer behavior. In the model one finds a consumer selecting from three different types of products: a Bruce Springsteen concert, an automobile, and a charitable contribution. In the field theory model, two key elements should be defined. First, the consumer's purchase process takes place within a **lifespace.** The lifespace is the totality of factors that influence the consumer at any given point in time.[15] Consumer theorists call these elements of the lifespace *environmental factors*. They include such forces as culture, subculture, economics, groups, other people, and the situation. In addition, those actions of marketers that the consumer is aware of fall within the lifespace. Some of the forces may conflict in moving the person toward a purchase. For example, friends of the consumer could exert personal influence to go to the concert while the person's family could oppose the idea and press the consumer to contribute to a charity. Economic factors may mitigate against buying a car. In contrast, a group pressure may be strong to own one. Field theory makes the important point that the elements of the lifespace are interdependent. Depending upon the buying pro-

Figure 1–3   A model of consumer behavior.

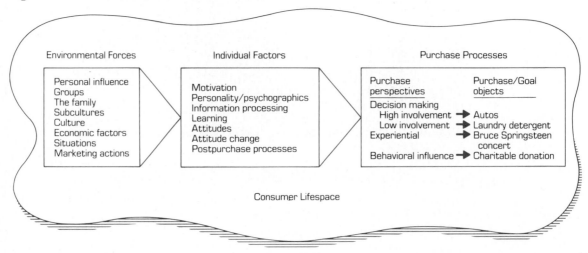

cess and upon the individual characteristics of the consumer, the various elements will combine in some manner to influence behavior.

The person himself or herself is also an important element of the model. The various personal factors that consumer behaviorists study include motivation, personality, psychographics, learning, information processing, attitudes, and post-purchase processes. These characteristics of the person will dictate which parts of the environment are in the lifespace and are likely to act on the consumer. If the consumer is not aware of some factor, such as a change in the price of the concert, it is not in the lifespace and cannot influence his or her behavior. Similarly, if the consumer has a personality characteristic, such as a high need for arousal, he or she may search out certain types of goal objects, such as hang gliding or attending rock concerts. In sum, the individual characteristics influence the consumer's selection of desired products, such as automobiles, concerts, and toothpaste. In addition, the personal factors control the nature of the lifespace. For example, an individual's personality and motivation characteristics will influence the extent to which he or she is aware of and responsive to the opinions of friends.

Three Consumer Purchase Perspectives

The consumer behavior model identified in Figure 1–3 also proposes that consumer purchases and actions tend to be marked by one of three general perspectives. These may be labeled the decision perspective, the experiential perspective, and the behavioral influence perspective.

The Decision-Making Perspective   During the 1970s and early 1980s, the dominant view of the consumer was as a decision maker. From this perspective, buying results from the consumer's first perceiving that a problem exists and then moving through a rational process of solving the problem. The **decision-making perspective** argues that consumers move through a series of rational steps when making a purchase. These steps include: problem recognition, search, alternative evaluation, choice, and postpurchase evaluation.

However, consumers do not always appear to move through each of the stages of the decision process with the same amount of intensity. Because of this, two general types of purchase decisions have been identified from within the decision-making perspective: extended decision making and routine decision making. Whether the consumer engages in extended or routine decision making depends largely upon that consumer's involvement in the purchase. Involvement refers to the extent of personal relevance that the purchase has for the consumer.[16] In many high-involvement decisions, the consumer moves through each of the stages of the decision process in a thorough fashion. In contrast, in low-involvement decisions the consumer is hypothesized to routinize the decision process, engage in a minimal search for information, and largely skip the alternative evaluation stage. The extended and routine decision processes are shown in Table 1–1.

As noted, consumers engage in an extended decision-making process for purchases they see as highly important. Such purchases could include autos,

Table 1–1   **The Decision-Making Perspective**

A. Extended decision-making process	B. Routine decision-making process
Step 1: Problem recognition	Step 1: Problem recognition
Step 2: Search	Step 2: Search (minimal search is performed)
Step 3: Alternative evaluation	Step 3: Choice
Step 4: Choice	Step 4: Postpurchase evaluation
Step 5: Postpurchase evaluation	

major appliances, and expensive consumer electronics, such as televisions, stereos, and computers. These purchases tend to be tied to the consumer's ego and to involve substantial amounts of financial, performance, and social risk. Thus, if something were to go wrong with the product, the consumer would be extremely concerned. In these instances it is rational to invest the time and energy to make as good a purchase decision as possible.

Routine decisions can also be viewed as highly rationally based. These decisions involve products that have little social, financial, or performance risk attached to them; therefore, it makes little sense to engage in extensive problem solving. Instead, the consumer attempts to make merely satisfactory decisions and thus minimizes effort in making the purchase. Consumers purchase many products at the grocery store through a routine purchase process. Thus, the search process for the products is minimal, a long process of evaluating alternatives is almost nonexistent, and the choice process among alternatives is quite simple.

When investigating the consumer from the decision-making perspective, researchers emphasize a number of psychological processes. In particular, researchers focus on the extent of information processing engaged in by the decision maker. (Information processing is discussed in Chapter 5.) **Information processing** refers to how a person takes in, analyzes, and interprets information from the environment. In addition, the researchers also focus on how product beliefs and attitudes are formed and changed (discussed in Chapters 7 and 8). In particular, the study of belief formation is important in the decision-making perspective, because belief formation about product characteristics is a key element in the buying process for both complex and routine decisions.

The Experiential Perspective   The **experiential perspective** on consumer buying proposes that in some instances consumers do *not* buy after a rational decision process. Instead, in certain instances products and services are bought in order to have fun, create fantasies, and achieve feelings.[17] Classified within the experiential perspective would be purchases made from impulse and purchases made to seek variety. Variety seeking occurs when consumers switch brands in order to lower boredom levels and obtain stimulation.[18] Many consumer services and products bought for leisure purposes have a strong experiential component to them, including such activities as going to rock concerts, symphonies, amusement parks, and movies. The goal of these leisure products is largely to create feelings among the consumers.

The study of affect (i.e., feelings) is an important aspect of the experiential perspective. In this approach, the starting point of the buying process is viewed as a strong positive affect, or feeling, towards a product, service, or idea. A number of authors have stressed the importance of affect as the starting point in consumer buying, and the experiential perspective captures this emphasis.[19]

Chapters of particular interest that pertain to the experiential perspective include those on motivation (Chapter 3), personality (Chapter 4), and attitudes (Chapter 7). Thus, rather than focusing on information processing, as does the decision-making perspective, the experiential perspective emphasizes the investigation of how feelings are formed.

The Behavioral Influence Perspective   In the **behavioral influence perspective,** the consumer's action does *not* result primarily from the formation of beliefs, as found in the decision-making perspective, or feelings, as in the experiential perspective. Instead, the consumer's action results from the direct influencing of behavior by strong environmental forces, such as cultural norms, the physical environment, or economic pressures. Thus, behavioral influence occurs when strong environmental forces create circumstances in which the consumer is propelled to perform some action without developing strong feelings or beliefs about the action. In this instance the consumer does not necessarily go through a rational decision process or rely on feelings to purchase a product or service. Instead, circumstances that encourage the occurrence of a particular behavior exist. Consumer researchers have used the term *behavioral influence* previously in describing how one person can influence another through the use of strong social norms.[20] In addition, what has been called "behavioral learning theory" also has close ties to the concept of behavioral influence.[21]

Behavioral influence may result from a number of sources. For example, it could occur as a result of the design of a building, which channels consumers in certain directions so that they confront specific products. Because of the design, the consumer has no choice but to physically move in a certain way. Behavioral influence could also result from norms and cultural values. Thus, in some instances a person may make a charitable donation, such as to the United Way, because the norms at his or her place of work dictate that such contributions should be made. Similarly, a person may feel compelled, as though by some unspoken law, to sing the national anthem at sporting events. In each of these instances, the behavior does not necessarily result from a decision process or from the operation of strong feelings towards a product or the action in which the person engages. Rather, the consumer is influenced to engage in the action by an external force.

Behavioral influence can also result from what is labeled **primitive consumption behavior.** Primitive consumer behavior consists of purchases and activities that exhibit personal spirituality, ancestral traditions, and communal methods of resource distribution.[22] Thus, primitive consumption involves "archaic processes," which dominated the consumption activities of premodern societies but are still practiced today. Such primitive consumption is influenced in particular by such environmental forces as culture, subculture, and the family. Because many of the primitive behaviors are guided by cultural values and norms, they are classified here within the behavioral influence category. Examples of primitive consumption behaviors include purchasing religious objects, such as Bibles, and buying leisure products because of ancestral traditions, such as upper-class white Anglo-Saxon Protestants engaging in such activities as sailing, fencing, and horse jumping.

Part II of the text on the environmental influences on consumption has particular application to the behavioral influence perspective. Such factors as the economy, culture, subculture, groups, and other people can place pressure on individuals to act in certain ways. In addition, Chapter 6 on learning is relevant. Certain types of learning involve the creation of behavior without the person first developing beliefs or feelings about the behavior.

A Cautionary Note

The consumer behavior model presented in this section makes the point that buying can be viewed from three broad perspectives—the decision-making, the experiential, and the behavioral influence perspectives. Readers should not interpret this trichotomy to mean that every consumer purchase can be categorized within one, and only one, of the categories. Indeed, it is likely that most purchases have some elements of each of the three perspectives. For example, at first analysis the purchase of a car would seem to be classified within the extended decision-making perspective. However, for many consumers the act of purchasing a car can be an impulse, based largely on strong, positive feelings. Similarly, the purchase of religious objects for some people may be done merely because it is expected of them, and thereby be classified in the behavioral influence category. Undoubtedly, however, the act may also result in part from deep feelings of love, so that it would be categorized within the experiential category.

The purpose of identifying three general perspectives on consumer buying is to help classify the buying behavior process so that it may be more easily studied and understood. In addition, whether a consumer buying process predominantly involves extended or routine decision making, experiential consumption, or behavioral influence can have a major impact on managerial and public policy making strategies. Additional discussion of the three approaches is found in Chapter 2 on consumer buying and the decision-making process.

SUMMARY

Consumer behavior is a broad field that studies how individuals, families, and groups acquire, consume, and dispose of goods, services, ideas, and experiences. The principles of consumer behavior are useful to business managers, government regulators, nonprofit organizations, and everyday people. In particular, for marketing managers knowledge of consumer behavior has important implications for environmental analysis, product positioning, segmentation of the marketplace, and design of the marketing mix. The high impact of consumer behavior on marketing management should not be surprising. Managers who follow the ideas flowing from the "marketing concept" view the consumer as the focal point of the marketing effort. Consumer behavior provides the knowledge base for the study of the consumer.

Consumer behavior is an applied discipline. It borrows theories and knowledge from other fields such as sociology, economics, and psychology. However, it is a discipline in its own right, and consumer researchers are developing their own body of knowledge which supplements that obtained from other fields.

The history of the consumer behavior field is short. Prior to 1960 a separate field did not exist; research done on consumers was performed by economists, psychologists, and sociologists. The developmental phase, which began in the early 1960s, ended in 1974 with the establishment of the field's own journal, the *Journal of Consumer Research*. From 1975 to 1981 consumer behaviorists focused heavily on consumer cognitive processes. They studied exhaustively such areas as attitudes, information processing, and decision making. Currently, consumer behaviorists are broadening their horizons to investigate relatively overlooked areas, such as motivation, physiological processes, and the sociology of consumption.

A consumer behavior model was developed and based partially upon field theory. The model states that individual consumer actions are influenced by various individual processes, such as motivation, information processing, personality, learning, and attitudes. The consumer resides within his or her lifespace, which is buffeted by environmental forces, including culture, subculture, economics, groups, other individuals, situations, and marketing communications of various types. The field theory perspective suggests that the various forces are interdependent and that an understanding of consumer behavior requires analyzing the entire environment faced by the consumer.

The consumer behavior model also presented three approaches for analyzing consumer purchase processses. The decision-making perspective until recently has been the dominant approach to understanding consumers. It argues that consumers move through a series of decision steps when buying a product or service. Two different versions of the decision-making perspective were described—extended decision making and routine decision making. The level of consumer involvement influences the extent of decision complexity. In contrast, the experiential perspective states that some purchases occur largely to obtain feelings and meet the needs of the consumer to experience fun and create fantasies. Finally, in the behavioral influence approach consumers are viewed as subtly forced to act in certain ways by pressures from the environment. Such pressures may come from the physical environment, from economics, from other people, and from cultural or sub-cultural forces. One example of such forces is found in primitive consumption behavior, in which a consumer acts because of spiritual beliefs, ancestral traditions, or communal agreements of how resources should be distributed.

Key Terms

Product differentiation
Consumer behavior
Product acquisition
Product disposition
Marketing
Exchange process
Consumer primacy
Environmental analysis
Marketing opportunity analysis
Product positioning
Segmentation
Marketing mix
Target markets
Theory

Public policy
Predisciplinary phase
Developmental phase
Cognitive era
Motivation research
Field theory
Lifespace
Decision-making perspective
Experiential perspective
Information processing
Behavioral influence perspective
Primitive consumer behavior

Review Questions

1. Define the term *consumer behavior*. Why is consumption viewed as a process?
2. Identify the reasons why an understanding of consumer behavior acts as a foundation for the development of marketing strategy and planning.
3. How can the study of consumer behavior assist managers in environmental analysis?
4. How can the study of consumer behavior assist managers in product positioning and product differentiation?
5. How can the study of consumer behavior assist managers in the segmentation of the marketplace?
6. Through what means does consumer behavior assist the marketing research function?
7. In what ways can the study of consumer behavior provide consumers, managers, and public policy makers with theories, facts, and an orientation?
8. What are the behavioral science fields from which

consumer behavior may draw theories and concepts?
9. Briefly identify and describe the four phases of the history of consumer behavior.
10. Draw a diagram of and label the consumer behavior model presented in the text.
11. Describe the three perspectives that can be used to analyze the consumer purchase process.
12. What are the environmental forces that may influence the consumer within his or her life space?
13. What are the various personal factors that moderate the influence of the environmental forces?
14. Discuss the two different types of decision-making processes that have been identified as falling within the decision-making perspective of consumer buying.

Discussion Questions

1. Consider the soft-drink industry. Through what means do companies such as Coca-Cola, Pepsi-Cola, Dr. Pepper, and others attempt to differentiate their products from those of other companies?
2. Define the concept of environmental analysis. Next, consider the use of electronic media, such as radio and television, by consumers. What environmental factors have influenced the use of these media by consumers over the past thirty years?
3. Define the concept of market segmentation. From your knowledge of the automobile industry identify as many different segments of customers as you can that auto manufacturers attempt to reach.
4. Define the concept of consumer primacy. Next, identify several ways in which marketers can demonstrate to customers the concept of consumer primacy. Finally, from your own buying experiences develop two to three instances in which marketers or retailers failed to follow the principle of consumer primacy.

5. Identify as many environmental factors as you can which a marketing manager for a national company that builds middle-income houses should consider. What are the managerial implications of these factors?

6. List five brand names of products that you use in the house. Evaluate the names to determine the extent to which each is memorable.

7. Consumer researchers are highly interested in the study of demographic trends. Identify three major demographic trends that may influence corporate market planning for marketers of golf clubs.

8. Identify three types of purchases you have made that were based mostly upon a careful, rational thought process. Briefly explain the nature of your thought process for each purchase.

9. Identify three purchases you have made that were based mostly upon a desire to obtain feelings and experiences. What feelings and experiences were you hoping to obtain from the purchase?

10. Identify three of your purchases that were made principally because of pressures from the environment. What was the nature of the pressure that encouraged each purchase?

11. Identify three of your purchases in which some combination of rational thought, desires for experience, and/or behavioral influence affected your purchase. Have you experienced decisions in which conflicts occurred among the three factors?

References

1. Bill Saporito, "Heinz Pushes to Be the Low-Cost Producer," *Fortune*, June 24, 1985, 44–54.
2. "What Killed Coffee?" *Marketing Communications*, March 1983, 19–22, 60.
3. U.S. Census of Population, P–25, no. 704.
4. Elizabeth C. Hirschman, "Innovativeness, Novelty Seeking, and Consumer Creativity," *Journal of Consumer Research*, 7, December 1980, 283–295.
5. Philip Kotler, *Marketing Management Analysis, Planning, and Control*, 4th ed., Englewood Cliffs, N.J.: Prentice-Hall, Inc., 1980, 21.
6. Bent Stidsen, Directions in the Study of Marketing," in *Conceptual and Theoretical Developments in Marketing*, Neil Beckwith et al. (eds.), Chicago: American Marketing Association, 1979, 383–398.
7. Kotler, *Marketing Management*.
8. Ibid.
9. Scott Ward and Thomas Robertson, "Consumer Behavior Research: Promise and Prospects," in *Consumer Behavior: Theoretical Sources*, Scott Ward and Thomas Robertson (eds.), Englewood Cliffs, N.J.: Prentice-Hall, Inc., 1973, 3–42.
10. John Sherry, "Some Implications of Consumer Oral Tradition for Reactive Marketing," in *Advances in Consumer Research, XI*, Thomas Kinnear (ed.), Ann Arbor, MI: Association for Consumer Research, 1984, 741–747.
11. Ward and Robertson, "Consumer Behavior Research."
12. Ibid.
13. Harold H. Kassarjian, "Field Theory in Consumer Behavior," in *Consumer Behavior: Theoretical Sources*, Scott Ward and Thomas Robertson (eds.), Englewood Cliffs, N.J.: Prentice-Hall, Inc., 1973, 118–140.
14. Marvin E. Shaw and Philip R. Costanzo, *Theories of Social Psychology*, New York: McGraw-Hill Book Company, 1970.
15. Shaw and Costanzo, *Theories of Social Psychology*.
16. Richard E. Petty and John T. Cacioppo, "Issue Involvement as a Moderator of the Effects on Attitude of Advertising Content and Context," in *Advances in Consumer Research, VIII*, K. B. Monroe (ed.), Association for Consumer Research, 1979, 20–24.
17. Morris B. Holbrook and Elizabeth C. Hirschman, "The Experiential Aspects of Consumption: Consumer Fantasies, Feelings, and Fun," *Journal of Consumer Research*, 9, September 1982, 132–140.
18. For a review of variety seeking, see Leigh McAlister and Edgar E. Pessemier, "Variety Seeking Behavior: An Interdisciplinary Review," *Journal of Consumer Research*, 9, December 1982, 311–322.
19. For example, see Werner Kroeber-Riel, "Emotional Product Differentiation by Classical Conditioning," in *Advances in Consumer Research, Vol. 11*, Thomas Kinnear (ed.), 1984, 538–543.
20. For example, see Peter H. Reingan and Jerome B. Kernan, "More Evidence on Interpersonal Yielding," *Journal of Marketing Research*, 16, November 1979, 588–593.
21. Michael L. Rothschild and William C. Gaidis, "Behavioral Learning Theory: Its Relevance to Marketing and Promotions," *Journal of Marketing*, 45, Spring 1981, 70–78.

PART I

Individual Consumer Processes

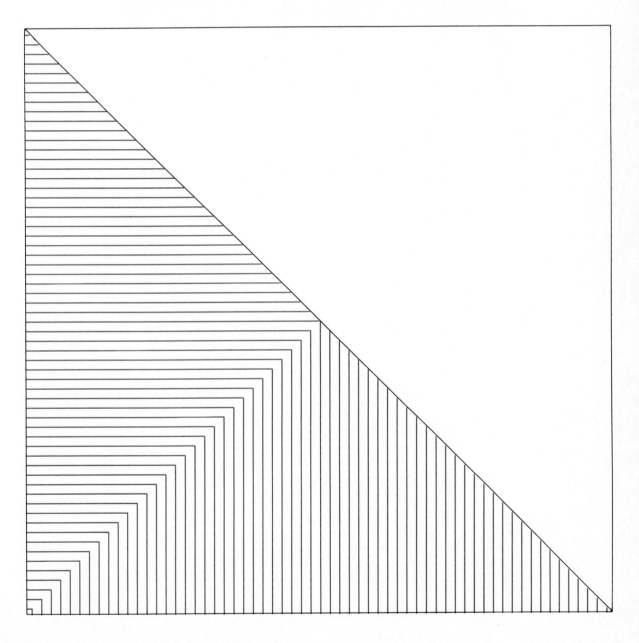

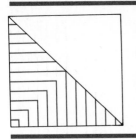

2
Consumer Buying:
The Decision-Making Process

On Buying Cars, Acting Like an Idiot, and Buying to Music

In the "buying guide" issue of *Consumer Reports* a consumer can find repair-record ratings for nearly every car model sold in the United States. For the last six model years, the cars are rated on a five point scale on seventeen different components—from the air conditioning to the transmission.

In addition, an overall trouble index, as well as a cost index, is computed. For each automobile as many as 2,600 separate bits of information may be transmitted to the reader. This is done for some eighty models. Only a person highly involved in the decision process to buy a car would attempt to analyze all of this information.

What do electronics engineers and computer technicians in Silicon Valley do for excitement? They go to an eighty-acre piece of poison-oak-infested land to play war games. Using CO_2 pistols designed to mark cattle with paint, the players play a game in which you are "dead" if shot with the paint. Why do intelligent people do it? Here are some quotes: "It really gives you a chance to act like an idiot." "It's like running a red light and a big truck is just about to hit you." "You get sweaty palms." "Out there you can yell, scream, call people slime puppies, chicken molesters, whatever."(a)

Have you ever noticed that many retailers play background music in their stores? Consumer researchers have found that music may influence buying behavior. In a study fast tempo and slow tempo music were played at various times in a supermarket.(b) The researcher found that shoppers tended to walk slower when the slow tempo music was played. Furthermore, sales volume increased by 38 percent during times when the slow tempo music was played. The customers seemed to spend more amounts of time looking for things to buy when in the presence of slow-paced music. Interestingly,

29

questionnaires revealed that the customers had no awareness of the effects of the music.

Buying a car, playing pretend war games, and reacting unconsciously to music illustrate three divergent perspectives of consumer behavior. These are the decision-making, the experiential, and the behavioral influence perspectives. Each is discussed in this chapter.

Portions based on (a) Erik Larson, "In Silicon Valley, Name of the Game is, Literally, Survival," *The Wall Street Journal*, May 22, 1984, 1, 14; and (b) Ronald E. Milliman, "Using Background Music to Affect the Behavior of Supermarket Shoppers," *Journal of Marketing, 46*, Summer 1982, 86–91.

INTRODUCTION

The consumer vignette that introduced the chapter illustrates three different perspectives on the consumer buying process, which were discussed briefly in Chapter 1. These divergent viewpoints may be labeled the decision-making perspective, the experiential perspective, and the behavioral influence perspective. The example from *Consumer Reports* depicts a decision-making view of consumer buying behavior. The information is provided to assist the consumer in making the most informed and logical decision possible in buying a car.

However, many consumer decisions do not follow a lengthy decision-making process or even any decision process at all. Instead, they are based upon the consumer searching for fun, sensations, or experiences. The example in the vignette of the executives playing war games with "ink guns" exemplifies a type of consumer behavior based upon the desire to have fun and experience strong emotions. As such, the second consumer buying perspective can be labeled the experiential approach.

A third perspective on why consumers buy also exists. Called behavioral influence, the idea is that in some cases consumers do not engage in activities as a result of a decision-making process or even the desire to experience fun and excitement. In this perspective consumers are viewed as acting because of the pressures of the environment. In such instances consumers may engage in activities without giving much, if any, conscious thought to why they are doing what they are doing.

The third example in the opening vignette illustrates the impact of behavioral influence on consumer behavior. In this instance the type of background music played in a supermarket was found to influence the pace that consumers moved as well as their buying behavior.[1] The research provided evidence that the music influenced behavior without the awareness of consumers.

Chapter 2 has two major purposes. First, the chapter seeks to introduce students to the three perspectives on consumer buying processes. Because much of the research in consumer behavior has focused on consumer decision making, the chapter will emphasize this perspective. Second, the chapter is written to provide a basis for integrating the remaining chapters in Parts I and II of the text. That is, by having an understanding of the three perspectives on consumer buying, one can more easily see the interrelationships among such individual concepts as motivation, personality and psychographics, learning, information processing, attitudes, and postpurchase processes. In addition, the perspectives show how the various environmental factors discussed in Part II of the text influence consumers.

THE DECISION-MAKING PERSPECTIVE

According to the decision-making perspective, consumers move through a series of steps when making a purchase. Shown in Figure 2–1, the five stages

Figure 2–1   Stages of the consumer decision process.

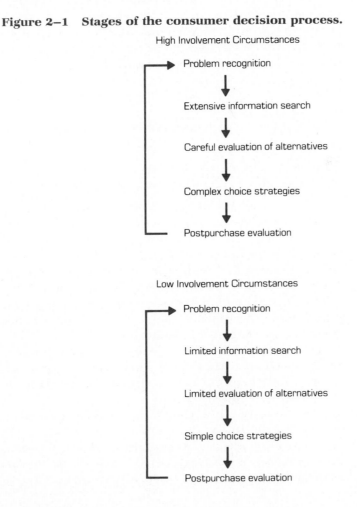

are: problem recognition, information acquisition, evaluation of alternatives, choice, and postpurchase evaluation.[2] The decision-making perspective has two alternative decision approaches. As shown in the top portion of Figure 2–1, in complex or extended decisions each of the stages is emphasized. However, the lower portion of the figure shows that in routine or limited decision making relatively little search behavior occurs. In addition, the alternative evaluation stage is largely absent from the decision process. Finally, the choice among alternative brands is done in a relatively simple manner in routine decision making. This section discusses each of the stages. However, it focuses in greater depth on the problem recognition stage and the search stage, because they are not covered elsewhere in the textbook. Differences between complex and routine decision making are mentioned for each of the stages.

As noted, the relative emphasis that consumers place on each of the stages depends in part upon whether the consumer is engaged in extended or routine decision making. In turn, the complexity of the **decision process** depends in part on the level of involvement of the consumer in the purchase. Involvement level has become a highly important concept in identifying the nature of the decision process and in developing managerial strategies to reach consumers. For these reasons consumer involvement is considered further.

Consumer Involvement

A wide number of definitions of **consumer involvement** exist.[3] Perhaps the most frequently used definition states that:

> involvement is the level of perceived personal importance and/or interest evoked by a stimulus (or stimuli) within a specific situation.[4]

Just what are the stimuli that may evoke differential levels of perceived personal importance? Such factors may originate from the product under consideration, from a communication received by the consumer, and from the characteristics of the situation within which the consumer is operating.[5] For example, as the product or service under consideration becomes more expensive, socially visible, and risky to purchase, it is likely that a consumer's involvement in the purchase would increase. Communications can also raise a consumer's involvement by skillfully arousing emotions. The situation can influence involvement by defining the context within which a purchase is made. For example, if the task definition is to buy a gift for an important person, such as a fiancée, the involvement of the purchaser is likely to increase. In addition, different consumers may react with divergent levels of involvement to various products, situations, and communications. Figure 2–2 diagrams the interrelationships among personality, product, communication and situation.

A critical problem in attempting to predict the involvement level of consumers is that of determining what influences "personal importance." One researcher suggested that personal importance results from the expected

Figure 2–2 **The factors influencing consumer purchase involvement. (Based in part on John H. Antil, "Conceptualization and Operationalization of Involvement," in *Advances in Consumer Research, XI*, Thomas C. Kinnear (ed.), Ann Arbor, MI: Association for Consumer Research, 1984, 203–209.)**

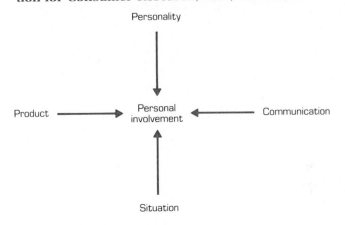

benefits and losses that can occur in any particular circumstance.[6] Thus, if the consumer believes that in a particular instance a great deal rides on making a good decision, then the consumer's involvement level is likely to increase.

What happens when a consumer's involvement level increases? First, some evidence suggests that under higher levels of involvement consumers begin to process information in a great deal more depth. Consumers are likely to give more diligent consideration to information relevant to the particular decision.[7] What this means is that consumers are more likely to think hard about a decision when it is made under high-involvement circumstances. In addition, higher levels of involvement are likely to lead consumers to engage in a more extended decision process and move through each of the decision stages in a more thorough manner.

As involvement level increases, consumers will tend to give more diligent consideration to the information they receive. Consequently, advertisers can develop more complex messages. The advertisement from Saab shown in Figure 2–3 illustrates this concept. Indeed, the headline of the advertisement (i.e., A Thorough Explanation of the 16-Valve Saab 900 Engine") immediately indicates to the reader that the message will be relatively complex. Saab can use such an advertising approach because it is likely that their target market consists of individuals more highly involved in the buying process.

Some authors have suggested that the type of decision process diverges sufficiently in **high-** and **low-involvement** circumstances to talk about two categories of decision making. Herbert Krugman was perhaps the first author to suggest that the decision process differs in high- and low-involvement cases.[8] As the involvement level decreases, consumers will tend to engage in more

Figure 2–3   Saab uses a detailed message to target buyers involved in extended decision making. (*Courtesy of Saab-Scania of America, Inc.*)

routine types of decisions. In such routine decision making one finds less search for information than in extended decision making. In routine decision making consumers are likely to deemphasize the alternative evaluation stage. Finally, they are likely to use simplified decision rules to make their choices.[9]

Components of the Decision Process

Because of the important effects of a consumer's involvement level on the decision-making process, it was important to discuss the concept prior to the detailed discussion of consumer decision-making processes. Now, however, we are ready to discuss the components of the consumer decision process—problem recognition, search, alternative evaluation, and postpurchase evaluation.

Problem Recognition   **Problem recognition** occurs when a discrepancy develops between an **actual** and a **desired state of being.** Typically consumer researchers seek to identify consumer problems by analyzing the factors that act to widen the gap between the actual and desired states. Thus, if the satisfaction with the actual state decreases, or if the level of the desired state increases beyond a tolerable amount, a problem may be recognized, which propels a consumer to action. Figure 2–4 diagrams how such a process may work and summarizes the factors that may influence either the actual or desired state.

FACTORS INFLUENCING THE ACTUAL STATE.   The factors influencing the actual state are concerned with the ability of the product or service to perform in a satisfactory manner. A variety of factors may cause the actual state to decrease below acceptable levels. A person could run out of a product,

Figure 2–4   The problem recognition process.

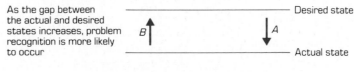

As the gap between the actual and desired states increases, problem recognition is more likely to occur

Desired state

Actual state

A. Factors lowering the level of the actual state
   1. Product depletion
   2. Product-use dissatisfaction
   3. Product availability
   4. Change in person's product requirements
   5. Product wears out or becomes out-of-style
   6. Marketing efforts

B. Factors raising the level of the desired state
   1. Cultural and subcultural factors
   2. Reference groups
   3. Changes in financial status
   4. Previous decisions
   5. Individual development
   6. Marketing efforts

such as gasoline or toothpaste. A product could wear out. The person could grow or gain weight so that a product, like clothing, no longer fits. A product may simply go out of style and not be up-to-date. Marketers can also take steps to create dissatisfaction with a competing brand by placing comparison advertisements that identify areas in which a competing product has problems, such as high price or a high failure rate.

FACTORS INFLUENCING THE DESIRED STATE. The desired state tends to be influenced by factors that affect the aspirations and circumstances of the consumer. Thus, such things as culture, subculture, reference groups, and lifestyle trends can cause a person to change his or her desired state. For example, if a person joins an organization, such as a fraternity, sorority, or corporation, the pressures of the social group may change the person's perception of the appropriateness of wearing certain types of clothing. When a student graduates from college, a whole new set of apparel requirements are imposed. Thus, the desired state changes, and needs develop for such things as nice suits, briefcases, and shoes, which would be considered totally inappropriate in a college environment. Other factors influencing the desired state include changes brought about by becoming older or by experiencing changes in one's financial situation. Previous decisions of the person can also affect the desired state. For example, if someone buys a house, a whole set of desires are created for new furniture, draperies, lawn products, and other items. Finally, marketers hope to influence the desired state of consumers by developing promotional campaigns that tie their product or service to popular lifestyle trends and show their product or service being used by highly attractive individuals.

Consumer Search Behavior After a consumer identifies a problem of sufficient magnitude to propel him or her to action, an **information search** process is begun to acquire information about products or services that may eliminate the problem. The investigation of the consumer search process is highly important to marketers. In particular, it influences a company's promotion and distribution strategies. For example, suppose that a company learns through marketing research that consumers buy its brand of product based on a routine decision process. Thus, consumers engage in highly limited amounts of external search prior to buying its brands. In such an instance it is crucial that consumers immediately think of the company's brand when a problem is recognized. To create such top-of-the-mind awareness high amounts of advertising are required so that the brand is recalled from long-term memory when a need arises. Such a strategy is used by fast-food companies, soft-drink manufacturers, and beer producers, and an example is presented in Highlight 2–1. When a consumer recognizes hunger or thirst, he or she is not going to engage in extensive search for a product to fulfill the need. Instead, the consumer is likely to choose the brand that immediately comes to mind. As a result, such companies spend huge amounts of

HIGHLIGHT 2–1

"Coors Is the One" Proved Successful

For products that involve little external search by consumers, a crucial problem is how to create awareness of the existence and qualities of the products. The goal of the marketing manager should be to have a sufficiently effective promotional program so that the product becomes one the consumer thinks of and considers.

The advertising industry has a tool that measures consumer awareness of advertising, called top-of-the-mind awareness. In the surveys a sample of consumers is asked to name the first advertisement that comes to mind overall or for a particular category of product, such as beer. Such surveys give some indication of promotional effectiveness, particularly when the size of the promotional budget is considered.

In February 1985 Coors replaced their "Best of the Rockies" advertising campaign with ads featuring an actor calmly talking about the characteristics of Coors beer and the factors that make it superior. Some of the points mentioned in the various ads included the fact that Coors only has one brewery so that quality can be controlled, that the water is naturally filtered by the earth so that it does not have to be purified, and that the beer is never heated to high temperatures. The ads avoided the common appeals of sex, emotion, and patriotism and stood out from the clutter. As a result, Coors was catapulted to first in advertising awareness soon after the campaign was started, replacing Budweiser, the perennial awareness leader.

Based in part on Scott Hume, "Survey: Coors Is the One," *Advertising Age*, May 27, 1985, 3, 87.

money on advertising to insure that their brands come to mind first, when a problem is identified.

Researchers have found that two types of consumer search processes exist—internal search and external search.[10] **Internal search** involves the consumer attempting to retrieve from long-term memory information on products or services that will help to solve a problem. In contrast, **external search** involves the acquisition of information from outside sources, such as friends, advertisements, packaging, *Consumer Reports*, or sales personnel.

INTERNAL SEARCH.   After a problem is recognized, consumers will engage in internal search prior to external search. Depending upon the type of problem encountered, the degree of internal search will vary. If the purchase process involves extensive problem solving, the consumer may actively search long-term memory for information on brand alternatives. If the consumer is in a low-involvement purchase process, internal search tends to be highly limited. When the purchase process involves an impulse or an induced purchase, it is likely that little or no internal search occurs. Rather than engaging in an information-processing task of searching through long-term memory for ideas, the consumer refers to his or her feelings or follows normative pressures.

When the purchase involves extensive problem solving or limited problem solving, consumers will engage in an internal search for information by attempting to retrieve from long-term memory information relevant to the

Figure 2–5   Categories of brands that consumers may retrieve from memory during internal search.

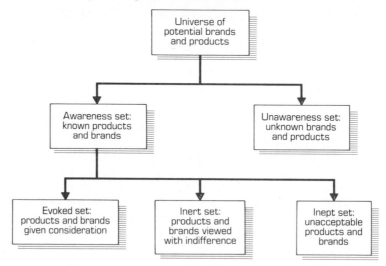

problem. One type of information that may be retrieved involves the brands that the consumer may or may not consider for purchase. Figure 2–4 identifies five different categories, into one of which a brand must fall.[11] As shown in Figure 2–5, internal search can be viewed as proceeding via a two-stage process. First, the consumer retrieves from long-term memory those products and brands of which he or she is aware. This **awareness set** is the subset of the total universe of potential brands and products available. The **unawareness set** consists of those brands that the consumer cannot recall from long-term memory or that were never placed into long-term memory. At minimum a company wants its brand to be a part of the awareness set. If consumers are unaware of a brand, they are unlikely to ever consider it unless they discover it in the external-search process. After identifying the awareness set, the consumer can be viewed as separating the awareness group into three additional categories—the **evoked set,** the **inert set,** and the **inept set.** The evoked set consists of those brands and products that are acceptable for further consideration. The inert set consists of the brands and products to which the consumer is essentially indifferent. The inept set consists of the brands and products that are considered unacceptable. Of course, the goal of a company is to have its brand placed in the evoked set and *not* placed in the inept set.

EXTERNAL SEARCH. As noted earlier in the chapter, external search involves the consumer soliciting information from outside sources. Table 2–1 identifies the four basic types of information that may be sought. In essence,

**Table 2–1   The Types of Information Sought Via
                External Search**

1. Alternative brands available.
2. Evaluative criteria on which to compare brands.
3. Importance of various evaluative criteria.
4. Information on which to form beliefs.
     Beliefs may be formed on attributes that brand alternatives
     possess.
     Benefits that various attributes provide.

a consumer engages in external information search in order to gain information so that attitudes may be formed and changed. As such, the consumer will search to identify what alternative brands are available. In addition, a consumer may seek to identify the various evaluative criteria on which the brands may be compared. Information may also be sought to help the consumer decide how important the various evaluative criteria should be in the decision. The consumer engaging in extensive external search will also seek to form beliefs about the various alternatives. In particular, information will be sought to form beliefs about the extent to which alternatives possess the attributes considered to be important. In addition, beliefs will be formed about the benefits that the various attributes provide.

FACTORS INFLUENCING THE DEGREE OF EXTERNAL SEARCH. Consumers may be viewed as engaging in external search for the purpose of obtaining sufficient information to identify and compare alternatives. One issue concerns the question of what factors influence the degree of external search. Economists have tackled this question and have argued that consumers will search as long as the marginal gains from search exceed the marginal costs of such a search.[12]

Another approach to predicting the amount of external search by consumers is to identify the type of purchase process in which they are engaged. In general, consumers will engage in heavy amounts of external search only when engaged in a purchase process that involves extensive problem solving. Such extensive problem solving will occur under high-involvement conditions. Table 2–2 identifies a number of factors associated with consumers engaging in extensive problem solving. The amount of external search will tend to vary directly with the amount of problem solving in which the consumer wishes to engage.

As can be seen in Table 2–2, three primary categories of factors influence the extent of problem solving and external search a consumer will pursue— factors associated with the risk of the product, factors associated with the characteristics of the consumer, and factors associated with the buying situation.

Table 2–2 Factors Associated with Consumers Engaging in Extensive Problem Solving

A. Factors associated with risk of product
   1. Financial risk
   2. Performance risk
   3. Psychological risk
   4. Time risk
   5. Physical risk
B. Factors associated with consumer characteristics
   1. Consumer knowledge and experience
   2. Personality characteristics
   3. Demographic characteristics
C. Factors associated with the situation
   1. Amount of time available for purchase
   2. Number of product alternatives available
   3. Store locations
   4. Information availability
   5. Antecedent states of consumer
   6. Social risk of situation
   7. Task definition

PRODUCT RISK FACTORS. In Chapter 3 on motivation the concept of perceived risk is discussed more fully. However, evidence exists to show that as the perceived risk of the product increases, consumers tend to engage in more extensive problem solving and search.[13] The types of risk associated with the characteristics of a product are: financial, performance, psychological, time, social, and physical. Thus, if a consumer recognizes a problem that can be solved only by a product or service involving high perceived risk, it is more likely that the consumer will engage in extensive problem solving.

CONSUMER FACTORS. The personality, demographic, and knowledge characteristics of the consumer will also influence the extent of problem solving and external-search behavior. For example, one researcher identified a group of consumers who perceived themselves as information seekers. This group was found to engage in more extensive external search prior to making a purchase.[14] Such personality characteristics as open-mindedness and self-confidence have been associated with greater amounts of external search.[15] Other researchers have found that the less experience consumers have had with a product category, the greater is their information-search behavior.[16] A number of studies have found that as consumers gain experience with a product category, their information-search behavior decreases. This relationship between experience and external search, however, occurs only for those with some minimal experience levels. Some evidence exists that if the consumer has had little or no experience with a product class, he or she may feel threatened by the experience and engage in less search.[17]

A number of demographic characteristics have been found to be associated with higher levels of consumer search behavior. Higher levels of external search have been found with people having increased amounts of education and income. Similarly, individuals in higher-status occupations tend to engage in greater amounts of external-search behavior.[18] Other researchers have found that as people grow older their search behavior tends to decrease.[19]

SITUATIONAL FACTORS. The characteristics of the consumer situation may also influence the amount of external search in which consumers engage. Thus, the amount of time available to make a purchase will influence the amount of possible external search. Such antecedent states as fatigue, boredom, and sickness are also likely to influence negatively the ability of consumers to engage in external search. If the social risk of the purchase is perceived to be high, consumers are more likely to engage in greater amounts of external search. Similarly, how the person defines the purchase task is also likely to influence external search. Thus, if the purchase is to be made for some type of important occasion, such as the wedding of a close friend or an important party for business clients, purchases will be made with care and with greater amounts of external search.

Another situational factor deals with the nature of the market situation faced by the consumer. Researchers have found that as the number of product alternatives available increases, a tendency to engage in greater amounts of search results.[20] Similarly, the number of stores available and their proximity will also influence the amount of external search. When stores are numerous and in close physical proximity, consumers will tend to engage in more external search.[21] As one would expect, consumers tend to engage in large amounts of external search when shopping in large malls where large number of stores exist in close proximity to each other.

A NOTE ON THE ECONOMICS OF SEARCH. A final point on external search should be made. It was noted earlier that from an economic perspective consumers should continue to search as long as marginal benefits outweigh marginal costs. Although it is difficult to quantify these concepts precisely, they should be considered by marketers. In general, the more costly it is for consumers to engage in external search, the less they will engage in this activity. A variety of factors can influence the cost of search, such as the physical proximity of stores, the cost of gasoline, and the value of the consumer's time. Furthermore, one can predict that the greater the benefits of search, the greater the external search will be. Factors influencing the benefits obtained from search include the number of product alternatives available, the amount of product differentiation that occurs in the marketplace, and the amount of experience the consumer has with the product category. If a number of different types of products are available in the marketplace and if they are highly differentiated, large benefits may be gained from external-search behavior. In contrast, as the consumer gains experience with a product class, the benefits of additional search—and, as a consequence, the search process—will cease. Thus, at some point in time the costs of additional search will exceed the benefits gained from additional search.

HOW MUCH SEARCH BY CONSUMERS?   Research has shown that consumers engage in surprisingly little external search, even when in extended problem-solving situations. For example, one study investigated the external-search behavior for refrigerators.[22] The author found that 42 percent of the respondents visited only one store. Furthermore, 41 percent considered only one brand. Another study found that in 77 percent of the cases consumers visited only one store when purchasing a small appliance.[23] One study of external search behavior for major appliances and automobiles found that "the amount of information sought by many buyers is small, even though information is accessible."[24]

Although the evidence shows that consumers engage in what appears to be abnormally low amounts of external search, one should not necessarily conclude that they are making purchases in an uninformed manner. Some evidence exists that the consumer self-report surveys used to gather such information may understate the actual amount of search by consumers. That is, when asked to describe their search process, many consumers forget some of the steps that they took in the search process.[25] In addition, in a number of instances consumers may have been quite experienced in the purchase of the product and simply not have needed to engage in large amounts of external search in order to make a purchase.

THE SEARCH PROCESS FOR AUTOMOBILES.   For most consumers the largest single purchase they will make, other than the purchase of a home, is an automobile. The purchase of an automobile tends to be a high-involvement process which entails substantial amounts of financial, performance, social, and time risk. Recently a number of studies have been performed that analyze the search process for automobiles. One of these investigated the factors that influence the amount of search.[26] The researchers identified the order of relative importance of five variables on the amount of search. The variables in their order of importance were:

1. Prior relevant knowledge—Those with the most knowledge searched the least.
2. The consumer's personality—Those consumers who had a strong desire to seek information tended to search more.
3. The number of alternatives available—The more brands available of the type sought by the consumer, the greater the amount of search.
4. Cost of search—The greater the cost of search, the less search occurred.
5. Frame of reference—Those who have a frame of reference for evaluating new information tended to engage in greater amounts of search.

One of the interesting findings of the study was that two types of consumer knowledge seem to exist. One type concerns the knowledge of specific attributes associated with the various makes of cars and knowledge of how to go about purchasing a new car. Consumers with high amounts of product and purchase-procedure knowledge engaged in lower amounts of search. The second type of knowledge concerned general information about cars and purchase decisions. Individuals who possessed high levels of general knowledge (but did not necessarily have specific knowledge about the attributes of specific makes of cars) tended to engage in larger amounts of external search. The reason for their higher amounts of external search may have been that they could more easily process new information and felt more comfortable obtaining new information.

A second study investigating the search process for automobiles focused on identifying psychographic profiles of consumers who engage in similar search patterns.[27] These clusters of consumers are identified in Table 2–3. The high-involvement nature of purchasing a car can be seen in the fact that only 26 percent of the respondents could be classified as low searchers. Also interesting is the finding that some 19 percent of the consumers were classified in the purchase pal assisted group. These individuals were the least experienced car shoppers and tended to bring along someone else who was perceived as more experienced in judging cars.

Alternative Evaluation   During and after the information-search process, consumers engage in an evaluation of the alternative brands. In the evaluation the consumer compares the brands identified as potentially capable of solving the problem that initiated the decision process. When the brands are compared, the consumer forms beliefs, attitudes, and intentions about the brands under consideration. Thus, **alternative evaluation** and developing beliefs, attitudes, and intentions are synonymous. Because Chapter 7 discusses in detail the development of beliefs, attitudes, and intentions, these concepts are touched upon only briefly here.

Some definitions are important in order to orient the reader to the forthcoming material. First, what is a belief? A **belief** is a perception of the extent to which some object (such as a product or service) possesses certain characteristics. These characteristics are called **attributes.** For example, an automobile may be evaluated on the extent to which a consumer believes it to have certain attributes, such as good fuel economy, low cost, good styling, and good handling. This type of belief is called an **object-attribute belief.**

Although many definitions of attitudes exist, the following definition tends to be used most frequently. An **attitude** is "the amount of affect or feeling for or against a stimulus."[28] Thus, an attitude implies that a consumer has developed a positive or negative feeling towards some object, such as a brand, a company, or even an idea.

Intentions are viewed as resulting from the formation of beliefs and attitudes. Thus an **intention** is the determination of a consumer to engage in some act, such as purchasing a product or service.

The nature of the alternative-evaluation process depends in part upon the involvement of the consumer in a particular purchase. When involvement is

Table 2–3   Profile of Shoppers for Automobiles

Cluster 1 (Low Search) (26%)

Spend least time of all clusters in search-related activities

Greatest prior purchase experience

Have owned more cars than average

More satisfied with previous purchases

Most certain would get a good deal without information search

More likely to know in advance the manufacturer and dealer from whom they wish to purchase

Reason for purchase more likely to be feeling that it is good to trade cars every few years

Older

Highest income of all clusters

Search for and purchase cars in a higher price range

Most likely of clusters to consider full-sized, four-door models

More likely to consider products made by Ford and General Motors (e.g., Cadillac)

Less likely to consider Chrysler products or imports

Cluster 2 (Purchase Pal Assisted) (19%)

Least experienced car shoppers

Have owned the fewest cars previously

Most likely to indicate a father was involved in decision

Tend to involve another who is perceived as knowing cars (purchase pal)

Express little confidence in their ability to judge cars

Likely to be less satisfied with most recent car purchase

May know manufacturer but not dealer from whom they will purchase

Largest percentage of single respondents in this cluster

Tend to work in clerical and sales jobs

Most likely to be buying because had no car or because they feel it is good to trade cars every few years

More likely to purchase a two-door model

Car purchased more likely than for any other cluster to be outside of original size and price set of models considered at the outset of formal search

Cluster 3 (High Search) (5%)

Spend the greatest amount of time (their own and others') in search activity

Have lowest confidence of any cluster in their ability to judge cars

Believe extensive information search is necessary to get a good buy

Least satisfied of all clusters with previous purchase

Post-purchase satisfaction with new car is below average

Tend to involve others in search activities, but these other individuals may have no particular expertise

Car actually purchased has the lowest average sticker price of all clusters

Less likely to have a trade-in or get a high trade-in price

Best educated of clusters but of moderate income

More likely than other groups to be female (although over half are male)

More likely to consider subcompacts, compacts, and hatchbacks

Likely to consider popular imports

Least likely of the clusters to select General Motors as the preferred manufacturer, although a majority still prefer GM products

Cluster 4 (Self-Reliant Shopper) (12%)

Spend the greatest amount of own time in search process but do not involve others in search

Consider a large number of automobile makes and models

Less likely to know in advance the dealer from whom car is purchased

Less likely to have a trade-in

Well educated with moderate to high income

Male

Most likely to be purchasing new car for fuel efficiency or because they want a car for a different purpose from that of previous car

Most likely to consider subcompacts and compacts

Most likely to consider imports, Ford products, and Dodge

Less likely than average to consider General Motors products

---

high, the consumer will tend to use an extended decision process and move through what is called the standard hierarchy of effects. In the standard hierarchy the consumer is viewed as first forming beliefs, then attitudes, and finally intentions. However, in low-involvement circumstances, the hierarchy

Table 2–3 *(continued)*

Cluster 5 (Retail Shopper) (5%)	Cluster 6 (Moderate Search) (32%)
Largest number of decisionmakers involved—especially the wife when she is not the principal decisionmaker (this group has the highest percentage of married individuals)	Devote below-average amount of time to search activities
	High certainty that they could obtain a good deal without information search
Unlikely to know dealer in advance	Very likely to know manufacturer in advance but not necessarily the dealer
Less likely to have a trade-in	Least likely to involve others in search process
Consider a large number of makes	Tend to be older males with higher income than average
Large amount of "other" involvement in the search process	Most likely to receive a high trade-in price
Well educated but not necessarily high income	Principal reasons for purchase are desire for greater fuel efficiency and feeling that it is best to trade cars every few years
Common occupations are managers, government officials, or proprietors	Most likely to consider four-door models
Principal reasons for new car purchase are desire for greater fuel efficiency or the fact that the old car quit working and needed replacement	Most likely to buy outside of initial price set
Pay highest average price of all clusters for car	Preferences for manufacturers well distributed among members of this group
Prefer intermediate-sized sedans made by GM or Ford (Oldsmobile and Pontiac are particular favorites)	
More likely to buy outside of initial manufacturer set but less likely to buy outside of original price set	

SOURCE: David Furse, G. Punj, and D. Stewart, "A Typology of Individual Search Strategies Among Purchasers of New Automobiles," *Journal of Consumer Research, 10*, March 1984, 417–431. Used by permission.

may change. When engaged in low-involvement decision making (i.e., a routine decision process), the consumer may only form a few rudimentary beliefs about a product or service and then develop little or no affect or attitude towards the decision object.[29] Indeed, under such low-involvement conditions, attitudes towards the object may form only after it is purchased or consumed. Thus, in routine decision situations the alternative-evaluation process is minimized. (Chapter 7 discusses beliefs, attitudes, and intentions in far more detail.)

The Consumer Choice Process After engaging in an evaluation of the alternatives, the consumer's next step in the buying process is to make a **choice.** Consumers make two different types of choices. They can choose between alternative *brands.* In addition, they can make choices between *stores.*

The study of consumer choice has generally focused on identifying the types of decision rules that people use to decide which alternative brands to purchase. Two broad categories of decision rules have been used to explain how consumers make choices among brands, and they are called compensatory and noncompensatory models of choice. Each type of model is based on how consumers deal with information about the attributes of the brands under consideration for purchase. In compensatory models of choice consumers are viewed as analyzing each alternative in a broad evaluative fashion.[30] All of the information on the attributes of a brand are combined into an overall judgment about one's preference for the brand. Such an evaluation is made for each of the brand alternatives. According to the compensatory model, the brand that has the highest overall preference is then chosen.

One aspect of compensatory models should be noted: that is, because a broad preference judgment is made, an alternative is *not* necessarily rejected because it has low ratings on any particular attribute. Thus, a consumer may rate a particular brand of automobile as poor in acceleration. However, because the car is rated more highly on other attributes and because judgment is based upon a global evaluation, the brand could still be chosen. The quality of having high ratings on some attributes that compensate for low ratings on other attributes is the basis for the name given to these models of choice— i.e., **compensatory models.**

As the name suggests, in **noncompensatory models** high ratings on some attributes may not compensate for low ratings on other attributes. A whole variety of noncompensatory models have been identified. They are used in either of two general sets of circumstances. First, these models may be implemented when consumers are engaged in a routine, low-involvement purchase process. Thus, rather than going through a long evaluation process, as is found with compensatory models, the consumer may take shortcuts to reach satisfactory rather than optimal decisions. Second, noncompensatory decision models are often used as preliminary screening devices to eliminate excess alternatives early in the decision process.

An example of the use of a noncompensatory model to bring the number of alternatives down to a manageable level is found in the purchase of automobiles. When initially faced with the decision to purchase a new car, a consumer has hundreds of alternatives from which to choose. The first thing that some people do is identify the key attributes the car must have. Thus, the person may decide that it needs to cost under $10,000, carry four people, and look sporty. In essence, the consumer has set arbitrary cut-off levels on three different attributes of the car. The attributes are cost, load capacity, and sportiness. Any alternatives not equaling or surpassing these cut-off points are eliminated. This type of noncompensatory decision rule is called a **conjunctive model.** By using such a choice rule, the consumer can quickly reduce the number of alternatives to a manageable level. Chapter 7 discusses several of the consumer-choice models that have been identified.

Postpurchase Processes   After a brand or service is purchased, a consumer moves into the **postpurchase phase** of the decision process. Figure 2–6 presents the major components of the postpurchase phase. These components are: product use, the formation of postpurchase attitudes towards the product, consumer complaint behavior, and finally product disposition. Each of these stages is discussed in more detail in Chapter 9, which focuses exclusively on postpurchase decision making. However, a brief description of the various components of the postpurchase process is useful.

Figure 2–6   The postpurchase process in consumer buying.

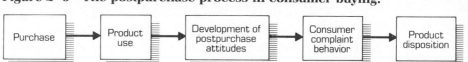

Product usage refers to how consumers go about consuming products and services in their everyday lives. Companies have certain assumptions about how consumers use their products, and these assumptions influence product design. Thus, in the early 1980s television companies began to recognize that television sets were being used by people to play video games. Because video games are best played on a higher-resolution screen, the manufacturers began to produce sets to match these needs.

The next step in the postpurchase phase is the development of attitudes related to the consumer's satisfaction or dissatisfaction with the product or service. The study of consumer satisfaction has grown into a large area of research. Some of the important issues discussed in Chapter 9 are how brand expectations are formed, the factors that influence the perception of the performance of a product or service, and the factors that influence the creation of feelings of satisfaction and dissatisfaction.

Consumer complaint behavior occurs as a result of feelings of dissatisfaction. Consumers have a number of means of voicing their complaints, from avoiding the future purchase of the product or service to instigating legal action. Studying the nature of consumer complaints is crucial because of their potentially devastating impact on sales and profits.

The last step in the postpurchase process is product disposition. Product disposition concerns what consumers do with a purchase after they have finished using it. A variety of alternatives are available, including throwing it away, renting it, and reselling it. The preferred means of disposition of a product by consumers can influence how a company designs a product. For example, one company tried producing a reusable mousetrap. The product was superior to traditional traps and cost only a marginal amount more. However, the product failed in the marketplace, because consumers wanted to throw away traps once they had successfully caught a mouse. The preferred means of disposition of a "once-used" mousetrap was totally inconsistent with one of the major design elements of the product. The result was failure in the marketplace.

THE EXPERIENTIAL PERSPECTIVE

The decision-making perspective of consumer buying has dominated the study of consumer behavior over the past twenty years. Within this perspective consumers are viewed as thinkers who actively process information about services and products in a rational, thoughtful manner. However, beginning in the early 1980s, an alternative view of the buying process began to emerge which emphasized the experiential side of consumption. According to the experiential view, consumers are feelers in addition to thinkers who consume many types of products for the sensations, feelings, images, and emotions that they generate.[31]

When researchers began to investigate buying processes based upon an experiential perspective, the types of products considered changed. When approaching consumer behavior from a decision-making perspective, researchers tended to focus on "functional" products, such as packaged goods, brands, and durables used by consumers to solve consumption problems. In contrast, from an experiential perspective products investigated include movies, art, novels, opera, and casinos.[32] The products offered in a disco setting are explored in Highlight 2–2.

One type of purchase that may be categorized within the experiential domain is **impulse buying.** Impulse purchases may be defined as a "buying action undertaken without a problem previously having been consciously recognized or a buying intention formed prior to entering the store."[33] Although little research has been done on the mechanism responsible for impulse purchases, it is likely that they result from the consumer seeing a product and reacting with an extremely strong positive affect towards it. The positive feelings lead to a desire to experience the product or service and result in its purchase. Impulse purchases occur frequently. Various studies have found that as many as 39 percent of department store purchases and 67 percent of grocery store purchases may be unplanned.[34]

Another type of purchase behavior that may be categorized in the experiential domain is that of **variety-seeking behavior.** Variety seeking refers to the tendency of consumers to buy spontaneously a new brand of product even though they continue to express satisfaction with the previously purchased brand. One explanation of variety seeking is that consumers are attempting to reduce boredom by purchasing a new brand.[35] The theory of

---

HIGHLIGHT 2–2

The Leisure Industry Markets Experiences and More

The discos of Manhattan provide a fascinating example of an unusual source of consumer stimulation. At the discos consumers are aroused through the visual and auditory experiences that await them. The flashing lights, high-intensity music, the "in" people, and the presence of alcohol and drugs make the night clubs an exciting place to spend a few hours.

At one of the clubs the most "action" is said to take place in the ladies' rest room. Here, men and women mingle with drinks while waiting for the stalls. It's considered unchic for the women to protest, and when a guy was asked why he was there, he responded, "It's a lot more interesting in here."

Based on Laura Landro, "Every-Night Fever: Manhattan's Discos Vie for Fickle Crowd," *The Wall Street Journal*, November 29, 1983, 1, 12.

Images of Consumer Behavior: A Pictorial Essay

This collage of photos and CLIO award winning print ads is the first of two sets of visual depictions of consumer behavior concepts. In this first section, the photographs and their captions identify many of the areas of consumer analysis discussed in Part I of the text.

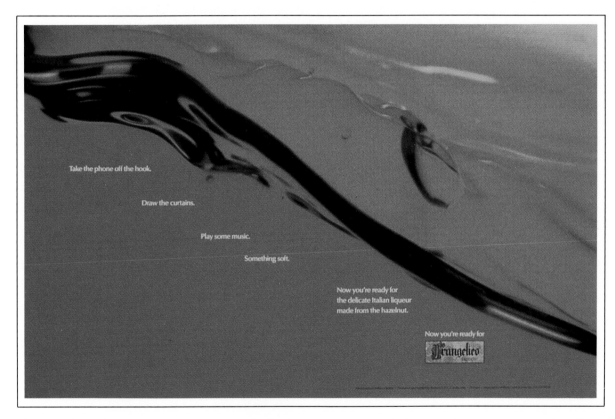

The experiential perspective on consumer behavior argues that consumers engage in many activities in order to experience feelings, fantasy and fun. Both the copy and the visual components of the above ad for Fra Angelica liqueur attempt to elicit emotions, feelings, and fantasy.

A second approach to understanding why consumers act as they do is the decision making perspective. Consumer decision making begins with the recognition of a problem. The CLIO award winning ad for Instapure Water Filter seeks to activate problem recognition.

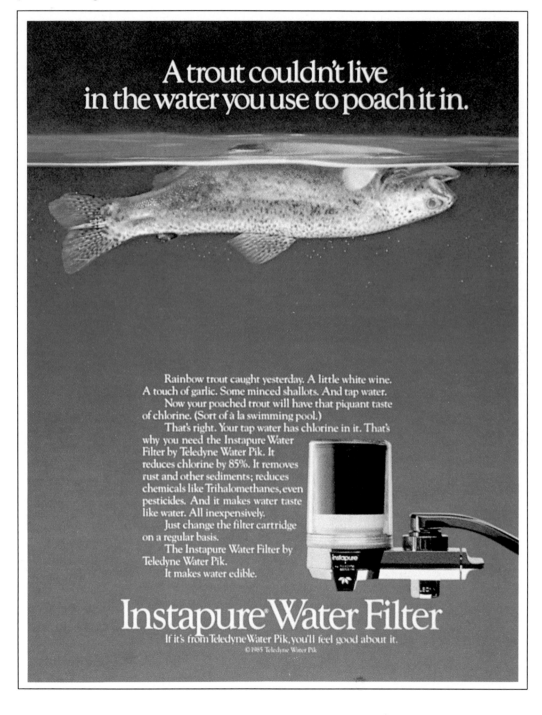

A third approach to the factors that influence consumers is called the behavioral influence perspective. As shown in the photo below, the design of the physical environment strongly influences the patterns in which people move and the places in which they congregate.

Reprinted Courtesy of *Oklahoma State* University Public Information Services

Perception.

Reality.

If your idea of a *Rolling Stone* reader looks like a holdout from the 60's, welcome to the 80's. *Rolling Stone* ranks number one in reaching concentrations of 18-34 readers with household incomes exceeding $25,000. When you buy *Rolling Stone*, you buy an audience that sets the trends and shapes the buying patterns for the most affluent consumers in America. That's the kind of reality you can take to the bank.

Rolling Stone

Part I of the text focuses on the individual consumer. One important point to recognize is that consumers' expectations influence how they interpret information. *Rolling Stone* magazine recognizes this problem, and has taken steps in its advertising to eliminate misconceptions about those who read it, as their ad by the Fallon McElligott Agency suggests.

Reprinted by permission of Yamaha International Corp.

Work on consumer motivation seeks to identify influences on individual behavior. Yamaha employs an achievement motivation theme in the guitar advertisement above.

When we make Prince Spaghetti Sauce, we give you a choice. Because no two people have quite the same taste. PRINCE

In order to influence consumer attitudes, advertisers will frequently use various types of message appeals. Humor is one message type, as illustrated in the ad above for Prince Spaghetti Sauce.

OPPOSITE: A particularly important area relevant to the individual consumer is information processing. Marketers go to great lengths to attract and hold attention—one element of information processing. One method of securing attention is by using contrast effects. In the ad for Bang and Olufsen's television set, produced by Bang and Olufsen [Hong Kong] Ltd., both the pictorial content and the pricing message contrast with consumers' expectations.

THE ART OF TELEVISION

MX2000 20 inch Stereo Television

Even the price is breath-taking
$8,800

Bang & Olufsen

Exclusively available at: G/F, Tak Shing House, 20 Des Voeux Road, Central (5-268800), 120G Ocean Terminal, Tsimshatsui (3-676944), 25 Chatham Road South, Tsimshatsui (3-686217).

Principles of learning apply to a variety of consumer behaviors. One form of learning occurs when people form associations between stimulii. The recent flurry of interest in purchasing modern art, as cited in a recent Wall Street Journal article, has not gone unnoticed by several advertisers. Both the Black and Decker ad, produced by the BBDO agency, and the Martex sheets and towels ad draw on associations between the aesthetic of their products and classic modern art. (Meg Cox, "Boom in Art Market Lifts Prices Sharply, Stirs Fears of a Bust," *Wall Street Journal*, November 24, 1986, 1, 27.)

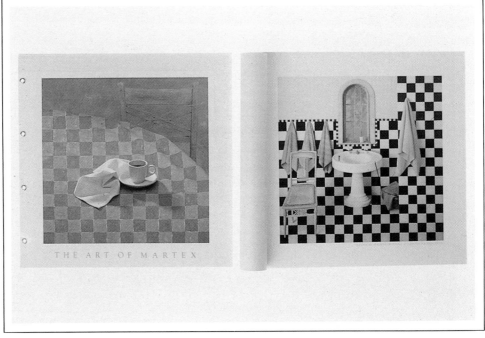

optimum stimulation has been proposed to explain this tendency to avoid boredom. Discussed more fully in Chapter 3, optimum stimulation theory posits that people have a need to maintain an appropriate level of activation.[36] If their activation falls too low or moves too high, they will take steps to change it. The switching of brands may be a method of increasing stimulation by bringing something new into a consumer's life.[37]

Variety-seeking behavior is classified with the experiential perspective because the consumer is buying the product in order to influence feelings. In other words, when consumers are bored, they are feeling suboptimal. By purchasing a new brand they are attempting to make themselves feel better. Thus, the product is bought partially for the experiences it is producing.

Because relatively little research has been done on experiential buying processes, the discussion of the experiential perspective must necessarily be shorter than that for the decision-making perspective. However, a number of sections of the forthcoming chapters are directly relevant to the investigation of experiential buying behavior. In particular, in the next chapter on consumer motivation several sections are pertinent, such as work on maintaining optimum stimulation levels, desires for hedonic experiences, and desires for leisure activities. In Chapter 4 on personality and psychographics, individual differences in the tendency to take a more rational or experiential approach to consumption are discussed. Furthermore, in Chapter 7 on attitudes a discussion of affective reactions has direct relevance to the experiential perspective.

In summary, work on experiential consumption is just beginning to be undertaken in earnest. Readers should not infer, however, that the paucity of research on the topic indicates that it lacks importance. On the contrary, gaining an understanding of the more emotional, nonverbal, experiential side of consumption is perhaps the major challenge of the present generation of researchers in consumer behavior.

THE BEHAVIORAL INFLUENCE PERSPECTIVE

From the decision-making perspective, consumer buying begins with the formation of beliefs about a product or service. In contrast, from the experiential perspective the buying process begins with the consumer developing strong emotional feelings about a product or service. In each case a factor within the consumer precedes the behavioral act of buying. However, evidence is beginning to accumulate that in some cases the dominant cause of a behavior may not come from within the consumer. Rather, outside forces may push the consumer into some action without strong beliefs or feelings preceding the behavior. The process is called behavioral influence when a behavior occurs without being preceded by strong beliefs or feelings and as a result of the effects of outside environmental forces.

A number of topics in Part I of the text on the individual consumer are pertinent to the behavioral influence perspective. For example, the principles of operant and classical conditioning, discussed in the chapter on consumer learning, are important means through which behavior may be influenced. The chapter on attitudes, beliefs, and behaviors is also relevant because it introduces the concept of "hierarchies of effects." Hierarchies of effects describe the buying process in terms of the sequence in which beliefs, feelings, and behavior occur. From the behavioral influence perspective, the sequence begins with a behavior occurring.[38] In contrast, in the experiential perspective the sequence begins with a strong affective reaction. Finally, according to the decision-making perspective, the sequence begins with the formation of beliefs.

The major portion of the text pertinent to the behavioral influence perspective, however, is found in Part II on the consumer environment. Within the environment a variety of forces exist that can directly influence consumer action. Some of the forces include cultural and subcultural pressures, group norms, and personal influence. For example, one person may influence another by subtly pointing out the cultural norm, called the norm of reciprocity, which states that if I do something for you, you should do something for me. In addition, a number of situational factors can influence behavior, such as the effects of time pressures and the type of consumer task (such as buying a gift) in which a consumer expects to engage. Also categorized as part of the situation are aspects of the physical environment, such as arrangements of seating in restaurants and the effects of music, which can influence consumers without their full awareness.

Managerial Implications

For the manager or public policy maker having an understanding of the buying process typically used by consumers to purchase products and services is crucial. One particularly important question concerns identifying which of the three decision processes consumers tend to use when purchasing the product or service offered by the company. The type of decision process used by consumers will have a major impact upon the marketing strategy of the firm.

Strategies in Extended and Routine Decision-Making Situations

As noted earlier in the chapter, consumers are conceptualized as moving through either an extended or routine decision-making process when viewed from the decision-making perspective. The type of decision process used depends in large part upon whether the consumer is in a high-involvement or a low-involvement state. Table 2–4 depicts how the marketing mix of a firm could be influenced if the product or service tends to be purchased via an extended or routine decision process.

Promotion   The type of decision process consumers use when purchasing a product influences both advertising and sales management strategy. In the

Table 2—4   Some Marketing Mix Strategies for Products Bought Via Extended and Limited Decision Processes

I. Extended Decision Processes
   A. Promotion strategy
      1. Sell product via skilled sales force
      2. Utilize strong persuasive arguments in messages
   B. Distribution strategy
      1. Utilize a more limited distribution system
      2. Insure that distributors are trained to provide outstanding service
   C. Pricing strategy
      1. Consider charging premium prices
      2. Avoid use of frequent sales
      3. Consider policy of price bargaining with customers
II. Routine Decision Process
   A. Promotional strategy
      1. Place greater weight on mass advertising to create sales awareness
      2. Use heavy amounts of message repetition
      3. Utilize likable/attractive endorsers
      4. Keep arguments in advertisements simple
   B. Distribution strategy
      1. Utilize an extensive distribution strategy
   C. Pricing
      1. Attempt to be low-cost producer
      2. Consider use of coupons and other price incentives to reach more price-conscious target groups

personal selling area, when the target segment uses an extended decision process, the firm should consider using a sales force to sell the product. Most products purchased under high-involvement circumstances have significant amounts of risk attached to them. In addition, the product or service is likely to be quite complex and/or difficult to understand. In order to reduce the perceived risk on the part of the consumer, a salesperson is often required to explain thoroughly the characteristics of the product or service and to reduce the various types of risk that the consumer may experience. For such products as autos, houses, stereos, televisions, and brokerage services, risk may take such forms as financial, performance, social, or physical risk. (In the next chapter the motivation to avoid various types of risk is discussed.)

The promotional strategy used to sell products purchased via routine decision making is quite different. Rather than relying on personal selling, mass advertising is more frequently employed. Products bought under low-involvement conditions tend to have less risk attached to them. They are frequently low-cost goods that can be distributed extensively and, therefore, require large amounts of advertising to support them.

Some generalizations regarding the advertising of high-involvement products can also be made. Recent research into how consumers react to advertising under high-involvement versus low-involvement conditions has been performed. The research indicates that when consumers are highly involved in a purchase, they attend to information related to the type of arguments presented in the message.[39] This suggests that managers should be highly concerned about content of messages that are delivered to high-involvement audiences. The research also found that under low-involvement conditions consumers tend to use what have been labeled **peripheral cues,** in their decision making. Peripheral cues are those bits of information not directly relevant to a decision, such as the likability or the physical attractiveness of the source of information. Thus, when consumers are in low-involvement circumstances, it may be best to focus on using highly attractive and likeable sources of information. In addition, under low-involvement conditions it is necessary to use high amounts of repetition of advertisements in order for them to have an impact.[40]

Distribution   The distribution of products and services purchased through an extended decision process is likely to be quite limited. Rather than employing a mass-distribution strategy, as found for many low-involvement products, the company may want to consider establishing their own dealers, as is the case with the automotive industry. Alternatively, the product could be sold only through particular department stores, such as the case with high-quality furniture manufacturers, such as Henredon. One important consideration in setting up the distribution system is to insure that it will provide excellent service both before and after the sale to buyers.

Because of the training required of the sales force, dealers, or retailers who sell the product, it is often impossible to distribute a high-involvement product extensively. Furthermore, because the product is bought after an extensive search process, having a limited distribution network is not a major liability, as it would be if the search process were highly limited. In addition, the establishment of a limited distribution network may give the impression of increased exclusivity of the product being sold.

Pricing   The pricing strategy for high- and low-involvement products is likely to be different. In particular, when consumers move through an extended decision process, they are more likely to use some type of a compensatory choice model. Thus, they may not immediately exclude a brand because it costs more than competitors. Furthermore, because consumers are often highly concerned with product quality in extended purchase situations, a higher price may actually lead to the perception that the product is of higher quality. As a result, firms may use a strategy of charging premium prices for such high-involvement products. Managers may also wish to consider avoiding the use of frequent sales, which may lower the perception of product quality. Finally, if skilled sales personnel are used, it may be possible to bargain the price selectively with customers. One currently finds such bargaining in the auto, stereo, housing, and even jewelry industries. Certainly such bargaining occurs in industrial purchasing where many if not most purchases are made via an extended decision process.

In contrast, price may be the single most important consideration when consumers are in low-involvement purchase situations. One research study found that among consumers who indicated that the purchase was unimportant, 52 percent said that price was the determining factor in making the purchase.[41] In many instances, the competition among brands purchased via limited decision processes is fierce, and becoming the low-cost producer may be the key element behind having a successful brand in the marketplace.

Strategies for Experiential Purchases

As noted earlier in the chapter, the types of products purchased tend to be different when purchase behavior is viewed from the experiential perspective. The focus is more likely to be on entertainment, arts, and leisure products, rather than on more functional consumer goods.[42] However, products can also be purchased for experiential purposes. For example, an automobile may be bought for the thrill of having one's head snapped back as the driver attacks the road. The advertisement shown in Figure 2–7 depicts the emphasis on experience in Pontiac's ad for the Grand Am SE.

As the advertisement for the Grand Am reveals, an important advertising objective may be to capture the experience the consumer will receive when using a product. An additional element of the experiential perspective is the recognition that products and services carry subjective symbolic meanings for consumers.[43] In particular, products such as flowers, jewelry, perfume, and after-shave lotion are bought largely for the meanings they provide. Thus, advertisements for the product should emphasize these symbolic elements. Advertisers of jewelry are frequent users of symbolism. For example, in the long-running advertising campaign for diamonds, De Beers uses such verbal statements as "This anniversary ask for her other hand" and "Give her the ultimate token of your love." In each case a diamond is symbolic of a man's love of a woman. The symbolism may also be transmitted via Freudian sexual imagery. An advertisement for jewelry from Avon depicted a blue Crayola crayon sticking through a gem-studded ring. The copy read, "Two Classics. One from Avon." The crayon piercing the ring is classic Freudian symbolism. (Chapter 4 on personality and psychographics discusses Freudian symbolism in more detail.)

Managers should also consider the extent to which their products are purchased on an impulse. Careful attention to where the product is placed in a store may influence the extent to which it is purchased via impulse. For example, many impulse items are placed at checkout counters in order to tempt consumers while they wait in line. The packaging of the product may also be particularly important in luring consumers into making impulse purchases.

Figure 2–7   Pontiac emphasizes the excitement one experiences when driving a Grand Am SE. *(Courtesy of the Pontiac Division of General Motors Corporation.)*

Exceeds the minimum daily adult requirement for driving excitement.

Introducing Grand Am SE. Aerodynamic. Monochromatic.
With a 3.0 liter multi-port fuel injected V6 and a rally tuned suspension that knows what to do with a road. Drive one often for fast relief from boredom.

PONTIAC GRAND AM
WE BUILD EXCITEMENT

**Strategies for
Behavioral
Influence
Purchases**

When a consumer acts because of behavioral influence, no conscious prior intention had been formed to engage in the activity. Furthermore, the consumer does not engage in the activity in order to experience fun, fantasies, or feelings. Rather, the behavior results from environmental forces propelling the consumer into doing something. Thus, from a managerial perspective the goal is to create an environment that makes the desired consumer actions more likely to occur.

The structure of the physical environment is perhaps the area most under managerial control that can be used to induce behaviors from consumers. The arrangement of aisles can funnel consumers to buy desired products. The use of textures, smells, and lighting can also create an atmosphere that elicits desired actions among consumers. For example, in one field study researchers investigated the effects of lighting on where people sat in a restaurant. They found that diners tended to sit in the darker areas facing the light. Other researchers have found that lighting affects how close people sit to each other. If the goal is have people sit close together, low lighting levels should be maintained.[44] Additional ways that the physical environment may influence consumers are discussed in Chapter 10 on situational influences.

The area of behavioral modification is also closely linked to the behavioral influence perspective. In Chapter 6 consumer learning processes are discussed, and the principles of classical and operant conditioning are presented. Managers may be able to use these principles to elicit desired behaviors from consumers. For example, in casinos the slot machines are a classic example of the effects of variable reinforcement schedules. A variable reinforcement schedule occurs when a reinforcement (a type of reward) occurs intermittently after a particular behavior. The behavior involved with slot machines consists of placing money in the machine and then pulling the handle. Players are intermittently reinforced for the behavior. That is, the players win infrequently, resulting in the reinforcement of money spilling from the machine. One of the characteristics of intermittent reinforcement is that the behavior is resistent to extinction (elimination). Thus, one can observe slot-machine players placing coins in the machines and pulling the handles for hours at a time with little or no reward experienced—a highly profitable outcome for casino owners.

SUMMARY

Three divergent perspectives can be used to examine the consumer buying process. The dominant approach in consumer behavior has been the decision-making perspective. From this perspective consumers are viewed as decision makers who make rational decisions regarding the products and services they buy. From within the decision-making perspective two different buying processes have been identified. First, when consumers are highly involved in the purchase, they will tend to engage in a lengthy decision-making process. In such high-involvement purchases consumers are described as moving through each of the five steps of the decision process in a sequential manner. The five steps of the decision process are: need recognition, information search, evaluation of alternatives, choice, and postpurchase evaluation.

In contrast to high-involvement situations, when consumers perceive little personal importance in the purchase, they will move through a limited decision process. The search stage will be minimized. In addition, the alternative evaluation stage may be largely skipped. Finally, in limited decision making the choice process will be much simpler than in high-involvement conditions.

Because of its importance in influencing the extent of consumer decision making, the concept of involvement has become quite important in consumer behavior. As a general rule, one can state that as the level of consumer involvement increases, the length and intensity of the consumer decision process increase. Consumer involvement is influenced by the type of product purchased, by the characteristics of the consumer, by the consumer situation, and by the nature of the communications the consumer receives. Involvement may be defined as the level of perceived personal importance and/or interest evoked by a product or service in a given situation.

The stages of problem recognition and search were particularly emphasized in the chapter because they are not covered elsewhere in the text. Problem recognition occurs when a sufficiently large discrepancy develops between an actual and a desired state of being. A variety of factors can raise and lower the level of both the desired and actual state.

The consumer search process consists of those steps taken to acquire information about the products and services that may eliminate the problem identified in the first decision stage. Two types of search have been identified. Internal search consists of the consumer searching through long-term memory for information on brands that may eliminate the problem. External search involves the consumer in seeking outside sources of information on what products may eliminate the problem.

From the experiential perspective consumers are viewed as searching for products and services that elicit sensations, feelings, images, emotions, and fun. Some industries are based around creating experiences for people. In particular the leisure industry exists in large part to provide experiences to people. The phenomenon of impulse buying also seems to result in large part from consumers attempting to gain new and different experiences.

The third approach to consumer buying is labeled the behavioral influence perspective. From within this perspective certain types of consumer behaviors are viewed as resulting from the effects of environmental forces rather than from the beliefs or feelings of consumers. In effect, behavior is induced by environmental pressures. Many of the effects of cultures, small groups, other people, and situations can be viewed as resulting from behavioral influence.

Key Terms

Decision process
Consumer involvement
High-involvement deci-
  sion making
Low-involvement deci-
  sion making
Problem recognition
Actual state of being
Desired state of being
Information search
Internal search
External search
Evoked set
Inert set
Inept set
Awareness set

Unawareness set
Alternative evaluation
Belief
Attributes
Object-attribute belief
Attitude
Intention
Choice
Compensatory models
Noncompensatory
  models
Conjunctive model
Postpurchase phase
Impulse buying
Peripheral cues
Variety-seeking behavior

Review Questions

1. Identify the three perspectives on consumer buying presented in the chapter. How do these perspectives differ from each other in their approach
   to understanding the factors that influence consumer buying?
2. From the decision-making perspective consumers are viewed as engaging in one of two types of
   decision making. Identify these two types of decision making and the factors that influence which
   type consumers use.
3. What are the stages of decision making through
   which consumers tend to move according to the
   decision-making perspective? How do these stages
   differ depending upon whether a consumer is engaged in high- or low-involvement decision making?
4. Define the concept of consumer purchase involvement. What are the factors that influence
   consumer purchase involvement?
5. Discuss the concept of consumer problem recognition. What are the factors that tend to influence the consumer's actual state and the consumer's desired state?
6. When a consumer engages in internal search, what
   are the various categories of brands that he or she
   might retrieve from long-term memory?
7. Discuss the factors that tend to cause consumers
   to engage in extensive problem solving and high
   amounts of external search.

8. From the perspective of an economist, what are
   the factors that influence the amount of external
   search in which a consumer will engage?
9. One study investigated the search process for automobiles. In their order of importance, what were
   the five most important factors that influenced the
   amount of search for automobiles?
10. What occurs during the alternative-evaluation
    process? How does involvement influence the type
    of hierarchy of effects through which a consumer
    may move?
11. What are the two general types of decision rules
    consumers may use when making choices?
12. What are the major components of the postpur-
    chase decision phase?
13. Contrast the experiential perspective with the de-
    cision-making view of consumer buying.
14. Contrast the behavioral influence perspective with
    the decision-making view of consumer buying.

Discussion Questions

1. Identify a consumer purchase you have made in
   which you engaged in an extensive decision process. What were the steps you went through in
   selecting the brand to purchase? To what extent
   did this series of steps match the high-involvement decision process discussed in the chapter?
2. Identify a consumer purchase you have made that
   was based largely upon an experiential buying
   process. What were the steps you went through
   in selecting the product or service in this case?
   What were the types of feelings and experiences
   you were seeking from the purchase?
3. Attempt to identify a recent purchase or activity
   that resulted largely from behavioral influence. To
   what extent did you have any feelings about the
   action? To what extent did you engage in any extensive amounts of search for the product or service purchased? What environmental factor was
   most responsible for the purchase or action?
4. Try to identify a consumer purchase or action in
   which more than one of the purchase processes
   was involved. Which of the processes were operating simultaneously? Which of the processes
   tended to dominate the decision?
5. List as many as possible of the consumer purchases of over five dollars that you have made over
   the past several weeks. Categorize these as to

whether they best fit into the high-involvement decision perspective, the low-involvement decision perspective, the experiential perspective, or the behavioral influence perspective. From which category did most of your purchases come?

6. To what extent do consumers characteristically use one of the purchase approaches more than others? To what extent do consumers show individual differences in their tendency to use one of the perspectives? For example, do some consumers tend to use a decision-making approach, whereas others tend to use an experiential approach in making their purchases?

7. How might advertising differ for products that are typically purchased under high-involvement conditions as opposed to products bought under low-involvement conditions?

8. Consider the product category of toothpaste. Identify your awareness set, evoked set, inert set, and inept set for the various brands of toothpaste which you can recall. What could a company do to move their toothpaste from the inert set to the evoked set?

9. *Why* would a company that markets razor blades be interested in encouraging consumers to engage in problem recognition? *How* might a company that markets razor blades encourage consumers to engage in problem recognition?

10. Under what circumstances would a company want consumers to engage in large amounts of search behavior? Under what circumstances would a company want consumers to minimize their search behavior?

References

1. Ronald E. Milliman, "Using Background Music to Affect the Behavior of Supermarket Shoppers," *Journal of Marketing*, 46, Summer 1982, 86–91.

2. For a lengthy description of the decision-making approach see James F. Engel and Roger D. Blackwell, *Consumer Behavior*, 4th ed., Chicago, Ill.: The Dryden Press, 1982.

3. For an excellent discussion of the various definitions of involvement see John H. Antil, "Conceptualization and Operationalization of Involvement," in *Advances in Consumer Research, XI*, Thomas C. Kinnear (ed.), Ann Arbor, MI: Association for Consumer Research, 1984, 203–209.

4. Antil, "Conceptualization and Operationalization."

For another view of involvement which emphasizes an information-processing approach see Anthony C. Greenwald and Clark Leavitt, "Audience Involvement in Advertising; Four Levels," *Journal of Consumer Research*, 11, June 1984, 581–592.

5. Antil, "Conceptualization and Operationalization."

6. Ibid.

7. Richard E. Petty, John T. Cacioppo, and David Schumann, "Central and Peripheral Routes to Advertising Effectiveness: The Moderating Role of Involvement," *Journal of Consumer Research*, 10, September 1983, 135–146.

8. Herbert Krugman, "The Impact of Television in Advertising: Learning Without Involvement," *Public Opinion Quarterly*, 30, 583–596.

9. Engel and Blackwell, *Consumer Behavior*.

10. James R. Bettman, *An Information Processing Theory of Consumer Choice*, Reading, Mass.: Addison-Wesley Publishing Co., Inc., 1979.

11. For information on the categories of brands that consumers may retrieve from long-term memory see F. May and R. Homans, "Evoked Set Size and the Level of Information Processing in Product Comprehension and Choice Criteria," in *Advances in Consumer Research, IV*, W. D. Perreault (ed.), Chicago, Ill.: 1977, 172–175.

12. Arieh Goldman and J. K. Johansson, "Determinants of Search for Lower Prices: An Empirical Assessment of the Economics of Information Theory," *Journal of Consumer Research*, 5, December 1978, 176–186.

13. Konrad Dedler, I. Gottschalk and K. G. Grunert, "Perceived Risk as a Hint for Better Information and Better Products: Some New Applications of an Old Concept," in *Advances in Consumer Research, VIII*, Kent Monroe (ed.), Ann Arbor, MI: Association for Consumer Research, 1981, 391–397.

14. R. Kelly, "The Search Component of the Consumer Decision-Making Process—A Theoretic Examination," in *Marketing and the New Sciences of Planning*, C. King (ed.), Chicago, Ill.: American Marketing Association, 1968, 273.

15. W. B. Locander and P. W. Hermann, "The Effect of Self-Confidence and Anxiety on Information Seeking in Consumer Risk Reduction," *Journal of Marketing Research*, 16, May 1979, 268–274.

16. See for example J. Swan, "Experimental Analysis of Predecision Information Seeking," *Journal of Marketing Research*, 6, May 1969, 192–197.

17. J. R. Bettman and C. W. Park, "Effects of Prior

Knowledge and Experience and Phase of the Choice Process on Consumer Decision Processes: A Protocol Analysis," *Journal of Consumer Research, 7,* December 1980, 234–248.

18. N. Capon and M. Burke, "Individual, Product Class, and Task-Related Factors in Consumer Information Processing," *Journal of Consumer Research, 7,* December 1980, 314–326.

19. J. Newman and R. Staelin, "Prepurchase Information Seeking for New Cars and Major Household Appliances," *Journal of Marketing Research, 9,* August 1972, 249–257.

20. D. R. Lehmann and W. L. Moore, "Validity of Information Display Boards: An Assessment Using Longitudinal Data," *Journal of Marketing Research, 17,* November 1980, 450–459.

21. G. S. Cort and L. V. Dominquez, "Cross Shopping and Retail Growth," *Journal of Marketing Research, 14,* May 1977, 187–192.

22. W. Dommermuth, "The Shopping Matrix and Marketing Strategy," *Journal of Marketing Research, 2,* May 1965, 128–132.

23. J. Udell, "Prepurchase Behavior of Buyers of Small Appliances," *Journal of Marketing, 30,* October 1966, 50–52.

24. Newman and Staelin, "Prepurchase Information Seeking."

25. J. Newman and B. Lockeman, "Measuring Prepurchase Information Seeking," *Journal of Consumer Research, 2,* December 1975, 216–222.

26. G. N. Punj and R. Staelin, "A Model of Consumer Information Search Behavior for New Automobiles," *Journal of Consumer Research, 9,* March 1983, 366–380.

27. D. Furse, G. Punj, and D. Steward, "A Typology of Individual Search Strategies Among Purchasers of New Automobiles," *Journal of Consumer Research, 10,* March 1984, 417–431.

28. L. L. Thurstone, "Comment," *American Journal of Sociology, 52,* 1946, 39–40.

29. M. Ray, "Marketing Communications and the Hierarchy of Effects," in *New Models for Mass Communications Research,* M. P. Clarke (ed.), Beverly Hills, Calif.: Sage Publications, 1973.

30. E. J. Johnson and J. E. Russo, "Product Familiarity and Learning New Information," *Journal of Consumer Research, 11,* June 1984, 542–550.

31. M. P. Venkatraman and D. J. MacInnis, "The Epistemic and Sensory Exploratory Behaviors of Hedonic and Cognitive Consumers," in *Advances in Consumer Research, XII,* Elizabeth Hirschman and Morris Holbrook (eds.), Ann Arbor, MI: Association for Consumer Research, 1985.

32. Holbrook and Hirschman, "Experiential Aspects of Consumption."

33. Engel and Blackwell, *Consumer Behavior.*

34. "Industrial Retail Selling Strategies Designed to Induce Impulse Sales," *Beverage Industry,* June 3, 1977, 6ff.

35. M. Venkatesan, "Cognitive Consistency and Novelty Seeking," in *Consumer Behavior: Theoretical Sources,* Scott Ward and Thomas Robertson (eds.), Englewood Cliffs, N.J.: Prentice-Hall, Inc., 1973, 354–384.

36. P. S. Raju, "Optimum Stimulation Level: Its Relationship to Personality, Demographics, and Exploratory Behavior," *Journal of Consumer Research, 7,* December 1980, 272–282.

37. For a review of variety seeking see L. McAlister and E. Pessemier, "Variety Seeking Behavior: An Interdisciplinary Review," *Journal of Consumer Research, 9,* December 1982, 311–322.

38. Ray, "Marketing Communications and the Hierarchy of Effects."

39. Petty, Cacioppo and Schumann, "Central and Peripheral Routes."

40. Ibid.

41. J. L. Lastovicka, "The Low Involvement Point-of-Purchase: A Case Study of Margarine Buyers," Paper presented at the first Consumer Involvement Conference, New York University, June 1982.

42. Holbrook and Hirschman, "The Experiential Aspects of Consumption."

43. S. J. Levy, "Symbols for Sale," *Harvard Business Review, 37,* July–August 1959, 117–124.

44. J. Meer, "The Light Touch," *Psychology Today,* September 1985, 60–67.

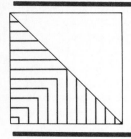

3

Consumer Motivation

Gambling and Consumer Motivation

In the 1980s the tourist attraction most frequently visited in the United States was the casinos of Atlantic City, New Jersey. Twenty-three million people visited the gambling parlors and lost $2 billion doing so. Gambling is a consumer behavior as much as buying toothpaste or automobiles. Two factors may account for the intoxicating effects of gambling—excitement and the incentive value of money.(a)

Gambling can make consumers aroused, and maintaining an optimum level of activation is a basic motivation. The feelings obtained from gambling can help to raise an individual's activation to a more comfortable level. For example, senior citizens flock to the Atlantic City casinos. One middle-aged woman, who takes her eighty-year-old mother to the casinos, stated, "Atlantic City is really a break for poor people. . . . It's something to look forward to instead of sitting home and waiting to die."(b)

Clearly, the possibility of winning big also attracts gamblers. Money is a potent incentive object that can motivate consumers to engage in quite unusual actions. In Dallas, Texas, a reporter as a joke had a gorilla, named Kanda, select winners of National Football League games. The ape immediately achieved success by compiling a 33–22–1 record. Soon the zoo was besieged with requests for interviews with the animal and callers asking, "Who's the ape got this week?" When the turmoil became too intense, the ape's prognostications were called off.(c)

Portions based on (a) Jeremy Geigelson, "How nine Casinos Go for the Jackpot," *Advertising Age,* October 17, 1983, M4–M8; (b) Ronald Alsop "Atlantic City Casinos Lure More Gamblers Away from Las Vegas," *The Wall Street Journal,* October 26, 1983, 1; and (c) "Ape's Career Days Are Soon Over," *The Daily O'Collegian,* December 2, 1983, 8.

INTRODUCTION

Consumers must have been highly motivated to have sought advice from a prognosticating ape. Just as bizarre is the sight of gamblers standing for hours pulling the levers of slot machines. In one month Resort's International casino counted 132,228,184 slot-machine pulls. A major medical problem at casinos is tendonitis of the shoulders of slot players.[1] These consumer behaviors illustrate two basic aspects of motivation that are discussed in the chapter. First, the idea that incentive objects, such as money or cars, can activate and direct consumers to action is a basic motivational concept. Second, consumers are motivated to seek fun and excitement. People take action to avoid being bored, and gambling is one source of arousal.

What Is Motivation?

Within a consumer behavior context, **motivation** refers to an activated state within a person that leads to goal-directed behavior.[2] Such goal-directed behavior could involve buying a product or service, making a complaint, or engaging in extensive search for information. The state within the person that leads to motivated behavior usually results from some unfulfilled need. **Needs** result from a discrepancy between an actual and a desired state of being. Note that the definition of a need is identical to that of the problem recognition stage of the decision process. In effect, problem recognition is the creation of a consumer need state.

Various generalizations have been made about the operation of needs. Thus, needs can be either innate or learned. They are never fully satisfied. If one need is fulfilled, another will spring up to take its place. If two needs are in conflict, people will tend to act to fulfill the more basic (i.e., the more physiologically based) need first.

Associated with needs are two additional concepts—drives and incentives. A **drive** is the physiological arousal that occurs when a need is felt. The arousal activates the person and can be measured through such means as monitoring the heart rate, blood pressure, and pupil size of consumers. Consumer **incentives** are the products, services, and people that are perceived as satisfying needs. The desire to obtain these incentives is what leads to the goal-directed behavior (i.e., motivated behavior). Interestingly, the mere presence of an incentive can cause a consumer's drive level to increase. Thus, for most people who eat red meat, the sight of a succulent piece of tender steak will cause a certain amount of arousal. Thus, incentives have two functions. They serve to activate or arouse the consumer to action. In addition, they direct behavior either towards or away from themselves.

As the last sentence implies, consumer incentives are not always positive; they can be negative and act to propel people away from them. An example of a negative consumer incentive might be dirt in a grocery store or the fear of being mugged. In each case an incentive object motivates the consumer to move away from it. People move towards positive incentives and away from negative incentives. The goal of the marketer is to develop products, services,

Figure 3–1 A simple model of motivation.

retail stores, packaging, advertising, and so forth that capitalize on these tendencies.

Figure 3–1 presents a simple model of motivation that captures the ideas discussed thus far. The figure depicts the sequence in which needs first create a motivated drive state. The drive state then causes goal-directed action to obtain incentive objects to satisfy the need. The incentive objects can be products, services, or even people. In addition, the presence of the incentive objects can itself create drive states.

Some General Theories of Motivation	Most textbook discussions of motivation focus on describing certain well-known broad theories, such as the Maslow's hierarchy of needs and Murray's list of social needs. (Figure 3–2 presents a brief review of the needs identified by Maslow and by Murray.) Indeed, by the time students take a consumer behavior course, they have usually had the Maslow hierarchy presented in four other classes. Very little research, however, has been performed on either of these theories, and the research that has been performed has not been supportive of them.[3] In contrast is one broad theory of motivation that has received substantial research attention—McClelland's theory of learned needs.

McClelland's Theory of Learned Needs David McClelland developed an important stream of research around the idea that three basic learned needs motivate people—the needs for achievement, affiliation, and power. Those with high **achievement motivation** seek to get ahead, to strive for success, and to take responsibility for solving problems. In one study McClelland found that 83 percent of students with a high need for achievement entered occupations noted for the ability to take risks, make decisions, and achieve great success, such as business management.[4]

McClelland seemed to view the **need for affiliation** in a manner similar to Maslow's belongingness need. Such a need motivates people to make friends, to become members of groups, and to associate with others. Those with a high need for affiliation tend to place the desire to be with others ahead of the need to succeed. For example, in one study subjects in an experiment were given the opportunity to choose a partner to assist them on a task. Those with a high need for achievement chose a partner based upon that person's demonstrated competence. In contrast, those with a high need for affiliation were more likely to choose their friends. Apparently, those with a high need for affiliation chose their partner more out of a desire to enjoy the experience than to succeed in the task.[5]

Figure 3—2   Needs identified by Maslow and Murray. (*Sources:* A. H. Maslow, *Motivation and Personality* (2nd ed.), New York: Harper & Row, 1970; and A. H. Murray, *Explorations in Personality*, New York, Oxford, 1938.)

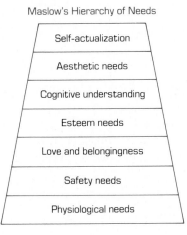

Maslow's Hierarchy of Needs

| Self-actualization |
| Aesthetic needs |
| Cognitive understanding |
| Esteem needs |
| Love and belongingness |
| Safety needs |
| Physiological needs |

Examples of Murray's Social Needs

Need	Definition
Abasement	Desire to accept blame, criticism, inferiority.
Aggression	Desire to use force, obtain revenge, injure.
Autonomy	Desire to be free, independent; to resist coercion, defy convention.
Deference	To admire and support superiors, praise, conform.
Exhibition	To excite, fascinate, shock, intrigue, amuse.
Nurturance	To support, comfort, help, give sympathy to a helpless being.
Order	To achieve cleanliness, order, tidiness.
Play	Desire to have fun, relax, participate in games and sports.
Sentience	Desire to obtain pleasurable feelings through the senses.
Sex	Desire to have erotic relationships, to have sexual intercourse.
Succorance	Desire to be nursed, supported, protected, consoled.

The **need for power** refers to the desire to obtain and exercise control over others. The goal is to influence, direct, and possibly dominate other people. The need for power can take two directions, according to McClelland. It can be positive and result in persuasive and inspirational power. It can also be negative and result in the desire to dominate and obtain submission from others.

Some research has investigated the relationship between McClelland's ideas and consumer behavior. For example, one study found that those with a high need for achievement tended to buy more outdoor leisure products, such as skis and boating equipment, than those with low need for achievement.[6] A clear prediction from McClelland's work is that products can be advertised with motivational themes derived from the three basic consumer motivations

Figure 3–3   Hilton seeks to link its image with an achievement motivation theme. *(Courtesy of Hilton Hotels, Inc.)*

Figure 3–4   Some midrange theories of motivation.

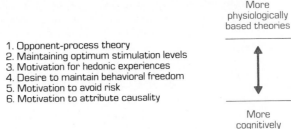

1. Opponent-process theory
2. Maintaining optimum stimulation levels
3. Motivation for hedonic experiences
4. Desire to maintain behavioral freedom
5. Motivation to avoid risk
6. Motivation to attribute causality

that he identified. The idea would be to analyze the characteristics of the heavy users of the product to determine their basic motivational structure. Advertising that places the product in such a context can then be developed.

An example of an advertisement that uses an achievement motivation theme is found in Figure 3–3, an ad placed in national magazines by Hilton. The purpose of the ad was to link Hilton to achievement by using the image of yacht racing and the effort required to be a winner in the competitive sport. The advertisement effectively portrays Hilton as a company that will work hard to cater successfully to the businessperson.

The trend over the past twenty years has been to move away from developing broad theories of motivation to creating more narrow "midrange" theories. Figure 3–4 lists the midrange theories of motivation discussed in this chapter. Their order of description moves from the more physiologically based theories (such as opponent process theory) to the more cognitively oriented (such as attribution theory). Each of the midrange theories of motivation discussed in the chapter has been supported through research, and one can be fairly confident of their validity.

MIDRANGE THEORIES OF MOTIVATION

The midrange theories discussed in this section have relatively narrow objectives. Each seeks to describe a particular type of motivational need and the implications of that need. Thus, opponent-process theory seeks to explain such phenomena as why people may feel exhilarated after a parachute jump or bad after a major success. Optimum stimulation level theory attempts to explain why some people seek thrills while others actively avoid them. The work in perceived risk attempts to explain the process through which people handle financial, physical, and other types of risk in their lives. Finally, attribution theory operates at a more cognitive level and seeks to explain how people determine the causes of their own and others' actions. In each case the goal is *not* to explain all of human motivation, but only a portion of it.

Opponent-Process Theory

A researcher made an interesting observation about the emotional reactions of parachutists. During their first free-fall, before the parachute opens, they may experience terror. They yell, their eyes bulge, their bodies go stiff, and they breathe irregularly. Upon landing safely, they at first walk around stunned, with stony-faced expressions. Then they begin smiling, talking, gesticulating, and showing every indication of being elated.

Why would someone who was in terror suddenly become elated? The answer seems to lie in a theory of motivation called the **opponent-process theory** of acquired motivation.[7] The basic idea behind opponent-process theory is that when a person receives a stimulus that elicits an immediate positive or negative emotional reaction, two things occur. First, the immediate positive or negative emotional reaction is felt. Next, a second emotional reaction occurs, which has a feeling opposite to that initially experienced. The combination of the two emotional reactions results in the overall feeling experienced by the consumer. Because the second emotional reaction is delayed, the overall experience consists of the consumer first experiencing the initial positive or negative feeling. After some time period, however, this feeling gradually declines, and the opposite feeling begins to be felt. Thus, the parachutists first felt extreme fear, but after landing the fear turned to its opposite emotion—elation. Figure 3–5 diagrams these relationships.

Figure 3–5 A diagram of the opponent-process theory.

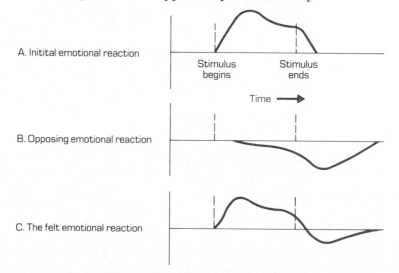

If the stimulus is positive, the initial emotional reaction will be positive. However, as shown in diagram B, the opposing negative emotional reaction begins to occur. The net result is shown in diagram C. Here the person is shown to feel positive initially. However, that feeling begins to decrease to the point at which a negative emotional state may occur. Finally, the person returns to the initial emotional state.

The idea that pleasure and pain often go together has been noted for many centuries. One example is a quote from Plato found in the work *Phaedo*.

> How strange would appear to be this thing that men call pleasure! And how curiously it is related to what is thought to be its opposite, pain! The two will never be found *together* in a man, and yet if you seek the one and obtain it, you are almost bound always to get the other as well, just as though they were both attached to one the same head. . . . Wherever the one is found, the other follows up behind.

Although opponent-process theory is quite simple, it has broad explanatory power. It can be used to account for a variety of consumer behaviors, such as drug addiction, cigarette smoking, jogging and marathoning, sauna bathing, and video game playing. For example, why would seemingly sane individuals go through the pain of running a marathon? The answer may be that through the operation of opponent processes, the pain that accompanies the endurance run is followed by physiological pleasure. When combined with the positive reinforcement from friends and acquaintances, the overall experience of marathoning may be viewed extremely positively.

Another concept closely related to opponent-process theory is that of **priming.** Priming occurs when a small amount of exposure to a stimulus (perhaps food, playing a video game, or watching television) leads to an increased drive to be in the presence of the stimulus. An example is the taste cravings consumers may get. After eating one potato chip, people find it extremely hard to stop and not consume more. The taste of the first potato chip activates the consumer such that the drive to consume additional chips is greater than the drive prior to eating the first one. The effects of priming may influence consumers in their consumption of drugs (e.g., cocaine and alcohol) and food (e.g., candies and coffee). Recently, attention has begun to be focused upon "binge" buying. Some consumers periodically go on buying binges in which they overspend markedly and buy articles of clothing they do not need. Other factors probably also account for this "deviant" consumer behavior, but the effects of priming particularly may result in consumers not being able to stop buying once they start.

A study was conducted to investigate the effects of priming on video game playing.[8] In the study college students rated their desire to play the video game Pac-Man at varying points in time. One group made their ratings after playing the game for ten minutes. Another group made their ratings after playing the game for three minutes. The results showed that the interest ratings made after playing the game for only three minutes were significantly higher than those made after playing for ten minutes. Furthermore, in comparison to ratings made prior to starting the game, ratings made after playing for three minutes were significantly higher. People wanted to play the game even more after playing for three minutes than they did before beginning to play the game. Figure 3–6 reveals the ratings of interest in the game after various time intervals for the two groups of subjects.

Priming may be understood from an opponent-process theory perspec-

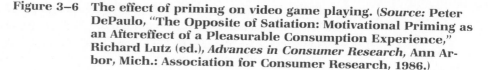

Figure 3–6   **The effect of priming on video game playing. (*Source:* Peter DePaulo, "The Opposite of Satiation: Motivational Priming as an Aftereffect of a Pleasurable Consumption Experience," Richard Lutz (ed.), *Advances in Consumer Research*, Ann Arbor, Mich.: Association for Consumer Research, 1986.)**

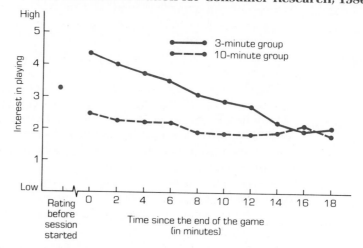

The three-minute group played Pac-Man for three minutes prior to giving their interest level in resuming playing. The ten-minute group played the game for ten minutes. The rating at the zero point gives their interest in resuming the game immediately after completing playing Pac-Man for either three minutes or ten minutes. Ratings of interest were then taken every two minutes.

tive. When the reinforcing stimulus is just beginning to be consumed, the opposite motivation has not had a chance to start building up. The experience then may be intensely pleasurable, resulting in a strong drive to continue.

Marketers intuitively use principles of priming on a regular basis. For example, providing samples in a supermarket is a classic example of priming. In one study it was found that providing free samples of doughnuts to grocery store shoppers resulted in consumers spending more than they had intended.[9] Interestingly, the effect was greater for shoppers classified as obese than for shoppers of more average weight. Two possible explanations may exist for the greater effects of priming on obese people. First, they may have been more sensitive to the taste of the food. Alternatively, the doughnut sample may have been perceived as smaller in size by the obese shoppers and not resulted in the formation of the opposite motivation—satiation.

Maintaining Optimum Stimulation Levels

The opponent-process theory of motivation is based upon a particular view of how the nervous system of people is organized. Thus, the theory is physiologically based. Another approach to motivation that is rooted in human physiology is the view that focuses on people's desire to maintain optimum levels of stimulation.

A growing body of research evidence indicates that people have a strong motivation to maintain an optimum level of stimulation. An **optimum stimulation level** is a person's preferred amount of physiological activation or arousal. Activation may vary from very low levels (a coma) to very high levels (severe panic). Individuals are motivated to maintain an optimum level of stimulation and will take action to correct the level when it becomes too high or too low.

Factors internal and external to the person may influence his or her level of stimulation at any given point in time. Internal factors include the individual's age, learning history, and personality characteristics. For example, people who prefer higher levels of stimulation score high on a scale that measures sensation seeking.[10] In order to maintain the high levels of stimulation required, sensation seekers are more apt to engage in such activities as parachute jumping, mountain climbing, and gambling. External factors influencing the stimulation level are those that affect the uncertainty and risk of the environment. Thus, if a person seeks a goal and some doubt exists as to whether the goal will be reached, his or her level of activation will tend to rise. People will attempt to manage their actions and the environment in order to maintain an optimum stimulation level. In other words, if their level of arousal is too high, they will take steps to lower it. Conversely, if their activation is too low, they will attempt to arrange their behavior to raise their stimulation level.

The motive of people to maintain an optimum stimulation level has implications for marketers, because a host of products and services exist that act to arouse or depress a person's activation level.[11] For example, various types of drugs exist to lower arousal levels (i.e., sleep aids) and to raise arousal levels (i.e., stimulants such as caffeine and amphetamines). A variety of leisure activities strongly influence levels of arousal, such as parachute jumping, white water rafting, and hunting. Indeed, the desire of consumers to attend sporting events is likely to be influenced in part by the need for excitement. Similarly, some rides at amusement parks are built to scare the customers. To determine your arousal-seeking tendencies, complete the scale found in Table 3–1.

The desire of people to maintain an optimum level of stimulation may account for some cases of spontaneous brand switching. Consumers will periodically change brands for no apparent reason. Thus, a housewife may use Tide detergent consistently for a long period of time and then suddenly buy another brand. When asked why she switched brands, she might say something like, "I just wanted a change." The likely cause of such spontaneous brand switching is that the consumer was bored and wanted to vary her everyday life in order to temporarily change her activation level. One study found that people who have a need for higher activation levels tend to engage in greater amounts of brand switching, to reveal greater innovativeness in product purchases, and to be greater risk takers.[12]

Table 3–1   A Scale to Measure Arousal-Seeking Tendencies

Directions: Answer each of the questions with a "yes" or a "no." The greater the number of "yes" answers you have, the more you tend to seek to be aroused.

1. I frequently change the pictures on my walls.
2. I enjoy seeing people in strange clothing.
3. I continually seek new ideas and experiences.
4. I get bored when I am always around the same people and places.
5. I enjoy doing foolhardy things just for the fun of it.
6. People view me as an unpredictable person.
7. I like surprises.
8. I enjoy having lots of activity going on around me.
9. I like a job that offers change, variety, and travel even if it involves some danger.
10. I enjoy dangerous sports like mountain climbing, airplane flying, and skydiving.
11. I feel restive when I am safe and secure.
12. I would like to try the group-therapy techniques involving strange body sensations.

SOURCE: Adapted from a scale developed by Albert Mehrabian and James Russell, *An Approach to Environmental Psychology*, Cambridge, Mass.: MIT Press, 1974.

The Motivation for Hedonic Experiences

Closely related to the need to maintain an optimum stimulation level are desires for hedonic experiences. For consumer behaviorists, **hedonic experiences** refer to the needs of consumers to use products and services to create fantasies, to gain feelings through the senses, and to obtain emotional arousal.[13]

The systematic study of hedonic consumption dates only from the late 1970s; however, it has roots in other areas of study. One is the motivation research that began in the 1950s. Motivation researchers tended to take a Freudian perspective in their interpretation of consumer behavior. They focused on the emotional reasons for people's consumption patterns and emphasized how products could be used to arouse and fulfill fantasies. (More will be said about Freudian ideas in Chapter 4 on personality.) In addition, the hedonic consumption approach borrowed concepts from sociologists on the symbolic nature of products. That is, products are not simply objective entities but also symbolize much broader concepts to consumers. Thus, diamonds are not merely carbon crystals but symbols of love and permanence.

Desires to Experience Emotion   The term *hedonism* usually refers to gaining pleasure through the senses. However, as used in the present context, the feelings consumers seek to gain may not be uniformly pleasurable. Consumers may seek to experience a variety of emotions, such as love, hate, fear, grief, anger, and disgust. At first thought it seems odd that someone would seek out negative experiences such as fear. As noted earlier, however, amusement parks are built in part to create fear. In particular, roller coasters exist to fan the flames of fear. Even their names are designed to instill fright, such as "Screamer" and "The Beast." Horror movies are created to frighten and disgust people. People go to movies and plays in part to experience secondhand the emotions of love, hate, and anger.

One particularly important point made by hedonic consumption theorists is that in some instances emotional desires dominate utilitarian motives in choosing products.[14] From a utilitarian perspective, why would a sane man give a woman a dozen roses? In 1986 the gesture would have cost forty dollars or so for something that would perish within a couple of days. Beyond their beauty, roses as a gift only make sense in terms of their symbolic value and the emotions created by such symbolism. (See Highlight 3–1.)

The types of products and services that hedonic consumption researchers investigate are different from those traditionally analyzed. Most consumer research has focused on packaged goods (e.g., toothpaste, beer, cigarettes, laundry detergent). Hedonic consumer research investigates such "products" as movies, rock concerts, the theater, dance, pornography, and sporting events. These products are intrinsically more emotionally involving than toothpaste or toilet paper. The choice of a hedonically relevant product tends to be based on its symbolic value and on the emotion it is most likely to elicit in the consumer. For example, a purely economic account of consumer behavior has a difficult task in explaining why some people buy an exotic sports car, such as a Porsche 928 or Ferrari. After all, the cost of car, along with its maintainance, insurance, and speeding tickets, makes the purchase highly

---

HIGHLIGHT 3–1

In the Mid-1980s Advertisers Turn to Emotional Themes

Beginning in 1979 with AT&T's "Reach Out and Touch Someone" campaign, advertisers began to stress the emotional benefits of a product or service rather than its functional benefits. A classic example of "emotional hard sell" was the campaign developed by Minute Maid orange juice. In one ad a young mother cuddles a newborn while her five-year-old son asks, "Who do you like better?" The mother responds, "I love you both." An off-camera announcer then intones, "He's got a new baby brother. Now he has to share your attention. You try to reassure him . . . you give him lots of love." The ad implies that you show "lots of love" by using the company's product.

Various ads in the mid-1980s talked about feeling (Maxwell House), touching (Cannon Mills, AT&T), and sharing (Hershey). In one of its commercials the slogan, "Cannon touches your life," was sung four times while its sheets, towels, and blankets were mentioned only once. As the ad director stated, "A towel is an insignificant thing until you relate it to a person's involvement with it."

Emotional themes, however, can be overdone. One ad agency head said, "You're playing with something that can be absolute garbage, sentimental slop. Everyone will start throwing up if it's overdone." Emotional overkill will occur when the themes don't match the product's qualities. The touching theme of Cannon towels matched and was a good campaign. In contrast, in an ad for White Cloud toilet paper a young girl, frightened by a thunderstorm, was calmed down after her mother talked to her about the product. Yuch!

Based on Bill Abrams, "If Logic in Ads Doesn't Sell, Try a Tug on the Heartstrings, *The Wall Street Journal*, April 8, 1982, 27.

uneconomical. Only when the purchase is viewed symbolically as representing power, thrill seeking, and youth does it make sense.

Perhaps the emotion that accounts for the largest amount of consumer buying is love—as it is experienced and as it is sought. The record industry is based largely around producing hit songs that almost uniformly deal with love. The themes found in the cosmetics industry tend to revolve around being attractive to the opposite sex. The use of perfumes and colognes is based largely on the objective of pleasing the senses of others. The clothing industry, and in particular makers of negligees, have the same objective. Indeed, on Valentine's Day, 1985, Americans were expected to spend $370 million on chocolates and $300 million on greeting cards.[15]

Desires for Leisure Activities   Another type of hedonic consumption rests on the desire to engage in leisure activities. The concept of leisure is multidimensional, and the research evidence indicates that a number of different needs propel people to seek leisure.[16] One of these needs is the desire to obtain an optimal stimulation level, as described earlier in the chapter. In addition, people appear to want to engage in nonwork activities for several other reasons. These include:

1. Desire for **intrinsic satisfaction.** Here the activity is viewed by the consumer as rewarding in and of itself. Thus, performing the activity does not have to lead to any other extrinsic rewards—monetary or otherwise. Some argue that the idea of intrinsic satisfaction is the key element defining leisure and that all other concepts merely explain how the intrinsic satisfaction is obtained.[17]
2. Involvement in the activity. The person is totally absorbed in the activity so that everyday life is forgotten. Thus, the consumer becomes so intensively engaged in a pleasurable activity that all else is screened from thought.
3. **Perceived freedom.** The person is free to engage or not engage in the activity. No coercion or obligation exists to force the person to engage in the activity. Thus, leisure experience can be conceptualized as operating on a continuum of obligation–discretion. Matters that a person is obligated to perform are categorized as nonleisure. In contrast, activities that a person is free to perform or not would be categorized as leisure.[18]
4. Mastery of the environment or of oneself. The person attempts to learn something well or to overcome some obstacle. The idea is to test oneself or to conquer the environment. One may particularly find mastery operating in leisure activities involving sports and intellectual games such as chess.
5. Arousal. Discussed earlier in the chapter, the need for arousal has been identified as a motivator of leisure activities. Seeking leisure activities that are novel, complex, and risky can temporarily raise the arousal levels of consumers, which may produce pleasurable feelings.

A recent factor analytic study investigated the dimensions of the leisure experience across a number of different activities.[19] The results revealed that three dimensions consistently emerged—intrinsic satisfaction, perceived freedom, and involvement. Other dimensions, such as arousal and mastery, tended to be activity specific. The authors also interpreted their data and other research as indicating that intrinsic satisfaction may be leisure in a personal sense.

Other authors, however, have placed more emphasis on product involvement as an important element of leisure. A product can be said to have **enduring involvement** when it relates to a consumer's needs, values, or self-concept.[20] A consumer can be said to have product enthusiasm at very high levels of enduring involvement. In such instances the ownership of a product may take on the characteristic of a hobby or leisure activity. In such instances products are not bought merely for their utilitarian value but also for their leisure value.[21] One can find enthusiasts associated with many different types of products, including autos, cameras, computers, wines, guns, horses, and many others.

The study of why consumers like to have fun, to play, and to seek out enjoyable activities represents the topic of experiential consumption discussed in the last chapter. Its study has been neglected even though leisure is a $200 billion-a-year industry. Individuals and families can spend a great deal of time and money engaging in activities that involve attempts to have fun. In part the lack of research effort on consumer experiential activities has resulted from the overemphasis of the field on the decision-making perspective. With a strong focus on rational choice processes, on how memory functions, and on the consumer decision process, a tendency exists to leave out the ideas that consumers also like to feel good, like to be aroused, like to be intrinsically motivated, and so forth.

The Motivation to Maintain Behavioral Freedom

One of the motivators of leisure activities mentioned in an earlier section was the desire to do things without being coerced by any external pressure, such as needs to conform to a company's dress codes. This motive to maintain behavioral freedom has broad implications for marketers and is an important consumer behavior concept. If the freedom to select a product or service is impeded, consumers respond by reacting against the threat. The motivational state resulting from the response to threats to behavioral freedom has been labeled **psychological reactance.**[22]

The term *reactance* describes the motivational state of the person whose behavioral freedom has been threatened. Thus, if a child is told that he or she cannot have a particular food, the child will usually respond by wanting it even more. Similarly, if a product is out of stock or in short supply, consumers' desire for it may well increase. Finally, if a salesman pushes a product too hard, the consumer may move against the sales pitch and actively avoid buying the product. In each case, a consumer perceives that his or her behavioral freedom is threatened. A reactance state results which motivates the consumer to move against the threat.

Two types of threats can lead to reactance. **Social threats** involve external pressure by other people to induce a consumer to do something. Examples might include pressing the consumer to buy a certain product, to go to a certain play, or to vote for a particular political candidate. If the pressure is too great, the consumer may react against it, resulting in a "boomerang effect." In such instances the consumer moves in the opposite direction intended by the person engaging in the social influence attempt. In the personal-selling area of marketing the problem of boomerang effects is great. Salespeople must take definite steps to persuade customers to buy their products. However, they cannot push too hard or risk alienating the prospect. A time-tested strategy is to give the customer the information so that he persuades himself that *this* is the right product to buy.

A second threat to behavioral freedom comes from impersonal sources. Generally, the **impersonal threats** are barriers that restrict the ability to buy a particular product or service. The barriers may result from a shortage of the product, from the possibility that someone else will buy the product, or even from a rise in its price. In each case, something comes between the consumer and the purchase of the product. The consumer's likely reaction is to reevaluate the product and want it even more. Even the decision to buy one product over another can result in the person's reevaluating the unchosen alternatives more positively.[23] The decision not to buy something threatens the freedom to choose and, therefore, results in an increase in the positivity of the person towards the alternatives. Such reactance is one reason why consumers often experience "buyer's regret" after making very large purchases. That is, after purchasing a product the freedom to buy other products is lost. Reactance then sets in, and the desire for unchosen, but attractive, alternatives increases. More will be said about buyer's regret in Chapter 9, "Postpurchase Processes."

Three basic requirements exist for consumers to experience reactance. First, the consumer must believe that he or she has the freedom to make a free choice in a given situation. If the general ability to make a choice is unavailable, perhaps because alternative products are unavailable, reactance will not occur. Second, a threat to the freedom must be experienced. Third, the decision must be one which is of some importance to the consumer.[24]

The Motivation to Avoid Risk

Suppose that you were suddenly given $10,000 which could be spent only for the purpose of paying for a ride on the space shuttle on its first commercial trip to an orbiting space station. What would be your thoughts? In all likelihood a couple of things would go through your mind. First, you might consider what could happen to you on the trip—becoming nauseated, getting an incredible "high," or even dying. Secondly, you might attempt to weight the likelihood that these various outcomes could occur. When you go through such a process, you are analyzing the **perceived risk** of the decision. As such, perceived risk may be defined as a consumer's perception of the overall favorability of a course of action based upon an assessment of the possible outcomes and of the likelihood that those outcomes will occur. As such, perceived risk consists of two major concepts—the positive or negative outcomes of a decision and the probability that these outcomes will occur.[25]

While engaged in their everyday activities, consumers are constantly faced with decisions that involve some uncertainty about an outcome. Examples of such decisions include buying products or services, determining where to go on a vacation, selecting a retailer from which to buy a product, deciding whether to go somewhere by auto, plane or train, and casting a ballot to determine whether a state should allow a nuclear power plant to be built. As can be seen, almost any decision a consumer makes involves uncertainty. A general rule found by researchers over the past twenty-five years is that people usually seek to avoid taking risks perceived as being too great. In general, consumers are risk averse in their actions.

Types of Consumer Risks   The first discussion of the concept of perceived risk appeared in the marketing literature in 1960.[26] Since that time, much of the effort of consumer researchers has focused on identifying the various **types of risk** about which consumers are concerned. Table 3–2 identifies seven different types of risk to which consumers may respond.[27]

The promotional work of marketers is often geared towards lowering the perceived risk of consumers. Advertisements may be used to point out how a particular product or service can lower risk. For example, insurance advertising stresses the reduction of financial risk. Automobile manufacturers such as Volvo mention the reduction of physical risk. Many personal-use product advertisements use a reduction-of-social-risk theme. Thus, products are available to avoid "ring around the collar," bad breath, and dandruff, which can cause social embarrassment. Deodorant ads frequently use a social-risk theme. Thus, one can even "raise your hand, if you're sure." The advertisement shown in Figure 3–7 uses such a social-risk theme. Headlined, "Gain Control, Never

Table 3–2   Types of Perceived Risk

1. Financial—Risk that the outcome will harm the consumer financially (e.g., will buying a car cause financial hardship?).
2. Performance—Risk that the product will not perform as expected (e.g., will the car really accelerate faster than a Porsche 928?).
3. Physical—Risk that the product will physically harm the buyer (e.g., will the car protect me in a crash?).
4. Psychological—Risk that the product will lower consumer's self-image (e.g., a swinging single wondering if she will look like a typical housewife if she buys this car?).
5. Social—Risk that friends or acquaintances will deride the purchase (e.g., will my best friend think that I am trying to show him up by buying a Porsche?).
6. Time—Risk that a decision will cost too much time (e.g., will buying a sports car cost me time because I have to tune it so frequently?).
7. Opportunity loss—Risk that by taking one action the consumer will miss out on doing something else he or she would really prefer doing (e.g., by buying a Porsche 928 I will miss out on buying several expensive oil paintings).

Figure 3–7   Gillette cleverly uses a social risk theme to promote a deodorant. *(Courtesy of The Gillette Company.)*

Let Them See You Sweat," the ad for Dry Idea deodorant suggests that a person loses social effectiveness if others observe him or her perspiring.

For each of the types of risk one can identify the two components of risk—the likelihood of loss and the amount of loss. Thus, suppose that the decision involved buying a car and deciding whether to get an adjustable-rate loan or a fixed-rate loan. With adjustable-rate loans the consumer gets a lower initial rate but takes the risk that interest rates may rise. If the rates rise, the consumer has to make larger monthly payments. In this instance, the possible outcomes can be identified, because the consumer can compute how much his or her monthly payments would change as interest rates go up or down.

The problem in assessing the risk of obtaining an adjustable-rate loan is that the likelihood of interest rates changing substantially is difficult or impossible to estimate. In fact, estimating the likelihood of most negative consumer outcomes is a difficult task at best. The information is simply not available in most cases. For example, how likely is it that the next time you buy a car, its engine will blow up within the first 50,000 miles? How likely is it that you will get lung cancer if you smoke cigarettes? How likely is it that a nuclear accident involving loss of life will occur if a nuclear power plant is built twenty miles from you? Exact answers to these questions cannot be obtained. Nonetheless, consumers will implicitly develop estimates of the likelihood of various events, a process to be discussed further.

Estimating the Likelihood of Negative Outcomes   One of the findings of behavioral scientists is that people are not very good at estimating the probability that negative outcomes will occur. For example, consider the following five pairs of events that could cause death:

1. Breast cancer versus diabetes.
2. Lung cancer versus stomach cancer.
3. Leukemia versus emphysema.
4. All accidents versus strokes.
5. Pregnancy versus appendicitis.

For each of the pairs of events, identify which of the two is the most likely to result in death. As it turns out, the negative events listed to the right (i.e., diabetes and so forth) are much more likely to cause death. In one study of people's impressions of the relative likelihood of these events causing death, less than 50 percent of the respondents accurately guessed the correct one.[28] The apparent reason for this inability to correctly estimate probabilities is that consumers make their guesses based upon how readily they can think of instances in which the negative outcomes occurred. Because different negative outcomes receive more publicity than others, the use of such a decision rule, based upon the availability of information in memory, often leads to erroneous conclusions.

Factors Influencing the Perception of Risk Researchers have found that a number of factors influence the amount of risk consumers perceive in a given situation. First, the characteristics of the individual consumer influence his or her perception of risk. Various researchers have found that personality factors can influence the extent to which a particular person will react to the risk in a given situation. The following personal characteristics have been found to be associated with a greater willingness to accept risk: higher self-confidence, higher self-esteem, lower anxiety, and lower familiarity with the problem. Individuals who tend to make choices from a wider range of alternatives also tend to see lower risk in a particular selection.[29]

Situational factors may also influence the perception of risk. For example, researchers have found that voluntary risks are more acceptable to people than involuntary risks.[30] Voluntary risks include such things as choosing to drive a car on a trip or choosing to go on a ski vacation. Involuntary risks include such things as having surgery or having a nuclear power plant near one's home. For voluntary activities consumers systematically perceive less risk than there really is. In contrast, for involuntary things consumers perceive more risk than is actually present.

Other researchers have found that consumers perceive that greater risk is involved in shopping through the mail than in shopping in a retail store.[31] As would also be expected, different amounts of risk are associated with purchasing different products.

How Do Consumers Reduce Risk? Because some degree of risk is inherent in nearly all decisions in which consumers engage, consumers must have some methods that help them make decisions with some confidence. One important finding is that consumers may compare their perception of the amount of risk present to some criterion of how much risk is acceptable. Thus, consumers may be conceptualized as comparing the perceived risk to the **acceptable risk.** If the perceived risk is greater than the acceptable risk, the consumer is then motivated to reduce the risk in some way or forego making the decision.[32]

What things do consumers do to reduce the amount of risk perceived in a decision? In general, all of the risk-reduction strategies involve taking some action to reduce the perceived likelihood that negative outcomes will occur. Following are six potential ways of changing such impressions:

1. Being brand loyal. Consumers tend to weigh their own personal experiences very highly in judging the likelihood that something will occur. If they have had success with a product, the belief that it will have satisfactory future outcomes is increased.
2. Buying through brand image. A certain feeling exists that if a company is nationally known and has a good image, it is less likely that negative outcomes will occur with its products.
3. Buying through store image. A certain feeling exists that if a store has a

very positive image, it is less likely that negative outcomes will occur with its products.

4. Seeking out information. Consumers can potentially reduce risk by obtaining information about brands or retail stores. They can read *Consumer Reports* or specialty magazines that evaluate the product. In addition, they can consult with friends or acquaintances who have had experience with the product or service. Further, they can attempt to test the product by borrowing it from a retailer or friend. Another type of information consumers can seek is simply reassurance. They may ask for such reassurance from salespeople or from friends. The goal is simply to have someone tell them that their decision is a good one.

5. Buying the most-expensive brand. Another strategy for reducing risk is to assume that the most-expensive model will have the greatest likelihood of having positive outcomes. The price-quality relationship has a major impact on many consumers.

6. Buying the least-expensive brand. A final strategy is to reduce financial risk by buying the least-expensive brand. In such instances consumers are likely to have low concern over other sources of risk, such as physical and performance risk.

The Motivation to Attribute Causality

As people move through their everyday lives, events happen for which they seek an explanation. Someone may insult them, a product endorser may strongly tout a brand of soft drink, or they may buy a product and be asked why they did so. In each case the individuals may seek to understand the cause for the action. Each person will want to identify why the other insulted him, why the endorser advocated buying the soft drink, and why he decided to buy one particular brand rather than alternative ones.

The explanation of the processes through which people make these determinations of the causality of action has been labeled **attribution theory.** According to attribution theory, people will attempt to determine whether the cause for action resulted from something internal or external to the person or object in question. Thus, if the referent is another person (e.g., the endorser) the attributor may ask whether the endorser recommended the product because he actually liked the product (an **internal attribution**) or because he was paid for endorsing it (an **external attribution**). Similarly, if someone asks the person why he bought a particular brand, he will seek to determine if the cause for action was something internal to the product (i.e., the product's good qualities) or something external to the product (i.e., pressure from a salesman or a temporary reduction in price).[33]

Describing the tendency of people to make attributions as a motivation is somewhat unusual, but precedent certainly exists. For example, Maslow discussed the need for cognitive understanding. Certainly, when a consumer makes an attribution, the purpose is to help achieve a cognitive understanding of why something occurred. More recently, researchers investigating the organization of the brain have suggested that our minds may have a modular arrangement. One of the modules has been called "the interpreter" by one proponent of the view. One function of the interpreter is to generate hypotheses about why things happen.[34] Thus, built into our brain functioning may be a "wired-in" need to make attributions.

People are motivated to make attributions as to the cause of actions in order to determine how to act in the future. Thus, if a consumer decided that an endorser advocated a product merely because he was paid, the consumer would tend to discount the message. That is, the consumer would not rely on the message as giving the endorser's real opinion. Such an attribution would likely result in the message having little or no impact on the consumer's attitude towards the product. Similarly, if the consumer were asked why he or she bought a product and realized that it was bought in spite of a high price, the tendency would be to make the attribution that he or she really liked the product. It is as though the consumer said to himself, "The product must be good, or why would I have bought it?" An internal attribution was made because the product was bought even though it had a high price.

Attribution theory is actually composed of a family of theories, each of which explains how people determine causality in various situations. Insufficient space exists to discuss each of the attribution theories, and only one will be examined—the person-perception approach of Harold Kelley.

Harold Kelley was one of the first social psychologists to articulate the basic ideas behind person perception. In one of his classic papers he developed two important concepts—the **augmenting principle** and the **discounting principle.**[35] The augmenting/discounting model is based upon the idea that people will examine the environmental pressures that impede or propel a particular action. If external pressures exist for someone to act in a particular way, the actions would be expected given the circumstances. The attributor will tend to believe that the actions were caused by the environment rather than by the person's actual beliefs, feelings, and desires. Thus, in such circumstances the action is discounted as representing the other's real beliefs. In summary, the discounting principle may be stated as follows: "The role of a given cause in producing a given effect is discounted if other plausible causes are also present."[36]

What happens if a person moves against environmental pressures to do something? In this instance the action would be unexpected given the circumstances. As a consequence, the observer will tend to believe that the person must have been highly internally motivated. The belief is augmented that the action represents the person's actual beliefs, feelings, and desires. An example of the augmentation principle would be a convicted criminal stating that prison sentences should be made longer in order to deter crime. Because the criminal made a statement that would be unexpected given the circumstances (i.e., he could harm himself if his advice were followed), the belief that the statement represents his true feelings would be augmented.

The augmenting/discounting model has frequent application to consumer behavior problems. Indeed, one of the major difficulties faced by marketers is how to avoid having consumers discount their messages. Consumers recognize that pressures exist to sell products and to make profits. Thus, when they watch advertisements on television or receive promotional messages from salesmen, they will tend to discount them as externally caused. Consumers are generally not particularly confident that promotional messages accurately describe the characteristics of products. For example, in 1985 a study found that over 59 percent of its respondents found "statistical" claims in advertisements to be unbelievable.[37]

As a result of consumers' tendency to discount messages, marketers frequently attempt to identify ways to create the impression that the message actually goes against the pressures of the environment. A classic example has been the advertisements run by the Lincoln/Mercury division of Ford Corporation. In the ads owners of Cadillacs evaluated the performance of Lincolns. After driving the Lincoln, a large percentage indicated that they preferred the Lincoln overall. In most cases, consumers expect people who own a particular car to like it better than other models. Why else would they have bought it? Thus, when the Cadillac owners report preferring Lincolns, the message is augmented so that the belief in its veracity is increased.

Figure 3–8 illustrates a case when a message would be augmented. In the ad R. J. Reynolds Tobacco Company advises young people not to smoke. Coming from a tobacco company, the message is certainly unexpected and seemingly against their best interests. The likely result is an augmentation in the belief of the trustworthiness of the company.

Another way to avoid consumer discounting of messages is to use man-on-the-street interviews. In this case, the impression is left with the audience that no external pressure existed for the seemingly randomly selected person to advocate the product. Therefore, discounting would not occur. Pepsi-Cola has run an effective campaign against Coca-Cola with its Pepsi Challenge series, in which people are asked to taste the two colas and give their preferences. With more people favoring Pepsi, the ads were successful in improving the brand's market share. In order to respond to the ads, Coke had their endorser, Bill Cosby, suggest that those taking the Pepsi Challenge deliberately chose Pepsi not because they preferred it but because they wanted to get on television. The goal of Coke was to give the audience a reason to discount the Pepsi message.

Managerial Implications

For managers the study of consumer motivation has importance for the development of the marketing mix. In particular, knowledge of consumer need structures—and especially those needs not being adequately met in the marketplace—can influence product development, distribution, promotion, and pricing decisions. For example, in the mid-1980s a need to achieve appeared to grip the United States. A number of causes were probably responsible for

Figure 3–8 **The augmentation principle is employed in this tobacco company's antismoking ad.** (*Courtesy of R.J. Reynolds Tobacco Co.*)

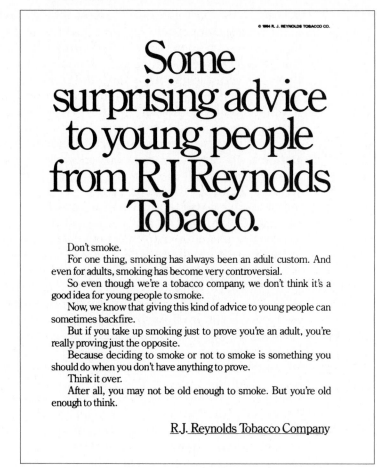

© 1984 R. J. REYNOLDS TOBACCO CO.

Some surprising advice to young people from RJ Reynolds Tobacco.

Don't smoke.

For one thing, smoking has always been an adult custom. And even for adults, smoking has become very controversial.

So even though we're a tobacco company, we don't think it's a good idea for young people to smoke.

Now, we know that giving this kind of advice to young people can sometimes backfire.

But if you take up smoking just to prove you're an adult, you're really proving just the opposite.

Because deciding to smoke or not to smoke is something you should do when you don't have anything to prove.

Think it over.

After all, you may not be old enough to smoke. But you're old enough to think.

R.J. Reynolds Tobacco Company

the emphasis on striving for success, achieving quality, and working hard. The deep recession of the early 1980s, the threat of high-quality foreign products to American industries, the 1984 Olympic games, and the aging of the population all may have contributed to the trend. The reaction of companies to the focus on achievement was to tie their products to achievement through their promotional campaigns. Examples include the linking of Vantage cigarettes to a "success" theme, the emphasis on quality among United States auto makers (e.g., Ford's slogan of "Where quality is job 1"), and a campaign by Smirnoff vodka that emphasized quality. In one of the ads a world-renowned violinist holds his violin and says, "When I play, I strive for the highest quality in my performance. I look for the same standards in my vodka . . . When it comes to Vodka, Smirnoff plays second fiddle to none."

Achievement motivation themes can easily be adapted so that mastery of the self is exhibited. Mastery of self is similar to the self-actualization need identified by Maslow. It stresses overcoming personal weaknesses to do the best one can. Bud Light beer used such a theme during the 1984 Olympic games in which one television ad had the copy, "The true message of the Olympics is not winning but bringing out the best in all of us." In the ad two farmers get up early in the morning and trudge out to a lonely road to watch a runner carrying the Olympic torch across the countryside to its destination in Los Angeles. In one of the programs accompanying the Olympic coverage a reporter noted that the advertising during the Olympics seemed to be operating on a "higher" level. Of course, he was right. Companies were attempting to tie their products to needs associated with the Olympics, such as achievement and mastery of the self. These are "higher" needs in comparison to the "lower-order" needs, such as Maslow's physiological and safety needs.

The problem for companies is that what they say in their advertisements must be matched by product performance. For example, if quality is stressed, the product must fulfill the expectations created by the message. This could become a major problem for U.S. auto manufacturers, who began to stress their products' quality in the mid-1980s. If their automobiles fail over time to meet the quality expectations created by the promotional messages, the long-term result could be even further erosion of consumer confidence in U.S. auto companies.

The midrange theories of consumer motivation have applications to a variety of managerial decision areas. The idea of priming found in opponent-process theory is particularly applicable to retailers. The giving away of food samples in grocery stores has already been discussed as an example of priming. Other examples could include providing access to the delicious smells from a bakery in a grocery store. Such smells could act as a priming agent to stir up hunger pangs and increase buying behavior. In department stores clerks at the cosmetics counter are instructed to spray perfume into the air every thirty minutes. Could this procedure act to prime customers to buy cosmetics? One also wonders if a priming strategy might involve sales personnel encouraging consumers to make a small purchase first. Perhaps this could prime them and increase the likelihood that they would make larger purchases. Much research needs to be done on the effects of priming on consumer behavior.

The recognition that consumers may seek to raise or lower their stimulation levels and may attempt to gain hedonic experiences is also managerially relevant. First, markets could be segmented based upon their need for activation. For example, one might hypothesize that buyers of sports cars are seeking stimulation, whereas buyers of full-size sedans are attempting to avoid stimulation. Such knowledge would have implications for advertising themes and personal selling tactics. Second, managers should identify the extent to which their product lines are purchased because of product enthusiasm. Enthusiasts appear to purchase products of interest in part because of their intrinsic interest in the products and also because the products relate to their needs, values, and self-concept. Such buyers seem to obtain a certain hedonic satisfaction with the product. These individuals are worthy of study because they may represent a class of product innovators as well as a source for new product and advertising ideas.

As noted earlier in the chapter, psychological reactance is an important problem for managers. Because many consumers are naturally wary of advertising and sales personnel, they may easily believe that their behavioral freedom is being threatened by strong messages. Identifying sales and advertising methods that do not activate feelings of reactance is an important managerial objective.

Another managerial area of interest is the assessment of the degree of risk that a target market perceives in a product or service. Managers should examine the various types of risk that consumers may perceive and identify those most relevant to the brand. Positive responses to the following questions are likely to result in consumers perceiving the brand to have significant amounts of risk:

- ☐ Is the product expensive for this target market?
- ☐ Do other people evaluate the purchaser based upon his or her choice of brand?
- ☐ Do consumers get ego satisfaction from owning the product?
- ☐ Do consumers perceive that they could be harmed physically by the product?
- ☐ Is the product likely to take up a lot of consumers' time?
- ☐ Do consumers have to give up purchasing other products or services in order to buy the one under consideration?

To the extent that one or more of the above conditions exist, managers should act to develop their marketing mix to influence consumer beliefs about the likelihood that a negative outcome could occur with the brand or service. Table 3–3 lists a number of these strategies, which run from pricing the product higher to providing warranties to distributing the product through high-image retailers.

It is also possible to develop advertising campaigns that focus on how a particular product or service can reduce consumer risk. General Motors has successfully used such a strategy in a campaign touting the safety of its vehicles. Focusing on the physical risk of driving an automobile, GM has forcefully pointed out the good safety record of many of its cars. Figure 3–9 represents one of the ads in the campaign.

Finally, managers should be concerned with the attributions that consumers make regarding the various actions of the company. In general, the company should make every effort to foster consumer beliefs that the positive

Table 3–3   Managerial Strategies to Lower Consumer Perceptions of Risk

1. Price product higher than average.
2. Give good warranties and guarantees.
3. Distribute through retailers with a high-quality image.
4. Use a high-quality sales force composed of people who can give reassurance.
5. Provide prompt service to lower time risk.
6. Obtain seals of approval (e.g., Underwriters Laboratories Approved).
7. Develop an extensive image-building campaign for company and product.
8. Provide hot-line numbers so consumers can get information.
9. Give free trials, test drives, etc. (e.g., "test drive an Apple").
10. Give lots of information about one's product through brochures, packaging, instructions, write-ups in magazines, and the sales force.
11. Possibly have trusted endorsers promote one's product or service.
12. Focus on developing good word-of-mouth communications about the product.

actions of the company are made because of its positive, ethical nature. Conversely, negative outcomes of the company's actions should be attributed to situational forces beyond the company's control. Of course, generating communications that will elicit such attributions is extremely difficult. Perhaps the most effective course of action is to manage so well that positive outcomes result because of the professionalism of the company and negative outcomes occur very rarely.

SUMMARY

Motivation refers to an activated state within a person that leads to goal-directed behavior. In a consumer behavior context marketers hope to create products that fulfill the needs initiating the goal-directed behavior. In effect, the goal is to establish products and services as incentive objects that act to fulfill consumer needs.

A number of general theories of motivation exist, such as the Maslow hierarchy, Murray's social needs, and McClelland's theory of learned needs. Although the VALs psychographic inventory (discussed in Chapter 4) is based in part on ideas taken from Maslow's hierarchy, in general neither the work of Maslow nor Murray has been supported by research. In contrast, work on McClelland's theory has been more extensive, such that his ideas on the effects of needs for achievement, affiliation, and power have been empirically documented.

The trend in the study of motivation over the past twenty years, however, has been to move away from general theories to more limited midrange theories of motivation. The midrange theories of motivation discussed in this chapter include: opponent-process theory, optimum stimulation level theory, motivation for hedonic experiences, the desire to maintain behavioral freedom, the motivation to avoid risk, and the motivation to attribute causality.

Figure 3–9   General Motors points out that their cars may reduce physical risk for drivers and passengers. (*Reproduced courtesy of General Motors Corporation.*)

These approaches to motivation are organized such that they move from more physiologically based theories to more cognitively based approaches.

The core concept forming the basis of opponent-process theory is that whenever a person receives a positive or negative stimulus, two processes are activated in a sequential manner. First, the process having the same affective content as the stimulus is elicited. Thus, if the stimulus is positive, initial feelings are positive. However, shortly after the initiation of the primary response, a second opposing response begins to occur. The overall feeling that results is the sum of the two processes. Thus, if a positive stimulus is felt, a person will initially feel pleasure. Over time, however, the positivity will gradually fade. Eventually, the opposing process will dominate, and the person will feel satiated and uncomfortable. Opponent-process theory can explain a wide variety of consumer actions, ranging from participation in daredevil sports, such as hang gliding, to consumption of drugs.

Work on maintaining optimum stimulation levels complements that on opponent-process theory. The research has found that people have a need to maintain an optimum level of stimulation and that they will take action to raise or lower their input of stimulation to maintain their desired levels. Thus, consumers may seek out amusement parks in order to raise their level of activation or consume alcohol to lower their activation.

Consumers have also been recognized as having a need to experience fantasies, feelings, and emotional arousal. The study of these needs represents the core of the experiential perspective on consumption. This need for hedonic experiences may well be an extension of the need to maintain an optimum stimulation level. One of the research findings is that consumers will in certain instances allow hedonic or emotional desires to dominate over utilitarian motives in choosing products. The types of products and services on which researchers focus tend to be different when the emphasis is on the experiential side of consumer behavior. Rather than investigating the buying of consumer durables and package goods, the focus tends to be on such "services" as rock concerts, dance, sporting events, and symbolic products, such as automobiles and jewelry.

Another midrange theory of interest to consumer researchers is reactance theory. Reactance theory states that consumers have a need to maintain their behavioral freedom. When this behavioral freedom is threatened, they will react in a manner necessary to restore it. Companies can act to threaten a consumer's behavioral freedom in a variety of ways, such as by having salesmen push customers too hard or by suddenly withdrawing a product from the marketplace, as in the case of Coca-Cola. When consumers feel their freedom threatened, they will take actions such as refusing to buy a product from a pushy salesman or filing lawsuits to have a product placed back on the market.

Although consumers will sometimes engage in high-risk activities, such as hang gliding to raise their activation levels, they generally seek to avoid risk. Researchers have identified a variety of consumer risks, such as financial, performance, and social risk. Two components of risk have been identified—the likelihood of a loss occurring and the amount of possible loss. Overall risk is assessed by combining these two perceptions. A number of factors have been found that influence the perception of risk, including the situation, the characteristics of the individual, and the nature of the product.

The perception of risk can be analyzed from a cognitive perspective. That is, one can investigate how consumers think about risk and its components. An even more cognitively based motivation is the desire to attribute causality. According to attribution theory, people attempt to identify why various things occur in order to have an understanding of the environment and of their own and others' actions. Marketers and consumer researchers should be concerned with identifying the attributions that consumers make in various situations. In particular, it is important to identify the attributions consumers make towards the actions of product endorsers and sales personnel. If consumers believe that these corporate representatives are giving information merely in order to sell the product rather than also to help and assist the consumer, it is likely that consumers will place low trust in the statements of such people.

Key Terms

Motivation
Needs
Drives
Incentives
Need for affiliation
Need for power
Opponent-process
   theory
Priming
Optimum stimulation
   level
Hedonic experiences
Intrinsic satisfaction
Perceived freedom

Enduring involvement
Psychological reactance
Social threats
Impersonal threats
Perceived risk
Types of risk
Acceptable risk
Attribution theory
Internal attribution
External attribution
Augmenting principle
Discounting principle
Achievement motivation

Review Questions

1. Define the concept of motivation. Draw the model of motivation presented in Figure 3–1 and indicate how needs, drives, and goal-directed action interrelate.
2. Identify the seven needs developed by Maslow.
3. Identify the three needs identified by McClelland.
4. Discuss how the opponent-process theory of acquired motivation can explain why someone becomes elated after making a parachute jump.

5. Define the concept of priming. How can it be used by retailers to increase sales?
6. Define the concept of optimum stimulation level. How can the desire to maintain optimum stimulation levels lead consumers to purchase products or engage in specific types of leisure activities?
7. What is meant by the term *hedonic consumption?* What types of products and services tend to fall into the hedonic consumption category?
8. Name four reasons why people engage in non-work leisure activities other than the desire to maintain optimum stimulation levels.
9. Define the concept of reactance. What factors can lead consumers to feel reactance?
10. Define the concept of perceived risk. Identify five of the seven types of risk to which consumers may respond.
11. Identify four of the five ways discussed in the text through which consumers may act to reduce risk.
12. What occurs when a consumer makes an attribution? Why are people motivated to make attributions?
13. Discuss what is meant by the augmenting and discounting principles.
14. A number of managerial strategies have been identified to lower consumer perceptions of risk. Identify six of these possible strategies.

Discussion Questions

1. Following are a number of slogans that have been used by corporations. Indicate which of the needs identified by motivation theorists each slogan best represents.
   a. "Be all that you can be" (U.S. Army).
   b. "Join the Pepsi generation" (Pepsi-Cola).
   c. "For all you do, this Bud's for you" (Budweiser).
   d. "Get a piece of the rock" (Prudential).
   e. "All my men wear English Leather, every one of them" (English Leather).
   f. "We have one and only one ambition. To be the best. What else is there" (Lee Iacocca for Chrysler).

2. You are on an advertising team assembled to develop a campaign for a new running shoe. Develop three slogans that could be used in an advertising campaign. Each slogan should illustrate one of the needs identified by McClelland.

3. Priming may be a potent method of encouraging consumers to purchase large amounts of a product. How could the following types of companies make use of priming—a sausage company, a movie distribution company, and an auto dealership?

4. Consider your own leisure activities. Which of your activities do you engage in to increase your level of activation and which to decrease your level of activation?

5. You are the marketing director for a company that makes camping equipment. Develop the copy for a print advertisement for a backpack. In the advertisement utilize three of the five reasons identified for people's desire to engage in nonwork activities.

6. Reactance can often cause problems for companies in their personal selling efforts. However, under some circumstances reactance may be beneficial to companies. Try to identify one or more of these instances.

7. Mail-order companies face a major problem because consumers perceive greater risk in purchasing from them. What are some steps that mail-order companies take to reduce the perceived risk among consumers?

8. What are some steps advertisers can take to convince consumers to attribute internal rather than external motivations to endorsers of products?

9. Make a list of your own leisure activities. What are the reasons you engage in each of these activities? Compare these to the reasons for people engaging in nonwork activities identified in the text.

References

1. Ronald Alsop, "Atlantic City Casinos Lure More Gamblers Away from Las Vegas," *The Wall Street Journal*, October 26, 1983, 1, 21.

2. Ernest Hilgard, Richard Atkinson, and Rita Atkinson, *Introduction to Psychology*, 6th ed., New York, N.Y.: Harcourt Brace Jovanovich, Inc., 1975.

3. Hilgard, Atkinson, and Atkinson, *Introduction to Psychology*.

4. David McClelland, "Achievement and Entrepreneurship: A Longitudinal Study," *Journal of Personality and Social Psychology*, April, 1965, 1, 389–392.

5. E. G. French, "Effects of the Interaction of Motivation and Feedback on Test Performance," in *Motives in Fantasy, Action, and Society*, J. W. Atkinson (ed.), New York, N.Y.: Litton Educational Publishing, Inc., 1958.

6. David H. Gardner, "An Exploratory Investigation of Achievement Motivation Effects on Consumer Behavior," M. Venkatasan (ed.), *Proceedings of Third Annual Conference*, Association for Consumer Research, 1972, 20–23.

7. Richard L. Solomon, "The Opponent-Process Theory of Acquired Motivation, *American Psychologist*, 35, August 1980, 691–712.

8. Peter DePaulo, "The Opposite of Satiation: Motivational Priming as an Aftereffect of a Pleasurable Consumption Experience," Richard Lutz (ed.), *Advances in Consumer Research*, 13, Ann Arbor, MI: Association for Consumer Research, 1986, 192–197.

9. Sandon A. Steinberg and Richard F. Yalch, "When Eating Begets Buying: The Effects of Food Samples on Obese and Nonobese Shoppers," *Journal of Consumer Research*, 4, March 1978, 243–246.

10. Marvin Zuckerman, *Sensation Seeking: Beyond the Optimum Level of Arousal*, Hillsdale, N.J.: Lawrence Erlbaum, 1979.

11. P. S. Raju, "Optimum Stimulation Level: Its Relationship to Personality, Demographics, and Exploratory Behavior," *Journal of Consumer Research*, 7, December 1980, 272–282.

12. Ibid.

13. Morris Holbrook and Elizabeth C. Hirschman, "The Experiential Aspects of Consumption: Consumer Fantasies, Feelings, and Fun," *Journal of Consumer Research*, 9, September 1982, 132–140.

14. E. Hirschman and M. Holbrook, "Hedonic Consumption: Emerging Concepts, Methods, and Propositions," *Journal of Marketing*, 46, Summer 1982, 92–101.

15. Chocolate Manufactures Assn. of U.S.A. and American Greeting Corporation, "What Price Love?," *Advertising Age*, February 14, 1985, 13.

16. Lynette S. Unger and Jerome B. Kernan, "On the Meaning of Leisure: An Investigation of Some Determinants of the Subjective Experience," *Journal of Consumer Research*, 9, March 1983, 381–393.

17. Seppo Iso-Ahola, *The Social Psychology of Leisure and Recreation*, Dubuque, IA: William C. Brown, 1980.

18. Douglass K. Howes, "Time Budgets and Consumer Leisure-Time Behavior," in *Advances in Consumer Research*, *IV*, William Perreault (ed.), Association for Consumer Research, Ann Arbor, MI: 1977, 221–229.

19. Unger and Kernan, "On the Meaning of Leisure."

20. Michael Houston and Michael Rothschild, "Conceptual and Methodological Perspectives on Involvement," in *1978 Educator's Proceedings*, S. Jain (ed.), Chicago, Ill.: American Marketing Association, 1978, 184–187.

21. Peter H. Bloch and Grady D. Bruce, "Product Involvement as Leisure Behavior," *Advances in Consumer Research*, *XI*, Thomas Kinnear (ed.), Ann Arbor, MI: Association for Consumer Research, 1984, 197–202.

22. Jack W. Brehm, *A Theory of Psychological Reactance*, New York, N.Y.: Academic Press, Inc., 1966.

23. Darwyn Linder and Katherine Crane, "Reactance Theory Analysis of Predecisional Cognitive Processes," *Journal of Personality and Social Psychology*, 15, July, 1970, 258–264.

24. Mona Clee and Robert Wicklund, "Consumer Behavior and Psychological Reactance," *Journal of Consumer Research*, 6, March 1980, 389–405.

25. A completely satisfactory definition of perceived risk has not appeared in the marketing literature. See the following article for a discussion of this problem: James Bettman, "Information Integration in Consumer Risk Perception: A Comparison of Two Models of Component Conceptualization," *Journal of Applied Psychology*, 60, 1975, 381–385.

26. Raymond A. Bauer, "Consumer Behavior as Risk Taking," in Robert S. Hancock (ed.), *Dynamic Marketing for a Changing World*, Chicago, Ill.: American Marketing Association, 1960, 87.

27. The first five risks in Table 3–3 were identified by Jacob Jacoby and Leon Kaplan, "The Components of Perceived Risk," *Advances in Consumer Research*, *III*, M. Venkatesan (ed.), Chicago, Ill.: Association for Consumer Research, 1972, 382–383. "Social risk" was identified by J. Paul Peter and Michael Ryan, "An Investigation of Perceived Risk at the Brand Level," *Journal of Marketing Research*, 13, May 1976, 184–188. "Opportunity cost" was identified by William Zikmund and Jerome Scott, "A Factor Analysis of the Multi-dimensional Nature of Perceived Risk," *Proceedings of the Southern Marketing Association*, Houston, Tex.: Southern Marketing Association, 1973, 1036.

28. Amos Tversky and D. Kahneman, "Availability: A Heuristic for Judging Frequency and Probability," *Cognitive Psychology*, 5, 1973, 207–232.

29. Thomas Pettigrew, "The Measurement and Correlates of Category Width as a Cognitive Variable," *Journal of Personality*, 26, December 1968, 532.

30. B. Fischhoff, P. Slovic, and S. Lichtenstein, "Which Risks Are Acceptable?" *Environment*, 21, January 1979, 17–38.

31. Homer Spence, James Engel, and Roger Blackwell, "Perceived Risk in Mail-Order and Retail Store Buying," *Journal of Marketing Research*, 7, August 1970, 364–369.

32. Donald Popielarz, "An Exploration of Perceived Risk and Willingness to Try New Products," *Journal of Marketing Research*, 5, November 1967, 368–372.

33. For an overview of the attribution process in consumer behavior, see Richard Mizerski, Linda Golden, and Jerome Kernan, "The Attribution Process in Consumer Behavior," *Journal of Consumer Research*, 6, September 1979, 123–140.

34. Michael S. Gazzaniga, *The Social Brain*, New York: Basic Books Inc, 1985.

35. Harold H. Kelley, "The Process of Casual Attribution," *American Psychologist*, 28, February 1973, 107–128.

36. Kelley, "The Process of Casual Attribution."

37. Nancy Millman, "Product Claims Not Believable," *Advertising Age*, March 15, 1984, 1, 32.

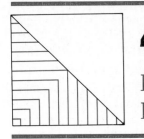

4

Personality and Psychographic Influences

Fear: An Individual-Difference Variable

What do the following people have in common? Ronald Reagan, Aretha Franklin, John Madden, Gene Shallot, Isaac Asimov, and Ray Bradbury? They all have suffered or are suffering from aerophobia, the fear of flying.

A phobia is an irrational, persistent fear of a particular object or class of objects. People can become fearful of almost anything, from snakes to elevators to riding in planes to flowers, open spaces, and three-legged stools. With an estimated one in nine adults suffering from some type of phobia, they can influence business. A 1977 survey found that the fear of flying strikes some 25 million Americans. The fear of open places keeps about one in twenty people from enjoying a visit to a shopping mall.

One variety of the debilitating problem called social phobias can take on many forms. Fear of public speaking, for example, is a social phobia. In other instances some men avoid going to football games because of the realization that they cannot urinate in the public stalls at halftime. Other people are afraid to go out to eat for fear of vomiting. If they do go out, they avoid menu items that look particularly noxious when vomited, such as spaghetti. Some individuals are afflicted with the belief that they will pass out in public. As a consequence, they wear the best-looking underwear in town, at least according to one sufferer.

A brief description of the panic a person feels when struck by a phobic attack will quickly eliminate any thoughts that phobias are trivial. One woman described a panic attack that she had in a supermarket as follows: "The food around me seemed piled so high, as if the aisles were closing in, and my head would start to swirl, and I'd just have to leave my cart right where it was and get out of there." A truck driver was afraid that he would stop his

91

semi in the middle of the Chesapeake Bay Bridge tunnel and jump off the bridge. The only way he could cross the bridge was to have his wife handcuff him to the steering wheel.

Phobias graphically illustrate how individuals can differ from each other. This chapter analyzes the "person variable" in consumer behavior, describing a number of ways in which market strategy can be influenced by such individual differences.

Based on "How Fearful Nonfliers, Dead Set Against Jets, Get By on the Ground," *The Wall Street Journal*, June 4, 1984, 1, 12; and "The Fight to Conquer Fear," *Newsweek*, April 23, 1984, 66–72.

INTRODUCTION

The consumer vignette introducing the chapter vividly illustrates the concept of individual differences. The idea is that two individuals may behave differently when they encounter exactly the same stimulus, such as a product, service, or advertisement. For most people, getting on an airplane entails no special thoughts or problems. However, for the approximately one in nine Americans who are aerophobic the experience is traumatic. Because aerophobics are encountered so frequently, many airplanes have begun to offer therapeutic courses to help passengers overcome their fears.

The treatment of consumer phobias is attracting the attention of corporations. The advertisement shown in Figure 4–1 was placed by the Upjohn Corporation in magazines as part of an effort to present the company as caring about consumers. The company is involved in research on the debilitating fear of open spaces. The ad effectively communicates the concern of Upjohn for such consumer problems and portrays a highly positive image for the company.

The analysis of individual differences began in psychology with the study of personality. Marketers have begun to borrow some of the personality theories from psychologists to assist them in identifying market segments and in developing the marketing mix. In addition, however, marketers have combined the analysis of personality with the study of lifestyles to develop a more managerially relevant approach called **psychographics.** This chapter will begin with an introduction to the personality area, focusing on the personality theories most frequently used by marketers. It will then discuss the newer area of psychographics. The chapter will conclude with some broad managerial implications of the study of individual differences in consumer behavior.

PERSONALITY AND CONSUMER BEHAVIOR

The word **personality** comes from the Latin term *persona* which means "actor's face mask." In a sense, one's personality is the "mask" worn as a person moves from situation to situation during a lifetime. Over the years many dif-

Figure 4–1   Upjohn emphasizes a caring approach through discussion of its research on agoraphobia. *(Courtesy of The Upjohn Company.)*

ferent definitions of personality have been proposed by psychologists. One of
the best from the consumer behaviorist's point of view states that personality
is

> the distinctive patterns of behavior, including thoughts and emotions, that char-
> acterize each individual's adaptation to the situations of his or her life.[1]

At a general level, the concept of personality has a number of characteristics.
First, in order to be called a personality, a person's behavior should show
some degree of consistency. That is, the behaviors must show a consistency
that distinguishes them from a person's random responses to different stimuli. Personality characteristics tend to be relatively stable across time rather
than short-term in nature. Second, the behaviors should distinguish the person from others. Thus, in the definition of personality just presented the
phrase "distinctive patterns of behavior" connotes the idea that to be called
a personality characteristic a set of behaviors cannot be shared by all consumers.

A third characteristic of personality is that it does interact with the situation. For example, one study found that the personality characteristic of
dogmatism interacted with the task definition of the situation to influence
the amount of innovativeness shown in the purchase of a gift. Dogmatism is
a social-psychological personality characteristic, and innovation proneness
refers to the tendency of a person to buy new or different products. A person
who is dogmatic tends to think rigidly and to have an intolerance for new
ideas. These characteristics can lead to quite different behaviors, depending
upon the situation. For example, one study found that when a gift was to be
bought for personal use, the higher the dogmatism of the purchaser, the less
innovative he or she was in selecting the gift. However, when a gift was purchased for another person, the pattern was reversed, such that the higher
the dogmatism the more innovative the purchase was.[2] Figure 4–2 shows the
interaction between dogmatism and the definition of the task.

A fourth aspect of the study of personality is that one should not expect
to be able to predict highly accurately an individual's purchase behavior from
single measures of personality.[3] Personality characteristics are not rigidly
connected to specific types of behavior. One cannot expect to predict how
many cans of peas a person will buy or the type of furniture a person will
own by looking at specific personality characteristics. The choice of a particular category of product or of a particular brand depends upon the interaction of personality, the situation, and the product. Within each of these categories, a variety of interacting forces may operate. For example, a number of
situational factors may simultaneously push and pull at the consumer. Thus,
the consumer may be under time pressure, may be buying a gift to be given
at a social occasion, and may be in a lousy mood. At the same time the
person may be very low in dogmatism but also very high in self-confidence.
The complexity resulting from the potential interaction of all of these factors
denotes well the idea that consumers must be viewed as a dynamic whole.[4]

Figure 4–2   **A personality-by-situation interaction. (*Source:* Kenneth Coney and Robery Harmon, "Dogmatism and Innovation: A Situational Perspective,"** *Advances in Consumer Research,* **William Wilkie (ed.)** *VI,* **Ann Arbor, Mich: Association for Consumer Research, 1979, 118–221.)**

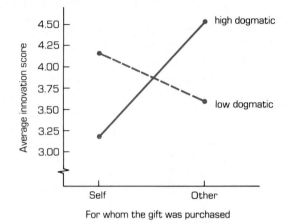

Simple stimulus-response connections between personality and purchase are unlikely to be found. In other words, a consumer researcher should not expect to find any one personality characteristic that predicts whether or not a consumer will buy a particular brand of peas at the supermarket.

For marketers four distinct approaches to personality have had an impact on developing the marketing mix and on segmenting the marketplace. They are psychoanalytic theory, trait theory, social-psychological and cognitively based personality theories, and self-concept theories.

Psychoanalytic Theory

Sigmund Freud's **psychoanalytic view** of personality has had a major impact on our understanding of mankind's makeup. Freud argued that the human personality results from a dynamic struggle between inner physiological drives, such as hunger, sex, and aggression, and social pressures to follow laws, rules, and moral codes. Furthermore, individuals are aware of only a small portion of the forces that drive their behavior, according to Freud. From his perspective, humans have a conscious, preconscious, and an unconscious mind. This idea—that much of what propels humans to action is a part of the unconscious mind and not available for scrutiny—revolutionized the perception of the human personality.[5]

The Structure of the Personality   According to Freud, the personality results from the clash of three forces—the id, ego, and superego. Present at birth, the **id** represents the physiological drives that propel a person to action. These drives are completely unconscious and are like a chaotic cauldron of seething excitations.[6] The id requires instant gratification of its instincts. As such, it operates on the **pleasure principle.**

The **ego** begins to develop as the child grows. The function of the ego is to curb the appetites of the id and helps the person function effectively in the world. As Freud stated, the ego stands for "reason and good sense while the id stands for untamed passions."[7] The ego was viewed by Freud as operating on the **reality principle.** Thus, it helps the person to be practical and to move efficiently through the world. Much of the ego's activities were viewed by Freud as conscious. However, through various **defense mechanisms** the ego helps to curb the unacceptable impulses of the id. Defense mechanisms are unconscious adjustments made by people to keep themselves from recognizing personality qualities or motives that might lower self-esteem or heighten anxiety.

The **superego** can be understood as the conscience, or "voice within" a person that echos the morals and values of parents and society. Only a small portion of it is available to the conscious mind. It is formed throughout middle childhood through the process of **identification,** according to Freud.[8] Identification is the normal process through which children acquire appropriate social roles through the conscious and unconscious copying of the behavior of significant others. The superego actively opposes and clashes with the id, and one role of the ego is to resolve these conflicts. The focus on the conflict between the id and superego is what classifies the psychoanalytic view of personality as a conflict theory.

Psychoanalytic Theory and Marketing   As noted earlier in the text, psychoanalytic thought had a major impact on marketing in the 1950s through the motivation researchers. In particular, advertising firms hired psychoanalysts on their staffs to help develop promotional themes and packaging to appeal to the unconscious minds of consumers. Psychoanalytic theory emphasized the use of dreams, of fantasy, and of symbols to identify the unconscious motives behind a person's actions. Marketers hoped that they could turn the tables and use symbols and flights of fantasy to propel people to buy products.

As noted, Freudian theory stresses the importance of fantasy to the human psyche. Advertisers frequently attempt to move consumers to fantasize about using the product or the consequences of using the product. A nice illustration of an advertisement that may invoke fantasies among consumers is portrayed in Figure 4–3. In the ad Chevrolet attempts to link driving a Monte Carlo SS with auto racing. The copy is designed in part to cause the reader to think of himself or herself as "unwinding" a twisty two-lane road.

A number of symbols exist in psychoanalytic theory that could be used by marketers. For example, **phallic** (male) and **ovarian** (female) **symbols** were thought to activate the release of sexual energy, or **libido.** Indeed, large numbers of books have been sold by sensationalizing the charge that advertising agencies place ovarian and phallic symbols in advertisements in order to

Figure 4–3 Chevrolet promotes fantasies of auto racing. *(Courtesy of the Chevrolet Division of General Motors Corporation.)*

generate sales by releasing such sexual energy.[9] Phallic symbols are represented by figures that are long and cylindrical, whereas ovarian symbols are
represented by figures that are round. In some instances it is quite clear that
companies make use of such symbols. For example, the concave shape of
Jovan perfume and the convex shape of Jovan aftershave appear to be highly
symbolic. However, little evidence exists to suggest that companies deliberately place such symbols in the drawings of ice cubes found in liquor advertisements.

According to psychoanalytic theory, people may also have a death wish,
which is symbolized by death masks. Death masks are facial covers that portray the contorted faces of people in unbearable pain. One author has argued
that liquor advertisers place death masks in the ice cubes of liquor advertisements in order to activate the death wish of heavy drinkers.[10]

Do advertising agencies really engage in such activities? The answer is a
qualified no. A college professor recently conducted a survey that asked advertising people if they ever deliberately embedded a subliminal message,
such as a word, symbol, or sexual organ not perceived at the conscious level,
in advertising artwork for a client. Ninety-six percent of the respondents said
they did not. When asked if they know of anyone doing it, 91 percent said
they did not.[11] Although the percentage admitting to awareness of the use of
embedded symbols in ads was low, it is somewhat surprising that anyone
admitted to the practice at all. One has to ask, however, whether portraying
the ideas symbolically can have any impact given the highly open use of sex
and violence in television and magazines today.

Some research has been performed to investigate the effects of embedding
sexual symbols in advertisements. The research has found little, if any, measurable impact of the symbols. In one study words such as ''sex'' were either
embedded or not embedded in photos of various foods, such as apples,
pretzels, cheese curls, cheese, and popcorn.[12] Advertisements were created
and then shown to student subjects. Overall, few significant effects were found.
Although the implant did significantly improve attitudes towards one of the
products—the cheese curls—one cannot make strong inferences from the
finding. This result could have occurred by chance. Indeed, out of twenty
different comparisons, in eleven instances attitudes were less favorable when
the symbol was present.

Clearly, the psychoanalytic approach to personality has had the greatest
impact on marketing through the research methods developed by Freud and
his followers. They developed projective techniques to assist psychologists in
identifying the unconscious motives that spur people to action. Examples of
the projective techniques include word association tasks, sentence completion tasks, and thematic apperception tests (TATs). (TATs are ambiguous
drawings about which people are asked to write stories.) Freud's major therapeutic tool was to have people lie on a couch and relax both physically and
psychologically and go through long sessions in which the therapist helped
them to bring down their defenses in order to understand more of their

unconscious motivations. Later, psychologists began to bring people together for group therapy. These two approaches have been translated by marketers into the use of **depth interviews** and **focus groups.** Depth interviews are long, probing, one-on-one interviews to identify hidden reasons for purchasing products and services. Focus groups are long sessions in which five to ten consumers are encouraged to talk freely about their feelings and thoughts concerning a product or service.

Trait Theory

The trait theory approach to personality attempts to classify people according to their dominant characteristics or traits. A **trait** is "any characteristic in which one person differs from another in a relatively permanent and consistent way."[13] Trait theories attempt to describe people in terms of their predispositions on a series of adjectives. As such, a person's personality would be described in terms of a particular combination of traits. Table 4–1 gives a list developed by a well-known trait theorist of sixteen traits on which a person could be described. Note, however, that many such lists have been developed by various authors. Indeed, one of the problems of trait theories is the huge number of traits that can be used to describe people.

Much of the early empirical work done in the 1960s by consumer behaviorists on personality involved the use of trait theories. Studies investigated the personality profiles of Ford versus Chevrolet owners,[14] of owners of convertibles versus compacts versus standard model cars[15], and of filter versus nonfilter cigarette users.[16] In general, the results of the studies were weak and inconclusive, and they were severely criticized.[17]

The criticism of the trait theories led to the realization that for the approach to be useful to marketers, the consumer characteristics selected for measurement should be carefully identified in terms of their relevance to the specific buying behavior investigated. The early studies relied on selected trait inventories used by psychologists for purposes that had nothing to do with buying behavior. In addition, researchers using a trait approach needed to recognize the importance of situational factors and assess the validity and reliability of their measures.[18] It also began to be recognized that studying

Table 4–1   Sixteen Personality Traits Identified by Cattel

1. Reserved vs. outgoing	9. Trusting vs. suspicious
2. Dull vs. bright	10. Practical vs. imaginative
3. Unstable vs. stable	11. Unpretentious vs. polished
4. Docile vs. aggressive	12. Self-assured vs. self-reproaching
5. Serious vs. happy-go-lucky	13. Conservative vs. experimenting
6. Expedient vs. conscientious	14. Group-dependent vs. self-sufficient
7. Shy vs. uninhibited	15. Undisciplined vs. controlled
8. Tough-minded vs. tender-minded	16. Relaxed vs. tense

Source: Adapted from R. Cattel, H. Eber, and M. Tatsuoka, *Handbook for the Sixteen Personality Factor Questionnaire*, Champaign, Ill.: Institute for Personality Ability Testing, 1970.

traits in isolation from other factors, such as consumer lifestyles, was not an effective method of predicting buying behavior. As such, the trait approach to personality assessment in marketing began to be integrated into a more general strategy of developing psychographic profiles of consumers. The psychographic approach is discussed later in this chapter.

Social and Cognitive Psychological Personality Theories

Early personality theorists, such as the psychoanalysts, tended to view the personality as resulting from biological factors. Somewhat later, researchers began to view personality as resulting from the *social nature* of people. These theorists believed that personality characteristics resulted from the consistent patterns of behavior that people show with regard to social situations. A number of these **social-psychological personality theories** have been used by marketers to help explain buyer behavior. For example, the personality concept of dogmatism, discussed earlier in the chapter, is social-psychologically based. The construct of dogmatism relates principally to the rigidity with which people approach the social environment. **Cognitively oriented personality theories** have been developed even more recently. These focus on identifying individual differences in how consumers process and react to information. In the following sections four of these social and cognitive psychological theories relating to personality are discussed briefly—three social-psychological theories (the CAD model, anxiety, and masculinity-femininity) and one cognitively oriented approach (tolerance for ambiguity).

The CAD Model   As noted earlier in the chapter, one of the criticisms of the use of personality theories in marketing is the tendency to borrow psychologically oriented theories that may be unrelated to consumer buying behavior. The **CAD** model was developed for the specific purpose of studying buying behavior.[19] CAD stands for "compliance, aggression, detachment." The personality scale was developed to assess the extent to which consumers are interpersonally oriented. Its formulation was based upon the work of the neo-Freudian psychologist Karen Horney. Like other neo-Freudians, Horney broke away from Freud by emphasizing the effects of social influences on the personality.

The CAD scale was based upon Horney's descriptions of people as varying along dimensions of compliance, aggressiveness, and detachment. Compliant people are classified as those who wish to be a part of the activities of others. Aggressive individuals wish to excel, to achieve success, and gain admiration. Finally, those who are detached wish to place emotional "distance" between themselves and others. The CAD approach can help marketers identify consumer segments and predict which consumers may be more or less prone to group influence. For example, one study found that men who rated themselves as more aggressive preferred a particular brand of men's dress shirts (Van Heusen) more than other brands, that highly compliant people were more likely to use mouthwash, that highly aggressive people used cologne more frequently than low-aggressive ones (presumably out of a desire to be noticed), and that highly aggressive men preferred manual razors whereas low-aggressive men preferred electric razors.[20]

Recent research, however, has pointed out some potential problems with CAD. In particular, the research has questioned the reliability and validity of the scale.[21] That is, questions exist as to whether the scale really assesses the personality concepts of compliance, aggression, and detachment or some other unknown constructs. This difficulty with the scale points to a major problem when researchers set out to design their own personality instruments. It takes thousands of painstaking hours and tens of thousands of dollars to develop and test a new personality instrument adequately. In many instances it may be best to borrow selectively existing scales that have been adequately tested and adapt them to the consumer behavior area of interest. Thus, while the CAD scale shows promise, it should be used with caution.

Consumer Anxiety   From time to time everyone experiences an occasion when he or she feels threatened by something. The feeling of threat results in emotional arousal and psychological discomfort. Such feelings of threat, psychological discomfort, and emotional arousal are components of anxiety. Researchers have identified two types of anxiety from which consumers may suffer.[22] **Trait anxiety** refers to the predisposition of a consumer to react with more or less anxiety to various situations. It is an individual-difference variable. Thus, people will react with different levels of anxiety to the same consumer situation. The second type of anxiety is called **state anxiety.** State anxiety is a temporary or transitory emotional state resulting from a specific situation. Thus, state anxiety is composed of the transitory unpleasant feelings that anyone would feel when threatened in some way. Although trait and state anxiety are considered to be two independent concepts, in one situation they are related. When faced with psychological or social stress, people with higher trait anxiety tend to reveal greater levels of the temporary state anxiety. Thus, in a particularly difficult purchase decision, one could expect a person high in trait anxiety to react with more feelings of threat than a person low in trait anxiety.

A variety of factors may act to threaten consumers. One of the major areas has already been discussed—risk perception. When consumers purchase a product, they may perceive that some amount of risk is involved in the purchase. The perception of such risk may result in the experience of anxiety. Figure 4–4 diagrams this relationship. Thus, when a consumer is engaged in some type of consumer choice, such as buying a product, he or she will experience some uncertainty and risk. The perception of risk will cause the consumer to feel anxiety. As a result of the anxiety, the consumer will seek to reduce the feeling of threat in some way. Notice in the figure that the uncertainty can occur before as well as after the choice is made.

A study was designed to test the relationship between decision conflict and anxiety.[23] In the study, individuals who had recently purchased appliances were interviewed to determine their level of state anxiety after the pur-

Figure 4–4 **The relationship between choice, perceived risk, and anxiety. (Based in part on William Locander and Peter Hermann, "The Effect of Self-Confidence and Anxiety on Information Seeking in Consumer Risk Reduction,"** *Journal of Marketing Research, 16,* **May 1979, 268–274.)**

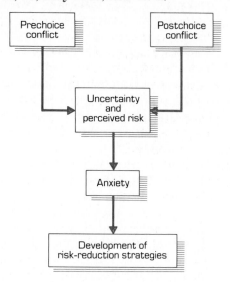

chase and to obtain a measure of the difficulty of the purchase decision. Difficulty was measured by asking the people how many stores they had visited and the number of brands they had considered. For a number of sound reasons the authors believed that decision difficulty or conflict would be greater for those individuals who visited more stores and considered more brands. The results showed a strong correlation $(r = .50)$ between state anxiety and decision conflict. The authors interpreted the relationship to indicate that the decision conflict tended to produce a temporary feeling of anxiety. Of course, it is also possible that individuals high in trait anxiety may have visited more stores and considered more brands as a risk-reduction strategy. However, regardless of which explanation is correct, the relationship between number of stores visited and anxiety shows the potential importance of considering this personality construct.

For managers the concept of consumer anxiety has straightforward implications. First, they should consider the level of anxiety that the purchase of their product or service produces. If consumers perceive a great deal of risk in making a decision, the manager should identify ways to help consumers lower the resulting anxiety. Such methods include using telephone hotlines, developing a trained sales force, and sending consumers postpurchase materials that may soothe their anxiety. Another approach is to assess the firm's target market to determine their trait anxiety. If the target market does suffer from chronic, high levels of trait anxiety, the same methods identified previously to lower anxiety could be utilized.

Masculinity-Femininity   Researchers in the mid-1970s began to investigate another social-psychological personality characteristic that deals with the tendency for people to reveal the characteristics of masculinity and femininity. One popular view held that masculinity and femininity are really two separate dimensions.[24] Thus, a person could be high in masculine characteristics and high in feminine characteristics simultaneously, and researchers developed **masculinity-femininity scales** to assess the characteristics. Figure 4–5 diagrams this idea. In the figure two axes exist—one for the masculinity dimension and one for the femininity dimension. The result is four possible personality types. The male-typed person rates high on masculinity and low on femininity. The female-typed person rates high on femininity and low on masculinity. The undifferentiated person rates low on both masculine and feminine scales. Finally, the **androgynous** person rates high on both masculine and feminine scales.

Although published research on masculinity-femininity in marketing has been scarce, the concepts do have potentially important applications. A number of authors have argued that sex roles in the United States are converging. That is, the jobs that people have and the activities in which they engage are less and less typed as either male-oriented or female-oriented. Both males

Figure 4–5   The two dimensions of masculinity and femininity.

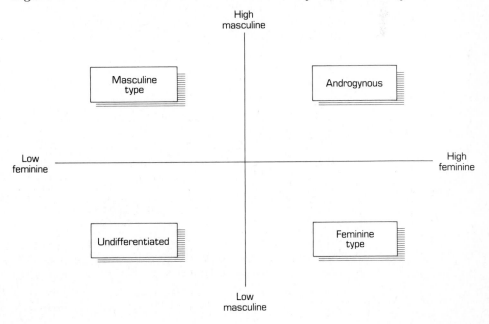

and females are doctors, lawyers, professors, assembly-line workers, nurses, and secretaries. Both females and males play basketball, golf, and tennis. Therefore, it may be possible for marketers to segment on the basis of an individual's sex-role orientation rather than his or her actual sex. Of particular interest are those individuals classified as androgynous. Either males or females can be androgynous, and such individuals have the capacity to show masculine characteristics or feminine characteristics as the situation demands. Thus, if the situation requires them to be nurturing and caring, they can display such feminine behaviors. In contrast, if the situation requires tough-minded, aggressive action, they can display such masculine characteristics.

One study did investigate consumers' sex-role orientations and their leisure activities.[25] The results revealed that in some instances the consumer's sex-role orientation predicted preferences for certain leisure activities better than their sex. In particular, the androgynous individuals tended to participate in and have higher preferences for certain activities than the other groups. These activities were watching documentaries on television, reading news-oriented magazines, and going to R-rated movies. Much additional research needs to be done, and the concept of masculinity-femininity has potentially important implications for marketers. Interestingly, products can also be sex-typed. For example, one study found that nylon underwear was perceived by consumers to be highly feminine, whereas pocket knives were viewed as highly masculine. Products seemed to be viewed as either highly masculine, highly feminine, or weak in both dimensions. Examples of androgynous products were not found in this particular study.[26]

Tolerance for Ambiguity   The concept of **tolerance for ambiguity** deals with how a person reacts to situations that have varying degrees of ambiguity or inconsistency.[27] Those individuals who are tolerant of ambiguity react to such situational inconsistency in a positive way. In contrast, those identified as intolerant of ambiguity tend to view situational inconsistency as threatening and undesirable.

Three different types of situations have been identified as ambiguous.[28] First, completely new situations about which a person has little information are considered ambiguous. Second, highly complex situations that tend to overwhelm a person with information have a high degree of ambiguity. Finally, situations that contain contradictory information are ambiguous. One can characterize these situations as: (1) novel, (2) complex, and (3) insoluble.

The personality construct of tolerance for ambiguity may influence people in a number of consumer tasks. For example, one study found that those categorized as tolerant of ambiguity reacted more positively to products perceived as new than those intolerant of ambiguity.[29] Such a result does make sense. When purchasing a new product, a consumer is encountering a novel situation, and those who are tolerant of ambiguity are more likely to react positively to such circumstances. From a manager's perspective the implications of this relationship are straightforward. When identifying a target market for a new product's introduction, managers should attempt to identify consumers who show a tendency to be tolerant of ambiguity.

A second area of application for the personality variable is in identifying those consumers who are most likely to search for information. One study investigated the factors that influence the extent to which consumers will search for information when making a product choice. One would predict that those consumers who are tolerant of ambiguity would be more likely to search for information as the choice task became more complex and as the products became more novel. The results supported these predictions. Those consumers identified as having a tolerance for ambiguity tended to search for information as the choice task became more complex and novel.[30] The implications of these results are quite interesting. It may be that individuals with higher tolerance for ambiguity may actually like to receive information about products. If this were found to be the case, it would have implications for promotional strategy. If the firm's target market consisted of large numbers of individuals who sought information, it would suggest that the company should develop lots of pamphlets, brochures, and other informative materials to accompany the product. In contrast, if the target market were composed of those intolerant of ambiguity, the strategy might involve giving relatively little information about the product. Perhaps in such cases more emotional appeals could be used. Of course, these are speculations that require additional research.

The Self-Concept in Consumer Research

The **self-concept** represents the "totality of the individual's thoughts and feelings having reference to himself as an object."[31] It is as though an individual "turns around" and evaluates in an objective fashion just who and what he or she is. Because people have a need to behave in ways consistent with their self-concept, this perception of themselves forms part of the basis for the personality. Such self-consistent behavior helps a person maintain his or her self-esteem and gives the person predictability in interactions with others.[32]

An important finding is that people have more than one self-concept. Table 4–2 presents six types of self-concept that have been identified. Two ver-

---

Table 4–2   Various Types of Self-Concept

1. *Actual self:* how a person *actually* perceives himself.
2. *Ideal self:* how a person *would like* to perceive himself.
3. *Social self:* how a person thinks *others* perceive him.
4. *Ideal social self:* how a person *would like others* to perceive him.
5. *Expected self:* an image of self somewhere in between the actual and ideal self.
6. *Situational self:* a person's self-image in a specific situation.

Source: Adapted from a discussion by M. Joseph Sirgy, "Self-Concept in Consumer Behavior: A Critical Review," *Journal of Consumer Research*, 9, December 1982, 287–300.

sions of the self appear in the various conceptualizations—the **actual** and the **ideal self-concepts.** The actual self-concept relates to how a person actually perceives himself. In contrast, the ideal self-concept denotes how a person would like to perceive himself or herself.[33]

The Self-Concept and Product Symbolism   In order to understand how the self-concept influences buying behavior, one must recognize that products may act as "symbols" for consumers. Symbols are "things which stand for or express something else."[34] Some writers have argued that the primary reason for buying many products is not for their functional benefits but for their symbolic value.[35] Others have written that consumers' personalities can be defined through the products they use.[36] Finally, many researchers believe that people view their possessions as an extension of themselves. In fact, various studies have found a relationship between the self-image of a person and certain products that he buys. Products for which such self-image/product-image congruence have been found include: automobiles, health products, cleaning products, grooming products, leisure products, clothing, retail-store patronage, food products, cigarettes, home appliances, magazines, and home furnishings.[37] Thus, there is ample evidence of the importance of **product symbolism.**

Just which products are most likely to be viewed as symbols by consumers? One might argue that the products consumers use to communicate themselves to others act as symbols. Such communicative products have three characteristics.[38] First, they must have visibility in use, such that their purchase, consumption, and/or disposition are readily apparent to others. Second, the product must show variability. That is, some consumers must have the resources to own the product while others do not have the time, financial, or other resources to possess it. If everyone owned the product or could use the service and if it were identical for everyone, it could not be a symbol. Third, the product should have personalizability. Personalizability refers to the extent to which a product denotes a stereotypic image of the average user. One can easily see how such symbolic products as automobiles or jewelry possess the characteristics of visibility, variability, and personalizability.

The importance of recognizing the symbolic nature of products is depicted in Figure 4–6. In the figure are three boxes representing a person's self-concept, an audience or reference group, and a product that acts as a symbol. The consumer may purchase a product that symbolizes a feature of his or her self-concept to the audience. As shown in the figure, in Step 1 the consumer buys a product that can communicate his or her self-concept to the audience, or reference group. The consumer hopes in Step 2 the audience will associate the desired symbolic qualities of the product with himself or herself. In Step 3 the consumer hopes that the reference group will perceive him or her as possessing these symbolic qualities.[39] Through the steps outlined consumers may be conceptualized as purchasing products in order to communicate symbolically various aspects of their self-concepts to others.

Figure 4–6   The communication of self to others via symbolic products.

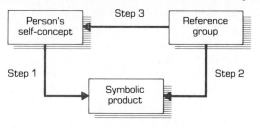

Step 1: Person buys product that is symbolic of self.
Step 2: Reference group associates product with person.
Step 3: Reference group attributes to person the symbolic
qualities of the product.

A Scale to Measure the Self-Concept and Product Image

One of the problems for the marketing researcher is how to assess the self-concept of consumers in a market segment and the image that they have of a brand. Ideally, one scale should be used to assess both product image and self-image, if the researcher is going to match optimally the segment to the product. One researcher developed a scale specifically for this purpose.[40] Shown in Table 4–3, the scale is composed of fifteen items that are presented in a

Table 4–3   A Scale to Measure Product Images and Self-Images[a]

1. Rugged	1	2	3	4	⑤	6	7	Delicate
2. Exciting	1	2	3	4	5	⑥	7	Calm
3. Uncomfortable	1	2	3	4	5	⑥	7	Comfortable
4. Dominating	1	2	3	4	5	⑥	7	Submissive
5. Thrifty	1	2	3	4	5	6	7	Indulgent
6. Pleasant	1	2	3	4	5	⑥	7	Unpleasant
7. Contemporary	1	2	3	4	5	6	7	Uncontemporary
8. Organized	①	2	3	4	5	6	7	Unorganized
9. Rational	1	2	③	4	5	6	7	Emotional
10. Youthful	1	2	3	4	5	⑥	7	Mature
11. Formal	1	2	3	④	5	6	7	Informal
12. Orthodox	1	2	3	4	5	6	7	Liberal
13. Complex	1	2	3	4	5	⑥	7	Simple
14. Colorless	1	2	3	4	⑤	6	7	Colorful
15. Modest	①	2	3	4	5	6	7	Vain

[a]Consumers are asked to rate either their actual, ideal, or social self-concept on the scale. They are then asked to rate one or more brands on the same scale. Brands whose pattern of responses most closely match a consumer's self-concept are expected to be preferred by a consumer.

Source: Adapted from Naresh K. Malhotra, "A Scale to Measure Self-Concepts, Person Concepts, and Product Concepts," *Journal of Marketing Research, 18,* November 1981, 456–464.

semantic differential format to consumers. (A semantic differential scale uses bipolar adjectives, such as light-heavy, on which a person rates something.) Researchers ask members of the target market to rate both themselves and various products on the scale. Brands rated in a manner similar to the consumer's rating of himself or herself are predicted to have an image that corresponds with the self-concept of the consumers. Although additional work needs to be performed to test the scale's reliability and validity, it does offer promise as an approach for assessing product image and consumer self-image congruity.

LIFESTYLES AND PSYCHOGRAPHICS

One of the major thrusts of the textbook is the identification of three major sets of factors influencing buying behavior—the product offering, the situation, and the person. The early portion of the present chapter on personality and psychographics focused on psychological approaches to the study of the person. The psychological study of individual differences has generally been called the study of personality. Marketers, however, do not have the time or resources to analyze an individual's personality as a psychologist would when performing therapy on a client. In addition, marketers tend to work at a group level rather than at the individual level, as a therapist would. Thus, the focus of marketers and consumer researchers has generally been on identifying the broad trends that influence how consumers live, work, and play. Such broad trends have been given the name consumer **lifestyles.**

Consumer Lifestyles

The concept of consumer lifestyle has been defined in a variety of ways. Lifestyle has been defined simply as "how one lives."[41] The term *lifestyle* can be used to describe different levels of aggregation of people. It has been used to describe not only an individual or a small group of interacting people but also larger groups of people, such as a market segment.[42] Thus, the concept of lifestyle denotes a set of ideas quite distinct from that of personality. Lifestyle relates to how people live, how they spend their money, and how they allocate their time. Lifestyle concerns the overt actions and behaviors of consumers. In contrast, personality describes the consumer internally. It delineates the consumer's "characteristic pattern of thinking, feeling, and perceiving."[43] In Highlight 4–1 trends in consumption activities as part of Americans' evolving lifestyles are explored.

Of course, the study of lifestyle and personality can be closely related. A consumer who has a personality categorized as highly risk averse will probably not indulge in a lifestyle that includes an occupation as a speculator in the futures market or leisure activities such as mountain climbing, hang gliding, and jungle exploration. Nonetheless, lifestyle and personality should be distinguished for two important reasons. First, they are conceptually distinct concepts. Personality refers to the internal characteristics of a person. In con-

HIGHLIGHT 4–1

A New American Lifestyle—Abstinence

Across a wide spectrum of consumption activities Americans have begun to practice good old Puritan values. Here are some of the trends.

- Per capita consumption of cigarettes is down by 39 percent since 1964.
- Per capita alcohol consumption is down.
- Per capita consumption of hard liquor is down, while consumption of wine is up.
- Per capita consumption of caffeinated coffee is down.
- Per capita consumption of beef is down.
- Per capita consumption of chicken is up.
- Per capita consumption of bottled water is up.
- Per capita consumption of diet soft drinks is up.

The reaction of companies hard hit by these lifestyle changes has been rapid. The maker of Bacardi rum has begun to run advertisements that make the point that a mixed drink with rum and orange juice contains no more calories and less alcohol than a five-ounce glass of white wine. In 1984 liquor companies spent $50 million on advertisements telling consumers to use alcohol in moderation. Broadcast companies faced with the threat of legislation designed to forbid television advertising of beer and wine have begun to run a spate of public service announcements warning against drunken driving. The National Beef Council spent $5 million in 1984 in an image campaign telling consumers that "beef gives strength."

The cause of these lifestyle changes is hard to pin down. The booming fitness trend could be part of the explanation. However, that does not explain why the sales of cholesterol-loaded cheese are exploding. It may have to do with the changing tastes of the baby-boom generation as they grow older. While the reasons are unclear for the abstinence trend, the bottom-line implications are devastating for companies who produce the "wrong" product.

Based in part on Brian Dumaine, "America's New Abstinence," *Fortune*, March 18, 1985, 20–23.

---

trast, lifestyle refers to the external characteristics of how a person lives. Although both concepts describe the person, they describe different aspects of the individual.

A second reason for the distinction between lifestyle and personality is that the process of distinguishing between the two has managerial implications. Some authors have argued that market segments can be too narrowly targeted if the target market is defined by personality too early in the process.[44] They recommend that marketers should segment the market sequentially by first identifying lifestyle segments and then by analyzing these segments for personality differences. By first identifying lifestyle segments that show consistent patterns of overt behavior in how consumers buy products, use their time, and engage in various activities, the marketer is apt to identify a large number of people with similar lifestyle characteristics. This first step of segmenting by lifestyle may be called "maximizing market potentials." The next step is to determine if the segment of consumers with similar buying and lifestyle characteristics is uniform with respect to personality characteristics.

A hypothetical example of the sequential segmentation of beer drinkers may help to clarify the concept. In the first phase of sequential segmentation lifestyle analysis is performed. Suppose that a lifestyle analysis of beer drinkers finds that they can be categorized according to their leisure activities. Further, suppose that four lifestyle segments are identified—inactives, television watchers, book readers, and outdoor-sports lovers. The imaginary analysis reveals that the heaviest beer drinkers are in the outdoor-sports-lover segment. In order to analyze this segment further, the second phase of the sequential analysis analyzes the group on personality variables. A sample of outdoor-sports lovers is given a series of personality scales. What might be found is that the outdoor-sports lovers differ substantially on one of the scales—masculinity-femininity. The heaviest beer drinkers of the group fall into the masculine category, followed by androgynous and feminine types. From a managerial perspective the strategy in reaching the groups would be quite different. For example, advertisements would direct different selling appeals to each of the three groups. In addition, the potential for creating different products for each of the segments would exist. Figure 4–7 illustrates the sequential segmentation strategy.

An important question, however, has not yet been addressed in the discussion on lifestyles and cognitive styles. How are they measured by mar-

Figure 4–7 Sequential segmentation by lifestyle and personality for heavy beer drinkers (a hypothetical example).

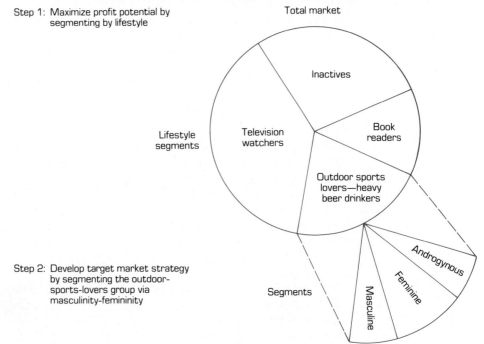

keters? That question, addressed in the next section, involves psychographic analysis.

The term **psychographics** means different things to different researchers. The term itself connotes the idea of describing (graph) the psychological (psycho) makeup of consumers. As such, psychographics would be used to identify the personality of consumers. Others identify psychographics with the assessment of consumers' activities, interests, and opinions (AIOs). In general, researchers tend to equate psychographics with the study of lifestyles.

The goals of psychographic research are usually of an applied nature. That is, psychographic research is used by market researchers to describe a consumer segment so as to help an organization better reach and understand its customers. Psychographic studies usually include questions to assess the sample members' lifestyles, their personalities, and even their demographic characteristics. In sum, psychographics is the quantitative investigation of consumers' lifestyles, personality, and demographics which is used to assist in marketing decision making.

Because of the applied orientation of psychographic analyses, a different set of questions generally will be formulated each time a new marketing problem is encountered. The questions can come from any source that seems relevant to the problem at hand. Questions may be borrowed from social-psychological personality scales, from cognitive scales, and from trait inventories. In almost all cases, questions to assess the demographic characteristics of the sample will be included. Thus, the age, sex, occupation, marital status, income, and other demographic variables will be obtained. In addition, questions concerning product usage will usually be asked in order to determine who the heavy, moderate, and light users of a product are.

Psychographics and AIO Statements   One of the features that distinguishes psychographic research from more traditional approaches is the use of questions called **AIO statements.** Standing for activities, interests, and opinions, AIO statements attempt to describe the lifestyle of the consumer through his or her activities, interests, and opinions. Activity questions ask consumers to indicate what they do, what they buy, and how they spend their time. Interest questions focus on what the consumers' preferences and priorities are. Opinion questions ask for consumers' views and feelings on such things as world, local, moral, economic, and social affairs. Table 4–4 lists questions representative of AIO items.

No hard-and-fast rules exist for developing AIO items. One dimension on which they frequently differ is their level of specificity. AIO questions may be highly specific and ask the respondent to provide information on his or her attitudes and preferences regarding a specific product or service. For example, a researcher for General Mills might be interested in consumer percep-

Table 4–4   Some Typical Questions Found in AIO Inventories

1. Activity questions
   a. What outdoor sports do you participate in at least twice a month?
   b. How many books do you read a year?
   c. How often do you visit shopping malls?
   d. Have you gone outside of the U.S. for a vacation?
   e. To how many clubs do you belong?

2. Interest questions
   a. In which of the following are you more interested—sports, church, work?
   b. How important to you is it to try new foods?
   c. How important to you is it to get ahead in life?
   d. Would you rather spend two hours on a Saturday afternoon with your wife or in a boat fishing alone?

3. Opinion questions (ask the respondent to agree or disagree)
   a. The Russian people are just like us.
   b. Women should have free choice regarding abortions.
   c. Educators are paid too much money.
   d. CBS Inc. is run by East Coast liberals.
   e. We must be prepared for nuclear war.

tions of Post Grape-Nuts, a breakfast cereal. The researcher might ask respondents to agree or disagree with the following highly specific questions:

I find Grape-Nuts to be too hard to chew.
Grape-Nuts remind me of the outdoors.
Eating Grape-Nuts makes me feel healthy.

On the other hand, AIO questions can be much more general. Some highly general questions that the researcher might ask the consumer to agree or disagree with include the following:

I consider myself an outdoor person.
I believe in world peace.
I think cities are where the action is.

Of course the researcher will have different purposes for asking the two types of questions. The highly specific questions will give the researcher information on what consumers think about the product and how that product relates to themselves. From such information products may be developed or changed and specific messages created. Indeed, unique selling propositions may be formulated. A **unique selling proposition** is a quick, hard-hitting phrase that captures a major feature of a product or service. For example, the makers of Wheaties have used for many years the unique selling proposition "The breakfast of champions." By asking people to describe through AIO statements the specific product, such unique selling propositions can be formulated.

The more general types of AIO questions also have a purpose. From these questions profiles of consumers can be developed. Such profiles can be used to obtain an understanding of the general lifestyle of a consumer segment that is being targeted. Based upon the profile, advertisers can develop ideas for the general themes of ads and for the setting within which to place an ad. For example, Highlight 4–2 presents a verbal profile of individuals who tend to have more driving accidents than average. As can be seen, the profile describes a distinctive person. If a marketer discovered that the accident prone tend to be heavy users of a particular product, it would be relatively straightforward to identify the promotional themes to appeal to this group from the profile. Thus, such themes might revolve around taking risks, doing things impulsively, and getting ahead in the future.[45]

The example of the accident-prone driver also reveals the importance of including demographic information when doing psychographic analyses. One of the best predictors of the tendency to have driving accidents is the age of the driver. The profile given in Highlight 4–2 does seem to describe the characteristics of a young adult. It would be important for the researcher to determine to what extent the lifestyle and personality characteristics of the consumer lead to accidents in addition to the mere fact that the consumer might be less than twenty-five years of age. Various statistical techniques, such as regression analysis and discriminant function analysis, could be used for such a purpose.

Psychographics and Purchase Activities   In addition to examining lifestyles via AIO statements, researchers can identify segments of consumers by assessing the types of purchases they make. In this instance, large numbers of people are surveyed about their purchase patterns. The data are then analyzed to find groups of people who exhibit similar patterns of purchase behavior. Table 4–5 identifies sixteen different segments of men based upon

---

HIGHLIGHT 4–2

A Profile of the Accident-Prone Driver

The accident-prone driver is defined as a person who has had two or more driving accidents in the past five years. Such drivers will tend to agree more frequently with such statements as, "I am the kind of person who will try anything once." They are also restless individuals who like to move from place to place. In general, they view themselves as having money problems and as being pressured by time. They tend to buy on impulse more frequently and view themselves as more of a "swinger" than those who have not had accidents. The accident prone tend to have more liberal ideas

and attitudes. For example, they are more likely to have attended an X-rated movie. Interestingly, they also like to watch disaster movies more than their less accident prone counterparts. Finally, the accident prone are more optimistic about the future than those without accidents. (Indeed, they may well have to be.)

Based on Table 4.9 in Sunil Mehotra and William Wells, "Psychographics and Buyer Behavior: Theory and Recent Empirical Findings," in *Consumer and Industrial Buying Behavior*, Arch Woodside et al. (eds.), New York: North-Holland, 1979.

Table 4–5 Lifestyle Categories of Men Based on the Products Bought Most Frequently

Category	Description	Products Bought Frequently
1.	The hard drinker	Whiskey, bourbon, scotch, vodka, beer, gin
2.	The car conscious	Car wax, polish, gasoline, antifreeze
3.	Candy consumer	Candy bars, hard candies, chewing gum
4.	Cosmopolitan traveler	Car rental, foreign trips, plane trips
5.	Electric shaver	Electric shaver, preshave lotion
6.	Cigar & pipe smoker	Cigars, cigarillos, pipe tobacco
7.	Dress conscious	Suits, shoes, dress shirts, sport shirts
8.	Well groomed	Hair tonic, after-shave lotion, mouthwash, hair shampoo
9.	Cold conscious	Cold tablets, cough drops, throat lozenges
10.	Photographer	Movie film, photographs, flash pictures
11.	Liquor & wine connoisseur	Rum, brandy, liquors, wines
12.	Old man	Hats, denture cream
13.	Hard-driving man	Gasoline and auto accessories
14.	Cocktail drinker	Bottled cocktails, cocktail mixer
15.	Regular shaver	Double-edged blades, stainless doubled-edged blades
16.	Deodorized man	Roll-on deodorant, spray deodorant

SOURCE: Lewis Alput and Ronald Gatty, "Product Positioning by Behavioral Life-Styles," *Journal of Marketing, 33*, April 1969, 67.

their particular buying habits. Although the categories appear somewhat oversimplified, they do offer some insight into the types of products that tend to be bought together. For example, the man who drives lots of miles in his car also tends to buy more car wax and polish. The man who smokes cigars is also likely to smoke a pipe. Such information can be extremely useful in developing ideas for promotional campaigns.

The VALS Psychographic Inventory Perhaps the most well developed psychographic inventory of consumers is the **VALS lifestyle classification scheme.** Developed by the Stanford Research Institute, VALS has been widely used by U.S. corporations to segment the market and to provide guidance for developing advertising and product strategy.[46] The ideas upon which the VALS approach is based were derived from the work of motivational and developmental psychologists. In particular, Maslow's hierarchy of needs played an important role in the development of the psychographic inventory. The influence of Maslow and of developmental psychologists led the originators of VALS to view consumers as moving through a series of stages that have been described as a double hierarchy. Shown in Figure 4–8, the hierarchy consists of four general categories of groups. These are: (1) the **need-driven** groups,

Figure 4–8   The VALS double hierarchy. (*Source:* Arnold Mitchell, *The Nine American Lifestyles*, New York, N.Y.: Macmillan Publishing Company, 1983.)

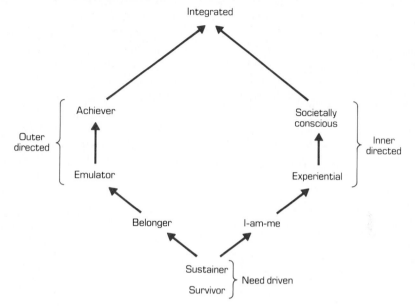

(2) the **outer-directed** groups, (3) the **inner-directed** groups, and (4) the **integrateds.**

THE NEED-DRIVEN GROUP. As can be seen in the Figure 4–8, the need-driven groups stand at the bottom of the hierarchy and are composed of two segments—the survivors and the sustainers. Survivors are marked by poverty, old age, poor health, and poor education. The sustainers stand above the survivors in the hierarchy. They are also marked by poverty and tend to be "angry, distrustful, rebellious, anxious, combative people who often feel left out of things."[47] They differ from the survivors, however, in that they have not given up hope. They tend to be younger than survivors and are frequently of a minority race. They are also psychologically different from the survivors. Sustainers are more self-confident, they do more planning, and they expect more of the future than do survivors.

THE OUTER-DIRECTED GROUP. At the next level in the hierarchy are two separate groups that have moved in different psychological directions. For the inner directeds, forces internal to themselves drive their actions. In contrast, the outer directeds focus on what other people think of them and gear their lives to the "visible, tangible, and materialistic." Neither group can be considered better off socially, financially, or psychologically. It is the focus of their thoughts and activities—either internal, to themselves, or external, to others—that sets the two apart.

Within the outer-directed group one finds three segments—the belongers, the emulators, and the achievers. The belongers are generally regarded as middle-class Americans. They desire to fit in rather than stand out. Most are white, possess middle incomes, and are middle-aged or over. They cherish the institutions of family, church, and country. This is the most "old-fashioned" and traditional of the VALS groups.

The emulators diverge substantially from the belongers. Emulators are intensively striving and seeking to get ahead by imitating the actions of those they consider richer and more successful than they. This group is highly ambitious, but they spend rather than save. As a consequence, they tend to be in debt. A major problem is that they do not really understand the values and lifestyles of the achievers whom they attempt to emulate.

At the peak of the outer-directed group are the achievers. These are the individuals who have built the system and are at the helm. These are the wealthy, successful Americans. They have high incomes and tend to be professionals. More than any other VALS group, they are self-employed. They tend to be conservative and Republican in political persuasion.

THE INNER DIRECTEDS. Rather than using the opinions of others as their reference point for their actions, inner directeds focus internally. These are introspective people who seek intense involvement in whatever they do. They tend to have been born after World War II, to hold professional jobs, and to have higher-than-average incomes. Politically they are usually independents. Three different inner-directed segments have been identified—the I-am-me's, the experientials, and the societally conscious.

The I-am-me group seems to be a group in transition from the views of their outer-directed parents to an inner-directed focus. In most cases the stay in this group is short—only a few years—and is marked by major shifts in emotions, feelings, and viewpoints. As one would guess, most are students and few have been married. Their average age is twenty-one. These are highly energetic individuals who are enthusiastic, daring, and eager to seek new ideas and possessions.

The second of the inner-directed groups is the experientials. These individuals seek direct, vivid experience in the things they do. It could be deep personal involvement in causes and issues, or it could be involvement in hedonism or activities requiring great exertion, such as rock climbing. They are independent and self-reliant people who are innovative. They have moderate incomes and are mostly in their late twenties.

The societally conscious represent the last of the inner-directed segments. This small group of about 13 million Americans is concerned with societal issues, trends, and developments. They are often involved in consumer issues. They tend to be successful, influential, and mature individuals.

Indeed, they are the inner-directed equivalent of the achievers. Their average age is forty. Most hold professional jobs and have high incomes. They are politically liberal and are driven by the social ideals about which they are highly concerned.

THE INTEGRATEDS. At the peak of the VALS inventory are the integrateds. A small group, they represent only 2 percent of the population. Approximating the self-actualized person about whom Maslow talked, the integrateds are mature, balanced people who have managed to put together the best of the characteristics of the inner- and outer-directed personality. Although the integrateds have the highest incomes of any of the VALS groups, their small numbers make them difficult to target successfully.

Buying and Activity Patterns of the VALS Groups   Because of the popularity of the VALS inventory, a substantial number of studies are available that describe the consumption and activity differences of the various VALS groups. Table 4–6 summarizes the results from a number of studies that have investigated the purchase patterns, activity patterns, demographics, and attitudes of the groups. As is readily observable, the psychographic segments differ widely in these areas.

One organization that has specifically used the VALS inventory to plan its marketing strategy is the Beef Industry Council. The beef industry has faced major problems in the 1970s and 1980s because of declining per capita consumption. One reason for the decline in beef consumption is that the price of beef has increased relative to that of its competitors, especially chicken. Another reason, however, is the changing lifestyles of Americans. Two changes in lifestyles have particularly harmed beef consumption. First, the increasing employment of women has resulted in less time available to cook traditional family meals. As a consequence, women (or men) simply do not have the time to spend several hours cooking roasts. The result is that 40 percent fewer roasts were served in 1984 than in 1968.[48]

In order to understand better these ominous trends in beef consumption, the Beef Industry Council authorized a survey of consumers to classify them into the VALS categories and to analyze their consumption of beef, lamb, fish, and other main-course items. Table 4–7 (see p. 120) provides an index of consumption of the eight VALS segments of beef, lamb, fresh fish, and chicken. As can be seen in the table, the survivors and sustainers simply do not consume much meat, probably because of limited financial resources. Achievers and the societally conscious in particular are heavy meat eaters in all categories. Again, it is quite likely that income plays a major role in explaining these results. That is, both groups have high incomes and can afford serving all types of meat, fish, and poultry. However, lifestyles also clearly influence the consumption patterns of these groups. In particular, the experiential segment eats very little lamb, whereas the I-am-me's eat much more than average.

Table 4–6   Some Selected Differences in AIOs Among VALS Groups

AIO Category	Survivors	Sustainers	Belongers	Emulators	Achievers	I-am-me	Experiential	Societally Conscious
Activities[a]								
Golf	0	100	54	62	162	162	108	85
Fishing	48	200	126	100	87	91	100	74
Go to museums	43	52	78	61	165	74	126	191
Watch TV game shows	233	225	158	108	42	17	42	50
Watch TV comedies	67	195	86	152	67	176	138	67
Read tabloids (e.g., *Enquirer*)	118	247	129	106	53	100	59	47
Read business magazines	36	64	100	36	186	100	114	157
Drink reg. soft drinks	112	112	82	171	94	176	94	59
Drink diet soft drinks	50	50	80	90	110	120	150	170
Demographics								
Size of group	11M	6M	57M	16M	37M	8M	11M	14M
Median age	66	32	51	28	42	21	28	37
Median household income	<$5,000	$11,000	$17,500	$19,000	$30,000	$10,000	$22,000	$25,000
Opinions								
Believe women should be in home	46%	32%	34%	9%	16%	7%	5%	2%
Experimental (not conventional)	15%	12%	6%	10%	7%	29%	33%	25%

[a]For activities 100 equals average rate of participation.

SOURCE: T. C. Thomas and S. Crocker, *Values and Lifestyles—New Psychographics*, Menlo Park, Calif.: SRI, 1981.

Figure 4–9   The story board for a beef ad targets active, contemporary adults, who represent particular psychographic groups. (*Courtesy of Beef Industry Council.*)

Table 4–7   A VALS Analysis of Meat and Fish Consumption[a]

	Beef	Lamb	Fresh Fish	Fresh Chicken	Turkey Breast
Survivors	64	21	62	69	41
Sustainers	77	54	111	93	62
Belongers	98	96	90	97	75
Emulators	102	62	111	107	63
Achievers	115	125	108	107	155
I-am-me	90	174	119	90	110
Experiential	95	36	79	100	85
Societally conscious	109	160	121	108	154

[a]Based on an index in which 100 is average. The respondents were asked to indicate if they had eaten the product in the last seven days.
SOURCE: T. C. Thomas and S. Crocker, *Values and Lifestyles—New Psychographics.* Menlo Park, Calif.: SRI, 1981.

Based in part upon the VALS analysis, the advertising agency of the Beef Industry Council recommended that their promotional activities should be targeted to active, contemporary adults. In VALS terms this group would be identified as the achievers and societally conscious. These groups were selected for targeting because they are growing in numbers, because the achievers and the societally conscious are opinion leaders, and because the I-am-me's and the experientials have somewhat negative attitudes regarding beef. An interesting question for the advertising agency is whether the lack of interest in reaching the belongers segment, who represent by far the largest market for beef, was a proper course of action. Figure 4–9 (see p. 119) presents a story board of one of the television ads targeted to these groups of individuals.

Managerial Implications

The analysis of the personality and psychographic characteristics of consumers has a number of important managerial uses. Perhaps most importantly such an analysis can assist managers in the segmentation of the marketplace. In addition, the study of individual consumer characteristics can assist in the development of the marketing mix, in the positioning of products, and in the development of media strategy.

Segmenting the Marketplace

Personality and psychographic analyses have two interrelated uses for marketing managers when they seek to segment the marketplace. First, the personality or psychographic categories may be used directly for segmentation purposes. Second, consumers may be initially segmented on other characteristics, such as product usage or social class, and then described via psychographic and personality analyses.

The VALS categories have been used to segment the marketplace directly. Companies or organizations, such as the Beef Industry Council, have identified one or more of the VALS lifestyle segments and targeted that group specifically. Thus, the Beef Council chose to target the inner-directed group and the achievers group. Anheuser-Busch has also used such a strategy in targeting beer drinkers. The company performed a psychographic analysis of the characteristics of drinkers and identified four major groupings—reward drinkers, social drinkers, indulgent drinkers, and oceanic drinkers.[49] Based upon the psychographic characteristics of these groups, the company could position, distribute, and price beer products to reach each of the groups most effectively. Even though the research was done over fifteen years ago, if one looks at the themes in Michelob advertising, it seems as though Anheuser-Busch is still attempting to reach the financially upscale person who is drinking as a reward for his or her achievements. In contrast, the Budweiser ads appear targeted to the social drinker, who is a young adult and is driven by ambitions.

Rather than using the psychographic or personality categories to segment the market, a firm may instead divide the market on such bases as demographics, social class, or product usage. Product usage is a frequent segmentation variable. In this case consumers are divided according to the frequency of their purchase or use of a product or service. Oftentimes three categories are developed—heavy, moderate, and light users of the product. Psychographics or personality variables are then used to described the segments. For example, one study divided consumers into the categories of heavy and light moviegoers.[50] As compared to nonmoviegoers, the heavy moviegoers were:

1. More achievement oriented.
2. More interested in traveling around.
3. Risk taking.
4. More interested in social activities.
5. More interested in magazines such as *Playboy*.
6. More swinging.
7. More apt to drink.
8. More likely to think that women should be able to smoke in public.
9. Less interested in religion.

Developing the Marketing Mix

Information on the personality and psychographic characteristics of consumer segments can also be invaluable for firms in the planning of the marketing mix. In particular, how the product is promoted should be guided in part upon the psychogenic and personality characteristics of the company's target market. For example, message development should be predicated upon such information. One study found that heavy beer drinkers like to take risks, play games of chance such as poker, act impulsively, like sports, reject old-fashioned institutions and moral guidelines, and take a highly masculine view of the world.[51] If one looks at the advertising of beer companies, such as Stroh and Miller, these elements can often be seen in commercials designed to be humorous. For example, in one of the Stroh's ads a group of men is out camping (a masculine kind of activity). They hear some noises and conclude that a grizzly bear is into the Stroh's beer. One of them takes off to get the beer from the bear (an impulsive and risk-taking thing to do). He returns safely, carrying one less case than he should have, and explains that he had to make a trade with the bear.

In one study researchers investigated the demographic and psychographic characteristics of the donors and nondonors of blood.[52] The results revealed that the typical blood donor tended to be a family man who had little self-esteem and avoided taking risks. He was concerned about his health because he had a rare blood type. In addition, he was religious and highly educated. The authors of the study concluded that the themes of advertisements and the handling of the donors should be based in part upon these characteristics. In particular, the effects of group pressure might be useful as a means of influencing such low self-esteem people.

In the personal-selling area, a number of companies are developing interactive computer programs to assist sales personnel in closing deals with customers. In some instances the programs were developed by psychologists and based upon theories of personality. For example, one program called "Sales Edge" was developed in part upon the Thurstone Temperament Scale. The program asks the salesman to answer a series of questions about himself and his client. It then prints out a set of tactics that the salesman can use in attempting to make the sale.

Product Positioning and Media Strategy

The psychographic analysis of consumers can also assist marketers in positioning products or services and in developing media strategy. As discussed elsewhere in the text, a brand may be positioned relative to competitors on the characteristics that consumers use to evaluate the products. Oftentimes the psychogenic or personality characteristics of a brand's target market can be used to determine the characteristics that the segment may prefer in a product. For example, when the Ford Pinto was first introduced, it was positioned as a "carefree, small, romantic" car. Researchers, however, found that Pinto buyers were not romantic, but practical and utilitarian. As a result, Ford repositioned the car as providing functional, economical transportation.[53]

Figure 4–10 presents an advertisement that attempts to reposition the potato as a diet food. The goal of the ad is to reach a lifestyle segment that is concerned with diet and nutrition. By using a humorous photograph to attract attention and hard-hitting copy, the ad is effective in positioning the potato as a potential diet food that consumers should consider.

Knowledge of the psychographic characteristics of a firm's target market can also influence media strategy. When promoting a product, a firm must determine the types of media over which to place its advertising. The goal should be to match the psychographic profile of the firm's target market to the profile of the viewers of the media in which advertising is placed. Thus, if the heavy users of a product exhibit particular psychographic or personality characteristics, the manager should want to find media and media vehi-

Figure 4–10 The Potato Board repositions its product as a diet food.
(Courtesy of The National Potato Board.)

cles whose audience shares these characteristics. For example, the readers of *Playboy* and of *Reader's Digest* reveal very different psychographic profiles. In contrast to those who receive the *Reader's Digest*, *Playboy* readers believe that their greatest achievements are still ahead, believe that movies should not be censored, go to church less frequently, and are more likely to believe that men would cheat on their wives if given the right opportunity.[54] If the heavy users of a product revealed a psychographic profile similar to the readers of either *Playboy* or *Reader's Digest*, the product manager should consider advertising in the periodical, assuming that the target group actively read it.

SUMMARY

Marketing managers are interested in the study of personality and psychographics because through these approaches information on the individual consumer is obtained. Purchases are made through the interaction of product factors, situational factors, and person (individual) factors. It is the individual who ultimately receives marketing communications. Thus, message, source, and channel effects all must be analyzed in terms of the individual who receives the communication. For the marketing manager information on personality and psychographics is useful for segmenting consumers, for developing marketing-mix strategy, for positioning products, and for designing media strategy.

The study of personality is typically done by psychologists, and personality is defined as the "distinctive patterns of behavior, including thoughts and emotions, that characterize each individual's adaptation to the situations of his or her life." Although marketers cannot expect to predict from personality the specific brands purchased by a consumer, marketers can gain an increased understanding of the factors that motivate and guide a consumer's purchases. Four different approaches to the study of personality were identified in the chapter—the psychoanalytic approach, trait theory, social-psychological theories, and cognitively based personality theories.

Psychoanalytic theory views the personality as resulting from the conflict among the id, the ego, and the superego. It has had a major influence on marketers through its contribution to the motivation researchers. In the trait approach to personality an attempt is made to classify people according to their dominant characteristics. Over the past ten to fifteen years the trait approach has been used extensively in psychographic studies of consumers in an effort to identify the cognitive style of consumers. The social-psychological approaches to personality investigate the consistent patterns that individuals reveal when interacting with others. Examples include the CAD model, consumer anxiety, and masculinity. Cognitive theories of personality focus on the characteristic manner in which individuals process information. The tolerance for ambiguity scale is an example of a cognitive personality approach.

The study of consumer self-concepts is also an important area of study relevant to personality. The self-concept is defined as the totality of a person's thoughts and feelings with reference to himself or herself as the object.

Evidence exists that many products are bought in part to reflect the self-concept of the consumer. As such, products become symbols representing the consumer's self to others.

Marketers have moved away from the study of personality to a greater focus on identifying the psychographic characteristics of consumers. One can define psychographics as the quantitative investigation of consumers' lifestyles, cognitive styles, and demographics, which together are used to assist in marketing decision making. The goal of psychographics is to describe individual consumers in a way that will assist managers in segmenting the marketplace, positioning products, and developing the marketing-mix strategy. Because of this highly applied purpose, marketing researchers will borrow from any source possible questions to be included in psychographic inventories.

As a general statement, psychographic inventories contain questions that assess three different aspects of consumers—their lifestyles, personalities and demographic characteristics. The term *lifestyle* refers to how people live, how they spend their money, and how they allocate their time. Generally, it is assessed by questions concerning a consumer's various activities, interests, and opinions. It concerns the overt actions and purchases of consumers. In contrast, personality refers to the characteristic patterns of thinking, feeling, and perceiving held by individual consumers. The personality of consumers is generally assessed through questions that focus on identifying consumer traits and consumer attitudes. Demographic questions are also asked in psychographic inventories in order to describe further the characteristics of individual consumers.

One of the most frequently used psychographic inventories is called VALS lifestyle classification scheme. In the VALS approach, consumers are divided into four broad groups of individuals—the need-driven group, the inner-directeds, the outer-directeds, and the integrateds. Numerous companies and organizations have used VALS to segment the market and to assist in the development of the marketing mix.

Key Terms

Psychographics
Personality
Psychoanalytic view
Pleasure principle
Ego
Id
Reality principle
Defense mechanisms
Superego
Identification
Phallic symbol
Ovarian symbol
Libido

Depth interview
Focus group
Trait
Social-psychological personality theories
Cognitively oriented personality theories
CAD
Trait anxiety
State anxiety
Masculinity-femininity scales
Androgynous

Tolerance for ambiguity
Self-concept
Ideal self-concept
Product symbolism
Lifestyle
AIO statements
Unique selling proposition

VALS lifestyle classification scheme
Need drivens
Outer directeds
Inner directeds
Integrateds
Actual self-concept

Review Questions

1. Compare and contrast the concepts of personality and psychographics.
2. Discuss the structure of the personality as developed by Freud.

3. In what areas has psychoanalytic theory had an impact on marketing?

4. Describe what is meant by trait theory. What has been the major problem with the use of trait theory by marketers?

5. From the perspective of the CAD model, what are three factors that influence personality. How might the CAD model be useful to marketers?

6. Indicate the two types of anxiety that have been identified by researchers. What is the relationship between anxiety and decision conflict?

7. What are the four personality types that result from looking at masculinity and femininity as separate dimensions? How might an understanding of these dimensions assist the marketing manager?

8. To what types of consumer tasks might the concept of "tolerance of ambiguity" be relevant? What types of consumer situations have been identified as ambiguous?

9. Define what is meant by self-concept. Identify five of the six different types of self-concepts.

10. Explain how consumers can communicate themselves to others via symbolic products.

11. A scale has been developed to measure product images and self-images. What are examples of the questions asked on the scale? What procedure must respondents go through in order to assess the relationship between product image and self-image?

12. Define the terms *consumer lifestyle* and *psychographics*.

13. What is meant by the term *sequential segmentation?*

14. Provide three examples of questions that would be classified as obtaining psychographic information on activities, interests, opinions.

15. Outline the basics of the VALS psychographic inventory.

16. What are the major managerial uses of personality and psychographics?

Discussion Questions

1. Think about your own tastes and preferences for food and automobiles. How do your preferences differ from those of your friends? Speculate on what personality differences might account for why your preferences are different from those other people.

2. Go through a magazine and look carefully at the print advertisements. Identify two instances of the possible use of Freudian symbolism in the ads. To what extent do you think people are influenced by these symbols?

3. One function of the superego according to Freudian theory is to create guilt. To what extent do advertisers attempt to use guilt as a mechanism to promote their products? Try to cite some specific examples.

4. Fantasy is a technique frequently used by marketers of perfumes, autos, and other products with a heavy symbolic emphasis. Rough out a print advertisement for a new perfume called "Temptation." Develop the ad so that it uses fantasy as a major theme.

5. In developing a trait profile of personality it is important to utilize adjectives that are closely associated with the product or service. Develop a ten-item trait sale that might be used to identify the trait characteristics of people who are heavy consumers of diet foods.

6. Consumers who possess higher-than-average degrees of trait anxiety may have preferences for particular types of products and services that they use to lower their chronic anxious feelings. Speculate on what types of products or services such individuals may seek out.

7. It may be possible to target products specifically to "masculine," "feminine," "undifferentiated," and "androgynous" people by carefully developing the marketing mix. Try to identify brands that have been targeted to each of these four categories of people.

8. Rate yourself on the scale provided in Table 4–3. Next, rate two of your material possessions that are particularly important to you on the scale. To what extent did you rate the material possessions in a manner similar to how you rated yourself?

9. Go through a popular magazine, such as *Newsweek* or *Time*, and identify advertisements that use products as symbols of the self. Describe the relationships you found.

10. Develop a psychographic inventory that might be used to distinguish between heavy and light users of video recorders.

References

1. Walter Mischel, "On the Future of Personality Measurement," *American Psychologist*, 32, April 1977, 2.

2. Kenneth A. Coney and Robert R. Harmon, "Dogmatism and Innovation: A Situational Perspective," *Advances in Consumer Research*, VI, William Wilkie (ed.), Ann Arbor, MI: Association for Consumer Research, 1979, 118–121.

3. Harold H. Kassarjian and Mary Jane Sheffet, "Personality and Consumer Behavior: One More Time," *American Marketing Association 1975 Combined Proceedings*, Series No. 37, Chicago, IL: American Marketing Association, 1975, 197–201.

4. Kassarjian and Sheffet, "Personality and Consumer Behavior."

5. For an interesting overview of psychoanalytic theory see Spencer Rathus, *Psychology*, New York, N.Y.: Holt, Rinehart, and Winston, 1981.

6. Sigmund Freud, "New Introductory Lectures," in *The Standard Edition of the Complete Works of Freud*, James Strachey (ed.), Vol. 22, London: Hogarth Press, 1964.

7. Freud, "New Introductory Lectures."

8. Ernest Hilgard, Richard Atkinson, and Rita Atkinson, *Introduction to Psychology*, 6th ed., New York, N.Y.: Harcourt Brace Jovanovich, Inc., 1975.

9. Wilson Bryan Key, *Subliminal Seduction: Ad Media's Manipulation of a Not-So-Innocent America*, Englewood Cliffs, N.J.: Prentice-Hall, Inc., 1973.

10. Key, *Subliminal Seduction.*

11. Jack Haberstroh, "Can't Ignore Subliminal Ad Charges," *Advertising Age*, September 17, 1984, 3, 42, 44.

12. John Caccavale, Thomas Wanty, and Julie Edell, "Subliminal Implants in Advertisements: An Experiment," *Advances in Consumer Research*, IX, Andrew Mitchell (ed.), Ann Arbor, MI: Association for Consumer Research, 1982, 418–423.

13. Hilgard, Atkinson, and Atkinson, *Introduction to Psychology.*

14. F. B. Evans, "Psychological and Objective Factors in the Prediction of Brand Choice," *Journal of Business*, 32, October 1959, 340–369.

15. R. Westfall, "Psychological Factors in Predicting Consumer Choice," *Journal of Marketing*, 26, April 1962, 34–40.

16. A. Koponen, "Personality Characteristics of Purchasers," *Journal of Advertising Research*, 1, January 1960, 6–12.

17. Harold Kassarjian, "Personality and Consumer Behavior: A Review," *Journal of Marketing Research*, 8, November 1971, 409–418.

18. Kassarjian, "Personality and Consumer Behavior."

19. Joel B. Cohen, "An Interpersonal Orientation to the Study of Consumer Behavior," *Journal of Marketing Research*, 4, August 1967, 270–277.

20. Cohen, "An Interpersonal Orientation."

21. Jon P. Noerager, "An Assessment of CAD—A Personality Instrument Developed Specifically for Marketing Research," *Journal of Marketing Research*, 16, February 1979, 53–59.

22. C. D. Spielberger, *Anxiety and Behavior*, New York, N.Y.: Academic Press, Inc. 1966.

23. Michael B. Menasco and Del Hawkins, "A Field Test of the Relationship Between Cognitive Dissonance and State Anxiety," *Journal of Marketing Research*, 15, November 1978, 650–655.

24. Sandra Bem, "The Measurement of Psychological Androgyny," *Journal of Consulting and Clinical Psychology*, 42, March, 1974, 155–162.

25. James W. Gentry and Mildred Doering, "Sex Role Orientation and Leisure," *Journal of Leisure Research*, 11, 2d Quarter 1979, 102–111.

26. Linda Golden, Neil Allison, and Mona Clee, "The Role of Sex Role Self-Concept in Masculine and Feminine Product Perceptions," *Advances in Consumer Research*, IV, William Wilkie (ed.), Ann Arbor, MI: Association for Consumer Research, 1979, 599–605.

27. Stanley Budner, "Intolerance for Ambiguity as a Personality Variable," *Journal of Personality*, 30, March, 1962, 29–50.

28. Budner, "Intolerance for Ambiguity."

29. Brian Blake, Robert Perloff, Robert Zenhausern, and Richard Heslin, "The Effect of Intolerance of Ambiguity Upon Product Perceptions," *Journal of Applied Psychology*, 58, October, 1973, 239–243.

30. Charles Schaninger and Donald Sciglimpaglia, "The Influence of Cognitive Personality Traits and Demographics on Consumer Information Acquisition," *Journal of Consumer Research*, 8, September 1981, 208–216.

31. Morris Rosenberg, *Conceiving the Self*, New York, N.Y.: Basic Books, Inc., Publishers, 1979.

32. Seymour Epstein, "The Self-Concept: A Review and the Proposal of an integrated Theory of Personality," *Personality: Basic Issues and Current Research*, Ervin Staub (ed.), Englewood Cliffs, N.J.: Prentice-Hall, Inc., 1980.

33. For an excellent review of the self-concept in consumer behavior see M. Joseph Sirgy, "Self-Concept in Consumer Behavior: A Critical Review," *Journal of Consumer Research*, 9, December 1982, 287–300.

34. Lloyd Warner, *The Living and the Dead*, New Haven, Conn.: Yale University Press, 1959.

35. Sidney J. Levy, "Symbols for Sale," *Harvard Business Review, 37*, July/Aug. 1959, 117–124.

36. William T. Tucker, *Foundations for a Theory of Consumer Behavior*, New York, N.Y.: Holt, Rinehart and Winston, 1957.

37. Russell W. Belk, Kenneth D. Bahn, and Robert N. Mayer, "Developmental Recognition of Consumption Symbolism," *Journal of Consumer Research, 9*, June 1982, 4–17.

38. Rebecca H. Holman, "Product as Communication: A Fresh Appraisal of a Venerable Topic," in *Review of Marketing*, Ben M. Enis and Kenneth J. Roering (eds.), Chicago, Ill.: American Marketing Association, 1981, 106–119.

39. Edward L. Grubb and Harrison Grathwohl, "Consumer Self-Concept, Symbolism, and Market Behavior: A Theoretical Approach," *Journal of Marketing, 31*, October 1967, 22–27. However, the author of the text conceived of these relations from the work of Fritz Heider on Balance Theory. See Fritz Heider, *The Psychology of Interpersonal Relations*, New York, N.Y.: John Wiley & Sons, Inc., 1958.

40. Naresh K. Malhotra, "A Scale to Measure Self-Concepts, Person Concepts, and Product Concepts," *Journal of Marketing Research, 18*, November 1981, 456–464.

41. Del Hawkins, Roger Best, and Kenneth Coney, *Consumer Behavior: Implications for Marketing Strategy*, Plano, Tex.: Business Publications, 1983.

42. W. Thomas Anderson and Linda Golden, "Lifestyle and Psychographics: A Critical Review and Recommendation," in *Advances in Consumer Research, XI*, Thomas Kinnear (ed.), Ann Arbor, MI: Association for Consumer Research, 1984, 405–411.

43. Ron J. Markin, *Consumer Behavior: A Cognitive Orientation*, New York, N.Y.: Macmillan Publishing Co., Inc., 1974.

44. Lifestyle has been distinguished from personality by Anderson and Golden (see ibid.). However, rather than the word *personality* they used the term *cognitive style*. The two terms, however, are nearly identical in this usage.

45. Sunil Mehrotra and William D. Wells, "Psychographics and Buyer Behavior: Theory and Recent Empirical Findings," in *Consumer and Industrial Buying Behavior*, Arch Woodside, Jagdish N. Sheth, and Peter D. Bennett (eds.), New York, N.Y.: North-Holland, 1979.

46. For an in-depth discussion of VALS see Arnold Mitchell, *The Nine American Lifestyles*, New York, N.Y.: Macmillan Publishing Co., Inc., 1983.

47. Mitchell, *The Nine American Lifestyles*, 6.

48. *1985 Meat Board Consumer Marketing Plan*, National Live Stock and Meat Board, 1985.

49. Russell Ackof and James Emshoff, "Advertising Research at Anheuser-Busch (1968–1974)," *Sloan Management Review, 16*, Spring 1975, 1–15.

50. Glen Homan, Robert Cecil, and William Wells, "An Analysis of Moviegoers by Life Style Segments," in Mary Jane Schlinger (ed.), *Advances in Consumer Research, II*, Ann Arbor, MI: Association for Consumer Research, 1975, 217–229.

51. Joseph Plummer, "Life-Style and Advertising Case Studies," in *Combined Proceedings, 1971 Spring and Fall Conference*, Fred Allvine (ed.), Chicago, Ill.: American Marketing Association, 1972, 294.

52. John J. Burnett, "Psychographic and Demographic Characteristics of Blood Donors," *Journal of Consumer Research, 8*, June 1981, 62–66.

53. Shirley Young, "Psychographic Research and Marketing Relevancy," in *Attitude Research Reaches New Heights*, Charles A. King and Douglas J. Tigert (eds.), Chicago, Ill.: American Marketing Association, 1971, 220–222.

54. Douglas J. Tigert, "Life Analysis as a Basis for Media Selection," in *Life Style and Psychographics*, William D. Wells (ed.), Chicago, Ill.: American Marketing Association, 1974, 179.

5

Information Processing

Marketers Nose in on the Perception of Smell

Consumers perceive the world through their senses, and the 2.4 billion-dollar fragrance industry is based largely on the sense of smell. A perfume is a complex product and may be composed of as many as eighty or ninety ingredients. The components in a bottle of $140-an-ounce perfume may cost only $3, making the margins of a successful product astounding.

Fragrances are added to literally hundreds of household products from soaps to toilet tissue to dishwasher detergent. One estimate has it that each of us comes into contact with fragrances added to products thirty times a day. Procter & Gamble, which doesn't sell perfume, has one of the best staffs of perfumists in the business.

One expert on smell noted that the sense is closely linked with feelings and emotions. The olfactory nerves are connected to the part of the brain that processes emotional information. Thus, whiffing the perfume or cologne that an old flame wore can stir up your emotions. Similarly, if a female boss, wearing Chanel No. 5, fires you from a job, the perfume is likely to have a negative impact on you forever.

Reactions to odors are highly subjective, however. The response to a perfume is affected by the time of day, the associations it triggers, and how the person feels. For these reasons advertising is crucial in defining the image of a perfume. Thus Charlie defines itself as the "gorgeous, sexy-young" fragrance. Midnight Musk described itself indirectly with an ad featuring a couple embracing in a romantic setting. The copy read, "My daddy always said nothing good happens after Midnight. Daddy was wrong." Colognes are increasingly becoming important to men as well. However, men's fragrances tend to be bought for them by women. Thus, Brut calls out for a woman to, "Make every day his Brut day . . . After shave, after shower, after anything."

The ultimate in perfumes was recently announced by Jovan. The perfume, called Andron, contains alpha-androstenol, a pheromone. The perfume is based on the finding that insects, fish, and mammals secrete chemical attractants, called pheromones, for purposes of sexual communication. In copy for a print ad, Andron asked, "Can a fragrance actually attract the opposite sex?" Their answer was, "Maybe."

Based on Margeret le Roux, "Psychology of the Senses: Nothing to Sniff At," *Advertising Age*, February 27, 1984, M–40; and "What Lies Behind the Sweet Smell of Success," *Business Week*, February 27, 1984, 139, 143.

INTRODUCTION

One of the most frequently reported problems encountered by marketers is getting prospects to receive, understand, and remember messages. The problem is particularly acute for advertisers. Millions of dollars can be spent developing and delivering a national campaign. If consumers fail to be exposed to the message, fail to understand it, or fail to remember it, the investment will be wasted. The study of how people receive, interpret, and remember information is called information processing. Formally, **information processing** may be defined as the process through which consumers receive stimulation, transform it into meaningful information, store the information in memory for later use, and retrieve the information for decision making.

The consumer vignette at the beginning of the chapter illustrates a number of points concerning information processing. In most instances when marketers discuss information processing, they refer to cases in which consumers are analyzing relatively complex messages received through the visual or auditory senses. However, people receive and process information through all of the senses—smell, touch, taste, hearing, and vision. Indeed, some products are differentiated from others almost entirely on the features of smell, touch, and taste. For example, in the toilet-paper industry the characteristic of "soft to the touch" has been the predominant advertised feature of the leading brands, such as Charmin and White Cloud. Of course the importance of the sense of smell to the perfume industry is obvious, as are the senses of taste and smell to the food and beverage industries. The taste test used in the Pepsi Challenge campaign allowed the soft-drink giant to make steady progress in catching up with Coca-Cola. Table 5–1 identifies the five

Table 5–1 The Senses and Some Industries Based on Them

Sense	Industry
Vision	Movie, television, photography, optical art, clothing
Hearing	Telephone, radio, music, hearing aid, noise control
Taste	Food, beverage
Smell	Perfume, food, deodorants (personal, household, industrial)
Touch (hot, cold, pain)	Clothing, pain relievers, air conditioning, massage

Figure 5–1   A simple model of information processing.

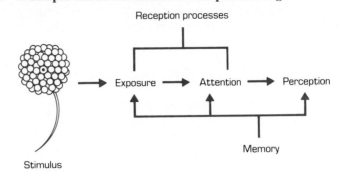

major senses of humans and some of the industries that are based to a large extent around them.

A second point made by the consumer vignette concerns the interrelationship of the concepts of sensation, perception, and memory. The perception of an odor is highly subjective. Marketers of perfumes attempt to influence how people perceive the odor by connecting other memories to their brand. Thus, when a woman smells Charlie perfume, her interpretation of the odor may be influenced by the advertising for the brand. If Revlon can cause consumers to associate the thought "gorgeous, sexy-young" with Charlie, the actual perception of the odor of the perfume may be influenced. Thus, perception is an active process influenced not only by the sensations received through the sense organs, but also by the memories elicited by the sensations.

Figure 5–1 presents a model of information processing. Three major topic areas are identified in the model as making up information processing—memory, reception, and perception processes. Reception refers to the factors that influence whether or not an individual decides to expose himself or herself to information and whether or not the information will be attended. **Perception** refers to the ways that people organize the information received and how they interpret this information so that it has meaning. Because of the large role played by memory in information processing, it is discussed first.

MEMORY PROCESSES

Researchers hold a number of different views on how memory functions. One frequently used approach hypothesizes that memory may be composed of three different components—**sensory memory, short-term memory,** and **long-term memory.**[1] Although the evidence is mixed as to whether the types of memories are stored in three separate locations in the brain, the multiple-store approach has a strong intuitive appeal.

Sensory Memory

The perception of a sight, sound, touch, or taste occurs because a stimulus activates nerve fibers in a person's sensory organs. Lasting only a fraction of a second, the sensory image of a stimulus consists of the immediate impression of the firing of the nerve cells. Because the nerve fibers fire for only very short lengths of time (in most cases for less than a second), the stimulus information will be quickly lost unless it is processed further.[2]

Short-Term Memory

Short-term memory is the site where information is temporarily stored while being processed. For example, when a consumer thinks about or simply passively views a television commercial, the cognitive processing may be thought of as occurring in short-term memory. Evidence indicates that both auditory and visual information can be stored temporarily in short-term memory. However, it is more common to encode the visual information into words or sounds for further processing.[3] This occurs in part because auditory stimuli can be maintained in short-term memory longer than visual stimuli.[4] Thus, if a consumer is in a high-involvement situation, the meaning of an advertisement will probably be interpreted through words, such as "this is a high-quality brand," or "I don't believe the person who endorsed this brand." Such interpretations are called **cognitive responses,** and these silent thoughts play a major role in determining the attitudes that a consumer will form about a brand.

Characteristics of Short-Term Memory   Short-term memory has a number of important characteristics. First, it has a limited capacity. As stated by psychologist George Miller, the average person has the ability to process only about seven plus or minus two chunks of information at a time.[5] A chunk may be conceptualized as a single meaningful piece of information. A chunk could be a single letter, a syllable (e.g., the syllable "thun" in the nonsense word "thunstofam"), or an entire word. This recognition that people can handle seven plus or minus two chunks of information at a time has been labeled Miller's Law.

The limited capacity of short-term memory means that it acts as a kind of bottleneck. If more information is received than the consumer can handle, some of it will be lost. Consumers will tend to react to such **information overload** by becoming aroused and by more narrowly focusing attention on only certain aspects of the incoming stimuli.[6] The consumer may simply make a random choice, not buy anything, or focus on the wrong product qualities for his or her decision. Information overload can easily occur in personal-selling situations in which a salesman is explaining the characteristics of a complex product. The uninformed consumer can quite easily be overwhelmed with facts. The consumer is likely to become aroused, nervous, and focus on narrow aspects of the product, which may or may not be appropriate. Such overarousal can lead to poor decisions and is often just the opposite of what the well-intentioned salesman had in mind. The problem of overloading consumers with information is a real one. Indeed, it has become a public policy problem in some areas, such as prescription and over-the-counter drugs, where literally pages of information may be given on the precautions in taking a drug.[7]

The amount of arousal felt by the consumer will influence to a certain degree the capacity of short-term memory.[8] In high-involvement situations the consumer is likely to be more aroused and more attentive, thereby expanding the capacity of short-term memory to its maximal extent. In contrast, under low-involvement conditions the consumer's arousal level is apt to be low, thereby focusing relatively little capacity on the stimulus. Advertisers generally maintain that the number of copy points that can be transmitted in an ad is limited to about three or four ideas. If copy points are viewed as analogous to chunks of information, this would indicate that in television advertising the cognitive capacity of consumers is quite low. This idea makes perfect sense when viewed from the perspective that most television advertising is done in low-involvement situations where arousal levels are low and little cognitive capacity is allocated to the task of processing the information in the ad. For companies advertising on television or radio the implication is direct—keep your messages simple.

Transfer of Information from Short- to Long-Term Memory   One of the functions of short-term memory is to assist in the transfer of information to long-term memory, where information is permanently stored. Some debate exists as to how long it takes to transfer a chunk of information into long-term memory. Evidence exists to indicate that it depends upon just how the information is to be recalled from long-term memory. If the goal simply involves recognizing that a stimulus has been seen, it may take only from two to five seconds for transfer if the information is processed. In contrast, if the information must be recalled without assistance at a later time, the transfer time is longer—from five to ten seconds for a single chunk.[9]

These differences in transfer times have important implications for marketers. When developing messages for consumers, the marketer should consider whether the consumer will be in a **recognition task** or a **recall task.** In a recognition task information is placed in front of a consumer. The task of the person is to judge whether the information has been seen previously. In a recall task the consumer must retrieve the information from long-term memory. Thus, in recognition tasks, memory recall is said to be aided; in recall tasks the retrieval of memories is unaided.

Grocery shopping frequently involves consumers in a recognition task. For example, if the product is of a low-involvement nature, such as laundry detergent, the shopper may merely scan the grocery store shelves for ideas on what to buy. In this case the shopper is engaging in a recognition task. The advertiser is interested in giving information to the consumer so that he or she will recognize that a brand they see on the shelf was advertised. For recognition to occur, the transmission time from short-term to long-term memory will probably be shorter than for recall tasks. As a consequence, the commercials used to advertise the brand may not have to be as long, be repeated as frequently, or attract as much attention from the consumer as when the consumer must recall the information without aid.

The packaging of Life cereal illustrates aided recall. The box contains a photo of Mikey taken from the highly successful advertising campaign in which Mikey, who hates everything, is shown to like the cereal. The photo of Mikey is easily recognized and will help the consumer retrieve from long-term memory the information in the advertisement. Figure 5–2 gives the storyboard of the popular advertisement.

In a number of instances the direct recall of a product name from memory may be required. For example, suppose that a person's vacuum cleaner suddenly breaks down. The consumer will attempt to recall from memory a list of brands from which to consider a purchase. This set of brands is called the **evoked set,** and it is crucial that a company's product be included in the evoked set in order for it to have a chance for consideration. Because the time required to transfer information from short-term to long-term memory is longer when unaided recall is required, the manufacturer may have to go to greater lengths to have consumers exposed to messages about its brand.

Just as the images contained in sensory memory are lost if not attended to, so too is the information contained in short-term memory. The evidence indicates that if information in short-term memory is not rehearsed, it will be lost within about thirty seconds.[10] One way such information is lost is through its replacement by other information in the limited storage capacity of short-term memory.[11] The finding that transfer of information from short-term to long-term memory may be impeded by the presentation of new information also has relevance to marketers. When consumers watch television or read a magazine, they are bombarded by dozens of advertisements competing for attention. The problem of too many ads has been called **clutter.** The findings of how information is transferred from short- to long-term memory indicate that clutter is a major problem for advertisers and that it probably acts to impede the ability of consumers to move information from temporary storage in short-term memory to permanent storage in long-term memory.

In addition to investigating how information is transferred from short-term to long-term memory, researchers have also analyzed how the two halves of the brain function. Highlight 5–1 discusses the area of brain lateralization.

Long-Term Memory

In contrast to short-term memory, long-term memory has an essentially unlimited capacity to store information permanently.[12] The stored information is largely semantic in nature. **Sematic concepts** are the meanings attached to words, events, objects, and symbols. Thus, long-term memory stores the meanings of words, symbols, and such along with the associations among various semantic concepts. Long-term memory also can store information in terms of its sequence of occurrence (episodic memory), in terms of its modality (e.g., visual, smell, touch senses), and in terms of its affective, or emotional, content.[13]

Figure 5–2 **Life cereal uses aided recall by drawing on the highly successful "Mikey" ad campaign depicted in the story board.** *(Courtesy of The Quaker Oats Company.)*

Relative Superiority of Picture Versus Word Memory An important finding from psychology and consumer behavior is that pictures are more memorable than their verbal counterparts.[14] Pictures appear to be more easily recalled and recognized than words. Visual material is particularly easily remembered if the objects to be remembered are perceived as interacting in

HIGHLIGHT 5–1

Split Brains and Consumer Behavior

Researchers have found that the human brain is divided vertically into two hemispheres. For people who are right-handed, the left hemisphere appears to control verbal processes and symbolic problem solving— i.e., the more rational components of behavior. In contrast, the right hemisphere appears to control emotions as well as spatial and imaginative impressions. Interestingly, in left-handed people, the roles of the right and left hemispheres may be reversed, as though the wiring of the brain were rearranged.

The effects of brain lateralization can be demonstrated. The speech center resides in the left brain. Also, the nerves of the right hand and arm are connected to the left brain. If someone attempts to balance a ruler in the right hand while reciting a poem, the recitation is impaired because of interference between the tasks occurring in the left brain. Conversely, if the ruler is balanced in the left hand, the recitation is done more easily.

A number of consumer actions appear to be associated with either left or right brain functioning. In particular, high-involvement consumer processes seem associated with left brain processes. In contrast, low-involvement consumer processes appear related to right brain processes. Thus, findings that repeatedly exposing consumers to a product may increase liking for it are consistent with right brain thinking. Similarly, visual and emotional information may influence consumers through right brain processes.

The differences in right and left brain functioning are just beginning to be understood. Further, this discussion is highly oversimplified. Nevertheless, the finding that humans have a split brain gives substance to greater study of the effects of emotions and imagination on consumer behavior.

Based on Flemming Hansen, "Hemispheral Lateralization: Implications for Understanding Consumer Behavior," *Journal of Consumer Research*, 8, June 1981, 23–35.

some way.[15] Thus, if an advertiser wanted to associate its product with a famous endorser, it would want to show the endorser actually using the product in everyday scenes.

The impact on memory of verbal and visual material is related to the involvement of the consumer at the time of the presentation of the material. The evidence indicates that verbally based material is best presented when the audience is highly involved and motivated to process the entire message sematically. In contract, visual information appears to be particularly effective when the audience is in a low-involvement state. Visual advertisements appear to require a lower number of repetitions than verbal information to achieve the same memorability.[16]

Memory Networks   Semantic memory appears to be organized such that information is placed into networks. Figure 5–3 presents a hypothetical example of a memory network for automobiles. The network is a series of memory nodes that represent the stored semantic concepts. The lines connecting the nodes indicate the associations that exist. Thus, suppose that the Corvette node were activated by someone mentioning that they plan to buy one. The activation of the node would result in a number of additional associations, such as a "sporty car that is fast, expensive, prestigious, and costly to

Figure 5–3   A memory network for automobiles.

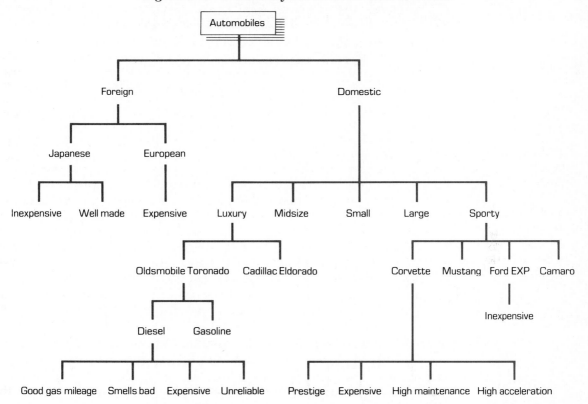

buy and maintain." Of course, different consumers will possess divergent memory structures such that the activation of a semantic concept could result in a quite different set of associations.

The relationship between the brands held in a consumer's long-term memory and the qualities of the brand are called **product-attribute associations.** These associations play an important role in forming the attitudes consumers hold towards various brands and can directly influence subsequent purchase behavior. The relationship between product-attribute associations, attitudes, and purchase behavior is discussed in more detail in Chapter 7 on attitudes. But it is important to note that marketers must know what associations consumers hold between brands and various attributes. For example, the associations between the Oldsmobile Toronado, diesel engines, and unreliability were a major problem for General Motors. Indeed, the company discontinued selling diesel engines in its cars in 1986.

The total package of associations that is brought to mind when a node is activated is called a schema. The complexity of the schema is indicative of the **cognitive differentiation** that the consumer has of a particular concept.

For example, in Figure 5–2 the consumer depicted has a relatively cognitively differentiated view of the Corvette. In contrast, the associations the person has with the Ford EXP are few in number, indicating a less cognitively differentiated view of the Ford product. For high-involvement purchases, such as automobiles, it is probably important to create increased cognitive complexity about a brand among the members of the brand's target market. Without a cognitively differentiated understanding of the high-involvement brand, the consumer may be reluctant to purchase it.

Memory-Control Processes

Although it is important for the marketer to understand how memory is structured, perhaps of greater importance is knowledge of the processes that people use to get information into and out of memory. Called **memory-control processes,** these methods of handling information may operate consciously or unconsciously to influence the encoding, placement, and retrieval of information.[17]

Rehearsal   After attending to a stimulus, an individual may want to do either or both of two things—maintain the information in short-term memory and/or transfer it to long-term memory. The process of **rehearsal** can involve the silent verbal repetition of the information. However, rehearsal can also result from the individual applying more energy to the task and focusing harder on the information in order to allocate more processing capacity to the task. An example of rehearsal is the silent repetition of a telephone number between the time one looks it up and the time when the number is dialed. The rehearsal allows one to maintain the number in short-term memory so that it can be retained until dialed. It also may result in the information being transferred to long-term memory, so that the number can be retrieved later.

Coding   Although rehearsal influences whether or not information is transfered from short-term to long-term memory, how the information is coded also has a great impact on the speed of transfer and on the placement of the information in memory. During rehearsal a consumer can simply repeat the stimulus over and over or attempt to link the stimulus to other information already placed into long-term memory. To the extent that the consumer can code information by drawing associations between it and information already in memory, the storage process is likely to be speeded up.

The development of brand names by marketers should be governed by a recognition that a **coding** process occurs. Some companies show an intuitive recognition of this principle and choose product names that describe in some way what the product does or what it is. For example, one can find Liquid Plumr, Head & Shoulders, Eraser Mate, Pudding Pops, and Love My Carpet. The goal is to help the consumer remember the name by giving him or her an easy way to code it. Thus, the marketer attempts to help the consumer encode the product's name by making it easy for the consumer to form associations between the product and its attributes or between the product and its task. Additional examples are presented in Highlight 5–2.

Remembering and Forgetting The act of remembering something is complex and consists of the control processes of **retrieval** and **response generation.** The retrieval process consists of the individual searching through long-term memory in order to identify within it the information desired to be recalled. In response generation the person constructs a response by actively reconstructing the stimulus.[18] The individual or consumer does not access stored replicas of the encoded stimulus information. Instead, traces of stimuli are activated and reconstructed into a recollection of the stimulus.

HIGHLIGHT 5–2

Developing Corporate and Product Names

Names and the associations they form can mean the success or failure of a brand or company. Consider the names Radio Shack and J. C. Penney. These names represent businesses whose combined revenues run into the billions of dollars. However, would you want to buy an expensive computer in a shack or try on a high-fashion dress in a place associated with "pennies"? After all, in the United States a penny is all but worthless. When Tandy began bringing out its powerful IBM-compatible business computers in 1984, company executives decided not to use the Radio Shack name that had been previously used on its computers. Instead, it was called the Tandy personal computer, in part to avoid the name stigma. When J. C. Penney began to change its merchandising strategy in the early 1980s to feature upgraded merchandise and designer names, experts wondered if the "Penney" name would support higher-class merchandise.

Corporations will go to great lengths to develop a suitable name for a new brand. In 1983 Frito-Lay began to test marketing a new potato-chip–type product that was thick and had ridges running in different directions on each side. The goal was to produce a product that "was of the earth . . . thicker . . . natural tasting."(a) The name O'Grady was chosen because consumers associated the name with such adjectives as "fun," "jovial," "happy-go-lucky," "hearty," and "big."

In the fall of 1984 Ford came out with a new, German-engineered car named the Merkur. The car was designed to compete against BMWs, and the name was selected to help consumers associate the car with its German heritage.(b) A key question was—and is—will Americans be able to remember a strange name that is hard to pronounce (Merkur is pronounced *mare-coor.)*?

How does a company go about picking a name? One expert gave the following rules:

☐ Make the name pronounceable.
☐ Make the name unique so that it can be remembered and recognized.
☐ Create a name that describes the product's benefits.
☐ Make sure the name has no negative connotations.
☐ Find a name that conveys the product's category (a car should not sound like a toothpaste).
☐ Try to find a name that translates well into foreign languages.(c)

Based on (a) Janet Guyon, "The Public Doesn't Get a Better Potato Chip Without a Bit o' Pain," *The Wall Street Journal,* March 25, 1983, 1, 12; (b) Melinda Grenier Guiles, "New Functional Luxury Car from Ford Faces Big Hurdles," *The Wall Street Journal,* June 7, 1984, 29; and (c) Walter Stern, "A Good Name Could Mean a Brand of Fame," *Advertising Age,* January 17, 1983, M-53.

The consumer uses logic, intuition, expectations, and whatever else is available to help reconstruct a memory.

Forgetting occurs when either the retrieval or response-generation process breaks down. In addition, retrieval failure can occur when the basis for the coding and placement of a piece of information is not accessed. Because memories exist within networks of stimuli, the memory may not be retrieved if the right network is not activated.

When response-generation failures occur, consumers will sometimes have errors of memory. One of the major problems of comparative advertising is that consumers may recall the wrong brand names. Thus, when an attempt is made to recall the advertised brand, both brands may be retrieved from memory. In generating the response the consumer will use whatever information is available to construct an answer. If the consumer last bought the unadvertised brand, this chunk of information could be activated, leading the consumer to recall the wrong brand name.

Marketers should attempt to assist the retrieval process by giving consumers a series of associations to hang onto brand names. The associations can be visual, musical, or semantically based. Examples of visual, musical, and sematically based methods of associating brand names with other stimuli may be found in a variety of consumer products. The use of cartoon characters to advertise products exemplifies a visual association. The Jolly Green Giant and the Pillsbury Doughboy are used by their parent companies to assist consumers in recognizing the product in the store after seeing it advertised on television. The musical jingles that accompany the advertising of many brands are used not only to help gain attention but also to attach associations with the product. Finally, the brand may be associated with various concepts semantically. For example, a company may want to attach the meaning of a certain concept to a brand through repetition. Over the years Maytag Corporation has stressed the reliability and desirability of its washers and dryers. Over time an association may form between the semantic concept of reliability and the brand.

In-store advertising attempts to activate visual and semantic associations held in long-term memory. Point-of-purchase (POP) displays are often used to attract the consumer's attention and help the consumer recall a brand name. The packaging of a product has the same goals. Perhaps the brand that has most effectively combined POP advertising and packaging to elicit associations is L'eggs pantyhose. Placing the hosiery product in POP displays and in distinctive egg-shaped packages helps the consumer to readily associate the national advertising with the brand in the store. The outcome is a product that has captured over 15 percent of the U.S. hosiery market.[19]

RECEPTION PROCESSES

Reception refers to the factors that govern the consumer's exposure to and amount of attention directed towards information in the environment. Memory plays a crucial role in determining what information a consumer receives. Thus, it influences which stimuli consumers expose themselves to and which information consumers will attend.

When discussing the reception process, two important concepts must be distinguished—sensation and attention. **Sensation** refers to the stimulation of a person's sensory receptors (e.g., nerves sensitive to light, sound waves, touch, etc.) and the transmission of the sensory information to the brain and spinal cord via nerve fibers. Thus, sensation is closely related to the exposure stage of the information-processing model found in Figure 4–1. On the other hand, **attention** refers to the allocation of mental capacity to a stimulus or task.[20] Attention is not an all-or-nothing process. It occurs after exposure to a stimulus and ranges from total inattention to a stimulus to a complete focus on the stimulus. The next two subsections discuss more fully the concepts of sensation and attention.

Sensation

The study of sensation refers to the investigation of the ways in which people in general react to the raw sensory information received through the sense organs. The goal is to analyze the raw response a person has to a stimulus prior to the individual attending to it, interpreting it, and giving it meaning. Thus, a person studying sensation might ask the question, "How loud does a sound have to be before it is detected?" or "How much difference in the level of the hem of a skirt must there be before a consumer can detect the difference?" The topic of sensation has a number of important applications to marketing, and in particular to the field of advertising.

As noted in the model presented in Figure 5–1, the exposure to a stimulus is the first step in the processing of information. With information exposure, a consumer's sensory organs are activated to some extent by the stimulation. If the consumer's sensory organs do not come into contact with the stimulation, the person cannot be said to have been exposed to the information. One characteristic of consumer information processing is its selectivity. Consumers will actively choose whether or not to expose themselves to information. For example, the concept of **selective exposure** is of great interest to advertisers. Particularly with the proliferation of cable television systems, consumers can, with the press of a button, switch channels instantaneously. Because a variety of cues are given to indicate that a commercial is coming, the consumer can anticipate it and make a decision about whether or not to watch the commercial. Unfortunately for advertisers, many consumers decide to switch channels in order to avoid watching the commercial. Thus, consumers selectively expose themselves to stimulation, resulting in a lowering of the effectiveness of the advertising dollars spent by companies.

Once a consumer is exposed to information, whether or not he or she goes beyond mere exposure to attend to actively and focus on the stimulus is determined by a number of factors. One determinant of whether or not a stimulus is actually detected is its intensity. The lowest level at which a stimulus can be detected fifty percent of the time is called the **absolute thresh-**

old. As the intensity of a stimulus, such as the loudness of an advertisement, increases, the likelihood that it will be sensed also increases. Advertisers have an incentive, therefore, to make their commercials as loud as possible without offending the consumer. Indeed, a common complaint by consumers is that television advertisements are louder than the programs that they accompany. Although the maximum intensity of sound coming from a commercial is no greater than that coming from a program, advertisers do take steps to create the sensation that the loudness is greater. Highlight 5–3 discusses some of these techniques. The goal of the advertiser is to create a stimulus loud enough to make the consumer recognize that something on which attention should be focused is there.

Also related to the concept of the absolute threshold is the controversial topic of subliminal advertising. The controversy centers on the issue of whether people respond to certain symbols and words that appear at stimulus levels below the absolute threshold. Highlight 5–4 briefly discusses the debate.

HIGHLIGHT 5–3

TV Ads Grab Attention with Sound

Every year television stations receive hundreds of complaints about the loudness of advertisements. However, federal rules forbid the practice of making ads louder than the programming. In addition, television stations always operate at the highest audio signal level allowed for reasons of efficiency. According to one NBC executive, no difference exists in the peak sound level of ads and programming. Given this information, why do commercials sound so loud?

The sensation of sound involves a variety of factors in addition to its peak level. Advertisers are skillful at creating the impression of loudness through their expert use of such factors. One major contributor to the perceived loudness of commercials is that much less variation in sound level occurs during a commercial. In regular programming the intensity of sound varies over a large range. However, sound levels in commercials tend to stay at or near peak levels.

Other "tricks of the trade" are also used. Because low-frequency sound can mask higher-frequency sounds, advertisers filter out any noises that may drown out the primary message. In addition, the human voice has more auditory impact in the middle frequency ranges (two to six kilohertz). Advertisers will electronically vary voice sounds so that they stay within such a frequency band. Another approach is to write the script so that lots of consonants are used, because people are more aware of consonants than vowel sounds. Finally, advertisers will try to begin commercials with sounds that are highly different from those of the programming within which the commercial is buried. Because people become adapted to the type of sounds coming from programming, a dramatic change in sound quality will draw viewer attention. For example, notice how many commercials begin with an upbeat song of some type.

The attention-getting property of commercials can be seen by observing one- to two-year-old children who happen to be playing around a television set. They will totally ignore the programming. However, when a commercial comes on their attention is immediately drawn to it because of its dramatic sound quality.

Based in part on John Koten, "To Grab Viewers' Attention, TV Ads Aim for the Eardrum," *The Wall Street Journal*, January 26, 1984, 33.

HIGHLIGHT 5–4

Subliminal Advertising: Does It Work?

In 1957 audiences at a movie theater in New Jersey were exposed to briefly presented messages that said, "Drink Coca-Cola" and "Eat popcorn." The messages were superimposed on the movie and presented so quickly that the audience did not consciously realize that the messages had appeared. Although no evidence was presented, the marketing firm that created the messages claimed that sales of the items increased dramatically.

The media and consumers were shocked. The *New Yorker* stated that people's minds had been "broken and entered." However, others saw potential in subliminal messages, and a radio station began broadcasting subaudible messages that "TV's a bore."

The term *subliminal* means below threshold. Thus, something that is subliminally perceived cannot be reported because it is below the individual's absolute threshold. However, there are those who argue that even though a stimulus cannot be reported, it can still influence behavior. According to this view, the end result of many sorts of stimulation may not be conscious recognition.

Three different types of **subliminal stimulation** have been identified—briefly presented visual stimuli, accelerated speech in low-volume auditory messages, and embedding or hiding sexual imagery or words in print advertisements. One author, in fact, has written two books claiming that advertisers intentionally embed erotic and death symbols in print advertisements. Indeed, if you look carefully at most print ads for liquor, it is possible to find various sexual organs and death masks in the drink glasses filled with ice.

Does subliminal advertising work? It is true that under certain, limited circumstances people may not realize that a message is influencing them. But concerning subliminal stimuli, the psychologist Timothy Moore said, "What you see is what you get." The effects of subliminal stimuli are extremely weak and most certainly are overridden by a host of other more powerful messages.

Why then can one find erotic stimuli in ice cubes? The likely answer is that the shapes appear for the same reasons that you can find faces, dogs, cats, and elephants in complex cloud formations.

Based on Timothy E. Moore, "Subliminal Advertising: What You See Is What You Get," *Journal of Marketing*, 46 Spring 1982, 38–47.

Difference Thresholds In addition to the absolute threshold, a **difference threshold** exists. The difference threshold is the minimum amount of difference in the intensity of stimulation that can be detected fifty percent of the time. The idea that people cannot always distinguish between two stimuli has marketing implications. Indeed, finding the **just noticeable difference (JND)** for the price of a product can be extremely important to a product manager. For example, if a company wants to raise the price of a product, it would be advantageous if consumers did not realize that a price rise occurred. If the price increase could be kept below the JND, consumers would not recognize the price increase, and sales would be less likely to be affected by the change. On the other hand, if the company wanted to discount the price of a product to increase sales, it would be important to identify the JND in order to insure that the price decrease was large enough to surpass the JND so that consumers would recognize that a meaningful reduction in the sales price had occurred. (Readers should consider potential ethical problems with such an analysis.)

One of the interesting aspects of the just noticeable difference is that it varies with the level of the stimulus in question. Discovered by the German scientist Ernest Weber, the relationship between the size of the JND and stimulus intensity has become known as Weber's Law. Weber's Law states that as the intensity of the stimulus increases, the ability to detect a difference between two levels of the stimulus decreases. Weber identified a formula that expresses these relationships:

$$JND = I \times K$$

where I is the intensity level of the stimulus and K is a constant that gives the proportionate amount of change in stimulus level required for its detection.

One rule of thumb of retailers is that markdowns must be at least 20 percent before consumers recognize them.[21] This 20 percent idea is equivalent to K, the constant in Weber's Law. Thus, if a diamond ring were priced at $400, it would have to be marked down by $80 ($400 × .20 = $80) for the sale to be meaningful. In contrast, if the diamond were priced at $4,000, the markdown would have to be $800 for the sale to be effective. The JND is much larger when the dollar values are higher.

A problem should be noted in applying psychological principles such as Weber's Law to consumer behavior problems. In some cases the idea of the principle applies quite well; however, the exact process through which it operates may not match precisely the consumer behavior context. For example, Weber's Law explains quite precisely the sensory impact of changes in the intensity of a stimulus. The question is, Does a change in sales price influence consumers at the sensory level or at a perceptual level where the information is being interpreted? Strictly speaking, Weber's Law would be misused if the sales-price change influenced people at the perceptual level rather than at the sensory level. Practically speaking, however, it makes little difference to the marketing manager whether or not the concept is being applied precisely. Weber's Law helps the manager to understand the relationship of the level of the stimulus to the amount of change required in the stimulus to make it noticeable—an important piece of marketing and consumer behavior information.

Table 5–2 identifies a number of marketing uses of the concept of the JND. Although marketers usually do not overtly state that they are going to use Weber's Law, they show evidence of implicitly understanding its implications. For example, Procter & Gamble has made no less than 19 changes in the wrapper of Ivory soap between 1898 and 1965.[22] The difference between any two of the changes was extremely subtle. However, when the 1898 and 1965 wrappers are compared, the differences are astounding. P&G made the changes in the wrapper so gradually that they probably stayed within the consumers' JND with each adaptation of the wrapper.

Table 5–2   Some Marketing Examples of the JND

Area of Application	Example of Use
Pricing	When raising the price, try to move less than a JND. When lowering price for a sale, move more than a JND.
Sales promotion	Make coupons larger than the JND.
Product	Make decreases in size of food product less than JND—e.g., shrinking of candy bars. When the word "new" is used, make sure product change is greater than JND.
Packaging	To update package styling and logo, keep within JND. To change image, make styling changes greater than JND.

The Adaptation Level Closely related to the concepts of the absolute threshold and the JND is that of **adaptation.** Everyone has experienced the process of adaptation before. When first sitting in a hot bath, one may think the steaming water is nearly unbearable. However, after a few minutes the water will feel quite pleasant. The change in sensation did not occur because the water got colder. It occurred because nerve cells adapted to the water's temperature and no longer fired signals to the brain telling it that the water was too hot. After an individual has had repeated experience with a stimulus, he or she will become bored with or accustomed to it. In order for the stimulus to have an impact on the consumer after adaptation has occurred, it must be changed in some way. Of course, the change must be greater than the JND of the stimulus.

Figure 5–4 presents what might be called a butterfly curve. (If you look hard, the humps could look like the wings of a butterfly.) What the curve shows is that the preference for a stimulus is at a moderate level at the point at which the person has adapted to it. However, the preference increases at both higher and lower levels of the stimulus. As the level of the stimulus moves too far from the adaptation level, though, the preference steadily decreases.[23]

The idea of the butterfly curve can be demonstrated by getting into that hot bath discussed earlier. After adapting to the bath by lying in it for five to ten minutes, its pleasure may be temporally increased by either adding cold or hot water to it. In either case the sensation of the water will be distinctly pleasurable because of the change in temperature.

The simple idea of the butterfly curve nicely explains why fashion trends are constantly changing. Consumers quickly become adapted to a certain look, and its pleasure falls. Designers will then modify the current look in

Figure 5–4   Butterfly curve.

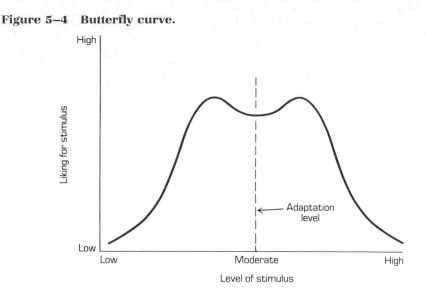

some relatively small way, and it will appear fresh and interesting because the stimulus has diverged from the adaptation level. The up-and-down movement of the hems of skirts over the years well illustrates the principle. Similarly, the width of men's ties and lapels shows the same confounded tendency to change.

Also, as predicted by the butterfly curve, unusual fashion looks are adopted slowly, because at first they are too far away from the adaptation level. When the rock group the Beatles first appeared on American television in the early 1960s, their long hair was horrifying to middle-class Americans. However, by the early 1970s the hairstyle worn by the Beatles early in the group's career was considered conservative.

Another consumer behavior phenomenon that the butterfly curve accounts for is **spontaneous brand switching.** Consumers show a nasty habit of periodically buying a new brand, even when nothing indicates that they are unhappy with the brand previously used. The phenomenon seems to occur most frequently for low-involvement products in which little difference exists between brands. Applying the concept of the adaptation level, consumers may switch brands because they have adapted to the brand most frequently used. Changing to a new brand moves the consumer off of the adaptation level, thereby providing some increment in the pleasure received from the product class. Companies seem implicitly to recognize the problem and frequently come out with "new and improved" versions of their products. By providing a "new" version of the product, the manufacturer may short-circuit spontaneous brand switching by arranging the situation so that the consumer can buy something that moves him or her off of the adaptation level while still using the same brand.

Attention

Marketers are vitally concerned with attention because it is a necessary step for information to be comprehended and placed into long-term memory. When a consumer attends to an advertisement, a public-relations piece of information, or a personal-selling communication, he or she is allocating mental capacity to the task. The more demanding the task or the more the person is interested in the task, the greater the amount of attention focused on it.[24] A computer analogy is often used to describe the process. Just as a computer has a certain amount of "core memory," consumers have a limited amount of capacity in short-term memory to handle information-processing tasks. The greater the complexity of the task, the greater the amount of short-term memory is allocated to it.

Attention can be activated either voluntarily or involuntarily.[25] **Voluntary attention** involves the consumer in actively searching out information in order to achieve some type of goal. A major aspect of voluntary attention is its selectivity. Through selective attention consumers identify the stimuli on which they will focus attention, based upon whether or not each stimulus matches their goals. Thus, someone who is interested in buying a car, some furniture, or an expensive camera will actively seek information about the product. When reading newspapers, he or she will be on the lookout to find advertisements and articles that deal with the product sought. Conversely, if the marketing communication is not perceived as matching a goal, the consumer will tend not to focus attention on it. Again, this is a major problem for advertisers on television and radio. Consumers may be exposed to the message but simply decide not to attend to the information contained in the communication.

In addition to voluntary attention, attention can be placed upon a stimulus involuntarily. **Involuntary attention** occurs when a consumer is exposed to something surprising, novel, threatening, or unexpected. Such a stimulus results in an autonomic response in which the person turns toward and allocates attention to the stimulus. This response, which the consumer cannot consciously control, is called an **orientation reflex.**[26] Because most advertisements to which consumers are exposed are unrelated to the goals of the audience, marketers go to some trouble to elicit the orientation reflex. Figure 5–5 illustrates a print advertisement that could elicit an orientation reaction through the use of novelty and surprise. The sight of the smiling orangutan attracts most people's attention to the advertisement for the Kodak film. The ad copy supports the picture with clever prose which will bring at least a small chuckle to even the most hard-nosed consumer.

With both voluntary and involuntary attention, cognitive capacity is allocated to the stimulus. When the individual attends to the information, he or she will reveal physiological arousal. The arousal will result in an increase in blood pressure, a quickening of breathing, a slight sweating of the hands, and dilation of the eye pupils, among other things. One way of assessing the impact of advertisements is to measure the arousal elicited when they are viewed. Devices that assess blood pressure, pupil dilation, and even the temperature of the eardrum have been used.

Figure 5–5   Kodak uses the principle of surprise in this photo. *(Courtesy of Eastman Kodak Company.)*

Marketers attempt to capture attention by varying the nature of the stimulus received by consumers. The goal is to activate the orientating response by adroitly creating stimuli that surprise, threaten, or violate the expectations of consumers. A number of stimulus factors can be used to achieve such a goal. The clever use of surprise illustrated in Figure 5–5 is an example. Movement can also activate the orientating reflex. Thus, on highways and in cities one finds retailers using neon lights that appear to move as the lights are turned on and off. Of course, the goal is to attract the consumer's attention to the hotel, bar, or whatever. Another stimulus factor is the size or magnitude of the stimulus. For example, all else equal, large print advertisements are more apt to be attended than small ones. A loud television commercial will more likely be processed than a soft one. Color can attract attention, particularly when amidst black and white print materials. The principle of contrast is also an important stimulus factor. Contrast occurs when a stimulus diverges substantially from the adaptation level of the consumer. A loud noise in a quiet room or a print ad with very little copy in a sea of verbose ads illustrates the concept of contrast.

PERCEPTUAL PROCESSES

As noted earlier in the chapter, perception refers to the process through which individuals organize and comprehend information. A crucial concept in consumer behavior is that marketers must focus their analysis on what consumers perceive rather than on what the marketing stimulus is. Different consumers may have divergent sets of mental impressions of the meaning of a stimulus, such as an advertisement.[27] Furthermore, consumers and marketers often react differently to a marketing stimulus. That is, because consumers often have experiences, expectations, lifestyles, and knowledge unlike the marketers who create marketing stimuli, their interpretations are apt to be quite different. Product failures can result from consumers perceiving the product in a way not anticipated by marketers. For example, consumers perceived Pringle's potato chips as processed and unnatural. These reactions were unanticipated by Procter & Gamble executives, in part because they focused on a different product quality—the snack's ability to be neatly stacked in cans.

The florist industry thrives on the divergent meanings attached to one type of basic stimulus—flowers. The perceiver of a bouquet of flowers can interpret their meaning in a variety of ways depending upon the circumstances. The flowers could represent a thank-you, part of a proposal of marriage, sorrow over a death or sickness, or a statement of love. The many meanings of something whose very nature is perishable and short-lived accounts for the $3 billion flower industry.[28]

In discussing perception two areas are of major importance—organization and comprehension processes. Organization deals with the way consumers identify the shapes, forms, figures, and lines in their visual world. In the comprehension process people draw upon their experience, memory, and expectations to interpret and attach meaning to a stimulus.

Perceptual Organization

What do you see when you look at Figure 5–6? The goal of the ad is to have consumers fill in the lines and recognize that the ad illustrates a bottle of whiskey. The fact that people will automatically fill in the lines illustrates one

Figure 5–6   The Gestalt principle of closure operates in this ad.
(Courtesy of John E. Seagram & Sons, Inc.)

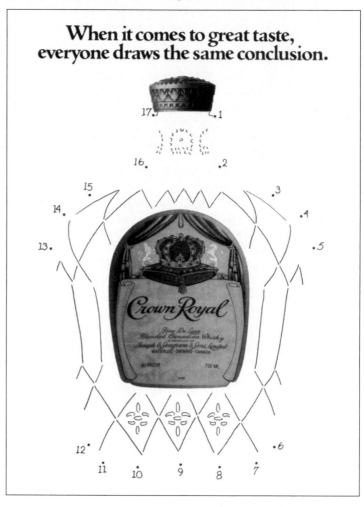

principle of **perceptual organization—closure.** People have a tendency to see a whole figure, even if there are gaps in it. They automatically try to make sense out of incomplete information by organizing it into a meaningful form. Much of the work on perceptual organization comes from the work of German psychologists active early in the twentieth century. Called **Gestalt psychologists,** these individuals attempted to identify the rules that govern how people take disjointed stimuli and make sense out of the shapes and forms to which they are exposed.

Figure 5–7 presents a number of the Gestalt rules of perceptual organization. Many of the rules deal with how people decide what things go together. For example, the rule of common fate states that elements that move in the same direction are assumed to belong to each other. Other rules applicable to the problem of deciding "what-goes-with-what" are similarity, proximity, and closure. Another area of Gestalt interest involves determining how people distinguish **figure and ground.** Example number 4 in Figure 5–7 illustrates what is called a reversible figure. At one moment the picture looks like two faces looking at each other. The next moment it looks like a vase. The image switches back and forth because the brain cannot decipher whether the black or the white portions of the drawing are the figure.

From a marketer's point of view, perceptual organization is generally applied to visual communications, such as print advertising, television advertising, and package design. For example, when drawing an ad, the artist will consciously or unconsciously use Gestalt principles in order to create the desired effect on the consumer. In particular, the artist will be attentive to the figure-ground concept. For the product to be noticed, it must stand out from the background of the print ad. Similarly, if the goal is to associate the product with something else desirable, such as a popular celebrity endorser, the principles of proximity, closure, and common fate could be used.

Figure 5–7   Some principles of perceptual organization.

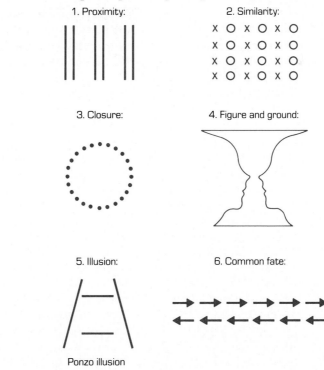

1. Proximity:

2. Similarity:

3. Closure:

4. Figure and ground:

5. Illusion:

Ponzo illusion

6. Common fate:

Comprehension

During and after attention to a stimulus, the consumer will attempt to gain an understanding of what it is and how he or she should react to it. In this **comprehension** stage people will retrieve from long-term memory information pertinent to the stimulus. In addition, expectancies regarding what the stimulus "should be like" are retrieved from long-term memory and used to help interpret it. The personal inclinations and biases of the consumer will also influence the interpretation of the stimulus. For example, ask two avid fans of opposing basketball teams how well the game was refereed. Quite likely the two will have very different views of the officiating because of the differences in the way they comprehended the game.

Although the principles of perceptual organization are applied unconsciously, the interpretive process occurs, at least in some instances, consciously. That is, when attempting to comprehend and understand the nature of a stimulus, consumers are aware that they are engaged in the task. In high-involvement situations in particular consumers will actively analyze the stimulus. This active processing of information seems to occur in short-term memory and involves the development of cognitive responses.[29]

Cognitive Responses Cognitive responses are the active thoughts that take any of a number of different forms. Three types frequently investigated by consumer researchers are counterarguments, support arguments, and source derogations. **Counterarguments** occur when the consumer begins to refute the claims of the message. **Support arguments** involve the consumer developing thoughts that support the message. The third type of response consists of thoughts that derogate the source of the information.[30]

An occasion when cognitive responses might be elicited would involve a consumer who actively searches for information concerning the repair records of various brands of automobiles being considered for purchase. A message received from *Consumer Reports* might result in support arguments, such as, "*Consumer Reports* has sure been right before." A message received from the automobile manufacturer might result in a source derogation, such as "the company is probably biased in the way they are presenting the information."

Assessing cognitive responses can help marketers understand how consumers are interpreting and comprehending the messages they receive. The measurement of the number of support arguments versus the number of counterarguments generated by a message has been shown to be predictive of the extent to which consumers accept a message.[31] What seems to happen is that when consumers are exposed to and attend to the message in a high-involvement setting, they react to it by actively interpreting the message. This interpretation involves the retrieval of information from long-term memory. To the extent that the retrieved memories are positive, the consumer will develop support arguments. However, if the retrieved thoughts are negative, the cognitive response is likely to involve counterarguments or source derogations. These cognitive responses then influence subsequent actions such as verbalizations about the product or actual steps taken to make a purchase. Further, the cognitive-response thoughts are likely to be stored in long-term memory. Thus, subsequent messages which pertain to the brand in question will tend to elicit the newly created responses stored in memory.

The Role of Expectations   A consumer's expectations will also influence the manner in which a consumer interprets marketing stimuli. **Expectations** are a person's prior beliefs about what should happen in a given situation. They can have a major impact on how consumers perceive information. A common problem for secondary brands with relatively small market shares is that consumers will misinterpret their advertising as actually coming from one of the market leaders. Because the market leaders spend so much more money on advertising, consumers begin to expect that the messages they receive are coming from the major brands. Thus, when an advertisement is received from a secondary brand, the consumer may not pay enough attention to it to recognize that it is not a major brand doing the advertising. It is as though the consumer were saying, "Gosh, what brand was that? Well, it must be brand *X* because you hear about it all the time."

An example of expectations influencing the interpretation of information occurred during the 1984 presidential elections. A labor leader who was speaking out for Walter Mondale during the primary elections pointed to a lack of substance in the proposals of challenger Gary Hart. To make his point the labor leader commented, "And as Burger King says, 'where's the beef.' " Of course, Burger King was not using the slogan "Where's the beef." It was Wendy's, a smaller chain that cannot do as much advertising as Burger King. The labor leader probably based his interpretation of the ad on his expectancy that Burger King did the advertisement.

Managerial Implications

The managerial implications of knowledge of how consumers process information are broad ranging. Such knowledge should impact management strategy in key areas of the marketing mix, including advertising, product and packaging policies, and pricing.

Advertising Implications

For advertisers a major problem concerns the consumer reception process. In particular, the tendency of consumers to screen selectively information to which they are exposed and to which they attend can dramatically lower the effectiveness of advertising dollars. In the early 1980s television executives began programming what became known as "The Big Event." These events were the miniseries such as *Roots* and *Shogun*, telecasts of major movies (e.g., *Jaws*), or telecasts of huge sporting events, like the 1984 Olympic games. Sanitation supervisors at water departments found that during these "events" water consumption fluctuated dramatically. Over a two- or three-minute period, many water-holding tanks were drained and the systems strained to capacity. Called the "flush factor," the sudden increase in water usage occurred during commercial breaks when consumers left their televisions to rush to their bathrooms. The flush factor illustrates the point that consumers watching television will selectively avoid exposing themselves to commercials and attend to other matters.[32]

Remote-control devices on television have proliferated with the influx of cable television systems. With such devices consumers can rapidly and easily change from one channel to another. Called "zapping" in the industry, about 6 to 19 percent of consumers at any one time are zapping commercials by remotely switching channels.[33] One study found that 64 percent of viewers with cable zap advertisements.

In 1984 a symposium was held by advertisers on the zapping problem and the related issue of audience erosion during commercial messages. The consensus appeared to be that an "erosion rate" of some 49 percent exists for television commercials. Thus, only six of every ten people watching a television program will actually observe any one commercial. The general response by professionals was that to reduce the **audience erosion** problem commercials would have to become more appealing. One executive commented that to prevent people from selectively avoiding commercials, advertisements would have to be made so well that people would want to view them.[34] Table 5–3 presents some other suggestions on how to deal with the audience-erosion problem.

Table 5–3 Methods to Reduce Problems of Audience Erosion

1. Format change	Place material in the interior of programs. Zapping occurs most at beginning and end of programs.
2. Spread commercials	Since consumers often switch from network shows to cable programming, place more ads on cable channels.
3. Strategic timing	Zapping frequently occurs after five to ten seconds of commercial are completed. Place important material early in commercials. Also, try to obtain first position in a series of commercials.
4. Budget more for print and other media	With audience erosion in television growing, why not place more emphasis on other media. *Reader's Digest* has run ads in trade magazines pointing out the erosion problem on TV.
5. Persuade networks to show fewer ads	Audiences may be reacting to commercial clutter and advertising overload by zapping commercials.

SOURCE: Extracted from Bernie Whalen, "$6 Billion Down the Drain!" *Marketing News,* September 14, 1984, 1, 37, 38.

In addition to the audience-erosion problem, advertisers have difficulties getting consumers to attend to messages even though they are exposed to them. A frequently used approach is to vary the characteristics of the communication in order to activate consumers' orienting responses. The use of some surprising or novel billboard or print ad would be an example. In many large cities billboards are now being produced in which the product appears to leap off the structure. Other ways of varying the stimulus consist of increasing its size or making use of contrast, color, or positioning.

The concept that consumers become adapted to stimuli has implications for both product and advertising strategies. Consumers will become adapted to a certain look, style, or message over some period of time. In order to keep product or service communications fresh, marketers should attempt to vary them periodically. Thus, Miller's Lite beer has bombarded consumers with the same message for years—i.e., it won't fill you up but tastes great. The message has not become boring because of the highly creative use of dozens of different advertisements in which various ex-jocks give the message in unusual circumstances. The net result is a long-running advertising campaign that propelled the beer into the number-one "light" beer position.

Problems in consumer comprehension of marketing communications also plague marketers. For example, the way in which people organize information for interpretation should be understood. The figure-ground principle is a case in point. Managers want their product to be the figure moving against the background of information in an advertisement. However, some advertisers make the mistake of letting their product slide into the background so that people focus attention on something other than the product. The use of highly attractive models in print advertisements can cause such a figure-ground misinterpretation. If the sexy model becomes the figure, the product may not be attended to, and the message may be ignored.

The ground against which the figure moves in an advertisement can be important, however, because it forms the context in which the message is interpreted. The context assists the consumer in interpreting the situation surrounding the use of the product. As such, the background of the ad can dramatically influence the product image acquired by consumers. For example, in an advertisement for Aviance Night Musk perfume, a woman is lying down so that only her bare legs are visible. Her right foot is positioned at the left knee, creating a triangular opening through which an attractive man can be seen in the background. The entire scene is colored with a sensual, pale yellow-orange hue. The context provided by the scene makes the interpretation of the perfume shown in the foreground unmistakable.

Also important to the interpretation of marketing communications are the expectations that consumers have prior to receiving messages. As noted earlier in the chapter, expectations are part of the filter through which people interpret information. In some instances a strong expectation can result in consumers not attending well to a stimulus and interpreting it on the basis of what is expected rather than what is actually there. This can result in consumers rating the performance of well-known brands higher than that of unknown brands that actually perform equally well, or in rating an unknown company more negatively than a known company that makes a product recall.[35]

The research on memory processes is having a major impact on how advertisers structure advertisements. For example, knowledge that short-term memory has limited capacity is consistent with advertisers limiting the number of copy points that they attempt to communicate in television and radio ads. Information on the superiority of visual memory, and in particular on how it can be tied to semantic memory by having pictures communicate the message, has resulted in some advertisers working carefully to communicate their message visually as well as verbally. Also, enhancing consumers' encoding of a message can make it easier for consumers to retrieve the message from memory. Jingles often serve such a purpose. Thus, Brim decaffeinated coffee commercials always have actors or actresses say, "Fill it to the rim, with Brim." Although the message can seem boring and repetitious, it effectively helps consumers encode the name of the brand by associating it with the rim of the cup from which they drink their coffee.

Product Strategy

Knowledge of consumer information-processing characteristics can also assist managers in product strategy. For example, as noted above, varying the characteristics of the product on a periodic basis can avert potential consumer boredom, which can result from consumers becoming adapted to the product's characteristics. The frequent appearance of "new and improved" product formulations probably represents just such a strategy.

Information on absolute and difference thresholds can also affect packaging strategy. Unless the intensity of a stimulus is strong enough or the change in stimulus is great enough, it is unlikely that consumers will be influenced. Why does the Campbell Soup Company package its pork and beans in a 20¾-ounce can while its major competitor uses a 21-ounce can? It may be because consumers do not notice the difference. After a twelve-month test, the candy company M&M/Mars found that increasing the size of its candy bars increased sales by 20 to 30 percent. As a result, the company changed nearly its entire product line. Bohemian brand beer lowered the quantity of beer in each bottle from twelve to eleven ounces. The cost savings were used to increase the ad budget and develop a fancier container. As a result, sales nearly doubled.[36] These examples illustrate how corporate strategy based on keeping changes within or beyond the difference threshold can have major influences on sales.

Pricing

As noted earlier in the chapter, Weber's Law has implications for managers in their pricing policies. In particular, when prices are raised, managers should attempt to stay below the "just noticeable difference." In contrast, when prices are lowered via coupons, a sale, a rebate, or some other means, the discount should be greater than the JND.

Another perceptual expectation that consumers have in some circumstances is the **price-quality relationship.** In normal circumstances the greater the price the less likely a consumer is to buy a particular product item. However, within certain ranges of price for a product, consumers may infer that higher prices are indicative of greater product quality.[37] The price-quality relationship is probably learned over time through such aphorisms as, "You get what you pay for." Although some researchers have argued that price is in fact a poor indicator of quality, recent evidence indicates that the relationship is highly complex because it depends upon the dimensions of quality that the researcher investigates.[38] One summary of the evidence on the price-quality relationship gave the following occasions when price may be used to indicate the quality of a product:

1. The consumer has some confidence that in the situation price predicts quality.
2. When real or perceived quality variations occur among brands.
3. When actual quality is difficult to judge through objective means or through brand name or store image.[39]

SUMMARY

Information processing is defined as the process through which consumers receive stimulation, transform it into meaningful information, store the information in memory for later use, and retrieve it for decision making. The area of study is particularly important for all marketing communications efforts. If consumers fail to receive marketing information, comprehend it improperly, or fail to remember it, a great deal of money and time will be lost.

Several areas make up the study of information processing. The reception process refers to the factors that govern the consumer's exposure to and amount of attention directed towards various stimuli. An important aspect of the reception process is the study of sensation. Sensations are the immediate impressions left by the firing of nerve fibers in response to the physical stimulation of the senses. Important aspects of the study of sensation include investigating absolute and differential thresholds and the adaptation level. Managers should be particularly aware of the tendency of consumers to expose and attend to marketing stimuli selectively.

Another important information-processing area is the study of perception. Perception refers to how consumers organize and comprehend information. Marketers must recognize that different people can perceive the same stimulus in quite divergent ways. Such perceptual differences can result from variations in expectancies, the types of cognitive responses that the information elicits from memory, and the peculiar ways in which different people organize information.

Memory is an important component of information processing because it acts to guide the reception and perception processes. Three separate types of memory may exist—sensory, short-term, and long-term memory. Short-term memory acts as a type of bottleneck in the information-processing system. It has a limited storage capacity for information of seven plus or minus two chunks of information. Further, unless information is transferred to long-term memory relatively rapidly, it will be lost from short-term memory. For these reasons consumers can easily be overloaded with information, particularly when they are investigating unfamiliar products or making difficult decisions. Various memory-control devices are used by people to encode, store, and retrieve memories. Some of these devices include rehearsing, coding, retrieving, and response generating.

For managers the study of information processing is particularly important in the areas of advertising, product design, package design, and pricing. Because advertisers are at the forefront of the marketing communications effort, they must be concerned with all areas of information processing. Those involved in packaging must be concerned with issues involving attention processes and information overload. Product decisions may be influenced by information on the adaptation level. Similarly, pricing decisions should be heavily influenced by considerations about whether consumers will perceive that a change in a price has occurred.

Key Terms

Information processing
Perception
Sensory memory
Short-term memory
Long-term memory
Cognitive responses
Information overload
Recognition task
Recall task
Evoked set
Clutter
Semantic concepts
Product-attribute associations
Schema
Cognitive differentiation
Memory-control processes
Rehearsal
Coding
Retrieval
Response generation
Reception
Sensation
Attention

Selective exposure
Absolute threshold
Difference threshold
Just noticeable difference
Weber's Law
Adaptation
Spontaneous brand switching
Subliminal stimulation
Voluntary attention
Selective attention
Involuntary attention
Orientation reflex
Perceptual organization
Closure
Figure and ground
Comprehension
Counterarguments
Support arguments
Expectations
Audience erosion
Price-quality relationship
Gestalt psychologists

Review Questions

1. Define the concept of information processing.
2. Distinguish the concepts of memory, reception, and perception.
3. What are the three types of memory that have been proposed? How do these differ?
4. What happens when information overload occurs?
5. What is the difference between a recognition and a recall task?
6. What is meant by the term *brain hemispheres*?
7. Compare the effectiveness of picture and word memory under high and low involvement. Are words more or less memorable than pictures?
8. What is a memory network?
9. Define three different memory-control processes.
10. What is the difference between sensation and attention?
11. What is meant by the term *reception*?
12. What are absolute and difference thresholds?
13. Discuss the concepts of selective attention and selective reception.
14. Define and give a marketing example of Weber's Law.
15. What is meant by adaptation level? How does it relate to the "butterfly curve"?

16. Is subliminal advertising effective? Why?
17. What are four of the five ways that marketers can attempt to capture consumer attention?
18. Identify five of the six principles of perceptual organization discussed in the text.
19. Define the term *cognitive response*. What are the different types of cognitive responses?
20. What is the relationship between expectations and perception?
21. What are four methods to prevent audience erosion?

Discussion Questions

1. Listen carefully to three television advertisements. Identify the number of "copy points" that can be found in each ad. To what extent do you think consumers will remember these points? What factors might influence the placement into memory of these copy points?
2. Go through a magazine and identify three print advertisements. Identify the number of copy points found in the ads. Compare the number of copy points found in the print ads to the number you observed in the television ads. What factors might account for any differences you found?
3. Describe two instances of consumer recognition tasks and two instances of consumer recall tasks. Do you find any differences in the advertising associated with the products identified in each instance?
4. It has been said that "one picture is worth a thousand words." Relate this aphorism to the capabilities of picture versus word memory. What are the implications for advertisers?
5. Draw a diagram of your memory network for fast-food restaurants.
6. Suppose that you had to develop a name for a new product. The produce is a soybean-curd (tofu) based desert, which uses real fruit in it, has no cholesterol, and does not bother people who have trouble eating milk-based products (a sizable portion of the population). Create several names for the product and identify how each utilizes the various memory-control processes.
7. Go to a grocery store and identify as many examples as you can of point-of-purchase advertising that effectively helps the consumer associate na-

tional advertising with the brand on the grocery shelves. What are the memory factors that make the POP displays more or less effective?

8. Select five products with different prices—ranging from less than a dollar to thousands of dollars. For each product indicate what you would consider to be the JND for a sales price. To what extent do you find that these exemplify Weber's Law?
9. To what extent do you think that clothing designers utilize the concept of the adaptation level? Would it make a difference in their behavior if they studied adaptation-level theory in detail?
10. Select three print advertisements. Identify as many instances as you can of examples of stimulus factors that are used to gain your attention.
11. Using the same three advertisements, identify as many instances as you can of examples of perceptual organization.
12. Again, using the same three ads, write down all of your cognitive responses to each. To what extent do you think the advertiser anticipated that you might develop cognitive responses?

References

1. Different models of memory have been identified in addition to the one presented here. For a review of some of these see James R. Bettman, "Memory Factors in Consumer Choice," *Journal of Marketing*, 43, Spring, 1979, 37–53.
2. George Sperling, "The Information Available in Brief Visual Presentations," *Psychological Monographs*, 74, No. 11, 1960, 498.
3. D. F. Fisher and R. Karsh, "Modality Effects and Storage in Sequential Short-term Memory," *Journal of Experimental Psychology*, 87, March, 1971, 410–414.
4. S. W. Keele, *Attention and Human Performance*, Santa Monica, Calif.: Goodyear Press, 1973.
5. George A. Miller, "The Magical Number Seven, Plus or Minus Two: Some Limits on Our Capacity to Process Information," *Psychological Review*, 63, March, 1956, 81–97.
6. Daniel Kahneman, *Attention and Effort*, New Jersey: Prentice-Hall, Inc., 1973.
7. A number of articles have been written on information overload. For example, see J. Jacoby, "Information Load and Decision Quality: Some Con-

tested Issues," *Journal of Marketing Research, 14,* November 1977, 569–573.

8. Kahneman, *Attention and Effort.*

9. Ibid.

10. Herbert Simon, *The Sciences of the Artificial,* Cambridge, Mass.: The M.I.T. Press, 1969.

11. Richard M. Shiffrin and R. C. Atkinson, "Storage and Retrieval Processes in Long-term Memory," *Psychological Review, 76,* 1969, 179–193.

12. For a more detailed description of memory and memory control processes see James R. Bettman, "Memory Factors in Consumer Choice," *Journal of Marketing, 43,* Spring 1979, 37–53.

13. Benton Underwood, "Attributes of Memory," *Psychological Review, 76,* November, 1969, 559–573.

14. Terry L. Childers and Michael J. Houston, "Conditions for a Picture-Superiority Effect on Consumer Memory," *Journal of Consumer Research, 11,* September 1984, 643–654.

15. For a review of this literature see Kathy A. Lutz and Richard J. Lutz, "Effects of Interactive Imagery on Learning: Applications to Advertising," *Journal of Applied Psychology, 62,* 1977, 493–498.

16. Terry L. Childers and Michael J. Houston, "Conditions for a Picture-Superiority Effect."

17. Bettman, "Memory Factors in Consumer Choice."

18. Bettman, "Memory Factors in Consumer Choice."

19. C. E. Curtis, "Nothing Beats a Great Pair of L'eggs," *Forbes, 126,* September 29, 1980, 72–73.

20. Kahneman, *Attention and Effort.*

21. Richard Lee Miller, "Dr. Weber and the Consumer," *Journal of Marketing, 26,* January 1962, 57–61.

22. See Leon G. Schiffman and Leslie L. Kanuk, Figure 6–1, in "Sequential Changes in Packaging that Fall Below the J.N.D.," *Consumer Behavior,* Englewood Cliffs, N.J.: Prentice-Hall, Inc., 1983, 140.

23. Flemming Hansen, *Consumer Choice Behavior,* New York, N.Y.: Collier Macmillan Publishers, 1972.

24. Kahneman, *Attention and Effort.*

25. Ibid.

26. Ibid.

27. These ideas have been expressed in the lens model of Egon Brunswick. An excellent series of papers concerning the work of Brunswick can be found in *The Psychology of Egon Brunswick,* Kenneth R. Hammond (ed.), New York, N.Y.: Holt, Rinehart, and Winston, 1966.

28. William Harris and Robert Teitelman, "Flower Power," *Forbes,* October 25, 1982, 75–76.

29. Peter Wright is credited with doing much of the early work on cognitive responses in marketing. For example, see Peter L. Wright, "The Cognitive Processes Mediating the Acceptance of Advertising," *Journal of Marketing Research, 10,* February 1973, 53–62.

30. The earliest work on cognitive responses was done by a psychologist, Anthony G. Greenwald, "Cognitive Learning, Cognitive Response to Persuasion, and Attitude Change," in *Psychological Foundations of Attitudes,* A. G. Greenwald, T. C. Brock, and T. M. Ostrom (eds.), New York, N.Y.: Academic Press, 1968.

31. Peter L. Wright, "Cognitive Responses to Mass Media Advocacy and Cognitive Choice Process," in *Cognitive Responses to Persuasion,* R. Petty, T. Ostrom, and T. Brock (eds.), New York, N.Y.: McGraw-Hill Book Company, 1978.

32. Bernie Whalen, "$6 Billion Down the Drain!" *Marketing News,* September 14, 1984, 1, 37.

33. "Background on Zapping," *Marketing News,* September 14, 1984, 36.

34. Whalen, "$6 Billion Down the Drain!"

35. John C. Mowen and Hal W. Ellis, "The Product Defect: Managerial Considerations and Consumer Implications," *The Annual Review of Marketing,* Ben Enis and Kenneth Roering (eds.), Chicago, Ill.: American Marketing Association, 1981, 158–172.

36. John Koten, "Why Do Hot Dogs Come in Packs of 10 and Buns in 8s or 12s?" *The Wall Street Journal,* September 21, 1984, 1, 26.

37. Kent B. Monroe, "The Influence of Price Differences and Brand Familiarity on Brand Preferences," *Journal of Consumer Research, 3,* June 1976, 42–49.

38. Chr. Hjorth-Anderson, "The Concept of Quality and the Efficiency of Markets for Consumer Products," *Journal of Consumer Research, 11,* September 1984, 708–718.

39. James Engel and Roger Blackwell, *Consumer Behavior,* New York, N.Y.: The Dryden Press, 1982.

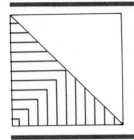

6
Consumer Learning Processes

The Consumer as Pigeon and Dog?

Do consumers act like pigeons and dogs? Apparently *The Wall Street Journal* thinks so. A few years ago a front-page article was headlined, "Why Are Auto Sales Strictly for the Birds? Ask Any Pigeon." A subtitle stated, "Much Like Random Rewards for Pecking, Car Rebates Teach Customers to Wait."

The article argued that the auto makers were unwittingly operantly conditioning consumers. Car buyers were acting like pigeons and responding to the on-again-off-again rebates as though the incentives were grains of corn. Because the rebates were announced aperiodically, consumers had learned to wait for them. As a consequence, when the rebate offers were withdrawn, sales dried up because consumers had learned to wait for the next rebate offer to appear.

Another article in *The Wall Street Journal* was headlined "Coca-Cola Turns to Pavlov." The first sentence read, "Do television commercials make people behave like Pavlov's dogs?" The article briefly described a classical conditioning approach used by Coke to test the effectiveness of commercials. As stated in the article, the company "attempts to evaluate how well a commercial 'conditions' a viewer to accept a positive image that can be transferred to the product."

Can consumers be conditioned to act like pigeons and dogs? The answer is yes and no. Consumers do learn via operant and classical conditioning principles. When properly used by managers, principles of operant and classical conditioning are practical tools that can influence sales. Can managers use these procedures to dupe "mindless" consumers? The answer to this question is a qualified no. Consumers are capable of engaging in the higher-level cognitive processing of information. They can plan, assess motives, and

161

engage in problem solving. We have little to fear that unscrupulous managers will on a massive scale take advantage of "mindless" consumers.

Based in part on Robert L. Simpson, "Why are Auto Sales Strictly for the Birds? Just Ask a Pigeon," *The Wall Street Journal,* December 15, 1982, 1, 24; and "Coca-Cola Turns to Pavlov . . . Car Buyers . . . 90 Second Ads," *The Wall Street Journal,* January 19, 1984, 31.

INTRODUCTION

Learning may be defined as a process in which experience leads to a relatively permanent change in behavior or the potential for a change in behavior. Learning results from experience, not from changes in physiology resulting from growth, injury, or disease. Thus, temporary states caused by ingesting drugs would not be classified as learning. Consumers, however, may experience learning but not reveal it through a change in behavior. Information may be stored in memory and yet not influence behavior because a situation to which the information is relevant fails to arise. For example, a consumer may learn a great deal about automobiles by watching television and reading advertisements in magazines. However, if the consumer lived in New York City and did not own a car, the learning could have negligible impact on his or her behavior.

Consumer researchers typically discuss three types of learning—**cognitive learning, operant conditioning,** and **classical conditioning.** Cognitive theorists focus on relatively complex forms of learning, such as how people retain verbal material (e.g., advertising messages), how people have insights, and how people plan. In addition to cognitive learning, however, people can also learn through the more basic, but no less powerful, means of classical and operant conditioning. Advertisers are particularly interested in the study of classical conditioning. They attempt to identify stimuli, such as messages, sights, or sounds, that will elicit positive reactions from consumers. Their goal is to associate their product or service with the positive stimulus, so that the product will elicit a similar positive reaction when the consumer thinks about or encounters it.

The principles of operant conditioning have importance to most marketing activities. Strategies involving advertising, pricing, personal selling, and sales promotion all can involve providing consumers with rewards and/or punishments which may influence their later behavior. The behavior of customers playing the slot machines at casinos well illustrates the effects of operant conditioning. Their incessant gambling, even in the face of staggering losses, their superstitious behavior, and their high levels of arousal all can be explained to a large extent via operant conditioning principles.

One outcome of learning can be the formation of a habit. A significant proportion of consumer purchases may be governed by the habitual purchase of the same brand of a product. Consumers may purchase the same brand over and over again because of either habit or brand loyalty. However, when brand loyalty is established, a positive attitude is also formed towards the brand so that it is liked more than comparable others. Companies court consumers in order to obtain their brand loyalty. The results of learning probably explain the reasons why some brands achieve high degrees of brand loyalty and others do not.

The vignette that opened the chapter illustrates how seriously companies take the learning process. No doubt Coca-Cola has invested large sums of money in their work on using classical conditioning principles to assess the likely effectiveness of advertisements. The auto rebate example points out the need for companies to examine carefully how they are rewarding consumers. The auto manufacturers set themselves up for problems by rewarding consumers for waiting to buy cars. It was not until the severe recession of the early 1980s ended and a strong economic upturn began that the effects of the conditioning were overwhelmed by other factors, such as a strong growth in personal income and consumer economic confidence.

In the following sections this chapter discusses the three major types of learning—cognitive learning, operant conditioning, and classical conditioning. In addition, it analyzes consumer buying habits. One habit of particular importance, brand loyalty, is singled out for attention. The managerial implications of each of these areas of consumer study will also be identified.

COGNITIVE LEARNING PROCESSES

As noted earlier in the chapter, cognitive learning involves such mental activities as thinking, remembering, problem solving, developing insight, forming concepts, and learning ideas. The field of study is closely related to that of information processing discussed in the last chapter. Indeed, those who study information processing are usually referred to as "cognitive psychologists."

Cognitive learning processes are particularly applicable to the promotional component of the marketing mix. For example, advertisements heavy in informational content often rely on cognitive learning for their effectiveness. A good illustration is found in the advertisement presented in Figure 6–1. In the ad the Beef Industry Council provides several important pieces of information concerning the nutritional value of beef. The goal of the ad is to cause consumers to associate lean beef with nutrition. The ad is strictly informational with no use of emotional appeals or of social reinforcers, such as attractive people eating beef. Therefore, it may be placed in the cognitive learning category.

Early Cognitive Theorists— The Gestalt Psychologists

Although cognitive learning is often associated with human thinking and information processing, some early researchers studied the cognitive abilities of apes. In the 1920s a German Gestalt psychologist, Wolfgang Kohler, investigated learning among chimpanzees. He found that one of his chimps, named Sultan, demonstrated a behavior that looked very much like insight. The chimp had already learned to take a stick and rake in bananas from outside his cage. One day Kohler placed a banana outside of the stick's reach. He also placed

Figure 6–1   This ad takes a cognitive learning approach by providing information on the nutritional value of beef. (Courtesy of Beef Industry Council.)

within the chimp's cage other sticks that could be fit end-to-end. After showing a great deal of frustration at not being able to get the banana, Sultan began fiddling with the sticks. All of a sudden in a spontaneous, insightful manner, the chimp fitted two of the sticks together and dragged in the banana. The sudden understanding of the relationship between joining the sticks and reaching the banana seemed to be explained only through reference to insight or to an "aha" experience.[1]

The Gestalt psychologists believed that biological and psychological events do not influence behavior in isolation from each other. Instead, people perceive the inputs from the environment as part of a total context. The work of the Gestalt psychologists was in marked contrast to other learning theorists in the first half of the twentieth century. In contrast to the view that man was a static organism who responded automatically to inputs from the environment, the Gestalt psychologists focused on the active, creative nature of learning and action.[2] As one noted consumer researcher stated,

> When we look at an automobile, we do not see glass and steel and plastic and bolts and paint. We see instead an organized whole, an automobile. And perhaps not even just an automobile but also comfortable transportation, prestige, status, and a symbolic sense of achievement. This is the familiar Gestalt dictum; the whole is different from, if not greater than, the sum of the isolated parts.[3]

The work of the Gestalt psychologists has important implications for marketers. A tendency exists for marketing researchers to perceive products in terms of their individual characteristics, such as price, color, features, and reliability. In contrast, consumers tend to perceive the product as an integrated whole. In isolation a particular color or style may be judged to be unacceptable. However, when seen in the overall context of a product, such as an automobile, the characteristic could be quite satisfactory. Thus, when considered in isolation, using plaid seats in a car might seem silly; however, when placed in a sports car the multicolor seats might fit quite well.

Another contribution of the Gestalt school is the idea that people do engage in problem-solving activities and have sudden bursts of insight. Consumer behavior has begun to emphasize low-involvement learning processes in the past few years, and many products or situations can activate the consumer so that he or she begins problem-solving activities. In fact, the advertising campaign for V-8 cocktail vegetable juice is based around the actors saying with sudden insight, "Wow! I could have had a V-8." Of course, the goal is to portray the actor as having the sudden "aha-experience" that rather than drinking that sweet soft drink, he or she could have had a healthful glass of V-8.

The Associationists

Other early work in cognitive learning was performed by researchers who believed in the **law of contiguity** and came to be known as **associationists.** The law of contiguity states that things that are experienced together become associated.[4] The earliest experimental work was performed in the late eighteenth century by H. Ebbinghaus, who discovered what came to be called the **serial position effect.** Shown in Figure 6–2, the serial position effect occurs when a list of items is to be learned. As can be seen, items in the beginning of the list and items at the end of the list are the most readily learned. In contrast, items in the middle of the list are learned much less rapidly.

One explanation for the serial learning effect is that the beginning and end of a list become anchors for learning. Because of limitations of short-term memory, people identify reference points for when to attempt starting or ending the learning process. Only limited amounts of information can be stored in short-term memory at a time, so only the items right around the beginning and end of the list are recalled readily. Items in the middle take many more repetitions of the material to be recalled.

The serial learning effect has important implications for marketers. Key information in advertisements should be placed at the beginning or end of the message. If important information is embedded in the middle of the communication, consumers may need more repetitions of the advertisement to learn the information.

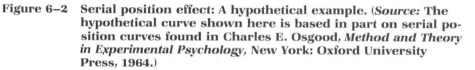

Figure 6–2   **Serial position effect: A hypothetical example. (*Source:* The hypothetical curve shown here is based in part on serial position curves found in Charles E. Osgood, *Method and Theory in Experimental Psychology*, New York: Oxford University Press, 1964.)**

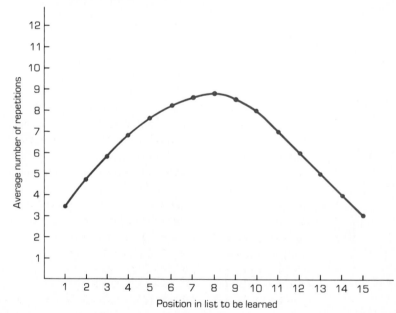

The curve shows the number of repetitions required to learn a fifteen-item list so that no errors occur.

In addition to studying how consumers learn lists of information, the associationists also investigated how consumers remember words that are to be associated with each other. Called **paired associate learning,** the task requires people to associate a series of response words with stimulus words. Thus, three pairs of stimulus and response words might be the following: Maytag–quality, Toyota–"Oh-what-a-feeling," and peas–Jolly Green Giant. In the task Maytag, Toyota, and peas would be the stimulus words, and subjects would be asked to recall from memory the respective response words—quality, "Oh-what-a-feeling," and Jolly Green Giant. An important finding in research on paired associate learning has been that learning is speeded up if the stimulus and response items can be readily associated with each other and are familiar.[5] In particular, if mental images can be developed between stimulus and response words, learning is more rapid.

The findings in paired associate learning tasks also have important implications for marketing communications. In many instances companies attempt to create associations between some concept and their product. The goal is to have the concept also retrieved from memory when their brand name is mentioned. Thus, Maytag wants the word "quality" retrieved when its name is mentioned. Similarly, Toyota would like to have the phrase "Oh-what-a-feeling," recalled when its name is mentioned. The findings of studies in paired associate learning suggest that for these associations to be learned most rapidly, the following conditions should be met:

1. The stimulus and response words should be easily pronounceable.
2. The person should be familiar with the stimulus and response words.
3. The stimulus and response words should be meaningful.
4. The stimulus and response words should be easily associated.
5. Visual images should be created to link the stimulus and response words together.[6]

Additional Issues in Cognitive Learning Theory

A number of additional topic areas should be addressed in regard to cognitive learning. Two particularly important areas are why people forget and how people learn through observation. In addition, cognitive learning researchers have investigated how people can improve their memories. Highlight 6–1 provides two of these memory improving techniques.

Forgetting   As noted in Chapter 5, **forgetting** occurs when either the retrieval or the response generation-process breaks down. Two factors that can cause problems in retrieval and response generation are **proactive interference** and **retroactive interference.** In each case, other material that has been learned interferes with the learning of new material. In the case of retroactive interference, new material presented after old material has been learned interferes with the recall of the old material. In some manner the learning of new material interferes with the retrieval from memory or in the response generation of the old material. With proactive interference, material

HIGHLIGHT 6–1

Some Tricks to Improve Your Memory

In the business world occasions exist in which a good memory can be important. In particular, the ability to remember the names of clients, colleagues, and distant acquaintances can help an executive present a highly competent image. Furthermore, being able to call someone by his or her first name after not having seen him or her for months or years can give the impression that an executive "really cares about people." Although it is true that some people simply have better memories than others, some tricks exist to help us improve our recall of information.

Perhaps the best way of assisting our memories is to develop mental images or pictures of what we want to remember. For example, when you meet an individual whose name you particularly want to remember, attempt to associate the name with some mental image. Say this person was named John Mowen. An effective mental image would be a lawn mower sitting on top of a toilet seat. Although the image would be

unflattering to the person, it would be an effective way of encoding the name so that it could be easily retrieved at a later point.

Mental imagery can also be used to recall long lists of items. Called the **method of loci,** the approach involves visualizing yourself taking a walk through a very familiar environment, such as your house or apartment. Each item on the list to be remembered is placed in some location. Thus, if you were trying to memorize the promotional mix, "advertising" might be hung on the coat tree in the entry hall, "personal selling" placed on the banister of the stairs, "sales promotion" hung from the chandelier at the top of the stairs, and "public relations" placed in the closet with the coats. The idea is to create a mental image of each item of the list in each location. When the list needs to be recalled later on, one merely follows the path from the coat tree to the banister to the chandelier to the closet and picks up each of the items to be remembered.

---

learned prior to the new material interferes with the learning of the new material.[7]

The effects of retroactive inhibition can be shown easily by learning material either right before going to bed or just after getting up in the morning. As shown in Figure 6–3, if a person learns material and then goes to sleep, little or no forgetting occurs while the person is asleep. In contrast, if the person remains awake between learning and testing, the new information causes an inability to recall the old material. For a student these results suggest that after studying for a test, he or she should either go directly to the test or try to sleep until the test in order to avoid any loss of recall of information.

Forgetting resulting from retroactive and proactive inhibition can create problems for marketers. A classic finding is that interference between sets of material to be learned increases as the similarity of their content increases.[8] On the basis of these findings in experimental psychology one can predict that if consumers receive a series of commercials for products in which similar types of claims are made, confusion will result and learning will be impeded. The problem of commercial clutter has already been discussed in Chapter 5. The work on retroactive and proactive inhibition suggests that clutter will be even worse to the extent that the competing commercials in-

Figure 6–3 **Effects of retroactive inhibition and sleep on forgetting.** (*Source:* **Data from J. G. Jenkins and K. M. Dallenbach, "Oblivescence During Sleep and Waking,"** *American Journal of Psychology,* **35, 1924, 605–612. Reproduced courtesy of University of Illinois Press.)**

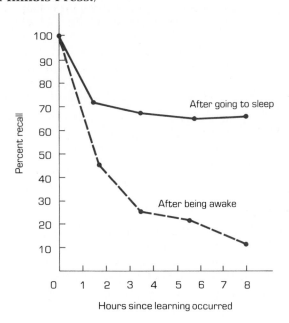

volve similar types of products or different products that use similar adjectives to describe their performance, such as high-quality, low-cost, or low-maintenance.

THE VON RESTORFF EFFECT. A finding of particular importance to advertisers has been called the **von Restorff effect.**[9] Experiments have shown that a unique item in a series of relatively homogeneous items will be recalled much more easily. It seems that with such unique items the effects of proactive and retroactive inhibition are minimized. The von Restorff effect immediately brings to mind the unique and sometimes bizarre commercials for Dr Pepper, which certainly stand out from the set of relatively similar commercials found on television today. The practice of many students of using Majic Markers to highlight important words and phrases in a chapter also illustrates the von Restorff effect.

THE ZEIGARNIK EFFECT. Another factor that influences whether something will be forgotten is the **Zeigarnik effect.** Named after the female German Gestalt scientist who discovered it, the Zeigarnik effect occurs when an individual is involved in a task and is interrupted.[10] If the recall of information is compared between a task that has been interrupted and one that has been completed, the findings consistently show that material in the interrupted task is recalled better. From a Gestalt perspective, the incompleted task creates a tension in the mind of the performer that persists until the task is completed. This tension causes the person to maintain memory traces of the material involved in the incompleted task.

Although specific work to test the Zeigarnik effect in advertising has not been done, the findings do have marketing implications. For example, if an advertiser creates a brief story that interests the consumer and then abruptly ends the story while leaving the consumer dangling, increased recall of the information in the story by the consumer may result. Levi Strauss and Company may have achieved this goal in an ad in which a young woman clad in Levi jeans is seen in front of a fence with a country house in the background. She looks at the house and yells, "Travis, you're a year too late!" The incompleteness of the ad and the mystery it involved created a great deal of conversation about the ad. It well illustrates the potential impact of the Zeigarnik effect.

Time and Forgetting Because of the operation of proactive and retroactive inhibition, the recall of verbal information decreases over time. Classic work by H. Ebbinghaus tracked the loss of recall over time.[11] Figure 6–4 shows the results of one of his experiments. After learning a list of nonsense words (e.g., xlp, mqv), the percentage of words remembered decreased dramatically at first and then leveled off over time.

The rapid forgetting that occurs immediately after learning has been shown to occur in advertising as well. In another classic experiment, Zielske had advertisements for a product run once a week for thirteen weeks.[12] At the end of the thirteen-week period, 63 percent of the housewives could recall having seen the ad. After thirteen weeks, no more ads were given, and forgetting showed the same pattern as that found seventy years before by Ebbinghaus. Forgetting occurred very rapidly at first and then leveled off. After twenty weeks, the recall of the ads had dropped to below 30 percent, and by the time nine months had passed less than 10 percent could remember the ads.

In addition to giving one group of housewives one ad a week for thirteen weeks, the researchers gave another group thirteen ads spaced four weeks apart. In this case the ability to recall the ads increased slowly, but at the end of the year some 48 percent could remember the ads. The difference between the group that had the ads bunched together and those who received the ads spaced over time has important implications for advertisers. If the advertiser wants to obtain rapid awareness of a product, a high frequency of ads over a short period of time will be effective. However, rapid forgetting after the burst of advertisements will occur. If the goal is to build long-term awareness of the ad, the commercials should be pulsed so that the ads are seen by consumers regularly over a long period of time. Often companies

Figure 6–4   **Relationship between time and forgetting. (*Source:* Data from H. Ebbinghaus, *Memory*, translated by H. A. Ruger and C. E. Bussenius. New York: Teachers College, 1913.)**

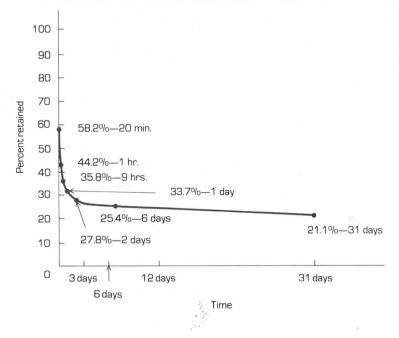

combine the approaches and use a high-intensity campaign to bring out a product and then pulse regularly after the introduction in order to maintain awareness.

Observational Learning

Another approach to learning links aspects of cognitive learning to another major type of learning—operant conditioning. Also called **observational learning** or social learning, the concept involves the finding that people will observe the actions of others in order to develop "patterns of behavior."[13] Such patterns of behavior can vary from the general approach that someone takes to handle frustration (e.g., yell at a clerk when a store runs out of a product) to the way someone learns to do specific things like riding a bicycle. Observational learning can influence a variety of consumer behavior activities, from learning how to use products to avoiding products to interacting with salespeople to reacting to violence on television.

Three important ideas have been mentioned as emerging from social learning theory.[14] First, social learning theorists view people as symbolic beings who can foresee the probable consequences of their behavior. People can anticipate the future and vary their behavior accordingly. Second, through **vicarious learning** people learn by watching the actions of others and the consequences of these actions. Social learning theorists particularly emphasize the importance of models in transmitting information through observational learning. (A model is someone whose behavior a person attempts to emulate.) Third, people have the ability to regulate their own behavior. Through this self-regulatory process people supply their own rewards and punishments internally by feeling either self-critical or self-satisfied.

OPERANT CONDITIONING PRINCIPLES

From a cognitive perspective, learning results from some change within a person's brain. Although not easily observable, the change is assumed to involve the existence of a memory trace, as postulated by the Gestalt psychologists, or the creation of new protein chains, as proposed by recent physiological psychologists. In contrast, the operant conditioning perspective actively avoids reference to any mentalistic processes. Indeed, the dominant figure and theoretician in the scientific movement, B. F. Skinner, opposed his students making any reference to such words as mind, thoughts, wants, needs, motivations, or personality. Skinner was even unhappy with the use of the word *learning* because for so many people it implies the operation of some internal mental operation.[15]

Just what is operant conditioning and what are operants? **Operants** are the naturally occurring actions of an organism in the environment. Dogs walk, bark, and sniff. Pigeons peck at objects. The human baby crawls, babbles incessantly, and loves to put things in his or her mouth. The initial cause of operants are from within the organism itself. They are *not* elicited reflexively by some stimulus.[16] Operants are often called **instrumental responses.** That is, the operants serve as instruments to obtain **reinforcements** from the environment. When a psychologist speaks of operant conditioning, he or she is referring to a change in the likelihood of an instrumental behavior occurring because of something that happened *after* it was emitted.

Formally, operant conditioning may be defined as a process in which the frequency of occurrence of a bit of behavior is modified by the consequences of the behavior.[17] Thus, when a consumer emits a behavior, such as buying a product, the consequences of the behavior will change the probability of that behavior occurring again. If the behavior is positively reinforced, say by the product performing well or by friends complimenting the person on his purchase, the likelihood of the purchase being made again will increase. If the behavior is punished, for example because the product failed or because friends ridiculed the purchase, the likelihood of making the purchase again will decrease. The concepts of operant conditioning have wide application to consumer behavior and marketing management. Of extreme importance to marketing managers is the analysis of the contingencies of reinforcement being received by consumers regarding the purchase and use of their product or service.

The analysis of the contingencies of reinforcement received by consumers refers to the study of all the reinforcers that follow the purchase of a product and that will influence the likelihood of that behavior occurring again. The vignette at the beginning of the chapter illustrated an occasion when auto manufacturers failed to analyze such contingencies of reinforcement. The behavior of buying a car was reinforced by the presence of the $500 and $1,000 rebates, thereby increasing the likelihood that cars would be bought in the future. However, when the rebates were removed, consumers were in effect punished for buying the car. Thus, over a period of time consumers were conditioned to buy autos when rebates were present and not to buy them when rebates were omitted. The outcome in the early 1980s was a boom-and-bust cycle in which the profit margins of the auto manufacturers were destroyed, resulting in huge operating losses.

Table 6–1 identifies eight key concepts of operant conditioning. A number of these are discussed further in the following subsections.

Reinforcement

As noted previously, a reinforcer is anything that occurs after a behavior and changes the likelihood that it will be emitted again by an organism. Consumer instrumental behaviors with which managers should be concerned include: purchasing a product or service, telling friends or acquaintances about a product's performance, writing or calling the company about product problems, and searching for the best product or the best price for a product. Three different types of reinforcers that influence the probability of recurrence of these various behaviors can be identified. A **positive reinforcer** involves giving a reward of some type immediately after a behavior occurs. The reinforcer acts to increase the likelihood that the behavior will be repeated. Giving consumers $25 if they will test drive a car is an example of a

---

Table 6–1   Some Basic Operant Conditioning Principles

Reinforcer: A stimulus that increases the probability of repetition of a behavior that it follows.

Positive reinforcer: A stimulus whose *presence* as a consequence of a behavior increases the probability of the behavior recurring.

Negative reinforcer: A stimulus whose *disappearance* as a consequence of a behavior increases the probability that the behavior will recur.

Secondary reinforcer: A previously neutral stimulus that acquires reinforcing properties through its association with a primary reinforcer.

Punisher: A stimulus whose presence after a response decreases the likelihood of the behavior recurring.

Shaping: A process through which a new operant behavior is created by reinforcing successive approximations of the desired behavior.

Extinction: A gradual reduction in the frequency of occurrence of an operant behavior resulting from a lack of reinforcement of the response.

Schedule of reinforcement: The frequency and timing of reinforcers form a schedule of reinforcement that can dramatically influence the pattern of operant responses.

SOURCE: These definitions are based on material found in *A Primer of Operant Conditioning* by G. S. Reynolds, Glenview, Ill.: Scott, Foresman, 1968.

positive reinforcer. Offered by Chrysler during the 1980–82 recession, the $25 reinforcer did increase the likelihood that consumers would test drive their cars.

A second type of reinforcer is a **negative reinforcer.** Negative reinforcers involve the removal of an aversive stimulus. A behavior that results in the elimination of something negative is reinforced and is more likely to occur again in the future. Examples of negative reinforcers are somewhat hard to find in marketing because their use would involve ethical problems. One example, however, might be a consumer deciding to buy insurance, a car, or whatever from a pesky salesperson simply in order to get the person off his or her back.

A **secondary reinforcer** is the third type of reinforcer. Early in one's life all reinforcers are of a primary nature. Such primary reinforcers are stimuli that are necessary for life and basic happiness, such as food, water, salt, and soft touching. Over a period of time, previously neutral stimuli, when paired with the presence of primary stimuli, will take on reinforcing properties similar to those of the primary stimuli. When this occurs, the stimuli become secondary reinforcers. Thus, if a mother coos softly just prior to touching her baby softly, over a period of time the soft cooing will in itself become reinforcing to the baby. Thus, a mother might unconsciously condition a baby to cry in order to be picked up. If the mother cooed each time she picked up the child, the cooing would become a secondary reinforcer leading the baby to emit behaviors simply to obtain the cooing.

In the marketing environment most reinforcers are of a secondary nature. A good performance by a product, a reduction in price, a friendly "hello" by a salesman are all examples of secondary reinforcers. Even though they are secondary reinforcers, they still may have a major impact on consumer behavior.

An operant behavior concept similar in nature to a reinforcer is that of a **punisher.** A punisher is any stimulus whose presence after a behavior decreases the likelihood of the behavior recurring. For a marketer a key goal is to avoid punishing consumers for using their product or service. The number of punishers in the environment to discourage product purchases is probably infinite. Some examples include poor product performance, ridicule of the product by friends, irritating actions or remarks by a salesperson, or stock outages of a product.

Extinction   Once an operant response is conditioned, it will persist as long as it is periodically reinforced. However, if the operant response goes without reinforcement for an extended number of occasions, it will tend to disappear. This disappearance of a response because of a lack of reinforcement is called **extinction.** Interestingly, immediately after the reinforcement ceases, the vigor of the response may actually increase. In humans the reaction would probably be called anger. Suppose that a salesman over the years has reinforced his customer for buying his product by taking him or her out to lunch each time his product was purchased. Suddenly the salesman decides that this is too expensive and quits providing the reinforcer. The initial reaction of the customer may be anger, and the eventual outcome could be the extinction of the buying response.

Schedules of Reinforcement   The way in which reinforcers are applied can have an enormous impact on the behavior of consumers. A reinforcer does not have to be applied each time a particular behavior is emitted in order to reinforce it. In these **intermittent schedules** the behavior is reinforced after a certain number of repetitions or after a certain length of time has passed. One outcome of using intermittent **schedules of reinforcement** is that the operant responses become more resistant to extinction. Thus, the reinforcer can be omitted for quite a number of cases, and the behavior will persist.

The auto rebate example introducing the chapter exemplifies an intermittent schedule. The auto rebates were placed on a variable interval schedule. That is, the timing of when the rebates went into effect varied. Sometimes a rebate was put in place relatively quickly after the last one went off. In other cases, a considerable length of time passed before a new rebate was initiated. The result was that consumers were conditioned to wait for rebates, and such behavior was resistant to extinction.

Discriminative Stimuli

Discriminative stimuli are those stimuli that occur in the presence of a reinforcer and do not occur in its absence. Because of the pairing of the discriminative stimulus with the reinforcer, the likelihood of the operant response occurring increases. The organism learns to emit the operant response when the discriminative stimulus is present and *not* emit the response when it is absent. There is nothing special about a discriminative stimulus. For example, the word *sit* has no particular impact on a dog until it is followed by a dog biscuit, if the animal sits on the floor. If the word is consistently followed by a reward after the behavior has appeared, it will come to gradually elicit the instrumental response of sitting.

Discriminative stimuli act as cues to inform an organism when a particular behavior is likely to result in a reinforcer. For marketers cues can be such things as brand names and symbols, which they try to create. The strategy of using "branded products" illustrates the managerial use of discriminative stimuli. Companies with broad product lines may identify prominently each product as being a part of the same brand. Thus, Campbell's Soup Company clearly displays its name on every one of its soup products in order to cue consumers that each is produced by the same company. The distinctive cans have become discriminative stimuli which indicate to consumers that their contents will be reinforcing. The use of corporate logos has a similar function. Figure 6–5 diagrams the relationship among the discriminative stimulus, the behavior, and the reinforcer.

Figure 6–5   The relationship among discriminative stimulus, behavior, and reinforcers.

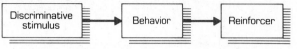

Stimulus Discrimination and Generalization

An important goal of companies is to have consumers differentiate their brands from those of competitors. Product differentiation is quite similar in nature to the operant conditioning idea of stimulus discrimination. **Stimulus discrimination** occurs when an organism behaves differently when in the presence of two stimuli. Thus, Procter and Gamble would like for consumers to discriminate between Crest toothpaste and their competitor Colgate toothpaste by buying Crest when in the grocery store.

When a consumer is reinforced for responding to a particular stimulus, the probability of the response occurring in the presence of other similar stimuli increases. **Stimulus generalization** occurs when an organism reacts similarly to two or more distinct stimuli. Suppose that a consumer was reinforced for buying a new type of coffee by really enjoying how it tasted. The next time the person is in the grocery store he sees that brand as well as other new brands. He then decides to try one of the other new brands. In this case, the buying response is said to have generalized from one brand to another. In general, the greater the similarity between stimuli, the greater the likelihood of stimulus generalization occurring.

In different situations marketers may seek to create stimulus discrimination and stimulus generalization. An example of stimulus discrimination is when high school seniors begin to discuss with parents and friends which university or college to attend. When the student brings up the name of various alternatives, other people react in some way to each possibility. These favorable and unfavorable reactions selectively reinforce some schools and punish the behavior of mentioning others. Over a period of time, the student is conditioned such that the alternative schools under consideration can be differentiated from one another.

Shaping Consumer Responses

Have you ever wondered how animal trainers are able to teach assorted animals, such as dogs, killer whales, and elephants, to do such bizarre tricks? Certainly, jumping through a hoop filled with fire is not a behavior that the average killer whale exhibits instinctively. The process through which animals are taught such amazing tricks is **shaping.** Through shaping totally new operant behaviors can be created by selectively reinforcing behaviors that successively approximate the desired instrumental response.

A brief example may help to clarify the shaping process. A few years ago I wanted to teach my dog, Troon, how to catch a Frisbee. The shaping process went as follows. First, Troon was introduced to the Frisbee by playing tug-of-war with it on the lawn. Troon loved to play tug-of-war, and this became the reinforcer that was used to control his behavior. After getting him accustomed to tugging on the Frisbee, I began to hold it out in order to get him to jump for it. He quickly mastered this behavior and would run and jump for the Frisbee with abandon. Each time that he successfully grasped the Frisbee from my hand without tearing my arm off, I reinforced him by playing tug-of-war with the Frisbee. After Troon learned to jump for the Frisbee, I began to drop it just before he took it from my hand. Each time he successfully caught it in the air, I reinforced him. If he failed to catch it, I did not reinforce him. Over a period of days Troon became progressively better at adjusting his jump to catch the Frisbee, as I gradually tossed it further and further away. After about a month of training I could throw the Frisbee as far as I wanted, and he would speed after it and catch it in midair. Importantly, he would always bring it back in order to be reinforced with the tug-of-war game.

It is also possible for companies to arrange contingencies so as to shape consumers. An example of such a shaping process to get a consumer to buy a car might go as follows. First, provide free coffee and doughnuts to anyone who comes into the dealership. Next, give five dollars to a licensed driver who will test drive a car. Third, give a $500 rebate to the person for buying the car. Finally, provide outstanding service to the customer when the car is brought in for maintenance. The ultimate behavior desired was repeat buying from the dealership (i.e., loyalty). To obtain the behavior, selected actions of the consumer that were related to the terminal behavior desired were reinforced.[18] Similarly, the act of buying a low-involvement product in a grocery can be shaped by first giving a free sample. The consumer will use the sample and be reinforced by its good performance. The consumer is next given a coupon in order to shape the behavior of buying the product in the store. Once this behavior is reinforced by the product's good performance, it can be maintained by giving additional, less valuable coupons. Over a period of time, the performance of the product may be the only reinforcer required to maintain the behavior of buying the product.[19]

Operant Conditioning and Marketing

As the above examples indicate, operant conditioning principles have wide application to marketing problems. The personal selling area in particular is a fruitful one in which operant conditioning principles may be used. A salesperson is in close enough contact with his or her clients to reinforce desired behaviors successfully. The skillful use of social reinforcers, such as compliments, pats on the back, and smiles, can create a situation in which the salesperson becomes a secondary reinforcer. In such a case the client may buy from the salesman as a means of being rewarded by having the salesman around. The skilled salesperson may also make use of monetary reinforcers through free lunches and the use of pricing discounts to shape the buying response.

In the sales promotion area the principles of operant conditioning also become important. As noted earlier, discounts, coupons, samples, contests, and so forth can be used to shape the behavior of buying the product. Indeed, the offering of prizes in sweepstakes has become a highly popular means of bringing customers into fast-food restaurants by companies such as McDonald's. In fact, sweepstakes influence consumers through the application of an intermittent schedule of reinforcement.

Advertising makes use of operant conditioning principles through vicarious reinforcement. Discussed in the last chapter, vicarious conditioning occurs when an individual observes the actions of someone else. If the observer's behavior changes as a result of the observation of the model, vicarious conditioning is said to have occurred. Thus, advertisers can show models successfully using a product and hope that the behavior of consumers will be affected through vicarious conditioning. Although vicarious conditioning is often thought of as a cognitive process because the observer does not receive the reinforcements directly, the principles of operant conditioning can explain its impact.

Perhaps the most important implication of operant conditioning principles to managers is in the area of product performance. How a product performs has strong reinforcing qualities. If it performs well and positively reinforces the buying behavior, the likelihood of the consumer repurchasing the product should increase. Conversely, if the product performs poorly, the consumer is punished, and the likelihood of a repurchase of the product diminishes.

CLASSICAL CONDITIONING

Would the background music played during a television commercial influence whether or not you bought the product advertised? An experiment found that the like or dislike for background music may actually influence consumer choice behavior.[20]

In the experiment college students were shown slides of either a light blue or a beige fountain pen. (The pens were exactly the same, and only the colors differed.) While the students saw the slides of one of the pens, music that they either liked or disliked was played in the background. (The "liked" music came from the movie *Grease*, and the "disliked" music was a one-minute piece of classical Indian music.) The students were later given a choice of getting free of charge either the color of pen with which the music was paired or the color of pen which had not been paired with any music. The results showed that when the popular music was played, 79 percent chose the pen with which the music was paired. In contrast, when the unpopular music was played, only 30 percent chose the pen associated with the music. The presence of music strongly influenced the students' preferences, depending upon whether the music was liked or disliked.

At the conclusion of the study the experimenter asked the students the reasons for their choices. Only 2 percent of the subjects gave the presence of the music as a reason for their choice. The influence of the music on the students in most cases took place without their awareness. The likely explanation for the effect of the music on the students' choice of ballpoint pens is a process called classical conditioning. First identified by the Russian physiologist Ivan Pavlov in the 1920s, classical conditioning is a primitive form of learning which affects the behavior of all animal species, from worms to dogs to humans.

Often called **respondent conditioning,** the process of classically conditioning an organism nearly always involves a stimulus that reflexively elicits some type of response. Pavlov discovered the phenomena when he was working with dogs. The dogs had the messy propensity to begin salivating profusely (the response) each time meat powder (the stimulus) was presented to them. The stimulus of the meat powder reflexively elicited the response of salivation. Humans also have a variety of such stimulus-response linkages. For example, puffing air into someone's eye elicits the response of blinking. Showing a sexy picture of someone elicits the response of a rise in blood pressure. Playing soothing music elicits the response of relaxation. The reflexive response elicited by the stimulus is called the **unconditioned response** (UCR).

When classical conditioning occurs, a previously neutral stimulus (called the **conditioned stimulus,** or CS) is repeatedly paired with the eliciting stimulus (called the **unconditioned stimulus,** or UCS). After a number of such pairings, the ability to elicit a response is transferred to the CS. The response elicited by the CS is called the **conditioned response** (CR). Figure 6–6 depicts these relationships. For optimal conditioning to occur, the CS should slightly precede the UCS in time.

In the experiments by Pavlov the presence of the meat powder (the UCS) was preceded by the ringing of a bell (the CS). After a number of such pairings, the mere ringing of the bell elicited the conditioned response of salivation (the CR). One can observe the same phenomenon in household pets. For example, in my household our dog, Troon, is fed at about the same time

Figure 6–6   The classical conditioning framework.

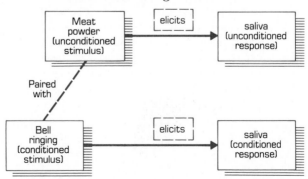

every day. About fifteen minutes before feeding time he becomes active and restless. When someone moves towards the cupboard to get his Gainesburgers, he starts wagging his tail. The sight of the Gainesburger and the sound of the crinkling of the paper as the burgers are dumped into his bowl result in intense salivation as he gallops down the hall to his dish. After every meal we have to mop up the floor behind him. In Troon's case, a series of conditioned stimuli were created—the time of day, the walk to the cupboard, the sight of the Gainesburgers, and the sound of the plastic wrap all came to elicit the conditioned response of salivation.[21]

In the music experiment described earlier in this section, the unconditioned stimulus was the positively or negatively regarded music heard by the students. The unconditioned response was the positive or negative emotional response to the music. Because the ballpoint pen was paired with the music, it became a conditioned stimulus. It, in turn, elicited a conditioned emotional response. Presumably, when the students were making their choice of pens, the emotional response elicited by the pen influenced their behavior. Thus, when the emotional response was negative, the pen was avoided. Conversely, when the emotional response was positive, the pen was actively sought. Highlight 6–2 explores some other influences of music on consumer behavior.

HIGHLIGHT 6–2

Music May Influence the Behavior of Consumers

Suppose that you were the manager of a chain of supermarkets. What would you do if you learned that by playing slow-paced music in your stores you could increase sales? An experiment actually found these results. Over a period of nine weeks, an experiment was conducted in a grocery store in which the tempo of music was varied. At various times customers heard either no music, slow-tempo music, or fast-tempo music. The results of the study revealed that significant differences existed between the slow-tempo music and the fast-tempo music. When the pace at which customers moved between two points was measured, it was found that those in fast-tempo conditions moved significantly faster than those in the slow-tempo conditions. Interestingly, daily gross sales volume was found to be significantly higher in the slow-tempo conditions. Indeed, sales were 38 percent higher in the slow-tempo conditions.

One cannot make wild generalizations from one study done in one grocery during one nine-week period. However, the results seem to show that music can strongly influence consumer behavior. Indeed, dentists have been said to play comforting music in the background while they drill on teeth in order to help their customers relax and raise their pain threshold.

What is the mechanism through which the situational variable of music influences behavior? One possibility is that people have been classically conditioned during their lives to respond to music in certain predictable ways. Thus, fast-paced music, when played in a grocery store, may elicit a response in which customers move faster. The fast pace, then, impedes buying. Similarly, slow-paced, pleasant music may relax patients in the dental office enough to raise their threshold for pain.

Based in part on Ronald E. Milliman, "Using Background Music to Affect the Behavior of Supermarket Shoppers," *Journal of Marketing, 46,* Summer 1982, 86–91.

In addition to classically conditioning a positive emotional response to the product, advertisements may act to draw attention to the product. This attention-drawing ability may be related to a phenomenon called **sign-tracking.**[22] Organisms have the tendency to attend to, orient themselves towards, and approach a positive reinforcer. In many instances unconditioned stimuli act as positive reinforcers. Research evidence exists to indicate that the ability of an unconditioned stimulus to draw attention to it is transferred to the conditioned stimulus. Thus, if a product can be paired with an unconditioned stimulus so that it becomes a conditioned stimulus, it may acquire the ability to draw attention itself. With the increasing commercial clutter found today, the ability of a product to induce people to engage in sign-tracking could be a major advantage in getting the message attended to and stored for later use.

Another concept of particular importance to marketers is that of **higher-order conditioning.** In higher-order conditioning, a conditioned stimulus can in and of itself act to classically condition another previously neutral stimulus. Indeed, most of the stimuli used by marketers to make products into conditioned stimuli are probably in and of themselves conditioned stimuli. For example, the pairing of a particular sports announcer, such as Curt Gowdy, with exciting sports events has made his voice a conditioned stimulus. Thus, when one hears Curt Gowdy, a certain degree of excitement is elicited. His voice can then be used as a stimulus to classically condition a product.

Requirements for Effective Conditioning

To classically condition a response most effectively, a number of requirements should be met.[23] First, to condition a neutral stimulus most effectively, it should precede the appearance of the unconditioned stimulus. The concept is that the conditioned stimulus needs to predict the occurrence of the unconditioned stimulus. Thus, in commercials the product should be shown prior to the appearance of the reinforcer used as the unconditioned stimulus.

A second finding is that classical conditioning is most effective if the product is paired consistently with the reinforcer. If the product is seen very frequently and the unconditioned stimulus very rarely, conditioning will be less likely to occur. This requirement implies that television advertising should be supported by a strong sales promotion effort. For example, if a celebrity endorser is used as the unconditioned stimulus in television advertising, his or her picture should be shown prominently with the product in point-of-purchase displays.

A third finding of importance is that classical conditioning is most effective when both conditioned stimulus and the unconditioned stimulus are highly salient to the consumer. Particularly in television commercials, the product and the reinforcer used as the unconditioned stimulus should stand out from the background of the advertisement and from the clutter of competing ads.

A number of the other characteristics of classical conditioning are similar to those found for operant conditioning. Like operant conditioning, classical conditioning is more likely to occur as the number of pairings increases. In addition, in a similar manner to operant conditioning one can find that extinction, discrimination, and stimulus generalization also occur.

LEARNING CONSUMER HABITS

In a variety of instances consumers reveal patterns of behavior that can only be called **habits.** A man or woman may be described as having a "bad smoking habit." A family may have the habit of turning on the nightly news during dinner. An executive may have the habit of playing golf every Saturday afternoon. A housekeeper may display **brand loyalty** through her habit of buying the same laundry detergent every month.

A Definition of Consumer Habits

Formally, a consumer habit may be defined as a behavior that displays a repetitive quality, persists through time, has positive feelings attached to it, and is difficult to alter. Psychologists who discuss the concept of habit tend to believe that when a habit is formed some quasi-permanent change in the organism has occurred.[24] One cannot look into a smoker's brain and find an entity called "a habit to smoke," but the implication is that something about the consumer's nervous system or brain has been altered.

What causes the formation of consumer habits? The likely explanation is that all three types of learning (cognitive, operant conditioning, and classical conditioning) probably contribute to the formation of a consumer habit. For example, from an operant conditioning perspective the contingencies of the environment shape a consumer such that particular behaviors are reinforced according to schedules that make them highly resistant to extinction. Consumers are also socialized into habits through operant and vicarious conditioning processes. Thus, habits can be created and influenced by the culture and the subcultures in which consumers live. The cultural ritual of watching television in the evening is a habit that has created multibillion-dollar business for television networks and advertisers.

The formation of consumer habits has a variety of implications for managers and public policy makers. For example, habits can result in consumers engaging in certain activities at certain times. Thus, the knowledge that millions of Americans have the habit of washing their hair every day has created a huge industry devoted to hair care. The fact that most consumers have the strong habit of driving their cars to work has made it extremely difficult to change such behavior during times when gasoline supplies are short. Other important public policy issues that involve consumer habits include smoking and eating too much of the wrong types of foods. Both of these problems have contributed substantially to the health-care problems of the United States.

Companies have begun to develop programs to help consumers break habits. For example, one popular program to help people give up smoking uses classical conditioning and operant conditioning learning principles. The ad shown in Figure 6–7 also discusses the problems of breaking the smoking habit. The ad notes that dependence on nicotine along with psychological, social, and physical factors contribute to the difficulty of stopping smoking. The "alternative source of nicotine to help alleviate tobacco withdrawal" is

Figure 6–7   Some companies promote products that help consumers break habits such as smoking. (Courtesy of Merrill Dow Pharmaceuticals, Inc.)

If you want to quit smoking for good, see your doctor

New knowledge about the smoking habit

Two major factors in cigarette smoking have long been recognized—psychological and social factors. Now research has clearly revealed a third important link in the habit—*physical dependence on nicotine*, which slowly but surely develops in many smokers. When people first start smoking, their bodies must get used to the nicotine. After smoking becomes a habit, their bodies may *depend* on getting nicotine.

Why a total program approach is needed to break the habit

When smokers try to quit, the body often reacts to the withdrawal of nicotine. This can result in craving for tobacco, restlessness, irritability, anxiety, headaches, drowsiness, stomach upsets, and difficulty concentrating.

Because these effects can defeat even a strong willpower, your chances of quitting successfully are greater with a program that provides an alternative source of nicotine to help alleviate tobacco withdrawal while you concentrate on breaking the habit.

How your doctor and Merrell Dow can help you succeed

If you are determined enough to sustain a strong effort, your chances of breaking the smoking habit are better than ever. Now your doctor can provide a treatment to help control nicotine withdrawal symptoms, materials to help you overcome the psychological and social factors, plus valuable counseling and follow-up. Merrell Dow has conducted extensive research into the smoking problem and is providing a wide range of support to health professionals.

Merrell Dow
Dedicated to improving the health of Americans

©1985, Merrell Dow Pharmaceuticals Inc., Cincinnati, Ohio 45242-9553.   5-4707 (B-1062)   MNQ-711B

the nicotine gum that is available only on prescription and is marketed by Lakeside Pharmaceuticals, a Division of Merrell Dow Pharmaceuticals, Inc.

A type of consumer habit that managers would like to create is brand loyalty. The next section discusses this important topic area.

Brand Loyalty

The president of the House of Seagram at a conference of liquor marketers warned his colleagues not to build the overall sales of their alcoholic products at the expense of brand loyalty. The strategy at Seagram's, according to the executive, was to raise prices on products in a continuous fashion and reinvest the profits in advertising. Through the heavy advertising, brand loyalty among consumers can be obtained. As the corporate president stated, "The goal of liquor advertising is more than getting a trial and repeat purchase of a product. . . . The consumer must *adopt* the brand. Until that, he's always vulnerable to competing brands."[25]

Having a large number of consumers "adopt" a brand, as though it were a pet or an important possession, is the goal of every brand manager. What the Seagram's president was suggesting is that adopting a strategy of price cutting to increase market share teaches consumers to look for the cheapest product available. In the short run such a strategy may increase market share, but it is unlikely to help profits over the long run. The Seagram's strategy was to build brand loyalty through advertising in order to teach consumers that their products are different from others and worthy of long-term consumer adoption.

An entirely differently strategy was developed by the chief executive officer of the home computer manufacturer Commodore International during the late 1970s and early 1980s. The executive, who later left Commodore to take over Atari, had a maxim: "We sell to the masses, not to the classes." The CEO felt that success in consumer electronics required the use of semiconductors. In turn, success in semiconductors requires a company to sell in quantity—something that can be achieved only by selling to the masses. Unlike the Seagram's president, the Commodore CEO viewed the masses as bargain hunters without any brand loyalty. As stated by the executive, "Whoever gives him [i.e., the consumer] the most for the money, this is what he is going to buy."[26]

Although the corporate strategies of the two companies were completely different, their executives had a similar view of consumers. That is, when a company competes on price as the major element that distinguishes its product from others, consumers reveal little brand loyalty. For Seagram's the answer was to focus on advertising to instill loyalty among the users of its brands. For Commodore the answer was to make sure that they were always the lowest-cost producer. This was accomplished by sharp-eyed attention to every detail to insure that no costs were greater than absolutely necessary.

Definitions of Brand Loyalty Two general definitions of brand loyalty have been developed. The first definition is based upon a consumer's actual

purchase behavior regarding the product. The most frequently used definition of brand loyalty in empirical research is called the proportion of purchases method. In this approach all of the brands purchased within a particular product category are determined for each consumer. The proportion of
purchases going to each brand is identified. Brand loyalty is then operation-
alized in terms of some arbitrary proportion of purchases going to a particular brand. For example, if more than 50 percent of the purchases went to a
particular brand during some time period, the consumer might be said to be
loyal to the brand.[27]

The problem with the behavioral measures of brand loyalty is that the
real reasons for the purchase of a product cannot be identified. A particular
product could be purchased because of convenience, availability, or price. If
any of these factors changed, consumers could rapidly switch to other brands.
In such instances consumers cannot be said to exhibit loyalty, because implicit in the idea of loyalty is that the consumer has more than a passing
infatuation with the brand.

The problems of the behavioral measures of brand loyalty clarify why it is
important to distinguish the concepts of brand loyalty and **repeat purchase
behavior.** With repeat purchase behavior the consumer is merely buying a
product repeatedly without any particular feeling for it. In contrast, the concept of brand loyalty implies that a consumer has some real preference for
the brand. As a consequence, another approach to assessing brand loyalty
was developed, based on the consumer's attitude towards the product, as
well as his or her purchase behavior. Thus, in order for a consumer to exhibit
brand loyalty, as opposed to simple repeat purchase behavior, the consumer
must actively prefer and like the product.[28] A complete definition of brand
loyalty follows:

> brand loyalty is (1) the biased (i.e., nonrandom), (2) behavioral response (i.e., pur-
> chase), (3) expressed over time, (4) by some decision-making unit, (5) with respect
> to one or more alternative brands out of a set of such brands, and (6) is a function
> of psychological (decision-making) processes.[29]

As would be expected, the definition of brand loyalty in a number of respects
matches that of the definition of a consumer habit. Consequently, it has a
number of implications for marketers. First, brand loyalty is not a random
event. Whether or not a consumer becomes loyal to a particular brand can
be controlled to some extent by the actions of a marketer. Second, mere verbal reports that someone is loyal to a product are insufficient to show brand
loyalty. Verbal reports taken on consumer surveys should be backed up with
records of the actual purchases made by the consumer. Third, to reveal brand
loyalty the repeat purchase behavior must be found over some lengthy period of time. Fourth, brand loyalty can be exhibited by decision-making units
in addition to individual consumers. For example, decisions may be made
jointly by husbands and wives such that they as a pair reveal brand loyalty.
Fifth, consumers may be loyal to more than one brand at a time. Out of a set

Table 6–2 Some Implications of Brand Loyalty for Marketers

1. Brand loyalty is not random. Marketers have influence over whether consumers become brand loyal.
2. Behavioral information on consumer buying is needed in addition to verbal reports in order to identify brand-loyal consumers.
3. For brand loyalty to exist the repeat purchase behavior must occur over a lengthy period of time.
4. Brand loyalty may be exhibited by decision-making units as well as by individuals.
5. Consumers may be loyal to more than one brand at a time.
6. Brand loyalty results from an evaluative process that follows from the outcomes of previous purchases.

of seven to ten competing brands, a consumer may be loyal to two or three while actively selecting out the others. Finally, brand loyalty results from some type of evaluative process that follows from the outcomes of previous purchases of the product. When a consumer has brand loyalty, he or she actively prefers the brand, is committed to the brand to some extent, and probably has developed positive feelings towards the brand. Table 6–2 summarizes these components of brand loyalty.

Brand Loyalty and Learning Theory In order to understand how the habit of brand loyalty is formed by consumers, one must return to the basic concepts of learning theory. One can identify how all three of the basic types of leaning can influence the development of brand loyalty. Because brand loyalty results from repeated experience with a product and because it is formed over a long period of time, studies to investigate the relative impact of various types of learning on its development have not been done. Thus, the linkages proposed in this section between the learning theories and brand loyalty are inferential in nature.

Perhaps the most important learning process influencing brand-loyalty formation is operant conditioning. Whether or not a consumer is rewarded for using a product is likely to influence most directly whether or not the brand will be repurchased. Recognizing this likely relationship between operant conditioning and brand loyalty has managerial implications. The positive reinforcements that a consumer receives after buying a product can come from a variety of sources. The product's performance certainly is one major source of rewards or punishers for buying the product. However, other influencers may be rewarding or punishing. For example, the reactions of friends, family, and opinion leaders will act to reinforce positively or negatively the purchase. Thus, a product could be performing quite well but attract few consumers who rebuy it because members of the consumers' reference group ridiculed them for buying the product. In contrast, the product may perform in a quite mediocre manner yet achieve brand loyalty because consumers were positively reinforced for purchasing it by their friends. Trendy products, such as the Izod and Polo shirts of the early 1980s, fit such an explanation. While the brands are in popular favor, consumers may exhibit high degrees of loyalty to them because of the reactions of their social group.

Explaining brand loyalty through operant conditioning ideas also suggests that manufacturers should investigate the reinforcing qualities of the retailers who sell and service a brand. If consumers find the experience of buying and having the product serviced positively reinforcing, the likelihood of repeat purchase behavior will likely increase. Thus, attention to how consumers are treated throughout the distribution channel is an important factor in creating and maintaining brand loyalty among consumers.

The adroit use of advertising may also act to reinforce the buying behavior of consumers. For example, after a consumer buys an automobile, seeing commercials on television for the car he or she bought may be highly reinforcing. If the commercial is well done and shows off the car in a highly positive way, the purchase of the car could well be reinforced. The use of commercials to reinforce consumer buying of a brand may explain why the president of Seagram's distillers felt advertising to be so important in creating brand loyalty.

Classical conditioning principles probably also act to facilitate or impede the formation of brand loyalty. Figure 6–8 shows how through classical conditioning a product could lead to positive affective feelings. In the hypothetical example the consumer initially buys "Get-It-On" cologne (the conditioned stimulus) and wears it on a date. While on the date, the consumer receives "very positive" overtures from the male or female companion. These reactions from the companion form the unconditioned stimuli that elicit the unconditioned response of "warm feelings of delight." Because of the pairing of the cologne with the unconditioned stimulus, the cologne is classically conditioned to elicit a conditioned response of "warm positive feelings." As a consequence, the mere thought of the brand name could lead to positive

Figure 6–8   Classical conditioning and brand loyalty toward "Get-It-On" cologne.

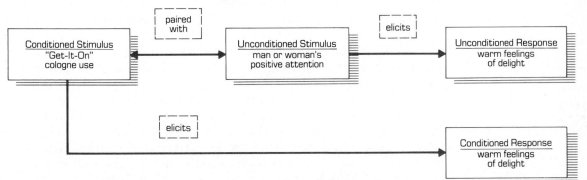

feelings. Thus, the positive feelings that occur when a person has a high brand loyalty may occur in part through the process of classical conditioning.

Undoubtedly, cognitive learning also plays an important role in the formation of brand loyalty. For example, through continued use the consumer becomes familiar with a product and forms a series of beliefs about how the product performs, what friends think about it, and how desirable its price, durability, and other characteristics are. Such beliefs are stored in long-term memory and are elicited when the brand name is mentioned or when the consumer must purchase a brand within the product's category. These beliefs are likely to have a major impact on purchase behavior because they are highly salient and available to the consumer. That is, because the consumer is familiar with the product, the beliefs are easily retrieved from memory and are highly influential. As a consequence, the beliefs formed through product usage are likely to influence strongly future purchase behavior. If the beliefs on an overall basis are positive, the product is more likely to be purchased. If the beliefs on an overall basis are negative, the product is less likely to be purchased.

Brand loyalty is also likely to be the result of the growth of a consumer habit. The repetitive behavior of buying a product over and over again fits the definition of a habit. In such a case, for whatever reasons, a consumer's learning history has converged such that the action of purchasing a particular brand has become ingrained to the point that it is a habit. When a product purchase becomes habitual, the consumer will tend to buy that product without going through any formal decision process. Upon recognizing that a need exists which the product fulfills, the consumer will take steps to purchase the product without formally comparing brands.

For a company that possesses large numbers of customers who buy its brands through habit, the goal will be to take steps to maintain the repetitive behavior. Thus, the company will not want to make dramatic changes in the marketing mix. Pricing, promotion, distribution, and product characteristics should remain relatively constant. When changes are made, they usually will consist of minor modifications of the marketing mix. Thus, a product change would probably involve minor improvements, which would be promoted and labeled as the "new improved" Tide or Wisk or Charmin or whatever.

Identifying Brand-Loyal Consumers   One important question asked by market researchers is whether a consumer group exists that is brand loyal across various types of products. Some evidence indicates that brand preferences are formed during childhood and adolescence.[30] If such preferences turn into loyalty among consumer segments, this would suggest that managers should begin targeting their customers early in their life cycles. However, as noted in Highlight 6–3, teenagers can be a difficult group to target.

The research evidence on brand loyalty, however, indicates that it is a product-specific phenomenon. Very little available evidence suggests that consumers exist who have a general tendency to be loyal. Thus, consumers

HIGHLIGHT 6–3

An Unloyal Consumer Segment: Teenage Girls

In 1982 Jane Evans headed the apparel division of General Mills Inc. One of the division's brands is Izod alligator shirts. One day she learned to her horror that 20 percent of the shirts were being bought by girls under twenty years of age. She immediately became concerned that at any time that portion of the business could disappear. Indeed, by 1983 it had.

Other brands victimized by the changing whims of teenage girls include Frye Boots and various designer jeans products. When interviewed on the topic, Ms. Evans stated, "It's a hazardous market; I don't think any responsible public corporation would deliberately go after it."

One marketing researcher said that using sophisticated survey research techniques to track the teenage market is next to impossible. "By the time you've finished a consumer survey, the picture has already changed." For example, a survey was done two years in a row to assess the favorite rock group of teenage girls. The group Stray Cats was reported by 36% of the girls to be one of their favorite groups the first year. The second year the group was barely mentioned. In 1983 the movie *Flashdance* created a demand for "torn-shoulder sweaters." However, by the time manufacturers could begin meeting the demand, the infatuation had ended.

The problem for companies is that the market is hard to ignore. Some estimates set the expendable income of the 12.8 million young women at $30 billion a year. Between jobs and allowances, and no mortgages or utility payments to make, their discretionary-spending ability is high.

Why do teenage women appear to have so little brand loyalty? The best answer seems to be because they have a highly fragile sense of self-identity. When combined with a tendency to act collectively, the outcome is turmoil for manufacturers who are trying to keep up with the constantly changing market.

According to one marketing researcher, one theme consistently produces good results with the teenage-girl segment—sex. Simply take a look at *Seventeen* magazine sometime to check this out for yourself.

Based on John Koten, "Teen-Age Girls, Alas, Are Big Spenders But Poor Consumers," *The Wall Street Journal*, November 9, 1984, 1, 12.

who are loyal in one product category may or may not be loyal in any other product category. Efforts to identify demographic, socioeconomic, or psychological characteristics related to brand-loyal behavior have generally been unsuccessful.[31] One variable that has been found to be predictive of brand loyalty is store loyalty. Consumers who are loyal to particular stores also tend to be loyal to certain brands.[32] It is possible that by repeatedly shopping at the same stores, consumers find a limited number of brands available for each product category. Thus, store-loyal consumers may be forced to buy certain brands because they are the only ones available in the stores where these consumers shop.

Managerial Implications

The basic learning processes discussed in the chapter have wide application to managerial and public policy problem areas. Cognitive learning, operant conditioning, and classical conditioning principles all have particular application to the promotional component of the marketing mix. In the areas of advertising and personal selling an understanding of consumer learning can have a positive impact on managerial decision making.

Cognitive Learning

A number of cognitive learning principles exist with which managers should be familiar. One of these is the serial learning effect. People tend not to learn as easily material that is placed in the middle of a list of information. For this reason advertisers should attempt to place key copy points at the beginning and at the end of commercials. The law of contiguity should also be remembered by managers. It states that things that are paired together tend to become associated. The implication is that advertisers should attempt consistently to pair the mentioning of a product or company name with key qualities, such as good service, high quality, low prices, or friendly service. Certain steps can be taken to increase the likelihood that the association will be made, such as using visual images (i.e., the Jolly Green Giant).

The concepts of observational learning are also relevant to decision makers. The impact of modeling on the behavior of consumers suggests that celebrities whom people admire would make excellent product endorsers. Indeed, the heavy use of celebrities to endorse products, particularly in the areas of sports equipment and products involving social approval (e.g., cars and perfume), builds on the importance of the modeling process. Because of the strong effects of modeling on young people, marketers must take responsibility in insuring that the behavior displayed by celebrities is consistent with those desired by society. For example, in late 1984 the television networks began to air a series of movies on teenage suicide. A number of groups expressed fear that teenage viewers of the shows would attempt to model the suicidal behavior of the actors and actresses in the television shows. Other research has shown that television violence can serve as a catalyst to actual violence by consumers.[33] There have been a number of cases of people who watched violence on television and then committed the very acts they had seen, including raping a girl with a bottle, setting a person on fire, and killing an elderly woman.[34] The ethical and social responsibility of the television networks in these instances must be carefully analyzed.

Operant Conditioning

In the personal-selling area operant conditioning principles have particular application to managerial decision making. A salesperson is in close enough contact with his or her clients to reinforce desired behaviors successfully. The skillful use of social reinforcers such as compliments, pats on the back, and smiles can create a situation in which the salesperson becomes a secondary reinforcer. In such a case, the client may buy from the salesperson as a means of being rewarded by having the salesperson around. The skilled salesperson can also make use of monetary reinforcers through free lunches, Christmas gifts, rebates, and the use of pricing discounts to shape the buying response. However, managers should be aware of potential unethical and even illegal behavior that can occur if the reinforcements turn into real or imagined bribes.

In the sales promotion area the principles of operant conditioning also become important. As noted earlier, discounts, coupons, samples, contests, and so forth may be used to shape the behavior of those buying the product. Indeed, the offering of prizes in sweepstakes has become a highly popular means of bringing customers into fast-food restaurants by companies such as McDonald's. In fact, sweepstakes influence consumers through the application of an intermittent schedule of reinforcement.

Problems can occur, however, if reinforcers are relied upon too heavily. Consumers may attribute their behavior to the reinforcer rather than to their liking for the product if the marketer is not careful. Thus, suppose that a marketer makes use of frequent price discounts to reinforce consumers for buying her company's brand. Consumers may attribute their buying to the discount rather than to the positive features of the brand. Thus, if the price discounts are discontinued, consumers may shift to other brands.[35]

Advertisers also make frequent use of vicarious reinforcement principles. Vicarious conditioning occurs when an individual observes the actions of someone else and the reinforcements that occur after the behavior. If the consumer's actions change as a result of the observation of the model, vicarious conditioning is said to have occurred. Thus, advertisers can show models (e.g., attractive and likable endorsers) successfully using a product and hope that the behavior of consumers will be affected through vicarious conditioning.

Perhaps the most important implication of operant conditioning principles to managers is in the area of product performance. How a product performs has strong reinforcing qualities. If it performs well and positively reinforces the buying behavior, the likelihood of the consumer repurchasing the product should increase. Conversely, if the product performs poorly, the consumer is punished, and the likelihood of a repurchase of the product diminishes.

Classical Conditioning

Much of the work done to investigate classical conditioning has been performed under carefully controlled laboratory conditions. Therefore, making authoritative statements about its effects in the "messy," uncontrolled real-world environment are difficult. However, the principles of classical conditioning do seem to apply and to explain the effectiveness of certain marketing actions.

For marketers perhaps the most important effects of classical conditioning involve the conditioning of emotional responses to brands. A variety of unconditioned stimuli may elicit positive emotional responses, such as sexy actors or actresses, patriotic music, exciting sporting events, or beautiful scenery. These positive emotional reactions are the unconditioned responses. By pairing a product (the conditioned stimulus) with the unconditioned stimulus, the product may gradually become a conditioned stimulus and elicit a positive emotional response. An excellent example of this process can be seen in television advertisements for Diet Pepsi in the mid-1980s. In these ads pictures of the Diet Pepsi can or bottle were followed by views of the scantily clad bodies of highly attractive men and women. Hard-driving background music enhanced the overall emotional impact of the advertisements for many people.

Brand Loyalty

As conceptualized in the chapter, brand loyalty results from the development of a strong consumer habit of purchasing the same brand repetitively. Brand loyalty appears to result from the basic consumer learning principles discussed in the chapter—that is, cognitive learning, operant conditioning, and classical conditioning. An important goal of managers should be to develop brand loyalty among customers for the product or service being offered. The key element in doing this appears to be the appropriate application of basic learning principles. If any one principle were to be singled out for emphasis, it would probably be operant conditioning. Consumers should receive positive reinforcement for using a brand. Such reinforcement can come through the performance of the product, the accolades of friends, and high levels of customer service from the company.

SUMMARY

Learning is a process in which experience leads to a relatively permanent change in behavior or the potential for a change in behavior. One can identify three major approaches to learning—cognitive learning, operant conditioning, and classical conditioning. The cognitive learning theorists view learning as primarily a mental process in which individuals form plans, have insightful experiences, and make associations without any need to talk about reinforcers. The area of cognitive learning is particularly important to advertisers in part because of its close relationship to the information-processing principles that are discussed in Chapter 5. Thus, such problems as how people forget are particularly important topics to advertisers who spend millions of dollars trying to get consumers to remember the names of their products. Two factors that influence forgetting are retroactive and proactive inhibition. In retroactive inhibition newly learned material interferes with the recollection of older material. In proactive inhibition, previously learned material interferes with the learning of new material. Another topic of importance to cognitive theorists is that of learning through observation. In particular, people show a tendency to model the behavior of others. Such imitative actions play a large role in consumer socialization. In addition, by using consumer role models in their commercials, advertisers attempt to use the modeling process to influence consumer buying behavior.

Another type of consumer learning is based upon operant conditioning. Operant conditioning occurs when an organism's behavior changes as a consequence of something happening after the behavior. Marketers must be particularly concerned about the rewards and punishments consumers receive while using their products or services. Important reinforcers that will influence consumer behavior include the performance of the product, the favorable and unfavorable information and reactions received from other people about products and services, and the positivity of the interactions consumers have with sales personnel.

Classical conditioning takes place in a manner different from that of operant conditioning. Whereas in operant conditioning the reinforcer comes after the behavior, in classical conditioning a stimulus of some type elicits a behavior, or unconditioned response. By pairing a previously neutral stimulus (the conditioned stimulus) with the eliciting stimulus, or unconditioned stimulus, the neutral stimulus will gradually come to elicit the response. Classical conditioning has implications for advertisers who wish to create positive feelings in consumers when they think of a particular product. As shown by one study, an unconditioned stimulus such as music may be able to be paired with the product so that the product becomes a conditioned stimulus. The result is the product eliciting positive feelings because of the previous pairing.

Closely related to the concept of learning is the development of consumer habits. A consumer habit is a repetitive behavior that persists through time, has positive feelings attached to it, and is difficult to alter. When a habit involves the frequent purchase of a product or service, it is called brand loyalty. Brand loyalty is more than simply repeat purchase behavior. When a consumer has brand loyalty, he or she also feels positively towards the product or service. Marketers have attempted to identify whether a segment of brand-loyal consumers exists. The research evidence, however, indicates that brand loyalty is a product-specific phenomenon. Consumers who exhibit loyalty to one type of product may or may not be loyal to brands in other product categories.

Key Terms

Learning
Cognitive learning
Classical conditioning
Operant conditioning
Law of contiguity
Associationists
Serial position effect
Paired associate learning
Forgetting
Proactive interference
Retroactive interference
Method of loci
von Restorff effect
Zeigarnik effect
Observational learning
Vicarious learning
Instrumental response

Operants
Reinforcements
Positive reinforcer
Negative reinforcer
Secondary reinforcer
Punisher
Extinction
Schedule of reinforcement
Discriminative stimuli
Stimulus discrimination
Stimulus generalization
Shaping
Respondent conditioning
Unconditioned response
Conditioned stimulus

Unconditioned stimulus
Conditioned response
Sign-tracking
Higher-order conditioning

Habit
Brand loyalty
Repeat purchase behavior

Review Questions

1. Define the concept of learning. What are the three types of learning that consumer researchers discuss?
2. Describe the Gestalt approach to learning.
3. A group of scientists called the associationists have investigated the law of contiguity. Discuss the law of contiguity, focusing on the findings from serial learning and paired associate learning.
4. Cognitive learning theorists have identified two factors that can lead to the forgetting of informa-

tion—proactive and retroactive interference. Define these concepts.

5. Briefly discuss the von Restorff effect.

6. Briefly discuss the Zeigarnik effect.

7. What is the relationship between time and forgetting?

8. What is meant by observational learning? What are three important ideas that result from its study?

9. Define operant conditioning and describe the process through which instrumental conditioning occurs.

10. Discuss the differential effects of positive and negative reinforcers.

11. What is meant by extinction?

12. What is meant by a schedule of reinforcement?

13. How are discriminative stimuli used by marketers?

14. Give an example of how a marketer might be able to shape a consumer response.

15. What are the primary differences between classical and operant conditioning?

16. What is the relationship among conditioned stimuli, unconditioned stimuli, conditioned responses, and unconditioned responses in classical conditioning?

17. Define the concept of a consumer habit. What learning processes may influence the development of habits?

18. What are the two major types of definitions of brand loyalty? What are four major factors that are considered in the complete definition of brand loyalty discussed in the chapter?

19. Identify two managerial uses for each of the theories of learning discussed in the chapter.

Discussion Questions

1. Sketch the ideas for a story board for an advertisement that applies Gestalt ideas to the impressions gained from an automobile. The idea is to present a consumer who thinks about the various product attributes but then realizes that the overall impression one gains of the automobile is much greater than the sum of the individual impressions.

2. Observe carefully several thirty-second or longer advertisements on television. At what points in time was the most important information placed in the advertisement?

3. The associations people form between various brands and other thoughts and feelings can tell a great deal about their impression of the product. List the first thoughts that come to your mind for each of the following brands: Crest toothpaste, Mercedes-Benz, Ford, Chrysler, and Ultra-Brite toothpaste. What do these thoughts indicate about your reactions to the brands?

4. From a cognitive learning perspective, what are the problems that commercial clutter can cause? Are there steps that managers might take to minimize the effects of clutter?

5. Sketch the outline of a television advertisement for a perfume product that makes use of the Zeigarnik effect.

6. Observational learning is an important means of socialization for children, teenagers, and adults. Consider the content of the popular television shows appearing on "prime time." What are the patterns of behavior that people may learn as a result of watching prime time television? Are there public policy implications that result from such an analysis?

7. What would you identify as the five major consumer reinforcers? To what extent can a salesperson use these to influence the behavior of prospective clients?

8. Try to remember the worst experiences you have ever had in a restaurant. What were the various ways in which you were punished for eating there?

9. One problem that many instructors face is how to get students to participate in classroom discussions. Develop a systematic plan in which reinforcers are applied to shape students into frequent classroom discussions.

10. Develop the outline of an advertising campaign for a new bath towel line, to include television commercials and point-of-purchase displays that make use of classical conditioning ideas. Make sure you identify the conditioned stimulus, the unconditioned stimulus, the conditioned response, and the unconditioned response.

11. Identify the product to which you have the most brand loyalty. Can you give examples of the strength of the loyalty? Discuss your loyalty from a learning theory perspective. In other words, describe the learning theory principles that may be responsible for your loyalty.

References

1. Wolfgang Kohler, *The Mentality of Apes*, New York, N.Y.: Harcourt Brace Jovanovich, Inc., 1925.

2. David Horton and Thomas Turnage, *Human Learning*, Englewood Cliffs, N.J.: Prentice-Hall, Inc., 1976.

3. Harold H. Kassarjian, "Field Theory in Consumer Behavior," in *Consumer Behavior: Theoretical Sources*, Scott Ward and Thomas Robertson (eds.), Englewood Cliffs, N.J.: Prentice-Hall, Inc., 1973.

4. Horton and Turnage, *Human Learning*.

5. Ibid.

6. Ibid.

7. Ernest Hilgard, Richard Atkinson, and Rita Atkinson, *Introduction to Psychology*, New York, N.Y.: Harcourt Brace Jovanovich, Inc., 1975.

8. Charles E. Osgood, *Method and Theory in Experimental Psychology*, New York, N.Y.: Oxford University Press, 1964.

9. Osgood, *Method and Theory*.

10. Ibid.

11. H. Ebbinghaus, *Memory*, Translated by H. A. Ruger and C. E. Bussenius. New York, N.Y.: Teachers College, 1913.

12. Hubert A. Zielske, "The Remembering and Forgetting of Advertising," *Journal of Marketing, 23*, January 1959, 231–243.

13. Albert Bandura, *Social Learning Theory*, Englewood Cliffs, N.J.: Prentice-Hall, Inc., 1977.

14. Hilgard et al., *Introduction to Psychology*.

15. B. F. Skinner, *Contingencies of Reinforcement: A Theoretical Analysis*, New York, N.Y.: Appleton-Century-Crofts, 1969.

16. G. S. Reynolds, *A Primer of Operant Conditioning*, Glenview, Ill.: Scott, Foresman and Company, 1968.

17. Reynolds, *A Primer*.

18. J. Paul Peter and Walter R. Nord, "A Clarification and Extension of Operant Conditioning Principles in Marketing," *Journal of Marketing, 46*, Summer 1982, 102–107.

19. M. L. Rothchild and W. C. Gaidis, "Behavioral Learning Theory: Its Relevance to Marketing and Promotions," *Journal of Marketing, 45*, Spring 1981, 70–78.

20. Gerald J. Gorn, "The Effects of Music in Advertising on Choice Behavior: A Classical Conditioning Approach," *Journal of Marketing, 46*, Winter 1982, 94–101. The Gorn study has received some criticism; see Chris T. Allen and Thomas J. Madden, "A Closer Look at Classical Conditioning," *Journal of Consumer Research, 12*, December 1985, 301–315. However, the experiment was successfully replicated by Calvin Bierley, Frances McSweeney, and Renee Vannieuwkerk, "Classical Conditioning of Preferences for Stimuli," *Journal of Consumer Research, 12*, December 1985, 316–323.

21. An excellent review of applications of classical conditioning and operant conditioning to marketing may be found in Walter R. Nord and J. Paul Peter, "A Behavior Modification Perspective on Marketing," *Journal of Marketing, 44*, Spring 1980, 36–47.

22. Francis K. McSweeney and Calvin Bierley, "Recent Developments in Classical Conditioning," *Journal of Consumer Research, 11*, September 1984, 619–631.

23. For an excellent discussion of classical conditioning, see McSweeney and Bierley, "Recent Developments in Classical Conditioning."

24. Osgood, *Method and Theory*.

25. "Instill Brand Loyalty, Seagram Exec Tells Marketers," *Advertising Age*, April 30, 1979, 26.

26. Susan Chace and Michael W. Miller, "Commodore's Tramiel Sharpens Competition in Small Computers," *The Wall Street Journal*, August 18, 1983, 1, 8.

27. For an excellent discussion of brand loyalty see James Engel and Roger Blackwell, *Consumer Behavior*, 4th ed., New York, N.Y.: The Dryden Press, 1982.

28. Jacob Jacoby and David B. Kyner, "Brand Loyalty versus Repeat Purchasing Behavior," *Journal of Marketing Research, 10*, February 1973, 1–9.

29. Jacob Jacoby and Robert W. Chestnut, *Brand Loyalty, Measurement and Management*, New York, N.Y.: John Wiley & Sons, Inc., 1978.

30. Lester Guest, "Brand Loyalty Revisited: A Twenty-Year Report," *Journal of Applied Psychology, 48*, April 1964, 93–97.

31. See, for instance, Ronald E. Frank, William F. Massy, and Thomas M. Lodahl, "Purchasing Behavior and Personal Attributes," *Journal of Advertising Research, 9*, December 1969, 15–24.

32. James M. Carmen, "Correlates of Brand Loyalty: Some Positive Results," *Journal of Marketing Research, 7*, February 1970, 67–76.

33. Bandura, *Social Learning Theory*.

34. Spencer Rathus, *Psychology*, New York, N.Y.: Holt, Rinehart and Winston, 1981.

35. Carol A. Scott, "The Effects of Trial and Incentives on Repeat Purchase Behavior," *Journal of Marketing Research, 13*, August 1976, 263–269.

7

Consumer Beliefs, Attitudes, and Behaviors

Some Unusual Product Attributes Lead to Success: Fast Ketchup, Tilted Radiators, and Stickum

The Hunt's ketchup product manager shook his head and groaned, "God, it made me angry. I winced every time I heard one of those."

He was referring to advertisements by Heinz ketchup, his major competitor, in which Hunt's tomato condiment was shown to burble out of bottles, glide through coffee filters, and slide down plates. In contrast, the competitor's product would ooze ever so slowly and be touted as the "slowest ketchup in the West" with "the taste that's worth the wait."

Why was the product manager so worried about how fast his ketchup "ran"? Consumers had come to perceive the thickness of ketchup as a highly desirable product quality. Indeed, after Heinz began to make slow-running ketchup, its market share rose steadily from 27 percent in 1963 to 48 percent in 1984. (a)

Would the tilt of a radiator make a difference to the owners of Corvettes? In late 1983 Chevrolet introduced its newly designed Corvette. The new model was faster and handled better than the car it replaced. However, it had one flaw. Instead of being tilted back thirty degrees, its radiator was vertical.

It seems that the new model has a much larger radar "signature." The result is that police radar screens can pick up the car at one-third greater distance than they could the older model. One hypothesis is that the older model's radiator was tilted back thirty degrees, which would bounce the radar beams into the air rather than back to the receiving antenna. One disgruntled buyer complained that he couldn't drive his new Corvette any faster than sixty-three miles per hour for fear of being caught. (b)

In 1977 3M Corporation began test marketing their Post-It notepads. The three-by-five-inch pieces of paper that you can stick on anything didn't fare well in early market tests. However, once the company began giving out free

196

samples to secretaries, sales took off. By 1983 its sales were $40 million a year and growing rapidly. (c)

The thickness of ketchup, the radar signature of a sports car, and the "stickability" of note paper are examples of "product attributes." Beliefs about such product attributes may influence consumer attitudes and behavior. On the other hand, in some cases actual experience with a product is required in order for beliefs and attitudes to form. This chapter on beliefs, attitudes, and behavior analyzes the relationship among these three important consumer behavior concepts and their managerial implications.

Based on (a) Betsy Morris, "Thwack! Smack! Sounds Thrill Makers of Hunt's Ketchup," *The Wall Street Journal,* April 27, 1984, 1, 17; (b) Mary Pitzer, "The '84 Corvette's Radiator Seems to Attract Undesirable Attention," *The Wall Street Journal,* September 29, 1983, 33; and (c) Lawrence Ingrassia, "By Improving Scratch Paper, 3M Gets New-Product Winner," *The Wall Street Journal,* March 31, 1983, 27.

INTRODUCTION

The ultimate goal of the market researcher is to understand and predict consumer buying behavior. The product manager seeks to use this knowledge in order to influence consumer actions or behaviors through the manipulation of the marketing mix. The primary consumer behavior of interest to the product manager is that of purchasing the product. However, other behaviors of interest include: searching for information, passing on information to another consumer (i.e., word-of-mouth communication), and visiting a retailer to inspect the product. In order to predict and influence such consumer behaviors, one must have an understanding of two important concepts—consumer beliefs and attitudes. Beliefs and attitudes are closely linked not only to each other but also to behaviors. The focus of this chapter is to provide the student with an understanding of their interrelationships and of how such an understanding can assist marketing managers and public policy makers.

THE CONCEPTS OF BELIEFS, ATTITUDES, AND BEHAVIORS

Consumer beliefs, attitudes, and behaviors, although distinct concepts, are closely linked together. In fact, in some cases attitudes can propel the consumer to engage in some type of behavior, such as buying a product. On the other hand, attitudes can result from the consumer's having made some type of purchase. However, prior to discussing how beliefs, attitudes, and behaviors are formed and how they are interrelated, the reader should have a good understanding of their definitions.

Defining Beliefs and Attitudes

Beliefs are the cognitive knowledge people have of the relations among attributes, benefits, and objects. Thus, in order to understand the nature of consumer beliefs, one must also understand the terms attributes, benefits, and objects. The consumer vignette that opened the chapter gave three illustrations of attributes. **Attributes** are the characteristics or features that an object may or may not have. Thus, an important attribute of the object, ketchup, is how fast it pours. **Benefits** are the outcomes that attributes may provide. The perceived benefit of slow-pouring ketchup is an increased richness of taste. Finally, **objects** are the products, people, companies and things about which people hold beliefs and attitudes.

Attribute-Object Beliefs   Three types of beliefs exist, and each involves, either directly or indirectly, product or service attributes. The first type of belief is an **attribute-object belief.** Attribute-object beliefs link an attribute to an object, such as a person, product, or service.[1] Thus, through attribute-object beliefs the consumer defines what he or she knows about something in terms of various attributes. Therefore, a consumer may form the beliefs that older Corvettes have tilted radiators, that Heinz ketchup is thick, and that Post-It notepads will stick to things.

Attribute-Benefit Beliefs   The characteristics on which consumers evaluate products are closely related to the benefits that they provide consumers. People seek out products and services to solve problems and fulfill needs. Thus, the attributes consumers seek are those that will help solve a problem or fulfill a need. This link between attributes and benefits represents a second type of belief, which may be called an attribute-benefit belief. An **attribute-benefit** is the consumer's perception of the extent to which a particular attribute will result in or provide a particular benefit. Thus, an attribute-benefit belief would be the perception that a thick ketchup is one that will have good taste and not run off of a hamburger bun. Table 7–1 gives examples of some attributes and their potential benefits in a hypothetical perfect sports car.

Object-Benefit Beliefs   The last type of belief is formed through the linkage of an object with a benefit. Thus, an **object-benefit belief** is a consumer's perception of the extent to which a particular product, person, or service will lead to a particular benefit. In the case of the older Corvette models, an object-benefit belief would be that these autos will allow a person to drive faster with a lower chance of being picked up by police. In the Heinz ketchup example, an object-benefit belief would involve the cognition that the product will have good taste and not make a hamburger bun soggy.

In Figure 7–1 an advertisement for Hasselblad cameras is presented. The ad attempts to create the object-benefit belief that Hasselblad cameras will not fail and will invariably provide exceptional photographs.

Figure 7–2 diagrams the relationships among a product, an attribute, and a benefit. The connection between the product and the attribute is the object-attribute belief discussed earlier. The connection between the attribute and the benefit is the attribute-benefit belief. To the extent that these beliefs are present, the consumer will draw an inferential belief that a particular

Table 7–1   Examples of Attributes and Their Benefits for the "Perfect" Sports Car

Attribute	Benefit
Quick acceleration	Creates thrills by snapping head back. Allows driver to pass more safely. Allows driver to navigate winding roads more quickly. Creates feelings of excitement and fun.
Superior handling	Allows driver to navigate winding roads more quickly. Heightens arousal when going fast around corners. Creates feelings of excitement and fun.
Small size	Helps improve acceleration. Improves gas mileage.
Good gas mileage	Lowers expenses.
Low sticker price	Lowers expenses
Good repair frequency	Saves money and time.
Futuristic styling	Makes owner feel good. Turns people's heads

product will provide the benefit desired. Thus, if a consumer believes that Hunt's ketchup has the attribute of thickness and also believes that the attribute of thickness leads to the benefits of good taste and a nonsoggy bun, the consumer is likely to infer that Hunt's ketchup will provide such a benefit.

Objects, attributes, and benefits are examples of what social psychologists call cognitive elements. **Cognitive elements** are those ideas consciously held by a person about people (including himself), objects, and qualities of objects (such as attributes and benefits).[2] Cognitive elements that are related to each other in some manner are formed into structures. For example, the cognitive elements of Hunt's ketchup (i.e., the product), the attribute of thickness, and the benefit of "won't run" form a structure. One property of cognitive structures is that people like for them to be consistent. That is, the cognitive elements should logically fit together in a way that does not violate commonsensical expectations.[3] Thus, in Figure 7–1 a consumer would logically expect that Hunt's ketchup would lead to the benefit of "not making a bun soggy," given that it has the attribute of thickness and that the attribute of thickness leads to "nonsoggy buns."

Attribute Importance   An important concept is that attributes differ widely in their importance to consumers. **Attribute importance** is determined by how closely attributes are tied to a consumer's self-concept. Discussed more fully in the chapter on personality and psychographics, the self-concept refers to the beliefs a person has about just who he or she is. If a consumer

Figure 7–1 **Hasselblad stresses the reliability of its cameras and thereby attempts to create an object-benefit belief.** *(Courtesy of Hasselblad, Inc.)*

A HASSELBLAD IS UNDENIABLY EXPENSIVE. SO IS A RE-SHOOT.

Inside or outside the studio—inside or outside the atmosphere, for that matter—the last thing you want on a shoot is a camera that lets you down.

A Hasselblad shouldn't give you any trouble.

Not after the trouble we take.

Every one of our cameras starts with a rugged aluminum shell and ends with a Carl Zeiss T* multi-coated lens.

Everything in between is then checked and re-checked thousands of times.

The time we spend making a Hasselblad naturally affects the money you spend buying one.

In exchange, you get a camera that takes beautiful pictures, time and time again.

No doubt that's why Hasselblads are the only cameras to have been on every one of NASA's manned space flights since 1962.

Of course, the Hasselblads used by NASA have been specially adapted and cost a bit more than the one shown here.

But when it costs billions of dollars to get to the location, you're hardly going to skimp on the camera.

HASSELBLAD
BUILT TO TAKE PRICELESS PICTURES

FOR FURTHER INFORMATION AND A FULL COLOR BROCHURE CONTACT VICTOR HASSELBLAD INC. DEPT
10 MADISON ROAD, FAIRFIELD, NJ 07006. TELEPHONE 201-227-7320.

Figure 7–2   How beliefs are formed among objects, attributes, and benefits.

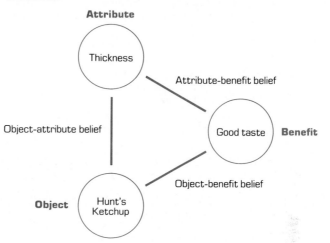

has a self-concept that includes the beliefs that he or she is a risk taker who loves speed and thrills, the tilt of a car's radiator could be relatively important. That is, a sports car that possesses the attribute may enable the person to act more easily to express his or her self-concept by traveling at high speeds with less harassment from police. On the other hand, if the consumer has a self-concept that includes the beliefs that he or she is a law-abiding individual, the tilt of a car's radiator would probably be very unimportant.

From a manager's perspective, it is crucial to identify the relative importance that a target market assigns to the attributes of a product. Thus, it took the Hunt's ketchup people years to realize the importance consumers attach to the thickness of the tomato-based condiment. Consumer beliefs that Hunt's ketchup did not have the property of thickness undoubtedly led directly to its falling market share over a twenty-year period. Thus, when marketing researchers attempt to evaluate consumer beliefs about products, they will include some type of measure of the importance their target market attaches to various attributes. An example of attribute importance and its impact on the film processing industry is found in Highlight 7–1.

Consumer Attitudes

The word *attitude* comes from the Latin term *aptus*, which means "fitness" or "adaptedness." By the eighteenth century the term had come to refer to bodily posture, and to this day the word *attitude* can mean something's general physical orientation with respect to something else. Late in the eighteenth century Charles Darwin used the word in a biological sense as a physical expression of an emotion. Indeed, well into the twentieth century researchers tended to link attitudes with physiological tendencies to approach or avoid something.[4]

HIGHLIGHT 7–1

What Product Benefits Do Consumers Seek in Film Processing?

In 1984 a shakeout occurred in the photo-finishing industry. No one was hurt more than Fotomat Corporation, which had to begin closing many of its drive-through outlets. In 1983 the company lost $23 million on sales of $187.5 million.

A number of factors caused problems for Fotomat and its competitors in the drive-through segment of the industry, such as Fox-Stanley. The problems centered on new competitors offering benefits to consumers, which the drive-through photo finishers could not do. Perhaps the most important new competitors were the miniphoto labs which could turn out high-quality pictures in an hour. Not only did they have the attribute of very high speed, they allowed customers to discuss their photography directly with the lab technicians. The president of one minilab firm said, the minilab's appeal is "the quality of the transaction." Another executive stated, "We don't believe the appeal is the fast service but the level of personal service."

The public's acceptance of the new minilabs has been rapid. The diffusion of this new innovation can be traced directly to its competitive advantage in providing benefits to consumers through service attributes that drive-through photo finishers cannot hope to achieve—quick service and the ability to talk directly to lab technicians.

Based on "One-Hour Film Processors Leave Photo Kiosks in a Blur," *Business Week*, January 23, 1984, 44.

Over the past thirty years the term *"attitude"* has been defined in numerous ways. The definition that best captures the ideas developed in this text was put forth by L. L. Thurstone, who was one of the originators of modern attitude-measurement theory. Thurstone viewed **attitudes** as "the amount of affect or feeling for or against a stimulus."[5] The idea that attitudes refer to affect or a general evaluative reaction has been expressed by many researchers, and the trend in recent years has been to link the concept to feelings rather than beliefs. Examples of some definitions of attitudes include:

1. Attitudes are likes and dislikes.[6]
2. The "major characteristics that distinguish attitude from other concepts are its evaluative or affective nature."[7]
3. Attitudes are the core of our likes and dislikes for certain people, groups, situations, objects, and ideas.[8]

It should be noted that some researchers have defined attitudes in terms of three separate components—cognitions (beliefs), affect (feelings), and conation (behavioral intentions).[9] However, such a conceptualization fails to distinguish these concepts properly, such that each has its own unique set of determinants.[10] Indeed, limited but growing evidence indicates that beliefs and feelings reside in completely different physiological systems.[11] Thus, beliefs may reside in a cognitive system influenced by cognitive learning principles. In contrast, feelings and affect may reside in the autonomic nervous system, which is affected more by classical conditioning and operant conditioning principles. As a result, the author has chosen to separate the definitions of beliefs and of attitudes. Beliefs refer to the cognitive knowledge consumers have linking attributes, benefits, and objects. In contrast, attitudes refer to the feelings people have about attributes, benefits, and objects.

Behaviors and Intentions to Behave

As noted earlier, the primary goal of the marketer is to understand, predict, and to a certain extent control the behavior of consumers. Thus, **consumer behavior** is everything that people do that is related to acquiring, disposing, and using products and services. Behaviors may be both overt and covert. Examples of **overt consumer behaviors** include: buying a product or service, providing word-of-mouth information about a product or service to another person, disposing of a product, and collecting information for a purchase. **Covert consumer behaviors** may be defined as the **intentions** consumers form to behave in a particular way with regard to the acquisition, disposition, and use of products and services. Thus, a consumer may form the intention to search for information, to tell someone else about an experience with a product, to buy a product or service, and to dispose of a product in a certain way.

HOW BELIEFS, ATTITUDES, AND BEHAVIORS ARE FORMED

Beliefs, attitudes, and behaviors may be formed in two distinct ways. The first is through **direct influence** in which a belief, attitude, or behavior is created without either of the other concepts occurring first. For example, a behavior could be induced without the consumer having formed strong attitudes or beliefs about the object toward which the behavior is directed. Similarly, an attitude can be created without the consumer having specific beliefs about the attitudinal object, such as a product or service, and without the consumer ever having bought the product. After a belief, attitude, or behavior is induced, a tendency exists for the concepts to build upon each other to form hierarchies. Thus, the consumer may first form beliefs abut a product, then develop attitudes towards it, and finally purchase it. In a similar manner, the consumer may first engage in the behavior of buying a product and then form beliefs and attitudes. The next two sections discuss the processes through which attitudes, beliefs, and behaviors are directly influenced and through which these concepts are formed into hierarchies of effects.

The Direct Influence of Beliefs, Attitudes, and Behaviors

Disparate processes cause the direct formation of beliefs, attitudes, and behaviors. Beliefs are formed primarily through cognitive learning principles. In contrast, attitudes appear to be formed through classical and operant conditioning principles. Less is known about the direct influence of behavior. Indeed, controversy exists as to whether one ever behaves directly without first having formed some attitude or belief about the object to which the behavior is directed. However, some evidence does exist that people will engage in behaviors because of environmental or situational factors. For example, a person may receive a free sample of toothpaste in the mail. In all likelihood, the consumer will engage in the behavior of using the sample without first developing firm beliefs or attitudes about the product.

Creating Beliefs Directly   As noted above, the direct formation of beliefs occurs through cognitive learning processes. As such, beliefs result from the information-processing activities of the consumer. Thus, information about the attributes of a product are received, encoded into memory, and later retrieved from memory for use. Figure 7–3 shows an advertisement for the Ford Escort which attempts to create specific attribute-object beliefs about the product. These beliefs are that the Escort has the attributes of a low number of scheduled maintenance operations, high gasoline mileage, a large amount of interior room, a smooth ride, high-quality workmanship, and a lifetime service guarantee. The goal of Ford and their advertising agency is to have consumers exposed to the ad, attend to it, place the information in short-term memory, transfer the information to long-term memory, and later retrieve the information for use.

The information-processing activities involved in cognitive learning can occur in either high- or low-involvement cases. In a high-involvement case the consumer is more actively processing information than in the low-involvement situation. That is, the consumer is actively engaged in attempting to solve a problem when highly involved in the decision task. The Ford Escort ad in Figure 7–3 is probably targeted to a highly involved consumer. In order for the consumer to take the time and effort to read the relatively long ad, he or she would have to be highly involved in a problem-solving task.

An example of an advertisement likely targeted to a low-involvement consumer is shown in Figure 7–4. Found in the magazine *Business Week*, the ad is targeted to the businessperson who is not going to take the time to investigate car-rental agencies exhaustively. In such a low-involvement case, the consumer receives information passively with relatively little information processing occurring. Note that the advertisement is quite simple, with only two pieces of information given: Budget has lots of Lincolns; the Lincolns can be obtained inexpensively for $39.95 a day. Through high amounts of repetition, members of the target market of the firm may gradually form the beliefs that Budget has Lincolns that can be rented inexpensively.

Forming Attitudes Directly   Earlier in the chapter, an attitude was defined as the amount of affect or feeling for or against a stimulus object, such as a person, product, company, or idea. Two mechanisms have been identified that explain how attitudes are formed directly. The first is through the processes of classical and operant conditioning. The second mechanism of attitude formation is through a process called **the mere exposure phenomenon.** These processes apply not only to attitude formation regarding objects but also toward advertisements, as discussed in Highlight 7–2.

Figure 7–3   **Ford attempts to create several attribute-object beliefs for the Escort.** *(Courtesy of Ford Motor Company.)*

CONDITIONING PROCESSES AND ATTITUDE FORMATION.   Attitudes may be created directly through both classical and operant conditioning. (For a detailed description of these, see Chapter 6.) From a classical conditioning perspective, an attitude is a conditioned response that can be elicited by a

Figure 7–4   Budget targets low-involvement consumers with a simple message. (Courtesy of Budget Rent a Car Corporation.)

conditioned stimulus. The emotional advertising, which one finds frequently used by advertisers, is based in part on such classical conditioning principles. For example, the "reach-out-and-touch-someone" campaign used by AT&T was highly successful in creating positive feelings among those who saw the

HIGHLIGHT 7–2

Another Type of Attitude: Attitudes Toward the Ad

In addition to developing attitudes toward an object, such as a brand, researchers have found that consumers can form attitudes toward advertisements.(a) Attitudes toward advertisements can result from a number of factors, including the content of the ad, the mood of the consumer, and the consumer's feelings about advertising.(b)

Recent research evidence has shown that the formation of attitudes toward ads can influence the attitudes consumers have toward brands. The suggestion is that positive feelings an advertisement generates can attach themselves to the brand being advertised. Importantly, these feelings seem to be transferred without the consumer necessarily forming beliefs about the brand. Thus, we have another example of the development of attitudes toward a brand without beliefs having been formed first.

Although the process that accounts for the transfer of positive attitudes from an ad to the brand has not been unambiguously determined, evidence exists to suggest that classical conditioning may be responsible. Thus, by pairing the positively viewed advertisement with a brand, some of the positive affect associated with the ad is conditioned to the brand.

What the research indicates is that advertisers should be concerned about producing ads that make consumers feel good. Some of these feelings may then be transferred to the product being advertised.

Based on (a) Andrew A. Mitchell and Jerry C. Olson, "Are Product Attribute Beliefs the Only Mediator of Advertising Effects of Brand Attitude?" *Journal of Marketing Research, 18,* 1981, 318–332; (b) Richard Lutz, Scott MacKenzie, and George Belch, "Attitude Toward the Ads as a Mediator of Advertising Effectiveness: Determinants and Consequences," *Advances in Consumer Research, X,* Richard Bagozzi and Alice Tybout (eds.), Ann Arbor, Mich.: Association for Consumer Research, 1983, 532–539.

ads. From a classical conditioning perspective, the sight of people communicating with friends and loved ones is an unconditioned stimulus that elicits the unconditioned response of positive feelings. The use of the AT&T service was paired with the unconditioned stimulus and after a number of repetitions could become a conditioned stimulus capable of eliciting a conditioned response of positive feelings.

The effects of the use of sex in advertising may be based in part on classical conditioning processes. Calvin Klein has made effective use of such a strategy. For example, in one advertisement by Calvin Klein a young woman is shown staring into the distance, clad in an unbuttoned, torn shirt, Calvin Klein jeans, and workman's gloves. In the ad the picture is the unconditioned stimulus that probably elicits certain feelings in its audience. Through the pairing of the Calvin Klein name with the picture, it may become a conditioned stimulus capable of eliciting similar, though muted, feelings.

Attitudes may also result from operant conditioning processes. For example, an individual may have a conversation with friends about various cars. During the conversation, the person may make statements about alternative models. The positive and negative responses of the friends will act to reinforce or punish the individual's evaluations. The positively reinforced evaluations are likely to recur, whereas the punished evaluations are likely to be suppressed. The social reinforcement of attitudes may be a major factor influencing their formation.

Vicarious conditioning also is a likely direct cause of attitude formation. The observation of important others expressing their feelings and evaluations of products may result in the target audience's modeling these actions. Through such a process a person may form his or her attitudes in part by taking on the attitudes of opinion leaders. Celebrity endorsers may have such an effect on consumers. Very popular endorsers, such as Bill Cosby or Victoria Principle, may influence the attitudes of their admirers through such a modeling process.

MERE EXPOSURE EFFECTS.   Another method through which feelings and evaluations may be formed involves repeated exposures with a stimulus. All else equal, through the mere exposure phenomenon, people's liking for something may increase simply because they encounter it over and over again.[12] The all-else-equal caveat is important. If the exposures with the stimulus are negative, the effect is less likely to be found. An interesting aspect of the mere exposure phenomenon is that it does not seem to be based on learning. The positive feelings created from repeated exposures can occur without the person consciously knowing or perceiving that the object is familiar.[13]

The effects of mere exposure should be distinguished from those of classical conditioning. Classical conditioning results from a stimulus eliciting a response. With mere exposure, no specific response can be identified. Instead, the mere repetition of a stimulus slowly changes the affective reaction of a person to it. The effects of mere exposure have important implications for marketers. By developing a corporate strategy to repeatedly have a product, its name, or its symbol encountered by consumers, the company may be able to subtly influence the feelings that large numbers of people have towards it. The omnipresence of the Coca-Cola name is an example. One sees it repeatedly flashed on television, at baseball parks, in theaters, in restaurants, on buses, and elsewhere. The effects of mere exposure may be one of the factors that have traditionally made Coke the leading soft drink.

Creating Behavior Directly   Consumer researchers have tended to view the behavior of buying a product or service as occurring after the formation of beliefs and attitudes. However, in certain circumstances behavior may be influenced directly without the consumer's having developed either beliefs or attitudes about the product. The direct influence of behavior tends to occur when strong situational or environmental forces propel the consumer to engage in a behavior. The ecological design of the physical environment is an excellent example of how behaviors can be directly induced.[14] Retailers and restauranteurs must pay particular attention to the physical layout of their buildings. The appropriate arrangement of aisles in a supermarket can move customers in desired directions past high-margin food and nonfood items. Similarly, the arrangement of seating in a restaurant can either enhance or detract from the ability of customers to interact during their meals, thereby influencing the rate of turnover of patrons during prime eating hours.

Some sales promotion tactics used by marketers are designed to influence behavior directly. As mentioned earlier in the chapter, free samples are given out in order to induce people to use the product. After the product is used, beliefs and attitudes may form. Contests have a similar impact. A consumer may purchase a product or service in order to become involved in a contest. The person may have few beliefs and little feeling regarding the product. Instead, the person engages in the buying behavior in order to stay in the contest. Again, beliefs and attitudes regarding the product may occur after its purchase.

Behaviors may also be influenced via societal norms and values. Much of what has been labeled **ancestral-based consumption** may be classified into the behavioral influence category. Ancestral-based consumption refers to the idea that some purchases result from ancestral traditions and ethnic group values and norms.[15] Thus, because of a cultural heritage of impoverishment, the black culture has come to value the free exchange of goods among related black families. Therefore, it has been argued within a black consumer's kin network what belongs to one tends to belong to all. Such behavior results largely because of group norms and values, rather than from specific beliefs and attitudes. Similarly, upper-class WASPs tend to be Episcopalian, Presbyterian, or Congregationalist. This behavior results largely from ancestral patterns. In many cases such individuals of Puritan descent became Congregationalists; if of Scottish descent, they became Presbyterian; or if of direct English descent, they became Episcopalian. The churchgoing behavior resulted from ancestral ties rather than beliefs and attitudes.[16]

Operant conditioning can also be used to influence behavior directly. Indeed, its proponents claim that people may not even be aware of conditioning when it occurs.[17] An example of the direct influence of behavior through operant conditioning is that of shaping. Discussed in Chapter 6 on learning, shaping occurs when reinforcers are skillfully applied so as to create new behaviors. Auto dealerships are skillful shapers of behavior. As a sales promotion tool, an auto salesperson may give coffee to a client for entering the showroom, offer the client $25 for driving the car, and provide a rebate of $500 for buying the car.

The direct influence of behavior has not received much attention from consumer researchers; thus, the frequency with which it occurs among consumers is unknown. However, future research may well show that a surprising number of consumer behaviors occur prior to the formation of specific attitudes or beliefs.

Hierarchies of Beliefs, Attitudes, and Behaviors

Although behaviors, attitudes, and beliefs can be formed in isolation, a tendency exists for them to be linked together into hierarchies of effects. **Hierarchies of effects** delineate the order in which beliefs, attitudes, and behavior occur, and several different hierarchies have been proposed. The factor that most directly controls which hierarchy is implemented appears to be the type of purchase process engaged in by the consumer. Table 7–2 identi-

Table 7–2   Purchase Processes and Their Possible Hierarchies of Effects

Purchase Process	Hierarchy of Effects
1. Extended decision making	Standard learning hierarchy: Beliefs—affect—behavior
2. Routine decision making	Low-involvement hierarchy: Beliefs—behavior—affect
3. Experience-based process	Experiential hierarchy: Affect—behavior—beliefs
4. Behavioral influence	Behavioral influence hierarchy: Behavior—beliefs—affect

fies four different purchase processes in which consumers may be involved and the hierarchy of effects associated with each process. A discussion of the purchase processes and their associated hierarchy of effects follows.

Decisions Involving Extended and Limited Problem Solving   Early consumer and advertising researchers proposed that beliefs about an object occurred first. Next, consumers developed affect (feelings) towards the object. Finally, consumers engaged in some behavior relative to the object, such as purchasing the product.[18] This pattern in which behavior follows affect which follows beliefs has been called the **standard learning hierarchy.**[19] The pattern seems to represent a logical process in which consumers first investigate a product in order to learn about its characteristics. Based on this information, they evaluate it and form feelings and an attitude. If the attitude is positive, they then purchase the product.

Beginning in the mid-1960s, however, consumer researchers began to recognize that many, if not most, consumer purchases do not follow the pattern of the standard hierarchy.[20] Researchers began to believe that in many cases products were purchased without consumers developing any feelings or affect. In such instances, it was proposed that consumers first form beliefs about a product, then purchase the product, and only after its purchase develop an attitude regarding the product.[21]

Why in some cases does the formation of an attitude occur after the occurrence of a behavior? The answer appears to lie in the involvement of the consumer with the product and the purchase situation.[22] As noted earlier in the textbook, involvement is defined as a state of motivation resulting from the act of purchase or consumption having high personal importance or relevance. As the amount of involvement in the decision increases, the consumer will tend to engage in increased problem-solving activities. The problem-solving activity will involve the consumer in extensively searching for information about alternative products or services that may be bought. As a result, a relatively large number of beliefs are likely to be formed about the alternatives. In addition, the consumer is likely to take the time to evaluate the alternatives and compare them. Through such activities, attitudes may be formed. With the formation of beliefs and attitudes, intentions to behave are likely to result, as is, ultimately, the action of purchasing the product or service. Thus, when the consumer is highly involved in a particular purchase decision, he or she will tend to engage in extended problem-solving activities and move through the standard learning hierarchy of belief formation leading to attitude formation leading to behavior. The links between level of involvement, attitudes, and behaviors are explored more in Highlight 7–3.

The flow of events is quite different when the consumer is in a low-involvement decision situation. In such a case, the consumer is *not* motivated to engage in extensive problem solving. Instead, the consumer moves through a **routine** or **limited decision process** such that only one or two alternatives are considered in a superficial manner. As a result, a limited number of beliefs are formed about the product alternatives. Furthermore, because the consumer does not evaluate the alternatives closely, attitudes tend *not* to be formed. Attitudes tend to occur only after the product or service is bought, and the consumer subsequently reflects back on how he or she feels about

---

HIGHLIGHT 7–3

When Do Attitudes Predict Behavior?

A classic problem for social psychologists and consumer researchers has involved explaining why the knowledge of consumer attitudes does not allow for a better prediction of actual behavior. In fact, early statements were highly pessimistic about the ability of attitudes to predict overt behavior.(a)

More recently, researchers have recognized that the issue is one of *when attitudes predict behavior*. One group of researchers argued that a variety of factors influence the extent to which attitudes predict behaviors.(b) One major factor concerns the degree of involvement of the consumer in the purchase decision. Attitudes are likely to predict behavior only under conditions of high involvement. Other factors relevant to the issue include:

1. *Measurement*. The measurement of the attitude should be reliable and valid. In addition, the measure of attitude should be at the same level of specificity as the measure of behavior. Thus, if the behavior involves buying a new Porsche in the next

six months, the measure should include a time parameter.
2. *Effects of other people*. The desires of other people towards the purchase, as well as the consumer's motivation to comply with these desires, will influence the extent to which attitudes predict behavior.
3. *Situational factors*. Situational factors, such as a shortage of time, holidays, sickness, and so forth, can intervene and cause attitudes not to predict behavior well.

Attitudes are related to behaviors; however, one must be careful to recognize the circumstances in which the relationship is most likely to be strong.

Based on (a) Allan Wicker, "Attitudes Versus Actions: The Relationship of Verbal and Overt Behavioral Responses to Attitude Objects," *Journal of Social Issues*, 25, Autumn 1969, 65; (b) Robert Cialdini, Richard Petty, and John Cacioppo, "Attitude and Attitude Change," *Annual Review of Psychology*, 32, 1981, 366.

it. The attitudes are formed through product or service use in low-involvement situations. Thus, when consumers have low involvement in a decision, they tend to engage in limited problem solving and move through what is called a **low-involvement hierarchy** consisting of belief formation–behavior–attitude formation.[23]

Experience-Based Processes   As discussed in Chapter 2, a second general consumer buying process is based upon the seeking of experiences. From this perspective the consumer may be viewed as engaging in a behavior because of a strong desire to obtain feelings and excitement. Such desires are unlikely to be cognitively based and probably result from affective states. In such instances the hierarchy of effects may be conceptualized as initiated by feelings or attitudes. Thus, a friend may ask you to go to a rock concert. Your decision would probably be based on the feelings that you have towards the group and going to the concert. If queried about the reason for going, you would be able to voice a series of beliefs. However, such beliefs would probably be far less influential than your feelings in the decision. Indeed, any belief statements you made might be voiced to justify the decision.[24]

Quite similar in nature to such experientially based decisions are impulse purchases. Impulse purchases have been defined as a "buying action undertaken without a problem having been previously recognized or a buying intention formed prior to entering the store."[25] Impulse purchases do frequently occur. Various studies have found that as many as 39 percent of department store purchases and 67 percent of grocery store purchases may be unplanned.[26] Impulse purchases have been described as "mindless reactive behavior."[27] Other researchers have noted that impulse purchases involve strong affective states. The behavior becomes somewhat automatic, has little intellectual control, and reveals a strong emotional content. As such, it is the antithesis of the rational consumption that one finds in high-involvement purchases and to a certain extent in low-involvement purchases.[28]

In one study of impulse purchases the researchers asked respondents in in-depth interviews to report on their feelings when they made impulse purchases.[29] Some of the statements are reported below:

> I was in Beverly Hills just walking around, not intending to buy, when I saw some shoes on sale. So I went inside and tried them on and they fit fine. At that time I thought about buying one pair, then I got the *feeling* I had to try everything. They were just calling to me.

> You suddenly feel compelled to buy something. It *feels* like getting an IDEA.

> It's a fast *feeling*, and if I don't get it right away, I'll think of reasons why I don't need it.

In each case, the purchase seems to have been preceded by the consumer's strong feeling that a product should be purchased. The affective state led directly to a behavior without the person forming beliefs or thinking very hard about the purchase. Indeed, it seems that in some cases consumers may act to repress thinking, which could dampen the feelings experienced. Thus, the hierarchy of effects for impulse purchases seems best described as moving from affect to behavior to beliefs.

Anecdotal evidence of the importance of affect in impulse purchases can be found in the buying behavior of young urban professionals (Yuppies). One article on Yuppies noted that their buying habits seemed to be based to a large extent on finding products that are new and interesting. One food retailer said that the keys to the Yuppie market are attractive displays. He noted, "We have people buy things because they look good in the refrigerator, like Martinelli's apple juice."[30] Another person, who owns a gourmet supermarket in Washington, D.C., said that for Yuppies a trip to his store "is like an outing." The favorite question of the group is, "What else do you have that's neat?"[31] Rather than belief formation driving the purchase, it seems that general feelings are referenced prior to the behavior of buying.

Purchases Based on Behavioral Influence   As discussed in the previous section, strong situational or environmental forces may propel a consumer to engage in buying behavior without the person having formed either feelings or affect about the object of the purchase. For example, a consumer may have the son or daughter of an acquaintance try to sell her packages of popcorn in order to raise money to go on a high school field trip. Because the consumer does not wish to offend her friend by saying no to the request, she buys the popcorn. The consumer had not formed any feelings or beliefs about the object of purchase, i.e., the popcorn. The behavior was induced through the operation of a norm which states that one should help out the children of one's friends when possible.

When behavior is induced directly through the operation of environmental or situational factors, the hierarchy of effects begins with the behavior. Whether feelings or beliefs follow the behavior in the hierarchy cannot be answered definitely at this time. One researcher has argued that the hierarchy may move from behavior to feelings to beliefs.[32] This has been called the "Do–Feel–Learn" hierarchy. Common experience does seem to support such a view. People can at times feel very good or very bad after a purchase. More is said about such postpurchase processes in Chapter 9.

Additional Comments on Hierarchies of Effects   Twenty-five years ago consumer behavior researchers had a simplistic, one-dimensional view of the relationship of beliefs, feelings, and behavior. Today, the view is highly complex with various authors proposing different hierarchies of effects operative under varying buying circumstances. Indeed, the current view may well be overly complex. For example, does it make sense to say that when a consumer is engaged in a routine decision process absolutely no affect exists prior to purchasing a product? Similarly, is it likely that in impulse purchases the consumer has formed no beliefs about the product?

Such reasoning leads to the realization that the various hierarchies of effects are highly idealized representations of consumer buying behavior. It is likely that regardless of the decision process involved, consumers will have some rudimentary beliefs and some vague attitudinal feelings about a product or service prior to buying it. What the various hierarchies of effects may provide is a feel for the relative emphasis of beliefs, attitudes, and behavior for various purchase processes.

What About Habitual Purchases? A large number of consumer purchases appear to be bought as a result of a habit rather than through a decision process, an experiential process, or a behavioral influence process. For example, one study found that consumers, when shopping for laundry detergent, spent a median time of only 8.5 seconds making their selection.[33] Clearly, very little information processing occurred during that brief time period.

A possible explanation for such a short decision process is that consumers entered the aisle knowing what they were going to buy. It is likely that they had bought the brand numerous times in the past. Furthermore, the buyers clearly had a positive attitude towards it. In the study, over 90 percent of the respondents had something positive to say about the brand purchased. Thus, habit probably played a large role in accounting for the purchase of the laundry detergent.[34]

A key question, however, is "What is the hierarchy of effects for a habitual purchase?" Researchers have not addressed this question, so one can only speculate. However, a likely explanation is that over time consumers come to evaluate certain brands in a highly positive manner. This positive global evaluation can be viewed as the initial step in the hierarchy when a habitual purchase is made. The behavior of buying the product then follows the possible affect.

The decision of which brand of detergent to buy moves the discussion of attitudes to a closely related area called consumer choice processes. The next section discusses this important topic area.

UNDERSTANDING HOW CONSUMERS MAKE CHOICES

To this point, the discussion of beliefs, attitudes, and behavior has focused on giving their definitions and providing an understanding of how they are formed. Missing from the discussion have been statements about how consumer beliefs and attitudes can actually be used to predict the brand of product or service consumers will choose. Consumers make many different types of choices, including which brand to select and which store to patronize. In addition, consumers make choices between disparate alternatives, such as whether to buy a car or go on a vacation and whether to spend or save.[35]

When consumers select among brand alternatives, they are making a choice. The evidence indicates that for most purchases consumers engage in very unsophisticated choice processes.[36] For the most part, consumers are simply interested in reaching satisfactory choices, rather than optimal ones. One can expect to find consumers attempting to make optimal choices only in the most important of their decisions. Indeed, some researchers have argued that consumers focus more on optimizing their time and effort expenditures than on optimizing their choices.[37]

How consumers go about making their choices clearly depends upon their involvement level in the purchase. For low-involvement, repetitive purchases, such as buying laundry detergent, consumers seem to use very simple choice tactics. These choice tactics include such approaches as: buying the product that you last purchased, buying the cheapest product, buying the brand that seems to have the best performance, or buying the brand that one's spouse tells you to buy.[38] Such simple tactics probably describe how most everyday shopping goods are purchased.

As the level of involvement in the purchase increases, however, choice processes may become more complex. At the highest levels of involvement consumers seem to act as though they are combining their beliefs about the attributes of the brands in a fairly sophisticated manner. Models of such high-involvement choice processes are called multiattribute attitude models. At somewhat lower levels of involvement, consumers seem to use slightly less sophisticated choice schemes. These are called heuristic models of choice. The next two sections discuss these two approaches to consumer choice.

Multiattribute Choice Models

As noted above, in high-involvement choice situations consumer decisions seem best described by what are called **multiattribute models.** These models identify how consumers may combine their beliefs about product attributes to form attitudes about various brand alternatives. The idea is that the brand toward which the consumer has the best attitude will be chosen. Note that multiattribute models assume that consumers are using the standard-hier-archy-of-effects model of beliefs leading to attitudes which lead to purchase behaviors. Also note that these multiattribute models are also describing how attitudes may be formed. That is, from their perspective attitudes are formed from the development of a series of beliefs about the attributes of the attitu-dinal object.

Two general varieties of multiattribute models have been identified. The first focuses on predicting the attitude that a consumer will form towards a specific attitude object, such as a product, service, person, or idea. The second type of model focuses on predicting the behavioral intentions of consumers to perform some type of action such as buying a product or service. The behavioral intentions model has appeared more recently than the atti-tude-towards-the-object models and in fact builds upon the earlier approach. The following two subsections discuss the two types of multiattribute models.

Attitude-Toward-the-Object Models   The multiattribute models that at-tempt to predict a consumer's attitude toward an object have identified three major aspects of a consumer's choice process. First, they obtain a measure of how the consumer rates the importance or the positivity of a particular attribute. This rating of importance is used to indicate how much weight a particular product characteristic is likely to have in reaching a decision. The second component of such multiattribute models is a belief rating of the extent to which a particular brand has the attribute under question. The purpose of the belief rating is to obtain a brand-attribute link. That is, the rating of the extent to which a particular brand possesses a specific attribute will give an indication of how high or low the brand rates on the attribute. The final component is a statement of how the ratings of importance of attributes and the ratings of beliefs are combined to form an overall attitude toward the brand or object. In nearly all of the multiattribute models, attitudes are viewed as resulting from a process in which the consumer first multiplies the belief ratings times the importance ratings for each of the attributes and then sums these outcomes.

A number of different multiattribute models have been proposed. Of those developed to assess attitudes toward an object, such as a brand, none has been shown to be superior to the others.[39] One model frequently used by consumer and market researchers is presented below. Algebraically the model is expressed as:

$$A_o = \sum_{i=1}^{n} B_i\, a_i$$

where

A_o = the overall attitude toward object o,

B_i = the belief of whether or not object o has some particular attribute or achieves some particular goal,

a_i = the evaluative aspect or importance to the consumer that o has the attribute or achieves the goal, and

n = the number of beliefs.[40]

Table 7–3 presents the results of a hypothetical consumer's evaluation of three sports cars—a Corvette, a Nissan 300 ZX Turbo, and a Porsche 944. This particular consumer is using four attributes on which to rate the cars—their styling, handling, cost, and acceleration. The evaluations (a_i) of the importance to the consumer of each of the attributes were obtained on an eleven-point constant-sum scale. Thus, the consumer divided eleven points among the attributes proportionate to their relative importance to him. Note that for this consumer styling was the most important attribute, followed by acceleration, handling, and cost. Beliefs about whether the sports cars possessed the attributes were obtained on five-point scales. Each scale was constructed so that 1 = very unlikely and 5 = very likely.

An inspection of Table 7–3 shows that the Corvette was rated as average on each of the attributes. That is, the particular consumer gave threes on

Table 7–3   A Hypothetical Multiattribute Evaluation of Three Sports Cars[a]

	Type of Sports Car[b]								
	Chevrolet Corvette			Nissan 300 ZX Turbo			Porsche 944		
Attribute	*a*	*B*	*a* × *B*	*a*	*B*	*a* × *B*	*a*	*B*	*a* × *B*
Great styling	5	3	15	5	2	10	5	5	25
Great handling	2	3	6	2	2	4	2	4	8
Low cost	1	3	3	1	5	5	1	2	2
High acceleration	3	3	9	3	4	12	3	2	6
$\Sigma B_i a_i$			33			31			41

[a]Ratings are purely hypothetical.
[b]Beliefs *(B)* were rates on 5-point scales where 1 = very unlikely to possess and 5 = very likely to possess. Evaluations of importance *(a)* were rated via a constant-sum scale such that the sum of the importance ratings across attributes equalled 11.

each of his belief ratings. In contrast, the 300 ZX was rated very highly on low cost and high acceleration. Unfortunately, it was not rated as highly on styling and handling. In contrast, the Porsche was rated very highly on styling and handling and relatively poorly on cost and acceleration.

When the importance and belief ratings are multiplied and these results summed, one gets the predicted overall attitude of the hypothetical consumer regarding each of the sports cars. As can be seen in the table, the Porsche obtained the highest score, followed by the Corvette, with the 300 ZX Turbo in last place. The computed attitude scores have meaning principally for comparison purposes. That is, one does not get much information by knowing that the Corvette had an attitude score of 33. It is only when one knows that the 300 ZX Turbo scored lower and the Porsche substantially higher that the score provides information. Based upon a comparison of the attitude scores, one would predict that the hypothetical consumer would have the most positive attitude towards the Porsche and would be more likely to buy it than the Corvette or 300 ZX.

The attitude-toward-the-object models have several limitations if they are to be used to predict behavior. Perhaps their most important deficit is that they fail to consider the attitude of the consumer in engaging in the behavior of purchasing a particular product. A person may have a positive attitude toward buying a Porsche 944 but never engage in the behavior of buying it. Factors that could lower the likelihood of purchasing it could be: the opinions of important other people; the thought of having to spend so much money on a sports car when it could be spent on something else, like a house; and the impact of various situational factors, such as time, on purchase behavior. For these reasons Fishbein and his colleagues developed a more elaborate model that predicted "intentions to behave" rather than simply attitudes toward an object.

The Behavioral Intentions Model The behavioral intentions model developed by Fishbein and his colleagues extended the basic multiattribute models in several ways.[41] Now called the theory of reasoned action, it proposes that behavior results from the formation of specific intentions to behave. Thus, the model does not attempt to predict behavior per se, but intentions to behave. A second extension of the earlier model was a construct called the **subjective norm.** The subjective norm (SN) assessed what the consumer believes other people think that he should do. In other words, SN introduces into the formulation the powerful effects of reference groups on behavior. The third change in the model involves the object to which attitudes are directed. Instead of assessing the consumer's attitude toward the brand itself, the model assessed the consumer's attitude toward the overt behavior of purchasing the product. The key difference in assessing attitude toward behavior rather than attitude toward the object is that the focus is on the consumer's perception of what the *consequences* of the purchase will be. When the consequences of the purchase are assessed rather than whether or not the product possesses certain attributes, the researcher has an enhanced ability to take into consideration factors that may act to impede intentions to behave. Considering the purchase of a sports car, some consequences of the purchase might be: buying the car will cause the person not to take a vacation, buying the car will cause the person to have to deal with obnoxious salespeople, and buying the car will involve the person in having to figure out how to get a loan at very high interest rates. Models that assess only the attitude toward the object have a difficult time measuring such factors.

Algebraically the behavioral intentions model is written:

$$B \approx BI = w_1(A_B) + w_2(SN)$$

where

B = behavior

BI = behavioral intention

A_B = attitude toward performing the behavior

SN = the subjective norm

w_1 and w_2 = empirically determined weights.

The weights (w_1 and w_2) are determined empirically through regression analysis. A_B and SN are obtained directly from consumers via questionnaires. In fact, A_B and SN are themselves indices that are obtained from other measures. Specifically, the attitude toward the behavior is obtained from the following equation:

$$A_B = \sum_{i=1}^{n} b_i\, e_i$$

where

A_B = attitude toward the behavior

b_i = the person's belief that performing the behavior will result in consequence i

e_i = the person's evaluation of consequence i

n = the number of beliefs.

Note that the equation is very similar to that used in other multiattribute models to obtain the attitude toward the object. The major difference is in the belief variable. Rather than assessing the belief that an object has an attribute, the behavioral intentions model assesses the person's belief that performing a particular behavior will result in a particular consequence. The equation for obtaining the subjective norm is:

$$SN = \sum_{j=1}^{n} NB_j\, MC_j$$

where

SN = subjective norm

NB_j = the normative belief that a reference group or person j thinks that the consumer should or should not perform the behavior

MC_j = the motivation to comply with the influence of referent j

n = number of relevant reference groups of individuals.

The subjective norm is calculated similarly to a belief. The normative belief is equivalent to a belief statement, and the motivation to comply is like an importance rating. Thus, for each person or reference group, these ratings are multiplied, and the result is added across all people or reference groups considered.

A number of researchers have tested the behavioral intentions model against the standard multiattribute models. In general, the results reveal that the behavioral intentions model is superior.[42] However, various authors have suggested that the model as specified may not be accurate. In particular, questions have arisen concerning the role of the subjective norm variable.[43]

Heuristic Models of Consumer Choice

The multiattribute models of consumer choice discussed thus far tend to be used when consumers are engaged in extended problem solving. In order for a consumer to act as though he or she considers a number of product attributes, weights the importance of these attributes, and assigns belief ratings to alternative brands (i.e., uses a multiattribute model), a great deal of information-processing effort is required. Such a task is complex and requires a large amount of cognitive effort on the part of the consumer. Because of the complexity of using a multiattribute approach, because of the limitations of

Table 7–4 Occasions When Choice Heuristics May Be Used

1. When decision involvement is low to moderate.
2. When consumers are in a limited problem-solving mode or are making a purchase out of habit.
3. When consumers seek to reduce the cognitive effort involved in reaching a decision.
4. When consumers are involved in high-involvement purchase but time constraints exist.
5. When consumers are in a high-involvement purchase, but the decision task is highly complex involving a large number of different brand alternatives.

consumer information-processing capacity, and because of the cognitive effort involved, consumers frequently take shortcuts in reaching a decision. Rather than seek perfect decisions, they are willing to arrive at merely satisfactory decisions. This process has been called **satisficing.**[44] In order to make choices given this desire to satisfice, consumers will frequently use **heuristics.** Table 7–4 gives a number of instances in which consumers are likely to use heuristics to make choices, or rules of thumb. Several of these heuristics are discussed further.[45]

The Affect-Referral Heuristic In the affect-referral heuristic, the consumer elicits from memory the overall recollection of his or her evaluation of an alternative. Thus, rather than examining attributes or beliefs about attributes, a holistic approach is used in which the consumer chooses the alternative about which he has the most positive feeling.

Affect referral was previously discussed as the likely explanation of how consumers make habitual purchases. When a product is bought through habit, a problem acts as a cue for the consumer to go through a memory search for possible products or services that will solve it. The first brand alternative to be recalled from memory that elicits positive feelings is likely to be the alternative the consumer will seek to purchase. This brand is also likely to be the alternative last used, as long as it reinforced the consumer by performing as expected.

The Conjunctive Heuristic In many instances, consumers are faced with a decision in which a large number of brand alternatives are available. For example, if one had attempted to select a personal computer in 1984, he or she could have chosen from over a hundred different brands. Clearly, it would be impossible to investigate every one of these brands, so a shortcut is needed to simplify the process. One such shortcut involves the use of the conjunctive heuristic. When the conjunctive heuristic is used, the consumer sets minimum cutoffs on each attribute that he or she wishes to investigate. If the product fails to surpass the minimum cutoff level, the alternative is rejected. The conjunctive heuristic is often used as an initial screening device to eliminate enough brands so that a more complex decision approach can be applied to the remaining alternatives.

An example of the use of a conjunctive decision rule might involve a consumer's attempt to select a personal computer. The consumer might decide to narrow his choices by eliminating all alternatives that cost more than $2,000 and that are not written up in *Consumer Reports* magazine. Note that when the conjunctive heuristic is used, negative information is weighted more heavily than positive information. It is not particularly important to a consumer using the conjunctive rule whether an alternative is the best on any one attribute. Instead, the consumer wants to make sure that an alternative is not rated poorly on any characteristic on which it is initially screened.

Lexicographic Heuristic Whereas the conjunctive heuristic is typically used to help the consumer reject unacceptable alternatives, the lexicographic heuristic helps the consumer identify the best alternative on the most important attribute. In order to use the lexicographic approach, the consumer is assumed to have an idea of the order of importance of the attributes on which he or she is evaluating a product. Thus, for a personal computer the order of importance of attributes might be: price, IBM compatibility, software availability, and service availability. After determining the order of importance of attributes, the consumer then rates all alternatives on the most important attribute. The alternative which is best on that attribute is then chosen. If a tie occurs, the consumer moves to the next attribute and selects the alternative rated best on that attribute, and so forth.

An example of an advertisement that could have been targeted to consumers who use a lexicographic choice process is found in Figure 7–5. The advertisement for Johnson's Baby Lotion provides four reasons for grown-ups to use the product. It is quite likely that marketing research was performed to identify the rank order of the most important product characteristics. The advertisement then was developed to show that the product possessed these attributes. Although other considerations probably influenced the development of the ad, it should effectively influence consumers using a lexicographic choice process, particularly if the qualities of "thick and rich" were most important to them.

Phased Strategies Consumers may also combine the use of the various heuristics. Thus, in a first phase a consumer may use a conjunctive model in order to reduce the alternatives considered to three or four. The consumer may then use a lexicographic approach or even a multiattribute model to make the final choice.

Which Choice Models Do Consumers Actually Use?

One study asked students to make choices among various automobile alternatives after being given seven attributes on which to rate the cars.[46] Table 7–5 presents the results. The study found that almost 61 percent of the time the students used a lexicographic model to make their choices. Next most frequently used was a compensatory model (32.4 percent). A phased strategy of using a conjunctive model to screen alternatives, followed by a compen-

Figure 7–5   This Johnson & Johnson ad could appeal to consumers who use a lexicographic heuristic to evaluate baby lotion. *(Courtesy of Johnson & Johnson Baby Products Company.)*

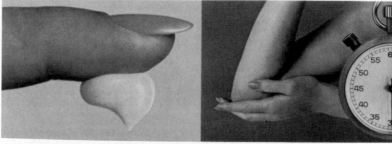

Four good reasons why *Johnson's* Baby Lotion is the perfect "grown-up" body lotion.

Thicker and richer than other lotions.

Absorbs fast. Goes to work instantly.

Unique combination of 10 skin softeners.

Leaves you feeling beautifully soft all over.

When it comes to keeping skin soft, *Johnson's* Baby Lotion has everything you want in a body lotion and more. Its super-rich formula gives a new beauty to your skin and leaves it with a healthy, youthful glow. In short, *Johnson's* Baby Lotion is a terrific body lotion. We've told you four good reasons why. But don't take our word for it. Just give it a try.

It's a perfect lotion for grown-up skin.

Johnson & Johnson

© J&J 1985

Table 7–5 Frequency of Use of Heuristics in Brand Choice

Type Heuristic	Verbal Description	Percent Using Approach
Conjunctive	I chose the car that had a really good rating on at least one characteristic.	0.6%
Lexicographic	I looked at the characteristic that was most important to me and chose the car that was best in that feature. If two or more cars were equal on that feature, I then looked at my second most important feature to break the tie.	60.7
Multiattribute model	I chose the car that had a really good rating when you balance the good ratings with the bad ratings.	32.1
Phased—conjunctive-compensatory	I first eliminated the cars with a really bad rating on any feature and then chose from the rest the one that seemed the best overall when you balance the good ratings with the bad ratings.	5.4
Other	(Category composed of several other types of heuristic models.)	1.8

SOURCE: Adapted from M. Reilly and R. Holman, "Does Task Complexity or Cue Intercorrelation Affect Choice of an Information Processing Strategy: An Empirical Investigation," in *Advances in Consumer Research*, *IV*, W. D. Perrault, Jr., (ed.), Atlanta, Ga.: Association for Consumer Research, 1977, 189.

satory approach, was used 5.4 percent of the time. These three strategies accounted for 98.2 percent of the choices. Although the study did involve a simulated buying situation and used students as subjects, it does indicate that consumers are likely to use choice heuristics frequently in their decision making.

Managerial Implications

The analysis of consumer beliefs, attitudes, and behaviors is of vital importance to marketing managers and marketing researchers. Indeed, much of what market research staffs do involves the analysis and prediction of beliefs, attitudes, and behaviors. The analysis of these concepts has importance to managers in four separate areas: (1) benefit segmentation, (2) competitive analysis, (3) development of the marketing mix, and (4) marketing opportunity analysis.

Benefit Segmentation

Benefit segmentation involves the division of the market into relatively homogeneous groups of consumers based upon a similarity of needs. Within the marketplace companies can often identify groups of people who seek particular benefits from products that can help satisfy specific needs. Thus, a consumer who has "computer phobia" has a need for a user-friendly computer. Apple developed a product that fulfills such a need—the MacIntosh.

Earlier in the chapter a discussion took place about three different types of beliefs—product-attribute beliefs, attribute-benefit beliefs, and product-benefit beliefs. (Figure 7–1 visually depicts these relationships.) When a set of consumers that has an unfulfilled need has been identified, the goal of a company should be to develop a product or position a product so that it is perceived by consumers as satisfying that need. In other words, the company wishes to establish a product-benefit belief. This goal can be accomplished by forming a product-attribute belief that the product has a particular attribute that leads to a particular benefit. Consumers probably will reason then that if the product possesses an attribute that will fulfill a need, the product will also fulfill the need.

A number of companies have built huge market shares for their products by establishing a strategy of focusing on how a product fulfills one particular consumer need. Procter & Gamble in particular has used the strategy successfully. For example, Crest toothpaste has built its dominant market share around providing one primary benefit—decay prevention. Similarly, Charmin toilet tissue has built its market share around providing the benefit of softness.

Competitive Analysis

An important job of the marketing manager is to track how his or her product compares to competitive offerings. The manager should compare his product to competing brands on the extent to which consumers perceive them as possessing particular attributes. Such a competitive analysis involves a comparison of the product-attribute beliefs held by consumers about competing products. If the product manager finds that his product is rated poorly in comparison to competitors on an attribute rated as important by consumers, actions are probably in order to correct the problem. Thus, the Hunt's ketchup manager worked hard to find a process to increase the thickness of his brand in order to match that of his chief competitor.

Perceptual Distortion of Product Attributes   Managers must also recognize that the product-attribute beliefs held by consumers may not match reality. For a variety of reasons, consumers may have an inaccurate impression of the extent to which a product possesses a particular attribute. For example, in some instances, such as when a brand has a low promotional budget, consumers may simply not be aware of the extent to which the product possesses an attribute. With this lack of information consumers may simply assume that the product ranks poorly on the attribute. In other cases, halo effects may cause consumers to expect that a product that is good on one attribute will also be good on other attributes. A halo effect occurs when consumers assume that because a product is good or bad on one product characteristic it will also be good or bad on another characteristic. Thus, a consumer who believes that Crest toothpaste is the best cavity-fighting toothpaste might also think that it also has the lowest abrasive qualities. In fact, other toothpastes have a lower tendency to abrade teeth.

Product Positioning   Another reason for comparing products on the extent to which they possess certain attributes is to aid the manager in positioning the product. A valid marketing strategy involves trying to position a product so that it provides benefits not provided by competing brands. If a brand is perceived by consumers as possessing the same basic attributes as other products, it is an indication that the product has not been differentiated from the competition. In such instances a repositioning of the brand may be called for. A classic example of the use of positioning strategy was followed by Apple Computer in the mid-1980s. With the entry of IBM into the personal computer field, a shakeout occurred, and many companies went out of business. The successful brands tended to run software that the IBM PC could also run. A major question for Apple was whether to produce an IBM compatible computer. The company shunned the advice of many analysts and decided to dissociate itself from IBM and position itself as an alternative that was highly user friendly. At the time of publication of this text the viability of the strategy is still in doubt.

Developing the Marketing Mix

The analysis of beliefs, attitudes, and their link to behavior can also assist the manager in the development of the marketing mix. Some considerations are briefly discussed in the following subsections.

Product Considerations   The analysis of consumer needs and the product qualities (i.e., attributes) that fulfill these needs can assist in product development. Such an analysis can lead to the identification of unfilled market niches. A classic recent example of such an approach was the marketing coup of Miller's Lite Beer. The company recognized in the late 1970s that male consumers were also becoming weight conscious. They developed a good-tasting beer with reduced calories and advertised it as a beer that "won't fill you up." The company successfully marketed a new product by recognizing that an opportunity existed to provide a beer with the attribute of "lower calories."

Promotion Considerations   The study of beliefs, attitudes, and their relationship to purchase behavior has major implications for promotional strategy. Of key importance is the type of buying process that the target market of the brand uses in buying products from a particular category. Table 7–6 summarizes some strategies that companies may use, depending upon the buying process involved.

   Each of the strategies outlined in Table 7–6 relates to the type of hierarchy of effect associated with the buying process governing the purchase. For example, in a high-involvement buying process, consumers are moving

Table 7–6 Some Promotional Strategies Based on the Type of Consumer Buying Process

Buying Process	Possible Promotional Strategies
High-involvement	Emphasize developing product-attribute and product-benefit beliefs through cognitive learning procedures. Can emphasize print advertising and personal selling. Help create affect through product demonstrations and advertising using classical conditioning procedures.
Low-involvement	Emphasize developing product-attribute beliefs through repetition of simple messages. Tie point-of-purchase displays into advertising. Place product and displays in high-traffic area.
Experiential/impulse	Emphasize the fun and feelings that can be obtained by experiencing the product or service. Emphasize creating affect through the classical conditioning of positive feelings towards the product.
Behavioral influence	Use sales promotion techniques, such as sweepstakes, rebates, samples, or coupons.
Habitual	Emphasize affect maintenance through advertising to support purchases. Use direct-mail advertising to owners to support their purchase and describe new offerings.

through the traditional learning hierarchy of beliefs–affect–behavior. Furthermore, they are most likely in such a case to engage in a more complex choice process, such as using a compensatory or a phased-choice strategy. In such instances, the company should focus on using cognitive learning principles to assist consumers in learning the brand's characteristics and how these will satisfy their particular needs. That is, the company should use advertising to assist the consumer in solving a problem and present the material in a way to help make the information-processing task easier. (Many of the principles involved relate to the problem of how to construct messages. Chapter 8 presents an in-depth discussion of the effects of various types of messages on consumers.) High-involvement media, such as magazines, can be used to present relatively complex product information. In addition, the creation of affect can be encouraged by also taking steps to create positive feelings towards the brands. Strategies to encourage the development of affect include advertising attractive models or popular celebrities with the product and by using emotional appeals as well as informational appeals in promoting the product.

In low-involvement situations, consumers are likely to use very simple decision rules to make their choices. In such instances, companies have to analyze carefully the attributes that consumers consider most important in reaching a purchase decision. Efforts should then be made to develop a product that possesses these attributes and then use promotion to emphasize this product-attribute linkage. Companies should also determine whether or not consumers are using a conjunctive choice approach as an initial screening device. If so, the company should insure that consumers will not eliminate the product from consideration because it falls below a minimum cutoff level on any of the attributes. In addition to this product design consideration, the company should attempt to develop a positive image for the product so consumers will assume that it will meet their minimum specifications.

The hierarchy of effects for both experiential and habitual decisions is likely to begin with the development of affect. In habitual decisions, the affect results primarily from the consumer having used the product frequently in the past. In such an instance, advertising and particularly direct mail can be used to reinforce these positive feelings. In order to create impulse purchases, the affect must be created prior to the purchase. The use of advertising to classically condition affect is one approach to create feelings. Perhaps even more important is the proper display of the product. In order to encourage the impulse purchase of products, the product must be attractively displayed in high-traffic areas.

A number of sales promotional techniques can be used to induce buying behavior directly. In recent years, techniques such as sweepstakes, coupons, and contests have become extremely popular as methods of inducing behavior without the consumer having first formed strong feelings or beliefs about the product.

Pricing and Distribution Strategies   The relationship of beliefs, feelings, and purchase behavior also has relevance for the pricing and distribution of the product. The product's price is in most cases one of the most important attributes evaluated by consumers. Managers should be highly aware of the role of price in the consumer's decision process. In some instances, consumers may be highly price sensitive (i.e., demand elastic), so that a high price relative to competitors will eliminate the product from consideration. In other cases, price can be used as a surrogate indicator of product quality. In such instances, a higher price may be viewed positively by certain segments. The price-quality relationship has been well established by researchers.[47] Consumers tend to use price as an indicator of quality when they have confidence that price in fact predicts quality, when they perceive there to be quality differences among competitors, and when quality is difficult to judge through some objective means or through the use of brand name or store image.

The method of product distribution is particularly affected by the type of buying process used by consumers to make product choices. When a high involvement decision process occurs, the product is often more costly. In order to reduce the perceived risk of the decision, many companies will emphasize the use of full-service dealers or retailers. Such full-service retailers will often emphasize personal contact with customers and high quality post purchase service for the product. In contrast, if the product choice process involves low consumer involvement or is based on impulse, intensive distribution is mandated. Thus, the product will be placed in as many retail stores as possible.

Marketing Opportunity Analysis

Another area in which the study of consumer beliefs, attitudes, and behaviors may influence managers is marketing opportunity analysis. As noted earlier in the text, marketing opportunity analysis involves the manager in attempting to identify how changes in demographics, lifestyles, and consumer preferences may lead to potential opportunities or problems. Of particular interest is how such changes in demographics or lifestyles may influence the benefits consumers seek from products. For example, consumers who have joined the lifestyle movement towards health will emphasize such food product attributes as low fat and cholesterol, low sugar content, and high fiber content. Of course, the problem for the marketing manager is to predict successfully such demographic and lifestyle trends so that products with the desired attributes can be designed.

Measuring Attitudes

A final managerial area of importance is the measurement of attitudes. Unless consumer attitudes are measured in a valid and reliable manner, they have little chance of predicting behavior. In general, the method of measurement selected will depend in part upon the type of attitude the researcher desires to assess. Thus, attitudes towards the object will likely be assessed through different scales than will attitudes towards the act or attitudes towards the advertisement. However, regardless of the specific type of attitude, a limited number of basic scales tend to be used by researchers.[48] These are briefly discussed next.

Rating Scales   These are general scales in which the consumer is asked to rate on a scale (usually consisting of five or seven points) his or her favorability towards something. An example might be—"Rate your overall attitude towards Bud Light Beer." The scale might be

Very favorable   1 2 3 4 5 6 7   Very unfavorable

Likert Scales   Likert scales are similar in nature to rating scales. However, they involve asking the consumer to indicate the amount of his or her agreement or disagreement with a statement, such as—"I strongly prefer Classic Coke to the 'new Coke.' "[49] The scale might be

Strongly agree   1 2 3 4 5 6 7   Strongly disagree

Semantic Differential   The semantic differential is often used to assess both consumer beliefs about objects and consumer attitudes. Subjects are asked to describe something by rating it on various scales anchored by opposite-meaning adjectives or statements.[50] Thus, the following scales might be used to assess consumer perceptions of New Coke:

```
Like    1  2  3  4  5   Dislike
Good    1  2  3  4  5   Bad
Strong  1  2  3  4  5   Weak
Sweet   1  2  3  4  5   Bitter
Smooth  1  2  3  4  5   Rough
```

The semantic differential can be used to draw profiles of how consumers view brands. Thus, the researcher could also ask the respondents to rate Classic Coke and Pepsi-Cola on the same scales. Graphs can then be made that visually depict how consumers perceive the brands. Work on the semantic differential has found that people often evaluate objects along three different dimensions—an evaluative dimension (e.g., good–bad, like–dislike), an activity dimension (e.g., fast–slow, active–passive), and a potency dimension (e.g., strong–weak, big–little). When constructing semantic differential scales, researchers should always consider including items that assess these three dimensions.

Constant-Sum Scales   In several attitude theories the researcher must assess respondents' ratings of the importance of an attribute. One commonly used approach to this problem is to use constant-sum scales. In such a scale respondents are asked to divide a certain number of points among attributes proportionate to the importance of each attribute. The number of points that may be assigned depends upon the number of attributes assessed. For small numbers of attributes, say four or less, eleven points may be used. For example, suppose that a researcher wanted to know the relative importance of the attributes of handling, gas mileage, acceleration, and roominess in sports cars. Respondents could be asked to divide eleven points among the attributes so as to best indicate the relative importance of each. A person who assigned five points to acceleration, three points to handling, two points to roominess, and one point to gas mileage is telling the researcher a great deal about the characteristics that he or she is looking for in a car.

Although a variety of other approaches exist to assessing consumer beliefs and attitudes, the brief descriptions just discussed give several commonly used approaches. It is important for managers and public policy makers to have a general understanding of scales that assess beliefs, attitudes, and intentions because such scales appear frequently in research reports.

SUMMARY

The study of the interrelationships among beliefs, attitudes, and behaviors is highly important to the marketing manager and the marketing researcher. Beliefs are the various ideas that consumers have about the extent to which a particular brand possesses various attributes and provides various benefits. Such beliefs may be formed from the exposure to and the processing of information obtained from advertising, friends, or experience with the product.

Over time, the beliefs that a person has about a brand may combine to form an attitude about the brand. The various multiattribute attitude models were designed to describe such a process. In addition, in cases in which the consumer is not highly involved in the decision process, the consumer may buy a brand based upon specific beliefs without having formed attitudes towards the brand.

As noted above, consumers hold beliefs about the extent to which a brand possesses an attribute or benefit. Product attributes are the characteristics that a product may or may not have. Product benefits are the positive outcomes that may result from product use. Particularly in high-involvement purchase situations, consumers may evaluate the importance that the various attributes of a product have for them. Managers should perform research to identify the attributes that their target market considers to be important. Such considerations can influence both product design and promotional strategy.

Consumer attitudes represent the amount of affect or feeling that a person holds for or against a stimulus object, such as a brand, person, company, or idea. Over time, attitudes may be formed because the consumer holds a number of either positive or negative beliefs about an object. Attitudes may also be formed through classical and operant conditioning principles. In addition, evidence exists that positive feelings can result from repeated exposures to a previously neutral stimulus. It seems that simply encountering a product, idea, or person over and over again can lead to more positive feelings.

Consumption behaviors have been discussed in two different ways. The first is through intentions to behave. Intentions to behave are the statements that consumers give when asked about the likelihood that they will engage in some behavior, such as buying a product, supporting a political candidate, or visiting a retail store. Intentions to behave are likely to be formed only when consumers are in high-involvement situations or are asked by a researcher, friend, or other person about their intentions. Actual consumer behavior involves an overt consumer action to purchase a product or service, visit a retail store, vote for a particular political candidate, and so forth.

Consumption behavior can result from a number of different processes, which appear to be governed in part by the type of buying process in which the consumer is engaged. When the consumer is in a high-involvement situation, behavior appears to result after beliefs are formed and attitudes are created. In low-involvement situations in which the consumer engages in limited decision making, behavior appears to occur after a limited number of beliefs are formed. In such a situation, attitudes appear to play a minor role in influencing behavior and are formed only after the consumer purchases and uses the product. In both impulse and habitual purchase situations, evidence exists to suggest that behavior results primarily from the consumer having positive affect and feelings toward the product. The impact of beliefs on behavior is minimal, and they are likely to be formed after the purchase is made. In other situations behavior may be influenced directly without the consumer having formed either beliefs or attitudes about the object to which the behavior is directed. Behavioral influence tends to occur in situations in which strong situational or environmental forces propel the consumer to engage in the behavior.

Another area of importance to managers and market researchers is how consumers make choices. In high-involvement, extended problem-solving situations, consumers appear to follow some type of multiattribute model in which high ratings on one attribute can compensate for low ratings on other attributes. In contrast, in limited decision-making cases, when the consumer is in a low-involvement situation, various choice heuristics may be used. Many of these choice heuristics involve the setting of cutoff points. If the product is rated below the cutoff point, it is eliminated from consideration. Such choice models are called noncompensatory because high ratings cannot compensate for low ratings that fall below the cutoff level. Identifying the type of choice model used by the firm's target market is an important task for managers. Both the design and the promotion of the product should be influenced by the type of choice process the firm's target market uses to select a brand.

Information on beliefs, attitudes, and their relationship to behavior has a variety of implications for marketing strategy. Of particular importance is the process of benefit segmentation. Benefit segmentation involves the division of the market into relatively homogeneous groups of consumers based upon a similarity of needs. In addition, the manager needs to engage in competitive analysis to determine how his product or service compares to that offered by competitors. Managers should also be aware that consumer perceptions of product attributes and benefits can be distorted through the impact of halo effects. The study of how consumers perceive a product in relation to competitors on various attributes can influence decisions on how to position it. In some circumstances, it may be wise to reposition products so that they do not compete directly against well-entrenched brands. Finally, the study of beliefs, attitudes, and behaviors can influence the design of the marketing mix.

Managers should also be familiar with basic attitude scales used by consumer researchers. Some of these scales include the semantic differential, Likert scales, constant-sum scales, and rating scales.

Key Terms

Product attribute
Beliefs
Attributes
Benefits
Objects
Attribute-object belief
Attribute-benefit belief

Object-benefit belief
Cognitive elements
Attribute importance
Attitude
Consumer behavior
Overt consumer behaviors

Covert consumer behaviors
Intentions
Direct influence
Mere exposure phenomenon
Ancestral-based consumption
Hierarchies of effect

Standard learning hierarchy
Routine (limited) decision process
Low-involvement hierarchy
Experientially based decisions
Habitual purchases

Consumer choice pro-
cesses
Multiattribute models
Attitude-toward-the-
object models
Behavioral intentions
model
Subjective norm
Satisficing
Heuristics

Affert-referral heuristic
Conjunctive heuristic
Lexicographic heuristic
Phased strategies
Benefit segmentation
Halo effect
Rating scales
Likert scales
Semantic differential
Constant-sum scale

Review Questions

1. Define the concepts of belief, attitude, and behavior.
2. Distinguish attribute-object, attribute-benefit, and
object-benefit beliefs from each other.
3. How does attribute importance relate to a consumer's self-concept?
4. What is meant by the idea that beliefs, attitudes,
and behaviors may form into hierarchies of effects?
5. What processes account for how beliefs are directly formed?
6. What processes account for the direct formation
of attitudes?
7. Why is it important for advertisers to assess a
consumer's attitude toward an advertisement?
8. Identify three ways in which behaviors may be induced without the formation of strong attitudes
or beliefs.
9. How do the hierarchies of effects differ in high-
versus low-involvement circumstances?
10. How do the hierarchies of effects differ in experiential versus behavioral influence circumstances?
11. Under what circumstances are attitudes most likely
to predict behavior successfully?
12. Why have impulse purchases been categorized
within the experiential perspective in the text?
13. What is meant by a multiattribute choice model?
Differentiate the attitude-toward-the-object model
from the behavioral intentions model.
14. Under what circumstances will consumers tend
to use heuristic models of choice?
15. Distinguish among the conjunctive, lexicographic, and phased-choice models.
16. Define the concept of benefit segmentation and

give an example of a company that has used this
strategy.
17. Give examples of four different types of scales that
can be used to measure attitudes.
18. How might a company's promotional strategy
change when the buying process involves low
rather than high involvement, and involves impulse purchases versus habitual purchases?

Discussion Questions

1. List as many attributes as you can that consumers
may seek in an automobile. You should be able to
identify at least fifteen attributes. Select five of these
attributes and identify the benefits consumers may
receive if the characteristics are present in an automobile.
2. Consider the sports car segment versus the family
car segment of the car market. Rank order the five
attributes that you think are most important for
each of the segments.
3. What are some of the methods that advertisers
use to persuade consumers that automobiles
possess the attributes claimed? Give specific examples when you can, such as Volkswagon having Wilt Chamberlin drive the Beetle to demonstrate its roominess.
4. An industry that has had problems in identifying
the benefits of its product to consumers is the
home computer industry. Identify the attributes
of home computers. What are the tangible benefits consumers can receive from these attributes?
Try to identify some means by which the benefits
of owning home computers can be communicated.
5. Rough out a print advertisement that seeks to influence consumer beliefs about two attributes of
a new soft drink. The specific attributes are: the
soft drink is composed of 90 percent real fruit juice,
and no sugar or artificial sweetener is added.
6. Consider the various advertising campaigns of
Coca-Cola over the last couple of years. What are
the means through which the company has attempted to influence attitudes directly via their
advertising?
7. Identify your favorite and least-favorite advertisements that have been recently broadcast. What are
the reasons for you having such a favorable attitude toward one set of advertisements and such

an unfavorable attitude toward the other? To what extent have these attitudes influenced your attitude toward the product and toward your buying behavior? Why or why not?

8. In an automobile purchase elements of extended decision-making and of experience-based decision making seem to exist. What are the things that an auto salesman can do to appeal to these two sides of the buying process?

9. Go to a grocery store and identify the various means through which marketers attempt to influence your feelings so that you will make an impulse purchase.

10. Think back to the last time you made a high-involvement purchase. Please explain in detail the choice process you used to make the purchase. Which of the choice processes discussed in the chapter did it most closely approximate?

11. For the product that you discussed in question 10, develop an attitude-toward-the-object model of the choice process. That is, list the various brands and attributes that you considered and give belief and importance ratings for each of the attributes of each of the brands.

12. Develop a series of questions to assess consumer perceptions of local fast-food restaurants. Develop questions illustrating each of the different types of scales that can be used to measure attitudes, beliefs, and behavioral intentions.

References

1. M. Fishbein and I. Ajzen, *Belief, Attitude, Intention, and Behavior: An Introduction to Theory and Research*, Reading, Mass.: Addison-Wesley Publishing Co., Inc., 1975.
2. This definition of cognitive elements borrows from two sources: W. A. Scott, "Conceptualizing and Measuring Structural Properties of Cognition," in O. J. Harvey (ed.), *Motivation and Social Interaction*. New York, N.Y.: The Ronald Press Company, 1963, 266–288; and Leon Festinger, *A Theory of Cognitive Dissonance*, Stanford, Calif.: Stanford University Press, 1957.
3. For a succinct summary of cognitive consistency, see Marvin E. Shaw and Phillip R. Costanzo, *Theories of Social Psychology*. New York, N.Y.: McGraw-Hill Book Company, 1970.
4. This brief history of attitudes was adapted from Richard Petty, Thomas Ostrom, and Timothy Brock, *Cognitive Responses in Persuasion*, Hillsdale, N.J.: Lawrence Erlbaum Associates, 1981.
5. Petty et al., *Cognitive Responses in Persuasion*, 31.
6. Darrel J. Bem, *Beliefs, Attitudes, and Human Affairs*, Belmont, Calif.: Brooks/Cole, 1970.
7. Fishbein and Ajzen, *Belief, Attitude, Intention, and Behavior*.
8. Phillip Zimbardo, E. Ebbesen, and C. Maslach, *Influencing Attitudes and Changing Behavior*. Reading, Mass.: Addison-Wesley Publishing Co., Inc., 1977.
9. Such a definition has been used by psychologists, (e.g., W. A. Scott, "Attitude Measurement," in G. Lindzey and E. Aronson (eds.), *The Handbook of Social Psychology* (2d ed., vol. 2), Reading, Mass.: Addison Wesley Publishing Co., Inc., 1968) and in consumer behavior textbooks (e.g., Henry Assael, *Consumer Behavior and Marketing Action*, Boston, Mass.: Kent Publishing Company, 1984.
10. T. M. Ostrom, "The Relationship Between the Affective, Behavioral, and Cognitive Components of Attitudes," *Journal of Experimental Social Psychology*, 5, January 1969, 12–30.
11. Robert A. Zajonc and Hazel Markus, "Affective and Cognitive Factors in Preferences," *Journal of Consumer Research*, 9, September 1982, 123–131.
12. Robert Zajonc, "The Attitudinal Effects of Mere Exposure," *Journal of Personality and Social Psychology Monograph*, 9, 1968, 2, pt. 2.
13. William Wilson, "Feeling More Than We Know: Exposure Effects Without Learning," *Journal of Personality and Social Psychology*, 37, June 1979, 811–821.
14. Walter Nord and J. Paul Peter, "A Behavior Modification Perspective on Marketing," *Journal of Marketing*, 44, Spring 1980, 36–47.
15. Elizabeth C. Hirschman, "Primitive Aspects of Consumption in Modern American Society," *Journal of Consumer Research*, 12, September 1985, 142–154.
16. Hirschman, "Primitive Aspects of Consumption."
17. For an excellent discussion of awareness in conditioning see Charles E. Osgood, *Method and Theory in Experimental Psychology*, New York, NY: Oxford University Press, 1964.
18. Michael Ray, "Marketing Communications and the Hierarchy-of-Effects," in *New Models for Mass*

Communications, P. Clarke (ed.), Beverly Hills, Calif.: Sage Publications, Inc., 1973, 147–176.

19. Robert Lavidge and Gary Steiner, "A Model for Predictive Measurements of Advertising Effectiveness," *Journal of Marketing*, 25, October 1961, 59–62.

20. Herbert Krugman, "The Impact of Television Advertising: Learning Without Involvement," *Public Opinion Quarterly*, 29, October 1961, 59–62.

21. Krugman, "The Impact of Television Advertising."

22. A variety of definitions of involvement have been proposed. For a good review, see John H. Antil, "Conceptualization and Operationalization of Involvement," in *Advances in Consumer Research, XI*, Thomas C. Kinnear (ed.), Ann Arbor, Mich.: Association for Consumer Research, 1984, 203–209.

23. For an excellent discussion of low-involvement decision making, see F. Stewart De Bruicker, "An Appraisal of Low-Involvement Consumer Information Processing," in *Attitude Research Plays for High Stakes*, John Maloney and Bernard Silverman (eds.), Chicago, Ill.: American Marketing Association, 1979, 112–130.

24. Such justifications would work through a self-perception process. See Bem, *Beliefs, Attitudes, and Human Affairs.*

25. James Engel and Roger Blackwell, *Consumer Behavior*, Chicago, Ill.: Holt, Rinehart and Winston, 1982.

26. "Industrial Retail Selling Strategies Designed to Induce Impulse Sales," *Beverage Industry*, June 3, 1977, 6 + .

27. E. Langer and L. Imba, "The Role of Mindlessness in the Perception of Deviance," *Journal of Personality and Social Psychology*, 38, September 1980, 360–367.

28. P. Weinberg and W. Gottwald, "Impulsive Consumer Buying as a Result of Emotions," *Journal of Business Research*, 10, March 1982, 43–57.

29. Dennis W. Rook and Stephen J. Hoch, "Consuming Impulses," *Advances in Consumer Behavior*, 12, E. Hirschman and M. Holbrock, (eds.), Ann Arbor, Mich.: Association for Consumer Research, 1985, 23–27.

30. "The Year of the Yuppie," *Newsweek*, December 31, 1984, 14–24.

31. "The Year of the Yuppie."

32. Michael Ray, "Marketing Communications and the Hierarchy-of-Effects."

33. Wayne D. Hoyer, "An Examination of Consumer Decision Making for a Common Repeat Purchase Product," *Journal of Consumer Research*, 11, December 1984, 822–829.

34. Peter Wright, "Consumer Choice Strategies: Simplifying Versus Optimizing," *Journal of Marketing Research*, 11, February 1976, 60–67.

35. Michael D. Johnson, "Consumer Choice Strategies for Comparing Noncomparable Alternatives," *Journal of Consumer Research*, 11, December 1984, 741–753.

36. Richard W. Olshavsky and Donald H. Granbois, "Consumer Decision Making—Fact or Fiction," *Journal of Consumer Research*, 6, September 1979, 93–100.

37. Hillel Einhorn, and Robin M. Hogarth, "Behavioral Decision Theory: Processes of Judgment and Choice," *Annual Review of Psychology*, 32, 1981, 53–58.

38. Hoyer, "An Examination of Consumer Decision Making."

39. Martin Fishbein, "The Search for Attitudinal-Behavioral Consistency," in *Behavioral Science Foundations of Consumer Research*, Joel S. Cohen (ed.), New York, N.Y.: Free Press, 1972.

40. Models similar to this may be found in Fishbein and Ajzen, *Belief, Attitude, Intention and Behavior;* and in F. Bass and W. Talarzyk, "Attitude Model for the Study of Brand Preference," *Journal of Marketing Research*, 9, February 1972, 93–96.

41. Ibid. Readers should note that the behavioral intentions model is now called the "theory of reasoned action." I have retained the older name to emphasize its focus on predicting behavioral intentions.

42. An example of articles finding the behavioral intentions model to be superior to attitude-toward-objects model is Michael J. Ryan and E. H. Bonfield, "Fishbein's Intentions Model: A Test of External and Pragmatic Validity," *Journal of Marketing*, 44, Spring 1980, 82–95.

43. R. J. Pomazal and J. J. Jaccard, "An Informational Approach to Altruistic Behavior," *Journal of Personality and Social Psychology*, 33, September, 1976, 317–326. Also see, M. J. Ryan and E. H. Bonfield, "The Fishbein Extended Model and Consumer Behavior," *Journal of Consumer Research*, 2, September 1975, 118–136.

44. Alan Newell and Herbert Simon, *Human Problem*

Solving, Englewood Cliffs, N.J.: Prentice-Hall, Inc., 1972.

45. This section on choice heuristics relies heavily on work by Peter Wright, "Consumer Choice Strategies."

46. M. Reilly and R. Holman, "Does Task Complexity or Cue Intercorrelation Affect Choice of an Information-Processing Strategy: An Empirical Investigation," in *Advances in Consumer Research, IV,* W. D. Perrault, Jr. (ed.), Atlanta, Ga.: Association for Consumer Research, 1977, 185–190.

47. For example, see Douglas J. McConnel, "Effect of Pricing on Perception of Quality," *Journal of Applied Psychology, 52,* August 1968, 331–334.

48. For a more complete discussion of the measurement of attitudes see Gilbert A. Churchill, *Marketing Research,* Hinsdale, Ill.: The Dryden Press, 1979.

49. R. A. Likert, "A Technique for the Measurement of Attitudes," *Archives of Psychology,* No. 140, June 1932.

50. C. E. Osgood, C. J. Suci, and P. H. Tannenbaum, *The Measurement of Meaning,* Urbana, Ill.: University of Illinois Press, 1957.

8

Communicating the Persuasive Message

CONSUMER VIGNETTE

Frightening and Laughing Your Way to Profits

"I remember hearing somebody say I was . . . dead, . . . I thought about Janice and Bobby, . . . Who'd take care of them now?" These words were whispered in a television commercial by a man on an operating table as the line on the oscilloscope went flat. After quick work by the medical personnel, the man survived. The goal of the sponsor of the ad was to scare people into buying life insurance. The campaign featured four commercials—a woman drowning, a volunteer fireman overcome by smoke, and a man rushed to a hospital in an ambulance, in addition to the surgery patient.

Wendy's one-liner, "Where's the beef," became the most-quoted saying of 1984. In the eight months after the launching of the "Where's the beef" campaign, the amount of beef sold at Wendy's restaurants increased by 20 percent. The company was able to point out humorously the importance of one hamburger attribute—the size of the burger in relation to the bun. Those three small words held great meaning to consumers, playing on the idea that in too many cases hamburger chains were promising more than they were delivering.

In each of these cases, a company developed a strategy to persuade consumers to do something by changing their beliefs and attitudes. Numerous methods of changing beliefs and attitudes exist, and this chapter identifies a number of these for readers.

Based in part on Bill Abrams, "New Prudential Ads Portray Death as No Laughing Matter," *The Wall Street Journal,* November 10, 1983, 33; and Amity Shales, "Wendy's Has No Beefs About Success of William Welter's Advertising Ideas," *The Wall Street Journal,* September 7, 1984, 39.

236

INTRODUCTION

Persuasion is omnipresent in our everyday lives. Radio and television commercials, print advertisements, and messages from sales personnel all seek to persuade us. In our encounters with friends and acquaintances, persuasive communications are commonplace. A friend who says, "Hey, there's a great new movie showing at the Bijou—do you want to go?" is engaging in a persuasion attempt.

What is **persuasion?** Persuasion is a process in which a communication is delivered in order to change beliefs and/or attitudes in a desired manner. Its purpose is to influence others so that they will engage in a desired behavior at some time in the future. The idea is that by changing beliefs and/or attitudes, behavior change will follow at some point in the future. This definition distinguishes persuasion from coercion. Coercion implies that the communicator is applying some type of reward (e.g., money) or punisher (e.g., threats) in a heavy-handed manner to force an action. Because coercive tactics tend to be either illegal (e.g., using bribes) or unethical, this topic will not be discussed.

The psychological processes that underlie persuasion can be categorized as to whether they occur under high or low consumer involvement conditions.[1] When persuasion occurs under *high-involvement* conditions, changes in beliefs tend to precede changes in attitudes. In addition, changes in attitudes tend to precede changes in behavior. In other words, the standard hierarchy of effects is in operation. One of the primary goals of communicators in such high-involvement situations should be to minimize the amount of counterargumentation that results from the message.

When persuasion occurs under *low-involvement* conditions, only limited attention is paid to the persuasive message. As such, through the repetition of the message, beliefs are slowly formed with minimal or no counterargumentation occurring. In the low-involvement situation, then, attitudes tend not to be formed until after the behavior occurs and the low-involvement hierarchy operates. In such circumstances, a primary goal of the communicator is figuring out how to have high repetition of the message without the consumer growing tired and bored with it.

In order to present the psychological processes that underlie the persuasive process, a model is presented in this chapter. The model shows the sequence of steps that occur in persuasion and the differences that occur in high- and low-involvement circumstances.

In addition to understanding the psychological processes at work, one must also investigate the communication factors involved in persuasion. In order to persuade someone to do something, four components are necessary—a source of information, a message, some channel of communication, and a receiver of information. Another purpose of the chapter is to discuss the various findings on how to optimize the effectiveness of persuasive messages through the adroit use of appropriate messages and channels of communication.

The introductory vignette illustrated two of the communications factors discussed in this chapter—the use of fear appeals and humor in messages. For example, Wendy's sought to make highly salient to consumers one attribute of the hamburger—the size of the patty. The goal of the ad was to increase the perceived importance of this product characteristic. Thus, through repetition and the use of humor, Wendy's was able to communicate an important concept and at least temporarily increase its market share. Humor is just one type of message characteristic. Creating fear is another approach to persuasion, and it was used effectively in the "deathbed" advertisements of the insurance company.

In the sections that follow, the chapter first presents a model of the persuasion process and discusses some of the psychological theories of persuasion. Next, the chapter identifies the various aspects of the communications process and their impact on persuasion. In particular, the effects of message and channel characteristics are emphasized. Finally, the managerial implications of the material on persuasion are discussed.

A MODEL OF THE PERSUASION PROCESS

Figure 8–1 presents a model of the persuasion process.[2] In the model one finds that a consumer first receives a communication. The term *communication* is defined broadly to include all aspects of the message, including the sender, the type of message given, and the channel through which it moves. Upon receiving the message, the consumer begins to process it. Depending on such factors as the message content, the nature of the consumer, and the situation that the consumer is in, the person will process it with higher or lower amounts of involvement.

Depending on the amount of involvement, belief and attitude change can be said to take one of two routes.[3] When high-involvement information processing occurs, the person is said to take the central route to persuasion. In contrast, when in low-involvement circumstances, the consumer is said to be engaging in a peripheral route to persuasion.

When attitude and belief change occur via the central route, the consumer is attending carefully to the message being received. The person will diligently consider the communication and compare it to his or her own attitudinal position. As a result, the consumer is likely to generate a number of **cognitive responses** to the communication. Based in part upon the extent to which the cognitive responses are supportive or nonsupportive of the message, the consumer will have belief change. Following the changes in beliefs, the consumer may then experience attitude change. Evidence exists that belief and attitude change that occurs through the central route is relatively enduring and predictive of behavior.[4]

Figure 8–1   A model of persuasion.

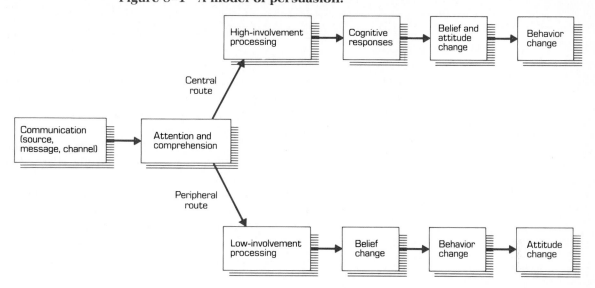

When the consumer engages in low-involvement information processing, he or she is said to be moving through the peripheral route to persuasion. In such instances, cognitive responses are much less likely to occur, because the consumer is *not* carefully considering the pros and cons of the issue and giving it diligent consideration. Instead, the consumer tends to use peripheral cues to determine whether to accept or reject the message, such as the type of source presenting it and the context in which the message was presented (e.g., a pleasant lunch). In such circumstances beliefs may change, but it is unlikely that attitudes or feelings will be influenced. Thus, measures of attitudes are likely to show them to be relatively temporary and unpredictive of behavior in such low-involvement circumstances.[5]

In summary, the model of persuasion depicts two important points about the persuasion process. First, the route to persuasion depends in part on the involvement of the consumer. In high-involvement circumstances a central route may be taken in which more information processing occurs. In contrast, in low-involvement circumstances a more peripheral route may be taken in which little information processing occurs. The second point the model communicates is that the hierarchy of effects is different depending upon the route to persuasion. In the central route the standard hierarchy of effects occurs (i.e., beliefs lead to attitudes, which lead to behaviors). In the peripheral route the low-involvement hierarchy occurs—i.e., beliefs are followed by behavior, which is then followed by the formation of attitudes.

THREE PSYCHOLOGICAL APPROACHES TO PERSUASION

In order to understand the persuasion process, it is useful to present three psychological theories. The first—the attitude-toward-the-object model—is familiar to readers because it was presented in Chapter 7. It is a useful way of understanding how to change beliefs and attitudes in high-involvement situations. The second model is labeled **balance theory** and is relevant to both high- and low-involvement circumstances. The final approach is called **social judgment theory,** and it specifically deals with the effects of involvement on persuasion. As considered in Highlight 8–1, however, attempts to persuade depend very much on the believability of advertising claims.

Persuasion and the Attitude-Toward-the-Object Model

In Chapter 7, a group of attitude models was discussed that postulates the attitudes that result from an overall evaluation of a consumer's belief system about an object or issue. Called attitude-toward-the-object models, they hypothesize that an attitude results from the formation of: (1) a rating of the importance of various attributes that an object may have, and (2) a rating of the person's belief that the object possesses the attribute.

In order to change an existing attitude, a communicator has several options. First, he can attempt to change the perceived importance of an attribute. The "Where's the beef" advertisements initiated by Wendy's International, in part utilized such a strategy. One goal of the ads was to make highly

---

HIGHLIGHT 8–1

Changing Attitudes Require Believable Ads

In 1984 *Advertising Age* conducted a study to determine the believability of various types of advertising claims. The 1,250 respondents were asked about the believability of three types of approaches—sample demonstrations, qualitative claims, and statistical claims. Of the three, only sample demonstrations reached the "neutral" category of believability. Both qualitative and statistical claims were rated as "somewhat unbelievable" overall.

The results of the study also found that females were more positive than males towards the believability of advertising. Also, the higher the income, the lower the respondents rated the product claims of advertisers. In addition, the study asked consumers to compare television advertising to "other" types of advertising. The results showed that the respondents rated the overall quality of television ads to be slightly lower than advertising overall. Ratings of television advertising decreased as income levels rose. Respondents were also asked to agree or disagree with the statement, "Advertising is generally trustworthy and honest." Among the respondents, 5 percent strongly agreed, 39 percent agreed, 6 percent were neutral, 35 percent disagreed, and 12 percent strongly disagreed. (Four percent failed to respond.)

The results of the study clearly indicate that changing attitudes is going to be tough when many consumers simply do not believe the claims made by advertisers.

Based on Nancy Millman, "Product Claims Not Believable," *Advertising Age*, March 5, 1984, 1, 32.

salient the size of the hamburgers from competing fast-food chains. If the importance of the attribute could be changed, there would be a good chance that the overall attitudes of consumers towards Wendy's would change.

Changing the importance of attributes is not easy, however, for communicators. The weight that consumers give to various types of information is closely related to their own personality structures and self-concept. Thus, if a person views himself as a person who eats very lightly, advertisements extolling the size of a hamburger probably will not have much influence in changing the importance of a size attribute.

Rather than attempt to change the importance of an attribute, another strategy involves introducing a new attribute. As is discussed later in the chapter, it is generally easier to influence weakly held beliefs and attitudes than ones that are strongly held. Thus, if a person essentially has no belief about the importance of a particular attribute, it may be possible to influence that importance rating. An example of a company attempting to add an attribute for evaluation is General Motors. In the 1980s the automobiles produced by GM began to receive excellent safety ratings by various automotive testing agencies. The company began to incorporate such information in its advertising as another reason why people should buy cars from GM.

A third way of influencing attitudes through a multiattribute model approach is to change the belief that an object has a particular attribute. This is probably the easiest of the three approaches, because a company can use a variety of methods to show that the particular characteristic of the product has changed. For example, the company could use demonstrations or trustworthy endorsers to show and explain the change. Again, General Motors can be used as an example of a company that has attempted to change consumer perceptions of the extent to which its products possess a particular attribute. The Chevrolet Division of General Motors Corporation developed a print advertisement designed in part to change beliefs about the nimbleness of the Corvette. Historically the Corvette was known as a fast car that possessed poor handling characteristics. In the ad, shown in Figure 8–2, the company sought to persuade consumers that the Corvette handles well by comparing its ability to steer and handle well under wet conditions to four other prestige sports cars. The ad effectively acts as a persuasion agent to change consumer beliefs about the handling of the sports car.

Table 8–1 summarizes the three methods of changing attitudes via compensatory processes.

Persuasion and Balance Theory

Another approach to changing attitudes involves the creation of a **cognitive imbalance** within the target of persuasion. The objective is to make use of the tendency of people to maintain cognitive consistency among the various ideas and concepts about which they think. Cognitive consistency is the name applied to the tendency of people to maintain a logical and consistent set of interconnected attitudes. Thus, by deliberately creating cognitive inconsistency, the skillful communicator can induce consumers to change their atti-

Figure 8–2   **This ad attempts to change consumers' beliefs about one attribute of the Corvette—its handling characteristics.** (*Courtesy of the Chevrolet Division of General Motors Corporation.*)

tudes in order to bring their cognitive system back into balance. In order to explain the mechanisms behind the operation of cognitive consistency, it is necessary to explain balance theory.

Balance theory was originated by one of the founders of social psychol-

Table 8–1   Three Methods of Changing Attitudes Via Compensatory Processes

Method 1
Change the perceived importance of the attributes.

Advantage: Can increase the attitude rating of a product or service without changing the product or service in any way.

Disadvantage: Very difficult to do because importance ratings are often tied to the consumer's self-concept.

Method 2
Change the product-attribute beliefs.

Advantage: Easier to do because the company can use demonstrations or trustworthy sources to present the message. Beliefs about the extent to which products contain attributes are not usually connected to a consumer's self-concept.

Disadvantage: May involve changing the product.

Method 3
Add a new attribute for consideration.

Advantage: Beliefs and attitudes are easier to change when they are weakly held.

Disadvantage: May involve changing the product or service. Requires extensive promotional efforts to get new information to target market.

ogy, Fritz Heider.[6] As originally conceived, the theory dealt with the cognitive relationships between an observer (o), another person (p), and an impersonal object (x). The idea of the theory is that the cognitive elements may form a unit in which each is linked to the other. Figure 8–3 shows an example of such a unit.

Two types of connections exist that join the cognitive elements within a unit—sentiment connections and unit connections. **Sentiment connec-**

Figure 8–3   An example of cognitive elements in a balance theory framework.

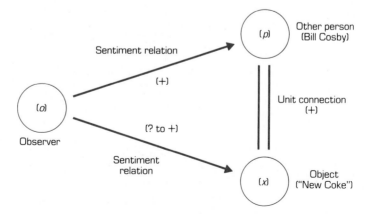

tions are identical in definition to the term *attitude* used in this text. Thus, sentiment relations are the observer's evaluations of other people and of other attitudinal objects. They are the positive or negative feelings that the observer may have towards the other person and the object. Sentiment connections are given a positive or negative algebraic sign depending upon whether the feeling toward p or x is positive or negative.

The second type of connection is called a **unit relation.** A unit relation occurs when the observer perceives that the person and object are somehow connected to each other. The factors that govern whether a person perceives such a connection are the same principles of perceptual organization discussed in Chapter 5 on information processing. Thus, p and x would be perceived as having a unit relation through such principles as proximity, similarity, continuation, and common fate. A positive unit connection indicates that p and x are perceived as related and as forming a unit. A null sign indicates that no relation exists between p and x. In such a case, the observer would not view the three elements as forming a unit, and no cognitive-consistency forces would operate.

The basic premise of balance theory is that people prefer to maintain a balanced state among the cognitive elements of p, o, and x, if they are perceived as forming a unit. A balanced state was defined by Heider as a situation in which the cognitive elements fit together harmoniously with no stress for change. Such "harmony" occurred when the multiplication of the signs of the connections between the elements resulted in a positive value. As shown in Figure 8–4, a balanced state would result from having three positive signs or from two negative signs and one positive sign. An imbalanced state would occur if one sign were positive and two signs were negative.

Figure 8–4   Examples of balanced and imbalanced states.

A. Balanced states

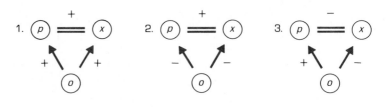

B. Imbalanced states

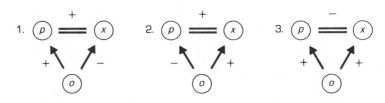

The key point made by Heider is that balanced states are preferred to imbalanced states. Further, if an imbalanced state is experienced, the person is motivated to change the signs of one or more of the cognitive relations. Through a type of unconscious, mental rationalization the person comes to view one or more of the sentiment and/or unit relations differently.

Although companies may not realize that they are using cognitive consistency procedures to change attitudes, one can identify numerous cases when their strategies employ principles of balance theory. Indeed, the use of celebrity endorsers to sponsor products fits balance model principles quite well. Companies strive to select endorsers who are viewed as positively as possible by consumers. From a balance theory perspective, they are attempting to maximize the strength of the sentiment relation between the observer (o) and the person (p). In addition, successful companies will attempt to create a unit connection between the endorser and the brand (x). Various ways of establishing this unit connection include:

1. Hiring endorsers who are known experts in using the product. For example, having a tennis star, such as Chris Evert Lloyd, endorse a company's tennis racket or tennis shoe.
2. Signing the endorser to long-term, exclusive contracts, so that the celebrity is associated only with the company's brand. Manufacturers of perfumes and cosmetics have long used such a strategy. For example, Shelley Hack for many years was associated only with Charlie perfume.
3. Having the endorser consistently wear or use the product whenever he or she is in public view, so that he or she is strongly associated with the product. Texaco Corporation has long used Bob Hope as a celebrity endorser. Mr. Hope apparently has taken his duties with Texaco seriously, occasionally mentioning Texaco in a positive way in such noncommercial appearances as those at a golf tournament.

A classic recent example of a company using a celebrity endorser is Coca-Cola's hiring of Bill Cosby to endorse New Coke. When the new Coca-Cola came out in early 1985, the immediate public reaction was quite mixed, and the Coca-Cola Company hired Bill Cosby to tout the taste of the product. The goal was to link Cosby (who was and is extremely popular) with the new product. With these strong positive connections, a tendency should have then existed for consumers to change their attitudes towards the product in a more favorable direction. The goal was to create cognitive imbalance. The hope was that consumers would achieve balance by changing their attitude towards the new Coca-Cola.

However, consumers do not always change attitudes as marketing managers plan. In general, one finds that consumers change the sign of the weakest connection in an imbalanced cognitive system.[7] Thus, people who were strongly against the new cola formulation may have changed their impression of Bill Cosby in an unfavorable direction or decided that Cosby really did not believe what he was saying about New Coke. Indeed, with Coca-Cola

Company introducing Classic Coke, it looks as though the strategy met with minimal success.

Social Judgment Theory and Persuasion

A third psychological approach influencing attitude change is social judgment theory. A key idea behind the theory is that the same factors that influence **psychophysical judgments** also influence attitude expression. Psychophysics involves the study of the ability of individuals to discriminate and categorize stimuli.[8] The work on "just noticeable differences" and on "absolute thresholds," discussed in Chapter 5 on information processing, are examples of psychophysical concepts.

From a social judgment perspective, when individuals must make a judgment about something, they compare the incoming message to their initial attitude, which acts as a **frame of reference** for the judgment. As such, judgment requires a discrimination or choice between the frame of reference and the alternative. The frame of reference, or initial attitude, is formed through experience and represents an individual's prior experiences, feelings, and interests on the issue in question. It acts as a type of anchor to which the issue in question is compared on the judgmental scale.[9] For example, a student may receive a communication from the university he or she is attending that tuition costs will be raised. The student will already have developed an attitude about the level of tuition at the university, which acts as the frame of reference to which new communications are compared. The question addressed by social judgment theory concerns how the student will perceive the communication and how it will influence the student's attitude towards the idea of a tuition increase.

Latitudes of Acceptance and Rejection   One of the findings of social judgment theory is that people form **latitudes of acceptances** and **rejection** around attitudinal frames of reference. Immediately surrounding this initial attitude is an area of acceptance. Communications falling within this range on the judgmental scale will tend to be assimilated. **Assimilation** refers to the idea that the communication will be viewed as more congruent with the position of the receiver than it really is, because it falls within the latitude of acceptance. In such instances, the receiver is likely to indicate that he or she agrees with the attitude statement. **Contrast effects** tend to occur when the attitude statement falls into the latitude of rejection. The latitude of rejection represents positions on the scale of judgment that are well outside of the latitude of acceptance. When an attitudinal statement is perceived as falling into the latitude of rejection, a contrast effect tends to occur. In such instances the attitude statement is rejected and may be viewed as more opposed to the position of the receiver than it really is.

Figure 8–5 diagrams latitudes of acceptance and rejection. The underlying judgment scale is the receiver's favorability or feeling towards the communication. Let us say that a consumer receives the communication that General Motors Corporation was using in 1985—"GM sweats the details." The message was part of a campaign to persuade consumers that GM was attend-

Figure 8–5   Effects of initial position on latitudes of acceptance and rejection.

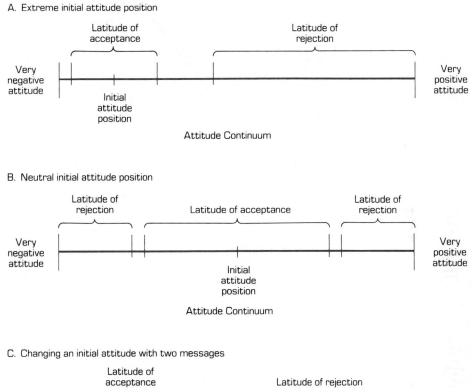

A. Extreme initial attitude position

B. Neutral initial attitude position

C. Changing an initial attitude with two messages

MA = Perceived position of Message A
MB = Perceived position of Message B
A = Assimilation effect for Message A (i.e., attitude moves toward message)
→
B = Contrast effect for Message B (i.e., attitude moves away from message)
←
X = The position of the message on the attitude continuum

ing to the "fit and finish" of its automobiles. If the statement falls within the receiver's latitude of acceptance, the statement may be assimilated such that the individual perceives it as closer to his or her initial attitude position than it really is. In contrast, if the message falls within the latitude of rejection, a contrast may occur so that it is perceived as further from his or her initial attitude position than it really is.

The Effects of Commitment to a Position and Involvement   One of the findings of researchers is that people differ in their ability to accept or tolerate positions different from their own. The results of a number of studies have indicated that strong commitment to a position resulted in a widening of the latitude of rejection and a narrowing of the regions of acceptance.[10] The level of commitment to an issue is associated with the extremity of the position held by the receiver. That is, if the receiver's initial position is either very positive or very negative, he or she will tend to be more committed to the position.

A second factor associated with the size of the latitudes of acceptance and rejection appears to be the level of involvement of the receiver. To the extent that the receiver is highly involved in the issue, the latitude of acceptance will be smaller and the latitude of rejection larger.[11] Examples A and B in Figure 8–5 exemplify the differences in the sizes of the latitudes of acceptance and rejection depending upon the initial position of the receiver.

The managerial implication of commitment and involvement is that persuasion becomes more difficult as levels of commitment and involvement increase. Consumers who are highly involved in a purchase will tend to exert greater energy in searching for information and in examining the information obtained. Consequently, they are better able to reject communications that contain information which does not match their desires. Such a conclusion meshes well with the findings that consumers who are highly involved tend to generate more **counterarguments** to messages. Although high commitment to a position also acts to narrow the latitude of acceptance, it probably works through a process different from that of consumer involvement in an issue. Rather than causing the consumer to engage in greater information processing, commitment may cause the consumer to engage in less cognitive effort. The result is that communications which do not seem to fit the frame of reference may be simply rejected outright without giving much thought to the ideas they contain. True believers in causes tend to show such tendencies. Thus, ardent antibusiness crusaders may reject any positive statements about American corporations simply because the communication is positive—i.e., it falls into their latitude of rejection.

Inducing Attitude Change   From a social judgment perspective the relation of the communication to the individual's initial frame of reference is crucial in determining whether the persuasive message will change that person's attitude. The results of a number of studies indicate that to have the best chance of creating attitude change, communications should fall just within the boundaries of the latitude of acceptance.[12] As shown in example C of Figure 8–5, if the message is perceived as falling just inside the latitude of acceptance (message A), the initial attitude, or frame of reference, may shift out to the message. In this manner the message is assimilated into the receiver's frame of reference, and in doing so actually shifts the initial attitude.

Messages that fall into the latitude of rejection may actually result in a contrast or **boomerang effect.** As shown in example C of Figure 8–5, the message perceived as in the latitude of rejection may result in a shifting of the initial attitude away from the message. In such an instance, the message would be rejected outright and cause the attitude to shift in the opposite direction from that intended.

The findings of social judgment theorists have major managerial implications. Perhaps most important is the idea that prior to developing persuasive communications marketers should conduct research studies to identify the initial attitude of the target group on the communication issue. Furthermore, pretests of potential messages should be performed to determine the reaction of the target audience to them. Identifying the exact locations of the regions of acceptance and rejection is difficult because they will vary from person to person, but it is possible to insure that messages that will result in boomerang effects are not created. Such a goal may sound easy to reach; however, in practice it is difficult because the natural tendency of firms is to create messages that are as strong as possible. Extreme messages are just the type that may cause the boomerang effect to occur. Rather than trying to induce large changes in the target audience with a single communication, a better goal is to attempt to change attitudes in small increments by creating messages just within the boundaries of the latitude of acceptance. Over time the audience may be moved slowly in the desired attitudinal direction.

MARKETING COMMUNICATIONS

Closely related to the topic of persuasion is that of marketing communications. As noted earlier in the textbook, most marketing and public policy communications are emitted for the purpose of changing attitudes and beliefs. Researchers have developed a **model of communications** in order to show the relationships among the various factors that influence the effectiveness and impact of persuasive communications.[13] Figure 8–6 presents one version of this model. The model proposes that five separate categories of factors control the effectiveness of communications: source characteristics, medium characteristics, message content, contextual factors, and audience characteristics.

As shown in Figure 8–6, persuasive communications begin with a source of information who encodes and delivers a message. A number of variables have been found to influence audience reactions to sources of information, including the source's expertise, likability, trustworthiness, and physical attractiveness. The source of information then encodes his or her ideas into a message. Numerous strategies exist for encoding messages. A communicator must think through such questions as whether a fear appeal should be used, whether a conclusion should be drawn at the end of the communication,

Figure 8–6   A communications model.

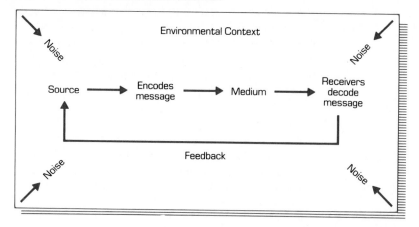

and whether the message should be one-sided or two-sided. The message is delivered through some medium of transmission. The medium could be face-to-face or via print, radio, or television. The characteristics of the medium will influence the interpretation of the message as well as how its information is processed. The message is then received by members of an audience, who decode and interpret the communication. Various characteristics of the audience can moderate the effects of persuasive communications. Such factors as personality, sex, intelligence, and involvement in the issue will mediate how receivers decode the information and react to the communication. Finally, the entire communication process takes place within a general environmental context. Various environmental stimuli may be present during the communication process to distract the audience, influence their mood, or act to create noise in the transmission of the message.

As is readily observed, the communications model presented above includes concepts derived from a variety of behavioral science areas. For example, the various source effects are discussed in Chapter 11 on personal influence. Similarly, the characteristics of the audience were discussed in Chapter 4 on personality and psychographics. Many of the contextual factors influencing communications are discussed in Chapter 10 on situational influences. Examples of these situational factors are physical surroundings, social context, temporary antecedent states (e.g., mood), task definition, and time.

The analysis of the remaining two categories of factors influencing the effectiveness of persuasive communications (characteristics of the message and of the medium) are best tackled in the present chapter. Possessing an understanding of both categories of factors is crucial for developing the most effective communication and then placing it in the most effective medium. The following two subsections discuss in turn messages and then medium characteristics.

Message Characteristics

The effects of message content and construction on receivers have been intensively studied by researchers. **Message content** refers to the strategies that may be used to communicate an idea to an audience. In contrast, **message construction** refers to such issues as where information should be placed in a message to get maximum impact and how often information should be repeated in a message. Various considerations in constructing a message and in developing its content are discussed below.

Developing Message Content   The logical first step in creating a message is to determine its content. That is, the communicator must identify the types of arguments that will be used to persuade the receivers of the information. A variety of questions exist for communicators to consider in developing message content. These include:

- ☐ How simple or complex should the message be?
- ☐ Should a conclusion be drawn?
- ☐ Should comparisons to competitors be made?
- ☐ Should the message be one-sided or two-sided?
- ☐ Is it appropriate to use a fear appeal?
- ☐ Is it appropriate to use humor?
- ☐ To what extent should statistics be used versus more vivid and concrete descriptions?

MESSAGE COMPLEXITY.   In order for a message to have any effect on a receiver, he or she must first be exposed to the message. In addition, the receiver must then *attend* to the information and *comprehend* it. (Note that exposure, attention, and comprehension are the information-processing steps discussed earlier in the text.) A factor that strongly influences the ability of receivers to comprehend the information is the **message complexity.** If the information is too complex, or worse yet, presented in a garbled, confusing manner, receivers are less likely to comprehend and be persuaded by the information. For example, in one study people received messages that argued for the desirability of sleeping less each night. Some received a comprehensible message, while others received a garbled, difficult-to-follow message. The results revealed that those who received the comprehensible message had more attitude change, regardless of the amount of sleep recommended and of the credibility of the source.[14]

DRAWING CONCLUSIONS.   Another question involving the developing of message content is whether the communicator should draw a conclusion for the audience. In a message the communicator may generate a number of arguments that support a particular position. These arguments may logically build on one another and lead to an inference that the audience should buy the product. Thus, an advertiser might state: "Our brand is built better, it will last longer, and it is priced lower than other brands." The conclusion that could be drawn is that the consumer should go out and buy it. The question, however, is, Should the communication expressly draw the conclusion and tell the audience to go out and buy the product or let the audience members draw the conclusion themselves?

Research on the effects of **drawing conclusions** is somewhat mixed. In one summary of the studies on the topic, it was suggested that the answer depended on the complexity of the message and the involvement of the audience.[15] If the message is relatively complex and/or if the audience is not involved in the topic, it appears that a conclusion *should be* drawn in the message. In contrast, if the audience is highly involved and the message is not particularly complex for that audience, it may be better to let the audience make the inference themselves.

COMPARATIVE MESSAGES. A **comparative message** is one in which the communicator compares the positive and negative aspects of his position to the positive and negative aspects of a competitor's position. The approach is frequently used by advertisers who may explicitly identify one or more competitors for the purpose of claiming superiority over them.[16] Since the early 1970s the Federal Trade Commission has encouraged the use of comparative advertising out of the belief that naming a competitor would assist consumers in evaluating a claim of superiority.[17] Comparative advertising has been argued to be useful for small companies who are trying to enter a market, particularly if their claims are based upon research done by independent third parties.[18] The opinion of many marketing managers was expressed by a Coca-Cola executive who said, "Comparative ads are good when you're new, but when you're the standard, it just gives a lot of free publicity to your competitors."[19]

Despite the logic and frequent use of comparative advertising, the research on its effectiveness has generally been negative. Studies have found that comparative advertising is no more effective than traditional advertising in influencing believability, credibility, attitude towards the brand, purchase intentions, or behavior.[20] Some researchers have suggested that what may inhibit the positive effects of comparative advertising in the research studies is the generation of counterarguments to the ads. That is, in the research studies the subjects tend to be in a high-involvement situation (i.e., they want to look good for the experimenters), and as a consequence they develop more counterarguments and resist the persuasive message.[21] It is quite possible that in the "everyday world" consumers are much less involved and consequently would engage in much less counterarguing to comparative ads.

In one recent research study, evidence for the effectiveness of comparative advertisements was found. The researchers noted that in most instances comparative advertising was initiated by a non-brand leader or challenger in a product category. The goal of the challenger is for consumers to consider its brand with the leader and be part of a consumer's evoked set. In an early study testing these hypotheses, the results were positive.[22] Thus, tentative evidence exists that comparative ads do result in consumers considering to a greater extent a challenger along with the brand leader.

In another recent study, researchers presented subjects with comparative ads favoring either a Scripto pen or a Paper Mate pen. The subjects were then given coupons so that they could buy either of the pens. The results revealed that the pen favored in the comparative ads (whether Scripto or Paper Mate) was purchased significantly more frequently.[23]

Comparative ads may take on many forms. Highlight 8–2 presents an unusual comparison of two brands of automobiles.

ONE- VERSUS TWO-SIDED MESSAGES. Somewhat related to the use of messages in which a competitor is also mentioned are messages in which both sides of an issue are mentioned. Figure 8–7 shows an advertisement that uses a two-sided message. The message from R.J. Reynolds Tobacco Company addresses the issue of "smoker's rights." In one column is information from the non-smokers' side and in the other column is information from the smokers' side of the issue. The result is a two-sided message which communicates effectively the idea that two viewpoints on the topic exist.

Research on the effectiveness of two-sided messages has shown the strategy to be an effective persuasion technique. Presenting both sides of an argument gives the appearance of fairness and may lower the tendency of consumers to counterargue against the message and the source. Particularly in cases in which the audience is unfriendly, when it knows that opposition arguments exist, or when it is likely to hear arguments from the opposition, two-sided communications may be effective.[24] In fact, the presentation and then the refutation of arguments that the "other side" may present can act as an effective **inoculation technique.** That is, by giving the audience the

---

HIGHLIGHT 8–2

A Different Type of Comparative Advertisement

On Wednesday, February 20, 1985, an advertisement appeared in *The Wall Street Journal* for the Saab Turbo. In the ad the Saab was compared to a car that cost more than $30,000 than it did—a Lotus. Of course, the point of the ad was not to induce high-rolling consumers to buy the Saab rather than the Lotus. After all, the cars exist in two completely different markets. The comparison was done to point out vividly the technical sophistication of the Saab. The headline of the ad read, "You don't have to go to Saab for a 4-valves-per-cylinder turbo engine. You could buy a Lotus instead."

The ad went on to point out that the Lotus goes from zero to sixty miles per hour in 6.6 seconds whereas the Saab takes 8.6 seconds (still very fast), that the Saab has 56.5 feet of cargo area as compared to Lotus's 8.2 cubic feet, and that the Lotus costs almost $30,000 more.

Not all comparative ads are developed to help the consumer choose between the products compared. Sometimes they are used to attract attention to and/or enhance the image of the lower-priced and possibly lower-quality brand.

Figure 8–7 **This ad uses a two-sided message.** (*Courtesy of R.J. Reynolds Tobacco Company.*)

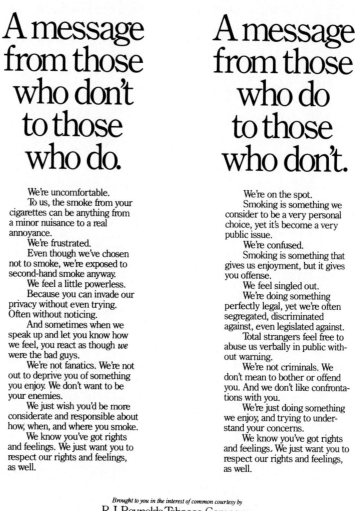

A message
from those
who don't
to those
who do.

We're uncomfortable.
To us, the smoke from your cigarettes can be anything from a minor nuisance to a real annoyance.
We're frustrated.
Even though we've chosen not to smoke, we're exposed to second-hand smoke anyway.
We feel a little powerless.
Because you can invade our privacy without even trying. Often without noticing.
And sometimes when we speak up and let you know how we feel, you react as though *we* were the bad guys.
We're not fanatics. We're not out to deprive you of something you enjoy. We don't want to be your enemies.
We just wish you'd be more considerate and responsible about how, when, and where you smoke.
We know you've got rights and feelings. We just want you to respect our rights and feelings, as well.

A message
from those
who do
to those
who don't.

We're on the spot.
Smoking is something we consider to be a very personal choice, yet it's become a very public issue.
We're confused.
Smoking is something that gives us enjoyment, but it gives you offense.
We feel singled out.
We're doing something perfectly legal, yet we're often segregated, discriminated against, even legislated against.
Total strangers feel free to abuse us verbally in public without warning.
We're not criminals. We don't mean to bother or offend you. And we don't like confrontations with you.
We're just doing something we enjoy, and trying to understand your concerns.
We know you've got rights and feelings. We just want you to respect our rights and feelings, as well.

Brought to you in the interest of common courtesy by
R.J. Reynolds Tobacco Company

other side's argument and then by showing how it is misleading or not substantiated, the communicator can help the audience resist the influence of the competitor.[25] The approach is described as an inoculation technique because the process of giving the arguments and then refuting them is analogous to giving someone a vaccine. The vaccine immunizes the recipient by giving him or her a very mild case of the disease, which builds body defenses against future attacks by the disease.

Another technique that may be effective is some cases is actually to disclaim superiority on some aspect of the product.[26] In one study, consumers were given information on a television set. One group of consumers received only positive information about the set. Another group received the same positive information, but also learned that the television did not have a device to change its brightness as the illumination of the room changed. Pilot tests had shown that particular feature not to be of much importance to the consumers. The inclusion of such a piece of negative information resulted in increased credibility of the overall message. It is likely that consumers found the provision of such information so unexpected that they attributed greater honesty to the entire communication.

Two-sided messages, however, are not always the most effective. In some instances only giving one side of an issue may result in the greatest attitude change. When the audience is friendly, when it is *not* likely to hear the other side's arguments, when it is not involved in the issue, or when it is not highly educated, one-sided messages may be more effective. In such instances, presenting the "other" side to a message may simply confuse the audience and weaken the effects of the arguments for the issue.[27] Because many of the purchases that consumers make occur in low-involvement circumstances, marketers should probably have good evidence from marketing research studies that a two-sided message is effective before using it.

FEAR APPEALS. The view of the extent to which fear-arousing communications persuade has changed considerably over the past thirty years. The first reported study on the use of **fear appeals** attempted to persuade consumers to brush their teeth more often. In the study, one group of high school students was shown gory slides of diseased gums and given messages that tooth infections can lead to heart damage, kidney damage, and other awful maladies. Other groups were given less gruesome messages. The results revealed that the more fear the messages created, the *less* behavior change was observed. These early results caused many researchers to conclude that fear appeals were ineffective in persuasion.[28]

More recently, however, fear appeals have been shown to be effective in producing attitude change when used under certain conditions. Indeed, by 1970 over twenty studies had been done revealing the effectiveness of fear-producing messages. The frequent use of fear by advertisers supports such research evidence. Companies that frequently use fear appeals are in such industries as life insurance, health insurance, burglar alarms, smoke alarms, automobiles, and even computers. Figure 8–8 shows an advertisement from Volvo that extols the virtues of the car in protecting its occupants in the event of a crash.

Commodore computer company created a furor among advertisers and

Figure 8–8   Volvo uses a not-so-subtle fear appeal in this ad. *(Courtesy of Volvo Cars of North America.)*

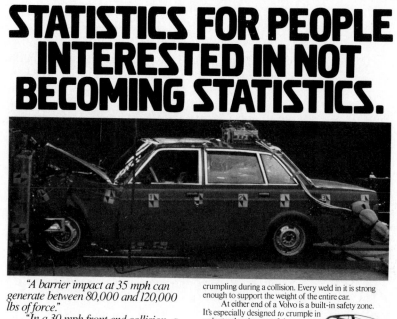

STATISTICS FOR PEOPLE INTERESTED IN NOT BECOMING STATISTICS.

"A barrier impact at 35 mph can generate between 80,000 and 120,000 lbs of force."

"In a 30 mph front end collision, a 165 lb man hits the windshield with a force of 3 tons."

"A 10 mph increase in impact speed from 30 to 40 mph means that 79% more energy must be absorbed."

Let a bunch of safety engineers slam enough cars into a wall and statistics like these begin to pile up. The more of them you have to work with, the safer the car you can build.

At Volvo, safety has always been a high priority.

So every year at our Technical Center in Gothenburg, Sweden, we destroy between 70 and 80 Volvos in crash tests. And the statistics we've gathered over the years have helped us make the kinds of innovations that have made Volvo the standard of safety for the automobile industry.

Our now famous steel "safety cage," for instance, surrounds the passenger compartment of a Volvo and is designed to keep it from

crumpling during a collision. Every weld in it is strong enough to support the weight of the entire car.

At either end of a Volvo is a built-in safety zone. It's especially designed *to* crumple in order to absorb some of the energy forces of a collision instead of passing them along to the occupants.

To make sure you have protection on all sides in a Volvo, we've placed tubular, steel anti-intrusion bars in all doors.

Even our steering column is designed to collapse upon impact and our laminated windshield is designed to remain intact.

Of course no car can protect you in a crash unless you're wearing the safety innovation that became standard equipment in Volvos back in 1959: the three point safety belt. (Statistics show that fifty percent of the deaths due to road accidents could be avoided if drivers and passengers were wearing them.) So if you're interested in not becoming a highway statistic, take a precaution the next time you take to the highway.

Be sure to fasten your safety belt.

And incidentally, it might be a good idea to be sure it's fastened to a Volvo.

VOLVO
A car you can believe in.

© 1984 Volvo of America Corporation.

columnists with its "train" commercial. In the commercial a hopeful young man is seen leaving for college from a train station. Leaving well dressed and optimistic in the first scene, the ex-student is shown returning as a disheveled failure. The announcer says, "This year 2 million families will send their kids off to college . . . but many of these kids won't be able to compete because they lack computer skills. A home computer can help. The Commodore 64 gives you more computer for less money than anyone else. Instead of saving for your kid's education, maybe you should spend a little for it."[29]

As the Commodore advertisement illustrates, fear appeals can come in a variety of forms. In fact, the types of fear appeals can be related directly to the various forms of *perceived risk* that consumers can experience. Thus, the risk of bodily harm has been used to generate fear by companies who sell the safety of burglar alarms and by auto manufacturers who advertise the crash protection of their cars. Fear of financial risk is used by insurance companies. Social risk is also used effectively to generate fears by a variety of companies. To a certain extent the Commodore advertisement built upon the idea of social risk. That is, if you son or daughter fails in college, you will look bad to your friends. Various companies selling deodorants, dandruff shampoos, and laundry detergents have successfully used fear appeals. By buying their products, consumers can avoid such "awful" maladies as "ring around the collar," they can "raise their arm if they're Sure," and they can scratch their heads without people snickering over their dandruff.

In order for fear appeals to be effective, researchers have found that the message should contain one or more of the following types of information. It should:

1. Give specific instructions on how to reduce the fear.
2. Provide an indication that following the instructions will solve the problem.
3. Avoid giving high-fear messages to audiences that feel highly threatened and vulnerable to the threat.
4. Avoid giving high-fear messages to audiences that feel inferior or low in self-esteem.

As noted by one set of authors, if these precautions are satisfied, "very frightening messages are almost always more persuasive than more factual appeals to reason."[30]

HUMOR IN MESSAGES. Like the use of fear appeals, the effectiveness of using **humorous messages** has been debated by marketing researchers. The use of humor in advertisements has varied over the years. One study published in 1973 found that as many as 42 percent of all television commercials used humor.[31] Although no studies have been done specifically to determine the percentage of humorous ads appearing since 1973, some industry personnel have referred to the 1970s as the "serious seventies." However, in the mid-1980s advertisements seemed to lighten up again with humorous campaigns, such as Wendy's "Where's the beef" ads. As one advertiser stated in February 1984, "I've been thinking very seriously about humor lately . . . The country is in a better mood, and I think the time could be right."[32]

Research evidence on the impact of using humor has been mixed. Three principle negative effects can result from using humor. Of most concern is the finding that using humor can reduce the comprehension of the message. For example, one study compared the recall of ad content in humorous ads to that in serious ads. The results showed that recall was significantly better in the serious version of the ad.[33] Another potential problem in using humor is that the life span of the ads may be shortened. Particularly if the humor is of a "gag" type, it may quickly fade and lose its positive effects. Humorous ads can also have unanticipated negative effects on various audiences. For example, shortly after Wendy's came out with its celebrated "Where's the beef" ads, the Michigan Commission on Aging sent a letter of complaint. The letter suggested that the commercial gave the impression "that elderly people, in particular women, are senile, deaf and have difficulty seeing . . . We are sure it was not your intent to insult older people. We hope, however, in the future you will avoid stereotyping the elderly."[34]

The problem of humor having unanticipated effects results in part from findings that different audiences may react in diverse ways to the same humor message. One study found that females may react more negatively to the injection of humor in ads than males.[35] Another study that reviewed the literature on humor found that a variety of audience characteristics mediate the effects of humor, including sex, race, national origin, personality, and social attitudes.[36] For example, one study investigated humorous liquor advertisements. It found that males reacted more to the ads than did females. In addition, blacks were found to respond less to the humorous messages than did Caucasians.[37]

Use of humor may have some liabilities, but it also provides some potential benefits. Perhaps most importantly, humor can attract attention to the advertisements. Although the attention-attraction properties of humor have been well documented, the context within which the message is placed does influence its attention-gaining properties. In one study, humorous ads and nonhumorous ads were placed in three different types of programming—documentary, action/adventure, and situation-comedy. The results revealed that the humorous ads had higher unaided recall than the nonhumorous ads in the documentary and action/adventure programming. However, when placed in the situation-comedy programming, the nonhumorous ads had greater unaided recall.[38] The authors interpreted the results as evidence of the importance of perceptual contrast. When the humorous ads were placed within the context of humorous programming, the ads were not as distinct as when placed within more serious programming. One can infer from these results that humorous ads will have attention-gaining properties only to the extent that the use of humorous ads does not become so widespread that they lose their distinctiveness.

The use of humor in advertising can also provide a number of additional benefits. One positive effect is that humor can act to distract the audience. As noted earlier, such distraction can have the negative effect of lowering comprehension. Distraction, though, may have a positive effect as well. It can act to lower the counterarguments of the audience.[39] For two reasons humor may lower counterargumentation. First, humor can put consumers in a positive mood. As noted in Chapter 10 on situational effects, positive mood can influence the tendency of consumers to buy. In addition, a positive mood can impede the formation of counterarguments. A second reason why humor may lower counterargumentation is that when humor is used, a portion of the consumer's short-term memory is allocated to thinking about the humorous aspects of the commercial. This leaves less cognitive capacity to process negative thoughts about the message. Interestingly, however, one study found that humor did not lower counterarguments as much for females as for males.[40] Clearly, additional research is needed in this area.

A final positive effect of the use of humor has been found. Evidence exists that humor can enhance the credibility of a source of information. In particular, research has shown that when commercials are perceived to be dull, adding humor may enhance the audience's perception of the source's credibility.[41] Table 8–2 presents some dos and don'ts advocated by one advertising professional on the use of humor.

Clearly, many companies perceive the benefits of using humor to outweigh its costs. An outstanding example of the use of humor in advertising is the portrayal of the Charlie Chaplin character in advertisements for the IBM Personal Computer. The long-running campaign uses the character to point out the features of a "serious" product in a humorous and entertaining manner. Figure 8–9 reveals one page of such an advertisement for the IBM PC.

VIVID VERSUS ABSTRACT INFORMATION. A well-established finding in psychology is that messages that use vivid, concrete words tend to have greater impact on receivers than messages containing more **abstract information.**[42] **Vivid information** tends to attract and hold attention as well as encourage the receiver to use his or her imagination. As such, vivid messages are more likely to be placed into long-term memory and later recalled than more pallid information.

What makes information vivid? Three factors have been found to increase the vividness of messages. First, to the extent that the message has emotional interest, it will tend to have a greater impact. One factor that will increase emotional interest is the **hedonic relevance** of the message to the receiver. Hedonic relevance refers to the extent to which the information has positive or negative consequences for the receiver. For example, if a consumer has purchased something and encounters a message in which a product recall of the product is announced, hedonic relevance exists, and the consumer is likely to attend closely to the information presented. A major goal of any promotional message should be to tie it as closely as possible to those things that are important to the target audience in order to generate increased hedonic relevance.

Table 8–2 Humor Can Sell

A variety of advertising executives have proposed various rules for using humor in advertising. Here is a list of dos and don'ts from one adman:

The Don'ts

1. Don't tell jokes because they wear out fast.
2. Never make fun of the product.
3. Don't use surprise endings; they surprise only once.
4. Don't make it hard for the viewer to figure out the humor.
5. Don't let the humor overwhelm the product.
6. Don't use humor when you can't figure out what else to do.

The Dos

1. Make the humor relevant.
2. Involve the audience in the humor early in the commercial.
3. Use the humor to sell the product's strong points.
4. Be charming, not funny.
5. Make humor simple and clear.
6. Integrate the humor with the message of the ad.

A number of highly successful advertising campaigns have been built around the use of humor. Below I have listed either a key phrase, a headline, or a key character from a well-known humorous ad campaign. See if you can recall the company doing the campaign. (The companies are listed under the list in reverse order.)

> Alex, you better be drinking your water.
> Tastes great; no, less filling.
> I can't believe I ate the whole thing.
> Lemon (headline on print advertisement).
> Hey, Vern, know what I mean.
> Are you surprised?
> Charlie Chaplin impersonator is the key character in the ad.
> Where's the beef?

(From bottom to top the companies were: Wendy's, IBM, NCR, Braum's Stores, Volkswagen, Alka-Seltzer, Miller Brewing Company, Stroh Brewery Company.)

SOURCE: Based in part on Anthony C. Chevins, "A Little Humor Carefully Used Can Work Wonders," *Journal of Broadcasting*, May 18, 1981, 22.

A second factor that will increase the vividness of a message is its concreteness. A concrete message gives a high degree of detailed, specific information about people, actions, and situations. For example, which of the following two statements has more impact?

1. Jack sustained fatal injuries in a car wreck.
2. Jack was killed by a semitrailer that rolled over on his car and crushed his skull.[43]

Clearly, the second statement uses more concrete words and has the greater impact. It has been argued that the high impact of certain books results from

Figure 8–9 IBM successfully uses humor to promote its PCs. (*Courtesy of International Business Machines Corporation.*)

their ability to use highly concrete, emotional information. For example, in the early 1900s Upton Sinclair's book *The Jungle* had a major impact on the United States public and was in part responsible for legislation that formed the Food and Drug Administration. Highlight 8–3 presents one excerpt from *The Jungle*. Note the concreteness of the words and feel the emotional impact that they carry. Good promotional messages should attempt to have such an impact, though, in a more emotionally positive way.

A final way to create more vivid, forceful messages is to make the information as close as possible to the receiver in terms of time, spatial proximity, and sensory proximity. A close proximity in time simply refers to using information that is as fresh and new as possible. For example, when a new product breakthrough occurs, it should be announced as quickly as possible. Spatial proximity refers to the idea of placing information in a context that is linked as closely as possible to the one experienced by the audience. Thus, if a product is targeted to one region of the country, television ads should be filmed in recognizable parts of the region. Sensory proximity refers to the concept of having the ideas in the message experienced firsthand by the audience or by someone else, such as an endorser, who can tell the audience firsthand what he or she experienced. One reason why automobile salesmen

---

HIGHLIGHT 8–3

An Effective Use of Concrete Imagery to Influence People

If one attempted to identify the ten most influential books in the United States during the twentieth century, one that would probably be on the list is Upton Sinclair's *The Jungle*. The book about the horrors of the meatpacking industry caught America's attention in the early 1900s and was responsible in part for the creation of the Food and Drug Administration. The following paragraph is taken from the book and exemplifies the use of vivid, concrete prose and its impact on people.

Some worked at the stamping-machines, and it was very seldom that one could work long there at the pace that was set, and not give out and forget himself, and have a part of his hand chopped off. There were the "hoisters," as they were called, whose task it was to press the lever which lifted the dead cattle off the floor. They ran along upon a rafter, peering down through the damp and the steam; and as old Durham's architects had not built the killing-room for the convenience of the hois-

ters, at every few feet they have to stoop under a beam, say four feet above the one they ran on; which got them into the habit of stooping, so that in a few years they would be walking like chimpanzees. Worst of any, however, were the fertilizer-men, and those who served in the cooking-rooms. These people could not be shown to the visitor,—for the odor of a fertilizer-man would scare any ordinary visitor at a hundred yards, and as for the other men, who worked in tank-rooms full of steam, and in some of which there were open vats near the level of the floor, their peculiar trouble was that they fell into the vats; and when they were fished out, there was never enough of them left to be worth exhibiting,—sometimes they would be overlooked for days till all but the bones of them had gone out to the world as Durham's Pure Leaf Lard. (1906, p. 117)

Based on Upton Sinclair, *The Jungle*, Cambridge, Mass.: R. Bentley, 1946.

are so anxious to get you to drive a car is to have you obtain firsthand sensory experiences of the car.

The overall impact of creating highly vivid messages is that the information is retained more easily in memory. Information that is concrete and promotes the use of imagination can increase recognition and recall.[44] The net result is that such messages are likely to have a greater persuasive impact on consumers.

Message Structure   Developers of messages must worry not only about their content but also about how the messages are structured. **Message structure** refers to how the source organizes the content of the message. For example, a major issue concerns where in the message important information should be placed. Research on what are called **primacy** and **recency effects** has tackled such a question. Another structural problem concerns how many times key pieces of information should be repeated in a message. Thus, in an advertisement how often should the brand name be mentioned?

PRIMACY AND RECENCY EFFECTS.   The terms *primacy* and *recency effects* refer to the relative impact of information placed either at the beginning or the end of a message. A primacy effect occurs when material early in the message has the most influence; a recency effect occurs when material at the end of the message has the most influence. The question is not trivial. Whether in a television commercial or in a formal presentation by a salesman, the communicator wants to insure that each piece of information has the maximum impact on the receiver. In addition, primacy and recency effects can occur when a series of messages is received. For example, when a number of commercials appear in succession on television, will ones at the beginning, middle, or end of the sequence have the most impact?

Like research on other aspects of the message, the findings on primacy and recency effects have been somewhat mixed. However, one classic study stands out as explaining *when* information placed early in a message or late in a message will have the most impact. What the authors of the study argued is that the material heard early in the message tends to be the most persuasive for the simple reason that it is heard first. However, this material also tends to be forgotten quickly. Consequently, material heard at the end of the message will be remembered relatively better if the message is long and the response is assessed soon after the message is given. In contrast, if a delay occurs between the message and when the measure of persuasion is taken, a primacy effect will tend to be found. This occurs because both parts of the message will have had time to decay substantially, and the intrinsically more persuasive early parts of the message will then predominate.[45]

The study presented above suggests that over the long haul primacy effects may predominate. Although such a conclusion must be regarded as highly tentative, one finding can be stated unequivocally. Material presented in the middle of a message is remembered the most poorly and will have the least impact. Research on serial learning presented in Chapter 6 on learning demonstrates the greater difficulty in retaining information placed in the middle of lists of material to be learned. Therefore, one can say with some confidence to communicators—try to avoid placing the important parts of a message in the middle of a communication.

REPETITION EFFECTS. In Chapter 6 on learning principles in consumer behavior, the importance of repetition was discussed. Whether for classical conditioning, operant conditioning, or cognitive learning, repetition of information must take place. With this knowledge in mind, the major question becomes one of how often the information should be repeated. Herbert Krugman has suggested that as few as three exposures to an advertisement may be sufficient.[46] Indeed, some evidence exists that too much repetition may result in consumers becoming increasingly negative towards the message. Such increased negativity has been called **advertising wear-out.** For example, in one study members of church groups received either one, three, or five exposures to an advertisement for a fictitious toothpaste during a one-hour television show. The results of the study revealed that the number of negative cognitive responses to the commercials increased as the number of repetitions increased.[47] Other research, however, has found results inconsistent with the study just mentioned. The researchers varied the content of each ad slightly. In this study the number of positive cognitive responses increased and the number of negative cognitive responses decreased as the message was repeated.[48]

One theoretical explanation of the effects of repetition proposes that two different psychological processes are operating as people receive repetitive messages. Called **two-factor theory,** in one process the repetition of a message causes a reduction in uncertainty and increased learning about the stimulus, resulting in a positive response. However, in the other process tedium or boredom begins to occur with each repetition. At some point the tedium will overtake the positive effects, and the receiver will begin to react negatively to the ad.[49] What two-factor theory suggests is that in order to avoid the negative effects of boredom, the communicator should vary the nature of the message slightly with each repetition. A number of highly successful advertising campaigns have used just such a strategy. By the end of 1984 the Miller Lite beer campaign had filmed its 100th different commercial. The basic content of almost every commercial was the same. One group of ex-athletes says, "Miller's tastes great," and the other says, "Miller's won't fill you up." What makes the commercials so successful and long-lasting is that the message is communicated in so many different, clever ways.

The Effects of the Medium and Context of the Message

Both the medium through which the message passes and the context within which the message is received can influence receiver reactions to the communication. The various media over which messages can be communicated are limited only by a communicator's imagination. Table 8–3 identifies some of these media. Although the media thought of first by many tend to be tele-

Table 8-3   Some Types of Media

Direct mail	Radio
Directory (e.g., Yellow Pages)	Specialty (e.g., pens, calendars, sweatshirts)
Magazine	Television
Movie (e.g., *E.T.*)	Television show (*Knight Rider* showing off a
Newspaper	Firebird)
Outdoor sites (e.g., billboards, balloons,	Theater
airplanes)	Transit
Point-of-purchase	

vision, radio, newspapers, and magazines, the list is actually much more varied. Direct mail is rapidly emerging as an important means of getting information to consumers. Specialty advertising involves placing short messages on various inexpensive trinkets, such as combs, golf tees, and calendars, which can be given away free of charge. Other media for communicating messages include transit vehicles, such as buses, trains, and even blimps, as well as placing logos on sweatshirts. Whereas advertisements have long been placed in movie theaters in Great Britain, the practice is just beginning to occur in the United States. With increasing frequency producers are beginning to charge companies for the use of their products in a movie. For example, the use of Reese's Pieces in *E.T.* increased the sales of that product substantially. However, the most effective transmission medium is probably that of face-to-face communications.

A number of factors act to influence the environment within which consumers receive a message. Included are such contextual factors as the nature of the physical surroundings, the presence or absence of other people, and the presence or absence of distractors. The next two sections discuss in turn some of the media and contextual effects that can influence communication persuasiveness.

Media Effects on Persuasion   Selecting the appropriate channel within which to place a message involves a number of considerations. Factors such as cost, the actions of competitors, media availability, and media restrictions should all be considered. From a consumer behavior perspective, however, four additional considerations are particularly important—**target-market match, media-message match, involvement match,** and the stage of the consumer decision process.

TARGET-MARKET MATCH.   Prior to selecting the appropriate medium and vehicle for a message, a manager should have detailed information on the characteristics of the target market. (A vehicle is the specific carrier of the message within a medium, such as using *Time* magazine within the magazine media.) Quite simply, different groups of people will tend to expose themselves to different media and to different vehicles within a medium. For example, people over the age of sixty-five tend to watch more television and listen to less radio than other groups within the general population.

Of course, the major objective of careful matching of media and media vehicle to target market is to reduce costs. Certain groups of people will tend to use certain media vehicles. For this reason radio stations, magazines, television stations, and newspapers, will develop careful profiles of their audience in order to demonstrate their suitability for reaching specific audiences. Managerially sophisticated magazines will even publish separate editions for the various segments of consumers who take their publication. *Time* magazine has over 125 different editions of its magazine which go out separately to carefully identified target groups, such as college students, doctors, and business executives and residents of particular regions, cities, and foreign countries.[50]

MEDIA-MESSAGE MATCH.   The type of media selected should also match the message. For example, a company that is promoting a product as highly reliable and trustworthy would probably want to avoid placing ads in vehicles whose trustworthiness might be questioned, such as the *National Inquirer.* The probable reason for such effects is that the media and vehicle form a context within which the message is evaluated. If the context within which the message is placed is trustworthy, some portion of that will carry over to the message itself.[51]

One study found that the type of message can interact with the media vehicle.[52] In the study, two different types of messages were created. One was a message that gave the "reason why" a product should be bought. The second message used an "image" format. The vehicles used were a "special interest" magazine, *Tennis World,* and a "prestige" magazine, the *New Yorker.* The results showed that for nonusers of the product, the prestige magazine was more effective in communicating product quality and image. However, the special interest magazine was more effective in communicating factual information. Such results support the idea that the media vehicle can establish a mood that influences the audience's receptivity to the message.

Some evidence exists showing that messages received via the print media may be perceived as more trustworthy. For example, a recent study investigated the relative effects of print, video, and radio formats on perceptions of messages announcing a product recall. The print media were perceived as more trustworthy and objective than the other modes of presentation.[53]

INVOLVEMENT-MEDIUM MATCH.   As noted earlier in the chapter, the level of involvement of the receiver influences his or her information-processing activity. The various media tend to encourage or discourage divergent levels of information processing. For example, it has been proposed that print is a high-involvement medium, whereas television is a low-involvement medium.[54] To the extent that the proposal is true, one should find that print media are better at communicating longer, more complex messages which require higher levels of information processing. In contrast, television, and to a lesser extent radio, should be better at communicating moods and feelings associated with "image" advertising. One study has supported the conjecture.[55] Subjects were given a persuasive communication via either videotape, audiotape, or written transcript. Two types of messages were given, either simple or complex. The results showed that television was the most persuasive when the message was simple. In contrast, the written transcript was most effective when the message was complex.

STAGE OF THE DECISION PROCESS. Consumers tend to use the various media for different purposes. If a consumer is late in the decision process and is about ready to make a product choice, he or she is unlikely to begin avidly watching television and listening to the radio in hopes of finding out where to purchase the product. Instead, the consumer will begin looking in newspapers, reading the Yellow Pages, and perhaps asking friends about where such a product can be found at a good price. As a consequence, retailers tend to use newspapers as the medium for announcing sales promotions of products and use the Yellow Pages to show the brands they carry.

When consumers are in the early stage of the decision process, they tend to be influenced more by television, radio, print, and billboard advertising. Generally, these media are used to keep the company's brand in the consumer's evoked set and to create or maintain a positive image toward the product. As such, these media are used relatively more frequently for image advertising. Although one will find sales promotions occasionally announced on television, it is usually for products in mass distribution that already have built a strong brand image. Examples include sales promotions by companies like McDonald's (e.g., a sweepstakes contest) or General Motors (e.g., $500 rebates).

Context Effects   The medium within which a message is placed can act as a context for the interpretation of the communication, yet a more general environmental context also exists. The various situational factors discussed in Chapter 10 form this environmental background against which messages are interpreted. Thus, time pressures will influence the ability of a consumer to attend to messages and process their information. The presence of other people may influence the ability of a person to attend to a message. Similarly, the mood of a consumer may influence his or her tendency to develop counterarguments to a message.

The physical surroundings have also been found to influence the persuasiveness of messages. One study found that a speech delivered in a comfortable lounge was more persuasive than one presented in a classroom.[56] Other researchers have found that messages accompanied by a pleasant song resulted in more persuasion than messages not accompanied by music.[57] Another study found that messages were more persuasive if the audience received the communication while they were consuming food and drink, but not after eating and drinking.[58] Taking a client out to lunch takes on new meaning in the face of this research evidence.

One possible explanation for the effects of pleasant surroundings and songs on persuasion is that they may act to distract the receiver of information. When the environment becomes cluttered with information that acts to divide a consumer's attention, the receiver will not be able to process the information fully. With less cognitive capacity available, the ability to develop counterarguments is likely to be diminished. A number of investigations have found that distraction will act to inhibit the formation of counterarguments and consequently increase persuasion.[59]

Managerial Implications

The study of persuasion and marketing communications is directly relevant to the promotional component of the marketing mix. A major reason for engaging in advertising, personal selling, sales promotion, and public relations activities is to change the beliefs or attitudes of a target audience through the delivery of a message by a source, who communicates through a medium of some type. The various theories and ideas discussed in the chapter give the manager a number of approaches for how to influence attitudes and beliefs.

The attitude-toward-the-object model is a good starting point. It shows the importance of consumer beliefs about the attributes that a brand possesses and the importance that the consumer attaches to these attributes in forming an overall attitude toward the brand. Thus, if the goal is to change attitudes toward the product, one approach is to attempt to influence such beliefs and importance ratings, which can be done in several ways. For example, comparative advertising could be considered. Showing that the brand is at least as good as the market leader on important attributes may result in a change of beliefs. Certainly the Pepsi Challenge advertising campaign used just such a tactic. The taste tests convincingly showed consumers selecting the taste of Pepsi-Cola over Coca-Cola. Consumer attitudes toward Pepsi slowly began to change, and the results began to show up in grocery stores, where sales of Pepsi inched past Coke in the mid-1980s.

Two-sided messages may also be used to change beliefs. Such appeals can increase the trust in the message so that information on the brand's attributes is subjected to less scrutiny. This tactic has been used in a series of advertisements by R.J. Reynolds Tobacco Company, as illustrated by Figure 8–6. Fear appeals may also be used to form beliefs about the effects of certain consumer actions. For example, the surgeon general's warning on the risks of smoking found on cigarette packages is placed in part to form a belief that cigarettes are dangerous to one's health. However, fear appeals may also have the effect of increasing the importance of a particular problem. Thus, the advertisement by Volvo of the smashed car, found in Figure 8–7, may influence consumer beliefs about the survivability of Volvos in accidents. It may also make highly salient to consumers the importance of the safety attribute in automobiles.

A particular problem faced by marketing managers is that of the tendency of consumers to develop counterarguments to messages. If measures can be found to reduce counterargumentation, the likelihood of consumers yielding to the communication increases. A number of the approaches to communication discussed in the chapter have the effect of lowering the number of cognitive responses. For example, research has shown that humor can decrease the number of counterarguments to the message. It is likely that two-sided messages may have the same effect. In addition, highly credible sources may have the effect of lowering the number of cognitive responses. Because cognitive responses tend to occur in high-involvement situations, managers should consider using these approaches in circumstances in which consumers are highly motivated to consider diligently the information received.

Marketing managers, as well as public policy makers, should have an understanding of concepts derived from balance theory and social judgment theory. Balance theory holds that attitudes can be changed by the communicator creating cognitive imbalance within the audience. In order to achieve such a goal, the attitude object that is to be connected to the brand must be viewed highly positively by consumers. The imbalance is created by connecting an extremely positive attitude object, such as a celebrity endorser, with a less positively evaluated brand.

One implication of social judgment theory is that managers should have a good understanding of the extremity of the attitudes of their audience. The research evidence indicates that extreme attitudes are much harder to change than more moderate ones. Thus, it makes sense to aim messages at groups of consumers whose attitudes are more neutral in valence. In addition, social judgment theory indicates that in order to change attitudes, one should attempt to use a "creeping strategy." That is, a series of messages should be targeted to be just within the latitude of acceptance of the audience. Because the attitude tends to be assimilated towards the message each time, the messages can gradually (in a creeping manner) be made stronger.

The material on communications also suggested some general rules for message construction. One is to place the most important material in the message at the beginning and the end of the message rather than in the middle. A second rule is to use vivid and concrete words rather than more abstract words. Furthermore, the manager should attempt to achieve moderate amounts of repetition of the message yet avoid having consumers receive the message so often that it wears out. Wear-out can be avoided by changing the message slightly each time. The classic example of such an approach is the commercials for Miller Lite beer, in which scores of different retired athletes have conveyed in many ways the message that the product "tastes great" and "doesn't fill you up."

Finally, managers should be concerned about the medium through which the message is transmitted. Managers should recognize that media vehicles can have an impact on the interpretation of the message. Furthermore, they should attempt to match the target market, the media, and the audience with the message.

SUMMARY

Persuasion is a process in which a change occurs in the beliefs or attitudes of a target person as a result of the delivery of a message. Persuasion can occur through two different psychological processes. In low-involvement cases persuasion results from the association of positive or negative feelings with an attitudinal object or behavior, or as a result of incidental learning. In such instances a more peripheral route to persuasion occurs, and the belief and attitudinal changes may be unstable. In contrast, in high-involvement processes persuasion is likely to occur through a central route. In this instance, the consumer is likely to diligently consider information relevant to the decision. As a consequence, the persuasion process will involve changes in the beliefs of the consumer, which lead to changes in attitudes, which in turn result in changes in intentions and behavior. When persuasion occurs through the central route, attitude and belief changes are more likely to result in behavioral changes.

When central routes to persuasion are used, attitudes may change as a result of any one of three factors. First, the importance of a particular attribute may change. Second, a new attribute may have been introduced for consideration. Third, the belief about an attribute may have been changed. Changing the beliefs about attributes is the easiest of the three approaches to persuasion.

When persuasion occurs in high-involvement situations, important mediating factors are the extent and type of cognitive responses that occur. Cognitive responses are the self-generated counterarguments, support arguments, and source derogations that may occur as a result of being exposed to a message. According to the model of persuasion developed in the chapter, such cognitive responses are likely to occur prior to belief and attitude change in high-involvement circumstances. In contrast, in low-involvement cases, it is less likely that cognitive response generation occurs prior to belief formation.

Balance theory also explains how attitudes may be changed. Balance theory is a type of cognitive-consistency approach. Cognitive consistency is the name applied to the tendency of people to maintain a logical and consistent set of interconnected beliefs. If one or more beliefs becomes inconsistent with the others, the person will unconsciously seek to change one or more of the beliefs in order to bring his or her cognitive system back into balance. From a balance theory perspective, communicators desiring to change an attitude may deliberately attempt to create cognitive imbalance. The hope is that the receiver will reorient his or her attitudes in a desired manner in order to achieve cognitive consistency.

Another psychological approach having relevance to persuasion is social judgment theory. The theory posits that people have latitudes of acceptance and rejection. A person's reaction to a message will depend in part on the regions within which a message falls. If the message falls within the latitude of acceptance, assimilation effects are likely to occur. In contrast, if the message falls in the latitude of rejection, contrast effects may occur.

In addition to analyzing the psychological processes influencing persuasion, the chapter also discussed two components of a general model of communications. The general model of communications consists of a number of components, including source, message, medium, receiver, feedback, noise, and environmental context. The chapter focused on the effects of various types of messages on receivers as well as on a number of the effects of the medium (channel).

Messages may have differential impact depending upon their content and on their structure. One content factor is the complexity of the message. Other content factors include whether conclusions are drawn, comparative messages are provided, the messages are one-sided or two-sided, fear or humorous appeals are used, and concrete or abstract information is included in the message. When studying message structure, the consumer researcher should focus on such factors as whether consumers may be influenced by primacy or recency effects. Another structural factor to consider is the amount of repetition required to influence the consumer.

The medium within which a message is placed can also influence consumer reactions. Those who seek to persuade should carefully match the channel to the target market, to the type of message delivered, to the involvement of the consumer, and to the stage of decision making the consumer is in when he or she receives the message. A number of contextual factors, such as time pressures and physical surroundings, can also influence the way that consumers interpret a message. In addition, background stimuli that act to distract the consumer can have major effects on whether or not cognitive responses are generated.

Key Terms

Persuasion
Central route to persuasion
Peripheral route to persuasion
Cognitive response
Balance theory
Social judgment theory
Cognitive imbalance
Sentiment connection
Unit relation

Frame of reference
Psychophysical judgment
Latitude of acceptance
Latitude of rejection
Assimilation effects
Contrast effects
Counterargument
Boomerang effect
Model of communications

Message content
Message construction
Message complexity
Drawing conclusions
Comparative message
One-sided message
Two-sided message
Inoculation technique
Fear appeals
Humorous messages
Vivid information
Abstract information
Hedonic relevance

Message structure
Primacy effects
Recency effects
Advertising wear-out
Two-factor theory
Target-market match
Media-message match
Involvement-medium match
Context effects
Support argument
Source derogation

Review Questions

1. Distinguish between the concepts of persuasion and coercion.
2. Draw the model of the persuasion process presented in the text. How does the persuasion process differ when it occurs through the central route as opposed to the peripheral route?
3. According to the attitude-towards-the-object model, what are the three ways in which attitudes may be changed?
4. Within balance theory what are sentiment and unit connections?
5. How can one tell if the cognitive elements within a balance theory framework are in balance?
6. What are three ways that may be used to try to create a unit connection between an endorser and a product?
7. What is meant by the terms *latitudes of acceptance* and *latitudes of rejection?*
8. What factors influence the width of the latitude of rejection?
9. From a social judgment theory perspective, how should a communicator attempt to create attitude change?
10. Draw the communications model presented in the text. Briefly discuss each of the components of the model.
11. Identify six of the different methods for varying message content presented in the text.
12. What are the reasons for and against using comparative advertisements?
13. When should a communicator consider using a two-sided message? A one-sided message?
14. What are the elements a message should have in order to be an effective fear appeal?
15. Identify the advantages and disadvantages of using humor in messages.
16. What are the three factors that tend to make messages more vivid?
17. Identify a potential theoretical explanation for why advertising wear-out occurs.
18. Identify the ways in which the nature of the media may influence persuasion.

Discussion Questions

1. Consider the advertising for the following brands of products: Pepsi-Cola, Volvo, McDonald's, IBM Personal Computers. Which of the ad campaigns would you consider to involve central routes and which involve peripheral routes to persuasion?

The next three questions are based upon the following idea. Over the past fifteen years American auto manufacturers have faced the problem that consumers perceive their autos to be of poorer quality than Japanese automobiles. Assuming that U.S. manufacturers have overcome the quality problems, how might they persuade consumers of this?

2. Sketch out an advertising campaign for the Ford Mustang to change consumers' perceptions of its quality, based upon the attitude-towards-the-object approach.
3. Sketch out an advertising campaign for the Mustang, based upon balance theory principles.
4. What are the implications of social judgment theory for the development of the two advertising campaigns?
5. You are the account executive for an advertising firm working on developing a comparative advertising campaign for the Chrysler New Yorker. The New Yorker's major competitors are the midsize and larger cars produced by General Motors and Ford—such as the Ford Grand Marquis, the Buick Le Sabre, and the Oldsmobile Delta 88. Try to sketch out a print advertisement that uses a comparative ad format. What things should you consider when developing the ad?
6. Identify three brands or types of products/services that you believe should use one-sided messages and three brands or types of products/services that you believe should use two-sided messages in their advertising. Explain your answers.
7. Go through magazines and find a print ad that uses a fear appeal. Criticize the ad based upon the criteria that have been identified as necessary for the creation of good fear appeals.
8. While you are watching television identify a commercial that uses humor. Discuss the effectiveness of the advertisement. What do you think were the advertising goals of the sponsors of the ad?
9. Write the copy of a print ad for the Porsche 944 directed to high-involvement consumers. In the ad use highly concrete words and imagery.
10. Consider the advertising for Mercedes cars versus

Charlie perfume. What are the differences in the types of media that the two brands might use? Considering television as a medium, in what types of programs might the two brands advertise? Explain your answers.

References

1. Richard Petty, John Cacioppo, and David Schumann, "Central and Peripheral Routes to Advertising Effectiveness: The Moderating Role of Involvement," *Journal of Consumer Research*, 10, September 1983, 135–146.
2. This model is based in part on work done by W. J. McGuire, "Personality and Susceptibility to Social Influence," in *Handbook of Personality Theory and Research*, E. F. Borgatta and W. W. Lambert (eds.), Chicago, Ill.: Rand McNally & Company, 1968.
3. Richard E. Petty, John T. Cacioppo, and David Schumann, "Central and Peripheral Routes to Advertising Effectiveness: The Moderating Role of Involvement," *Journal of Consumer Research*, 10, September 1983, 135–146.
4. Robert B. Cialdini, Richard Petty, and John Cacioppo, "Attitude and Attitude Change," *Annual Review of Psychology*, 32, 1981, 357–404.
5. John Cacioppo, Stephen Harkins, and Richard Petty, "The Nature of Attitudes and Cognitive Responses and Their Relations to Behavior," in *Cognitive Responses in Persuasion*, Richard Petty, Thomas Ostrom, and Timothy C. Brock (eds.), Hillsdale, N.J.: Lawrence Erlbaum Associates, 1981, 31–54.
6. Fritz Heider, *The Psychology of Interpersonal Relations*, New York, N.Y.: John Wiley & Sons, Inc., 1958.
7. M. J. Rosenberg, "An Analysis of Affective-Cognitive Consistency," in *Attitude Organization and Change*, M. J. Rosenberg, C. I. Hovland, W. J. McGuire, R. P. Abelson, and J. W. Brehm (eds.), New Haven, Conn.: Yale University Press, 1960, 15–64.
8. Marvin Shaw and Philip Costanzo, *Theories of Social Psychology*, New York, N.Y.: McGraw-Hill Book Company, 1970.
9. Shaw and Costanzo, *Theories of Social Psychology*.
10. For example see M. Sherif and C. Hovland, "Judgmental Phenomena and Scales of Attitude Measurement," *Journal of Abnormal Psychology*, 48, 1953, 135–141; and M. Sherif and C. Hovland, *Social Judgment: Assimilation and Contrast Effects in Communication and Attitude Change*. New Haven, Conn.: Yale University Press, 1961.
11. See, for instance, C. W. Sherif, M. Sherif, and R. Nebergall, *Attitude and Attitude Change: The Social Judgment-Involvement Approach*, Philadelphia, Pa.: W. B. Saunders Company, 1956.
12. For an excellent discussion of social judgment theory see Shaw and Costanzo, *Theories of Social Psychology*.
13. C. I. Hovland and I. L. Janis, *Personality and Persuasibility*, New Haven, Conn.: Yale University Press, 1959.
14. Alice Eagly, "The Comprehensibility of Persuasive Arguments as a Determinant of Opinion Change," *Journal of Personality and Social Psychology*, 29, 1974, 758–773.
15. Bertram Raven and Jeffrey Rubin, *Social Psychology*, New York, N.Y.: John Wiley & Sons, 1983.
16. Kanti V. Prasad, "Communications Effectiveness of Comparative Advertising: A Laboratory Analysis," *Journal of Marketing Research*, 13, May 1976, 128–137.
17. Gerald Gorn and Charles Weinberg, "Comparative Advertising: Some Positive Results," *Advances in Consumer Research*, X, Richard Bagozzi and Alice Tybout (eds.), Ann Arbor, Mich.: Association for Consumer Research, 1983, 377–380.
18. William Wilkie and Paul Farris, "Comparison Advertising: Problems and Potential," *Journal of Marketing*, 39, November 1975, 7–15.
19. "Creating a Mass Market for Wine," *Business Week*, March 15, 1982, 108–118.
20. Gorn and Weinberg, "Comparative Advertising."
21. William Swinyard, "The Interaction Between Comparative Advertising and Copy Claim Variation," *Journal of Marketing Research*, 18, May 1981, 175–186.
22. Gorn and Weinberg, "Comparative Advertising."
23. Z. S. Demirdjian, "Sales Effectiveness of Comparative Advertising: An Experimental Field Investigation," *Journal of Consumer Research*, 10, December 1983, 362–364.
24. See, for example, studies by Russell Jones and Jack Brehm, "Persuasiveness of One-and Two-Sided Communications as a Function of Awareness: There Are Two Sides." *Journal of Experimental Social Psychology*, 6, 1970, 47–56; Alan G. Sawyer, "The Effects of Repetition of Refutational and Suppor-

tive Advertising Appeals," *Journal of Marketing Research,* 10, February 1973, 23–33.

25. Carl Hovland, Arthur Lumsdaine, and Fred Sheffield, *Experiments on Mass Communication,* New York, N.Y.: John Wiley & Sons, Inc., 1949, 182–200.

26. Robert B. Settle and Linda Golden, "Attribution Theory and Advertiser Credibility," *Journal of Marketing Research,* 11, May 1974, 181–185.

27. G. C. Chu, "Prior Familiarity, Perceived Bias, and One-Sided Versus Two-Sided Communications," *Journal of Experimental Social Psychology,* 3, 1967, 243–254.

28. Raven and Rubin, *Social Psychology.*

29. Brad Danzig, "Ally Execs Derail Commodore Criticism," *Advertising Age,* October 31, 1983, 64.

30. Raven and Rubin, *Social Psychology.*

31. Brian Sternthal and C. Samuel Craig, "Humor in Advertising," *Journal of Marketing,* 37, October 1973, 12–18.

32. John Koten, "After Serious '70s, Advertisers Are Going For Laughs Again," *The Wall Street Journal,* February 23, 1984, 29.

33. Joan Cantor and Pat Venus, "The Effects of Humor on the Recall of a Radio Advertisement," *Journal of Broadcasting,* 24, Winter 1980, 13–22.

34. Michael Norman, " 'Where's the Beef?' All Over Town," *New York Times,* February 11, 1984, Sec. L., 32.

35. H. Bruce Lammers et al., "Humor and Cognitive Responses to Advertising Stimuli: A Trade Consolidation Approach," *Journal of Business Research,* 11, June 1983, 182.

36. Sternthal and Craig, "Humor in Advertising."

37. Thomas J. Madden and Marc Weinberger, "The Effects of Humor on Attention in Magazine Advertising," *Journal of Advertising,* Summer Issues, 11, #3, 1982, 8–14.

38. John H. Murphy, Isabella Cunningham, and Gary Wilcox, "The Impact of Program Environment on Recall of Humorous Television Commercials," *Journal of Advertising,* 8, Spring 1979, 17–21.

39. P. Kelly and Paul J. Solomon, "Humor in Television Advertising," *Journal of Advertising,* 4, Summer Issues, 1975, 33–35.

40. Lammers et al., "Humor and Cognitive Responses."

41. Sternthal and Craig, "Humor in Advertising."

42. This section relies heavily on material found in Richard Nisbett and Lee Ross, *Human Inference: Strategies and Shortcomings of Social Judgment,* Englewood Cliffs, N.J.: Prentice-Hall, Inc., 1980.

43. Nisbett and Ross, *Human Inference.*

44. Ibid.

45. Norman Miller and Donald Campbell, "Recency and Primacy in Persuasion as a Function of the Timing of Speeches and Measurement," *Journal of Abnormal and Social Psychology,* 59, 1959, 1–9.

46. Herbert Krugman, "Why Three Exposures May Be Enough," *Journal of Advertising Research,* 12, December 1972, 11–14.

47. George E. Belch, "The Effects of Television Commercial Repetition on Cognitive Response and Message Acceptance," *Journal of Consumer Research,* 9, June 1982, 56–65.

48. J. L. McCullough and Thomas Ostrom, "Repetition of Highly Similar Messages and Attitude Change," *Journal of Applied Psychology,* 59, June 1974, 395–397.

49. D. E . Berlyne, "Novelty, Complexity, and Hedonic Value," *Perception and Psychophysics,* 8, November 1970, 279–286.

50. For a detailed breakdown of all the various editions of *Time* and other magazines that are available, see *Consumer Magazine and Farm Publication Rates and Data,* Skokie, Ill.: Standard Rate & Data Service, Inc.

51. Gert Assmus, "An Empirical Investigation into the Perception of Vehicle Source Effects," *Journal of Advertising,* 7, Winter 1978, 4–10.

52. Charles Winick, "Three Measures of the Advertising Value of Media Context," *Journal of Advertising Research,* 2, June 1962, 28–33.

53. David Jolly and J. C. Mowen, "Product Recall Communications: The Effects of Source, Media, and Social Responsibility Information," in *Advances in Consumer Research, XII,* E. Hirschman and M. Holbrook (eds.), Ann Arbor, Mich.: Association for Consumer Research, 1985, 471–475. Also see William Dommermuth, "How Does Medium Affect Message?" *Journalism Quarterly,* 51, 1974, 441–447.

54. Herbert Krugman, "The Impact of Television Advertising: Learning Without Involvement," *Public Opinion Quarterly,* 29, Fall 1965, 349–356.

55. S. Chaiken and A. Eagly, "Communication Modality as a Determinant of Message Persuasiveness and Message Comprehensibility," *Journal of Personal-*

ity and Social Psychology, 34, October 1976, 605–614.

56. T. Biggers and B. Pryor, "Attitude Change: A Function of Emotion-Eliciting Qualities of the Environment," *Personality and Social Psychology Bulletin, 8,* 1982, 94–99.

57. M. Galizio and C. Hendrick, "Effect of Music Accompaniment on Attitude: The Guitar as a Prop for Persuasion," *Journal of Applied Social Psychology, 2,* 1972, 350–359.

58. J. Dabbs and I. Janis, "Why Does Eating While Reading Facilitate Opinion Change? An Experimental Inquiry," *Journal of Experimental Social Psychology, 1,* May 1965, 133–144.

59. For example, see R. E. Petty, G. L. Wells, and T. C. Brock, "Distraction Can Enhance or Reduce Yielding to Propoganda: Thought Disruption Versus Effort Justification," *Journal of Personality and Social Psychology, 34,* November 1976, 874–884.

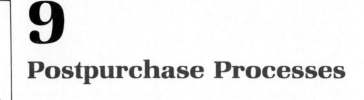

9

Postpurchase Processes

The Dissonance After Buying a New House

A number of years ago, my wife and I decided to take jobs at another university. Knowing that we would buy a house in the new town, we began an extensive process to identify the characteristics of the "perfect" home.

For financial and time reasons, it was decided that only one person could go to the new city to search for the home, and I got this important task. After arriving and going through about ten possible homes, I quickly narrowed the choice to two houses. The houses were priced the same and about the same size, but there the similarities ended.

House A was next to the country club. It was immaculate. The furniture was beautiful; the yard was cut; the floors shined; I felt really good in the house.

House B was a pit. The furniture was twentieth century garage sale; the yard was a mess; the curtains were torn; even the toilets were filthy. I felt bad.

The problem was that house B had nicer features. The rooms were better arranged. It was on a small lake. It had built-in furniture. Furthermore, according to the multiattribute model that we had developed, we should have had a more favorable attitude towards house B.

I called my wife and described the houses. After hearing that house B had a bay window, she said, "There's no choice, buy house B!" I then calmly explained that I felt much better in house A. Always logical, my wife responded that once we cleaned up the house and moved in our furniture, everything would be fine.

The next day I made an offer on house B. It was accepted, and the papers were signed. Then the next day came, and I was in agony. I knew I had blown it. As the realtor drove me to the airport, I told him how awful I felt.

The realtor patted me on the back and told me that I had made a great purchase. He said that I was merely having a case of buyer's regret and that most people went through it.

Suddenly, a flash hit me. I was experiencing cognitive dissonance. I then proceeded to explain to the realtor all about cognitive dissonance and how this buying situation would certainly create it. He responded by saying that it still sounded like buyer's regret to him.

So there I was, traveling in a car, feeling awful, and realizing that my understanding of buyer's regret was having no ameliorative effects.

Well, what happened? We eventually arrived in the new town, moved in our furniture, and repainted the house. Further, as cognitive dissonance theory suggests, we grew to like and even love the new house.

INTRODUCTION

After a brand is chosen, the consumer moves from the prepurchase to the postpurchase phase of the consumer buying process. As discussed in Chapter 2, the major components of the postpurchase phase are: product use, the formation of postpurchase attitudes towards the product, consumer complaint behavior, and finally product disposition. Of particular importance is the formation of attitudes of satisfaction and dissatisfaction towards the product after the purchase. Such attitudes influence complaint behavior and product disposition. In addition, they are an important determinant of the development of brand loyalty. Because of its importance, the discussion of postpurchase consumer attitudes will be emphasized.

The introductory vignette to the chapter illustrated an important aspect of the postpurchase process. Consumers do not always feel good after making some types of purchases. As is discussed later in the chapter, after making larger, more important purchases, consumers may experience a state of cognitive dissonance. The result is psychological discomfort resulting from having serious doubts about whether a particular alternative should have been purchased. The real estate agent described in the vignette recognized the phenomenon and called it buyer's regret. Indeed, he exerted some effort to help me resolve these highly negative feelings. However, because dissonance is an emotional state, even my knowledge of its cause did little to lower my discomfort.

The sections that follow discuss the various stages of the postpurchase process. They begin with a brief analysis of product usage, followed by longer sections on the development of postpurchase satisfaction, consumer complaint behavior, product disposition, and finally the effects of reactance and dissonance.

PRODUCT USAGE

Understanding how consumers go about using products in their everyday lives is important to brand managers. Assumptions about how people use products influence both their design and promotion. For example, it has long been assumed that people do the dishes by putting dishwashing detergent in the sink, filling the sink with water, and then washing the dishes. Procter & Gamble hired a firm to observe consumers and their dishwashing habits.[1] The company placed television cameras in homes and recorded the daily activities of the families. One of the findings was that most people no longer fill their sink with sudsy water. Instead, they squirt the dishwashing liquid directly onto the dishes and pots and pans. This behavior probably results from the fact that with the prevalence of dishwashing machines the number of dishes done by hand is small. Knowledge of such information could assist the company in new product development. For example, a less-concentrated detergent is needed if it is squirted directly onto the dishes.

That the observation of how consumers use products can lead to the development of new market offerings is illustrated by another example from Proctor & Gamble. During the 1960s, P&G researchers noted that consumers were beginning to wash more loads of laundry while using lower temperature water. Recognizing that these changes resulted from the introduction of new, artificial fabrics that required colder water temperatures, the company developed a new product that could be used in all water temperatures. The product was Cheer, which went on to garner a sizable share of the laundry detergent market.[2]

Another area in which information on product usage can be important is in avoiding product liability problems. Consumers have a nasty habit of finding unintended uses of products. Examples include using doors of ovens as a stepping stool, using lawnmowers as hedge trimmers, and pouring perfume over candles to make them scented. In each of these cases, consumers were injured while misusing the products and then sued the companies under product liability laws. Although the way these products were used may seem rather bizarre, in each case the plaintiff won the lawsuit. Companies must design a product so that it is safe in the use for which it was designed. In addition, companies must take steps to investigate unintended uses for their products and either design them for safe use or provide warnings that they should not be used in certain applications.[3] For example, one can find warnings all over aluminum stepladders warning consumers not to stand on the top of the ladders and to avoid using them near electrical lines.

THE DEVELOPMENT OF POSTPURCHASE ATTITUDES

After a consumer buys and uses a product, he or she will tend to develop attitudes towards the product—**postpurchase attitudes.** These attitudes take the form of feelings of satisfaction or dissatisfaction with the performance of the product. Researchers have tended to view **postpurchase satisfaction/dissatisfaction** as emotional feelings that result from the confirmation or disconfirmation of expectations about how the product should perform.[4] A model of the manner in which feelings of satisfaction or dissatisfaction are formed is shown in Figure 9–1. Based upon the use of a particular brand, as well as upon the use of other brands in the product class, consumers may be viewed as developing two different types of beliefs. Consumers may form *expectations* about how the brand should perform and beliefs about how the brand *actually* performed. Consumers are then conceptualized as comparing **actual product performance** with **expected product performance.** If performance falls below expectations, emotional dissatisfaction results. If performance is above expectations, emotional satisfaction occurs. If performance is not perceived to be different from expectancies, confirmation occurs. Although insufficient research has occurred in this area, when expectations and actual performance coincide, the consumer may not consciously consider his or her level of satisfaction. Quite simply, the consumer may not think much about his or her feelings about the product in such circumstances.[5]

Figure 9–1 **The formation of consumer satisfaction/dissatisfaction. (Adapted from a discussion in R. B. Woodruff, E. R. Cadotte, and R. L. Jenkins, "Modeling Consumer Satisfaction Processes Using Experience-Based Norms,"** *Journal of Marketing Research,* **20, August 1983, 296–304.)**

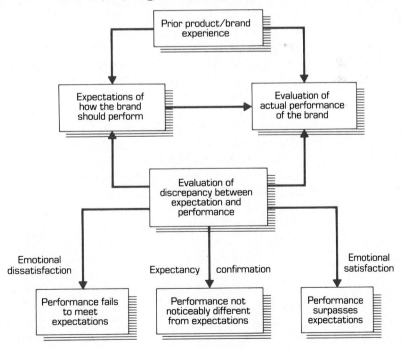

The Formation of Brand Expectations

Brand expectations can be viewed as forming a type of adaptation level. As such, the expectations become a standard against which the actual performance of the product is assessed.[6] A number of factors will influence the level of performance expected of a product. These are discussed briefly.

Product Factor Influences Factors associated with the product itself will influence the nature of the expectancies and how it will perform. A consumer's prior experiences with the product, its price, and its physical characteristics all influence how consumers expect it to perform. Thus, if the product has a high price and/or if it has performed extremely well in the past, consumers will expect it to meet high performance standards.

Promotional Factors How the company promotes the product through its advertising and through the communications of sales personnel will influence the performance expectations of consumers. For example, a company that advertises a product as having extremely high reliability is acting to set a standard against which its product will be judged by consumers. By setting such a high standard, the company risks creating consumer dissatisfaction if the product is perceived by consumers as not performing up to those standards.

The advertisement shown in Figure 9–2 illustrates how a company can create expectations. The ad from American Express forms the expectation that if billing problems occur, someone will be able to use their "judgment and initiative" to solve the problem.

The Effect of Other Products Another set of factors influencing consumer expectations of performance involve their experiences with other products of a similar nature. These experiences with the product class may result in the formation of norms or standards about the level of performance that a particular brand should be able to achieve.[7]

The idea that expectations of a particular product's performance are influenced by experience with other products is an important one. Consumers do not develop expectancies in a vacuum. They will use whatever information is available. An excellent example of such a process has occurred in the automobile industry. In the late 1970s and 1980s the Japanese exported to the United States automobiles that achieved quality levels substantially higher than that of American cars. In effect, the Japanese shifted the adaptation level of American consumers to a higher level, resulting in increased expectations of U.S. consumers regarding American cars.

Chrysler Corporation has attempted to utilize the high consumer expectations regarding the quality of Japanese cars. Chrysler imports from Mitsubishi of Japan a car that is marketed by the Dodge and Plymouth divisions. In the print ad shown in Figure 9–3, Chrysler makes the point that the Colt DL and Premier are of Japanese origin with the headline, "Refine your Japa-

Figure 9–2   American Express attempts to create service expectations.
(Courtesy of American Express, Inc.)

Figure 9–3   **Chrysler emphasizes the Japanese origins of two of its cars to create expectations of quality.** *(Courtesy of Chrysler Corporation.)*

nese." Of course the goal is to create the expectation that these cars will provide superior satisfaction because of their Japanese origins.

Characteristics of the Consumer   A fourth set of factors influencing expectations of performance concerns the characteristics of the consumer. Some consumers simply expect more of products than others and, consequently, set higher standards. In other instances, various consumers may have wider latitudes of acceptance around the adaptation level than others. Consumers with very narrow regions of acceptance could be expected to be more easily dissatisfied than those with broad regions of acceptance.

Factors Influencing the Perception of Actual Performance

Like the development of expected performance, the perception of actual performance will also be influenced by a number of factors. One way of viewing the formation of beliefs about actual performance is through a type of multiattribute model. That is, the consumer evaluates the product on a variety of attributes and then assesses its performance on each of the attributes. These evaluations are then combined to form an evaluation of the product's performance level. As some authors have noted, however, ratings of performance level may not coincide with reality. The consumer's prior experiences with the brand and his or her prior attitudes towards the brand may influence the perception of the product's performance. Similarly, it has been found that expectations of brand performance can actually influence perceptions of that performance. It is for this reason that a line has been drawn in Figure 9–1 that links expectations of performance to evaluations of actual performance.

The Creation of Satisfaction/ Dissatisfaction

The amount of satisfaction derived from the evaluation of a product or service results from an evaluation of the amount of discrepancy between actual performance and expected performance. If actual performance is perceived to be lower than expected performance, feelings of dissatisfaction result. If actual performance exceeds expected performance, feelings of satisfaction result. When no discrepancy exists between actual and expected performance, **expectancy confirmation** results.[8] Expectancy confirmation is a positive state for the consumer. However, because it consists of actual performance matching the adaptation level of what is expected, it is likely that expectancy confirmation will not motivate the consumer to form strong feelings of satisfaction. Such strong feelings are likely to be elicited only when actual performance deviates markedly from expected performance.[9]

Perceptions of Equity Another approach to predicting the satisfaction/ dissatisfaction that someone obtains from a product purchase is through **equity theory.** A number of researchers have argued that people will analyze the exchange between themselves and someone else to determine the extent that it is equitable or fair.[10] Equity theory holds that people will analyze the ratio of their outcomes and inputs to the ratio of the outcomes and inputs of the partner in an exchange. If the person perceives that his or her ratio is unfavorable in relation to the other member of the exchange, the individual will tend to have feelings of inequity. The equation below shows these ratios:[11]

$$\frac{\text{Outcomes of } A}{\text{Inputs of } A} \approx \frac{\text{Outcomes of } B}{\text{Inputs of } B}$$

Thus, the outcomes that person *A* receives from an exchange divided by the inputs of person *A* to the exchange should equal the outcomes of person *B* from the exchange divided by the inputs of person *B* to the exchange. To the extent that the ratios are perceived as unequal, particularly when unfavorable to the consumer doing the evaluation, dissatisfaction is proposed to result.

Just what are some examples of outcomes and inputs to a consumer exchange? **Inputs** are the information, effort, money, or time exerted to make an exchange possible. **Outcomes** are the results of the exchange. In other words, outcomes are the benefits and liabilities received from the exchange. They could consist of gaining savings in time, of having a product or service perform in some desired way, or of receiving some level of compensation.

A number of authors have investigated equity theory in consumer behavior. For example, one study looked at the exchange process between the consumer and an airline.[12] For the consumer, his or her inputs to the exchange consisted primarily of the money paid for the ticket. The consumer's outcomes consisted of the quality of the service received on the trip and the speed with which the airline gets the consumer to his destination. The results of the study revealed that if consumers perceived their inputs to be large because they paid a higher-than-average fare, they tended to be dissatisfied with the service. Similarly, if they perceived that their outcome was poor, because, for example, their flight had been delayed for two hours, they also revealed more dissatisfaction.[13]

Readers should note that equity proposes a different process through which satisfaction/dissatisfaction occurs than does the expectancy disconfirmation model presented in Figure 9–1. Equity theory suggests that feelings of satisfaction/dissatisfaction result from the feeling that a social norm has been violated. In other words, a norm exists that each party to an exchange should be treated fairly or equitably. Thus, satisfaction occurs when the ratios of outcomes and inputs are equal. In contrast, in the expectancy confirmation model satisfaction/dissatisfaction results from the comparison of actual performance to expected performance. As noted by one researcher, satisfaction/dissatisfaction can result from either process. It remains for future research to examine how consumers combine feelings of equity or inequity with feelings of expectancy confirmation to obtain global feelings of satisfaction or dissatisfaction.[14]

One approach by companies to increase consumer satisfaction is through the use of warranties. Highlight 9–1 discusses such a strategy.

CONSUMER COMPLAINT BEHAVIOR

Once a consumer perceives that he or she is dissatisfied with a product or service, the problem arises as to what to do about it. If the consumer decides to take action, five alternative courses are available. The consumer can:

HIGHLIGHT 9–1

Using Warranties to Increase Consumer Satisfaction

For many companies the fight to satisfy consumers continues after the purchase is made. One approach to help maintain consumer satisfaction and stem consumer complaints is the use of warranties.

Warranties are guarantees that include some means for the consumer to obtain redress for a product or service problem. A warranty can be one factor consumers use in determining which brand to choose. Thus, prior to a purchase a warranty can reduce consumer fears of financial and performance risk. After a purchase, a warranty can encourage consumers to take some action to correct product or service problems.

For example, Holiday Inns began a program to offer customers their money back if their accommodations were not satisfactory. One of the company's corporate officers stated:

> Before we started offering the guarantee there was a good chance someone might leave one of our hotels mad without telling us what was wrong. That probably meant that we'd lose them forever as customers.

In the year after the guarantee program, the evaluations became increasingly positive. Not only were customers more satisfied, but the service of the company also improved.

Based on John Koten, "Aggressive Use of Warranties is Benefiting Many Concerns," *The Wall Street Journal*, April 5, 1984, 33.

---

1. Stop buying the product/service or stop using the store.
2. Engage in negative word-of-mouth communications to friends.
3. Complain to the business, to private agencies, or to government.
4. Seek redress from the business.
5. Take legal action to obtain redress.[15]

The actions of not patronizing the brand or store, of telling friends about the problem, and of complaining are straightforward responses to product/service problems. When a consumer seeks redress to dissatisfaction, he or she takes steps to obtain some type of refund. The refund could be in the form of money or through a new product.

Studies of consumer **complaint behavior,** however, have shown that a minority of dissatisfied customers actually take overt action to complain. For example, one study found that among a sample of 2,400 households about one in five purchases resulted in some degree of dissatisfaction. In less than 50 percent of these instances of dissatisfaction did the buyer take action. The type of action taken by consumers depended in part on the type of product/service purchased. For low-cost, frequently purchased products fewer than 15 percent of consumers were found to take some action. In contrast, for household durables and automobiles, over 50 percent of consumers were found to take some action if they were dissatisfied. The type of product that most frequently activates consumers' responses to dissatisfaction is clothing. As many as 75 percent of those experiencing dissatisfaction with clothing took some form of complaint action.[16]

In general, the models of consumer complaint behavior have identified two major purposes for complaining.[17] First, consumers will complain in order to recover an economic loss. They may seek to make an exchange of the problem product for another product. They may seek to get their money back either directly from the company/store or indirectly through legal means. A second reason for engaging in some type of complaint behavior is to rebuild the person's self-image. Particularly when the self-image of a consumer is tied to the purchase of a product, dissatisfaction with the product will lower the person's self-image. In order to raise his or her self-image, the consumer can engage in such activities as negative word-of-mouth communications, stop buying the brand, complain to the company or Better Business Bureau, or take legal action. In general, the self-image maintenance aspects of consumer complaint behavior have been insufficiently studied by researchers and companies.

Factors Influencing Complaint Behavior

A number of factors have been found to influence whether or not consumers will complain. As noted above, the type of product or service involved will influence the tendency to complain. As the cost and social importance of the product rise, the tendency to complain usually increases. Authors have suggested that complaint behavior is related to the following variables:

1. The level of the dissatisfaction of the consumer.
2. The importance of the product to the consumer.
3. The amount of benefit to be gained from complaining.
4. The personality of the consumer.
5. To whom the blame for the problem is attributed.
6. The attitude of the consumer towards complaining.
7. The resources available to the consumer for complaining.
8. Previous experience with the product and with complaining.[18]

The above variables are logically related to complaint behavior. Thus, the greater the dissatisfaction of the consumer, the greater the tendency to complain. Similarly, as the product increases in importance to the consumer, complaint behavior increases. Consumers with a positive attitude towards complaining will complain more. Similarly, if the consumer can attribute the blame for the product or service problem to a specific company or store, complaint behavior is more likely to occur. The ability to complain requires certain resources, such as time, the ability to write letters, or the personal power to confront an employee of a firm and make him or her listen to a problem. Previous experience may be associated with increased complaint behavior because people with higher levels of experience know how to go about contacting appropriate authorities and are less bothered by such a task.[19]

As a general statement, researchers have not been particularly successful in relating demographic factors to consumer complaining behavior.[20] One study looked at education, income, age, and experience with the product and their relationship to complaining behavior. The results revealed that experience with the product was by far the most closely related to the tendency to complain.[21] More recent research found a modest relation between age, income, and complaining behavior.[22] Consumers found to engage in complaining behavior after experiencing dissatisfaction tended to be younger and to have higher incomes.

Other investigators have looked at a number of personality variables and their relationship to complaining behavior. Some evidence exists that individuals higher in dogmatism (close-mindedness) and self-confidence were more likely to complain.[23]

Corporate Reactions to Consumer Complaining　Surprisingly, evidence exists that many companies do not make systematic efforts to investigate the extent of consumer satisfaction/dissatisfaction with their products or services. For example, one survey of food marketers found that 60 percent had little or no idea of the satisfaction of consumers with their products.[24] However, consumer-oriented firms do make special efforts to track consumer satisfaction/dissatisfaction with their products and services. The use of toll-free consumer hot-line numbers is becoming increasingly popular for this purpose. Companies such as Procter and Gamble, Whirlpool, and 3M have used such numbers effectively. Because of the expense and personal importance of automobiles, problems with them result in frequent complaints. Auto companies have responded by establishing regional service representatives whom consumers can call if satisfaction cannot be gained from the auto dealer. In fact, Ford, Chrysler, and GM have established some type of quasi-independent panel to arbitrate consumer complaints.

PRODUCT DISPOSITION

Although the study of how consumers dispose of the products they purchase is fundamental to consumer behavior study, little research has been performed in the area of **product disposition.** Figure 9–4 presents a taxonomy of the ways in which consumers can dispose of products.[25] Basically, a consumer has three alternative dispositional strategies after a product has been used for some period of time—keep it, get rid of it permanently, or get rid of it temporarily. Each of these alternatives has suboptions. For example, if the product is kept, it can still be used, converted to a new use, or stored. (Conversion to a new use could include such things as using an old toothbrush as a cleaning device.) Similarly, if the product is to be removed permanently, a number of options exist. The product can be thrown away, given away, traded, or sold.

Table 9–1 presents the results of a study that investigated the disposition decisions for six different products.[26] One clear pattern in the results is that as the value of the product increases, consumers revealed a tendency to dispose of the product through a means that maximizes the value returned.

Figure 9–4   A taxonomy of product disposition. (Adapted by permission, from J. Jacoby, C. Berning, and T. Dietvorst, "What About Disposition?" *Journal of Marketing, 41,* **April 1977, 23.)**

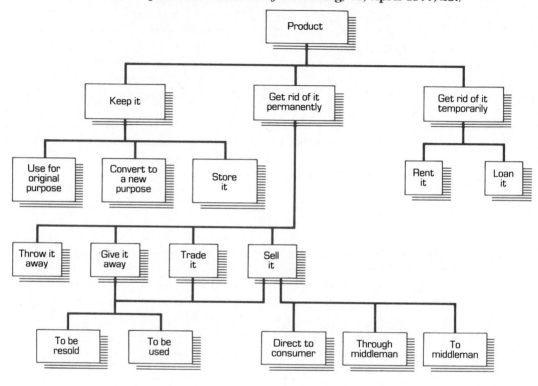

Table 9–1   Disposition Decisions of Six Test Products

	All Products	Stereo Amplifier	Wrist Watch	Tooth-brush	Phono Record	Bicycle	Refrigerator
Converted	7.9%	1.6%	1.8%	17.2%	9.6%	1.5%	7.5%
Stored	12.7	—	28.7	—	32.8	3.1	—
Thrown away	39.7	11.5	30.6	79.7	43.2	17.3	22.6
Given away	17.1	31.1	23.1	—	9.6	40.2	19.3
Sold	11.5	42.6	5.6	—	—	17.3	25.8
Rented	0.7	—	0.9	—	—	—	3.2
Loaned	0.3	—	—	—	—	1.5	1.0
Traded	5.3	4.9	5.6	—	0.8	3.2	20.4
Other	4.8	8.3	3.7	3.1	4.0	15.9	—

SOURCE: J. Jacoby, C. Berning, and T. Dietvorst, "What About Disposition?" *Journal of Marketing,* April 1977, 26. Used by permission.

Thus, refrigerators and stereo amplifiers were less frequently thrown away and more frequently sold.

The disposition of products should be of concern to marketing managers. For some types of products a thriving aftermarket exists which can cut into sales of new products. For example, sales of used textbooks can severely lower the overall sales for a publisher. Although students benefit in the short run by having to pay less for used books, it may actually be harmful in the long run. That is, the cost of new textbooks is increased because fewer new books are sold and because new editions must be brought out sooner. Another enterprise based on product disposition is the used-car market. The used-car market is extremely large, and hundreds of thousands of people make their living buying and selling used cars. With publications such as *Consumer Reports* rating which used cars are best, new-car buyers are beginning to consider the possible resale value of new cars.

THE EFFECTS OF REACTANCE AND DISSONANCE

When a consumer is making a brand choice, he or she may have feelings of anxiety about making the purchase. Immediately before making the choice a person can feel a great deal of conflict about whether or not to make a purchase or about which brand to buy. Similarly, shortly after making an important purchase, the consumer may experience severe feelings of anxiety and doubt about whether the correct purchase was made. Real estate professionals call such an experience **buyer's regret.** The negative feelings, which can occur both before and after a purchase, are caused by the psychological processes of **reactance** and **dissonance.** Because they tend to operate in circumstances in which a salesperson is involved, it is important that sales personnel and companies have a good understanding of them.

Predecisional Reactance

When a consumer compares brands, a negative affective reaction may occur if the individual perceives that his or her behavioral freedom is being threatened. As discussed in Chapter 3 on motivation, such threats to behavioral freedom can result in reactance. But how can the prospect of making a choice cause a person to believe that behavioral freedom is being lost? When a consumer must make a choice between two or more brands, one of the choices must be given up. Particularly, if the choice is important and involves a high degree of financial and social risk, the threat of giving up one of the choices can create a reactance state. The feelings of reactance, in turn, will lead the person to reevaluate positively the alternative that the person was about to give up.

A classic study was performed on the evaluation of alternatives prior to making a choice among decision alternatives.[27] In the study individuals had to choose which of two people would give to them a highly confidential interview concerning personal matters. Ratings of preferences for the two interviewers were taken at various time intervals prior to the point in time when the decision had to be made. The results showed that as the time prior to the decision decreased, the ratings of the two interviewers converged. Reactance theory can explain such a convergence of feelings for two alternatives. Basically, each time the decision maker begins to commit himself or herself to an alternative, reactance is created because the freedom to choose the other alternative is lost. As a result, high degrees of decision conflict occur, and the feelings towards the two alternatives converge.

If the feelings about two important alternatives tend to converge prior to the decision, what happens to these feelings immediately after the decision? Some evidence exists to suggest that shortly after an important decision an individual may experience reactance in the form of buyer's regret. One study investigated the postdecisional feelings of Army recruits who had just chosen their occupational specialties—an extremely important decision with potential life-and-death consequences.[28] The recruits were asked to rate their feelings about their decision at varying amounts of time after the choice. Shortly after the decision the ratings of their choice decreased, indicating that the recruits were having second thoughts about it. While research on the predecisional and postdecisional effects of reactance have not been performed in the consumer area, it is likely that a similar effect would be found. Thus, after an important purchase consumers may reevaluate the unchosen alternative so that it is actually viewed as superior to the chosen alternative. This state of affairs, in which an unchosen alternative is rated more highly than a chosen alternative, is highly aversive and is called cognitive dissonance.

Postpurchase Cognitive Dissonance

In the introductory vignette the experience of buying a house was discussed. My feelings the day after purchasing the house were similar in nature to those of the recruits soon after they selected their occupational specialties. In circumstances in which reactance occurs and the unchosen alternative is viewed more favorably than the alternative selected, the consumer becomes psychologically uncomfortable. I experienced it as an awful feeling making me almost sick to my stomach. This state of psychological discomfort that may occur after an action is called cognitive dissonance.

Cognitive dissonance is closely related to the balance processes discussed in Chapter 8. It is basically an imbalanced state that results when a logical inconsistency exists among cognitive elements. Leon Festinger, the originator of dissonance theory, stated that "two elements are in a dissonant relation if, considering these two alone, the obverse of one element would follow from the other."[29] In the introductory vignette the cognitive elements were the knowledge that I bought a house I didn't like and that I am a careful, prudent decision maker. These two ideas were in conflict and created a dissonant state.

How Do People Resolve Dissonance? According to Leon Festinger, the experience of dissonance is an aversive state, and people will act to reduce it. After purchasing a product, three different means exist for reducing dissonance.

1. Break the link between the person's self-concept and the product by returning the product or complaining about it.[30]
2. Add new information by reading material relevant to the purchase.
3. Psychologically reevaluate the desirability of the chosen alternative in a positive direction and the desirability of the unchosen alternative in a negative direction.

The first alternative has quite negative implications for the brand. If a person seeks to lower dissonance by returning the product or by engaging in negative word-of-mouth communications, the company will lose one or more sales of the product. In the second alternative the consumer seeks to resolve the cognitive imbalance by obtaining greater amounts of information. The third approach to handling dissonance is reevaluating the desirability of the chosen alternative. In this case the consumer lowers the psychological imbalance by gradually changing the perception of the brand purchased and the brand(s) not purchased. Thus, feelings towards the brand chosen become more favorable, and the feelings towards the brands not chosen become less favorable.

A number of consumer researchers have investigated the predictions of dissonance theory. In one study consumers had to choose between a number of different record albums.[31] In the high-dissonance condition, the albums were all rated relatively highly. In the low-dissonance condition, one of the albums was clearly preferred by most of the participants. In the high-dissonance conditions, preference for the chosen album increased after the purchase, whereas preference for the album not chosen decreased after the purchase. In the low-dissonance situation, preferences remained essentially unchanged after the purchase. This finding supports the third means of dissonance reduction mentioned previously. In fact, the reevaluation of the chosen alternative in a favorable direction is a common means of reducing dissonance.

The record album experiment just mentioned illustrates one of the necessary conditions for a person to experience cognitive dissonance after a purchase. Table 9–2 presents six factors that influence the degree of dissonance

Table 9–2 Factors Associated with the Creation of Cognitive Dissonance

1. Two or more alternatives are rated similarly in overall favorability.
2. Two or more alternatives, although rated similarly, are perceived to differ on specific attributes.
3. The person has free choice.
4. The person is committed to the decision.
5. The person is highly involved in the purchase.
6. The tendency of the person is to experience dissonance.

experienced.[32] The first two factors are interrelated. In order to experience dissonance the person must have similar feelings about two or more of the preferred alternatives. If one of the brands is clearly superior to the others, no dissonance will be felt. However, a second condition also exists. The brands perceived to be similar must also be rated differently on different attributes. In other words, if the brands are perceived to be similar in every way, it would not make any difference which was chosen. However, if one is good in some areas and not so good in others, and the other brand is good in the areas in which the first is poor (or vice versa) a great deal of conflict will be felt.

The remaining conditions necessary for dissonance are quite logical. The consumer must be able to choose freely among the alternatives. If he or she is forced to choose one brand, say because of price or availability, dissonance will not be experienced. Further, the person must be committed to the decision. If it is possible to back out of it at any time, dissonance will not be felt. Another important factor is that the purchase must be a highly involving one that involves substantial perceived risk. The risk could be financial, social, time, performance, or others. In such instances it becomes important to make the best choice, and people are more likely to feel conflict in their decision. Finally, individual differences have been found to exist in experiencing dissonance. That is, some consumers will feel greater conflict and doubt about their purchases than others.

Figure 9–5 diagrams the potential effects of reactance and dissonance on a purchase in high-involvement, free-choice circumstances. Note that prior

Figure 9–5   The effects of reactance and dissonance before and after purchase.

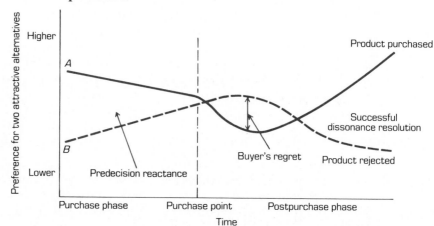

In this example product *A* was purchased. Dissonance was reduced satisfactorily such that the buyer preferred product *A* some time after making the purchase.

to the purchase, predecision reactance may cause a convergence of preferences for the two alternatives. Further, immediately after the purchase reactance may cause a phase of buyer's regret. If buyer's regret occurs, the unchosen alternative is rated more highly than the brand purchased and feelings of cognitive inconsistency result. In order to relieve the effects of the cognitive dissonance, over a period of time the consumer may cognitively reorganize his or her attitudes about the alternatives. Thus, in order to reach the preferred state of cognitive consistency, the favorability toward the purchased product increases and the favorability toward the foregone product decreases.

From a managerial perspective the recognition of the effects of dissonance and reactance is important. It is likely that if the conditions are ripe to cause dissonance, the consumer may also have a tendency to experience reactance. This could result in the consumer having difficulty choosing between brands and being more likely to experience a severe case of buyer's regret. As noted earlier in the chapter, dissonance and reactance tend to occur when consumers buy products sold by sales personnel. That is, sales personnel tend to be used to sell high-involvement products, such as homes, automobiles, and computers. Sales personnel should be aware of the effects of reactance and dissonance and take steps to minimize their negative impact. For example, the real estate agent mentioned in the introductory vignette helped the author to overcome his buyer's regret over the purchase of a house. His approach involved pointing out to me that people frequently have second thoughts after buying a house and patting me on the back for having bought such a beautiful house and getting such a good price for it.

Some companies have developed systematic programs to contact consumers after their purchase. For example, in the mid-1980s Honda, Ford, and Audi had a program of contacting consumers in the first year after making a purchase to check on the buyers' satisfaction and to assist the buyers if any problems existed. Such programs may help consumers resolve their postpurchase anxieties.

Managerial Implications

Managers and public policy makers should take an active interest in the postpurchase process for two basic reasons. First, consumers may factor into their decision process information on how a company will treat them after a purchase. Thus, in reaching a buying decision for high-involvement products, such as durables, consumers may consider such factors as the length of warranty, the presence or absence of service contracts, and whether a toll-free hot line exists so that the company can be reached in case problems occur. A second reason for being concerned with postpurchase processes is that they influence the consumer's satisfaction with the purchase. Dissatisfied consumers tend not to repurchase the product, spread negative word-of-mouth information, and even file lawsuits against the company.

As an overall statement, one can say that perhaps the most important goal of managers relevant to postpurchase processes is to attempt to insure the postpurchase satisfaction of consumers. The factor most relevant to postpurchase satisfaction is the satisfactory performance of the product. If the expectations of the consumer regarding product performance are not fulfilled, it is likely that dissatisfaction will result. Conversely, if the product meets expectations, or even better surpasses expectations, the consumer is rewarded for his or her purchase. As operant conditioning principles suggest, in such instances the likelihood of the consumer repurchasing the product should then increase.

In order to insure that product performance meets or exceeds expectations, managers should carefully analyze quality control as well as the promotion of the products. In other words, the product may perform below expectations either because it is produced or designed poorly or because the promotional materials have promised more than it can deliver. In addition, other factors can influence performance expectations. These include the performance of competitive products, the characteristics of the target market segment, and the price of the product.

In some instances companies may attempt to capitalize on the dissatisfaction of customers of other corporations. The goal is to create a state in which customers recognize that a problem exists with some aspect of the product or service they have purchased. An excellent example of this strategy is found in the advertisement by Wang shown in Figure 9–6. In the ad Wang makes the point that IBM withdrew its support for one of its computer systems. The ad attempts to reach IBM customers by indicating that Wang can both solve the problem and provide an easily updated system.

A second means of maintaining postpurchase satisfaction is by providing outstanding levels of service. Indeed, many purchase decisions are based upon expectations that the company will provide excellent service after the sale. IBM has been successful in part because of the high levels of service that the company traditionally has offered.

Managers should also consider consumer perceptions of equity. The question should be asked, Do my customers feel as though they are being treated equitably? In answering this question, the manager should identify how consumers view the inputs and outcomes of the two parties in the exchange process. Of particular concern to the manager is whether consumers recognize all of the inputs the company has to the transaction.

In particular, certain service industries have problems with consumers not recognizing the quantity of input by service providers to the transaction. For example, in the real estate industry many home sellers complain that the real estate commissions are too high. In a seller's market their home, which they sell for $100,000, may only be on the market for a month or so. Because

Figure 9–6   Wang attempts to capitalize on possible consumer dissatisfaction with other brands. (*Courtesy of Wang Laboratories, Inc.*)

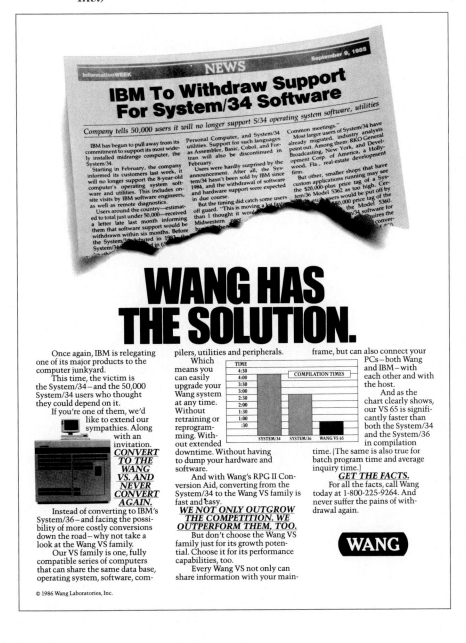

they see relatively little of the real estate agent, they perceive her inputs to be very small in relation to her outcomes, i.e., the 6 percent commission she receives.

The problem for real estate professionals is that many if not most of their activities go unobserved by home sellers. The home seller is not aware of all of the contacts an agent may make that do not result in the bringing of prospective buyers to the house. Furthermore, most sellers are unaware that much of the 6 percent commission goes to the broker, who has to pay for secretaries, rent, and various other fees. By prudently making the seller aware of these hidden costs, the real estate agent may increase the satisfaction of the seller with the exchange.

When complaints do occur, managers should have mechanisms in place to handle them. Highlight 9–2 describes one highly effective means of handling complaints–the "800" toll-free number. The presence of warranties is another way for consumers to have their complaints handled. Recently, another approach has been developed that can diminish the ill feelings resulting from product problems—the service contract.

Buying a service contract is somewhat like buying insurance. The cus-

---

HIGHLIGHT 9–2

How to Increase Satisfaction by Giving Consumers a Way to Complain—the "800" Number

What do Avis, Kentucky Fried Chicken, General Electric, and Clairol have in common? They all have implemented consumer hot lines via toll-free "800" numbers as a way for consumers to air their gripes.

Consumer hot lines can do a number of things for a corporation. One major benefit is that they can personalize the large corporation. As one General Electric executive stated, "Major companies, including GE, have become somewhat faceless. . . . We're trying to put a face on the company and make a large company like a small one."

Another benefit is happier customers. One expert on consumer complaints argued that hot lines can increase brand loyalty. He noted that only about 4 percent of dissatisfied customers complain. Instead, they simply stop buying the product and then bad-mouth the company. A hot line can break the cycle by encouraging a customer to complain.

A third benefit of the hot line is that it can actually reduce warranty costs. Many routine problems can be handled over the phone, avoiding lengthy mailed communications. Because responding by phone is one-third the cost of responding by letter, savings may result.

Consumer hot lines, however, do have some problems. They are expensive. One three-minute call costs about 3 dollars. They can also backfire. Consumers quickly become irate if all they receive are busy signals or are placed on hold for long periods of time. In addition, companies may receive unusual requests. For example, Kellogg's had to discontinue their toll-free number for Frosted Flakes when kids kept asking for Tony the Tiger.

However, for most consumer goods firms the toll-free number is becoming a necessary part of the marketing effort. Indeed, without it firms may be at a competitive disadvantage.

Based on Bill Abrams, "More Firms Use '800' Numbers to Keep Consumers Satisfied," *The Wall Street Journal*, April 7, 1983, 29.

tomer pays a premium to guarantee that over some period of time certain problems which occur with a product will be fixed by the manufacturer or retailer. Service contracts have been adopted strongly by auto manufacturers. In 1983 Ford had some 2.2 million contracts written on its vehicles. One Ford executive stated that "We've found a customer with a service contract is twice as likely to buy from the dealer again and is twice as likely to be a satisfied customer."[33]

Some of the automobile companies have developed a fourth way of dealing with consumer complaints. They have put into place third party arbitration programs. For example, General Motors has developed a program in which consumers can present their automobile problem to an unbiased third person who then decides exactly how the problem should be remedied.

Managers should also be aware of the effects of reactance and dissonance on consumers. When consumers are engaged in a high-involvement purchase in which they must choose between several alternatives and in which they have free choice as well as commitment, the conditions are ripe for reactance to cause them to lower their evaluation of the chosen alternative. As a result, they will feel dissonance. Because reactance can cause consumers to be dissatisfied with the purchase, managers should consider how they can help consumers resolve in a favorable way the dissonance produced.

One thing consumers can do when experiencing dissonance is search for additional information. The information sought can be either positive or negative regarding their purchase.[34] One strategy that companies may implement is to try to contact consumers after their purchase. This strategy has been used by Ford, Honda and Audi.

Researchers have investigated the effectiveness of following up purchases with favorable information about the product. In one study, consumer researchers investigated the effects of either sending letters, calling customers, or doing nothing after a purchase of a refrigerator.[35] The letters and phone calls thanked the customers for making the purchase and reassured them that they had made a wise purchase. The results revealed that sending a letter reduced doubt or dissonance in comparison to those who received no information. However, people who received a phone call actually had higher levels of doubt. The telephone call may have been so unusual that it actually frightened the buyers. These results show that dissonance may be reduced by carefully constructed communications made after the purchase.

Public policy makers also have a major interest in the postpurchase satisfaction of consumers. If they find that consumer satisfaction becomes too low, they may become interested in developing regulations that could possibly ameliorate the problem. Of course, in most instances managers seek to avoid the encroachment of government, and the possibility can be a strong force for industries to set up standards that all companies are supposed to follow.

The Council of the Better Business Bureaus, Inc., has compiled information on the types of industries that receive the most complaints. Table 9–3

Table 9–3   The Top Ten Complaint Categories by Type of Business

Type of Business	Percentage of Total Complaints
1. General mail-order companies	23.4%
2. Franchised auto dealers	5.9
3. Magazines ordered by mail	2.9
4. Miscellaneous home maintenance companies	2.9
5. Home furnishing stores	2.9
6. Auto repair shops	2.6
7. Department stores	2.3
8. Miscellaneous automotive	2.2
9. Television service companies	1.8
10. Dry cleaning/laundry companies	1.8

SOURCE: Adapted from data in Kevin Higgins, "Mail Order Industry Is Fighting the Old, Sleazy Image on Several Fronts," *Marketing News, 17,* July 8, 1983, 1, 12.

presents the top ten complaint categories by type of business. The table shows that mail-order companies received the largest numbers of complaints, followed by auto dealers. With the rapid growth of the direct-mail industry, one should not be surprised to find regulators stepping in with proposed regulations to end abuses. (Chapter 19 discusses the public policy implications of consumer behavior in detail.)

SUMMARY

The postpurchase phase of the consumer buying process consists of four stages—product use, the formation of postpurchase attitudes, consumer complaint behavior, and product disposition. The postpurchase phase has a major impact on whether consumers will repurchase the product. In addition, expectations of how they will be treated in the postpurchase phase may influence actual buying decisions.

The product-usage stage of the postpurchase process has received relatively little attention by consumer researchers. However, it is important. Consumers do not always use products in the ways expected by manufacturers. As discussed further in Chapter 19, product misuse is the major cause of consumer injuries. In addition, the study of product usage can give ideas for changes in current products or for new products.

The satisfaction or dissatisfaction that consumers feel during and after product use form the postpurchase attitudes of buyers. Feelings of satisfaction may be viewed as resulting from either of two possible processes. One process is expectancy confirmation. When the expected performance of the product fails to met expectations, emotional dissatisfaction may be said to result. When performance meets expectations, a consumer may be said to have expectancy confirmation. The consumer will probably be satisfied with the purchase, but will probably not think much about it. It is when performance surpasses expectations that emotional satisfaction is likely to result from the purchase. The performance expected of a product or purchase is influenced by the nature of the product, by promotional factors, by the effects of other products, and by the characteristics of the consumer.

The satisfaction with a purchase may also be influenced by feelings of inequity. Such feelings of inequity may occur when consumers perceive that the ratio of their outcomes to inputs is inferior to another's ratio of outcomes to inputs. The other person could be a retailer, a service agent of some type (such as a real estate agent or stockbroker), or even another consumer. Inputs are the information, effort, money, time, and other resources with which the two parties enter the exchange. Outcomes are the benefits and liabilities that result from the exchange for each party.

If a consumer feels dissatisfied with a purchase, he or she may engage in consumer complaint behavior. Complaints can take many different forms, from simply not buying the product or service again, to telling friends about the problem, to making verbal or written complaints, to seeking redress from the business or from the legal system. Consumers complain for either of two reasons. They may complain in order to recover economic loss. In addition, they may complain as a means of restoring their self-concept, which may be injured to some extent as a result of the product or service problem.

Research into consumer complaining reveals that most consumers are satisfied with their purchases. Of those who are dissatisfied, the percentage who take some action to resolve their problem depends upon the type of product purchased. For low-cost household items as few as 15 percent of consumers appear to take some action. However, for socially visible products, such as clothing, the percentage rises to about 75 percent of consumers taking some action. Corporations need to monitor consumer complaint behavior and have programs installed to deal with complaints. Some approaches to stem complaints include the use of warranties, service contracts, consumer hot lines, and regional service representatives.

The final phase of the postpurchase process is product disposition. Consumers can dispose of products in three general ways. They can keep the product for later use, they can get rid of it permanently, or they can get rid of it temporarily by renting it or loaning it out. Managers should be aware of the various means of disposition used by consumers. For certain consumer durables, such as automobiles, how much a consumer can get for a product when he or she finishes using it is an important factor in selecting a brand. Some auto manufacturers, such as BMW, stress in their advertising the high resale value of the cars. In other instances, regulations may exist regarding how products are to be disposed. Particularly in the industrial area, a variety of hazardous chemicals must be disposed of in highly specific and often expensive ways.

Closely related to the area of postpurchase attitudes is that of the effects of reactance and dissonance on consumers. Reactance may cause consumers to view a newly purchased product somewhat negatively. In some instances this may be combined with an elevation of feelings towards an unchosen alternative. These feelings result from the fact that by making a choice, the consumer's behavioral freedom to choose has been restricted. These feelings resulting from reactance can then lead to cognitive dissonance. The dissonance occurs when the consumer perceives that he or she has chosen an inferior alternative. The result is psychological discomfort.

Dissonance can be resolved in any of three ways. The consumer can return the product or call off the deal. The consumer can attempt to add new information about the purchase. Finally, the consumer can reevaluate the alternatives in order to bring his or her feelings back into consonance. Of course, managers hope that the third option occurs for consumers. In order to assist consumers in reevaluating the chosen alternative in a more favorable direction, some companies have begun to communicate with consumers after the purchase in order to positively reinforce them for their choice.

Key Terms

Postpurchase attitudes
Postpurchase satisfaction
Postpurchase dissatisfaction
Actual product performance
Expected product performance
Brand expectation
Expectancy confirmation
Equity theory

Outcome
Inputs
Complaint behavior
Product disposition
Reactance
Dissonance
Buyer's regret
Emotional dissatisfaction
Emotional satisfaction
Expected product performance

Review Questions

1. What factors influence the formation of postpurchase satisfaction and dissatisfaction?
2. Identify the factors that influence the formation of brand expectations.
3. How do feelings of equity influence satisfaction/dissatisfaction with an exchange?
4. How does the equity approach to understanding postpurchase satisfaction differ from the expectation confirmation approach?
5. What are the actions a consumer may take when he or she is dissatisfied with a product or service?
6. What are the two major reasons why consumers complain?
7. To what extent do consumers take overt action to complain when they are dissatisfied?
8. Eight factors have been identified that influence consumer complaining. Identify six of the eight factors.
9. Discuss the various ways in which consumers may dispose of a product.
10. What are the effects of reactance on the predecisional preference for brands that are actively being considered for purchase?
11. What is the effect of reactance on preferences immediately after a purchase?
12. Define the concept of cognitive dissonance. What are its effects on postpurchase feelings?
13. What are the factors necessary for the formation of dissonance?
14. What are some actions companies may take to help resolve postpurchase dissonance?
15. Identify four actions companies can take to help insure postpurchase satisfaction.

Discussion Questions

1. While you have probably never tried to use a lawnmower to trim a hedge, you probably have used products in unintended ways. Think back upon your own behavior and identify instances in which you have misused products. (For example, did you ever stick a knife into a toaster without unplugging it first?) Did your consumer misbehavior result in any problems? Could the manufacturer have done anything to prevent you from your actions?
2. Look through a magazine at the print advertisements. What kinds of expectations did the ads

create, such as beliefs regarding product performance, postpurchase satisfaction, or social benefits of owning the product? To what extent do you believe that the products will fulfill these expectations?

3. What are some of the actions the real estate industry might take as part of an effort to create consumer beliefs that an equitable relationship exists between the sellers of homes and the real estate agent?

4. Equity theory predicts that consumers will analyze their purchases in relation to similar purchases made by other consumers. Identify one or two instances in which you compared the outcomes of a purchase you made to the outcomes of a similar purchase made by another consumer. What were the bases for comparison that you used? Did any feelings of inequity/dissatisfaction result from the comparison?

5. List several occassions when you expressed some type of consumer dissatisfaction. On the occassions when the retailers could do something about it, was the outcome satisfactory? What could the retailers have done to improve the outcome?

6. To what extent have you or would you consider the resale value of a car prior to purchasing it? Go to a bookstore and find one of the magazines that gives you resale values of automobiles. Based upon resale value, which of the following sports cars would you purchase—Nissan 300ZX, Mazda RX7, Porsche 944, or Chevrolet Corvette?

7. Thinking about the sports car that you found in question 6 to have the highest resale value, how might its manufacturer make this point when promoting the car? Please describe any advertising you have seen mentioning the resale value of an automobile or other product.

8. According to reactance theory, as the time when a decision approaches the preference between two closely evaluated alternatives will tend to converge. From a personal-selling perspective, what are some actions that a salesman might take to keep this convergence of preferences from occurring?

9. The statement was made in the introductory vignette of the chapter that the purchase of the house had all of the ingredients to create high levels of cognitive dissonance. Discuss the purchase of the house and how it illustrates the six factors associated with the experience of dissonance identified in Table 9–2.

10. Think back upon one or two major decisions you have made in the past, such as buying a car or selecting which college or university to attend. Did you experience reactance prior to and immediately after the decision? How much dissonance did you feel after making the decision? How was the dissonance resolved? Please explain your answers.

References

1. "Meanwhile, P&G Is Losing One of Its Best Customers," *The Wall Street Journal*, May 1, 1985, 31.

2. J. A. Prestbo, "At Procter and Gamble, Success Is Largely Due to Heeding Consumer," *The Wall Street Journal*, April 29, 1980, 23.

3. For a review of many of these problems see John C. Mowen and Hal Ellis. "The Product Defect: Managerial Implications and Consumer Implications," *The Annual Review of Marketing*, Ben Enis and Kenneth Roering (eds.), 1981, 158–172.

4. R. B. Woodruff, E. R. Cadotte, and R. L. Jenkins, "Modeling Consumer Satisfaction Processes Using Experience-Based Norms," *Journal of Marketing Research*, 20 August 1983, 296–304.

5. Woodruff, Cadotte, and Jenkins, "Modeling Consumer Satisfaction Processes."

6. R. L. Oliver, "A Cognitive Model of the Antecedents and Consequences of Satisfaction Decisions," *Journal of Marketing Research*, 17 November 1980, 460–469.

7. Woodruff et al., "Modeling Consumer Satisfaction."

8. Oliver, "A Cognitive Model."

9. Woodruff et al., "Modeling Consumer Satisfaction."

10. J. S. Adams, "Toward an Understanding of Inequity," *Journal of Abnormal and Social Psychology*, 67, 1963, 422–436.

11. The equity ratio shown has been criticized and is given primarily for pedagogical purposes. See John C. Alessio, "Another Folly for Equity Theory," *Social Psychological Quarterly*, 43, September 1980, 336–340.

12. R. P. Fisk and C. E. Young, "Disconfirmation of Equity Expectation: Effects on Consumer Satisfaction with Services," *Advances in Consumer Research, XII*, E. C. Hirschman and M. B. Holbrook (eds.), Ann

Arbor, Mich: Association for Consumer Research, 1985, 340–345.

13. For other studies of equity in consumer behavior see J. W. Huppertz, S. J. Arenson, and R. H. Evans, "An Application of Equity Theory to Buyer-Seller Exchange Situations," *Journal of Marketing Research, 15*, May 1978, 250–260.

14. J. E. Swan and Alice Mercer, "Consumer Satisfaction as a Function of Equity and Disconfirmation," in *Conceptual and Empirical Contributions to Consumer Satisfaction and Complaining Behavior*, Sixth Annual Conference, H. Hunt and R. Day (eds.), Bloomington, Ind.: Indiana University 1982, 2–8.

15. R. Day, "Extending the Concept of Consumer Satisfaction," in *Advances in Consumer Research, IV,* W. D. Perreault (ed.), Ann Arbor, Mich.: Association for Consumer Research, 1977, 153.

16. A. Andreason and A. Best, "Consumers Complain—Does Business Respond?" *Harvard Business Review, 55*, July–August 1977, 93–101.

17. R. E. Krapfel, "A Consumer Complaint Strategy Model: Antecedents and Outcomes," *Advances in Consumer Research, XII,* E. Hirschman and M. Holbrook (eds.), Ann Arbor, Mich.: Association for Consumer Research, 1985, 346–350.

18. E. L. Landon, "A Model of Consumer Complaint Behavior," in *Consumer Satisfaction, Dissatisfaction, and Complaining Behavior*, Ralph Day (ed.), Symposium Proceedings, School of Business, University of Indiana, Bloomington, Ind., 1977, 20–22.

19. See K. Gronhaug and G. Zaltman, "Complainers and Noncomplainers Revisited: Another Look at the Data," *Advances in Consumer Research, VIII,* K. Monroe (ed.), Ann Arbor, Mich.: Association for Consumer Research, 1981, 83–87.

20. Gronhaug and Zaltman, "Complainers and Noncomplainers Revisited."

21. Ibid.

22. W. O. Bearden and J. B. Mason, "An Investigation of Influences on Consumer Complaint Reports," *Advances in Consumer Research, XI,* Thomas Kinnear (ed.), Ann Arbor, Mich.: Association for Consumer Research, 1984, 490–495.

23. See J. Faricy and M. Maxio, "Personality and Consumer Dissatisfaction: A Multi-Dimensional Approach," in *Marketing in Turbulent Times*, E. M. Mazze (ed.), Chicago, Ill.: American Marketing Association, 1975, 202–208; and W. O. Bearden and J. E. Teel, "An Investigation of Personal Influences on Consumer Complaining," *Journal of Retailing, 57*, Fall 1981, 3–20.

24. R. C. Stokes, "Consumer Complaints and Dissatisfaction," speech before Food Update Conference, The Food and Drug Law Institute, April 1974, Phoenix, Ariz.

25. J. Jacoby, C. K. Berning, and T. F. Dietvorst, "What About Disposition?" *Journal of Marketing, 41*, April 1977, 23.

26. Jacoby et al., "What About Disposition?"

27. D. Linder and K. Crane, "A Reactance Theory Analysis of Predecisional Cognitive Processes," *Journal of Personality and Social Psychology, 15*, July 1970, 258–264.

28. E. Walster, "The Temporal Sequence of Post-Decisional Processes," in *Conflict, Choice, and Dissonance*, L. Festinger (ed.), Stanford, Calif.: Stanford University Press, 1964, 112–127.

29. L. Festinger, *A Theory of Cognitive Dissonance*, Stanford, Calif.: Stanford University Press, 1957, 13.

30. E. Aronson, "Dissonance Theory: Progress and Problems," in *Theories of Cognitive Consistency: A Sourcebook*, R. Abelson, E. Aronson, W. McGuire, M. Rosenburg, and P. Tannenbaum (eds.), Chicago, Ill.: Rand McNally, 1968, 5–27.

31. L. LoSciuto and R. Perloff, "Influence of Product Performance on Dissonance Reduction," *Journal of Marketing Research, 6*, August 1967, 186–190.

32. For an excellent discussion on the factors required to experience dissonance, see C. A. Insko and J. Schopler, *Experimental Social Psychology*, New York, N.Y.: Academic Press, 1972.

33. Roger Howard, "Keeping the Market Securely Covered," *Advertising Age*, June 6, 1983, M–38.

34. R. Lowe and I. Steiner, "Some Effects of the Reversibility and Consequences of Decisions on Post-Decision Information Preferences," *Journal of Personality and Social Psychology, 8*, April 1968, 172–179.

35. S. Hunt, "Post-Transactional Communication and Dissonance Reduction," *Journal of Marketing, 34*, January 1970, 46–51.

PART II

The Consumer Environment

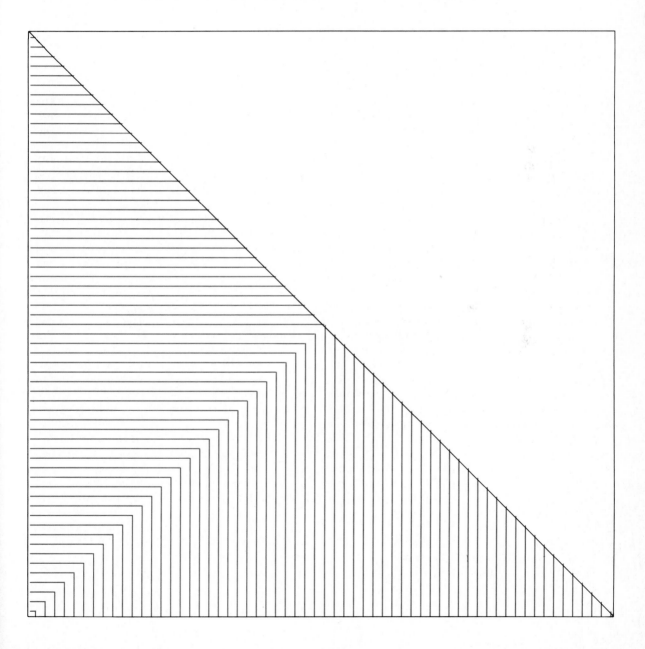

Images of Consumer Behavior: Part II

Part II of the text focuses on identifying the environmental forces that influence consumers. Various types of situational factors bridge the study of the individual and the investigation of the environment. One situational factor is the task definition that occasions an action, such as giving a gift or making a purchase. The Heineken ad below depicts the use of one special occasion—Christmas—to influence consumers' buying behavior. If not gift giving, what might the ad be suggesting about Heineken and the holiday season?

The source of information may influence how a consumer responds. Various types of sources exist, such as famous personalities, cartoon characters and even animals. The Dogmor ad below, produced by Ogilvy and Mather, uses a dog to endorse its message to consumers.

"I was a Mexican hairless terrier until I tasted new Dogmor with vitamin enriched grrravy."

You know at one time I had no luck at all with the fairer sex.

I don't know what it was but they would take one look at me, turn tail and I'd never see them again.

I tried everything to boost my appeal, but nothing seemed to work. When the wig and false moustache failed, I tried tempting them with tacos. I tried lying under a sombrero. I even gave up eating chili. But I was barking up the wrong tree.

My desire for feminine company burned within, but it wasn't enough to warm up the cold winter nights.

Then one day my human brought home a bag of Dogmor with vitamin enriched grrravy. Do you know that it took just one mouthful of that delicious Steak 'n Kidney flavour with its 27 essential ingredients, and I could feel my appeal increasing.

Maybe it was Dogmor's vitamin enriched grrravy that did the trick. All I know is that from that moment on, I knew I would never again have to stay at home on a Saturday night. My social life has blossomed and my phone number is hot property around the neighbourhood.

Just the other day a French Poodle asked me over for the afternoon.

Believe me, a siesta was the last thing she had in mind.

New Dogmor
with vitamin enriched grrravy.
Puts hair on a dog's chest.

Reprinted Courtesy of *Oklahoma State* University Public Information Services

Consumers are influenced by a variety of groups and sometimes seek out occasions to be a part of a crowd. This photo portrays the excitement of people watching a football game.

Rambo and Kid B. King Syma

OPPOSITE: The family is a particularly important socialization agent for children. In addition, however, the media and its fictional characters also influence the values of our youth, as shown in the photo.

Subcultures are an important basis for the segmentation of the market by firms. For example, religious groups may form subcultures. The two ads below for the Episcopal church are targeting another subculture—women—in order to differentiate the church from other denominations.

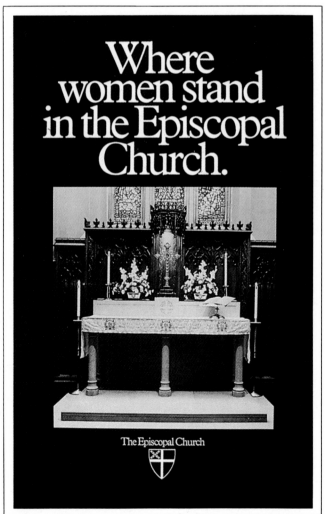

In the church started by a man who had six wives, forgiveness goes without saying.

The Episcopal Church

Reprinted courtesy of the Episcopal Ad Project

Where women stand in the Episcopal Church.

The Episcopal Church

Consumers are influenced by the values and symbols of the culture in which they live or with which they identify. In the Colombian coffee ad on the left, and the New York Air ad on the right, can you identify the symbols used and the values with which they are identified?

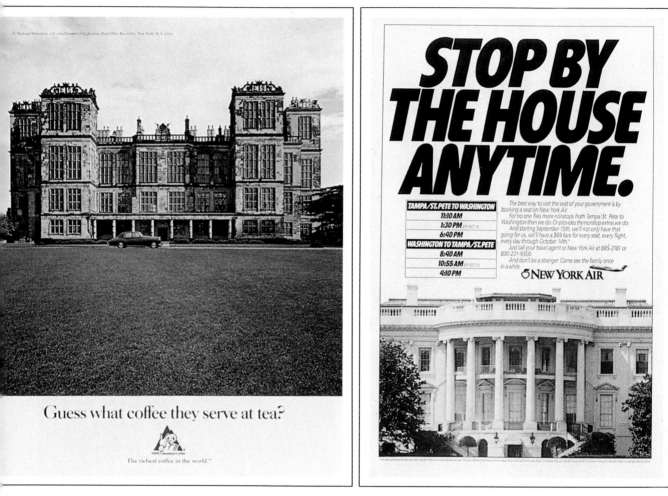

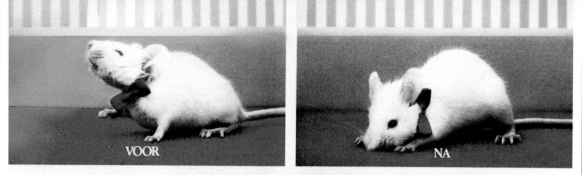

VOOR   NA

EEN ALLERGISCH MUISJE NEEMT MEN NIET BIJ DE NEUS.

Voor wie het kleinste stofje al te veel is is er maar één echte oplossing · de onveranderlijke kracht van de COMPUTER CONTROL stofzuiger van Philips.

Hij is even wendbaar als een muisje en met één lichte vingerdruk regelt u de steel tot op de millimeter waardoor geen hoekje onbereikbaar blijft. Daarom hebben we die steel MAGIC TUBE genoemd. En vermits deze computergestuurde stofzuiger even gevoelig is als het gevoeligste muizeneusje, heeft hij een exclusief filtersysteem dat bovendien, dankzij de AFS 2000 filter de lucht van de uitlaat filtert en bijna alle geniepige stofjes de pas afsnijdt. De Philips COMPUTER CONTROL moet je in huis hebben want het kleinste stofdeeltje is nog te veel voor de neus van een allergisch muisje.

DE COMPUTER CONTROL STOFZUIGER VAN PHILIPS.

PHILIPS

DE TECHNOLOGIE START MET STIL   PHILIPS LOOPT VOOROP

International marketing is becoming increasingly important for U.S. firms. Understanding how consumers differ in foreign cultures is an important consideration, as the Philips Consumer products ad produced by J. Walter Thompson, Brussels, (above) entitled "We Can't Fool the Nose of an Allergic Mouse," and the ad (right) for ECCO Newport, "May We Present" both suggest.

Får vi presentera Eccos nya fina modesko.

Innehåller inget som är hårt, styvt och stumt.

Bara sånt som är mjukt, skönt och bra för fötterna.

Samtidigt så läckert designad att du kan segla fräsch och välklädd genom livets flesta skeden.

Ecco Newport heter den.

Gjord i äkta skinn och med spänstig och slitstark sula som alla andra Ecco.

Finns i storlek 35–47 i vårens färger.

Prova Ecco Newport!

NEW·PORT

SAFETY BELT EDUCATION CAMPAIGN
PUBLIC SERVICE SPOTS

Please discontinue use after December 31, 1986.

"PRE CRASH"   (CNTD-5230)   30 SECONDS

VINCE: After this joy ride, I'm out of the crash dummy business for good.

LARRY: But, Vince, it's a great job. Heck, they'd have to pry me away from it.

VINCE: Anybody home? Larry, they do pry you away. LARRY: Oh, yeah.

VINCE: For years, I've been eating steering wheels. For what? LARRY: To prove how safety belts save lives.

VINCE: But thousands die every year in car accidents 'cause they don't buckle up.

LARRY: Vince, we're dummies. We don't wear safety belts.

VINCE: Larry, you really know how to hurt a guy. Hit it.

ANNCR. (VO): You could learn a lot from a dummy. Buckle your safety belt.

"POST CRASH"   (CNTD-5330)   30 SECONDS

VINCE: That's it -- I'm history -- end of the road.

LARRY: You can't quit, Vince. No crash dummy takes out a utility pole like you do.

VINCE: Larry, for years I've been proving how safety belts save lives. But nobody's listening.

LARRY: Sure they are. VINCE: Yeah, that's why thousands die in car accidents every year.

I feel like I'm banging my head against the wall.

LARRY: Come on, Vince. Tomorrow's the big day. Two compacts. Head on.

VINCE: High speed? LARRY: Could save a life. VINCE: I'll be there. LARRY: Yeah!

ANNCR. (VO): You could learn a lot from a dummy. Buckle your safety belt.

Volunteer Advertising Agency: Leo Burnett U.S.A.
Volunteer Coordinator: Susan Leick, McDonald's Corp.

The study of consumer behavior has direct application to public policy issues. The story board for the Ad Council, depicted above, employs a humorous message from an unusual source to encourage safety belt use. (Ad Council Ad for U.S. Department of Transportation)

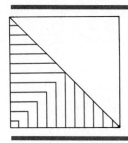

10
Situational Influences

Bok Choy Wah-Wahs Create Buying Panic

Holidays are prime gift-giving situations, and during Christmas 1983, American households were in turmoil. A $29 present was in short supply, and parents began doing strange things. In Miami, Florida, the police were called in when hundreds of shoppers began trampling each other. In a West Virginia town, 5,000 shoppers appeared at one store when it advertised that a supply of the gift was available. In some places shoppers began arriving at 3 A.M. to get in line. One man flew to London to find the gift. (a)

Rumors began to spread. A radio announcer, as a joke, announced that a B-29 bomber would make an airborne delivery of 2,000 of the gifts to Milwaukee County Stadium. A dozen people fell for the gag and showed up to catch the sensations as they fell from the sky.

The extent of the gift's popularity could be seen in the want ads. In the Boston *Globe* one could find twenty-two ads in one day for the gift. Prices went as high as $3,000. An ad in the Chicago *Tribune* offered to trade two tickets to the Rose Bowl for the present. An ad in the Washington *Post* stated, "Brother and Sister, will not separate family, best offer over $2,000." (b)

The product even began to be traded like a security in an over-the-counter market. At one time the bid price was $40 and the sell price was $50. The broker who set up the market got the $10 difference in the prices. (c)

The company marketing the product was Coleco Industries. Production actually began in China, where it was called "bok choy wah-wah." The stitching and stuffing of the product were done in China because of the country's cheap but highly skilled seamstresses. However, a problem faced by Coleco was that in the autumn and spring, the seamstresses left work to harvest the rice crop. From China the product went to Hong Kong, where the heads were molded and yarn hair put on. The CEO of the Hong Kong manufacturing facility called the product the ugliest doll he had ever seen.

Well, what does "bok choy wah-wah" mean? You guessed it—cabbage doll. The sixteen-inch dolls came with birth certificates and adoption papers. No two dolls were alike. The name Cabbage Patch came from the old wives' tale that babies come from the cabbage patch. In 1983 Coleco was estimated to have shipped 2.5 million of the dolls and could have sold many more were it not for production limitations. Furthermore, the doll was still popular in 1986, and the line had been expanded to include clothing and strollers for the dolls. (d)

Based on (a) "Doll Sales Cause Pandemonium," *The Daily O'Collegian*, Tuesday, November 29, 1983, 14; (b) "Patch"-Doll Mania Hits Wants Ads," *USA Today*, December 19, 1983, 1; (c) "Oh, You Beautiful Dolls," *Newsweek*, December 12, 1983, 78-85; (d) Adi Ignatius, "Cabbage Patch Dolls, Believe It or Not, Begin as Bok Choy Wah-Wahs in China," *The Wall Street Journal*, Thursday December 8, 1983, 36.

INTRODUCTION

The consumer vignette just presented illustrates how situational factors can affect consumers. **Consumer situations** are those temporary environmental and personal factors that form the context within which a consumer activity occurs. The buying panic brought on by the introduction of the Cabbage Patch dolls resulted from a confluence of situational events. First, the dolls were introduced several months prior to Christmas—an important gift-giving situation. Christmas provided the immediate reason for buying the doll. Second, the dolls were in short supply. When people began to ask for them, they found that the dolls were not always available. The situational factor of short supply raised consumers' liking for the dolls. The press began to publicize the doll, further increasing consumer desires for the product. Finally, the sight of other shoppers clamoring for the dolls enhanced the buying mood of shoppers and contributed to the "manic" nature of the shoppers' actions. In sum the series of situational factors converged to create a product stampede.

A consumer situation is composed of those factors that: (1) involve the time and place of a consumer activity, (2) influence buying behavior, and (3) do not include the consumer's personal long-term characteristics or the product's features. Consumer situations are relatively short-term events or happenings and should be distinguished from the environmental and personal factors having a more long-lasting quality. Examples of situations include the physical surroundings, social surroundings, time, the task definition, and antecedent states—all of which are described more in Table 10–1. These situational characteristics influence people in a number of different consumer activities, such as receiving communications about products or services, purchasing the product, consuming the product, and disposing of the product.

Table 10–1   Five Types of Consumer Situations

1. *Physical surroundings:* the concrete physical and spatial aspects of the environment encompassing a consumer activity.
2. *Social surroundings:* the effects of other people on a consumer in a consumer activity.
3. *Task definition:* the reasons that occasion the need for consumers to buy or consume a product or service.
4. *Time:* the effects of the presence or absence of time on consumer activities.
5. *Antecedent states:* the temporary physiological states and moods that a consumer brings to a consumption activity.

The study of situations has important implications for managers. Products may be defined by the situations in which they are used. Watches, for example, are positioned and segmented in part based on usage situations. One can find formal watches, sports watches, everyday watches, and specialty watches (e.g., a diving watch). Thus, groups of people are identified with an unfulfilled situational need, such as a watch to be used to time yourself while jogging. A product is then developed to fit the needs of that situation, e.g., a durable timepiece with a stopwatch capacity. Finally, promotional materials are created that clearly position the product in reference to its situational use and to its competitors.

In addition to segmentation and positioning, the study of situations has a variety of other managerial uses. People may obtain information on products only in specific situations, e.g., via the radio in a car while commuting. Thus, how products are promoted can be influenced by the situational variations in information reception. Similarly, certain products may be bought only in certain situations, e.g., as a gift. Such information has an impact on pricing, promoting, and distributing the product. In summary, the study of the situation is an important aspect of the job of product managers.

SITUATION-PERSON-PRODUCT INTERACTIONS

Three major categories of factors influence the buying of products and services—the consumption environment, the consumer's personal characteristics, and the marketing offering. For two reasons the concept of the consumer situation stands at the crossroads of these three elements. First, consumer situations are one component of the consumer environment. Such situational factors as the physical surroundings, time, the task definition, and the social surroundings of the activity are elements of the consumer environment. Second, consumer situations also can interact with the personal factors that influence consumption and with the type of product being offered. Providing students with an understanding of how two different factors can interact to influence consumers is an important goal of this section of the chapter.

An interaction may occur when two or more factors influence consumers simultaneously. The factors are said to be interacting when their combination causes a consumer to behave differently than he or she would if the two factors were not combined. An example of a person-situation interaction was found in a research study that investigated the innovativeness of consumers when they were buying gifts either for themselves or for others.[1] In the study two factors were investigated. The first was the type of situation. A gift was bought either for someone else or for the consumer himself or herself. The second consumer factor was a personality characteristic of the buyer—either dogmatic or nondogmatic. The results revealed that the gift occasion interacted with the personality characteristic of consumers. The more dogmatic (close-minded) the consumer was, the more likely he or she was to buy innovative gifts for *others.* In contrast, when the gift was bought for personal use, the opposite pattern occurred. As dogmatism increased, the likelihood of buying an innovative gift decreased, if it was purchased for personal use. The combination of the factors resulted in consumer actions different from those that would have occurred if the factors were not combined.

The situation can also interact with the marketing offering. In a situation-by-product interaction different products are viewed as useful in different situations. Thus, the product Gatorade would be seen by most consumers as appropriate in situations in which a consumer has worked up a great thirst, such as after a competitive tennis match. On the other hand, drinking a quart of Canada Dry ginger ale after a hard workout sounds perfectly awful. In contrast, Gatorade would be an inappropriate mixer at a fashionable party, whereas Canada Dry ginger ale would be quite appropriate. Thus, the factors of type of product and type of situation interact so that in one situation one product would be favored, whereas in a different situation the other product would be preferred.

The relative contribution of situation, person, and product to consumer buying behavior has been investigated.[2] Table 10–2 summarizes the findings of a number of studies. As can be seen, the situation itself explains very little purchase behavior across the various products. It is the interaction of the situation with the product and the person that accounts for a reasonable fraction of consumer buying behavior. In fact for beverage products the interaction of the product and the situation accounted for almost 40 percent of the change in consumer purchases.

An important point to observe in Table 10–2 is that the impact of the situation on consumer buying varied substantially across types of product. For beverages and meat products, the situation and its interactions accounted for over 30 percent of the change in consumer buying. Situations, however, accounted for less than 10 percent of the variation in motion picture attendance. In that case a product-by-person interaction predominated. Indeed, this makes sense. A decision to go see a motion picture would seem to be governed largely by a person's preferences and the type of movies playing.

Table 10–2   Relative Effects of Situation, Person, and Product on Consumer Buying

Source of Influence	Type of Product					
	Beverages	**Meats**	**Snacks**	**Fast Foods**	**Leisure Activities**	**Motion Pictures**
Person	0.5%	4.6%	6.7%	8.1%	4.5%	0.9%
Situation	2.7	5.2	0.4	2.2	2.0	0.5
Product	14.6	15.0	6.7	13.4	8.8	16.6
Product × situation	39.8	26.2	18.7	15.3	13.4	7.0
Person × situation	2.7	2.9	6.1	2.2	4.0	1.9
Product × person	11.8	9.7	22.4	20.1	21.2	33.7
Product × situation × person	a	a	3.4	a	a	a
Unexplained variance	27.8	36.4	35.6	38.7	46.1	39.4

[a]The studies did not calculate the variance. The percentages are how much variance each of the sources of influence accounted for.

Source: Adapted from R. W. Belk, "Situational Variables and Consumer Behavior," *Journal of Consumer Research*, 2, December 1975, 160.

A discussion of types of situations and their influence on consumers follows.

THE PHYSICAL SURROUNDINGS

Physical surroundings refer to the concrete physical and spatial aspects of the environment encompassing a consumer activity. Researchers have found that such stimuli as colors, noise, lighting, and the spatial arrangements of people or objects can influence a variety of behaviors. For example, one study investigated the impact of music on the purchase process.[3] In the study two types of music were tested to see how they would affect supermarket shoppers. Over a period of nine weeks either no music, slow-tempo music, or fast-tempo music was played. The results showed that people walked slower or faster depending on whether fast or slow music was played. This was an interesting result, but did it translate to the bottom line? The answer was yes! Sales volume was significantly higher when slow-tempo music was played. Sales on a daily basis increased by 38 percent when a slower-cadenced music was played. Interestingly, when customers were asked questions about their awareness of the music, no differences were found. The effects of the music, therefore, seemed to operate at a level below consciousness. Companies have developed products, such as Muzak, to provide music in the working and shopping environment. Figure 10–1 presents an advertisement that highlights the advantages of music in the environment.

The supermarket study is interesting because it demonstrates that the physical environment can influence buyer behavior. However, one should not immediately generalize and say that all retail stores should play slow-paced

Figure 10–1   **Muzak positions its product as a productivity booster.** *(Courtesy of Westinghouse Broadcasting and Cable, Inc. "Muzak®" is a registered trademark and service mark of Muzak.)*

music. There may be consumption situations in which fast music would be more appropriate. For example, restaurants that have low margins and depend on high volume must have a high occupant turnover rate. In this case playing fast-paced music may speed up customers, thereby, making their seats available for other customers more quickly.

Crowding is another aspect of the physical environment. Crowding occurs when a person perceives that his or her movements are restricted because of limited space. The experience can result from too many people, from a limited physical area, or from a combination of the two.[4] The concept has particular relevance to retailers who must decide how to arrange floor space. When consumers experience the effects of crowding, a number of different outcomes can occur.[5] Consumers may react by reducing their shopping time, by altering their use of in-store information, and by decreasing their communication with store employees. Potentially, it may increase shopper anxiety, lower shopping satisfaction, and negatively affect store image.

As with the case of music, though, in some circumstances crowding may be beneficial. Particularly when consumers are seeking an "experience," such as a sporting event or a rock concert, the feeling of crowdedness may enhance the overall impact. In reality there is probably some optimum level of crowding for each consumer situation. For example, when dining out one has an uncomfortable feeling if the restaurant is nearly empty. Conversely, if the restaurant is so full that you are jostled and receive poor service, the experience is equally negative. The optimum level of crowding is somewhere between the two extremes.

Physical surroundings influence consumer perceptions through the sensory mechanisms of vision, hearing, smell, and even touch. As such, the surroundings have important implications for building a store image. If a retailer wants to portray an upscale image, it is crucial that the surroundings match such an image. Thus, colors, shapes, music, scents, and temperature blend to express upper-class taste. Uncomfortably hot temperatures, unpleasant smells, and loud colors and noises would not be appropriate for a hairstyling salon attempting to cater to wealthy customers.

The perception of bodily safety is another factor controlled in part by the physical surroundings. Providing ample, nearby parking, adequate outdoor lighting, and open spaces enhances the feeling of security for shoppers. The presence of such physical attributes could increase night-time shopping, particularly among the elderly, who are highly conscious of their vulnerability to crime.

The impact of the physical environment on consumers perhaps has its greatest effects on the managerial actions of retailers. In three areas the physical environment influences consumer perceptions of and buying in retail stores—the store's location, layout, and atmosphere.

Effects of Store Location

Those in real estate sales have a rule of thumb which states that the primary factors influencing the value of a piece of property are—location, location, and location. Those who study retailing echo this point, because location's contribution to store choice has received a large amount of research.

Store location influences consumers from several perspectives. How large a trading area within which a store is located affects the overall number of people who are likely to be drawn to it. The analogy of a planet's gravitational effects has been used to predict how many people will go outside of their town's boundaries to shop in other cities. Called the **gravitational model,** the formulation proposes that trading areas act like planets and attract outside shoppers in proportion to the relative populations of the towns in question and to the square of the inverse of the distance between the towns.[6]

Other research has found that the selection of which shopping center a consumer will patronize is influenced by the distance to the shopping center from the person's residence. A number of factors have been found to influence shopping center choice, such as price and variety. Nonetheless, one general rule is that the farther away a shopping center is, the less likely a person is to patronize it.[7]

In addition to actual distance, perceived distance also makes a difference. Research has shown that consumers have "cognitive maps" of the geography of a city. Interestingly, the perceptual maps of the locations of retail stores may not match the actual relationships. Such factors as ease of parking, the merchandise quality, and the ease of driving to the shopping center can make the distance seem shorter or longer than it actually is.[8]

Store Layout

Stores are layed out to facilitate customer movement, to assist in the presentation of merchandise, and to help create a particular atmosphere. The overall goal is to maximize profits by increasing sales through a cost-effective store design. **Store layout** influences consumer reactions and buying behavior. For example, the placement of aisles influences traffic flow. The location of items and departments relative to traffic flow can dramatically influence sales. In one case an appetizer-deli section was moved from the rear of a grocery store to a high-traffic area near the store's front. Sales in the department increased over 300 percent. This was significant because the profit margins were substantially higher in the deli than in other departments in the rest of the store.[9]

How seating arrangements are designed can dramatically influence communication patterns. It has been argued that airport terminals are designed to discourage people from talking comfortably to each other. Chairs are bolted down and placed so that people cannot face each other and converse from a comfortable distance. The reason for the antisocial arrangement of furniture in airports is presumably to drive people into airport bars and cafeterias, where space is arranged more comfortably—and where customers spend money.[10] As noted in Chapter 2, store location and layout may directly influence consumer actions without the prior formation of beliefs or attitudes.

Atmospherics

A store's atmosphere results from the combination of predominantly physical elements that influence a consumer's feelings and/or behaviors. In addition, store atmosphere can deliver a message to consumers, such as "this store has high-quality merchandise." Thus **atmospherics** is a more general term than "store layout" and deals with how managers can manipulate the design of the building, the interior space, the layout of the aisles, the texture of the carpets and walls, the scents, colors, shapes, and sounds experienced by customers. These elements are pulled together well in the definition developed by Philip Kotler, which describes atmospherics as "the effort to design buying environments to produce specific emotional effects in the buyer that enhance his probability of purchase."[11]

A store's atmosphere can be viewed as one component of its image. A variety of factors combine to create a store image, such as:

- ☐ The merchandise.
- ☐ The store's service.
- ☐ The clientele.
- ☐ The store's convenience.
- ☐ The store's promotional activities.
- ☐ The store's atmosphere.[12]

Atmosphere, then, is that component of the image resulting from the physical characteristics of the store.

Researchers have argued that store atmosphere influences the extent to which consumers spend beyond their planned levels in a store.[13] The store's atmosphere influences a shopper's emotional state, which then leads to increased or decreased shopping. The emotional state is made up of two dominant feelings—pleasure and arousal.[14] The combination of these elements in turn results in the consumer either spending more or less time in the store.

Figure 10–2 diagrams these relationships. When the atmosphere arouses the consumer (say, from bright colors and a strong scent) and positive emotions also exist, the buyer will tend to spend more time in the store and have an increased tendency to affiliate with people.[15] Such a situation is likely to result in increased buying. In contrast, if the environment is not pleasurable, increased arousal could result in decreased buying. Research by psychologists has shown that when people become aroused, their dominant tenden-

Figure 10–2 Atmospherics and shopping behavior. (Adapted from a discussion in Robert Donovan and John Rossita, "Store Atmosphere: An Environmental Psychology Approach," *Journal of Retailing, 58,* **Spring 1982, 34–57.)**

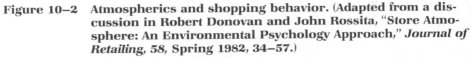

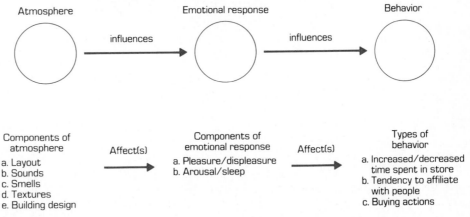

cies are more likely to occur. If the dominant tendency is to leave the store, increased arousal will tend to increase the desire to leave.

The finding that fast-tempo music results in decreased buying among grocery store shoppers could also result from changes in customer arousal. That is, fast-paced music may arouse the shoppers. Because most grocery stores have an unsightly appearance and because many grocery shoppers view the experience negatively, fast-tempo music increases the likelihood that they will follow their preferred response—i.e., leave the store.

Although Philip Kotler and some others have emphasized the effects of atmospherics on emotions, the behavioral influence perspective on consumer behavior suggests that atmospheric elements of the environment may also influence behavior directly. In particular, the layout of buildings and the design of traffic corridors in cities may directly influence the movements of consumers without their behavior first being influenced by either beliefs or feelings.

A variety of other studies have found that a building's atmosphere influences its inhabitants. Psychologists have found that surroundings can influence the mental outlook of people.[16] Some have suggested that increasing the number of windows and the sunlight admitted to rooms can actually improve people's mood. Observers have found that as illumination in a tavern increases, the noise level rises. Lowering the noise level and illumination increases the length of time customers will spend in a bar.[17] Even something as simple as carpeting can influence people. Administrators have reported that students are more restrained in carpeted hallways and classrooms, presumably because the atmosphere has been altered.[18]

In summary, the spacial arrangements found in a retail store have important consumer behavior effects. The effects of space can be summarized in four statements:

1. Space modifies and shapes consumer behavior.
2. Retail store space affects consumers through the stimulation of the senses.
3. Retail stores are like other aesthetic surroundings and affect perceptions, attitudes, and images.
4. Stores can be programmed through space utilization to create desired customer reactions.[19]

From a managerial perspective atmospherics is particularly important to retailers. Atmospherics becomes progressively more important to the extent that the product is *bought* and *consumed* on the retailer' premises. Compare the atmosphere of retailers who sell liquor. Those who encourage consumption on the premises will go to great lengths to provide an atmosphere conducive to socializing. Those who only sell the product could care less about the atmosphere they provide and often have a "warehouse" atmosphere.

In addition, atmosphere becomes increasingly important as the number of competitors increases, as the differences in product and price decrease among the competitors, and as the market becomes segmented on lifestyle and social class differences.[20] A retail store's atmosphere can be used as a tool to differentiate one retailer from another and to attract specific groups of consumers to whom the feelings derived from the atmosphere appeal.

SOCIAL SURROUNDINGS

Social surroundings refer to the effects of other people on a consumer in a consumption situation. Thus, the information provided in later chapters on group effects and on personal influence has direct application to the social situation. For example, the presence of a group can result in conformity pressures on a consumer. If a college student belongs to a fraternity or sorority, certain pressures will exist to purchase particular brands of beverages, clothing, and even automobiles. Similarly, the presence of others may result in a person taking on a role that he or she would not adopt otherwise. If an older brother or sister happens to take his or her younger sibling on a shopping excursion, the elder child suddenly has a leadership role requiring more responsible behavior than if he or she were shopping alone.

As noted earlier, consumer situations can influence people in each type of consumer activity. The social surroundings are no different. Knowledge that the **consumption situation** will involve the presence of other people can dramatically influence a consumer's actions. For example, the type of snack foods which someone will buy is affected by the knowledge that others will be present when the snacks are consumed. One author found that light/salty snacks tended to be bought in part as something to have around the house if friends should drop buy.[21]

The presence of others can influence a consumer within the **purchase situation.** Tupperware parties exemplify how other people can influence buying behavior. In fact, one can view a Tupperware party as a carefully orchestrated concert whose purpose is to place social pressure on those who attend to buy the merchandise. Auctions are also designed in order to create a situation in which the presence of others influences buying behavior. By having consumers compete against each other to purchase the goods being sold, additional psychological elements are brought into play. In addition to being concerned about the quality and price of the goods, the bidders become concerned with the actions of competitors. In many cases the motive of defeating the competitor by outbidding him or her can lead to exhorbitant prices being paid. (See Highlight 10–1 for an example of the impact of an auction on purchase behavior.)

Finally, other people can also influence the impact of the **communications situation** on the consumer. For example, the presence of others in a room is likely to lessen the degree to which a television viewer pays attention to the advertisements that cross the screen. In a personal-selling situation, the presence of a friend could lower the impact of the sales presentation.

On Auctions and Tupperware Parties

Consumers sometimes place themselves in situations designed to encourage them to spend. Two classic examples of such contrived situations are auctions and Tupperware parties. Each has a number of similarities. People are invited who have a buying interest. The potential buyers tend to compete with one another for purchases. Finally, the people running the events are trained to encourage competition among the buyers and to create a buying mood.

The powerful buying stimulus of auctions has been felt personally by the author of this text. A few years ago I went to an auction at which some Navajo rugs were to be sold. I went early to look them over and decided that they weren't really what I wanted. One, however, seemed okay as long as I didn't pay more than $150 for it. The bidding started slowly and soon only two bidders, in addition to myself, were competing. When the bidding got to $425, I decided to put in one more bid of $450. If those other guys wanted the rug at more than that price, they were crazy!

As it turned out, they weren't crazy. I got the rug for $300 more than I had wanted to pay for it.

When you go to auctions, pick a maximum price you are willing to pay and stick to it!

Selected studies on conformity, to be discussed further in Chapter 13, found that many people would conform to the views of a group even when they knew objectively that the group was wrong. However, if only one other member of a group concurred with the subject in the experiments, the group conformity effect was lost.[22] It is likely that if a friend is brought along, he or she would have a similar effect during a sales presentation. That person could act to buttress the views of the buyer against the sales message of the seller.

Social motives can be a reason for why people go out and shop.[23] Shopping can be an important social experience for consumers. While on a shopping excursion, one can meet new people and possibly make friends with them. "Experts" on how to meet members of the opposite sex claim that the grocery store is a prime location to make contacts for future dates. Shopping can also be used as a device to share experiences with a close friend. In fact, shopping for clothing almost requires two people. One person tries on the clothes while the other acts as a delivery boy to fetch different sizes, colors, and styles.

For hobbyists shopping can be an occasion to associate with others having similar interests. The similar other could be a customer or a salesclerk. People who are serious hobbyists and into tropical fish, sewing, model airplanes, crafts, and so forth can usually find friendly individuals in hobby shops catering to their product needs. Other social situations sought by consumers include peer group attraction and dominance. In any community certain retailers become the spot where friends go to meet. It could be a record store, an ice cream parlor, a bowling alley, or whatever. In such cases the product sold is almost irrelevant. The important thing is that a space exists for a group to meet.

Chapter 3 discussed the concept of motivation. One motivator of people discussed in that chapter is the need for power.[24] Consumers can fulfill a need for power or dominance by visiting retailers who use salespeople. The customer can easily obtain dominance over the salesperson because of their divergent roles. For those with a need for power such an experience can be quite gratifying.

From a retailer's perspective, it is usually of benefit to encourage the social aspects of shopping. One study found that when a shopper is with others, he or she visits more stores and makes more unplanned purchases.[25] In fact, many products would not exist unless people gathered into social groupings. A small industry exists to supply party needs, including companies that make noise makers, party napkins, and specialized mixers. Even for a basic beverage such as beer, many of the contexts in which it is consumed are social in nature. In an inventory of beer-drinking situations, half of the items dealt with social situations, such as:

☐ Entertaining close friends at home.
☐ Giving a party.
☐ Attending a social event for which you bring your own beverages.
☐ Going to a tavern after work.
☐ Going to a restaurant or lounge on Friday or Saturday night.
☐ Taking a camping trip, beach trip, or extended picnic.[26]

THE TASK DEFINITION

The reasons why people buy and consume a product or service are varied. These buying purposes form what is called the consumer's **task definition,** or the situational reasons for buying or consuming a product or service at a particular time and place. Examples of such buying purposes are plentiful. A purchase could be occasioned by some type of gift situation, such as Christmas, a birthday, graduation, or a wedding. The reason for buying a beverage could be to satisfy thirst, to get "high," or to stay awake. In fact, the number of ways for consumers to define the task situation is probably infinite. It is up to the skilled marketing manager to identify such buying reasons that are not adequately met by existing products.

Closely related to the task definition is the usage situation. Usage situations form the context in which a product is used and can control the product characteristics sought by consumers.[27] The usage situation of camping places a set of requirements on the properties of eating utensils, food packaging, bedding, and shelter. These requirements center around the need for light weight, portability, and durability. The task definition of "going camping," therefore, is a situational factor that will influence the design of products. Those who choose the situation of living outdoors for short periods of time can become a profitable market segment, as Coleman Company, Inc., has discovered.

Occasion-Based Marketing Opportunities

One problem for marketers is that a product can become locked into one usage situation, thereby severely limiting its market potential. Through habit consumers may come to use a product in a particular situation and not consider it appropriate for other situations. Orange juice is a perfect example. By convention, orange juice has become associated with breakfast. Although nutritious and tasty, the beverage has not been adopted by consumers as a thirst-quenching beverage in a way that rivals the soft drinks. The orange juice trade association has spent millions trying to redefine the task definition of the beverage. The campaign based around the theme, "Orange juice isn't just for breakfast anymore," has brought national attention to the thirst-quenching aspects of the beverage, and only time will tell whether or not consumers will change their dietary habits.

Other examples of companies or trade associations attempting to change the usage situations of products are numerous. Turkey manufacturers have attempted to persuade Americans to eat the big birds on occasions other than Thanksgiving and Christmas. In fact, the uneven pattern of demand for the bird causes major production problems for turkey growers. Another example is the beef industry. In an attempt to broaden the situational usage of the product, the beef trade association has sponsored commercials suggesting that beef makes a good breakfast meat.

In other cases the usage situation of products will change spontaneously as a result of relatively long-term consumer lifestyle changes. For example, athletic footwear and clothing traditionally have been worn for the purpose of competing in a sport. With the fitness trend of the late 1970s and 1980s, athletic wear became fashionable for everyday use. Running shoes became status symbols. The company Nike, Inc., grew rapidly by providing shoes and clothing to a generation that wanted to look athletic even if the individuals were not actually so.

The ability of companies to recognize new or overlooked usage situations can result in the discovery of profitable market segments. In the mid-1980s the personal computer boom struck the United States. However, because of extreme competition, profit margins for the manufacturers were extremely thin. Many small companies flourished, however, not by making personal computers, but by tailoring the computer and accompanying software to specific businesses with unique needs. These small companies developed a vertical marketing approach in which they attempted to fulfill all of the computer needs of the small business. By using a computer made by a large manufacturer, such as IBM, Digital, Apple, or Tandy, and by developing their own software, these companies could carve out marketing niches by computerizing churches, lumberyards, and medical offices. Such companies had a specific task definition for the computer, and the small entrepreneurial computer companies stepped in to fill this need.

Gift Giving

An important ritual in most societies is the giving and receiving of gifts. By engaging in the ritual pattern of giving–receiving–giving back, people build reciprocal relations. Bonds of trust and dependence are formed which assist the parties in their everyday lives.[28] It has been suggested that gifts reflect various status hierarchies, denote rights of passage, such as graduations, and influence the socialization of children through the formation of sex roles (e.g., little boys receive toy soldiers). In Western countries, like the United States, gift giving has important economic benefits. In retail stores 30 percent of their sales occur during the Christmas season. More importantly, Christmas buying has been estimated to account for 50 percent of their yearly profits. Conservative estimates are that 10 percent of all retail sales in North America are for gifts.[29]

Retailers recognize the importance of gift giving to their profits and take full advantage of the many gift occasions that have been prescribed by society. Table 10–3 provides a partial listing of the occasions when some type of gift is expected by children, husbands, wives, and acquaintances. Because of the profits involved in having these gift-giving occasions proclaimed nationally, companies go to some lengths to create new ones. The company Red Calliope Associates has worked to have September 9 declared "Expectant Mother's Day." Not surprisingly the company sells coordinated nursery products. In fact, the company achieved some success when in 1982 the mayor of Los Angeles issued his official proclamation of "Expectant Mother's Day."[30]

Gift-giving occasions naturally influence the task definition. As a consequence, the behavior of consumers is influenced by whether a purchase is made as a gift or as a self-purchase. In some instances the consumer's involvement in the purchase has been found to be greater for gifts. In one research study it was found that when the products were not highly involv-

Table 10–3   Gift-Giving Occasions

A. Various religious days	D. Legislated days
1. Christmas	14. Thanksgiving
2. Easter	15. Halloween
3. Hanukkah	16. Mother's Day
4. Confirmations	17. Father's Day
5. Christenings	18. Grandparent's Day
B. Birth-related days	19. Children's Day
6. Birthday	20. Valentines
7. A child's birth	E. Leaving and coming
8. Baby shower	21. Going on trip—bon voyage
9. Expectant Mother's Day	22. Return from a trip
C. Wedding-related days	23. Retirement
10. Weddings	24. Graduations
11. Wedding shower	F. Miscellaneous
12. Wedding anniversary	25. Return for a favor
13. Wedding engagement	26. House warming
	27. Sympathy
	28. Hostess gifts
	29. Congratulations

ing (e.g., buying bubble bath or a blanket), consumers indicated that they visited more stores and spent more time in information search if the purchase was a gift.[31]

The type of gift situation, as well as the type of product, can influence a consumer's involvement in the purchase. For example, the wedding of a close friend will involve the consumer in greater search and will lead to more expensive, higher-quality presents than an occasion such as a thank-you for someone who watched your house for a couple of days. Thus, it is not always the case that gifts for others result in greater search and effort than gifts bought for oneself. If the gift situation involves, for example, buying a toaster for a distant relative's son's graduation, time spent in search is likely to be low.[32]

Other researchers have found that people were more conservative when buying gifts for their spouses than for themselves.[33] The reason is that they perceived much greater risk in buying for their spouses instead of themselves. Somewhat similarly, another study found that small electrical appliances, when purchased as a gift, were bought at stores with a higher-quality image.[34] Buying a product at a department store can lower the perceived risk of the purchase and represents a conservative approach to purchasing products.

Research on what people give as gifts has found that clothing is the most popular item, followed by jewelry, sporting goods, homemade items, and phonograph records and tapes.[35] Researchers in Britain have investigated the reasons people give. The reasons in their order of frequency were:

- ☐ To obtain pleasure.
- ☐ To show friendship/love.
- ☐ To do the expected thing.
- ☐ To give pleasure.
- ☐ To show appreciation.
- ☐ Because of sentimentality.
- ☐ Other reasons [36].

In summary, the consumer's reason for making a purchase strongly influences his or her buying behavior. For example, when a consumer is buying clothing, the task definition specifies the attributes the article should possess. Thus, compare the qualities of women's clothing designed for the purpose of: swimming, sunbathing, interviewing for a job, going to class, and going to a formal party. For the product manager identifying the tasks in which consumers are involved can result in opportunities to design new products or to reposition established brands.

TIME AS A SITUATIONAL VARIABLE

Ben Franklin in his *Advice to a Young Tradesman* said, "Remember that time is money." It was not until the mid-1970s that *time* was recognized to be an important consumer behavior variable. Since then, however, some authors have even suggested that time may be the most important variable in consumer behavior because it plays a role in so many theoretical areas.[37] For example, as discussed earlier in the text, definitions of brand loyalty should include a specific statement of what period of time is being considered. Similarly, studies of the diffusion of innovations require the consideration of how rapidly in time a new product or service is adopted. In learning theory, which was discussed in Part I of the text, an important concept is that rewards must be given in close time proximity to a behavior in order to be effective. These examples represent only a few of those found in consumer behavior where time is an important variable.

Time can be analyzed from three different perspectives; (1) individual differences in the conception of time, (2) time as a product, and (3) time as a situational variable.

Individuals and Time

At the individual level various consumers may use time differently. People can use their time in four different ways—work, necessities, home work, and leisure.[38] These groupings are arranged on a continuum of obligatory to discretionary uses of time. People have little control over when and how long they work. Somewhat more control exists concerning necessities, such as how long one sleeps and when one eats. The amount of effort spent on maintaining a clean, attractive place to live (i.e., home work) is much more variable. In fact, families in which both spouses work tend to spend less time on "household production." Finally, people have the most discretion in how they use their leisure time. Research has shown that leisure time is strongly affected by outside situational variables, such as the weather.[39]

In one study researchers related consumers' perceptions of time to their lifestyles. Table 10–4 compares thirteen lifestyle characteristics of people hav-

Table 10–4   Time Orientation and Lifestyles

Past Orientation	Future Orientation
1. Cautious shopper	Consumption oriented
2. Cautious	Adventurous
3. Stationary	Mobile
4. Conservative	Innovative
5. Morally rigid	Morally flexible
6. Detached	Involved
7. Financially pessimistic	Financially optimistic
8. Insecure	Secure
9. Negative about work	Positive about work
10. Homebody	Cosmopolitan
11. Content	Ambitious
12. Indifferent to cars	Car conscious
13. Opinion follower	Opinion leader

SOURCE: Adapted from Robert Settle, Pamela Alreck, and John Glasheen, "Individual Time Orientation and Consumer Life Style," Working Paper, San Diego State University, 1977.

ing a past orientation to those having a future orientation. In general, those who focused on the past agreed with statements like, "I dread the future," "Things are changing too fast," and "Modern life is anxiety ridden." Future-oriented consumers agreed with statements like, "The new styles turn me on," and "I work hard most of the time."[40] As one can see in the table, the future oriented would be a much better target market for companies introducing new products. Their innovativeness, tendency to see themselves as opinion leaders, their consumption orientation, and their mobility make them a logical target group. How individuals view time is even influenced by their culture.[41] Highlight 10–2 discusses how different cultures may view time in diverse ways.

HIGHLIGHT 10–2

My Time Is Not Your Time

The amount of time available to consumers is an important situational variable. However, the discussion of time assumes a particular cultural perspective. Not everyone views time in the same way. Indeed, three separate ways of viewing time may be identified.

Linear-Separable Time   The type of time on which most Americans and Western Europeans run is "linear separable." People on "Anglo" time have a set of perceptions not shared by much of the rest of the world. Time is viewed as divided into a past, present, and future. It can be divided up and allocated for specific tasks. Anglos speak of time as being spent, saved, wasted, and bought. For them, time is like a ribbon that stretches into the future. The objective is to spend time appropriately in the present so that the future will be better. A heavy future orientation exists. Activities are enjoyed not as ends in themselves but as means to an end.

Circular-Traditional Time   People on circular time tend to be regulated by the natural cycles of the seasons, sun, and moon. For them time does not stretch into the future. Rather, it is circular, such that the future offers neither joy nor fear because it will be much like the present. People operating on circular time tend to do today only things that have to be done today. In the Spanish culture this is called *mañana*. You put off what can be put off and do what has to be done. An-

glos who are engaged in international marketing often have a great deal of trouble dealing with people who run on circular time. They do not see a relation between time and money and have a habit of not appearing on time for meetings or of trying to accomplish several tasks at one time.

Procedural-Traditional Time   People on procedure time tend to have little written history and are governed by the task rather than by the time. If asked when a meeting will occur, the response will be, "When the time is right." When asked how long will it take, the response might be, "When the meeting is over." Because native American Indian culture follows such a pattern, the phenomenon has been called "Indian" time. This view of the world results in extremely loose time schedules. Such individuals see no connection between time and money, and the idea of wasting time is irrelevant. The task is the key.

   Based on these divergent approaches to time, it is clear that when time is categorized as a situation, we are referring to "Anglo time." Factors that might influence the buying behavior of Anglos would likely have much less influence on people running on "Indian time."

Based on Robert Graham, "The Role of Perception of Time in Consumer Research," *Journal of Consumer Research*, 7, March 1981, 335–342.

**Time as a
Product**

Of course, time can also be a type of product. Many purchases are made in order to buy time. Appliances such as microwave ovens, disposals, and trash compactors exist in part for the purpose of saving time. Fast-food restaurants have flourished because consumers have a need to obtain nourishment while on the go. A name has been given to one who engages in such behavior—the time-buying consumer.

Corporations frequently use the time-saving qualities of their products as a key promotional idea. For example, the advertisement from Perception Technology shown in Figure 10–3 illustrates this concept. Using the bold

Figure 10–3   The time-saving qualities of this product are the key promotional idea in the ad. (*Courtesy of Perception Technology.*)

"Customer Service...One moment please."
"Order Department...One moment please."
"Checking Department...One moment please."
"Credit Verification...One moment please."
"Reservations...One moment please."
"Inventory Control...One moment please."
"Central Dispatch...One moment please."
"Sales Department...One moment please."
"Traffic Department...One moment please."
"Switchboard...One moment please."

Stop wasting time on every routine call your staff has to answer.

Perception's Voice Response eliminates the problems of disgruntled customers and unproductive staff. Voice Response gives your computer a human voice so it can answer customer's and salespeople's regular requests for information.

Your customers and salespeople need only a Touch-Tone telephone to access available data base information. This system is ideal for heavy traffic applications. Unusual or complex calls are switched automatically to a staff person for manual assistance.

Accurate, efficient, convenient, and timely communication are the results. And lower telephone, personnel and equipment costs. And happier customers.

Don't wait one more moment, please. Call today for more information.

PERCEPTION TECHNOLOGY
The Leader in Voice Response Technology
Shawmut Park
Canton, MA 02021-1409 (617)821-0320
TLX 948146 PTC CTON

As appearing in Business Week, February 17, 1986

headline, "Stop wasting time on every routine call your staff has to answer," the company effectively makes the point that their computerized voice response system can lower costs by saving time.

Time as a Situational Variable

Time may be a factor that influences the consumer's conduct in a given situation. In such cases time is an independent variable, or a factor that affects the actions of consumers.

Generally, the situational characteristic of time that influences consumers is its availability. How much time a consumer has available to do a task, such as buying a product, will influence the strategy used to select and purchase it. In particular, information search is influenced by the time available. Researchers have found that as time pressure increases, consumers will spend progressively less time searching for information. In addition, the utilization of available information will decrease, and negative or unfavorable information will be given more weight in a decision when time pressures are severe.[42] Other research has found that the longer the length of time since the last purchase, the more a consumer will engage in searching for product information. Similarly, the longer a consumer is committed to use the product, the greater will be the external search for information about competing products.[43]

Time can also interact with other variables to influence purchase behavior. For example, how long a person has gone since his last meal has been shown to influence how much he buys at a grocery store.[44] Impulse purchases occur when people are hungry and the aisles seem to be lined with temptations. As noted by the researchers, when people shop while hungry, their . . .

imagination readily places potatoes and onions around roasts and transforms pancake mix into a steaming, buttered snack.[45]

Interestingly, in the above research on hunger and food shopping, a situation-by-consumer interaction occurred. The food buying of shoppers classified as overweight was not affected by how long they had gone since their last meal. The effect of buying more when hungry occurred mainly for people of average weight. The authors interpreted the results as indicating that overweight consumers fail to use internal cues to determine their hunger. Rather, they use the presence of food to determine how much to buy and consume.[46]

Another way that time may influence consumers has been labeled **time compression.** The idea is that through electronic means radio or television commercials may be compressed so that they last a shorter length of time. Through electronics this may be accomplished without distorting the voice pitch and the balance between pauses and speech. The procedure simply speeds up the pace of the action without distortion.

Early research on time compression found that word transmission could be increased by 50 percent—to about 280 words per minute—with little loss of comprehension on the part of listeners. Some studies have found that speech rate influences how listeners perceive the speaker. For example, in one research study slow speakers were given relatively negative evaluations and normal to fast talkers were rated more positively.[47] More recent research however, in which advertisements were compressed by 20 percent, found minimal viewer responses to the procedure. Some evidence exists that time compression may interfere with the processing of the information in the commercial so that recall is poorer. Some evidence also shows that the formation of both positive and negative attitudes was inhibited.[48]

Managerial Implications   Concepts related to time can be used to segment the market and develop the marketing mix. For example, the finding that consumers have different time orientations can be used as a segmentation variable. As noted earlier, future-oriented consumers may be early adopters of products. Furthermore, the types of promotional themes would likely be very different for a future-oriented person as compared to a past- or present-oriented consumer.

The relationship of time to purchase and use situations also has importance to managers. Some products may be bought while people are in a rush. Facilitating the speed with which such products are purchased could give a competitive edge. The drive-through windows at fast-food restaurants would be an example. In many areas of the United States gasoline stations are adding a line of staple foods and "fast" foods. Consumers can thus save time by filling themselves and their cars up simultaneously.

Other products are used in situations in which time is short or is important. In such cases the product's design should encourage ease and quickness of use. Frozen foods have become popular in part because they are quick to prepare. In the mid-1980s food companies began to market gourmet frozen foods, such as Le Menu by Campbell's Soup Company.

ANTECEDENT STATES

The situational factor of **antecedent states** is discussed last because it concerns the temporary physiological and mood states that a consumer brings to a consumption situation. It naturally bridges the individual consumer, discussed in Part I of the text, and the consumer environment, discussed in Part II of the text. Examples of antecedent states include such **physiological states** as hunger, thirst, and lack of sleep, as well as the consumer's mood. **Mood states** are temporary variations of how people feel and range from happy feelings to neutral mood states to very negative feelings.

Physiological States

An example of a temporary physiological state influencing buying behavior was given in the last section. Consumers who shop for groceries while hungry are in danger of making unnecessary impulse purchases.[49] Burger King Corporation has tried to take advantage of hunger urges in its advertising.

Using a musical theme in which a chorus sings, "Aren't you hungry, aren't you hungry for a Burger King now," television ads show a delicious-looking hamburger and suggest that the audience hurry down to buy one. The idea is to activate consumers' hunger pangs and tie the name Burger King directly to these urges. Gatorade has pursued a similar strategy but has focused on the temporary state of thirst. In the ads athletes dripping with sweat are shown gulping down Gatorade directly from the bottle. Again, the goal is to tie graphically the beverage to the physiological state it is designed to remedy.

These temporary physiological states probably influence buying by changing the "feeling" component of the hierarchy of effects, which was discussed in Chapters 7 and 8. Such feelings are partially physiological in nature and may cause the consumer to become aroused. The arousal can in fact be measured in a variety of ways, such as by changes in pupil size or blood pressure.

When a person is in the presence of food while hungry, feelings about the food are likely to be increased by the physiological state. Thus, when hungry, someone who enjoys red meat will see a porterhouse steak as even more appetizing than usual. These unusually positive feelings will then lead to an increased likelihood of purchasing the food product. Similarly, if a shopper happens to be thirsty while in the store, the physiological state is likely to influence positively feelings about assorted thirst-quenching beverages.

Temporary Mood States

Mood states have also been found to influence consumer behavior. In marketing the work on mood has been predominantly survey-based research. In one survey people were asked why they shopped. Two of the reasons given were that they wanted to alleviate either depression or loneliness.[50] In such instances consumers were expressing the idea that they were using the shopping and purchasing experience to influence their temporary mood state.

Psychologists have done studies in which they investigated the effects of mood on gifts to charities, to others, and to themselves. In these studies, though, the researchers actually influenced the mood of subjects. After creating either positive or negative moods in the subjects, the researchers then took measures of how the changes in mood state affected behavior.

In one mood change study, a group of second- and third-grade children were asked to think of something that made them very happy. Another group was asked to think of something that made them feel very sad. A third group was asked not to think of anything in particular. This process of having people think of happy or sad things has been shown to influence effectively a person's mood state. After having their mood influenced, the children were given a chance to help themselves to candy from a treasure chest. The results revealed that in comparison to the control group, those with either a *positive* or a *negative* mood took more candy for themselves.[51] Figure 10–4 shows the results of the study.

What the results of the mood study show is that people tended to reward themselves when they felt either good or bad. The mediator of the phenom-

Figure 10–4   Effects of moods on self-reward. (Data from D. Rosenham, B. Underwood, and B. Moore, "Affect Moderates Self-gratification and Altruism," *Journal of Personality and Social Psychology, 30,* **October 1974, 546–552.)**

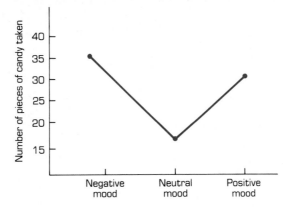

enon appears to be the *affective* component of attitudes—the same concept suggested as the explanation for why hungry people buy more in a supermarket. As stated by the authors of the mood study,

> When one is feeling good, one tends to be more generous to oneself.[52]

However, the phenomenon extends beyond self-generosity. A positive mood state also results in people being more generous to others as well.[53]

Why did the children who were sad also indulge themselves more? The reason seems to be that they took more candy in order to make themselves feel better. Importantly, the impact of negative moods seems to extend to how much one person will help another. In general, the research evidence shows that people over the age of six will help others more when they are feeling bad than when they are in a "neutral" mood state. Again, the reason seems to be that people know that it makes them feel good to help others. When a person feels bad, he or she will seek out ways to feel better and will consequently help others more.

The psychological studies on mood have not been replicated in a consumer setting. Thus, one cannot be sure that mood will influence the buying of products in the same way it affects the taking of candy or the giving away of coupons that can be used to obtain a prize.[54] It is likely, however, that buying gifts for oneself is influenced similarly. People seem to enjoy buying for themselves when they feel either good or bad. It is also likely that people will buy more for others when they are feeling good. It is easy to be altruistic when one is feeling positive about things.

But will people give more gifts to others when they are feeling bad? The evidence is less clear here. While people may seek to give to others to make themselves feel better, it is also the case that when one feels bad, he or she may think less about others, try to conserve resources, and help only himself or herself.[55] Clearly, more experimental research needs to be done on the effects of mood on buying behavior.

From a managerial perspective the mood research has several implications. A primary goal of customer-oriented retailers should be to influence positively the mood of customers who enter the store. To the extent that customers can be made to feel good, their tendency to buy for themselves and others should increase. Such positive mood states could result from the development of a store atmosphere that appeals to customers, from the training of skilled salespeople who can develop rapport with customers, and from the display of merchandise that appeals to customers in terms of quality, price, and display.

DEVELOPING SITUATIONAL INVENTORIES

Because situations influence consumer behavior on such a broad scale, it is important to be able to define and categorize them precisely. A **situational inventory** should be useful across a wide variety of products and should specify the common situations that influence consumer actions. In reality such an inventory is probably impossible to achieve.

Two approaches have been used in the development of situational inventories. **General inventories** attempt to classify all situations that affect consumers into a set of simple categories. In one approach all situations were defined in terms of three elements—pleasure, arousal, and dominance.[56] Pleasure deals with whether people feel good or bad about something. Arousal pertains to whether the situation, such as viewing a basketball game or reading a book, makes people feel active or passive. Dominance deals with whether people are more likely to feel powerful or weak in a given situation.

The applications of the pleasure-arousal-dominance formulation to consumer behavior have been sparse. Early attempts to apply the classification scheme to consumer behavior met with little success.[57] More recently the taxonomy was applied to customer activities in retail stores. Here evidence of the utility of the scheme was obtained. In particular, the dimensions of pleasure and arousal influenced consumer in-store buying intentions. Thus, to the extent that the store environment caused shoppers to be more aroused and to feel more pleasant, they:

1. Expressed more enjoyment in shopping.
2. Spent more time browsing.
3. Were more willing to talk to sales personnel.
4. Tended to spend more money than planned.
5. Expressed a greater likelihood of returning to the store.[58]

Some authors have criticized the general approach to classifying situations as irrelevant to marketing. In their view situations are product specific. Thus, situations that might influence the choice of snack foods are totally

Table 10–5   A Situationally Based Beer Inventory

1. Entertaining close friends at home.
2. Giving a party at home where the guests include people you know at work and friends you come in contact with only once or twice a week.
3. Going to a tavern after work.
4. Going to a restaurant or lounge on a Friday or Saturday night.
5. Watching a sports event or some favorite TV show.
6. Attending some social event for which you are asked to supply your own refreshment.
7. Engaging in some sports activity or hobby such as golf, bowling, softball, or fishing.
8. Taking a weekend or vacation camping trip, beach trip, or extended picnic.
9. Working at home on the yard, house, or car.
10. Simply relaxing at home.

SOURCE: Data adapted from William Bearden and Arch Woodside, "Consumption Occasion Influence on Consumer Brand Choice," *Decision Sciences, 9,* April 1978, 273–284.

different from those that would influence the choice of cosmetics.[59] According to this view, situational inventories must be product specific.

Much of the research on consumer situations has used **product-specific inventories.** For example, one study investigated the effects of situations on choice of fast-food restaurants.[60] The results showed that the restaurants chosen did depend on the type of situation. Four situations were identified:

1. Lunch on a weekday.
2. Snack during a shopping trip.
3. Evening meal when rushed by time.
4. Evening meal with the family when not rushed.

Wendy's, for example, was found to have a higher proportion of choices for the evening meal when people are not rushed for time. Burger Chef was more likely to be visited for lunch on a weekday than at other times.

In another study the occasions when beer is consumed were examined. The ten circumstances identified are found in Table 10–5.

The major problem with the product-specific approach to designing situational inventories is cost. Because no two inventories are alike, an entire new set of research studies will have to be done for each product. The studies are time-consuming and expensive to perform. However, until it can be demonstrated that a general inventory can provide the managerial answers demanded by marketers, the product-specific taxonomies predominate.

Managerial Implications

The study of the situations in which a product or service is used can have important managerial implications. What follows is an outline of how product managers should approach the issue of incorporating the study of situations into their product planning.

Step 1: Identify the various occasions in which the product is used. Consider the types of situations, including the task definition, the physical surroundings, the effects of time, antecedent states, and the social surroundings.

Step 2: Determine the impact of the situations and the occasions in which the product is used through market surveys. In particular, identify what proportion of the product's sales are based on the product, the product-use situations, the person, and the interaction of product/person, product/situation, and situation/person.

Step 3: Consider appropriate segmentation and positioning strategies based upon how the product is affected by situational influences. For example, Bristol-Myers recognized that their pain-relieving product, Excedrin, was limited in use to certain situations. In particular, the product was inappropriate for use before bedtime. Its aspirin content upset some people's stomach, and the caffeine it contained kept people awake. Therefore, they developed a new product, Excedrin PM, which contained a sleep aid and a different type of pain reliever. The new product was positioned as a pain reliever for nighttime use.

Step 4: Develop the marketing mix based upon how the product-use situation, the communication situation, and the product-purchase situation affect consumers.

Step 5: Keep in mind the following general findings about how situations affect consumers. (a) When brand loyalty is high, the situation will have less impact on brand choice.[61] (b) The higher the level of product involvement, the less likely it is that situational factors will determine behavior.[62] (c) The closer in time the usage situation is to the purchase, the more the situation will influence brand choice.[63] These situations that are closely linked in time to purchase behavior have been called facilitators. (d) The situations in which a product is to be used will influence consumer attitudes towards the product. Therefore, when doing surveys consider carefully specifying the situation when measuring consumer attitudes.[64]

When going through the above managerial steps, it is particularly important to focus on how consumer situations can influence market segmentation, product positioning, and the development of the marketing mix.

Below are brief examples of how situations can influence the product, price, promotion, and distribution components of the marketing mix.

Product: The situations in which a product will be used can influence its design. For example, look at the design of women's bras. The characteristics vary depending upon whether the situation involves participating in an athletic competition, wearing a low-cut dress to a cocktail party, or wearing a business suit to a board meeting.

Price: How products are priced may even vary by situations. For example, it is likely that in certain situations people are highly price inelastic.

That is, because of the situation, they are not particularly concerned about how much something costs. An example is weddings. Here the price of formal wear, gifts, and such may be higher than on other occasions because people are less prone to concern themselves with pricing issues.

Distribution: The situational factor that most influences product or service distribution is *time.* Consumers experiencing a shortage of time will want to be able to obtain products quickly and with minimal effort. The drive-through windows at fast-food restaurants are examples of a distribution system that allows customers to obtain their burgers, fried chicken, and such rapidly. Mail-order, telephone-order, and computer-ordering systems for products have been developed over the years so that consumers do not have to take the time physically to go to a retail store to make a purchase.

Promotion: How companies advertise their products and services is influenced by the *communications situation* consumers are in when they receive messages. One communications situation that companies frequently take advantage of to advertise is when consumers are at sporting events. Go to almost any minor league or major league ballpark and you will find billboard advertisements displayed all over the ballpark. The messages are short, simple, and direct, which fits the situation of watching a baseball game with friends. Conversely, the situation of reading a magazine alone at home is such that more complicated messages are possible. Thus, print ads in magazines tend to be longer and more detailed.

SUMMARY

Consumer situations are those short-term environmental and personal factors involving the time and place of a consumer activity that influence buying behavior. Examples of situational factors that influence consumers are the physical surroundings, social surroundings, the occasion for which a product is bought (task definition), and the consumer's temporary physiological and mood states (antecedent states). These situations can influence consumers when they receive communications about a product or service, when they make a purchase, and when they use the product or service. Information on situational influences on consumer behavior helps managers in segmenting the market, positioning the product, and designing the marketing mix.

The situation can influence consumers directly in their buying behavior. However, most often the situation will interact with the product and/or the individual characteristics of consumers to influence buying behavior. For example, situations interact strongly with the type of product for beverages. The type of beverage bought for a party (task definition) will be quite different from that bought for quenching thirst (antecedent state).

The impact of the physical surroundings on consumers is particularly important for retailers. Effects of store layout, atmospherics, crowding, music, and store location are all examples of how the physical environment can affect consumers. Social motives influence why people shop, their involvement in the purchase, and their conformity to the tastes and preferences of others. The task definition deals with the reasons why a product or service is bought. One can think of the task definition in terms of the occasion that spurs a purchase, such as a gift occasion, a party, or even a type of meal (e.g., breakfast and orange juice). Usage occasions can be utilized as a potent segmentation tool, such as Sony's Walkman radios to be used while running.

Time influences consumers predominantly through its availability. Hundreds and perhaps thousands of new products have been successfully developed for the purpose of saving time. Finally, antecedent states concern the temporary physical and mood states that influence consumer buying behavior. Whether people are happy or sad, hungry or thirsty, can influence their attitude about the purchase and how much they buy.

Because of the importance of situations on consumers, marketing researchers have begun to develop situational inventories. Two types of inventories have been developed—general inventories and product-specific inventories. Currently, the product-specific inventories are proving to be more valuable to managers.

Key Terms

Consumer situations
Crowding
Physical surroundings
Store location
Gravitational model
Store layout
Atmospherics
Social surroundings
Consumption situation
Purchase situation
Communications situation
Usage situation

Task definition
Time compression
Antecedent states
Physiological states
Mood states
Situational inventories
General inventories
Product-specific inventories
Person-situation-product interactions
Time as a consumer situation

Review Questions

1. Define the concept of a consumer situation. What are the five types of situations that have been identified?
2. Give an example of a situation-by-person interaction. Give an example of a situation-by-product interaction.
3. For which types of products does one find most of the variance in buying accounted for by product-by-situation interactions? For which types of products does one find most of the variance in buying accounted for by product-by-person interactions. (Hint—look at Table 10–2.)
4. The effects of music on shoppers is one example of how the physical surroundings can influence buying. Identify five other means through which the physical surroundings can influence buying.
5. What are the effects of a store's location on consumer store choice?
6. What are five factors that influence consumers' perceptions of a store's image?
7. Draw the model of how atmospherics influences shopping behavior presented in Figure 10–2. What are the components of store atmosphere?
8. How can the effects of other people influence the consumption situation, the purchase situation, and the communications situation?
9. Define the term *task definition*. A number of gift-giving situations have been identified. Indicate five categories of gift-giving situations.
10. Identify four of the six reasons why people give gifts as mentioned in the chapter.

11. Identify and give examples of three ways in which *time* may influence consumption activities.
12. To what extent can time compression be used to improve consumer reactions to verbally presented communications?
13. Define the concepts of *antecedent states*. What are two types of antecedent states and how might each influence consumption?
14. What are the two types of situational inventories that have been developed? What are the benefits and liabilities of each?

Discussion Questions

1. The shoe industry is segmented to a large extent upon the usage situation of the product. Identify as many different usage situations as you can for which manufacturers have created different types of shoes.
2. The situation can interact with the type of person and with the type of product. Give an example of each. (Hint, think about your own characteristics and preferences and about those of someone else who is quite different. Compare how each of you responds to various types of situations and products.)
3. Draw a diagram of the grocery store with which you are most familiar. Identify the specific physical features of the store that are designed to move customers in specific patterns and to encourage customers to purchase specific products.
4. From your own experience think of two instances of consumer behavior settings in which large numbers of people were present. To what extent did you find that the presence of people enhanced the overall consumption experience? What are the circumstances in which large numbers of people detract from the consumption experience?
5. Draw a map of your community. Place on the map the location of where you live and where you attend college. Now draw in the locations of the retailers you most frequently patronize. Do you find any relationship between the location of the retailers and the location of your residence and college?
6. Considering all of the components that help to create a store atmosphere, describe in one or two paragraphs the atmosphere of two popular eating

or drinking establishments in your community. To what extent do you think the atmosphere of these establishments was consciously created?
7. List all of the gifts you have given to people over the past year. What was the occasion that prompted the giving of each of these gifts? In which instances did you purchase a product that was designed specifically to be given as a gift?
8. Identify five products and/or services that differentiate themselves from competition based upon whether they save or use up time. How do these products communicate this benefit to consumers? Try to identify a new product or service that could be marketed as saving the time of college students. To what extent is there a market for products and services that help you "use up" time?
9. Suppose you were an advertising executive assigned the task of developing a campaign for a company that sells exotic coffees. Your task is to design an advertising campaign based upon the idea that people drink coffee because of their good or bad moods. Develop a print ad carrying out this task.
10. Develop a product-specific situational inventory for the situations in which greeting cards might be given.

References

1. K. A. Coney, "Dogmatism and Innovation: A Replication," *Journal of Marketing Research*, 9, November 1972, 453–455.
2. R. W. Belk, "An Exploratory Assessment of Situational Effects in Buyer Behavior," *Journal of Marketing Research*, 11, May 1974, 156–163.
3. Ronald E. Milliman, "Using Background Music to Affect the Behavior of Supermarket Shoppers," *Journal of Marketing*, 46, Summer 1982, 86–91.
4. Daniel Stokols, "On the Distinction Between Density and Crowding: Some Implications for Future Research," *Psychological Review*, 79, May 1972, 275–277.
5. G. Harrell, M. Hutt, and J. Anderson, "Path Analysis of Buyer Behavior Under Conditions of Crowding," *Journal of Marketing Research*, 17, February 1980, 45–51.
6. William J. Reilly, *Methods for the Study of Retail Relationships*, Austin, Tex.: Bureau of Business Research, University of Texas, 1929, 16.

7. James Bruner and John Mason, "The Influence of Driving Time Upon Shopping Center Preference," *Journal of Marketing, 32,* April 1968, 57–61.

8. R. Mittelstaedt et. al., "Psychophysical and Evaluative Dimensions of Cognized Distance in an Urban Shopping Environment," in *Combined Proceedings,* R. C. Curhan (ed.), Chicago, Ill.: American Marketing Association, 1974, 190–193.

9. "Store of the Month," *Progressive Grocer,* October 1976, 104–110.

10. Robert Sommer, *Personal Space: The Behaviorial Basis of Design,* Englewood Cliffs, N.J.: Prentice Hall, Inc., 1969.

11. Philip Kotler, "Atmospherics as a Marketing Tool," *Journal of Retailing, 49,* Winter, 1973–74, 48–64.

12. Jay Lindquist, "Meaning of Image," *Journal of Retailing, 80,* Winter 1974–75, 29–38.

13. Robert Donovan and John Rossiter, "Store Atmosphere: An Environmental Psychology Approach," *Journal of Retailing, 58,* Spring 1982, 34–57.

14. Albert Mehrabian and J. Russell, *An Approach to Environmental Psychology,* Cambridge, Mass.: The M.I.T. Press, 1974.

15. Donovan and Rossiter, "Store Atmosphere."

16. Abraham Maslow and N. Mintz, "Effects of Aesthetic Surroundings," *Journal of Psychology, 41,* 1956, 247–54.

17. Sommer, *Personal Space.*

18. Ibid.

19. Ron Markin, Charles Lillis, and Chem Narayana, "Social-Psychological Significance of Store Space," *Journal of Retailing, 52,* Spring 1976, 43–54.

20. Kotler, "Atmospherics as a Marketing Tool."

21. Russell Belk, "An Exploratory Assessment of Situational Effects in Buyer Behavior," *Journal of Marketing Research, 11,* May 1974, 160.

22. Solomon E. Asch, *Social Psychology,* Englewood Cliffs, N.J.: Prentice-Hall, Inc., 1952.

23. E. M. Janbes, "Why Do People Shop?" *Journal of Marketing, 36,* October 1972, 47.

24. D. C. McClelland, J. W. Atkinson, J. Clark, and E. Lowell, *The Achievement Motive,* New York, N.Y.: Appleton Century Crofts, 1953.

25. Donald H. Granbois, "Improving the Study of Customer In-Store Behavior," *Journal of Marketing, 32,* October 1968, 28–33.

26. William Bearden and Arch Woodside, "Consumption Occasion Influence on Consumer Brand Choice," *Decision Sciences, 9,* April 1978, 275.

27. Peter R. Dickson, "Person-Situation: Segmentation's Missing Link," *Journal of Marketing, 46,* Fall 1982, 56–64.

28. C. Levi-Strauss, *Structure Elementaires de la Parente,* Paris: Presser Universitaires de France, 1954.

29. C. S. Belshaw, *Traditional Exchange in Modern Markets,* Englewood Cliffs, N.J.: Prentice-Hall, Inc., 1965.

30. "Expectant Mother's Day," *Sales and Marketing Management,* May 16, 1983, 22.

31. Keith Clarke and Russell Belk, "The Effects of Product Involvement and Task Definition on Anticipated Consumer Effort, *Advances in Consumer Research, VI,* William Wilkie (ed.), Ann Arbor, Mich.: Association for Consumer Research, 1979, 313–317.

32. Clarke and Belk, "The Effects of Product Involvement."

33. E. W. Hart, "Consumer Risk Taking for Self and Spouse," unpublished Ph.D. dissertation, Purdue University, 1974.

34. A. Ryan, "Consumer Gift-Giving Behavior: An Exploratory Analysis," in D. Bellinger and B. Greenberg (eds.), *Contemporary Marketing Thought,* Chicago, Ill.: American Marketing Association, 1977, 99–104.

35. Sharon Banks, "Gift-Giving: A Review and an Interactive Paradigm," *Advances in Consumer Research, VI,* William Wilkie (ed.), Ann Arbor, Mich.: Association for Consumer Research, 1979, 319–324.

36. B. Lowes, J. Turner, and G. Wills, "Patterns of Gift-Giving, in *Exploration in Marketing Thought* G. Wills (ed.), London: Bradford University Press, 1971, 82–102.

37. F. M. Nicosia and R. Mayer, "Toward a Sociology of Consumption," *Journal of Consumer Research, 3,* September 1976, 65–76.

38. Laurence Feldman and Jacob Hornik, "The Use of Time: An Integrated Conceptual Model," *Journal of Consumer Research, 7,* March 1981, 407–419.

39. Jacob Hornik, "Situational Effects on the Consumption of Time," *Journal of Marketing, 46,* Fall 1982, 44–55.

40. Robert Settle, Pamela Alreck, and John Glasheen, "Individual Time Orientation and Consumer Lifestyle," *Faculty Working Paper,* San Diego State University, 1977.

41. Robert Graham, "The Role of Perception of Time in Consumer Research," *Journal of Consumer Research, 7,* March 1981, 335–342.

42. Peter Wright, "The Harassed Decision Maker: Time Pressures, Distractions, and the Use of Evidence," *Journal of Applied Psychology, 59,* October 1974, 555–561.

43. James Engel and Roger Blackwell, *Consumer Behavior,* New York, N.Y.: The Dryden Press, 1982.

44. R. E. Nisbett and D. E. Kanouse, "Obesity, Food Deprivation, and Supermarket Shopping Behavior," *Journal of Personality and Social Psychology, 12,* August 1969, 289–294.

45. Nisbett and Kanouse, "Obesity, Food Deprivation."

46. Ibid.

47. William Apple, Lynn Streeter, and Robert Krauss, "Effects of Pitch and Speech Rate on Personal Attributions," *Journal of Personality and Social Psychology, 37,* May 1979, 715–727.

48. Mary Schlinger, Linda Alwitt, Kathleen McCarthy, and Leila Green, "Effects of Time Compression on Attitudes and Information processing," *Journal of Marketing, 47,* Winter 1983, 79–85.

49. Nisbett and Kanouse, "Obesity, Food Deprivation."

50. E. M. Tauber, "Why Do People Shop?" *Journal of Marketing, 36,* October 1972, 47.

51. D. L. Rosenhan, B. Underwood, and B. Moore, "Affect Moderates Self-Gratification and Altruism," *Journal of Personality and Social Psychology, 30,* October 1974, 546–552.

52. Rosenhan and Underwood, "Affect Moderates."

53. B. Moore, B. Underwood, and D. Rosenhan, "Affect and Altruism," *Developmental Psychology, 8,* January 1973, 99–104.

54. D. Kenrick, D. Baumann, and R. Cialdini, "A Step in the Socialization of Altruism as Hedonism," *Journal of Personality and Social Psychology, 37,* May 1979, 747–755.

55. Rosenhan et. al. "Affect Moderates Self-Gratification."

56. Albert Mehrabian and James Russell, *An Approach to Environmental Psychology,* Cambridge, Mass: MIT Press, 1974.

57. P. Kakkar and R. J. Lutz, "Toward a Taxonomy of Consumption Situations," *Combined Proceedings,* Chicago Ill.: American Marketing Association, 1975, 206–210.

58. Robert Donovan and John Rossiter, "Store Atmosphere: An Environmental Psychology Approach," *Journal of Retailing, 58,* Spring 1982, 34–57.

59. Henry Assael, *Consumer Behavior and Marketing Action,* Boston, Mass.: Kent Publishing Company, 1981.

60. Kenneth Miller and James Ginter, "An Investigation of Situational Variation in Brand Choice Behavior and Attitude," *Journal of Marketing Research, 16,* February 1979, 111–123.

61. William Bearden and Arch Woodside, "Consumption Occasion Influence on Consumer Brand Choice," *Decision Sciences, 9,* April 1978, 273–284.

62. Keith Clarke and Russell W. Belk, "The Effects of Product Involvement and Task Definition on Anticipated Consumer Effort," *Advances in Consumer Research, VI,* William Wilkie (ed.), Ann Arbor, Mich.: Association for Consumer Research, 313–318.

63. Brian Sternthal and Gerald Zaltman, "The Broadened Concept: Toward a Taxonomy of Consumption Situations," in *Broadening the Concept of Consumer Behavior,* Gerald Zaltman and Brian Sternthal (eds.), Ann Arbor, Mich.: Association for Consumer Research, 1975, 144.

64. Miller and Ginter, "An Investigation of Situational Variation."

Personal Influence and Word-of-Mouth Communication

Create Positive Word-of-Mouth Communications About Your Product

In 1983, the movie *Educating Rita* was released on a low promotional budget. About a teacher who fell in love with a student, the movie became one of the twenty-five top money-makers for the year. What caused the movie to surprise its producers and the movie critics? Positive word-of-mouth communications. Consumers liked the movie and told their friends about it.(a)

The ability of one person to influence the buying behavior of another is strong, and companies attempt to encourage the process. In 1983 Ford launched a new, sleek, rounded version of its Thunderbird model. One part of the marketing strategy was to build word-of-mouth communication among opinion leaders. To do this Ford mailed invitations to 406,270 executives to drive the T-Bird for a day. Of those who took Ford up on the offer, 80 percent said they would recommend the car to a friend. The word-of-mouth campaign was in part responsible for the 200 percent improvement in sales of the Thunderbird.(b)

Other companies have tried similar strategies. Elsewhere in this text the book *Megatrends* is discussed. Warner Books, the publisher of the hugely successful text, began its promotional efforts by sending 1,000 copies of the book free of charge to chief executive officers of Fortune 500 companies. The goal was to have these individuals recommend to others that they read it.(c) Similarly, Gillette sent 60,000 samples of their Eraser Mate erasable-ink pens to U.S. Senators, English teachers, bankers, and others when the product was introduced in 1979.(d)

The reasons for the importance of word-of-mouth communications are numerous. They include the fact that people trust the disinterested opinions of their friends. In addition, the firsthand experience of others carries more weight in the decision process than information received over the various media. Finally, information from others often can be gained quickly and easily, making the search process shorter and less time consuming. Word-of-mouth promotion is a phenomenon that consumer goods companies must take seriously.

Based on (a) Eileen Prescott, "Word-of-Mouth: Playing on the Prestige Factor," *The Wall Street Journal,* February 7, 1984, 32; (b) Meg Cox, "Ford Pushing Thunderbird with VIP Plan," *The Wall Street Journal,* October 17, 1983, 35; (c) Prescott, "Word-of-Mouth;" and (d) Stephen Morin, "Influentials Advising Their Friends Sell Lots of High-Tech Gadgetry," *The Wall Street Journal,* February 28, 1983, 23.

INTRODUCTION

Personal influence refers to the concept that one individual may intentionally or unintentionally influence another in his or her beliefs, attitudes, or intentions about something. The object of influence could be any one of a number of things, such as the characteristics of a product, a company's image, a salesperson's honesty, or a retailer's pricing policies.

This chapter discusses personal influence from the perspective of one consumer influencing another either directly or indirectly. Direct personal influence occurs through word-of-mouth interaction. In word-of-mouth interaction two individuals are interacting with each other about something. Indirect personal influence occurs when the two parties are not interacting together. The impact of a celebrity endorser on consumers is an example of indirect personal influence. In addition, highly respected consumers may be imitated by others. Thus, others will observe the clothing, automobile, household furnishings, and other possessions of influencers and seek to buy them in order to be similar to these fashion leaders.

Personal influence is pervasive and has a major impact on consumers. One survey of consumers asked what factors influenced their purchase of sixty different products. The results revealed that referrals from others accounted for three times the number of purchases as did advertising.[1] Another study done after World War II found that word-of-mouth influence was twice as effective as radio advertising, four times more effective than personal selling, and seven times as effective as newspapers and magazines.[2] Other research found that two-thirds of new residents in a community found their doctor through discussions with others.[3]

A **negativity bias** also operates in word-of-mouth communications. Negative information is given more weight than positive information by consumers when they make decisions to buy a product or service. One piece of negative information about a product or service will influence a consumer more than will one, two, or even three pieces of positive information. For example, one study of a new coffee product found that after receiving positive information 54 percent tried the product. However, after receiving negative information only 18 percent tried it.[4] A number of reasons have been offered for the disproportionate influence of negative information. A likely explanation is that because most products are pretty good, negative information is a rather rare occurrence. When it does occur, it then takes on greater importance because of its high saliency. Further evidence of the clear impact of negative word-of-mouth communications is presented in Highlight 11–1.

Why Does Personal Influence Occur?

The omnipresence of personal influence results from the needs of both the sender and receiver of the information. The receiver may desire information because he or she fails to believe the advertisements and sales messages received in the marketplace. The receiver may be seeking additional information in order to lower anxiety about a seemingly risky purchase. When receivers are highly involved in a purchase decision, they will tend to go through a longer search process for a product or service. A part of this search process may include asking friends and "experts" about various alternatives. In these

---

HIGHLIGHT 11–1

Negative Word-of-Mouth Communications Can Devastate Product Sales

Word-of-mouth communications can break a product. Sales of General Motor's X-body cars fell 35 percent between 1981 and 1982. During the period, sales of all new cars fell only 6.4 percent. When introduced in 1979, over 500,000 of the cars were sold. Sales peaked at over 700,000 units. However, by 1983 sales were down to 269,000 units. One cause of the dramatic decline in sales was the negative word-of-mouth communication about the various problems of the car and in particular its rear-wheel brake difficulties.

The X-body models have been recalled by General Motors more than any other car model. Five defects brought recalls even before the car went on sale. By early 1983 the number of recalls of the model stood at fifteen. However, the most devastating negative piece of information was that in the early models of the car the rear-wheel brakes had a tendency to "lock up." Critics claimed that the car could go out of control and cause serious accidents unnecessarily. *Consumer Reports* rated the 1980 and 1981 models as "worse" or "much worse" than average in their frequency-of-repair ratings.

Was the auto model as bad as the sales decline would indicate? Probably the answer is no. General Motors did refine the car, and the records of later models were highly improved. In fact, one department of the U.S. government ordered 17,000 of the X-body models.

However, despite later positive information on the car, the negative communications about the car predominated. After a long string of problems with his Citation, one owner had the trunk collapse on his head due to a defective gas cylinder. In his letter to the president of General Motors, the motorist asked rhetorically, "Do you think I'll ever buy a Citation again? Do you think I'll ever recommend that car to anyone?" You be the judge of the impact on sales of hundreds of thousands of people saying that to their friends.

Based on Douglas Sease, "X-Cars, Once GM's Pride, Getting a Shoddy Reputation with Owners," *The Wall Street Journal*, March 3, 1983, 23; and Roger Rowand, "GM Model Falls Short of X-pectations," *Advertising Age*, June 21, 1984, 46.

high-involvement situations personal influence will occur with increased frequency. In three additional cases consumers may be motivated to seek the input of others in a purchase.[5] First, when products are highly visible to others, the consumer will tend to be more involved in the purchase and seek the advice of others. Second, if the product is highly complex; and third, if it cannot be easily tested against some objective criterion, the opinions of others may be sought. Again, in each case the consumer is in a high-involvement buying situation.

The process of influencing others also fulfills the needs of senders of information. The ability to provide information and to sway others in their decisions provides a person with feelings of power and prestige. Influencing others can also help the influencer erase doubts about his or her own purchase. By persuading another to buy a product that the influencer just purchased, the sender can ease his or her own anxieties about the purchase. In addition, by providing information to others, a sender can increase his or her involvement with a group. Thus, providing information acts to increase social interaction and the general cohesion of the group.[6] Finally, a person can engage in personal influence attempts in order to derive some benefit. An endorser may be attempting to persuade consumers to buy a product. A salesman may be trying to close a sale. A child may be attempting to persuade his or her mother or father to buy a bicycle. Table 11–1 summarizes the factors that increase the likelihood that personal influence will occur.

The consumer vignette that introduced the chapter illustrates how seriously managers view the personal influence process. The costs to Ford Motor Company and its dealers to mail over 400,000 invitations to executives and to loan out the Thunderbirds certainly went into the millions of dollars. The negative word-of-mouth information about General Motors' X-body cars was responsible in part for a 35 percent decline in sales in one year. For companies of less financial stability than General Motors, such a precipitous sales decline could result in bankruptcy.

Table 11–1   Factors Causing Personal Influence to Occur

A. The Needs of the Sender of Information
  1. Gain feelings of power and prestige
  2. Erase doubts about his or her own purchase
  3. Increase involvement with a desirable person or group
  4. Obtain a tangible benefit
B. The Needs of the Receiver of Information
  1. Seek information from sources more trustworthy than those who endorse products
  2. Lower anxiety about possible "risky" purchase
    a. Risk can result from the product because of its complexity or cost
    b. Risk can result from the buyer's concern about what "others" will think
    c. Risk can result from the lack of an objective criterion on which to evaluate the product
  3. Lower time spent in search of information

The study of personal influence is important to managers in four areas. First, investigating word-of-mouth communication is crucial to the success of many products. The success of service offerings is particularly dependent upon positive word-of-mouth communications. Second, opinion leadership is a type of personal influence process. Finding and influencing opinion leaders is an important early step in introducing new products. Third, successful personal selling relies upon knowledge of the factors that influence consumers in one-on-one sales situations. A variety of influence techniques have been developed which can be used and misused by industrial and consumer salespeople. Finally, the study of personal influence is important for assisting advertisers in determining the characteristics they should seek in their product endorsers.

TRANSMISSION OF PERSONAL INFLUENCE

A question of interest to marketers and sociologists concerns how mass communications flow from person to person. Two issues are involved in the question. How does information move from the mass media to the general population, and are there opinion leaders who mediate this movement of information? This section addresses both questions. First, the three approaches to the transmission of personal influence are analyzed—the trickle-down theory, the two-step flow model, and the multiflow model. Second, the issue of opinion leadership is discussed.

Models of Personal Influence

The **trickle-down theory** holds that trends, and particularly fashion trends, begin with the wealthy. In order to distinguish themselves from lower classes, the wealthy adopt styles of clothing and attitudes that separate them from the lower classes. The lower classes then attempt to emulate the wealthy by copying their actions. In this way the fashions and behaviors of the wealthy "trickle-down" to the lower classes. The problem with the trickle-down theory is that in actuality relatively little communication occurs between the classes. As Chapter 16 on social class discusses, most communications occur between people in the same social class. In addition, in today's mass-communication culture, information on fashion is transmitted almost instantaneously. Thus, the information is much more like a flood than a trickle.

A second approach to the transmission of personal influence is the **two-step flow model,** which is depicted in Figure 11–1. This approach has been criticized as being overly simplistic for some of the same reasons as the trickle-down theory. The two-step flow model posits that mass communications first influence opinion leaders, who then influence followers. Rather than viewing the influence as occurring between the social classes, the approach regards the influence as horizontal within a class. Thus, within a social class opinion leaders who influence a large group of passive followers are hypothesized to exist. The two-step flow model, however, has been shown to be overly sim-

Figure 11–1   The two-step flow model.

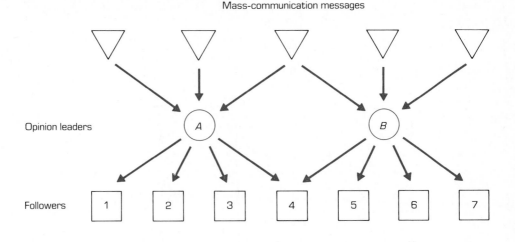

Mass-communication messages

Opinion leaders

Followers

plistic. No passive group of followers has been identified. Similarly, opinion leaders have been found to be different for different products.

The approach that appears to represent the flow of personal influence best is the **multistep flow** approach. Figure 11–2 diagrams the model. In this approach information is transmitted by the mass media to three distinct sets of people—opinion leaders, gatekeepers, and followers.[7] Each type of person is viewed as having the capability of giving information to the other categories of people. The **opinion leader** is the person who influences others about the particular piece of information transmitted by the mass media. The gatekeeper is an individual who has the capability of deciding whether or not others in a group will receive information. That person's opinions may or may not influence the others, however. The followers are those who are influenced by the opinion leader or by the information provided by the gatekeeper.

The multistep flow model recognizes a number of important pieces of information. They are:

1. Mass communications can directly reach nearly everyone in the population.
2. For some products certain individuals, the opinion leaders, will be able to influence a group of followers. However, for different products the role of opinion leader and follower may be reversed.
3. Another group of individuals, the gatekeepers, can chose whether or not to provide information to opinion leaders and/or followers.
4. Communications can be transmitted back and forth between the three groups.

Figure 11–2 The multistep flow model.

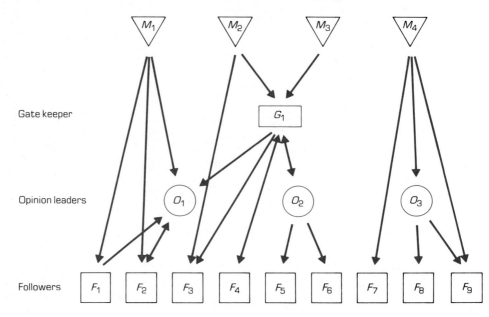

Although the multistep flow model downplays the overall impact of opinion leadership, it still plays an important role in influencing the purchase of many products. Some of the findings on opinion leadership are discussed in the next section.

Opinion Leadership

Opinion leaders are those people who influence the purchase decisions of others. As the multistep flow model suggests, however, opinion leaders do not influence a passive group of followers. Indeed, the evidence indicates that opinion leadership is specific to the product category and situation. Within a single product category, such as appliances, packaged goods, or household furnishings, an opinion leader may influence others across a number of different products. For example, one study found that people who were opinion leaders for small appliances were also opinion leaders for large appliances.[8] However, opinion leadership does *not* seem to occur across product categories. Thus, another study found that no overlap of opinion leadership occurred across unrelated product categories, such as fashion and public affairs.[9]

Strong evidence exists that opinion leadership is influenced by the situation. Discussed in Chapter 10, examples of situations include how such factors as time, the type of task, the physical surroundings, and the presence or absence of others can influence consumers. Research has shown that opinion leadership tends to occur in situations that somehow involve the product category about which opinion leadership occurs. For example, one study found that word-of-mouth communications about Maxim coffee tended to occur in situations that involved food, such as talking about the brand during a coffee break.[10]

Characteristics of Opinion Leaders Marketers have attempted to identify the characteristics of opinion leaders. However, these efforts have met with limited success. The most clear-cut finding is that opinion leaders tend to be involved with the product category. They are interested in the product category, tend to read special interest magazines about it, and are more knowledgeable about the category. Some evidence exists that opinion leaders may be more self-confident and socially active than followers. Opinion leaders may also have a somewhat greater social status than followers; however, they do belong to the same peer group as followers. Finally, they tend to be more innovative in their purchases than followers, but they are *not* the consumers who are "product innovators."[11] Attempts to find demographic and personality characteristics that pinpoint opinion leaders have in general *not* been successful.[12]

Comparing Opinion Leaders and Product Innovators In a variety of respects opinion leaders and **product innovators** are similar. Product innovators are the small set of people who are the first to buy new products. In a study of physicians, innovators and opinion leaders were found to be similar in a number of ways.[13] As compared to followers or noninnovators, they were more highly socially integrated into the medical community, they were more oriented to their professional goals than to their patients, they read larger numbers of medical journals, they shared offices with other physicians, and they tended to attend more medical conferences. Both innovators and opinion leaders showed a pattern of being highly active in their profession, of communicating with other doctors frequently, and of keeping up with new happenings in the medical literature.

Although innovators and opinion leaders share a variety of similarities, the evidence is that on some key characteristics they are different people. The innovator may be described as an adventurer who strikes off on his or her own to buy new products. In contrast, the opinion leader is like an editor who can influence others but who can never be too far away from the goals, values, and attitudes of those whose opinions are being influenced.[14] Thus, innovators are individuals who are less integrated into social groups and feel freer to break group norms by adopting new products very early in their life cycle. In contrast, opinion leaders are more socially integrated and exert their influence in part because they do not espouse beliefs that are widely divergent from those of the group.

SOURCE CHARACTERISTICS

When one person gives information to another, a variety of factors will influence the impact of the communication. One of these factors pertains to the characteristics of the person who is the source of the communication. Understanding the factors influencing the effectiveness of sources of information is extremely important to marketing managers. For example, in personal selling the salesperson acts as a source of information. His or her effectiveness depends in part upon how he or she "comes across" to the client. Similarly, a frequent approach used by advertisers is to hire endorsers to advocate a product or service. In one study that investigated 243 commercials, over 38 percent used some type of endorser.[15]

Just what is a source of information? Many researchers view the term *source* very broadly. Thus, a source can be a person (e.g., Bill Cosby), a company (e.g., Coca-Cola), a media vehicle (e.g., *Time* magazine), or most any other entity.[16] For the purposes of this chapter, however, the concept of a source is discussed in terms of an individual who is presenting information about some topic. Indeed, much of the research done on source effects has used a person, rather than some other entity, as the source. This research, done over the past thirty years, has identified a number of source characteristics that affect the ability of one person to influence another. These characteristics include the source's credibility, physical attractiveness, and likability.

Source Credibility

The concept of **source credibility** has long been recognized as an important element in determining the effectiveness of a source. Source credibility tends to be defined in terms of its two components—source expertise and source trustworthiness.[17] That is, the greater the expertise of the source and the greater the trustworthiness of the source, the more likely an observer is to label the source as credible. **Source expertise** refers to the extent of knowledge the source is perceived to have about the subject on which he or she is speaking. **Source trustworthiness** refers to the extent that the source is perceived to provide information in an unbiased, honest manner. Recent research by the author of this text has found that expertise and trustworthiness make an independent contribution to source effectiveness. That is, a spokesperson can be perceived as an expert and still be untrustworthy. Similarly, a spokesperson can be perceived as lacking expertise and be perceived as highly trustworthy.[18] The implication of this work is that if someone is perceived to be trustworthy, he can influence an audience, even if he is perceived to have relatively little expertise. Similarly, even though someone may be perceived to be untrustworthy, if she is perceived to be an expert, she will tend to have some persuasive ability.

The research on source credibility has shown that in most cases a highly credible source is more effective than a less credible source.[19] Highly credible sources have been found to:

1. Produce more positive attitude change toward the position advocated than less-credible sources.
2. Induce more behavioral change than less credible sources.
3. Enhance the ability to use fear appeals, which involve physical or social threats.
4. Inhibit the creation of counterarguments to the message.

The evidence, therefore, indicates that high-credibility sources are generally more effective than low-credibility sources. The credible spokesperson can change attitudes and behaviors. In addition, such a person enhances the effectiveness of the use of fear appeals. For example, American Express adroitly uses Karl Malden in their commercials for traveler's checks. After presenting a brief story about someone who lost their traveler's checks, Malden asks, "If you lost your checks, what would you do? What would you do?" Of course the idea is in part to scare consumers into buying American Express traveler's checks. Karl Malden is effective because his television background as a hard-nosed cop increased the believability of the message.

The use of credible endorsers is also effective because they can reduce counterargumentation. The idea is that in many cases consumers will develop their own thoughts in response to a message. These thoughts are called **cognitive responses** and may be either positive regarding the message (support arguments) negative towards the message (counterarguments) or concern the characteristics of the source (source derogations).[20] When a highly trustworthy and expert endorser is used, however, people tend to lower their defenses and not think up as many cognitive responses. Because highly credible sources tend to inhibit the development of counterarguments, they *may* be more persuasive than less credible sources.

Are highly credible sources always more effective than less credible sources? The answer is a clear *no!* In certain circumstances moderately credible sources may cause more attitude change than highly credible sources. In particular, in cases in which the audience is already favorably predisposed to the message, a lower credibility source can induce greater persuasion than a highly credible source.[21] The reason for this surprising finding lies in the nature of the cognitive responses developed by the receiver of the message. If an individual is already predisposed to a message, the natural tendency is to develop support arguments for the message. If a source has moderate rather than high credibility, the receiver may summon up these support arguments in order to bolster his or her beliefs. However, if the source is highly credible, no reason exists to bring up support arguments, and the attitude may not change. Under such circumstances a moderately credible source may actually be more effective than a highly credible source.

A recent study supported the idea that source credibility affects the cognitive responses generated by the audience, which in turn affects persuasion.[22] In the study a persuasive message was given by either a highly credible source or a moderately credible source. In one case the sources advocated that the audience buy a microcomputer. In another case the sources advocated that the audience lease a microcomputer. Pretesting had shown that the audience was favorably predisposed to leasing the computer and unfavorably predisposed to buying the computer. As expected, the moderately credible source caused greater attitude change in the lease condition than in the buy condition. The explanation was that support arguments would likely be generated in the lease condition, because the audience was favorable to the position. As a result, when the source was only moderately credible, the development of favorable cognitive responses was not impeded and attitudes became more positive. In contrast, the counterarguments that occurred in the "buy situation" were not impeded by the moderately credible source, and attitudes shifted in a negative direction.

In the mid-1980s advertisers began to emphasize the use of highly expert endorsers. In particular, it became popular to use the chief executive officers (CEOs) of companies to endorse their products. The trend was begun in large part by Lee Iacocca, the CEO of Chrysler, who almost single-handedly brought the company back from bankruptcy. Figure 11–3 shows one print ad done by the tough-talking CEO. Other CEOs who have endorsed their products in the 1980s include Frank Perdue for his Perdue chickens, Frank Borman for Eastern Airlines, Victor Kiam for Remington razors (remember his saying, "I liked the razor so much, I went out and bought the company"), Bill Marriott for Marriott Hotels, and David Mahoney trying harder for Avis.

Although little research has been done to compare the effectiveness of the use of CEOs to other types of endorsers, such as actors or sports stars, some evidence does exist that when a CEO speaks out, people may find him or her more trustworthy and more likely to use the product endorsed.[23] A possible explanation is that consumers sense that a CEO must really believe in the product to go on television to endorse it. Perhaps the most successful of the CEO endorsers is Victor Kiam, who turned the company around from a $30 million loss and doubled the market share of Remington shavers to 40 percent.[24]

The Physical Attractiveness of the Source

To discern the importance of physical attractiveness one has only to watch television or look at print advertisements. Most television and print ads use physically attractive people. Indeed, a requirement for news reporters on television seems to be that they are physically attractive.

The research on the impact of physical attractiveness generally supports what we see around us every day. In general, the research has shown that physically attractive communicators are more successful than unattractive ones in changing beliefs.[25] In addition, people tend to form positive stereotypes about physically attractive people. For example, one study found that college men and women expected physically attractive people to be more sensitive, warm, modest, happier, and so forth. Indeed, the results of the study were summarized as, "What is beautiful, is good."[26]

In the advertising area some research has been done on the physical at-

**Figure 11–3   Corporate CEOs such as Lee Iacocca are increasingly used
to promote their companies in ads. (*Courtesy of Chrysler
Corporation.*)**

tractiveness of endorsers. However, the research has generally concerned the
use of "sexually suggestive" models rather than physically attractive models.
The research has shown that attractive models may facilitate recognition of
advertisements.[27] However, in general the use of highly sexually explicit ads
has been found to result in a mixed response regarding their effectiveness.
For example, one study found that the presence of physically attractive and

partially clad models influenced an automobile's image in a favorable manner.[28] The same study also suggested that if the erotic nature of the ad was too high, it actually harmed recall of the ad, when the recall was measured a week after the person saw the ad. Another study found that physical attractiveness may interact with other variables.[29] In the study high and low physically attractive people endorsed either a coffee product or a perfume/cologne. The results showed that attractiveness produced greater intentions to buy the product when the product was related to sexual appeal, i.e., was the perfume. In contrast, if the product had nothing to do with attracting the opposite sex, (i.e., the product was coffee) the unattractive source had more impact. Subjects in the study may have inferred that physically attractive endorsers would know something about perfume but have little knowledge of coffee. Although other explanations are possible for these results, they clearly indicate that using physically attractive models may not be appropriate for some types of products, such as coffee.

As noted by one investigator, much research needs to be done before final conclusions can be drawn on the impact of physical attractiveness on consumer reactions in marketing settings, and the use of artificial laboratory settings may cause more rational processing of information and impede the effects of physical attractiveness on consumers.[30] A recent study investigating the effects of source attractiveness found that if the physical attractiveness was matched to the product, such as using an attractive person to endorse a shaving razor, it would be highly effective in influencing attitudes.[31] Indeed, the study concluded by quoting Aristotle: "Beauty is greater recommendation than any letter of introduction."

Likability of the Source

The study just mentioned, which quoted from Aristotle, also suggested that likability and physical attractiveness are two different concepts. As such, **source likability** refers to the positive or negative feelings that consumers have towards a source of information. The tennis player John McEnroe has been used as an example of someone who is considered physically attractive but unlikable.[32] Developing a definition of the concept of likability is a difficult task, because it is probably different for each person. In general, however, likability probably most closely relates to the extent to which another person is viewed as behaving in a way that matches the desires of those who observe him or her. Thus, a person may be likable because he or she acts or espouses beliefs that are similar to those of the audience.[33]

The concept of likability has received little study in the consumer behavior literature. However, it is clearly important. For example, how can one explain the phenomenal success of the celebrity endorser Bill Cosby without reference to the idea of likability. Figure 11–4 shows an ad for Cosby endorsing Texas Instruments computers. Cosby has also endorsed products from the Ford Motor Company and Jell-o products for General Foods Corporation. He was used heavily by Coca-Cola to counter the Pepsi challenge by pro-

Figure 11–4 Bill Cosby has been the most popular celebrity endorser in recent years. (*Courtesy of Texas Instruments, Inc.*)

TI's Magic Wand Speak & Learn.™
The more it does for them, the more it will do for you.

And does it do a lot! Texas Instruments made the Magic Wand Speak & Learn more than a learning aid. It's a complete educational activity system. With books on subjects from math to music that expand your potential for aftermarket sales.

Customers keep coming back for the products that help their children learn. Spelling, reading, geography ...Magic Wand makes them fun. It not only speaks; it entertains with songs and exciting sound effects.

Children pass an electronic wand over the bar code that's printed beneath the words in every book. Magic Wand then says the words as the child sees them. As he or she grows, an expanding library takes the child from basic preschool activities to a wealth of subjects and exercises—bringing customers back to you for more.

The low cost and wide appeal of Magic Wand talking books make them as attractive to parents as they are to children. Titles from *Mr. Rogers®*, *PicturePages®*, *Spider-Man®** and the *Berenstain Bears*™ will have customers asking for the books by name.

They're all supported by strong national advertising, new self-demonstrating POP, newsletters and the ever-powerful Cosby.

Ask your Texas Instruments representative about the Magic Wand Speak & Learn. Then learn how much it can do for you.

*PicturePages is a trademark of PicturePages, Inc.
**The Amazing Spider-Man and the distinctive likeness thereof is a trademark of the Marvel Comics Group, a division of Cadence Industries Corporation and is used with permission.

Copyright ©1983 Texas Instruments

TEXAS INSTRUMENTS
Creating useful products and services for you.

Come see us at the Summer CES at McCormick West, Booth #5000.

nouncing that "Coke Is It" prior to the reintroduction of Coke Classic in 1985. For many reasons Bill Cosby is liked very much by consumers, as evidenced by his number-one-rated television show and his role as the most effective endorser of the 1980s.

TECHNIQUES OF PERSONAL INFLUENCE

Thus far the discussion of personal influence has focused on the transmission of information via word-of-mouth and on the opinion leaders who affect the behavior of others. Another approach to studying personal influence investigates the techniques one person can use to cause another to act in a desired manner. The techniques have been implemented by charities, by honest salesmen, and by everyday people to induce others to comply with their requests. As Highlight 11–2 shows, even intimidation can sometimes be effective. Unfortunately, the techniques also can be used by unscrupulous individuals to gain their own illicit ends. In the following subsections four of these techniques are discussed—ingratiation, the foot-in-the-door, the door-in-the-face, and even-a-penny-will-help.

HIGHLIGHT 11–2

Influence Through Intimidation?

During the early 1980s a whole series of books were published on how to succeed by intimidating others. The books suggested that how you dressed, walked, and talked influenced your ability to gain a power advantage over others.

The act of intimidating an opponent has reached the level of an art, as in sports. A great relief pitcher, Ryne Duran, pitched for the New York Yankees in the late 1950s. Duran would walk to the mound wearing glasses that looked like the bottoms of Coke bottles. He would start his warm-up pitches by throwing one of his fire-balling pitches over the catcher, umpire, and backstop. Reputed to have severe drinking problems, Duran had the combination of a lack of sight, a reputation of craziness, and a super-fast ball, which made him almost unbeatable. Batters would come to the plate more worried about their lives than about hitting the ball.

The consumers of sports, the fans, can also be intimidators. They are one of the reasons that home teams win more often than visiting teams. For example, at football games the home crowd can drive the visiting team to distraction with blaring horns and loud chants. The Florida State football team faced such a problem when they played their traditional rival—Louisiana State. When opponents had the ball, LSU's fans passed a deafening cheer from section to section around the stands, like a verbal baton. In order to foil the verbal barrage, the Florida State team began practicing with the loudspeakers blaring out the offending cheers. The practice helped the players to screen the distracting noise at game time, and the Florida State team began to win on a regular basis at LSU.

Is winning through intimidation something that can be practiced by salespeople? Probably the answer is no. One cannot bully customers into buying. However, just as salespersons can make judicious use of ingratiation tactics, so may they subtly use tactics to gain a slight power edge over clients. Such tactics may include knowing a great deal about their own product line as well as the *client's* business. In addition, they include dressing appropriately and being able to explain clearly why the customer should buy their products.

Based in part on C. R. Creekmore, *Psychology Today*, July 1984, 40–44.

Ingratiation Tactics

The term **ingratiation** refers to self-serving tactics engaged in by one person to make himself or herself more attractive to another.[34] In this case attractiveness refers to the overall positivity or negativity with which one person views another. An ingratiator builds on the knowledge that as the attractiveness of one person increases, the likelihood of another complying with his or her wishes increases. It is a subtle way of obtaining increased power over another person. Of course, everyone attempts to make herself or himself more attractive to favored others. With ingratiation, however, the efforts are manipulative and calculating.

A number of different ingratiation techniques are available for use. A common denominator among the tactics of ingratiation is that in each case the ingratiator subtly rewards the target.[35] Examples include:

□ *Appearing to be similar to the target.* One of the strongest findings in the social sciences is that people like others who are similar to them. Thus, a skillful ingratiator will attempt to assess the target and identify rapidly the person's attitudes, opinions, and interests. The ingratiator will then modify his or her own statements to match the perceived beliefs of the other. If successful, the target will perceive the ingratiator to be similar and consequently like him or her more.

□ *Conforming to the target's wishes.* One way to building the ego of another is to agree with him and conform to his wishes. In this manner the target is made to feel important by the ingratiator. The conformity subtly rewards the target and consequently builds the importance of the ingratiator to the target.

□ *Offering compliments, gifts, and so forth.* The ingratiator can build power by directly rewarding the target through compliments (e.g., you solved that problem brilliantly) or through gifts (e.g., picking up a lunch tab). Figure 11–5 illustrates the use of a gift as an ingratiation technique. The ad by De Beers, the huge diamond company, shows a younger woman responding positively to the gift of a diamond by an older man. Implied in the copy is the thought that if this man wants to keep this "young thing," he had better shower her with expensive gifts.

□ *Expressing liking.* People tend to like others who like them. If the ingratiator can persuade the other that he or she is viewed with genuine affection, the target is likely to return the liking.

□ *Asking advice.* By asking for advice, the ingratiator makes the other feel as though he or she is respected. This is a more indirect method of telling the other that he or she is liked.

Ingratiation tactics are effective methods of achieving increased power in a short-term relationship, such as a personal-selling situation. Indeed, one of the primary tactics of the skilled salesperson is to create a "close relationship" with the client. A major problem can occur, however, if the ingratiator

Figure 11–5 An ingratiation technique operates in this ad promoting the giving of diamonds as gifts. *(Courtesy of De Beers Consolidated Mines, Inc., and N W Ayer, Inc.)*

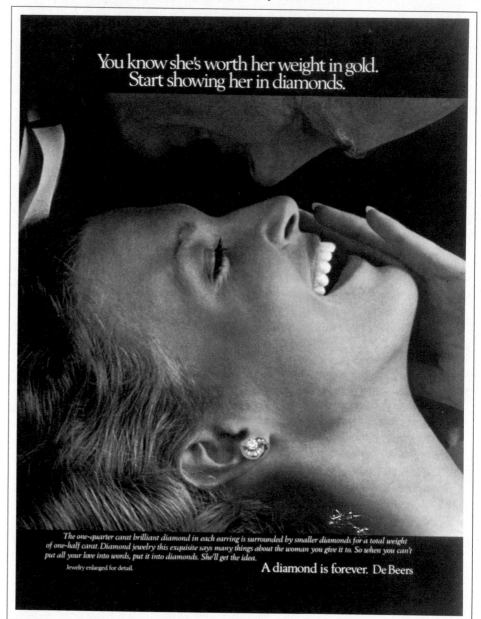

is caught in the attempt to manipulate the target. If the target recognizes that he or she is being deliberately manipulated, the influence attempt is likely to boomerang, resulting in a *loss* rather than a *gain* of power. An **ingratiator's dilemma,** therefore, exists. The ingratiator cannot be too obvious in his or her attempts to reward the target. On the other hand, for the approach to be successful the target must be rewarded in some way.[36]

The likelihood of the ingratiator being caught is quite high in a sales situation. A natural power difference exists between the prospect and the salesperson. The prospect knows that the salesperson wants to make a sale and is wary of his or her influence attempts. Thus, the successful salesperson must come across as sincere and nonmanipulative.

The Foot-in-the-Door Technique

An old saying exists that the if a successful salesman can merely get his foot in the door, he can make the sale. As it turns out, the adage has scientific support. A requester can increase the likelihood that a prospect will say yes to a moderately sized request if the person can be persuaded first to say yes to a smaller request. Thus, by getting a prospect to let him in the door, the skilled salesman has persuaded him or her to capitulate to a small request. The task of selling the person the product then becomes that much easier.

The **foot-in-the-door technique** operates through a **self-perception** mechanism. That is, by complying to the first, small request, the prospect forms an impression that he or she is the type of person who does such a thing. Later, when the second request is made, the person is more likely to agree to the request, out of the need to be consistent with that self-perception.[37]

The foot-in-the-door technique has been shown to influence people in a wide variety of settings. For example, in comparison to control groups, those who were asked to do something very small first more frequently agreed to give blood, to count traffic for a fictitious safety committee, and to complete market research surveys. Thus, one study found that people who were first contacted over the phone and asked a few short questions were later more likely to complete a long written questionnaire than people who had not been contacted on the phone first.[38]

A number of areas of application exist for the foot-in-the-door technique in marketing. Thus far it has most frequently been used as an approach to increase the response rate to market research surveys. A more important area of use, however, is likely to be personal selling. The task of selling a product consists of a series of steps. To the extent that the salesperson can persuade the client to agree to small initial requests first, the task of making the final sale is likely to be that much easier. For example, if a stockbroker can persuade a potential client to visit her office, the task of selling that person stock should be substantially easier, because the buying of the stock is consistent with the previous behavior of going to visit the broker.

The Door-in-the-Face Technique

In the foot-in-the-door technique a small initial request is followed by a larger request. The **door-in-the-face technique** operates by again making an initial request. However, instead of being very small, request is extremely large. In fact, it is so large that no one would be expected to comply to it. Again, the two-step approach results in a greater degree of compliance to the second request, in comparison to control groups that do not receive an initial request. Areas for which the door-in-the-face technique have been found to increase the rate of compliance include asking people to complete marketing surveys, to take juvenile delinquents to the zoo, and to count automobiles for a traffic-safety committee.

The self-consistency mechanism that accounts for the effectiveness of the foot-in-the-door technique would suggest that the door-in-the-face should be ineffective in increasing compliance rates. After all, if a person first says no to a request, from a self-consistency perspective he or she should also say no to a second request. A completely different explanation accounts for the door-in-the-face—the **norm of reciprocity.**[39] The norm of reciprocity states that if a person does something for you, you should do something in return for that person. The norm helps to grease the wheels of society by insuring that efforts to help someone else will not go unrewarded. When the door-in-the-face is implemented, the norm is illicitly invoked. That is, the requester makes the large request and never expects the person to comply with it. He or she then makes the smaller, moderate-sized request. The requester attempts to make it appear that he or she has given up something when the smaller request is made. The target then feels as though he or she must return the favor. The only possible way of reciprocating the imaginery gift is to say yes to the second request.

The door-in-the-face has more limited applications than does the foot-in-the-door. Because it is based on the operation of the norm of reciprocity, the second request must be a smaller portion of the first request. Thus, if the large request is to complete a long survey, the second request should involve completing a shorter version of the survey. A second limitation of the door-in-the-face approach is that the same person must make both requests. The target must be made to feel that the requester is actually giving up something in the second request. If a different requester makes the request, nothing is perceived to be given up. A final difference is that the second request must immediately follow the first in the door-in-the-face procedure. The two requests can be made even a week or two apart with the foot-in-the-door. However, to create the impression that a concession is being made, the two requests must be close in time (certainly within an hour or so) when the door-in-the-face is implemented.

Even-a-Penny-Will-Help Technique

The foot-in-the-door and the door-in-the-face are based upon the norms of self-consistency and reciprocity, respectively. The **even-a-penny-will-help technique** is based upon the universal tendency for people to want to make themselves "look good." Most often used in charity contexts, the approach operates by asking the target to give money and by tacking on the phrase "Even a penny will help" at the end of the request. Because everyone has a penny, the person would look foolish in saying no to the request. Thus, the person must say yes. The problem is that the target cannot simply give a penny, because he or she would look completely foolish. Thus, the person will tend to give whatever is normatively appropriate for the situation and the charity.

Research investigating the technique has found that the total amount given to charities increases when the technique is used. Although individuals give slightly less money on average in comparison to those who did not receive the request, the larger number of people giving something more than compensates for the slightly smaller individual contributions.[40]

It is important to recognize that the compliance tactic can be implemented in many ways in addition to merely saying "Even a penny will help." A marketing researcher could ask the respondent to complete a survey and add the phrase "Even answering a question or two would help." A sales person making a "cold call" could state "Even two minutes of your time would be appreciated." The adaptations of the technique are limitless.

In addition to the four compliance techniques mentioned, skilled salespeople may also use other approaches. One of these is based on using principles of perceptual contrast and is discussed in Highlight 11–3.

HIGHLIGHT 11–3

Use Contrast Principles to Influence Others

Here is an experiment for you to try sometime when you are really bored. Take out three large pans. Put very hot water in one, very cold water in another, and room temperature water in the third. Now, plunge one hand in the hot water and one hand in the cold water at the same time. Keep your hands in the water until you can't take it any longer. Then, quickly place both hands in the pan of room temperature water. What you will find is that the hand that had been in the cold water feels very hot, and the hand that had been in the hot water feels very cold. You have just experienced firsthand the sensations that result from a contrast effect.

Contrast effects are a perceptual phenomena which can be used by skillful influencers. Adept salespeople at better clothing stores often use such contrast ef-

fects. For example, they know that a person is much more likely to buy ties, shirts, sweaters, belts, and shoes after they have bought a $400 suit than before they buy the suit. What happens is that after spending $400 on the suit, a $15 tie or a $40 sweater does not seem that expensive. A contrast occurs between the expensive suit and the less expensive accompaniments, making the sweater and tie seem low priced.

In a similar manner, realtors will sometimes take prospects to overpriced "shacks" prior to taking them to the house that they really want to sell. The contrast between the "shack" and the target house makes the latter much more attractive.

Based on Robert Cialdini, "The Triggers of Influence," *Psychology Today*, February 1984, 40–45.

Managerial Implications

Knowledge of personal influence factors is vital to much of the promotional effort of the firm. The study of how information is transmitted from person to person and of how opinion leadership works is important to the firm in developing strategy, particularly for products early in the product life cycle. The study of the influence of sources of information is important to the advertising effort, to the development of the personal characteristics of the sales force, and to the use of corporate personnel in public relations efforts, such as making speeches at civic functions. The study of compliance techniques can possibly make the personal-selling effort more effective.

Implications of Information Transmission

Having an understanding of the multistep flow model and of opinion leadership can assist marketers in planning advertising strategies. The multistep flow model holds that communications flow to opinion leaders, followers, and gatekeepers. With information flowing freely among the three sets of people, the marketer should attempt to target advertising to each group. In particular, advertisers should insure that their messages reach followers as well as opinion leaders, because the follower may initiate the conversation with the opinion leader about the product category. Thus, when promoting a product, such as a camera, the advertising firm should place information in media vehicles that are likely to be read by opinion leaders, such as magazines devoted to photography. In addition, advertisements should be placed in media vehicles likely to be ready by followers, such as *Newsweek*.

The ability of managers to target and influence opinion leaders directly is difficult because their demographic characteristics are so similar to those of followers. However, the rewards of successfully targeting opinion leaders are so great that the effort can be cost-effective. One approach is to look for "natural" opinion leaders. For example, county extension agents, hair stylists, local golf professionals, and others who have special expertise about a product category will act as opinion leaders. Marketers of sporting equipment will sometimes hire top local amateurs as consultants and provide them with the use of their brand of raquetball racket or golf ball in the hopes that the local "star" will influence others to buy the product.

Another approach to targeting opinion leaders directly is through special interest magazines. Thus, a maker of golfing equipment could advertise in *Golf Magazine* and *Golf Digest* in an attempt to get information to potential opinion leaders.

In a few instances companies have attempted to create opinion leaders. For example, Canada Dry set up a board of socially prominent women to serve their products at parties. The idea was to get their products into the hands of people "who make things happen."[41] In another case a record company attempted to shape a "hit" by creating opinion leaders. The company invited influentials in high schools (e.g., cheerleaders, class presidents) to serve on a panel to evaluate rock records. In several instances records became popular in the trial cities while not reaching the top ten in other cities.[42]

Companies have also attempted to stimulate word-of-mouth communications through the use of mysterious or controversial commercials. For example, Levi Strauss developed an advertisement in which an attractive female, clad in tight Levi jeans, drives up to a gate of a house located in a large field. She turns to the house and yells, "Travis, you're a year too late." The advertisement created a great deal of word-of-mouth conversation about the mystery of what had happened and of just what the woman wanted. Similarly, Calvin Klein created intense word-of-mouth conversation with its suggestive ads for jeans. For example in one of the ads the actress Brooke Shields says, "Nothin' gets between me and my Calvins."

Knowledge of opinion leadership has two additional implications for managers. First, when doing product testing, opinion leaders should be specifically sought for inclusion in the tests. These are the individuals who will influence others, and their views of the product should be analyzed. Second, when sending samples through direct mail as part of the introductory phase of a new product, efforts should be made to identify potential opinion leaders for receiving the samples. In each case the manager is trying to include opinion leaders in the product development and promotional efforts early in the life cycle of the product.

Implications of the Study of Source Influence

As noted above, the study of the factors that influence the effectiveness of sources of information is important to advertising, personal selling, and public relations. A new trend in the use of sources is to license cartoon and comic book characters to place on products. One estimate is that by 1990 the retail sales of licensed products will reach $75 billion.[43] In effect, the cartoon character acts as a source of influence to persuade millions of children and adults to purchase products.

Another recent trend is a movement away from reliance on celebrities to endorse products. One survey showed that only 19 percent of consumers felt that celebrities and athletes increase their interest in products. Half of the respondents believed that celebrities do the commercials only for the money.[44] Such a belief would seriously impair the trustworthiness of the celebrities. In fact, according to the Screen Actor's Guild, its members rely on advertising jobs for 48 percent of their income. In order to evaluate consumer impressions of celebrities companies turn to what are called Performer Q ratings.[45] These are measures of how well liked celebrities are among consumers. The question is, though, whether likability is enough. In 1983 Alan Alda was the most-liked actor. However, his endorsements of Atari computers did little for the company. As the work on source effects suggests, expertise and trustworthiness are also important characteristics of the source.

As a general statement, the following rules should be employed when identifying the characteristics of sources of information. All else equal, the source should be perceived by consumers as:

1. Having expertise on the topic.
2. Being likable.
3. Being trustworthy.
4. Being similar to the audience.
5. Being physically attractive, as long as it pertains in some way to the product or service.
6. Actually believing in the product.

Implications of Compliance Techniques

The various compliance techniques discussed in the chapter can be used by companies in personal-selling efforts. However, each of the four compliance techniques has a Machiavellian aspect to it. The requester is attempting to manipulate the target by utilizing powerful societal norms or by using knowledge concerning how people can make themselves more attractive to others. The foot-in-the-door technique uses the norm that people should be consistent in their behaviors. The door-in-the-face technique uses the norm of reciprocity. The even-a-penny-will-help approach borrows on the concept that people have a need to maintain a positive image in front of others. The ingratiation tactics illicitly use knowledge of the factors that make one person more attractive to another in order to gain power in a short-term relationship. Because these tactics involve the conscious attempt to manipulate another, the manager must be concerned about the ethical implications of their use.

Suppose that you were a marketing researcher and a company contracted with you to perform a large survey. Further, suppose that a clause in the contract stated that if the response rate were over 50 percent, you would receive a bonus. The thought of using one or more of the techniques would probably cross your mind. If you chose the door-in-the-face one, you would have the interviewers first ask the respondents to complete a very long questionnaire. After the respondent refused, the interviewer would ask in a hurt voice if he or she would be willing to complete a few of the "key" questions. Of course, these are the questions you wanted to have completed all along. The interviewer in effect lied to the respondent.

A strong argument can be made that a "law of marketing research" is that interviewers should never *lie* to respondents. Because surveys take up the time of respondents, marketing researchers have a responsibility to treat them with total respect. Fortunately, the ability to abuse the tactics of compliance is limited. In each case the problem of the boomerang effect exists. If the requester is caught in his or her subterfuge, good will is lost and a dissatisfied consumer results.

In summary, each of the four compliance tactics can increase the likelihood that targets of influence will comply with the wishes of requesters. They are particularly useful in the personal-selling area. Charitable organizations and religious groups can also use them to increase the likelihood that people will make contributions. In addition, they may be implemented by marketing researchers as a method of increasing the response rate to surveys. A key question, however, concerns whether or not an implicit code of ethical conduct is being broken when the tactics are implemented.

SUMMARY

Personal influence refers to the concept that one person may intentionally or unintentionally influence another in his or her beliefs, attitudes, or intentions concerning a product, service, or idea. Personal influence results from both the needs of the sender of information and the needs of the receiver of information. Personal influence forms the basis around which word-of-mouth information flows through the marketplace. Such word-of-mouth communications are in part responsible for the success or failure of new products and for the distribution of negative information about an existing product. A negativity bias exists such that information on product problems strongly influences the actions of consumers.

Several models have been developed to explain how personal influence is transmitted. The trickle-down model holds that information moves from the upper classes to the lower classes. The two-step flow model holds that mass communications first influence opinion leaders, who in turn influence followers. In the multistep flow model information is viewed as moving from the mass media to gatekeepers, opinion leaders, and followers. The approach holds that communications can pass back and forth between the three groups of people and that in different situations the members of the groups may interchange.

Opinion leaders are important to companies because they in part control the positivity or negativity of the information that followers receive. Although different people will tend to be opinion leaders for different product categories, some common factors do characterize opinion leaders. In general, opinion leaders tend to be heavily involved in and knowledgeable about the product category. Opinion leaders share some common characteristics with product innovators, such as being active in professional groups and interested in the product category. However, the opinion leader tends not to be the earliest buyer of the product and is more prone to follow the norms of various social groups.

In studying personal influence an area of particular importance is that of source effects. A source can be a person, a company, a media vehicle, or even a cartoon character. Three groups of factors govern the effectiveness of sources—their credibility, physical attractiveness, and likability. Source credibility has been found to be based upon consumer perceptions of the expertise and trustworthiness of the communicator. In general, the higher the credibility of the source, the greater the effectiveness of the communication in changing beliefs, attitudes, and behaviors. However, in certain circumstances a moderate credibility source may be more effective. In conditions where the audience is already favorably predisposed to the communication, using a moderately credible source rather than a highly credible one may be most effective.

The physical attractiveness of the source is also a variable that should be considered by managers. The research generally indicates that highly physically attractive sources are superior to less attractive sources. However, it is important for the attractiveness to match the product or service. If the product or service is totally unrelated to physical attractiveness, using beautiful people may not be appropriate. Indeed, it is possible that using a beautiful person could be harmful with some products, such as coffee, because it may be assumed by an audience that those who look good would know nothing about the product.

The likability of a source is another factor for managers to consider. The concept of likability is difficult to define precisely, but it seems to occur when consumers perceive that the source acts in a way that supports the desires and beliefs of the audience. Although some endorsers, such as John McEnroe, have been successful even though they are not generally perceived as likable, the characteristic is in general something that a manager would prefer an endorser or a salesperson to have.

Another area relating to personal influence concerns various compliance techniques. These techniques allow the influencer to affect the actions of a target individual without the target consciously changing his or her attitudes about a product or purchase. Ingratiation tactics involve the influencer engaging in tactics to make himself or herself more attractive to the target. Through this method the ingratiator gains a small power advantage, which can be used to further his or her desired ends. The foot-in-the-door technique operates through the influencer making two requests. The first, small request is followed by a moderately sized request. The door-in-the-face technique also uses two requests; however, in this case the first request is very large, and the second request is of moderate size. Both techniques result in increased levels of compliance to the second request. The foot-in-the-door approach works because of a self-perception mechanism. The door-in-the-face technique works through the norm of reciprocity. Another compliance technique, even-a-penny-will-help, operates by asking the target to do something so small that the person must comply or face possible ridicule. However, the target ends up doing more than requested in order to avoid looking bad for having done so little.

The study of personal influence and word-of-mouth communications has a number of managerial applications. The various techniques of influence can be used in personal-selling and marketing research applications. (e.g., inducing people to complete surveys). The goal of the salesperson is to increase the likelihood that clients will say yes to sales presentations through the use of techniques such as ingratiation, the door-in-the-face, and the foot-in-the-door. However, managers should recognize that these techniques are manipulative and can backfire if the client perceives that the salesperson is employing them. In addition, the ethics of their use should be considered.

Managers should also be aware of the impact of word-of-mouth communications on product success. Indeed, steps can be taken to enhance the likelihood that opinion leaders will spread positive information about the product. The actions of Warner Books in sending a thousand copies of *Megatrends* to CEOs exemplifies such an approach. Managers should also be aware of the devastating effect of negative information on products. Periodic consumer surveys are employed by many companies to assess the current word-of-mouth information about their product.

Key Terms

Personal influence
Negativity bias
Trickle-down theory
Two-step flow model
Multistep flow model
Opinion leader
Product innovators
Source credibility
Source expertise
Source trustworthiness
Cognitive response
Source likability

Ingratiation
Ingratiator's dilemma
Foot-in-the-door technique
Self-perception
Door-in-the-face technique
Norm of reciprocity
Even-a-penny-will-help technique
Perceptual contrast

Review Questions

1. Define the concept of personal influence. What are the two types of personal influence that may occur?
2. What is the negativity bias in word-of-mouth communications?
3. Indicate the various needs within the sender and the receiver that can cause personal influence to occur.
4. Identify the three models that describe how personal influence is transmitted through the population. Which of the models appears to be the most accurate? Why?
5. What are the characteristics of opinion leaders? How are opinion leaders and product innovators similar? How are they different?
6. Identify the characteristics of sources that tend to influence their effectiveness.
7. Discuss the concept of source credibility. What are the benefits of using highly credible sources? Are more highly credible sources always more effective than less credible sources? Why?

8. Delineate the benefits and problems of using physically attractive sources of information.
9. Discuss four means people can use to ingratiate themselves with others. What is meant by the term *ingratiator's dilemma?*
10. What are the steps in implementing the foot-in-the-door influence technique? Explain the psychological mechanism that appears to be responsible for the technique's effectiveness.
11. What are the steps in implementing the door-in-the-face influence technique? Explain the psychological mechanism that appears to be responsible for the technique's effectiveness.
12. Why does the even-a-penny-will-help technique work?
13. How can contrast effects be used in personal-selling situations?

Discussion Questions

1. Think about some of the products or services that you have purchased for the first time. Examples might include a stereo receiver, a meal at a good restaurant, an appointment with a medical doctor or an automobile. To what extent did word-of-mouth communications influence the brand, place, or person you chose? How important was the word-of-mouth information in comparison to other inputs, such as those from sales personnel, product literature, and third-party information, such as reading *Consumer Reports?*
2. Various models of personal influence have been developed, such as the trickle-down theory, the two-step flow model, and the multistep flow model. Thinking about the purchases you make and about the people with whom you interact, try to draw and label a diagram of the flow of information

among these various people about products and services. (Hint: use Figures 11–1 and 11–2 to get yourself started.) Which of the models does your experience seem to support?

3. Suppose that you were a marketing manager for a regional brewery. How successful do you think a strategy would be of attempting to reach opinion leaders with communications so that they will pass these messages on to followers and, thereby, influence their behavior?

4. Suppose that you are an advertising agency account executive charged with the responsibility of finding an endorser for a new toothpaste. What would be the considerations in attempting to find a person who could act as a spokesperson for the toothpaste product?

5. List four celebrities who are currently endorsing products. How effective do you perceive them to be? What is the role of their expertise, trustworthiness, likability, and physical attractiveness in making them more or less effective?

6. Ingratiation is a device frequently used to influence others. Describe the various ingratiation tactics an automobile salesman could use and their possible impact on customers.

7. You are working in the marketing department for a firm that does market surveys. Your boss tells you that he wants to use the foot-in-the-door technique to increase the response rate to telephone interviewers. He asks you to develop the specific wording for telephone surveyers to use, which incorporates the foot-in-the-door technique. The research in question involves a ten-minute survey on the use of dishwashing detergent. Write out the specific words that the interviewers should use.

8. Do the same thing as found in question 7, except write the words that would be used to implement the door-in-the-face technique.

9. Identify three types of sales situations in which contrast principles might be used. Identify specifically how the salesperson would make use of perceptual contrast to increase the likelihood of making a sale in each sales context.

10. Discuss the ethical implications of using the various compliance techniques identified in the text. Are some of the techniques more ethical than others?

References

1. Stephen P. Morin, "Influentials Advising Their Friends Sell Lots of High-Tech Gadgetry, *The Wall Street Journal*, February 28, 1983, 23.

2. Elihu Katz and Paul Lazarsfeld, *Personal Influence*, Glencoe, Ill.: The Free Press, 1955.

3. Sidney Feldman and Merlin Spencer, "The Effect of Personal Influence in the Selection of Consumer Services," in *Proceedings of the Fall Conference of the American Marketing Association*, Peter Bennett (ed.), Chicago, Ill.: American Marketing Association, 1965, 440–452.

4. Johan Arndt, "Role of Product-Related Conversations in the Diffusion of a New Product," *Journal of Marketing Research*, 4 August 1967, 292.

5. Thomas Robertson, Joan Zielinski, and Scott Ward, *Consumer Behavior*, Glenview, Ill.: Scott, Foresman, and Company, 1984.

6. Ernst Dichter, "How Word-of-Mouth Advertising Works," *Harvard Business Review*, 44, November–December 1966, 148.

7. Henry Assael, *Consumer Behavior and Marketing Action*, Boston, Mass.: Kent Publishing Co., 1983.

8. Charles W. King and John O. Summers, "Overlap of Opinion Leadership Across Product Categories," *Journal of Marketing Research*, 7, February 1970, 43–50.

9. Katz and Lazarsfeld, *Personal Influence*, 332–334.

10. Russell Belk, "Occurrence of Word-of-Mouth Buyer Behavior as a Function of Situation and Advertising Stimuli," in *Combined Proceedings of the American Marketing Association*, Series No. 33, Fred C. Allvine (ed.), Chicago, Ill.: American Marketing Association, 1971, 419–422.

11. Everett M. Rogers, *Diffusion of Innovations*, 3d ed., New York, N.Y.: The Free Press, 1983, 281–284.

12. Thomas Robertson and James Myers, "Personality Correlates of Opinion Leadership and Innovative Buying Behavior," *Journal of Marketing Research*, 6, May 1969, 168.

13. James Coleman, Elihu Katz, and Herbert Menzel, *Medical Innovation: A Diffusion Study*, Indianapolis, Ind.: The Bobbs-Merrill Co., Inc., 1966.

14. Robertson, Zielinski, and Ward, *Consumer Behavior*.

15. Terrence Shimp, "Methods of Commercial Presen-

tation Employed by National Television Advertisers," *Journal of Advertising, 5,* Fall 1976, 30–36.

16. Richard Petty, Thomas Ostrom, and Timothy Brock, *Cognitive Responses in Persuasion,* Hillsdale, N.J.: Laurence Erlbaum Associates, 1981.

17. Carl Hovland, Irving Janis, and Harold Kelley, *Communication and Persuasion,* New Haven, Conn.: Yale University Press, 1953, 35.

18. Josh Weiner and John Mowen, "The Impact of Product Recalls on Consumer Perceptions," *MOBIUS: The Journal of the Society of Consumer Affairs Professionals in Business,* Spring 1985, 18–21.

19. For an excellent review of the material on source credibility see Brian Sternthal, Lynn Phillips, and Ruby Dholakia, "The Persuasive Effect of Source Credibility: A Situational Analysis," *Public Opinion Quarterly, 42,* Fall 1978, 285–314.

20. Peter Wright, "Cognitive Processes Mediating Acceptance of Advertising," *Journal of Marketing Research, 10,* February 1973, 53–62.

21. Brian Sternthal, Ruby Dholakia, and C. Leavitt, "The Persuasive Effect of Source Credibility: Tests of Cognitive Response," *Journal of Consumer Research, 4,* March 1978, 252–260.

22. Robert Harmon and Kenneth Coney, "The Persuasive Effects of Source Credibility in Buy and Lease Situations," *Journal of Marketing Research, 19,* May 1982, 255–260.

23. Joseph Poindexter, "Voices of Authority," *Psychology Today,* August 1983, 53–61.

24. Poindexter, "Voices of Authority."

25. Shelley Chaiken, "Communicator Physical Attractiveness and Persuasion, *Journal of Personality and Social Psychology, 37,* August 1979, 1387–1397.

26. Karen Dion, E. Berscheid, E. Walster, "What Is Beautiful Is Good," *Journal of Personality and Social Psychology," 24,* December 1972, 285–290.

27. Robert Chestnut, Charles LaChance, and Amy Lubitz, "The Decorative Female Model: Sexual Stimuli and the Recognition of Advertisements," *Journal of Advertising, 6,* Fall 1977, 11–14.

28. M. Steadman, "How Sexy Illustrations Affect Brand Recall," *Journal of Advertising Research, 9,* March 1969, 15–19.

29. Michael Baker and Gilbert Churchill, "The Impact of Physically Attractive Models on Advertising Evaluations," *Journal of marketing Research, 14,* November 1977, 538–555.

30. W. Benoy Joseph, "The Credibility of Physically Attractive Communicators: A Review," *Journal of Advertising, 11,* Summer 1982, 15–24.

31. Lynn R. Kahle and Pamela Homer, "Physical Attractiveness of the Celebrity Endorser: A Social Adaptation Perspective," *Journal of Consumer Research, 11,* March 1985, 954–961.

32. Kahle and Homer, "Physical Attractiveness."

33. Herbert Simon, Nancy Berkowitz, and John Moyer, "Similarity, Credibility, and Attitude Change," *Psychological Bulletin, 73,* January 1970, 1–16.

34. E. E. Jones, *Ingratiation: A Social Psychological Analysis,* New York, N.Y.: Appleton-Century-Crofts, 1964.

35. Edward E. Jones and Harold B. Gerard, *Foundations of Social Psychology,* New York, N.Y.: John Wiley & Sons, Inc. 1967.

36. Jones, *Ingratiation.*

37. Peter H. Reingen and J. B. Kernan, "Compliance with an Interview Request: A Foot-in-the-Door, Self-Perception Interpretation," *Journal of Marketing Research, 14,* August 1977, 365–369.

38. Robert A. Hansen and Larry M. Robinson, "Testing the Effectiveness of Alternative Foot-in-the-Door Manipulations," *Journal of Marketing Research, 17,* August 1980, 359–364.

39. John C. Mowen and Robert Cialdini, "On Implementing the Door-in-the Face Compliance Strategy in a Marketing Context," *Journal of Marketing Research, 17,* May 1980 253–258.

40. Robert Cialdini and David Schroeder, "Increasing Compliance by Legitimizing Paltry Contributions: When Even a Penny Helps," *Journal of Personality and Social Psychology, 34,* October 1976, 599–604.

41. Cited in Henry Assael, *Consumer Behavior and Marketing Action.*

42. Joseph R. Mancuso, "Why Not Create Opinion Leaders for New Product Introductions?" *Journal of Marketing, 33,* July 1969, 20–25.

43. Joanne Cleaver, "Starring 'Mickey Mouse' On Marketing Team," *Advertising Age,* June 6, 1985, 15–16.

44. Ronald Alsop, "Jaded TV Viewers Tune Out Glut of Celebrity Commercials," *The Wall Street Journal,* February 7, 1985, 35.

45. Alsop, "Jaded TV Viewers."

12

Group Processes

Groups and the RCA Videodisk Failure

In 1984, RCA abandoned its efforts to introduce a new concept in television entertainment—the videodisk. Estimated to have cost the company $780 million, the videodisk research, development, and marketing efforts encompassed a fifteen-year period.(a)

The videodisk was a phonograph-like record that provided a high-quality television picture. The company anticipated that movies and instructional shows would be popular on the disks. However, several unanticipated factors substantially reduced the total market potential of the product. Each of the factors involved some aspect of group processes.

One expectation of the RCA marketers was that the videodisks would be bought with the large-screen televisions that were beginning to be sold in the mid-1970s. These mammoth TV sets made a family's living room into a movie theater. A report by a consulting firm predicted that by the year 1980 there would be almost no movie theaters left in the United States, because of the effects of big-screen televisions.(b) What the consulting firm and RCA failed to realize is that people go out to the movies in part to be with a large group. Going to the movies is a social occasion—a chance to see others and be seen. These qualities cannot be obtained in the family living room.

Similarly, one motivation for watching network television is the ability to share the viewing experience with others the next day. People will not give up watching network television in part because of the desire to talk about the programs that they watched the night before. When the videodisk is viewed, the consumer cannot watch television, thereby missing out on the camaraderie the next day. This need for affiliation limited the market potential of the videodisk.

In the end, however, it was the success of the video recorder that caused the demise of the videodisk. The videodisk was substantially cheaper than the video recorder, giving it a relatively higher market potential. However, during the early 1980s the prices of video recorders plunged to well under $500, and they became competitive with the videodisks.

A major topic area under group behavior concerns how innovations, such as the videodisk, are adopted by members of the population. One factor that governs the diffusion of innovations through a population is the extent to which the new product has a relative advantage over its competition. With the lowering of the price of the video recorders, the videodisk lost its one relative advantage. The ability of the video recorder to record information from the television was too much of a handicap for the videodisk to overcome.

Based on (a) "Videodisc Dream Is Over: RCA," *Advertising Age,* April 9, 1984, 4, 68; and (b) John Naisbitt, *Megatrends,* New York, N.Y.: Warner Books, 1982.

INTRODUCTION

Why is it that restaurants usually add a 15 percent tip to the bill when more than four or five people eat together? Why is it that Procter & Gamble, McDonald's, and other large corporations are constantly beseiged with rumors about their products? Why is it that members of many fraternities and sororities tend to wear similar clothes? Each case exemplifies a different way in which group processes influence consumers. Groups give a lower percentage tip because each member feels less responsibility to provide a fair share. Rumors illustrate the phenomenon of the diffusion of information through a population. The similarities of ideas and dress among fraternity and sorority members illustrate the concept of reference group influence.

A **group** may be defined as a set of individuals who interact with one another over some period of time and who share some common need or goal.[1] Each consumer belongs to numerous groups, each of which may have some impact on his or her buying behavior. For example, a college student is likely to be a member of a series of groups. Families, sororities and fraternities, dorms, student organizations, and clubs are examples of groups. The family group, which is discussed in detail in Chapter 13, is particularly important because it has a major impact on the socialization of an individual.

Types of Groups

Sociologists have developed a variety of terms to describe the various types of groups a person may belong to, aspire to join, or avoid. Table 12–1 provides a brief definition of the various groups. These include reference groups, primary and secondary groups, and formal and informal groups. Each type of group has importance to the marketing manager.

Reference Groups **Reference groups** are perhaps the most important to the manager, because they are used by consumers to form their values,

Table 12–1 Types of Groups

Reference Group: A group whose values, norms, attitudes, or beliefs are used as a guide for behavior by an individual.

Aspirational Group: A group to which an individual would like to belong. If it is impossible for the individual to belong to the group, it becomes a symbolic group for the person.

Dissociative Group: A group with whom the person does not wish to be associated.

Primary Group: A group of which a person is a member and with whom that person interacts on a face-to-face basis. Primary groups are marked by an intimacy among their members and by a lack of boundaries for the discussion of various topics.

Formal Group: A group whose organization and structure are defined in writing. Examples include labor unions, universities, and classroom groups.

Informal Group: A group that has no written organizational structure. Informal groups are often socially based, such as a group of friends who meet frequently to play golf, bridge, or party together.

beliefs, and attitudes about the consumption process. Reference groups form a point of reference to which consumers can compare themselves with others in order to determine the correctness of their attitudes and behaviors.[2]

The term *reference group* is a broad one that encompasses a number of more specific types of groups. The common factor among the various types of reference groups is that each is used by the consumer as a point of reference to evaluate his or her actions, beliefs, and attitudes. One type of reference group is the aspiration group. **Aspiration groups** are those sets of people to whom a consumer hopes to belong. Therefore, an aspiration group can become a reference group for a consumer. One can see the effects of aspiration groups on college students in the spring of their senior year. At this point in time they are interviewing for jobs. Their aspiration group has suddenly changed and along with it their clothing—from jeans and cutoffs to business suits.

A **dissociative group** is another type of reference group. In this case, though, the consumer wishes to separate himself or herself from the group. The dissociative group still acts to form a point of reference; however, it is a point with which the consumer wants to avoid being associated. Such separation from a group can occur when individuals are striving to move into higher social classes. They may attempt to avoid buying the products and services used by the dissociative reference groups, i.e., the social class that the consumer is attempting to leave. For example, a person who wishes to move into the upper middle class may want to avoid bowling groups or groups involved in selling Tupperware, because of their association with the lower-middle class.

Other Types of Groups A number of other types of groups exist. These may or may not form reference groups for the consumer. For example, groups may be classified as either formal or informal. A **formal group** has an organizational structure that is likely to be defined through charts and membership rosters. A written code of conduct is likely to exist. The American Marketing Association and the Association for Consumer Research are examples of formal groups. **Informal groups,** as their name implies, are much less organized. They may be a neighborhood group of friends or a teenage clique. Although rules and norms may exist in an informal group, they will not be codified in writing.

Another type of group is the **primary group.** The factor that denotes this group is the frequent face-to-face interaction of its members.[3] Families and coworkers in an office would be examples of primary groups. Because of the close contact of the members of a primary group, one of the prime characteristics of its functioning is the desire of members to have satisfaction with the relationships among the people of the group.

A key point regarding the various types of groups is that they are *not* mutually exclusive. For example, a formal group may or may not be a reference group. A person could be in a formal group in the business where he or she works and actively be attempting to leave it. In this case the group could be a dissociative reference group. On the other hand, the person may not be influenced at all by the group because he or she does not expect to be in the job for very long. In such a case, the group may not be used as a reference and would have less influence on the person's behavior. Reference groups are a very important base for some types of products, though this can lead to marketing problems. Highlight 12–1 presents some examples of products being linked to reference groups.

Groups Are More Than the Sum of Their Parts

A major reason for studying groups is that when people enter a group they will frequently act differently than when they are alone. For a variety of reasons the interaction and the expectation of interactions among people modifies their behavior. As noted in the consumer vignette that introduced the chapter, the expectation of talking about the network programs limited the total market for the RCA videodisk. Similarly, the desire to be a part of a group at a theater makes the downfall of large movie theaters unlikely.

A study on shopping behavior illustrates the impact of groups on consumers. In the study the purchases of consumers were examined based upon the size of the shopping group they were in.[4] The results showed that when the consumers shopped alone, they tended to make their purchases as planned. However, as the size of the group increased, they tended to move away from making their planned purchases. In groups of three or more the number of shoppers who made more purchases than planned increased by almost 100 percent. Similarly, the number of shoppers who purchased less

HIGHLIGHT 12–1

Mary Kay Cosmetics: A Group-Based Company

Until 1983 Mary Kay Cosmetics was a Wall Street darling. With sales growing rapidly the stock jumped 670 percent between 1973 and 1983. The company uses a sales force of women. To be successful the company must constantly recruit new entries into its sales force, because it is the new recruit who makes substantial orders from the company.

The problem occurred during 1983, when the number of new recruits began to fall rapidly. So did the stock price, falling over 65 percent in a six-month period.

A number of factors were responsible for the decline in recruitment. The increasing number of women working full-time jobs began to draw new recruits from part-time selling. The improved economy in 1983 made it less necessary for additional members of the family to engage in part-time work. The added money in a family's budget allowed women to buy higher-priced cosmetics.

However, a more fundamental reason could ac-count for the falling of recruits and may bode ill for the entire direct–home-selling market. Individuals who join companies such as Avon, Tupperware, Amway and Mary Kay tend to sell through a network of relationships. The women sell to their family, friends, and neighbors. In other words, sales are made to people within the seller's reference group. However, with increasing rates of divorce, with people moving more frequently from neighborhood to neighborhood, and with people changing jobs regularly, the pool of people to whom a person can sell cosmetics and household products is reduced substantially.

Companies that use an in-home, direct-sales approach tend to do best in closely knit, ethnic neighborhoods. With the numbers of such areas dwindling, the future of companies like Mary Kay does not look as bright as it once did.

Based on Dean Rotbart and Laurie P. Cohen, "The Party at Mary Kay Isn't Quite So Lively, As Recruiting Falls Off," *The Wall Street Journal*, October 28, 1983, 1, 25.

than planned increased by almost 100 percent. Table 12–2 shows these percentages.

HOW GROUPS INFLUENCE CONSUMPTION

Groups influence consumers through a variety of means. Reference groups affect people through norms, through information, and through the value-

Table 12–2   Effects of Group Size on Shopping Purchases

Purchases	Size of Shopping Group	
	Person Alone	**Three or More**
No items planned or purchased	3.7%	0.0%
Fewer purchases than planned	15.1	31.3
Purchases as planned	58.9	26.6
More purchases than planned	22.3	42.1

Source: Data from Donald H. Granbois, "Improving the Study of Consumer In-Store Behavior," *Journal of Marketing*, 32, October 1968, 28–32.

expressive needs of consumers. In addition, groups influence consumers by other means. Within groups certain roles can form which dictate the types of behaviors to be expected in various situations. A person who happens to be filling such a role will be expected to act in a manner dictated by the role requirements. Groups can also influence consumption through conformity pressures. Through various means groups can make their members follow their wishes and, thereby, influence consumption. Finally, groups can influence consumers through social comparison processes. Each of these topics is discussed further.

Normative, Value-Expressive, and Informational Influence

A **norm** is a behavioral rule of conduct agreed upon by over one half of the group in order to establish behavioral consistency within the group. Norms are rarely written down but are nonetheless generally recognized as standards for behavior by members of a group. They represent shared value judgments about how things *should* be done by members of the group.[5] **Normative influence** occurs when norms act to influence behavior. For example, the effects of unwritten corporate dress codes depict the impact of normative influence on the clothing purchased by employees. Similarly, norms can influence what and how much a person eats or drinks at a party and even the type of car that is bought. Many college professors feel that it would be nonnormative to buy a Cadillac or Lincoln automobile, because to many of them buying such cars represents an ostentatious show of wealth. Indeed, one study compared the consumption patterns of professors and businessmen.[6] The results indicated that in comparison to businessmen professors exhibited less of a tendency to engage in conspicuous consumption. Further, the study found that the norms of informal faculty groups tended to oppose conspicuous consumption and that these norms were responsible for the less-conspicuous buying behavior of the professors.

Groups can also influence consumers by providing them with information and encouraging the expression of certain types of values. **Informational influence** affects individuals when the group provides highly credible information that influences the consumer's purchase decisions. **Value-expressive influence** affects consumers when they sense that a reference group has certain values and attitudes pertaining to the consumption process. Because the person wishes to be a part of the group and to be liked by the members, he or she will be influenced by these values and attitudes. Figure 12–1 shows an advertisement illustrative of the use of value-expressive influence. In it a group of "young urban professionals" (Yuppies) are shown together after work, enjoying themselves and smoking cigarettes. The idea is to use the target market's reference group to show that it is okay to smoke—a type of value-expressive influence.

The three types of reference group influence can affect the consumption behavior of employees in organizations. A company a person works for is a formal group and probably also a reference group. In addition, those who are members of a corporate department to which an employee aspires represent

Figure 12–1   This ad uses a value-expressive influence by focusing on the target market's reference group. *(Reprinted by permission of Philip Morris, Incorporated.)*

an aspiration group. Different companies have divergent sets of norms, values with which their employees are expected to comply. For example, the dress codes of a company may be enforced quite strictly, and the normative pressure to comply can be quite strong. IBM Corporation has clear-cut norms about how their employees should dress when on the job. These expectations directly affect the purchase patterns of clothing among IBM employees.

In a company, value-expressive influence can affect the choice of an automobile and how employees spend their recreational hours. In an effort to be liked and to be similar to important others in the company the employee may take up bowling or golf in order to fit into the corporate culture. Similarly, the employee may select an automobile that symbolizes the values of the corporation. Thus, an executive working for a "high tech" company may select a car that symbolizes the technological emphasis of the company, such as a BMW.

Informational influence will tend to occur when an individual obtains facts from a reference group. Thus, the executive might ask colleagues working in the firm about the qualities of alternative automobiles and about their experiences with them.

In each of the above cases, the corporate group influenced an employee's consumption behavior. The same types of effects can occur if the group involved is a church, a family, a softball team, or a set of neighbors who socialize together.

Roles

Both formal and informal groups have a variety of positions that people fill. A position has a specific status attached to it; thus, a person's position describes his or her place in the social system. For example, in Chapter 13 the family is discussed in terms of the various buying roles that are present, such as decision maker, buyer, influencer, and disposer of the product. Each position is a type of **role** into which various family members step.

A role consists of the specific behaviors expected of a person in a position. Thus, when a person takes on a role, normative pressures exert influence on the person to act in a particular way.[7] An important role in consumer behavior is that of the decider. This person makes the final decision concerning which brand to chose. In industrial buying settings identifying the decider is crucial. Often times it is an individual outside of the purchasing department who must take responsibility for the outcome of the buying decision. Reaching this individual with the promotional message can make the difference in whether or not a sale is made.

The term **role-related product cluster** has been given to the set of products necessary for the playing of a particular role. For example, to play the role of a cowboy requires the purchase of boots, jeans, and a hat that match the role. Such roles can move in and out of favor as lifestyles change. In the early 1980s the cowboy role was in fashion. By the mid-1980s the role of business executive became popular. The resulting penchant for shorter haircuts and conservative dress affected a variety of industries.

A classic study relevant to the role-related product cluster idea was performed in the 1950s. In the study groups of housewives were given shopping lists that a "homemaker" had prepared. The two shopping lists were identical except for whether each contained the entry of drip-grind coffee or of instant coffee. The homemaker who bought the ground coffee was described by the respondents as "practical and frugal." In contrast, the woman who had bought the instant coffee was seen as lazy, short-sighted, as an "office girl who is living from one day to the next in a haphazard sort of life."[8] Although the study has been criticized, it does indicate that in 1950 instant coffee was not a part of the role-related product cluster of someone who was a good homemaker. Interestingly, the 1950 study was repeated in the 1970s, and the results were dramatically different. The user of instant coffee was then described favorably, whereas the user of ground coffee was viewed as "old fashioned."[9]

For marketing managers the task of identifying those products that match the roles of consumers can be a profitable endeavor. For example, the role-related product cluster of a successful executive's office might include a secretary, a personal computer, a window on an upper floor, and an exercising device in the corner. An advertising campaign for the exercise equipment could tie symbolically its product to the rest of the product cluster as necessities for the upward-moving business person.

Conformity Pressures

Conformity may be defined as a "change in behavior or belief toward a group as a result of real or imagined group pressure."[10] Two types of conformity can be identified. The first is simple **compliance,** in which the person merely conforms to the wishes of the group without really accepting the group's dictates. The second is **private acceptance,** in which the person actually changes his or her beliefs in the direction of the group. A number of factors will increase the conformity pressures of a group, and these are identified in Table 12–3.

Table 12–3 Factors Influencing the Conformity Pressures of a Group

A. Properties of the Group
  1. Cohesiveness
  2. Size
  3. Expertise
  4. Group's view of product's salience
B. Properties of the Person
  1. Information available to person
  2. Attractiveness of the group to person
  3. Person's need to be liked
  4. Type of decision the person faces

Factors Within the Group Leading to Conformity   Notice in Table 12–3 that conformity pressures can result from the properties of the group as well as from the needs of the person. Three aspects of a group influence the conformity pressures felt by its members. The first is its cohesiveness. *Cohesiveness* refers to how closely knit the group is. A group to which its members have a high degree of loyalty and identification will exert greater influence on its members. Thus, some firms, such as IBM, pride themselves on being highly cohesive. As a consequence their ability to influence the behavior of employees both on and off the job is high.

The *expertise* of the group also affects conformity pressures. Because consumers are members of many groups, several different groups may have input into a particular purchase decision. The group whose members have more expertise relevant to the decision will have greater influence on the purchase.

The *size* of the group has also been found to influence decisions, particularly when the group is of a transient nature. In a classic series of experiments a psychologist, Solomon Asch, had people view a series of lines and judge which of the lines on one card matched the length of a line on another card. The task was quite simple, and when done alone the subjects made almost no errors. However, in the experimental conditions the researcher had confederates estimate the relative length of the lines prior to the subject doing so. These confederates, who actually worked for the experimenter, systematically gave a wrong answer. To the experimenter's surprise the subjects in 37 percent of the cases agreed with the confederates' judgments. The impact of the group was found to vary with the number of confederates. The likelihood of the subjects agreeing with the confederates increased until the size of the group reached about four people. After the group size got to four people, the impact of adding more individuals to the group was minimal.[11]

Factors Within the Person Leading to Conformity   The ability of a group to make a person conform depends upon the nature and needs of the person as well as the properties of the group. One such personal factor is the amount of information that the person has for a decision. Thus, when little information is available for the decision or when the information is ambiguous, the group will have more impact on the consumer's decision. For example, in an experiment that was modeled after the "line experiments" done by Asch, consumer subjects rated their preferences for suits of clothes. When confederates of the experimenter first gave their choice, the subjects tended to select the same suit of clothes as the confederates.[12] However, the suits were all essentially identical so that the information on which the decision was based was highly ambiguous.

The attractiveness of the group and the person's need to be liked by the group often work together to create conformity pressures. In most cases the more the person wants to be a part of the group, the more he or she also wishes to be liked by its members. In such circumstances the individual will tend to conform to group norms and pressures in order to fit in as well as possible. An example of these ideas may be found in work done during World War II to encourage consumers to eat organ meats, such as liver, kidneys, and hearts. The research found that the most effective means of encouraging consumers to eat such less desirable cuts of meat was to have neighborhood discussions.[13] Although numerous factors could explain the positive results of the neighborhood discussions, one likely explanation is that the attractiveness of the group and the desire to be liked helped to increase conformity.

The type of decision is a final factor that will influence the amount of conformity pressure felt by the person. Several studies have suggested that when a product is highly salient and conspicuous to others, conformity pressures will increase. For example, in one case researchers found that for products such as color televisions, automobiles, home air conditioners, refrigerators, insurance and physicians references, the group had a major impact on the decision.[14] The first two products, color televisions and autos, exemplify the concept that conspicuous consumption decisions are affected by conformity pressures. The remaining products, however, are not highly salient purchases to other people. The likely explanation for their inclusion is that inadequate information is available, and the group is used to obtain information on where to purchase insurance and on which physician to select. An additional likelihood is that such purchases are viewed as having a high degree of risk, leading the consumer to seek additional information from outside sources.

Social Comparison Processes   Another way in which groups influence consumers is through a need by people to assess their opinions and abilities by comparing themselves to others. The process through which people evaluate the "correctness" of their opinions, the extent of their abilities, and the appropriateness of their possessions has been called **social comparison.**[15] Thus, in addition to using groups to obtain factual information, consumers use groups to determine where they stand in terms of their opinions, abilities, and possessions.

Two approaches are used by consumers to obtain ability and opinion information. The first is through **reflected appraisal.** In this process the consumer examines the manner in which others in a reference group interact with him. Thus, if the other person responds fondly to the person, compliments the person, and generally treats the person well, the individual will conclude that he is acting correctly. In contrast, if the other person responds negatively, the person will conclude that he is doing something wrong.

The second method of obtaining social comparison information is through **comparative appraisal.** Whereas in reflected appraisal the person must interact with others, in comparative appraisal interaction is unnecessary. The consumer evaluates his own relative standing with respect to an attitude, belief, ability or emotion by observing the behavior of appropriate reference others.[16]

An important point regarding social comparison processes is how a consumer selects an appropriate group to which she will compare herself. The evidence indicates that people will compare themselves to others who are at about the same level on the given attributes rather than to someone who shows great differences. Thus, a college professor is more likely to assess the appropriateness of the car he or she drives by comparison with other faculty members rather than with the corporate managers with whom he or she consults. This has been called the "extent of co-orientation" shared by the individuals. The more the individuals are co-oriented (i.e., similar on relevant characteristics, such as income, job, social status as well as similar regarding the ability, opinion, or belief in question), the greater will be the tendency for one to compare himself or herself to the other.[17]

The ideas behind social comparison theory have been tested in a consumer setting.[18] Using cosmetics as the type of product, the researcher found that consumers sought information from their peers in order to determine their relative standing. They tended to seek information from friends to whom they were similar rather than from friends to whom they were dissimilar. In addition, reference group influence was strong when a high degree of similarity among members occurred on characteristics relevant to the purchase. This was strong evidence for the hypothesis that co-orientation increased the need to socially compare oneself with others.

One implication of this need of consumers to socially compare themselves to similar others has to do with the diffusion of innovations, which is discussed later in the chapter. To the extent that a new product is adopted by individuals with similar value orientations and who are likely to be communicating among each other, the product should diffuse rapidly through the population. In contrast, if the product is adopted by people with different orientations, the product can be predicted to diffuse slowly.[19]

THREE TYPES OF GROUP PHENOMENA

Groups influence consumers in a variety of ways, a number of which were discussed in the last section. In addition to providing norms and roles and creating conformity pressure, groups also change the way people react to information. Groups can influence the way people make decisions and the speed with which they do tasks. In addition, groups can cause people to act for their short-term benefit at the expense of long-term group and individual liabilities. These processes are labeled group shifts, social facilitation, and social traps and fences phenomena.

Group Shifts

Many aspects of **group shifts** have been investigated. For example, about twenty years ago psychologists began studying a highly perplexing group phenomenon—the risky shift. In the early studies researchers gave groups or individuals decision dilemmas and compared their choices. These early results revealed that groups tended to select the riskier alternative. For example, in one situation a man of moderate means was described as receiving a small inheritance. Groups and individuals had to decide how he should invest the money. The groups more often recommended that he invest the money in risky securities which might produce larger gains than in conservative blue-chip stocks. Later research found that conservative as well as risky shifts could occur. For example, one study investigated an interesting type of consumer behavior—racetrack betting. These researchers found that groups were more cautious in placing bets than individuals at the track.[20] The tendency of groups to cause people to shift their decisions, either in a more cautious or a more risky decision direction, is called the group polarization phenomenon.

A variety of explanations have been offered for the group polarization phenomenon. One factor accounting for group shifts is the information transmitted during group discussion of the problem. During the course of discussion arguments are made for various decisions. The decision alternative receiving the greatest number of arguments typically is chosen.[21]

Another explanation for the group polarization phenomenon is called the cultural value hypothesis. Researchers have found that the shifts are almost always in the direction to which the individuals are already leaning. Thus, the interaction of the members tends to emphasize this initial predisposition of the individual members. The social interaction then reinforces such predispositions and moves the group decision to a more extreme position than the average of the individual decisions.[22]

Group polarization effects have been shown to influence consumer decisions. For example, researchers found that shifts occurred among groups of housewives for decisions involving financial and socio-psychological risk.[23] In another study consumer scenerios were developed to assess group shifts for six different types of risk—financial, physical, social, time, functional, and psychological.[24] The results showed that group polarization effects occurred for some types of risk and that men and women differed in the types of shifts that occurred. For example, groups of women revealed risky shifts for social decisions, and men revealed cautious shifts for functional decisions.

The study of group shifts in consumer behavior and marketing has been neglected. For example, Chapter 13 focuses on the family. Many types of consumer decisions made within the family are made jointly by the husband and wife, with children often having input. Researchers have failed to investigate whether group shifts could occur within such family decisions. Another area in need of research is industrial buying behavior. Here the key question is, To what extent does group polarization influence the corporate purchasing practices? Indeed, one possible explanation of the phenomenal success of the IBM Personal Computer is that cautious shifts occurred among industrial purchasing agents. That is, why take risks buying less well known brands when IBM has a product, even though the others may provide more power and capabilities for the dollar?

Social Facilitation

Social facilitation is one of the earliest phenomena discovered by social psychologists. In 1898 Triplett discovered that adolescents could turn fishing reels more quickly when someone else was present than when alone. The results were interpreted as indicating that somehow the mere presence of others caused a change in the performance of an individual.

A number of theories have been advanced to explain why simply having others present affects the actions of individuals. One likely explanation is that the presence of others increases the drive or arousal of an individual.[25] The higher arousal level increases the likelihood that the person's dominant response tendency will occur. Thus, the heightened arousal will invigorate the actions of a person reeling in a fishing rod and increase the speed with which the reel is turned.

The effects of social facilitation are not always positive, however. The presence of others will increase the speed with which a person works only on relatively simple tasks. For difficult, complex tasks, however, the speed is actually decreased. Similarly, on complex tasks the presence of others can decrease the level of performance.[26] The greater levels of arousal resulting from having other people present appear to impede high levels of performance on complex tasks.

At this point in time consumer researchers have not investigated social facilitation. However, the arousing presence of groups clearly has implications for consumer purchasing behavior. For example, when making a major purchase such as a car, the presence of a salesman and other purchasers could act to influence the information processing of the consumer merely by their presence. Because selecting a car and making a price deal with the salesman are complex tasks, the presence of others could negatively affect the performance of the consumer. Other occasions in which social facilitation effects could occur are in family decision making and industrial purchasing situations. Finally, the presence of other shoppers could have an impact on individuals in department or discount stores. Chapter 10, which discussed the effects of situational factors on consumers, analyzed the impact of crowding on consumer purchase behavior.

Highlight 12–2 further explores the effects of groups on consumer behavior by discussing a phenomena called *social loafing*.

Social Traps and Fences

New England villages in the 1700s were organized around a commons area or pasture where everyone could graze their cattle freely. Because their pasture was a free good, people took advantage of the opportunity by gradually increasing the number of cattle that they placed in the commons area. Over a period of time the number of cattle would increase to the point that they overwhelmed the grass resources of the commons area, and it would be reduced to a large mud hole. Researchers have recognized that the "commons dilemma" is but one example of an entire class of group problems and have labeled them **social traps**.[27]

HIGHLIGHT 12–2

Why Do Groups Give Lousy Tips?

Have you ever noticed that most restaurants simply add a 15 percent gratuity to the bill when groups of larger than five or six people have dinner? The reason this policy is enforced is that when people conglomerate into a group, their tipping behavior changes. As each additional person is added to the group, the total tip given by the group tends to decrease. This phenomenon has been called "social loafing," and it affects a broad number of tasks in which groups may engage.

The tendency of people not to tip as much or work as hard when in a group was demonstrated in a series of experiments. In the studies different numbers of people were placed into groups and asked to pull a rope together, clap their hands as loudly as they could, or shout as loudly as they could. As additional people were added to the group, the individual performance of each member of the group *decreased.* The larger the group, the less effort each person contributed to the group goal. Furthermore, the reduced results were

not caused by problems in coordinating a large number of people. Additional studies showed that in fact the reduced performance resulted from decreases in effort by individual team members.

A number of reasons probably account for such social loafing. It could be that some members perceive that others are not working hard enough. As a result, they slacken their efforts. It is also possible that in larger groups lower goals are set than in smaller groups. Perhaps the most likely possibility is that a "diffusion of responsibility" occurs when people get into larger groups. In other words, the relationship between one person's effort and the overall outcome is lost. Thus, individuals don't feel a responsibility to exert high amounts of effort.

Based on Bibb Latane, Kiling Williams, and Stephen Harkins, "Many Hands Make Light the Work: The Causes and Consequences of Social Loafing," *Journal of Personality and Social Psychology*, 37, June 1979, 822–832.

Several conditions are necessary for a social trap to occur. First, in most instances social traps involve some kind of resource. In the commons dilemma the resource was the grass of the grazing land. Other resources that may involve social traps are water, vegetation, animals, and the atmosphere. A second condition is that the resource is replenishing itself at some rate. Rivers and oceans can eliminate pollution, grass will grow, and animals will reproduce. The third condition is that the people using the resource are interdependent. That is, the individuals are "tapping the same pool" of the resource. Thus, in the commons dilemma the townspeople were all using the same pasture. Finally, for the trap to be set the individuals must have relatively easy access to the resource.

With the presence of the four conditions the stage is set for the operation of the trap. What can happen is that each person operates for his or her own gain by drawing upon the resources of the pool. This could involve grazing cattle, trapping lobsters, killing whales, or spewing pollutants into a river, lake, or atmosphere. At first the actions of a few individuals have little impact because the resource can replenish itself. However, if too many begin to use it, they can overwhelm its rate of replenishment. In the worst case the resource can be totally destroyed. Lakes can go dead, species can be exterminated, and even deserts can be created, as in Africa today. In summary, in a social trap each person acts to obtain an individual short-term gain that results in a long-term group and individual loss.

The **social fence** works similarly to a social trap; however, the actions of the group members are for a different purpose. In a social trap people take an action in order to obtain some benefit—e.g., fatten their cattle. In a social fence people *avoid* taking some action because the action would cause some temporary harm. The problem is that by not taking the short-term action, a long-term group loss results.

An example of a social fence has been described as follows.[28] A large number of weekend travelers were returning to the city from the beach on a two-lane highway. The road was extremely busy, with traffic moving bumper-to-bumper in both directions. A pickup truck dropped a mattress into one of the lanes, and immediately a long traffic jam resulted. People waited in line for thirty minutes prior to reaching the point where the mattress lay in the road. Upon reaching the mattress, each person had one of two options. He or she could get out of the car and move the mattress to the shoulder of the road or drive the car around the mattress. Of course, if one driver took the time to pick up the mattress the traffic jam would be remedied. However, the additional time it would take to stop and move the mattress, particularly after spending thirty minutes in a traffic jam was too much, and each driver would simply steer carefully over to the shoulder of the road and proceed. The trap occurred because no one person would accept the personal inconvenience to help the others.

Examples of social traps and fences abound. In particular, social traps often occur in areas that relate to public policy issues. Overfishing is a classic social trap. In the mid-1980s the lobster population began to fall dramatically off the coast of New England. Individual trappers were operating for their own short-term gain at the possible expense of totally depleting the resource for many years. Another example of a social trap is occurring in Tulsa, Oklahoma. In Tulsa an air pollution problem occurred because motorists were taking off the catalytic converters on their cars. Each motorist did this to obtain the short-term benefit of increased gas mileage and power in his or her car. The thousands of motorists acting for their own individual benefit resulted in a major air pollution problem for the city.

Social fences also operate in the business sphere. Investing in research and development has short-term negative consequences for most companies. Specifically, it lowers profit levels in the short term because the costs of such activities must be expensed in the quarter in which they occur, due to accounting rules. The incentive is *not* to invest in research and development in order to maximize short-run profits. The problem is that when thousands of companies fail to invest in research and development, a national problem results because the future benefits of the research efforts are lost.

Consumer researchers have not investigated social traps and fences, although they certainly occur among groups of consumers. For example, the failure of consumers to report product problems when they occur is an example of a social fence. Such inaction can allow unscrupulous companies to operate without law enforcement authorities becoming aware of their existence. An example of a social trap is occurring in Texas, Oklahoma, and Kansas, where farmers and ranchers are pumping water from aquifers faster than it can be naturally replenished. A potential disaster is lurking because the overpumping will eventually curtail farming in an important agricultural region. The social trap occurs because the short-term benefits propel each farmer to pump enough water to meet his own needs. However, the large numbers of farmers, all pumping to satisfy their own needs, results in the dramatic lowering of water tables. The study of consumer traps and fences is an area worthy of additional research.

DIFFUSION PROCESSES

Thus far the discussion of groups has focused on small aggregations of people. Reference groups will normally consist of less than twenty-five or so people. Groups, however, can be much larger. For example, a *market* can be viewed as a group of people composed of hundreds of thousands and even millions of consumers. The discussion of social traps and fences began this shift in the discussion to aggregations of larger numbers of individuals. This section on **diffusion processes** tackles an even broader set of group phenomena. The term *diffusion* refers to the idea that substances or even ideas can gradually spread through a medium of some type and reach a state of equilibrium. For example, if a drop of colored water is placed into a fish tank, it will gradually diffuse until it is evenly dispersed throughout the entire tank. Similarly, contagious diseases also may be viewed as diffusing through the population.

In marketing and consumer behavior the "thing" being diffused is generally an *idea* or *product* of some type. The medium through which it is diffused is the population of people that makes up a consumer market. In this section three different types of diffusion phenomena are discussed. The first is the diffusion of innovations. It concerns the factors that influence how innovative products become accepted and adopted by consumers. The second is the problem of how rumors spread. Corporations are plagued by rumors about their products, and understanding the process of rumor spread and control is important for large companies. Finally, the section covers the topic of consumer mass hysteria. Occasionally, large numbers of people get involved in huge money-making schemes which can end in terrible busts. Examples include the tulip bulb craze in Holland in the sixteenth century and the Mississippi land scheme in the seventeenth century.

The Diffusion of Innovations

The study of the adoption process of new products is an important one for marketers. In order to grow a company must continually improve existing products and periodically develop new products for the changing marketplace. The study of product adoption is also important because of the relatively low success rate of new products, where estimates are that about 50 percent of new products fail.

A product innovation is defined as a product that has been recently introduced and is perceived by consumers to be new in relation to existing products or services. Indeed, to be advertised as new, according to a proposal once made by the Federal Trade Commission, a product would have had to be in distribution for less than six months. Other factors also are relevant to whether a product is perceived as new in the marketplace. Perhaps most important is the extent to which it changes the behavior of consumers. A product that fails to alter the behavior or lifestyle of consumers cannot be described as new or innovative. In contrast, a product that causes consumers to engage in entirely new lifestyle patterns, such as those resulting from the introduction of the television, are certainly highly innovative.

Types of Innovations   Categories of innovations have been developed based upon the extent to which the behavior of consumers is influenced by the new product. The categories are part of a continuum and are shown in Figure 12–2. The three categories are labeled **continuous, dynamic continuous,** and **discontinuous.** Continuous innovations have the least impact on consumers. They are usually modifications of existing products to improve performance, taste, reliability, and so forth. An example would be the change-over of General Motors from round automobile headlights to square headlights in the 1970s. The new product had no real impact on the behavior of consumers, but it was important in the marketplace to the auto company.

Figure 12–2   A continuum of product innovations and their behavioral impact.

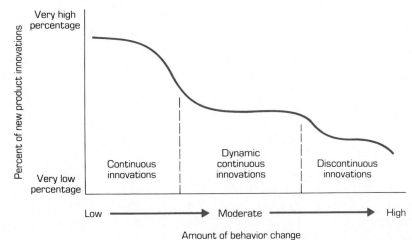

Changing the headlights was one way that the company could differentiate its models from those of other companies.

A dynamic continuous innovation will influence the lifestyles of consumers to some degree. The dynamic continuous innovation generally involves some major change in an existing product. An example would be the building of diesel engine automobiles. Diesel engines require a new set of maintenance requirements and fuel-filling procedures for consumers. Other examples of dynamic continuous innovations include the introduction of the first compact cars, of microwave ovens, and of heat pumps for residential housing.

Discontinuous innovations are those that produce major changes in the lifestyles of consumers. They come along much less frequently than the dynamic or continuous innovations. Examples include computers, televisions, radios, air conditioning, and airplanes. In each of the above cases, the innovation changed how people live. For example, radio and television changed dramatically how people spend their leisure hours. In the future one can anticipate that products from the biotechnology revolution will likely have discontinuous properties.

Remember, however, that the categories of continuous, dynamic continuous, and discontinuous innovations are on a continuum. That is, the impact on behavior of various new products labeled "dynamic continuous" could be quite different. Also note in Figure 12–2 that the percentage of new products in the continuous category is much greater than in the dynamic continuous grouping, which in turn is much greater than in the discontinuous set.

Factors Influencing New Product Success Most new products that reach the consumer do work. However, for various reasons over 50 percent of them fail within the first couple of years. A number of principles have been suggested as necessary for the success of new products:[29]

1. *Relative advantage.* The product must do something better, cheaper, or more reliably than other products on the market. As noted in the consumer vignette at the beginning of the chapter, one reason for the failure of the RCA video disk was that it failed to have a relative advantage over video recorders.
2. *Compatibility.* The innovation needs to be consistent with the lifestyle, social system, and norms of the target market. For example, when solar heating was introduced in the mid-1970s, as a response to the energy crisis, it was hailed as an answer to skyrocketing fuel bills. However, the active solar systems failed to catch on, in part because they required the homeowner to control the system actively. The prospect of having to clean solar panels, service the system, and turn solar panels to achieve optimum output went against the lifestyle of Americans, who had grown accustomed to not having to think about whether their house would heat itself automatically when it turned cold.

3. *Complexity.* Generally, the less complex a product, the faster it will be adopted and the greater the chances of its success. The high complexity of active solar systems was one reason for their failure. In the 1980s the single most important factor that made personal computers popular among the general public was that software was developed which made their operation much less complex.
4. *Trialability.* The easier it is for consumers to use the product and experience its benefits firsthand, the greater its chances for success. The high trialability of microwave ovens is one reason for their phenomenal success. A salesman can demonstrate in the showroom of a department store the ability of a microwave to cook a potato in eight minutes.
5. *Observability.* If consumers can see others successfully using the product, its adoption will be more rapid and its success more likely. In such cases social comparison can occur and lead consumers to believe that they should have the product because other consumers have it. When a new product is highly observable, it can take on the characteristics of a status symbol. To a certain extent buying video games had such a characteristic among teenage boys during the early 1980s.

Above all else a new product must fulfill the needs of a target market. After determining that the product does fulfill needs, the five qualities of observability, trialability, complexity, compatibility, and relative advantage should be thoroughly investigated prior to bringing a new product to market.

The Diffusion Pattern   Figure 12–3 identifies the normal pattern of how innovative products diffuse through the population. Note that the pattern

Figure 12–3   The shape of the diffusion process.

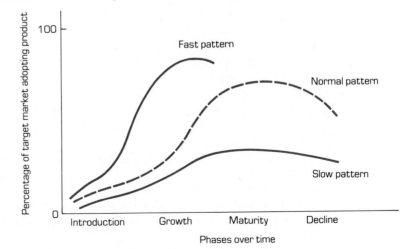

looks very similar to the familiar product life cycle concept. Indeed, only one key factor distinguishes Figure 12–3 from depictions of the product life cycle. The difference is that the product life cycle is based upon *actual sales,* whereas the diffusion process is based upon the *percentage of potential adopters within a market who adopt the product over time.*

The curve that describes the diffusion process in Figure 12–3 is S-shaped. During the introductory phase, the percentage of consumers adopting the product is small and slowly accelerating. As the product moves into the growth stage, the percentage accelerates, and the curve bends upward rapidly. During maturity, the growth slows until it turns negative when the decline begins to take place.

The exact shape of the curve depends upon a number of factors. If the innovation is adopted very quickly, the fast pattern found in Figure 12–3 results. If the adoption rate is slow, the pattern becomes much flatter and more drawn out. A number of factors affect the rapidity with which an innovation is adopted and, as a consequence, the shape of the curve. These include the characteristics of the product, the characteristics of the target market, and the amount of marketing effort exerted by the company.

CHARACTERISTICS OF THE PRODUCT. The same factors that influence the likely success of an innovation also influence the rapidity with which it is adopted. Thus, to the extent that it fulfills a need, is compatible, has a relative advantage, has low complexity, has observable positive features, and is easily tried, the product will be adopted more quickly.[30]

CHARACTERISTICS OF THE TARGET MARKET. Products targeted to different target groups will have divergent adoption patterns. For example, products that appeal to younger, change-oriented individuals will often be quickly adopted, but also run the risk of rapidly moving into decline. The sales of video games showed just such a pattern. Bought predominantly by teenage males, video game sales experienced phenomenal growth during the early 1980s, only to collapse when the thrill wore off. In general, the more socially integrated the target group, the quicker will be the adoption process. For example, a study of doctors found that doctors who had the most social contacts among other doctors were more likely to adopt a new pharmaceutical product.[31]

EXTENT OF MARKETING EFFORT. Companies can influence the growth curve of a product by the quality and extent of marketing effort. One of the reasons for the success of the IBM Personal Computer was the sheer weight of marketing effort that the massive computer company could place behind the product. Starting with no sales in 1980, the company by 1984 was dominating the personal computer market.

Various researchers have attempted to predict the shape of the diffusion curve by using mathematical models. One well-known model for predicting the adoption of durable goods stated that the adoption curve was based on the number of innovators who would initially try the product and on the number of imitators who bought the product because the innovators had bought it. By combining information on innovation and imitation propensities with knowledge of the total market potential of the product and of how many people had previously bought the product at various times, a good prediction of sales of various home appliances could be made.[32]

An example of an extremely fast diffusion process is a fad. Highlight 12–3 discusses the problems inherent in marketing a fad product.

Categories of Innovators   One of the important problems faced by marketers of innovative products is identifying the characteristics of people who buy the product early in its life cycle. Names have been given to groups of individuals who adopt new products at various stages of the product life cycle, and these are shown in Figure 12–4. Five different categories of adopters have been identified. The innovators are those who make up the first 2½ percent of the buyers of a new product. The early adopters make up the next 13½ percent of buyers, followed by the early majority (the next 34 percent), the late majority (the next 34 percent), and last the laggards (the last 16 per-

---

HIGHLIGHT 12–3

Fads—New Products Requiring Hustle

A **fad** is a product based on fashion and novelty rather than on fulfillment of a basic consumer need. A few of the fads that have surfaced in the market place over the past few years include pet rocks, Deely Bobbers (antennae-like springs with balls worn on top of the head), and the Wacky Wallwalker (a slimey spider that climbs down walls).

A *Wall Street Journal* article described the process that two entrepreneurs of fads use to sell their short-lived products. The marketers have a rule of 90 that they follow. They have 90 days to make and ship the product and 90 days to sell it out. As one stated, after 90 days "profits are eaten by inventory costs. We never stick around for the last dollar. . . . Pigs in our business get killed."

The best fads are inexpensive, action oriented and cute, according to these experts. Kids are particularly tough to market to because once they learn to play a game, the novelty has worn off and the product isn't touched. Once a fad "takes" among kids, it must wait for another generation to appear before it can be marketed again. Witness the "hoola-hoop," which makes a new appearance in the marketplace periodically.

A success for the entrepreneurs was Mr. T's Puzzle, which sold during the Christmas of 1983. The initial cost to produce the first 200,000 puzzles was over $250,000, which they had to finance themselves. As one of them said, "Banks don't understand us, . . . We jump from deal to deal, and they can't react as fast as we can."

Their general rule for deciding if a potential product has the makings of a good fad is to watch kids play with it. If kids play with something for more than 30 minutes, it has potential.

Based in part on Jennifer Bingham Hull, "Fad Merchants Hustle to Sell Tomorrow's Big Craze Today," *The Wall Street Journal*, November 17, 1983, 33.

Figure 12–4 Categories of adopters.

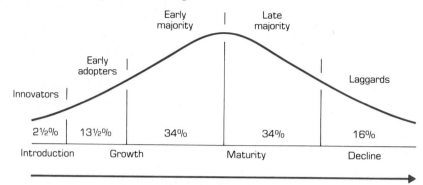

cent). Despite a great deal of research effort, little progress has been made in identifying a profile of consumer innovators that can be used to predict those who will first adopt the product. The evidence indicates that innovativeness seems to be product specific. Thus, different people will be the first to buy different types of new products. It has also been found that people who are innovative tend to be opinion leaders in that product category. The demographic and personality characteristics of opinion leaders and innovators were discussed at greater length in Chapter 11 on personal influence and word-of-mouth communication.

The Diffusion of Rumors

Rumors can be more than simply a headache for corporations. They can result in lost sales and profits. In addition, the process of halting their spread through the population can take up enormous amounts of time for corporate officials—time that could be spent on profit-producing activities. Since 1978 rumors have created major problems for such corporate giants as Xerox, Procter and Gamble, and McDonald's. In 1978 the rumor began to spread that the dry toner used by Xerox in its copiers caused cancer. In 1979 Procter and Gambler began to be plagued by the rumor that the firm avows Satanism. Flyers printed among conservative Protestant congregations noted that the P&G symbol contained a sorcerer's head and thirteen stars—a sign of Satan. McDonald's Corporation has also been hit by the Satan rumor. However, even more disturbing has been the fiction that the company adds ground worms to their hamburger meat.

Types of Rumors Sociologists and psychologists have identified a number of different types of rumors.[33] **Pipe dream rumors** represent wishful thinking on the part of the circulators. They are positive hopes concerning something that is going to happen, such as how much the Christmas bonus will be in a corporation. "Hot tips" in the stock market exemplify the pipe dream.

Individuals will circulate grandiose information about the prospects for a stock. The public may begin to buy the company's shares based upon the *hope* that a fortune can be made.

Another type of rumor is the **bogie.** Bogies are fear rumors that spook the marketplace. These are the type that have plagued Xerox, McDonald's, and Procter & Gamble. A bogie demolished the first king-sized menthol cigarette, Spud, in the 1940s.[34] A rumor spread that a leper worked in the plant where the brand was packaged. In six months the cigarette had disappeared from the marketplace.

Rumors can also be self-fulfilling. In this case the rumor is based on a perception of what could happen in the future if something else were to occur. "Bank runs" are examples of self-fulfilling rumors. It is true that if all of the depositors in a bank suddenly withdraw their money, any bank would fail. In bad times this knowledge can "spook" people and result in the very behavior that the people were afraid would occur. Indeed, runs on banks occurred in the early and mid-1980s, forcing the closings of a number of banks across the United States.

Rumors can be premeditated. In this case individuals with something to gain set out to spread rumors that will help them financially or otherwise. Such premeditated rumors can spread through the stock market and cause short-term shifts in the value of companies, which unscrupulous individuals can use to make money. Procter & Gamble believed that its Satan rumors resulted in part from the salespeople of a competing firm distributing the flyers describing the firm's supposed Satanic activities. The company took the unprecedented step of filing lawsuits against five individuals.[35]

Finally, rumors can be spontaneous, occurring when people seek explanations for unusual events. One author suggested that the ground worm rumors striking McDonald's may have begun when a consumer found "tubular" matter in some hamburger.[36] Such matter could easily result from a small blood vessel not being ground up very well. In order to explain the material, the consumer leaps to the conclusion that the tube must have been a worm.

Causes of Rumors The causes of rumors may be found in part in the various types of rumors just described. Rumors may be caused by an individual or group deliberately setting out to create a false idea. Rumors can result from wishful thinking among a group of people. Rumors can result spontaneously from an individual attempting to explain some unusual event or happening. In addition, however, the right environment is required for rumors to be nourished so that they will move through the population. The two factors that seem to be required are *uncertainty* and *anxiety.* Rumors generally occur and spread most rapidly when times are bad—when people are down, uncertain about their future, and anxious about what will happen to their dreams. Thus, it is not surprising that the rumors that struck Mac-Donald's and Procter & Gamble were at their worst during the severe recession/depression that struck the United States between 1980 and 1983.

Rumors have been studied for many years now. Immediately after World War II research on the topic was popular because of the many rumors that occurred during the war. For example, when meat shortages occurred in the United States, rumors sometimes circulated that whole sides of beef were being thrown in the garbage at a nearby military camp. One important insight into rumors was that they are born and circulated based upon the importance and the ambiguity of a situation. A formula was developed to express the relationship:[37]

$$Rumor = Ambiguity \times Importance$$

How to Respond to Rumors One expert on rumors has suggested that companies should go through a series of actions if a rumor strikes them:[38]

Step 1: Ride out the rumor.
Step 2: Trace its origins.
Step 3: Treat it locally.
Step 4: Rebut it with facts, but don't deny the rumor before the public hears about it.

The core idea among these suggestions is to avoid having the company spread the rumor by publicizing it. By keeping the rumor local, by trying to trace its origins and eliminate its sources, the problem may be kept in check. An example of the use of facts to combat rumors may be found in the actions of Life Savers, the maker of Bubble Yum bubble gum. A rumor began circulating that the gum contained spiders' eggs in it. After doing a telephone survey and finding that the rumor was spreading rapidly and after knowing that the news media had published the story, the company took out full-page ads in newspapers. The ads were headlined, "Somebody is telling your kids very bad lies about a very good gum." The ad went on to refute the rumors. The media praised the open methods of the firm, and the rumor died.[39]

To say that rumors "die" is an overstatement, however. They are rarely eradicated completely. Procter & Gamble's Satan rumor was still resurfacing in the mid-1980s, some six or seven years after it began. One executive with P&G stated, "Rumors are like matter. They can't be destroyed."[40] In fact, they can move from company to company. The worms-in-hamburger talk was such a divergent rumor—as it struck Wendy's prior to jumping on McDonald's, the industry leader.

A possible problem, however, should be noted with the use of refutational strategies to eliminate rumor problems. A study was done to investigate the earthworm rumor and McDonald's hamburgers.[41] The authors found that when the rumor was refuted with facts (e.g., red worms cost five dollars per pound and could not possibly be used) the negative impression of McDonald's remained. Because a refutational strategy mentions the rumor, the consumer is reminded of the *negative* information in the rumor. One way around the problem may be to give the facts without mentioning the rumor. McDonald's has in fact done this with a major promotional campaign that advertises the fact that the hamburgers are made with 100 percent pure beef. No mention of any rumors is made in the advertising campaign.

Urban legends, a phenomenon related to rumors, are considered in Highlight 12–4.

Consumer Crowd Behavior

In a number of circumstances consumers can show the same kinds of behavior as found in the actions of hysterical crowds. In such instances consumers become irrational and do things, as a part of the crowd, that they would never do alone. During the Christmas of 1983, consumers exhibited such crowd behavior. The Cabbage Patch dolls became so important to shoppers that mobs literally formed outside of department stores when news spread that the store carried the dolls. In a number of instances people were in-

---

HIGHLIGHT 12–4

Urban Legends: Modern Folklore That Can Hurt Sales

"Say, did you hear the story about the little old lady who had just washed her pet poodle. Well, the dog had a cold; and because she wanted to dry it quickly she put it in her microwave oven. Ten minutes later she found the poor thing, cooked from the inside out."

The "microwaved-pet" anecdote is one example of a number of **urban legends** that float around the country, often for years. Urban legends are realistic stories about incidents that are reputed to have occurred recently. Similar to folktales and old legends, they will usually have some type of twist or moral to them. For example, the microwaved-poodle tale warns us of the problems of too much technology.

Urban legends are diffused through the population much like rumors. However, they are longer and more specific and often are related to local happenings. They may even incorporate local rumors. Even the mass media will help to circulate the legends as something that really occurred. For example, the following story was carried in an Ann Landers column and is called the "Nude Housewife." A woman was doing her laundry in her basement when

she impulsively decided to take off her soiled housedress and put it in the machine. Her hair was in rollers, and the pipes overhead were leaking. She

spotted her son's football helmet and put in on her head. There she was, stark naked (except for the football helmet) when she heard a cough. The woman turned around and found herself staring into the face of the meter reader. As he headed for the door his comment was, "I hope your team wins, lady."

Unfortunately, urban legends can affect corporations. One such story involved a K-Mart store in Dallas, Texas. A woman was described as looking for some fur coats that had been imported from Mexico. When she put her hand in one of the pockets, she felt a sharp pain. After a few minutes her arm was turning black and blue. Later that day her arm had to be amputated because of a snake bite. One of the local newspapers tried to investigate the legend to see if it was true. They checked hospitals, insurance people, and even a person to whom it was supposed to have occurred. The woman had heard the legend but had understood that the snake was in a basket of fruit.

The legend capitalizes on American xenophobia and on the dangers of falling for terrific bargains.

Based on Jan Harold Brunvand, "Urban Legends, Folklore for Today," *Psychology Today*, June 1980, 50–62.

jured, and police had to be called in to control the unruly shoppers. In European and South American countries, spectators at important soccer events have been known to turn into mobs. In several instances hundreds of people were killed by mobs forming among the supporters of opposing teams.

The factors that cause normal consumers to form into crowds are still not understood completely. Gustav Le Bon, a Frenchman, in 1896 suggested that people go into hypnotic trances when they are part of a mob such that a collective mind is formed. A more likely explanation is that the mass of people are brought together by some idea or event of great importance to them. Such a large grouping causes a high degree of physiological arousal among each of the members. The high arousal results in the tendency of each member of the crowd to act on his or her dominant idea or tendency. Because a similar idea brought the group together, the individuals within the crowd are likely to share the common tendency to action. Unfortunately, in many instances the dominant tendency involves aggressiveness, although it could also be the urge to buy, as in the case of the Cabbage Patch dolls. When combined with the fact that in a crowd each person becomes inconspicuous, individual responsibility is lost. Thus, the usual norms that control behavior do not apply. The result is an unruly, highly aroused group of people who are not acting as individuals and are not subject to the standard norms that control behavior. The result can be riots, runs on banks, or panic buying of a product in short supply.

A concept related to crowd behavior is that of popular delusions. Popular delusions are similar to broad-based rumors that propel people to act in quite irrational ways. In many cases the actions involve wishful thinking that a fortune can be made. Two such infamous examples are the "tulip bulb mania" and the "Mississippi scheme."[42]

Tulipmania The tulip was introduced into Europe in the sixteenth century. Gradually, their ownership became a status symbol for men of means. However, the hysteria did not envelop Europe until the middle classes "caught the craze." In Holland the mania was particularly acute. Everyone began to get involved in the tulip trade. Highly prized varieties of the bulb were sold for astronomical prices. One trader was offered twelve acres of building ground for a single bulb—a huge price in a land consisting mostly of marsh. In other cases people were known to invest entire fortunes on the purchase of forty tulip roots.

Inevitably the bust occurred. The rich no longer bought the tulips to place in their gardens. Rather, they bought them so that they could be resold at a profit. Finally, some recognized that the folly would end. As the mania changed to fear, the price of the bulbs began to fall. In six weeks time the value of a single bulb could fall 1,000 percent, and still it could not be sold. Fortunes were lost as fast as they were gained. Those who profited by getting out early had to hide their money for fear of bodily harm.

The Mississippi Scheme   In the 1700s France was not in good shape financially, and commerce was lagging. The son of a Scottish banker, John Law, entered the country as part of his flight from the death penalty for having killed a man in a duel over a love affair. Law had studied banking extensively and in 1716 persuaded the French Regent to start a national bank and use paper money. The bank quickly prospered and two years later Law persuaded the French monarchy to begin development of the Mississippi basin and Louisiana, which were then French territories. The Mississippi Land Company was formed, and shares of stock were sold. Law promised to return to shareholders 120 percent of their investment in dividends in the first year.

The response to the company was overwhelming. The price of its shares shot up, sometimes rising 10 or 20 percent in a few hours. At the height of the buying panic, the company was worth twice as much as all of the gold and silver coin in the country. Inevitably, however, the bubble burst. People realized that the company had no assets and that no gold and silver had been found in Louisiana. In a matter of a few months the shares of the company had decreased by 99 percent of the peak worth. John Law was driven from the country.

Why did the French people and its monarchy fall for such a scheme? Law was a successful marketer. He paraded American Indians draped in gold and silver through the streets. Engravings of the "Louisiana mountains" bursting with gold, silver, and precious stones were distributed. Through wishful thinking and simple greed, people fell for the story.

Do not be misled in thinking that because Tulipmania and the Mississippi scheme occurred so long ago that such "busts" do not repeat themselves regularly. After the "crash of 1929" the shares of General Motors and General Electric declined 94 and 96 percent respectively. In a stock market fall during 1971–72 the shares of Polaroid and other well known companies fell over 90 percent. Similar horror stories were told during the 1980–82 recession/depression. Popular delusions are still with us and unlikely to go away.

Managerial Implications

A knowledge of the principles of group behavior is important to marketing managers for several reasons. One major area of application concerns the motivation and control of employees within the firm. Understanding how roles, norms, and reference groups influence people can influence decisions concerning compensation schemes, the handling of employee problems, and the development of corporate operating procedures. For example, many high technology companies like to foster a very creative entrepreneurial atmosphere. Thus, the companies provide many employees with stock option plans and have very relaxed norms concerning working hours and appropriate dress.

Such companies deliberately attempt to develop corporate norms that will appeal to the "looser" work habits of creative computer people.

A number of companies have built their marketing efforts directly around the use of group conformity pressures. In particular, Tupperware is sold via parties in the homes of their sales force. Groups of friends and acquaintances are invited to the home where games are played and the products are displayed. Conformity pressures to buy can become quite intense. Value-expressive influence occurs because the people at the party know each other and for the most part want to be a part of the group. Informational influence is also present because the salesperson will have a "canned" talk on the quality of the products offered. Finally, a norm to buy can develop after a couple of orders are taken. A person who fails to buy can feel that she simply came to the party for a good time and not to "help out" the party's sponsor.

Knowledge of diffusion processes is also important to managers, particularly those involved in marketing new products. Product managers need to identify just what type of innovation their new product is—continuous, dynamic continuous, or discontinuous. They need to investigate the extent to which it has a relative advantage over competitors and is compatible with the values and lifestyle of their target market. Furthermore, the manager needs to assess the product's complexity, trialability, and observability. Through such analysis the marketing manager can get a feel for the likely growth curve of the product. Will the product be a slow starter that must be nurtured for a substantial length of time, or will a strong marketing effort allow it to start fast?

New products that are of a continuous nature and that are breaking into an existing market have the potential to be fast starters. Figure 12–5 shows the sales growth of COMPAQ Computer Corporation. The COMPAQ computer was a continuous innovation—the first competitor to be compatible with the IBM Personal Computer and also be portable. With a market already established and a product that possessed all of the attributes necessary for success (i.e., observability, trialability, and so forth), it became in its first year the most successful company in the history of American business.

In order to achieve rapid early growth, a company must back a new product with a strong marketing effort. Procter and Gamble is well known and feared for entering established markets with new products that have some new advantage. Their products are continuous innovations, but they do have a clear relative advantage over their competitors. For example, a P&G subsidiary, Duncan Hines, brought to market a new cookie that was chewy rather than crunchy. Tasting very much like cookies right from the oven, the new product rapidly gained market share in what had previously been a "dull" market. In mid-1984 P&G introduced a new product, Always. Competing in the nearly one-billion-dollar feminine hygiene market, P&G advertised the product as having the advantage that it "breathed" and therefore helped women feel drier. In order to achieve a rapid growth curve, P&G was expected to spend $100 million in advertising in its first year on sale.[43]

Figure 12–5   The product in this ad represents a continuous innovation with a fast growth curve. *(Courtesy of COMPAQ Computer Corporation.)*

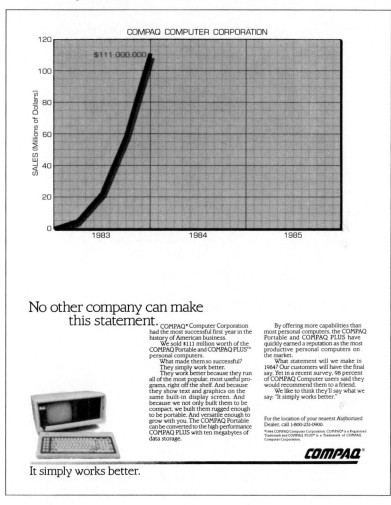

In addition to analyzing the characteristics of the product in order to identify how quickly it can penetrate the market, the manager should also analyze the characteristics of its target market. In particular, those who will buy the product early in its life cycle, the innovators, should be scrutinized carefully. Such individuals should be targeted specifically in the introductory phase of the product, because they will become the opinion leaders for the product in the future.

Another diffusion phenomenon of great importance to managers is that of rumors. As noted earlier, rumors tend to strike industry leaders and once started are difficult to eradicate. Avoiding and fighting rumors requires a total company effort. It starts by insuring that products are made to the highest standards so that rumors are not given any foundation on which to start. For example, the cancer scare surrounding Xerox's copier toner resulted from early tests showing that a material supplied by an outside company contained traces of a possibly carcinogenic compound. Although the problem was quickly corrected, the resulting rumor died slowly.[44]

SUMMARY

A group is a set of individuals who interact with one another over some period of time and who share some common need or goal. Groups are important to study because they are more than simply the sum of their parts. By virtue of being in a group, consumers will act differently than if they were alone. A variety of different types of groups that may have an impact on consumption exist. They include reference groups, aspiration groups, dissociative groups, formal and informal groups, membership groups, and primary groups. Such groups influence the behavior of consumers directly through informational influence, normative influence, and value-expressive influence. In addition, groups develop roles that consumers will fit and thereby control their buying behavior. Finally, groups exert conformity pressures through various means in order to change the behavior of consumers to fit the groups' norms.

Groups can influence consumer decision making and performance on tasks as well. *Group shifts* is a term that describes the tendency of groups of individuals to reach decisions that systematically differ from those reached by individuals. Depending upon the circumstances, the group decision can be more conservative or more risky than the individual decisions. Social facilitation refers to the fact that when a person performs a task in front of other people, the person will become more highly aroused. The increased arousal can improve performance when the task is easy, but it can harm performance when the task is complex. Social traps and fences refer to the idea that when a large number of individuals all do something that would help each individually, the results can be negative for all. The social trap occurs when the individuals act for their short-term benefit and consequently hurt the group in the long term. The social fence occurs when the individuals avoid doing something that would be negative in the short term but that would benefit the group in the long term.

Diffusion processes illustrate cases when ideas, products, or emotions spread through a large number of people. Consumer behaviorists are particularly interested in the factors that influence how innovations are adopted by consumers. Factors that influence the rate of adoption include the type of innovation, the characteristics of the target market and the extent of the marketing effort. Rumors and crowd behavior are two additional types of diffusion phenomena. Rumors can be major threats to companies and have even resulted in the demise of products. Crowd behavior in which consumers act quite irrationally occur periodically. In such instances panics can occur, leading consumers to stampede into buying binges or even to become violent.

An understanding of group processes can influence the decisions of managers. Some companies, such as Tupperware, base their marketing efforts in large part around the effective use of group-conformity pressures. When marketing new products, companies find that the study of the diffusion of innovations can be quite important in order to determine the degree and type of marketing effort to place behind the products. Having an understanding of how and why rumors spread can save a company thousands of hours of time in fighting the rumor and possibly avert the unnecessary loss of sales. All in all, the study of groups is an important and neglected area of consumer behavior.

Key Terms

Group
Reference group
Formal group
Informal group
Primary group
Aspiration group
Dissociative group
Norms
Informational influence
Normative influence
Value-expressive influence
Roles
Role-related product cluster
Conformity
Compliance
Private acceptance
Social comparison

Reflected appraisal
Comparative appraisal
Group shift
Social facilitation
Social traps
Social fences
Diffusion processes
Continuous innovations
Dynamic continuous innovations
Discontinuous innovations
Fads
Rumors
Pipe dream rumors
Bogies
Urban legends
Membership group
Categories of innovators

Review Questions

1. Define the concept of the group and identify the various types of groups.
2. Why is it that "groups are more than the sum of their parts"? Cite a specific example of how the buying patterns or actions of people differ when they engage in the activity as part of a group rather than as an individual.
3. Indicate how groups influence people through normative, value-expressive, and informational influence.

4. Define the concept of role. What are some examples of "role-related product clusters"?
5. Identify the various characteristics of the product and the properties of the person that can lead to conformity to group pressures.
6. How can social comparison processes influence consumers?
7. What is a group shift? What is a likely explanation for why group shifts occur? What types of consumer decisions might be influenced by group shifts?
8. What is it called when the mere presence of others influences the action of a person? What is most likely the process responsible for this phenomenon?
9. How do social traps and social fences differ? Give an example of a social trap and a social fence.
10. Why is it that groups often give very poor tips in restaurants?
11. What is meant by the term *diffusion*. In a consumer behavior context what is it that is diffused?
12. What are the various types of product innovations that have been identified?
13. What are the factors that can influence new product success by affecting the rate of diffusion?
14. What is meant by the term *diffusion pattern?* What are the factors that influence the type of diffusion pattern displayed by a product?
15. Identify the five categories of adopters and the relative size of each category.
16. What are the various approaches to dealing with corporate rumors? Identify four different types of rumors.

17. What are two reasons why consumers may act differently when they form into crowds? Cite two examples of extreme behaviors that have occurred when consumers have formed into crowds.

Discussion Questions

1. List the various reference groups that have an impact on you and categorize them into aspiration, dissociative, primary, and informal groups. Try to rank them as to their importance in influencing your consumption behavior. On what types of products, if any, do these groups influence your consumption?

2. Groups develop norms in order to help them function more smoothly. Consider the classroom situation at your university or college. What are the norms that guide the behavior of instructors as well as students in the classroom?

3. Groups can affect consumption through both value-expressive and informational influence. What are some examples of value-expressive and informational influence that could affect fraternity or sorority members in their purchase of an automobile and of a stereo?

4. What products would be considered as part of a role-related product cluster for a college student and for a young mother and father with a new baby?

5. Consider the various groups of which you are a member. In which of these groups are conformity pressures the greatest? Why is this the case?

6. Suppose that you are a member of a buying center for a large, highly conservative corporation. Most major purchase decisions are reached through a consensus process among five members of the group. In the current instance your group must decide whether to purchase a complex and expensive computer system from an established firm that charges high prices or from a smaller, but competently run firm that charges lower prices. What would the group polarization phenomenon say about the likely decision?

7. Suppose that your company installs computer systems and helps to train the users. Your company policy is to have an expert train the company's computer users by randomly selecting one of its employees and instructing that person while others stand around and watch. What would the concept of social facilitation say about the effectiveness of such a strategy?

8. In early 1986 the price of oil on the world market began to fall dramatically. Apparently each of the members of OPEC began to increase substantially their oil production levels. How does this series of events illustrate the operation of a social trap for the oil exporting countries?

9. Consider the following three products—compact disk record players, pump toothpaste dispensers, and the computer. Classify each of these as to their type of innovation. What type of diffusion pattern would you describe each as having? Please justify your answers.

10. Identify a recent rumor that involves corporations or their products. What should the company be doing to squash the rumor?

11. Consider the Mississippi scheme and Tulip-mania. How likely is it that these kinds of consumer mass hysteria could occur today? Can you cite any examples of similar instances, though probably tamed-down versions, that have occurred in the past ten years?

References

1. Michael S. Olmstead, *The Small Group*, New York, N.Y.: Holt, Rinehart and Winston, 1962.
2. H. H. Hyman, "The Psychology of Status," *Archives of Psychology*, 38, No. 269, 1942.
3. C. H. Cooley, *Social Organization*, New York, N.Y.: Schocken Books, Inc., 1962.
4. Donald H. Granbois, "Improving the Study of Consumer In-Store Behavior," *Journal of Marketing*, 32, October 1968, 28–32.
5. Marvin E. Shaw, *Group Dynamics*, New York, N.Y.: McGraw-Hill Book Company, 1971.
6. James N. Porter, "Consumption Patterns of Professors and Businessmen," *Sociological Inquiry*, 37, Winter 1967, 255–265.
7. Shaw, *Group Dynamics*.
8. M. Haire, "Projective Techniques in Marketing Research," *Journal of Marketing*, 14, April 1950, 649–656.
9. F. E. Webster and F. von Pechman, "A Replication of the Shopping List Study," *Journal of Marketing*, 34, April 1970, 61–63.
10. Charles A. Kiesler and Sara B. Kiesler, *Conformity*,

Reading, Mass.: Addison-Wesley Publishing Co., Inc., 1969, 7.

11. Solomon E. Asch, *Social Psychology*, Englewood Cliffs, N.J.: Prentice-Hall, Inc., 1952.

12. M. Venkatatesan, "Experimental Study of Consumer Behavior Conformity and Independence," *Journal of Marketing Research, 3*, November 1966, 384–387.

13. Kurt Lewin, "Group Decision and Social Change," in *Readings in Social Psychology*, Theodore M. Newcomb and Eugene Hartley (eds.), New York, N.Y.: Henry Holt, 1947, 41–47.

14. V. Parker Lessig and C. Whan Park, "Promotional Perspectives of Reference Group Influence, Advertising Implications," *Journal of Advertising, 7*, Spring 1978, 41–47.

15. Leon Festinger, "A Theory of Social Comparison Processes," *Human Relations, 7*, May 1954, 117–140.

16. Edward Jones and Harold Gerard, *Social Psychology*, New York, N.Y.: John Wiley & Sons, Inc., 1967.

17. Festinger, "A Theory of Social Comparison Processes."

18. George P. Moschis, "Social Comparison and Information Group Influence," *Journal of Marketing Research, 13*, August 1976, 237–244.

19. Moschis, "Social Comparison."

20. R. E. Knox and R. K. Safford, "Group Caution at the Race Track," *Journal of Experimental Social Psychology, 12*, May 1976, 317–324.

21. Helmet Lamm and David G. Myers, "Group-Induced Polarization of Attitudes and Behavior," in *Advances in Experimental Social Psychology, 11*, Leonard Berkowitz (ed.), New York, N.Y.: Academic Press, Inc., 1978, 145–195.

22. Lamm and Myers, "Group-Induced Polarization."

23. Peter Reingen, "The 'Risky Shift in Ad Hoc and Natural Consumer Groups: A Test of the Polarization Hypothesis and a Majority Rule Explanation," in W. D. Perreault (ed.), *Advances in Consumer Research, IV*, Ann Arbor, Mich.: Association for Consumer Research, 1977, 87–92.

24. Maureen Coughlin and P. J. O'Connor, "Risk Shifting in Joint Consumer Decision Making," *Advances in Consumer Research, XI*, Thomas Kinnear (ed.), Ann Arbor, Mich.: Association for Consumer Research, 1984, 165–169.

25. R. B. Zajonc and S. M. Sales, "Social Facilitation of Dominant and Subordinate Responses," *Journal of Experimental Social Psychology, 2*, April 1966, 160–168.

26. Charles Bond and Linda Titus, "Social Facilitation: A Meta-Analysis of 241 Studies," *Psychological Bulletin, 94*, September 1983, 265–292.

27. John Platt, "Social Traps," *American Psychologist, 28*, August 1973, 641–651.

28. Platt, "Social Traps."

29. Everett M. Rogers, *Diffusion of Innovations*, 3d ed. New York, N.Y.: The Free Press, 1983.

30. E. M. Rogers and F. F. Shoemaker, *Communication of Innovations: A Cross-Cultural Approach*, New York, N.Y.: Holt, Rinehart and Winston, 1971.

31. James Coleman, Elihu Katz, and Herbert Menzel, *Medical Innovation: A Diffusion Study*, Indianapolis, Ind.: Bobbs-Merrill, 1966.

32. Frank M. Bass, "A New Product Growth Model of Consumer Durables," *Management Science, 15*, January 1969, 217.

33. Excellent articles about rumors and their impact on business may be found in Robert Levy, "Tilting at the Rumor Mill," *Dun's Review*, July 1981, 52–54 and James Esposito and Ralph Rosnow, "Corporate Rumors: How They Start and How to Stop Them," *Management Review*, April 1983, 44–49.

34. Robert Levy, "Tilting at the Rumor Mill."

35. "Proctor and Gamble Rumor Blitz Looks Like a Bomb," *Advertising Age*, August 9, 1982, 1, 68.

36. James Esposito and Ralph Rosnow, "Corporate Rumors: How They Start and How to Stop Them".

37. G. W. Allport and L. Postman, *The Psychology of Rumor*, New York, N.Y.: Holt, Rinehart and Winston, 1947.

38. Levy, "Tilting at the Rumor Mill".

39. Ibid.

40. Ibid.

41. Alice Tybout, Bobby Calder, and Brian Sternthal, "Using Information Processing Theory to Design Marketing Strategies," *Journal of Marketing Research, 18*, Feb. 1981, 73–79.

42. These examples of popular decisions and many others can be found in the book Charles MacKay, *Extraordinary Popular Delusions and the Madness of Crowds*, New York, N.Y.: Harmony Books, 1980.

43. Janet Neiman, "Major Always Effort Marks P&G's Return," *Advertising Age*, May 28, 1974, 3, 63.

44. Levy, "Tilting at the Rumor Mill."

13

The Family and Households

Grazing for Dinner—A New Family Eating Style

A variety of factors are changing the consumption habits of the American family. The dramatic increase in the number of two-career families, the increase in the number of after-school activities of children, and the rise in the number of frozen foods in single-serving containers have combined to create a new eating trend—grazing.

Grazing was defined by one executive of Uncle Ben's (the rice producer) as "each individual in the household going through the kitchen at mealtime and grazing through the refrigerator and the cabinets, pulling together various foods to make a meal."(a) The executive noted that the grazers will use whatever is on hand to form spontaneous combinations of food.

The term *grazing* apparently was coined to describe people's habits when salad bars were first introduced. The sight of people lining up and carefully picking over assorted leaves, fruits, nuts, and stalks reminded some of sheep grazing for food in a pasture. The term has stuck and now refers to the habit of people to avoid sitting down for a full meal that required several hours of preparation time. Such meals simply do not fit the lifestyle of many families in the 1980s.

Grazing is also affecting the restaurant business. Childless, two-income couples often eat out for dinner. It is common for these "yuppies" (young, urban professionals) to order two or three different appetizers, a bottle of wine, and a couple of desserts and then share everything. In response, restaurants are adding more appetizers.

Doubtless the invasion of microwave ovens into 30 percent of American kitchens has increased the grazing trend. Even established companies are getting into providing forage for grazers. In 1984 Campbell's Soup Company announced plans to test-market soups packaged in plastic containers, rather

398

than metal cans. The soup will be "ready-to-eat," so that it can be popped directly into a microwave oven, heated and eaten. A metal can is hard to open, cannot be microwaved, and simply fails to fit the time-constrained life of the grazer. Sound economic reasons also exist for Campbell's to switch cans. The plastic containers are expected to be cheaper to produce.(b)

Grazing represents one important outgrowth of changes in the nature of the family. Trends toward couples having two incomes, having fewer or no children, having meals on the run—and divorcing more often—all are factors that make grazing a popular affair. Indeed, one survey found that over one-third of the families in the U.S. eat less than six meals a week together. Families are less frequently taking the time to sit down and eat together.

Based on (a) Trish Hall, "A Sheepish Trend: U.S. Eating Patterns Become Animalistic," *The Wall Street Journal,* April, 6, 1984, 1, 20; and (b) "Canning Campbell's Can," *Newsweek,* April 9, 1984, 84.

INTRODUCTION

For most people the family is their most important primary group. Through family interactions an individual develops many of his or her values, attitudes, and opinions. Thus, the family not only shapes an individual's personality and general view of others but also influences his or her values and attitudes about religion, achievement, leisure, and consumption. In addition, the family is an important consumption unit in and of itself. Most high-involvement purchase decisions involve input from more than one person. To some extent the entire family gets involved in such decisions as which car to buy, where to go on vacation, and what kind of house or apartment to have. Family members may even express preferences in low-involvement decisions, such as the types of food to serve or the kind of toilet tissue to buy. Some have argued that the family should be the primary focus of study in consumer behavior.[1]

The term *family* is actually a subset of a more general classification—the **household.** Households are composed of all those people who occupy a living unit. Examples of households include:

Roommates living in an apartment.
An unmarried couple living together.
A husband and wife with children.
Husband, wife, children, and grandparents living under one roof.
Two couples sharing the same house in order to save money.

The key similarly among all of the examples is that the group must live in the same residence. Based upon the above definition, a husband, wife, and children who live together are a household as well as a family.

A number of different types of families exist. The **nuclear** family consists of a husband, a wife, and their offspring. The **extended** family consists of the nuclear family plus other relatives, such as the parents of the husband or wife. Because of the high divorce rate in the United States, a growing number of single-parent families constitute households.

In many societies a husband and wife are expected to reside with one or the other of their parents. In the United States and Canada, children from middle-class families tend to strike off on their own to form families away from their parents. Such a trend has been called the detached nuclear family structure. As noted by some researchers, the detached nuclear family is associated with the following characteristics:

Free choice of mates.
Higher levels of divorce.
Increased residential mobility.
Entry of large numbers of women into the labor force.
Lower responsibility of children to care for their parents in their old age.[2]

Over the past two decades major changes have occurred in the United States and Canada in the nature of households and families. New living arrangements have begun to be established which profoundly affect the number and size of households and families. Many of these changes are discussed in the next section on the demographics of households.

THE DEMOGRAPHICS OF HOUSEHOLDS

Trends in such demographic characteristics as the number of marriages, the divorce rate, and the birth rate all represent changes in household structure. A household consists of a group of people living under one roof. Thus, a household could be a traditional family of husband, wife, and kids. However, it can also consist of a single individual, roommates sharing an apartment, or couples cohabiting.

Table 13–1 provides a breakdown of the various types of households and how they have changed between 1970 and 1985. Overall, household formation has been increasing, particularly "nontraditional" households. Between 1970 and 1985 households headed by married couples increased by only 12.6 percent. In contrast, households headed by single men and single women increased by 81.4 and 84.1 percent respectively. The greatest gains, though, occurred in the numbers of nonfamily households—101.6 percent between 1970 and 1985. People living alone and unmarried couples living together increased dramatically. Indeed, individuals living with a nonrelative increased by over 218 percent. Another notable feature in Table 13–1 is the decrease in the number of married couples with children at home. Because of the aging of the baby boom generation, married couples with children at home decreased by over 5 percent between 1970 and 1985.

The growth in the number of households occurred at the expense of the size of the average household. Between 1970 and 1982 the average household size fell from 3.14 to 2.72 persons, and average family size fell from 3.58 to

Table 13–1   Household Change: 1970–1985 (in thousands)

	1970		1985		Change 1970–1985
	Number	**Percent**	**Number**	**Percent**	**Percent**
Total households	63,401	100.0%	86,789	100.0%	36.9%
Family households	51,456	81.2	62,706	72.2	21.9
Married couples	44,728	70.5	50,350	58.0	12.6
a. With own children					
<18 at home	25,532	40.3	24,210	27.9	−5.2
b. Without own children					
<18 at home	19,196	30.3	26,140	30.1	36.2
Female-headed, no spouse	5,500	8.7	10,129	11.7	84.1
Male-headed, no spouse	1,228	1.9	2,228	2.6	81.4
Non-family households	11,945	18.8	24,083	27.7	101.6
a. Living alone	10,851	17.1	20,602	23.7	89.9
b. Living with nonrelative	1,094	1.7	3,481	4.0	218.2

SOURCE: Based on data found in: Arthur Norton, "Keeping Up With Households," *American Demographics, 5,* February 1983, 17–21; and, Cheryl Russell and Thomas Exter, "America at Mid-Decade," *American Demographics,* 8, January 1986, 22–29.

3.25 persons.[3] Reasons for the trend to smaller households lie in an increasing divorce rate, decisions of young people to leave home prior to marriage, and the tendency of older people to maintain their own homes after other family members are gone.

The number of nonfamily households has increased dramatically since the early 1970s. Most contain only one person, but cohabiting adults are becoming more common. Households maintained by unmarried couples are sometimes called **POSSLQs,** or "partners of the opposite sex sharing living quarters." From 1970 to 1982 the number of POSSLQs quadrupled to nearly 1.9 million.[4]

A trend to later marriage is another factor linked to the decreasing size of households. In 1966 the average male was 22.8 years old and the female 20.5 years old at the time of first marriage. By the 1980s the ages had moved to 24.8 years for men and 22.3 years for women. The number of women aged 25 to 29 who have never been married has doubled since 1970. In fact, in 1985 58.5 percent of women aged 20 to 24 had never married—up from 50 percent in 1980.[5]

The trend to later marriage has a number of implications. First, it means that more people will remain single. Second, it means that fertility rates will decrease. Older couples simply have more trouble conceiving than younger couples. Later marriages also increase the chances for premarital pregnancies because women are "at risk" longer prior to marriage. Finally, by remaining single longer, young people have more time to "invest" in themselves. They have time to pursue educational and work goals.

Divorce is a growing fact of life for couples in the 1980s. In the late 1970s it was estimated that 35 percent of new marriages would end in divorce. That estimate has since been raised to 50 percent.[6] The average length of marriage prior to a divorce was six years in 1983. The result is a large increase in the number of single men and women caring for children under 18 years of age. Between 1970 and 1982 this number increased by over 100 percent.[7]

What is likely to occur to the size of households in the late 1980s and 1990s? Some analysts believe that households will in fact start to increase in size again. Factors that could increase household size exist. The baby-boom generation is beginning to have children, and birthrates are beginning to creep up. If the country continues its trend to become more conservative, we may see fewer divorces, more births, and children staying with parents longer. Finally, if the economic climate should become worse, household size could increase as families pull together to conserve resources.

The size and composition of households have important implications for marketers, particularly those involved in strategic planning. Large increases in the number of households place increased demands on the housing and appliance industries. The increased demand resulting from the rapid increase in the number of households in the 1970s could partially explain why the price of homes increased so much during that time period. Shrinking household size also results in different housing needs. Smaller houses can be built, and condominiums and townhouses become more popular due to their compact size. Such trends occurred in the 1970s and early 1980s. In particular, single-family homes decreased in size. However, the extra amenities, like fireplaces and central heating and cooling, were retained. Although the size of houses shrank, their quality did not.

Increases in the number of single people have implications for marketers of personal care products. Growth of companies like Fabergé and Gilette in the 1970s and early 1980s could in part be attributed to increased numbers of single people demanding personal grooming products. Single people simply use more hairspray, deodorant, perfume, and so forth because they are competing for members of the opposite sex. Therefore, a premium is placed on physical appearance. Highlight 13–1 discusses other reasons for the importance of singles as a market segment.

Similarly, an increasing divorce rate creates a demand for particular sets of products and services. When a person is divorced, he or she becomes single and personal care requirements may increase. In addition, after a divorce child-care services become more important, as do time-saving devices, such as microwave ovens.

Strategic decisions need to include projections of household size. Decisions on whether to build new production facilities, on what new products to develop, and on potential acquisition candidates to consider may be influ-

HIGHLIGHT 13–1

Singles: A Highly Valued Market Segment

During the 1970s, the number of single people exploded. By 1980 59 million people were single in the United States, and the number was growing four times faster than the general population.

According to *Sales and Marketing Management*, the singles market consists of unmarried people from eighteen to thirty-four years of age. Their interests form a lifestyle that includes greater-than-average participation in activities like motorcycling, joining health clubs, sailing, and particularly downhill skiing. They also are heavy magazine readers and light television viewers. SRI International, a research firm, calls them the "I-am-me" group. This group describes themselves as preferring to spend rather than save, as unconventional, and as experimental.

The key question is, What will happen to the singles of the 1970s in the mid and late 1980s? It would not be surprising to find the swingers becoming more sedate, choosing different activities, such as tennis and golf, and revealing a more conservative lifestyle.

Based in part on the article "Singles: A Go-Go-Go Market," *Sales and Marketing Management*, October 25, 1982, 41.

enced by this demographic variable. For example, if household size increases between 1987 and 1995, the demand for larger cars and houses will probably increase. People like to have a car large enough to accommodate all of the household members. Indeed, the popularity of Japanese cars in the 1970s and early 1980s may have been due in part to decreasing household size, in addition to the frequently mentioned reasons of the cars' better gas mileage, lower prices, and higher quality. Such considerations should be factored into the immediate and long-term plans of automakers. In particular, decisions concerning the mix of large and small cars that will be built should be based in part on household size projections.

THE FAMILY LIFE CYCLE

The **family life cycle** refers to the idea that families may move through a series of stages in a developmental fashion. Thus, a family may begin as a married couple and moves through phases in which young children are born, the children grow older and eventually move out, and finally the couple grows old. Some authors have suggested that rather than calling the phenomenon the "family life cycle" it should be called "family careers."[8] In one instance researchers suggested that that the career stages should be labeled as follows: sexual experience, marital, parental, and adult-parent.[9] The family life cycle may also be criticized because in many instances individuals may have more than one type of cycle. Some people are never married and move through a different set of stages. Divorce can cause people to move through the cycle a second time or result in the individual moving through the same type of cycle as a single person. Most consumer behaviorists, however, have retained the term "family life cycle" as best representing the idea that people go through identifiable stages in their lives and that a cycle recurs as grown children later marry and procreate.

As suggested above, a number of factors has changed the family life cycle over the past several decades. The declining number of children born within each family, the high divorce rate, the rising number of couples who never have children, and the changing roles of husbands and wives all influence the exact nature of the family life cycle. Thus, when the family life cycle is discussed, a number of groups of people are omitted, such as cohabiting couples, couples who are separated but not divorced, and women or men who have never been married and are raising children.

A Modernized Family Life Cycle

Table 13–2 presents an updated view of the family life cycle.[10] Composed of five distinct stages, the model attempts to include a number of categories not previously found, such as divorceés and middle-aged individuals without children. The stages are described briefly in the following discussion.

1. *Young Single.* The young single has left high school and is either in college or beginning to work. With the number of teenage marriages declining and the average marital age increasing, the number of young singles has been increasing. Such individuals have relatively high discretionary incomes and tend to spend substantial amounts on personal care items, transportation, and certain luxury goods, such as stereos. They make up about 10 percent of the population.
2. *Young Married Without Children.* Making up about 3 percent of the pop-

Table 13–2 A Modernized View of the Family Life Cycle

Stage	Percentage of U.S. Population
1. Young single	8.2%
2. Young married without children	2.9
3. Other young	
Married with children	17.1
Divorced with kids	1.9
Divorced—no kids	0.1
4. Middle-aged—35 to 65	
With children	33.0
No dependent children	5.5
No children	4.7
Divorced—no kids	0.3
Divorced—with kids	1.9
5. Older 65+	
Married—spouse present	5.2
Unmarried—no spouse present	2.0
All other	17.2

SOURCE: Adapted from Patrick Murphy and William Staples, "A Modernized Family Life Cycle," *Journal of Consumer Research, 5,* June 1979, 16.

ulation, this group is in a life phase that some call the "honeymoon" or "establishment" period. Traditionally, the period until children arrive has lasted about two years; however, the length of the honeymoon has been increasing because of contraceptives and women feeling a need to establish their careers prior to having children. Young marrieds can establish financial security for themselves because of the possibility of having two paychecks. One often finds them buying homes and traveling prior to the arrival of children.

3. *Other Young.* This category accounts for the remainder of young adults under thirty-five years of age. The three subgroups composing the category are married with children, divorced with no children, and divorced with children. The largest is composed of *couples with children.* Accounting for about 17.1 percent of the total U.S. population, this group is large. Because the wife sometimes drops out of the work force when children are born, the financial affairs of this group are tight. The divorce rate among young marrieds is high. Indeed, over 60 percent of the divorces that occurred in 1976 involved women under thirty years of age.[11] In total about 2 percent of the population is composed of *divorced young adults*, the vast majority of whom have had children.

4. *Middle-Aged.* The middle-aged group accounts for about 46 percent of the population and like the young adults is composed of a number of subsegments. By far the largest is those *families with dependent children* (33 percent). The lifestyle of the family in this group tends to center around the children and their schooling. Discretionary income is higher than for those with younger children because the careers of both spouses have moved forward. Furthermore, it is more likely that if the wife did not work when the children were younger, she has gone back into the labor force. The next largest group consists of a family whose children are no longer dependent (5.5 percent). Those who have married and do not have children represent 4.7 percent of the population. These groups have previously been described as in the "empty-nest stage." Those middle-aged couples who have been divorced account for 2.2 percent of the population. The group that is expanding the fastest in this category is middle-aged couples without children. Highly educated women who live in urban areas are the most likely not to have children.[12] Those couples without children have extremely high discretionary incomes.

5. *Older stage.* About 7.2 percent of Americans are age sixty-five or older, and this group has been growing rapidly. Among this group about 72 percent of the people are married. Their characteristics and needs match those of the elderly consumer discussed in Chapter 14.

The consumption patterns of families in the various family life cycle stages can be quite divergent. Thus, as the number of families present in each of the stages changes (usually as a result of demographic trends), marketing opportunities may appear. Table 13–3 summarizes a number of differences

Table 13–3   Consumption Patterns of Families in Life Cycle Stages

Stage	Consumption Patterns
1. Young single	Outdoor sporting goods, sports cars, fashion clothing, entertainment and recreation services
2. Young married with no children	Recreation and relaxation, insurance, home furnishings, travel, home appliances, high purchase rate of durables
3. Young married with children	Baby food, clothing, and furniture; starter housing, insurance, washers-dryers, medical services/supplies for children, toys for children
4. Middle-aged With children at home	Children's lessons (piano, dance, etc.) large food purchases (respond to bulk buying deals), dental care, higher-priced furniture, autos, and housing; fast-food restaurants
With no children at home	Luxury products, travel, restaurants, condominiums; recreation, make gifts and contributions, high discretionary incomes, solid financial position.
5. Older (married or single)	Health care, home security, specialized housing, specialized food products, recreation geared to the retired, generally cash poor.
6. Divorced	Money-saving products, frozen foods, rental housing, child care, time-saving appliances and foods; cash poor.

in the consumption characteristics of families in the various life cycle stages. As can be seen in the table, the presence or absence of children to a large extent dictates the families' activities. Estimates in 1983 were that the total cost of raising a child can be over $200,000 (in 1980 dollars).[13] Thus, much of a family's disposable income is spent on fulfilling the children's needs. Furthermore, children require investments in time as well as money. Leisure time also tends to revolve around the children's activities.

A number of studies have investigated the changing consumption patterns of specific products or services through the family life cycle. For example, the tendency to eat out in restaurants was found to vary quite dramatically.[14] The group most likely to eat out was single adults, followed by married couples without children. The group least likely to eat out was young marrieds with children under two years of age. As the children gradually got older, the family was progressively more likely to eat out. Singles were more than twice as likely to eat out in the evening as families with small children at home. Why do young children inhibit eating out? The night when this paragraph was written the author and his wife went out to eat with their one- and three-year olds. The energy required to get the kids to the car, to harness them into their safety seats, to supervise the three year old and feed the one-year old, and to ensure that damage was not done to the restaurant or other customers was enough to deter us from a similar endeavor for several months into the future.

In another study researchers investigated telephone expenditures across various phases of the family life cycle.[15] The lowest expenditures on long-distance calls were made by young singles. In comparison, families with young teenagers made more than three times the number of long distance calls. It seems that teenagers like to reach out and touch others frequently.

The energy use of families in various stages of the family life cycle has also been investigated.[16] The results showed that the least energy was consumed by young singles, followed by middle-aged singles. The most energy was consumed by middle-aged couples with children and young marrieds with children. What the data seem to show is that as the number of people in the household increased, the family used more electricity, natural gas, and gasoline.

Family Life Cycle Versus Age

An interesting question concerns whether family life cycle stage or age better predicts consumption patterns. Overall, the evidence favors the family life cycle as the superior predictor. Until an individual reaches old age, such factors as the presence or absence of children and of a spouse will overwhelm the age variable as a predictor of consumption. For example, in one study it was found that the family life cycle was a better predictor of the following aspects of a family's consumption activities—income, indebtedness, home ownership, and purchase of new cars.[17] However, with old age, physical problems take on increasing importance, and consumption patterns begin to be geared toward dealing with these infirmities. It has also been found that age is an important variable in predicting the purchase of luxury products. The likely reason is that with increasing age, discretionary income rises—at least until retirement.[18]

An International Family Life Cycle?

The family life cycle has been investigated in other countries. One study analyzed the effect of family life stage on the amount and type of household expenditures among Norwegian households.[19] Table 13–4 shows the proportion of income spent by Norwegian families in the various life stages on a variety of goods. The patterns match relatively closely those found for American families. For example, bachelors and newly marrieds were found to spend the greatest percentage of their income on transportation. The patterns then changed so that for the remainder of their life cycle stages food became the major household expense. The rise in food expenditures matches American household experiences. However, the large proportion spent by Norwegian families on food is substantially higher than that by Americans. A second

Table 13–4 Economic Resource Situation and Composition of Consumption Expenditures by Households in Different Stages of the Life Cycle

Stage of Family Life Cycle	Criteria	Resource Situation	Composition of Consumption Expenditures	Gift-Giving
Bachelor	Young single (less than 40).	Low-income, one-person households; early stages of career.	Overspend on restaurants, cars, and recreation; spend little on food, housing, furniture, and appliances.	Fairly high amount allocated to gifts because of high discretionary income.
Newly married	Young couples without children (main income earner less than 40).	High income; two income earners.	Spend more than Bachelors on food, housing, furniture, and appliances, but less on restaurants.	Spend relatively less than Bachelors, in spite of higher income; need money to establish the household.
Full nest I	Young (main income earner less than 40) couples with children (less than 16).	Lower income than former group because more likely to have one income earner.	Overspend on food and housing while spending less on cars and restaurants.	Like former group.
Full nest II	Older (main income earner 40 or more) couples with children (less than 16).	Higher income than former group; members more likely to be further in career and have two incomes.	Overspend on food, furniture, and appliances (second generation), and recreation.	Like the former two groups.
Empty nest	Older (main income earner 40 or more) couples without dependent children (less than 16)	High income.	Overspend on recreation, beverages and tobacco, furniture, and appliances.	High degree of gift-giving.
Solitary survivor	Older (40 or more) single	Relatively low income; High proportions of retired and low-education persons.	Overspend on food, housing, and medical care. Spend little on cars, recreation, and restaurants.	High degree of gift-giving because most of own needs are met.

Source: Data from John Arndt, "Family Life Cycle as a Determinant of Size and Composition of Household Expenditures," *Advances in Consumer Research, VI,* William Wilkie (ed.), Ann Arbor, Mich.: Association for Consumer Research, 1979, 129.

difference between Norwegian and American households is the lower amount spent by Norwegians on medical costs.

A Challenge to the Family Life Cycle

A recent study, however, challenged the family life cycle as an important factor controlling family consumption patterns.[20] The authors investigated the clothing expenditures of families. In addition to collecting information on the stage of the family life cycle, they collected a variety of socioeconomic and demographic information. Their results revealed that a measure of income was the best predictor of clothing expenditures. Although stage of family life cycle did increase the predictive ability, its contribution was extremely small.

The effects of controlling for the socioeconomic variables can be found in Table 13–5. In the table the bachelor stage is used as the base to determine how much more or less is spent on clothing in the other stages. If one does not take out the effects of income and other variables, one finds that married parents with older children spend 260 percent of what bachelors spend on clothing. However, if the socioeconomic variables are accounted for in the analysis, one finds that young single parents spend 142 percent of what bachelors spend on clothing, by far the largest percentage of any life cycle stage. Thus, with the effects of such variables as household income controlled in the analysis, young single parents spend more of their available income on clothing than any other group.

The clothing study indicates that income and other variables such as education and occupation should be accounted for before assuming that the

Table 13–5   Family Clothing Expenditures and the Life Cycle

Life Cycle Stage	Clothing Expenditures as a Percentage of Young Bachelor Spending	
	Model without Socioeconomic Variables	**Model with Socioeconomic Variables**
Bachelor (base variable)	100	100
Newly married	165	87
Married with young children	214	98
Young single parent	161	142
Middle-aged with older children	260	102
Middle-aged without children	152	81
Married older	66	78
Single older	37	80

SOURCE: Data adapted from Janet Wagner and Sherman Hanna, "The Effectiveness of Family Life Cycle Variables in Consumer Expenditure Research," *Journal of Consumer Research, 10,* December 1983, 281–291.

family life cycle controls how consumers spend their money. However, the study investigated only one variable—clothing. Quite possibly for other products, such as housing, automobiles, or food, the family life cycle would be a more important predictor of consumption patterns.

FAMILY ROLE STRUCTURE

One key point about consumer behavior is that the buyers and users of a product may be different. For example, most men's underwear is bought by women. Similarly, wives and girlfriends purchase 70 percent of the fragrances and colognes used by men.[21] Crayola, maker of children's writing instruments, had advertised mostly on children's television on Saturday mornings. After examining who really bought their products and their media habits, Crayola shifted the advertising to women's magazines.[22] It was the mothers who were initiating and making the purchases, not the children.

The examples of cases in which buyers and users of products differ illustrate the point that within any small group individuals will take on different roles in order to help the group function more smoothly. Because of its permanency and importance to its members, a family will develop a highly organized set of roles. A number of different types of roles exist within most families. These are: instrumental and expressive, internal and external, and purchase-process roles.[23]

Instrumental and Expressive Roles

In most small groups two different sets of needs exist. One deals with the problem of achieving certain goals and completing tasks to reach these goals. The person who leads the group to achieve the instrumental goals is thought of as the leader of the group. Traditionally, the male has taken on the **instrumental role** in the family by providing financial leadership and by taking on the primary responsibilities for such things as driving the car, tending the household budget, and purchasing the family's major assets, such as a house.

The second type of goal involves a group's need to have someone help maintain the group and provide emotional support for its members. The individual taking on such expressive functions—that is, the **expressive role**— within the group is the social leader. In traditional families the female has tended to be the expressive leader. She has been responsible for the children and for making the home into a pleasant and comfortable place to live.

With the dramatic increase in the number of working women and with expectations changing about what men and women should do, the rigidity with which the above roles are held is breaking down in American families. In 1985 estimates were that 61 percent of married women in the United States with children under 18 were employed or seeking jobs.[24] Currently in a significant portion of cases the husband and wife work different shifts. In such cases, both the male and female must take on expressive and instrumental roles when on family or work duty. As one "split-shift" husband commented, "I may be closer to my kids because I have been Mom and Dad."[25] Finding

HIGHLIGHT 13–2

Buying and Saving Time in the Family

When a family consists of two working parents, major time problems exist. Who has the time to do the many household tasks, such as cleaning, cooking, paying bills, bathing children, and transporting children to doctors, dance lessons, and baseball practice? Traditionally, these tasks have fallen upon the wife as the keeper of the household. However, when the wife works, the ability to perform all of these tasks while being on the job for eight or more hours is nearly impossible.

Some researchers have suggested that a family adjusts to the employment of the wife by making increased use of "time-saving" devices, such as mail-order catalogs, appliances, and in-home shopping and cleaning services.

A study recently investigated how families with working wives handle the time crunch. The authors found that working wives do *not* substitute capital equipment for their efforts. Working wives did not use more products and services than nonworking wives to decrease their time commitments to the home. The working wives did not spend less time in volunteer activities than nonworking wives. The employed also did not substitute the efforts of other family members for their own work. The employed wives did not sleep less than nonworking wives.

How did the working wives handle the time crunch? The main means of handling the problem was that working wives engaged in fewer leisure activities than nonworking wives. Families with working wives also tended to purchase more meals away from home, to use disposable diapers more often, to engage in less housework, and to reduce the amount of time taken to care for family members.

Based on Sharon Nickols and Karen Fox, "Buying Time and Saving Time: Strategies for Managing Household Production," *Journal of Consumer Research, 10,* September 1983, 197–208.

the time to perform all of one's duties is difficult in two income families. Highlight 13–2 discusses how families buy and save time.

Internal and External Roles

A second distinction in family role structure deals with those functions internal and external to the family. **External roles** involve communications and involvement with people outside of the family. **Internal roles** consist of those duties inside the family. In traditional marriages these roles are also split along male-female lines. Even the division of labor in and around the house tends to have such an internal-external dimension. The woman is expected to prepare food and do the laundry and the housework. The husband works on the yard and the car and takes out the trash—all duties that take place outside of the house. Of course, these are the roles found in the traditional marriage; although, many couples are trying new divisions of labor. Also, in the growing number of single-parent families formed after divorce these roles will tend to be borne by one person or shared by the adult and children.

Purchase Roles

In the buying and using of products family members also take on a variety of roles. Eight of these **purchase roles** are listed below:

1. *Influencers:* Members of the family who attempt to affect the product choice by giving information and advice.

2. *Gatekeepers:* Family members who have the ability to control information available to a decision maker. Parents take on the role of **gatekeepers** when they control the times and types of television programs that children watch.

3. *Deciders:* The family members who have the power to make the decision of when and what to buy.

4. *Buyers:* The family members who actually make the purchase. Buyers and deciders may be different people. For example, a teenager may be given the responsibility of deciding what kind of car to buy and even when he or she can purchase it. However, the parent is actually the person who negotiates with the dealer and pays for it.

5. *Preparers:* These family members adapt the product so that it can be used by others. Food preparation, sewing, and garden work come under the heading of ''preparation'' activities.

6. *Users:* Users are those who consume or use the products and services purchased and/or prepared by others in the family.

7. *Maintainers:* Those who provide for the upkeep of the house, yard, auto, and so forth have the role of ''maintainer.''

8. *Disposers:* The disposer of a product or service determines when to discontinue its use and determines what to do with it. For example, the person who decides that an auto no longer meets the needs of a family would be classified as the disposer.[26]

Figure 13–1 shows a flow chart of the various roles that exist in the purchase of an automobile by an executive woman, who is married. The family is real, and the roles describe the behavior of the family members. The behavior patterns described are nontraditional, because the executive woman in this case takes on the roles of decision maker and purchaser. However, with more women in the work force, such a pattern is increasing. As shown in Figure 13–2, auto manufacturers are targeting such women in print ads.

FAMILY DECISION MAKING

During the course of everyday living, thousands of decisions are made by family members. Some of the decisions are highly important, such as selecting which car to buy, where to move, and where to go on vacation. Other decisions are more mundane, like what to have for dinner or what should be planted in the garden. One major question for consumer researchers has been determining which family members have the most influence on various household decisions.

An important early effort in identifying the relative influence of family members on household decisions was performed in Belgium.[27] The classic study identified four role specialization dimensions in the buying of products—wife dominant, husband dominant, autonomic, and syncratic. Some of the characteristics of these dimensions are:

Figure 13–1 Nontraditional car purchase by a woman who is an executive and a wife.

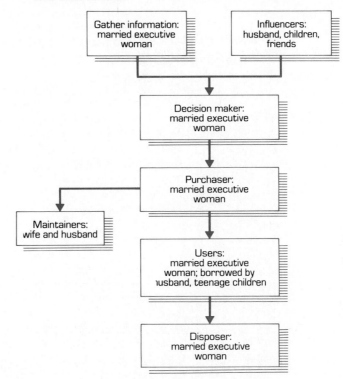

1. *Wife dominant*—decisions in which the wife plays a largely independent role in deciding what to buy.
2. *Husband dominant*—decisions in which the husband plays a largely independent role in deciding what to buy.
3. *Autonomic*—decisions of lesser importance which either the husband or wife may make independently of the other.
4. *Syncratic*—important decisions in which the husband and wife participate jointly.

Figure 13–3 depicts the four decision classifications and how some types of product purchases were found to relate to the decisions. For example, it was found that a major husband-dominated purchase was life insurance. **Syncratic decisions** tended to be made for vacations, children's schooling, housing, and living room furniture. Wife-dominated decisions included the buying of cleaning products, kitchenware, and food. **Autonomic decisions** were made for garden tools and alcoholic beverages.

As shown in Figure 13–3, the amount of role specialization results from the relative importance of the decision to the marriage partners. The two

Figure 13–2   Automakers are increasingly targeting women buyers.
(*Courtesy of Ford Motor Company.*)

Figure 13–3   **Marital decision-making role specialization. (Based on research by Harry Davis and Benny Rigaux, "Perception of Marital Roles in Decision Processes,"** *Journal of Consumer Research, 1,* June 1974, 51–62. *Note:* **For clarification purposes, the axes of the figure have been changed from those found in Davis and Rigaux.)**

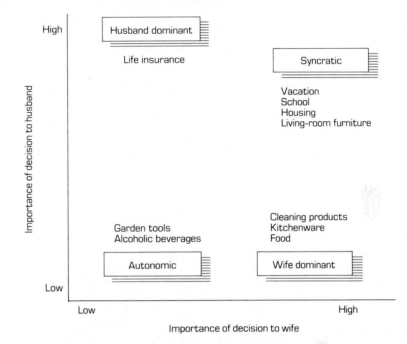

axes of the graph in the figure are, therefore, labeled "importance to the husband" and "importance to the wife" respectively. (Readers should note that the axes of the figure were changed from those found in the original Belgian study. They were relabeled for clarification purposes.) Thus, when the decision is important to both partners, it tends to be made syncratically. When it is important to only one of the partners, it is dominated by the partner who cares. When the decision is not particularly important to either partner, it is made autonomically.

The Belgian study was conducted in the early 1970s. Because of the changes that have occurred in society since that time and because it was conducted in Europe, the conclusions as to the types of decisions that are syncratic, autonomic, and so forth may not be applicable in the United States or Canada today. For example, the decision to purchase insurance is rapidly becoming much more of a shared responsibility. With the costs of housing climbing rapidly in the 1970s and 1980s in more and more cases two incomes are required to purchase a home. Therefore, insurance is required on both lives, and its purchase has become much more of a syncratic decision.

Family Decision Stages

Just as there are different purchase roles, there are also a number of different steps in a decision to buy a product or service. The amount of influence exerted by the husband, wife, and children will vary depending on the stage of the decision process. In the Belgian study three such stages were identified—problem recognition, search for information, and final decision.[28] These authors found that as the **family decision stage** moved closer to the final choice, the role specialization in general became more syncratic.

Another study investigated who had the most influence in the buying process of automobiles and furniture.[29] The buying process for automobiles was divided into six steps:

1. When to buy.
2. How much money to spend.
3. What make to buy.
4. What model to buy.
5. What color to buy.
6. Where to buy.

Similarly, the furniture decision had six steps:

1. What pieces to buy.
2. How much money to spend.
3. Where to buy.
4. When to buy.
5. What style to buy.
6. What color and fabric to choose.

For the automobile purchase most of the decision stages tended to be dominated by the husband. Only concerning what color to buy did the wife consistently share in the decision or dominate the decision. The results for the furniture purchase were quite different. Here the wife tended to dominate all phases of the decision except for the issue of how much money to spend. An interesting aspect of the study was that each spouse stated an impression of his or her own influence. In most cases close agreement existed in the perceptions of the spouses. The only exception was a tendency of wives to indicate less often that they dominated the furniture purchase.

Another study investigated the influence of marriage partners in home purchase decisions.[30] The decision elements investigated in the study were: residence selection, floor plan, style, price, location, and size. In all cases syncratic decisions predominated. Only on the issue of price did the husband dominant mode approach the joint decision mode. Although syncratic decision making did predominate, on a number of dimensions (floor plan, style, and size) substantially more wife-dominated decisions were made than husband-dominated decisions. Thus, when decisions were not made syncratically, (i.e., for floor plan, style, and size) the wife tended to dominate the decision. The study also investigated the amount of agreement between husbands and wives. The authors found that disagreements tended to occur because husbands were willing to admit dominance in a decision (whether by themselves or their wives), and the wives were less willing to admit that one partner dominated a decision.

The Role of Children in Family Decision Making

The studies just mentioned tended to ignore the role of children as influencers, decision makers, and users of products and services. Clearly, though, children do make a difference in family decisions in such areas as the types of foods to buy, vacations, and eating out. One study investigated the vacation decision process for couples and families.[31] The results revealed that families with children tended to have less response consensus and more husband-dominated decisions than did couples. Although children did not dominate the decision process, they had the potential to form alliances with either the husband or wife to produce a "majority" decision.

The influence of children on the purchase of breakfast cereals has been extensively investigated. Researchers have found that children make requests for breakfast cereals more frequently than for other product categories.[32] Other researchers have found that almost one-half of mothers interviewed at grocery check-out counters mentioned that their child had asked for a breakfast cereal. A relation between Saturday morning television viewing and cereal requests has been found such that the greater the amount of television viewing the greater the tendency to make requests for specific cereals.[33]

Figure 13–4 shows the flow of parent-child interaction in breakfast cereal selection, based upon the findings of a large-scale study in twenty supermarkets.[34] The results are quite interesting and show a number of surprising results. For example, parents tended to yield more often when the child demanded a cereal than when the child requested a particular cereal. However, when the parent invited a cereal selection, he or she tended to agree with the child's selection much more frequently, and about 90 percent of the time as compared to 71 percent when the child demanded the cereal.

The age of the child was also found to influence the yielding of mothers to requests for cereals.[35] The results of the supermarket study also showed that as the child gets older the parent tends to initiate the choice of cereal more often. Furthermore, the percentage of occasions when conflict occurs tends to be at a maximum when the children are between the ages of six and eight. Data were also analyzed to determine if sex of the child or the social class of the parent affected the trends. The results showed that sex had little effect. However, the social class of the family was related to the occasions of child unhappiness. Working-class families tended to have more frequent occasions when child unhappiness occurred.

The way in which children asked for a product was found to influence the parental response in another study.[36] The study involved 400 mothers with children between two and ten years old. Somewhat surprisingly the researchers found that mothers said yes more often when a child asked for a product because he or she saw it on television or because it also had a prize or premium attached to it. Least effective was a request based on the

Figure 13–4 **Flow of parent-child interaction in breakfast cereal selection. (Adapted by permission, from Charles P. Atkin, "Observation of Parent-Child Interaction in Supermarket Decision Making," *Journal of Marketing, 42*, October 1978, 43.)**

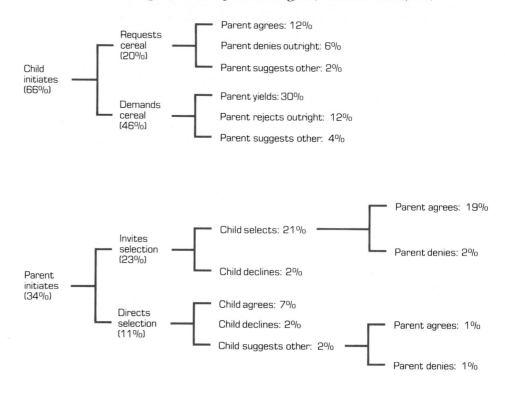

idea that other kids have it. Asking for the product because it was healthful also did not in general receive positive responses from the mothers. These results are shown in Table 13–6.

Power and Conflict Resolution in the Family

Like in all small groups, families face the problem of determining who gets what he or she wants (i.e., dealing with *power relations*) and of how to resolve conflicts. The concept of power refers to the ability of an individual in a social relationship to obtain his or her will, even when resisted by others.[37] Power is obtained from a variety of sources, which include:

1. *Economic resources*—The partner making the greatest economic contribution tends to have the most power.
2. *Cultural and subcultural definitions*—According to the prevailing culture one partner may have the most power. In many cultures for example, the male is expected to be dominant.

Table 13–6   Percentage of Positive Responses by Mothers to Children's Requests

Nature of Request from Child	Percentage Positive Response by Mother
Wanted a gift found in box	46.7%
Saw it on television	46.7
Asks for product	33.7
Puts product in cart	27.5
Uses health appeal	27.0
Wants boxtop	26.0
Says others use it	23.2

SOURCE: Data adapted from Pat Burr and Richard Burr, "Parental Responses to Child Marketing," *Journal of Advertising Research*, 17, December 1977, 17–20.

3. *The importance of the issue*—If something is highly important to an individual, that person becomes more committed and tenacious.
4. *Personal resources*—Factors such as personality, physical attractiveness, and competence on the issue influence the amount of power possessed.
5. *Interactional techniques*—The negotiation style, assertiveness, and skill that a person brings to an interaction will influence his or her degree of power.
6. *Degree of interpersonal dependence*—The person least committed to the other will tend to have a power advantage.
7. *Control over decision making*—The person who tends to make and implement decisions will tend to have the greater power.[38]

In addition to these seven **power sources,** a number of additional aspects of the concept should be noted. Power relations in a family are not static; they will change with the age of its members, their economic contributions, and so forth. Power is a multidimensional concept that includes a process, outcomes, sociocultural variables, and personal variables. Finally, power is also based on the perceptions of people as well as on objective reality. Give-and-take relationships exist in which low power in one sphere may be compensated for by greater power in another.

Closely related to the concept of power is that of conflict resolution in families. Power can be used both to cause and to avoid conflict. However, the use of power strategies will often occur when some type of disagreement occurs between family members. A recent study investigated a variety of influence strategies that spouses may use to resolve conflicts and achieve their own goals.[39] The author identified six types of influence strategies that a spouse could employ—expert, legitimate, bargaining, reward/referent, emotional, and impression management. (These are described in Table 13–7.) After interviewing ninety-eight couples, the researcher classified individuals into six groups based upon the amount and type of influence strategy used. Descriptions of the groups follow.

Table 13–7   Influence Strategy Approaches

Strategy	Example of Strategy
Expert	Relating the discussion to other similar decisions on which the influencer has shown expertise
Legitimate	Convincing other to accept influencer's judgment because men (women) know more about such things
Bargaining	Asking other to give in on this decision in return for influencer giving in on another decision
Reward/referent	Attempting to please other prior to decision in order to influence him or her on the decision
Emotional	Using tactics such as the "silent treatment"
Impression management	Misleading the person on other alternatives in order to convince him/her

SOURCE: Adapted from Rosann L. Spiro, "Persuasion in Family Decision Making," *Journal of Consumer Research, 9,* March 1983, 393–402.

Noninfluencers. Consisting of 22 percent of the respondents, this group was marked by a general lack of influence attempts. When influence was used, it was usually based upon expertise.

Light influencers. The largest subgroup (35.9 percent), light influencers focused on the use of expertise and impression management. Overall, the number of influence attempts by this group came in between those of "noninfluencers" and the other groups.

Subtle influencers. Making up about 19 percent of the sample, this group tended to use the reward/referent strategy and the expert strategy. They tried to "butter-up" their partner as a way of gaining power.

Emotional influencers. A small group (about 7 percent), these people focused on using reward/referent influence and on withdrawing affection and approval.

Combination influencers. Representing 10 percent of the sample, this group made liberal use of all of the influence strategies.

Heavy influencers. Another small group (about 7 percent), the heavy influencers tended to make frequent use of all of the strategies.

The researcher found that these influence strategies (particularly the "subtle approach) were used when a spouse was attempting to avoid conflict. The use of influence strategies by the wife was also greatest when she contributed a higher percentage to the family income.

CHILDHOOD CONSUMER SOCIALIZATION

As noted earlier in the chapter, one reason for the family's importance is its role as a socialization agent. Socialization may be defined as the process by which individuals acquire knowledge, skills, and dispositions that enable them to participate as members of society.[40] The general concept of socialization can be narrowed to that of **consumer socialization.** Consumer socialization refers to the "processes by which young people acquire skills, knowledge, and attitudes relevant to their functioning as consumers in the market-place."[41]

Understanding how individuals are socialized into consumers is important for several reasons. First, an understanding of the factors influencing consumer socialization can provide information to marketers that may be useful in designing marketing communications. Second, public policy decisions concerning the rules and regulations of the marketing of products to children should in part be based on an understanding of the consumer socialization process. For example, one key question concerns how advertising affects children. During President Carter's administration the Federal Trade Commission nearly promulgated regulations that would have severely limited the ability of companies to advertise to children. The regulations were based in part on research suggesting that advertising can influence children's product preferences.

A Model of Consumer Socialization

Figure 13–5 presents a simple model of consumer socialization.[42] It suggests that consumer socialization is based upon three components—background factors, socialization agents, and learning mechanisms.

Background factors are the environmental influencers that the text has been discussing thus far. They include such variables as the consumer's socioeconomic status, sex, age, social class, and religious background.

Socialization agents are those individuals directly involved with the consumer, who have influence because of their frequency of contact with the consumer, importance to the consumer, or control over rewards and punishments given to the consumer. Examples of socialization agents include parents, brothers and sisters, peers, teachers, the media, and media personalities, such as athletes, movie stars, and rock stars.

Figure 13–5   A model of consumer socialization.

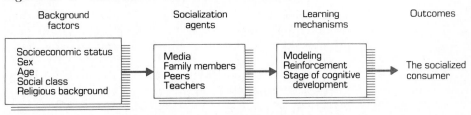

The impact of socialization agents and background factors on consumer socialization has been investigated. In an important early study, the factors of family, mass media, newspaper readership, school, peers, age, social class, and sex were analyzed.[43] The study found that the family was important in teaching the "rational" aspects of consumption. The amount of communication in the family about consumption was also related to how often the adolescents performed socially desirable acts, such as giving to charities.

The amount of television viewing was found to have a major impact on socialization in the study. Greater television viewing was associated with the learning of the "expressive" aspects of consumption. Thus, high television viewing seemed to encourage consumption for emotional reasons, rather than for more rational reasons. In contrast, adolescents who read newspapers were found to possess a number of consumer skills. However, the newspaper readership could have resulted from the presence of these skills, rather than causing them.

Peers were found to be an important socialization agent. They contributed particularly to the expressive element in which one buys for materialistic or social reasons (e.g., buying to keep up with the "Joneses"). For teenagers buying to impress or be like others was clearly important. However, interaction among peers also was related to an increased awareness of goods and services in the marketplace. The school, though, was found to have very little influence on the socialization process. For whatever reasons, formal consumer education in school was unrelated to measures of consumer socialization.

Learning mechanisms are those processes through which a person retains information from the environment. Ultimately, the socialization process is based upon what the child *learns.* In Chapter 6 learning was discussed in detail. The consumer socialization process is based upon two major types of learning—modeling and operant conditioning. Modeling involves the imitation of the acts of others. In this instance the consumer observes the actions of others and potentially the outcomes of the actions. The child could imitate the behavior of the model for several reasons. If the behavior leads to a positive outcome for the model, the child will be more likely to engage in the act. A child will also be more likely to engage in the act if the model is someone who is liked or important.

A second mode of learning involves the reinforcements that the child receives for his or her various consumption-related actions. Behaviors that have received praise or that have resulted in positive outcomes will tend to be repeated. Conversely, consumption actions that bring ridicule or a negative outcome are less likely to be repeated. The agents of socialization mentioned earlier are important mediators of the positive and negative reinforcers. A parent or a schoolmate through a compliment or a negative comment can have a strong impact on a child's view of a consumption behavior. For example, if a child contributes to a charity or buys a particular brand of product and a respected peer laughs at the action, the child may avoid that particular behavior in the future. The ridicule punished the child for the action, making it less likely to occur in the future.

Social scientists have argued that what is learned early in life has an important and lasting effect on people. In areas such as criminology and psychiatry theorists have noted that behaviors shown early in life tend to persist into adulthood. Some evidence exists that consumption behaviors learned early in life also persist. Studies have found that brand loyalty may be transmitted from parents to offspring and that favored brands may persist for periods of twelve years or longer.[44] Little research has been done in this important area. However, if early childhood consumption experiences and training are as important as such studies suggest, it behooves us to analyze carefully just what kinds of consumers we are training our children to be.

A recent review article summarized many of the findings on childhood socialization.[45] The author noted that parents play an important role in childhood socialization, especially in providing information on the rational aspects of consumption. However, the influence of parents is situation specific. Their impact varies across the stage of the decision process, across various types of products, and across various personal characteristics, such as age, socioeconomic class, and sex of child.

Although the influence of parents on childhood socialization is situation specific, adult couples have more to say about the initial question of whether to have children. Highlight 13–3 discusses the question from an economic perspective.

HIGHLIGHT 13–3

To Have Children or Not: An Economic Decision?

During the 1970s, the fertility rate plummeted to less than the replacement rate in the United States. Many reasons account for the decision by millions of American couples to have fewer or no children. The large increase in working women no doubt has played a role in the trend. The widespread acceptance of birth control devices doubtless has also contributed. However, the high cost of having children also could explain in part the reluctance of couples to start families. Viewed from this perspective, having a child is similar to the purchase of any large consumer durable.

Estimates vary, but the figure of $278,000 for boys and $295,000 for girls is a good estimate of the cost of raising a child and putting him or her through college (based upon 1982 dollars). Although the figure is astronomical, it makes sense when all of the costs of raising a child are included. You may ask why it costs more to raise a girl than a boy. Boys eat more than girls (particularly during the teenage years), but girls have greater entertainment, travel, clothing, and personal effects needs. In addition, our society requires that the wedding costs be born by the girl's family—not an inconsequential expense. Some feminists argue that a part of the greater cost of raising girls is that our society subsidizes the cost of leisure for boys through sports programs run by cities and schools that are unavailable to girls. As a consequence, girls are enrolled in expensive music, dance, and gymnastics lessons more frequently than boys.

Based on Carrie Tuhy, "What Price Children?" *Money*, March 1983, 77–84; and "Facing Up to the High Cost of Kids," *Changing Times*, April 1983, 28–32.

Managerial Implications

An understanding of the family can assist the marketer in a number of important tasks. Changes in the demographics of families and households can present new marketing opportunities. Marketers should track such key indicators as divorce rates, the number of children born, household size, and the average marital age. A related factor is the pattern of employment of household members. What percentage of husbands, wives, and children are working in some capacity? If a marketer can anticipate changes in such demographic trends, it may be possible to enter a new market prior to the competition and catch the most lucrative phases of the life cycle of that market. For example, the decrease in the size of families during the 1970s presented an opportunity to food companies. With many single individuals and couples in the market, demand grew for frozen and canned foods to come in smaller containers. Campbell's Soup Company recognized the trend and developed single-serving soups. Such actions helped the company maintain its preeminant market share of the soup industry.

The number of families in the various stages of the family life cycle should also be tracked carefully by marketers. Those families in a particular life cycle stage are market segments that can be targeted. As illustrated in Table 13–3, the consumption patterns of people in various stages of the family life cycle differ. As the numbers of families increase or decrease in the various stages, through changes in demographic patterns, demand for products will shift. In the late 1980s the baby-boom group will be moving into the "middle-aged" category of the family life cycle. During this phase, food purchases will increase. Because the earnings of families in this stage are high, more will be spent on furniture, housing, and such. Forward-thinking companies should anticipate such trends and begin to position themselves to take advantage of the likely changes in demand for certain food products and durable goods.

Changes in the family also can influence the marketing mix. In particular, the rapid increase in the number of working women has dramatically changed the way marketers attempt to reach them. The time demands on working women mean that the distribution system has had to be adjusted so that retail stores are open weekends and at night. Mail-order purchasing has increased in popularity due to the desire of working couples not to have to leave home after a day at the office to take extended shopping trips. Products have had to be designed to appeal to working women with different needs. For example, companies in the clothing industry have introduced suits and shirts for working women which last and do not go out of style every year. The Victory company has its president, Mary Sprague, featured in its ads. Wearing one of her shirts and ties, she states in the ad that her shirts work on the working woman. The ad copy states, "When you buy a *Victory* shirt, you know that the President of the company does more than stand behind her product. She stands in it."[46]

Of course promotion has also changed with the increasing employment of women. American Express is one company that has wholeheartedly pinpointed women with its promotional campaign. The company first thought of targeting working women with its credit cards in the mid-1970s. However, the company was afraid that doing so aggressively would turn off their male customers. In one of their first ads to women, they had a macho-looking guy with a cigar stating, "It's time women got their own American Express Card and started taking me to dinner." The company was so afraid of frightening off men that they would not show the entire body of a woman. In an ad called the "headless horsewoman" by some, the company showed the torso of a woman with the copy, "To get anywhere in business, it takes a little application." Of course, the idea was to encourage women to apply for the card. However, the company was too timid to even show her head in the ad.[47] Today, American Express is one of the most sophisticated of advertisers to women. For example, in one recent ad a woman is shown walking out of a sporting goods store in a two-piece suit and carrying a briefcase and a lacrosse stick. The copy reads, "The American Express Card. It's part of a lot of interesting lives."

The family also has importance for public policy, and marketers must be aware of potential changes in rules and regulations affecting the marketing mix. The American culture is a child-oriented one, and how children are socialized is important to most parents as well as society. Thus, the impact of television and television advertising on children is an important issue. Companies should be aware of these concerns and take steps to insure that their promotional activities do not offend parents or regulators. Another area of importance to companies is the safety of their products. Massive recalls of unsafe children's products have been ordered in the past by the Consumer Product Safety Commission. Product testing to insure that products are safe for children's use is crucial.

In summary, understanding the family and the way in which it is changing is important for marketers. What are some of the factors most likely to influence the future characteristics of the family? Some factors important to the future of the family include:

1. *The amount of leisure time available to the family.* As the amount of time spent working by members of the family increases, the available leisure time changes. Increasing numbers of working wives and working adolescents decrease leisure, whereas the shortening of the work week increases the time available.

2. *The amount of formal education.* Increased amounts of education among family members change product preferences and increase the desire for individualism. A potential trend is to increase the amount of time that children spend in school. Educators are becoming concerned that a gap exists between the educational achievement of American children and those in foreign countries—particularly Japan. Thus, proposals are being circu-

lated to increase the number of hours per day and the number of days per year that kids go to school.

3. *The number of working married women.* Discussed previously in the chapter, the presence of a working wife changes substantially the consumption patterns of a family.

4. *Life expectancy.* Americans are living longer. Such increases in life expectancy affect the monetary needs for retirement and the product needs after retirement.

5. *Family size.* During the 1970s family size decreased. In the early 1980s it began to rise again. Anticipating such changes will affect decisions on matters such as how large cars, houses, and food containers should be.

6. *Social and cultural trends.* Over the past twenty years the women's movement and the physical fitness trend have had a major impact on the family. There is no guarantee that these trends will still be with us five or ten years from now. Anticipating new trends and how they affect the family is what companies should be doing.

SUMMARY

Families and households are two of the basic types of consumption units. Households consist of all those living under one roof. They may or may not be related persons. Two important types of families are the nuclear family, consisting of husband, wife, and offspring, and the extended family, consisting of the nuclear family plus grandparents and other kinfolk. The tracking of the demographics of families and households is important for marketers. Such factors as family size, age of marriage, the divorce rate, and the number of employed women and men all have an influence on family purchase patterns.

The family life cycle is another idea of importance to marketers. Families can be viewed as moving through a series of stages in a developmental fashion. As the parents grow older and the children, if any, age and leave, the family's purchase patterns change. Single individuals and couples without children have very different spending habits as compared to a family with a couple of teenage children. Marketers should track the number of households in various stages of the family life cycle and analyze projections of how the distribution may change in the future. For example as the number of young single individuals decreases between 1985 and 1995, the manufacturers of motorcycles will experience problems. Not only will total demand probably decrease but also the features desired on a bike will change. It should be noted, however, that income differences change along with the family life cycle. Many of the changes in consumption patterns may be explained by income differences that occur between the life cycle stages.

When trying to reach families, marketers should realize that a set of roles exists within the family. Such roles include instrumental, expressive, internal, and external. These relate to which individuals in the family focus on tasks, emotional needs, internal family requirements, and outside communications.

Different purchase roles may also be identified, such as influencers, gatekeepers, deciders, buyers, and users.

The various roles help to determine how families make decisions. Decisions within the family can be classified into four different categories—wife dominant, husband dominant, autonomic, and syncratic. These categories refer to the extent to which the husband and wife act independently versus together in making purchases. Research has shown that decision making tends to become increasingly shared as the decision stage moves from problem recognition to search to purchase. Children, though, should not be left out of family decision making. For certain types of products and services, the presence of children as well as their requests can influence the purchase decision.

Another factor that influences family decision making is how power is shared within a family and how conflicts are resolved. Power can be obtained from a variety of sources, some of which are: economic means, cultural definitions, and degree of interpersonal dependence. Different people have also been found to use various techniques to resolve conflicts in order to get their own way, such as using emotional appeals, rewards, or bargaining.

One important function of the family should not be overlooked—the socialization of children. Consumer socialization is the process of learning the skills, knowledge, and attitudes that enable a person to function as a consumer. This learning takes place within the context of background factors, such as the individual's social class, religious background, and socioeconomic status. In addition, the process is influenced by socialization agents such as the media, family members, peers, and teachers, Finally, the learning can occur through several means, such as modeling and reinforcement.

An understanding of the aspects of the family discussed thus far can assist managers in several ways. Tracking demographic and life-cycle changes can pay off through finding marketing opportunities and avoiding marketing mistakes. Understanding the family decision process can be important to marketers in designing the marketing mix. Finally, knowledge of consumer socialization may help managers anticipate changes in the consumer regulatory environment.

Key Terms

Household
Nuclear family
Detached nuclear family
Extended family
POSSLQs
Family life cycle
Instrumental role
Expressive role
Internal roles
External roles
Purchase roles

Gatekeeper
Syncratic decision
Autonomic decision
Family decision stages
Power sources
Consumer socialization
Background factors
Socialization agents
Learning mechanisms
Public policy

Review Questions

1. Differentiate the terms *household* and *family*. Identify three different types of families.
2. Between 1970 and the present, the demographics of households changed dramatically. Identify four major changes in household composition that occurred over this time period.
3. Identify what changes occurred in the following areas between 1970 and the present: households headed by single men and women, numbers of nonfamily households, average household size, average age of marriage, and divorce rates.

4. Identify the stages of the modernized family life cycle presented in the text.

5. How do consumption patterns change as people move through the stages of the family life cycle?

6. Is age or the family life cycle a better predictor of consumption patterns? Why?

7. Both family life cycle stage and income influence purchase patterns. What happens to the proportion of family income spent on clothing at various life cycle stages, when the analysis controls for the effects of differences in income?

8. Identify and briefly discuss three types of roles that exist within families.

9. Four role specialization dimensions have been described regarding family decision making. Identify these dimensions and indicate possible purchases that would fall within each dimension.

10. Researchers have investigated the purchase steps for both furniture and automobiles. What decision steps are common to both types of purchases?

11. Children have an important influence on family decision making. What are the major types of decisions on which children influence their parents?

12. Identify five factors that tend to influence the power relationships within a family.

13. Six influence strategies within families were identified in Table 13–7. Name four of these strategies.

14. Draw the diagram of consumer socialization presented in the text.

15. What are the primary learning mechanisms that control the consumer socialization process?

Discussion Questions

1. Consider the changes in household size over the past twenty-five years. How have these changes probably influenced the automobile industry and the housing industry?

2. Ask two female friends and two male friends what they think is the proper age for marriage. How do these ages match the average age at which couples got married in the 1960s and the early 1980s?

   What do you think will be the trend in the age of marriage over the next ten years?

3. Consider the various life cycle stages discussed in the chapter. How is the size of the various stages likely to change over the next ten years? What industries are likely to reap positive effects from these changes? What industries are likely to experience problems?

4. Think about your own family. Which individuals in your family have the roles of gatekeeper, influencer, decider, buyer, and preparer? To what extent do these roles change across different product categories?

5. As noted in the chapter, the research on marital decision-making role specialization was performed many years ago. Identify what you see as husband dominant, wife dominant, autonomic, and syncratic purchases for middle-class Americans today.

6. How mothers (and fathers) react to the requests of children in grocery stores is an interesting problem. Go to a grocery store and eavesdrop on two parent-child interactions. What type of requests did the child make? How did the parent handle the requests? To what extent did the requests seem to result from the influence of advertising?

7. Consider the power relations that exist in your own family. Who tends to hold the most power? To what extent does the power change across situations? Why are the power relationships arranged as they are?

8. In recent criminal court cases the defense has argued that the defendant should be found innocent of a crime because he was influenced to commit the crime by viewing it on television. To what extent do you think that television is a socialization agent of children? To what extent do you believe that television can cause people to commit antisocial actions without recognizing the gravity of their actions?

9. Compare the brands of products that you prefer to those your parents prefer. To what extent do they coincide? To what extent do you attribute these similar preferences to the socialization process?

10. The decision of how many children to have is an important one. What are the factors that you think you will consider or that you are now considering relevant to having children? To what extent do you personally believe that consumer researchers can view children as a "consumption item"?

References

1. Harry L. Davis, "Decision Making Within the Household," in *Selected Aspects of Consumer Behavior: A Summary from the Perspective of Different Disciplines*, Washington, D.C.: National Science Foundation, 1977, 73–97.
2. Gerald Zaltman and Melanie Wallendorf, *Consumer Behavior: Basic Findings and Managerial Implications*, New York, N.Y.: John Wiley & Sons, Inc., 1983, 168.
3. Arthur Norton, "Keeping Up with Households," *American Demographics*, 5, February 1983, 17–21.
4. Norton, "Keeping Up with Households."
5. Cheryl Russell and Thomas Exter, "America at Mid-Decade," *American Demographics*, 8, January 1986, 22–29.
6. Norton, "Keeping Up with Households."
7. Ibid.
8. Roy H. Rodgers, "Improvements in the Construction and Analysis of Family Life Cycle Categories," Ph.D. diss., University of Minnesota, 1962.
9. Harold Feldman and Margaret Feldman, "The Family Life Cycle: Some Suggestions for Recycling," *Journal of Marriage and the Family*, 37, 1975, 277–287.
10. Patrick E. Murphy and William A. Staples, "A Modernized Family Life Cycle," *Journal of Consumer Research*, 5, June 1979, 12–22.
11. Paul Glick and Arthur Norton, "Marrying, Divorcing, and Living Together in the U.S. Today," *Population Bulletin*, 32, Washington, D.C.: Population Reference Bureau, Inc., 1977.
12. Glick and Norton, "Marrying, Divorcing."
13. Carrie Tuhy, "What Price Children?" *Money*, March 1983, 77–84.
14. Spring 1976 Target Group Index, *Axiom Market Research Bureau*, referenced in Del Hawkins et al., *Consumer Behavior: Implications for Marketing Strategy*, Plano, Tex.: Business Publications, Inc., 1983.
15. A. Marvin Roscoe and Jagdish Sheth, "Demographic Segmentation of Long-Distance Behavior: Data Analysis and Inductive Model Building," in *Third Annual Conference of Association of Consumer Research*, M. Venkatesan (ed.), Association for Consumer Research, 1972, 262.
16. David Fritzsche, "An Analysis of Energy Consumption Patterns by Stage of Family Life Cycle," *Journal of Marketing Research*, 18, May 1981, 227–232.
17. John B. Lansing and Leslie Kish, "Family Life Cycle as a Dependent Variable," *American Sociological Review*, 22, October 1957, 512–519.
18. *Expenditure Patterns of the American Family*, New York, N.Y.: National Industrial Conference Board, 1965.
19. Johan Arndt, "Family Life Cycle as a Determinant of Size and Composition of Household Expenditures," in *Advances in Consumer Research*, VI, William Wilkie (ed.), Ann Arbor, Mich.: Association for Consumer Research, 1979, 128–132.
20. Janet Wagner and Sherman Hanna, "The Effectiveness of Family Life Cycle Variables in Consumer Expenditure Research," *Journal of Consumer Research*, 10, December 1983, 281–291.
21. P. Sloan, "Matchabelli Name Readied for Men's Fragrance Line," *Advertising Age*, September 18, 1978, 3.
22. "Research, High TV Costs Push Crayola into Print," *Advertising Age*, September 18, 1978, 3.
23. David Loudon and Albert J. Della Bitta, "Consumer Behavior: Concepts and Applications," New York, N.Y.: McGraw-Hill Book Company, 1984.
24. Cheryl Russell and Thomas Exter, "America at Mid-Decade," *American Demographics*, 8, January 1986, 22–29.
25. Joann S. Lublin, "Couples Working Different Shifts Take on New Duties and Pressures," *The Wall Street Journal*, March 8, 1984, 29.
26. The eight family roles were discussed by Leon Schiffman and Leslie Kanuk, *Consumer Behavior*, Englewood Cliffs, New Jersey: Prentice-Hall, Inc., 1983, 321.
27. Harry L. Davis and Benny P. Rigaux, "Perception of Marital Roles in Decision Processes," *Journal of Consumer Research*, 1, June, 1974, 51–62.
28. Davis and Rigaux, "Perception of Marital Roles."
29. A. Shuptrine and G. Samuelson, "Dimensions of Marital Roles in Consumer Decision Making: Revisited," *Journal of Marketing Research*, 13, February 1976, 87–91.
30. Gary M. Munsinger, Jean Webe, and Richard Hansen, "Joint Home Purchasing Decisions by Husbands and Wives," *Journal of Consumer Research*, 1, March 1975, 60–66.
31. Pierre Filiatrault and J. R. Brent Ritchie, "Joint Purchasing Decisions: A Comparison of Influence

Structure in Family and Couple Decision-Making Units," *Journal of Consumer Research*, 7, September 1980, 131–140.

32. Scott Ward and Daniel Wackman, "Children's Purchase Influence Attempts and Parental Yielding," *Journal of Marketing Research*, 9, August 1972, 316–319.

33. For a review of this literature see Charles K. Atkin, "Observations of Parent-Child Interaction in Supermarket Decision-Making," *Journal of Marketing*, 42, October 1978, 42–45.

34. Atkin, "Observations of Parent-Child Interaction."

35. Ibid.

36. Pat Burr and Richard Burr, "Parental Responses to Child Marketing," *Journal of Advertising Research*, 17, December 1977, 17–20.

37. Gerald McDonald, "Family Power: The Assessment of a Decade of Theory and Research, 1970–1979," *Journal of Marriage and the Family*, 44, November 1980, 841–854.

38. McDonald, "Family Power."

39. Rosann L. Spiro, "Persuasion in Family Decision Making," *Journal of Consumer Research*, 9, March 1983, 393–402.

40. David A. Goslin, "The Nature of Socialization," in *Handbook of Socialization Theory and Research*, D. A. Goslin, (ed.), Chicago, Ill.: Rand McNally, 1969.

41. Scott Ward, "Consumer Socialization," *Journal of Consumer Research*, 1, September 1974, 1–14.

42. Various authors have developed models of the socialization process; see Gilbert A. Churchill and George Moschis, "Television and Interpersonal Influences on Adolescent Consumer Learning," *Journal of Consumer Research*, 6, June 1979, 23–35.

43. George Moschis and Roy Moore, "Decision Making Among the Young: A Socialization Perspective," *Journal of Consumer Research*, 6, September 1979, 101–112.

44. L. P. Guest, "Brand Loyalty—Twelve Years Later," *Journal of Applied Psychology*, 39, December 1955, 405–408.

45. George P. Moschis, "The Role of Family Communication in Consumer Socialization of Children and Adolescents," *Journal of Consumer Research*, 11, March 1985, 898–913.

46. Susan Roy, "Victory Seamlessly Slits the Three-Piece Set," *Advertising Age*, April 2, 1984, 32, 33.

47. Nancy Josephson, "Interesting Lives Are in Their Cards," *Advertising Age*, April 2, 1984, M–10, M–11.

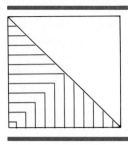

14

Age and Sex Subcultures

The Baby Boomers Grow Affluent

In 1970, the United States imported only sixty-eight thousand European luxury cars. By 1982 the figure had risen over sixfold. Today the European onslaught continues. The cars are bought by people ten to twenty years younger than those buying Lincolns and Cadillacs. The young affluents view the American luxury cars as "old people's cars."(a)

To reach these young, affluent professionals, magazines began changing their format. *Apartment Life* was renamed *Metropolitan Home* and began to feature expensive furniture. (It had once featured a story on how to build a table from a garbage can lid.) *House and Garden* dismissed twelve of its editors, almost tripled its price, and began to target families in the $50,000+ income range. As one irate editor said after being fired from a magazine undergoing an upgrading, "You can't pick up anything without a damn wine column these days."(b)

This emphasis on reaching younger, affluent people began in the early 1980s and is likely to remain strong over the coming ten years. A major reason is that the baby-boom generation, born between 1946 and 1964, is reaching their thirties and forties, a time during the life cycle when incomes are rising rapidly. In addition, the group is highly educated, professional, and forming two-income families. The effects of the maturing of the baby boomers on marketers are broad. From shaking out the soft-drink industry to hurting the market for blue jeans to increasing the demand for luxury products, the baby boomers are a force to be reckoned with.

Portions are based in part on (a) Charles Stevens, "European Luxury Cars Capturing a Growing Share of U.S. Market," *The Wall Street Journal,* May 6, 1983, 2; and (b) Daniel Machalaba, "More Magazines Aim for Affluent Readers," *The Wall Street Journal,* October 14, 1982, 31, 39.

WHAT IS A SUBCULTURE?

The United States is composed largely of immigrants from throughout the world and their descendents. Although an "American" culture does exist, the melting pot has not created a homogeneous mass of people out of the hodge-podge of settlers. A culture is a way of life of a particular society. However, within the overall culture of the United States and other countries, such as Canada, subgroups exist that retain some of the values, beliefs, and symbols of their culture of origination. These groups form subcultures that can become important target markets for marketers. For example, the need of Jews to have kosher food makes them a tempting target for marketers willing to control adequately the preparation of food products. (The concept of culture is discussed in detail in Chapter 17.)

In addition to originating from immigration, subcultures can also develop from "naturally" occurring subdivisions within a society. All societies reveal such subgroups, which may be based on age, social class, and regional differences. In each case some factor causes differences in values and lifestyles sufficient to create a subculture. Thus, in the United States a combination of retirement, common physical problems, and similar housing needs has resulted in the development of the elderly subculture.

A **subculture** may be defined as a subdivision of national culture, based around some unifying characteristic, such as social status or religion, whose members share similar patterns of behavior that are distinct from those of the national culture.[1] Numerous demographic characteristics have been used to identify subcultures, including:

Nationality (e.g., Hispanics, Italians, Poles).
Race (e.g., blacks, Indians, Chinese).
Region (e.g., New England, Southwest).
Age (e.g., elderly, teenager).
Religion (e.g., Catholic, Jewish).
Sex (i.e., male, female).
Social class (e.g., upper class, lower class).

Although subcultures are often described via demographic variables, one must distinguish subcultures from demographics. When one speaks of cultures or subcultures, the focus is on how groups of people behave. The concern is with the groups' beliefs, actions, symbols, and so forth. People do not necessarily belong to a subculture because they are young or old, black or Chinese, rich or poor. In contrast, demographics merely describe the physical characteristics of a population of people. The reason why a marketer might speak of a black subculture is that a demographic characteristic conveniently describes those blacks who have similar behavior patterns.

Individuals are simultaneously members of a number of subcultures. For example, a black person could also be an entertainer, Jewish, and possess only one functioning eye, like the entertainer Sammie Davis, Jr. Mr. Davis does not fit the image that many people may hold of the black subculture. Thus, when defining a subculture, a marketer will usually utilize a combination of demographic variables to define the group. Rather than targeting Hispanics in general, for example, the marketer might target Hispanic males who are middle-class and under forty years of age, as does Adolf Coors in their beer advertising.

Marketers have identified as specific target markets a number of subcultures. In this chapter the consumption and demographic characteristics of several such groups are discussed. They include subcultures based on the demographic classifications of age (the baby-boom generation and the elderly) and of sex (the subculture of women). Chapter 15 discusses several additional subcultures based on the demographics of race (blacks), nationality (Hispanics), religion (Jews and Fundamentalist Protestants) and region.

AGE SUBCULTURES

As a person moves through his or her life cycle, predictable changes in values, lifestyles, and consumption patterns occur. A five-year-old has a completely different set of needs from a twenty-year-old, who in turn has different needs from a sixty-five-year-old. Because various age groupings of consumers have similar values, needs, and behavioral patterns, and because people in the groupings will attempt to cluster together, they form subcultures that may constitute important market segments. Furthermore, as the numbers of people in age categories change because of variations in birthrates, new marketing opportunities may result.

An analysis of age trends is important to marketers for two additional reasons. First, highly accurate measures of the age composition of the population exist. Thus, homogeneous groups of people can be identified—an important segmentation requirement. Second, the age profile of the population can be projected into the future more easily than most other demographic factors, such as income or occupation. Such projections allow marketers to recognize potential marketing opportunities years in advance, which greatly simplifies the planning process.

Over the coming years two age groupings will become increasingly important—the baby-boom generation and the elderly. Although some debate may exist as to whether the **baby-boom generation** actually forms a subculture, sufficient lifestyle similarities exist among the huge group of Americans born between 1946 and 1964 that the group has a large impact on marketers and the economy as a whole. The elderly also are becoming important as a market segment because of the rapidly increasing size of the group.

The Baby Boomers

The United States is currently experiencing fundamental changes in the age characteristics of its population. The major reasons for the shifts in the age of Americans over the next forty years lie in the dramatic changes in birthrates over the last half century. During the Great Depression of the 1930s a "birth dearth," or **baby bust,** occurred. The number of children born to the average woman during her lifetime, or the **fertility rate,** dropped to the replacement level of 2.1 births. Total births dropped 25 percent.[2]

The Depression birth dearth was followed by the post–World War II baby boom. Here the fertility rate shot past 3.8, and the total number of births increased by one-third over Depression levels. The baby boom lasted through 1964. It, however, was followed by another baby bust. Caused by changes in the technology of birth prevention (e.g., the birth control pill) and by changes in lifestyle (e.g., the emergence of the working woman), the baby bust sent fertility rates plunging to as low as 1.8 in 1976—a rate far below replacement level.[3]

This series of changes in the birthrate created a huge bulge of people. This bulge has been described as like a "melon being digested by a boa constrictor."[4] As the years pass the bulge moves, growing older and changing the nature of the marketplace. Table 14–1 gives an overview of the U.S. population between 1970 and 2000. In 1970 the majority of the baby boomers were between five and fourteen years of age. Marketers of soft drinks and fast foods were ecstatic over the hordes of teenyboppers clamoring for their products. By the year 2000, though, the baby boomers will be in their mid-thirties to mid-fifties. As described in the vignette at the beginning of the chapter, such consumers tend to be affluent and will have a new set of product needs and wants. One estimate is that by 1990 more than 18.2 percent of households will have inflation-adjusted incomes of over $40,000 as compared to 10.9 percent in 1983.[5]

As income expands, people change their spending habits. One survey found that when income moved from middle to upper levels, spending increased by over 80 percent on such items as clothing, house furnishings, floor coverings, and recreation. Spending increased by less than 40 percent for food at home, utilities, major appliances, and vehicle operations. The single item with

Table 14–1   Projected U.S. Population to the Year 2000

	Millions			Percent Change	
	1980	**1990**	**2000**	**1980–90**	**1990–2000**
Under 5 years	16,020	19,437	17,852	21.3%	−8.2%
5–14	33,896	35,758	39,153	5.6	9.5
15–19	20,609	16,777	19,727	−18.4	17.6
20–29	39,848	38,122	33,367	−4.3	−12.5
30–39	31,275	40,178	38,416	28.4	−4.4
40–49	22,817	31,220	39,899	37.4	27.8
50–59	23,069	21,838	29,991	−5.6	37.3
60–64	9,797	10,360	10,151	6.1	−2.0
65 +	24,927	29,824	31,822	19.7	6.7
Total	222,159	243,513	260,378	9.6%	6.9%

Source: Data from U.S. Census of Population, P–25, no. 704.

the largest increase when incomes jumped to high levels was recreation. People take many more trips, stay in more expensive hotels, and participate in more expensive hobbies, such as golf.[6] Manufacturers must place special attention on the marketing mix when dealing with the affluent, thirty- to forty-nine-year-old market. Below are several generalizations about the mix when marketing to this group.

Product. Focus on quality. The group is not afraid of prestige products. They are investment oriented in purchases.

Price. Try to provide value. High prices will not scare off these consumers if they believe that they are receiving a better product.

Distribution. The group is highly concerned with service, in part because of their lack of time. Specialty shops will do well.

Promotion. The group reads more magazines and watches less television than average. They know puffery when they see it. Maintaining good taste will be important, especially when women are featured in the ads.

One of the prime marketing requirements for consumer goods firms (ie., clothing, food, entertainment, etc.) is the tracking of the baby-boom generation. As their tastes and preferences change with the passing years, the fortunes of manufacturers are dramatically affected, as discussed in the example in Highlight 14–1. Indeed, a marketing law might be phrased as "Those who live by the baby boom shall die by the baby boom."[7]

HIGHLIGHT 14–1

Levi's and the Baby Boomers

Levi Strauss, Inc., the maker of Levi's Blue Jeans, used the baby-boom generation to catapult it to being the world's largest clothing manufacturer. Established in 1853 by a Bavarian immigrant, the company first sold denim jeans to farmers, miners, and cowboys. Until the mid-1950s the company was only modestly successful.

The events that moved the company to the fast track were two movies in the mid-1950s—*Rebel Without a Cause* and *The Wild One*—in which leading actors wore Levi jeans. The jeans became an antiestablishment symbol. During the turbulent 1960s jeans became a worldwide uniform of the baby-boom generation. The jeans were banned in American schools and smuggled behind the Iron Curtain. Between 1962 and 1977, the height of the years when baby boomers were eight to eighteen years old, the company's sales and profits expanded twenty times over.(a)

But companies that live by the baby boom die by the baby boom. By the late 1970s the baby boomers were moving into their twenties. Something more sophisticated was needed. Designer jeans suddenly caught on, and Levi's unparalleled growth was halted. By the early 1980s profits were down 25 percent. In response to the lagging profits, Levi closed plants and realigned management. The company became marketing oriented and brought out new clothing products, such as a line of maternity wear. However, even by 1985 the profit picture had not turned around. The company may have to wait until the 1990s for a profit turnaround, when the sons and daughters of the baby boomers reach their teenage years.(b)

Based in part on (a) Landon Jones, "The Baby Boom Consumer," *American Demographics*, February 1981, 28–35; and (b) Marilyn Chase, "Levi Emerges from Recession with Plan," *The Wall Street Journal*, September 23, 1983, 16.

In the early 1980s soft-drink manufacturers were clamoring to develop new marketing appeals to attract the aging baby boomers. In particular, 7-Up was causing panic among the cola companies by first promoting 7-Up as *not* having caffeine and then arguing that the beverage is "natural," containing no artificial color or additives. The objective was to differentiate 7-Up from other soft drinks to appeal to the health-conscious baby boomers. The tactic worked and 7-Up's market share began to rise.

For similar reasons fast-food restaurants, like McDonald's, began to add breakfast menus in the 1980s in order to attract working people. Why? Their traditional target market of five- to seventeen-year-olds would decline by more than one-half million people during the 1980s.[8] As indicated in Highlight 14–2, the dairy industry has also had to cope with changes in demographics.

The Graying of America

A second major demographic trend related to age is the graying of America. This aging of the population will be the dominant demographic factor for the foreseeable future. As of 1980 the median age of the U.S. population was thirty years old. By 1990 the ratio of those over thirty to those under thirty is expected to jump to 124 people over thirty for every 100 under thirty. By the year 2000 the ratio should move to 145 and by the year 2030 should reach 176.[9] Barring global war or other disasters, the population of those under thirty will never again be as large as it was in 1983. By the year 2020 those over sixty-five will outnumber teenagers two to one.

A number of factors influence the accuracy of age projections. The birthrates, mortality rates, and immigration rates all influence the projected population and its characteristics in the years ahead. Unfortunately, each is difficult to predict accurately.[10] Birthrates are influenced by the technology available to prevent births as well as by cultural values and lifestyle patterns. **Mortality rates** have been falling since the 1970s. Life expectancy increased by three years during the 1970s, and projections are that they will increase another two to three years in the 1980s. By 1990 it is estimated that men will live on average seventy-two years and women eighty-one years. Because of

---

HIGHLIGHT 14–2

The Demographics of Milk Consumption

Changing consumer tastes and preferences have dramatically influenced the dairy industry. In 1930 the average American consumed 819 pounds of milk a year. In 1960 the consumption had dropped to 653 pounds. By 1981 the figure was down to 541 pounds.* This 33 percent decline can be attributed largely to two changes in demographics. First, fewer Americans now live on farms than in the 1930s. (Farm families drink a great deal of milk because it is plentiful and cheap.) Second, the U.S. population is substantially older than in 1930. People simply drink less milk as they grow older.

*Daniel Chasen, "Milk," *Science 83*, July–August 1983, 66–74.

the striking difference in the life expectancy of men and women, an aging population means more women. Elderly women will increasingly form an important market segment for marketers to target. Indeed, of those over eighty-five years old, women outnumber men by almost two and one-half to one.[11]

Immigration will also influence the age distribution of the population. Immigrants, whether legal or illegal, tend to be younger, and recently more of them have been of Spanish and Indo-Chinese origin (e.g., Vietnamese and Cambodian). Immigrant women have high birthrates. It has been estimated that the Hispanic population grows at a rate of 1.8 percent a year in comparison to .6 percent a year for the entire United States population.[12] Because of the youth of the immigrants and their higher fertility rates, immigration is the single most important factor retarding the aging trend of the U.S. population.

The Mature Consumer

Just who is the **mature consumer**? No specific age is associated with becoming "mature," elderly, a senior citizen, or reaching one's "golden years." However, a series of events occur around the age of sixty-five that set the aging consumer apart from younger people. At about the age of sixty-five retirement has occurred or is being anticipated. In all likelihood income will be reduced and become relatively fixed, making inflation a threat. Health concerns become more important at about this age, and close friends begin to die.

On two major dimensions mature consumers—here defined as age sixty-five or older—differ from younger people. First, in certain ways they process information differently. Second, they reveal a variety of consumption differences from younger consumers.

Information-Processing Characteristics   An entire chapter (Chapter 5) was devoted to information processing. But it is appropriate here to describe briefly the differences between mature and younger consumers in their memory functions and in their abilities to acquire and use information. One major problem for people sixty-five and older is the decrement that occurs in their sensory systems. In particular, their vision and hearing tend to become impaired with age. For example, vision problems make it difficult for many elderly people to function effectively at night, which leads them to shop more during the day. Similarly, as people age they tend to become far sighted and require bifocals. Reading fine print on product packages may become extremely difficult. Some authors have suggested that the inability to read small print may be the reason why older consumers show less familiarity with nutrition labeling, open dating, and unit pricing.[13]

Research has indicated that the ability to solve problems declines steadily as a person ages, particularly once a person enters his or her seventies. In particular, the speed with which the elderly are able to use information decreases with age.[14] Evidence also exists that the ability to acquire new information rapidly decreases with age, particularly when interference from the environment (e.g., noise) is present. However, other authors have concluded that if the elderly are given sufficient time to make decisions and to take in and handle information, there is little, if any impact of age on learning or memory.[15]

The changes in information-processing abilities indicate that marketers should be concerned with how much time the elderly are given to make a decision. Providing additional time for information processing—for instance, by making an advertisement longer or by a salesperson going slowly—may assist older consumers. In addition, marketers should pretest the way the information is organized. Some research has shown that the elderly organize information differently from younger adults.[16]

Perhaps the greatest problem faced by the elderly that influences their consumption activities is the decrement that occurs in motor skills. The inability to walk, to write, to talk clearly, and to drive can severely impede an individual's freedom of activity. In many cities companies are now providing a variety of services to the elderly to help them overcome these age-related handicaps. Examples of such services include in-home food delivery, yard and house cleaning, fix-up services, and nursing care.

Consumption and Activity Patterns of the Mature Consumer   Table 14–2 identifies how the elderly differ from younger consumers on a number of dimensions. In terms of shopping, those over sixty-five shop more fre-

Table 14–2   Consumption and Buying Habits of Mature Consumers as Compared to Younger Consumers

1. Shopping behaviors
   a. Shop more frequently
   b. Spend less per shopping trip
   c. Shop less often at night
   d. Use coupons
   e. Pay with cash—not credit cards
   f. Shop less at discount stores
2. Media habits
   a. Watch 60 percent more television, particularly daytime
   b. Read more newspapers
   c. Listen to less radio, particularly FM
3. What they want from retailers
   a. Courteous treatment
   b. Personal assistance
   c. Delivery service
   d. Rest facilities (e.g., benches)

SOURCES: Adapted from K. L. Bernhardt and T. C. Kinnear, *Advances in Consumer Research, III,* Ann Arbor, Mich.: Association for Consumer Research, 1976, 449–452; and Zarrel Lambert, "An Investigation of Older Consumers' Unmet Needs and Wants at the Retail Level," *Journal of Retailing, 55,* Winter 1979, 43.

quently but spend less per shopping trip. They also shop less frequently at night. They use more coupons, pay with cash rather than credit cards, and shop less frequently at discount stores.

From retailers the elderly expect high amounts of personal attention. They seek courteous treatment by sales personnel. They also desire delivery service and rest facilities, such as benches and chairs, more than younger age groups. As a group the elderly are less physically active than younger consumers. As a consequence, they watch more television, particularly in the daytime. They read more newspapers but listen to FM radio less.

Table 14–3 identifies some industries that will be positively and negatively influenced by an aging U.S. population. Industries providing for the health needs of the elderly will flourish. People over sixty-five spend two and one-half times the amount spent by the general population on health-care services.[17] The elderly are also among the largest spenders on stocks, bonds, furs, jewelry, and expensive clothing.[18] Companies involved in nursing care, drugs, and hospital services will find increased demand for their products and services as the elderly population increases.

As a group the elderly consider themselves younger than their age would indicate. In one study the authors identified a number of "ages" in addition to chronological age, such a "feel-age," "look-age," and "do-age."[19] Most of the elderly believed themselves to be younger than their years would indicate. Thus, when asked how old they are based on how they feel, what they

Table 14–3   The Graying Revolution: Its Impact on Selected Industries and Products

Positive Impact	Negative Impact
Drug	Soft drinks
Ulcer	Fast foods
Laxative	Diapers
Heart	Movies
Health care	Single-family housing
Alcohol facilities	Toys
In-home convalescence	Selected physical sports
Nursing home	Basketball shoes
Hospitals	Football supplies
Beer industry	Selected magazines
Coffee	*Parents*
Liquor	*Rock*
Condominium housing	Child care
Selected sedate sports	
Golf	
Bowling	
Selected magazines (e.g., *Over Fifty*)	
Travel	
Leisure time	

do, what their interests are, and how they look, most responded with an age lower than their chronological age. Interestingly, the tendency was more pronounced as the chronological age increased. Thus, in every category people in their eighties felt relatively younger than people in their fifties. Thus, a person fifty-five might feel *five* years younger than his or her "true" age, while someone eighty-five would feel *ten* years younger.

A second study that focused on the age people "feel" also found that people tend to feel *thirty* to *thirty-nine* years old, regardless of their ages.[20] People under the age of thirty feel older than their actual years. Most fifty-year-old people still felt themselves to be *thirty-five.* The study also had some other interesting findings. In comparison to a person the same age, an individual tended to feel younger if he or she was working rather than retired, had teenagers in the household, lived in the Pacific region, was a college graduate, or had an upper income.

One major finding concerning the elderly is that they are cautious consumers. Older people have been found not to risk being wrong for the sake of acting fast. They do things in their own time and pace.[21] In addition, it has been found that the higher the perceived risk, the less likely the elderly are to try a product.[22]

A number of researchers have maintained that the elderly are *not* a single market. In terms of shopping behavior, the elderly can be divided into six segments:[23]

1. Saver-planners.
2. Brand loyalists.
3. Information seekers.
4. Economy shoppers.
5. Laggards.
6. Conspicuous consumers.

Others have segmented the sixty-five-and-older market on the basis of lifestyle and have found four groups:[24]

1. Experimental—like to try new things.
2. Getting away—want to leave the "rat race."
3. Social—want to make new friends.
4. Family—focus on doing things with extended family.

Somewhat surprisingly, marketers have been late in recognizing the size and buying ability of the elderly consumer. The tendency is to view all elderly as having a limited income and thus limited ability to make discretionary expenditures. However, the overall elderly consumer market is now over $100 billion and growing rapidly. Furthermore, although the fixed income of many elderly couples is low, they may have large amounts of savings in reserve that can be used to splurge.

Slowly, though, marketers have begun to target the older consumer. Food and health companies in particular have begun to design products specifically for the older consumer. Timex has begun to market digital blood-pressure measuring devices, Campbell's Soup has come out with a line of low-sodium foods, Bulova has designed watches with easy-to-read dials, and at least four magazines have emerged for the senior citizen—*50 Plus*, *Modern Maturity*, *Seniority*, and *Golden Years.* Companies like Sears, De Beers, and AT&T have deliberately started using older people in their advertisements. Freedent gum began a major advertising campaign in the early 1980s shouting the message that Freedent does not stick to most dental work. In 1983 the septuagenarian John Houseman was named endorser of the year for his commercials for Smith-Barney brokerage services and other companies.

Marketing to older consumers requires sensitivity, however. The elderly are concerned about their self-image. Procter and Gamble has had problems advertising its product Attends, which is a type of diaper for incontinent adults. Heinz introduced "senior foods," which were strained foods for adults. The product failed when the target market bought baby food instead, ostensibly for grandchildren, in order not to admit that they used strained foods.[25]

As the U.S. population grows older a number of marketing opportunities will occur. In the cosmetics industry the focus has moved to skin care and the prevention of lines and wrinkles. Companies recognize that by the year 2000, forty-five- to sixty-four-year-olds will account for about 23 percent of the population and 91 percent of its discretionary income.[26] Marketers started battling for their piece of the pie in the early 1980s. In 1982, for example, over $53 million was spent just on media advertising of these products. Men have not been neglected by skin-care marketers either. Increasingly, one finds new moisturizing products aimed at the maturing-male market.

SEX-BASED SUBCULTURES

The differences in values and lifestyles of men and women are most vividly seen in highly traditional cultures, such as those in Moslem countries. In the Moslem culture women are expected to clothe their entire bodies, remain near or in the home, and work exclusively in the home. In the American culture men and women for the most part have similar educational and occupational opportunities. However, physical and social differences distinguish the groups, making each a distinct subculture that can be targeted by marketers. Because the female subculture has been examined most thoroughly, this section will focus on women in the marketplace. The targeting of men will unfortunately be given less emphasis because relatively little has been written on reaching this important target market.

Targeting the Female Subculture

On a variety of dimensions women form a subculture distinct from men. Women tend to have lower self-confidence and tend to take less risks than men.[27] They are generally cautious concerning risks associated with the products they buy, their own physical safety, and war on a national level. A manifestation of such risk aversion can be seen in the problems that President Reagan had with women voters in the 1984 election. Reagan was much less popular with women than men, largely because of women's fears that Reagan would lead the United States into war.

Differences in anatomical form and function are one reason why the sexes separate into distinct subcultures. Women bear the principle reproductive burden due to the fact that they, not men, become pregnant. Thus, a whole set of norms and behavioral expectations, have formed around the roles of mother and father in the American culture. Thus, women tend to take on the major child-care responsibilities. In addition, the menstrual cycle sets up a series of product needs for women that men do not share.

A second difference between men and women concerns their divergent social needs. Whether from differences in biological makeup or socialization, women are more group oriented than men. Woman tend to seek out groups of other women and in these groups enjoy sharing advice and developing a sense of closeness and warmth. In contrast, when men come together, the tendency is to tease each other and poke fun at the foibles of their friends.[28] Advertisements by Miller's Lite beer cleverly capitalize on the penchant of men to tease and joke. Each ad in the long-running campaign had the same message, i.e., drink Lite beer because "it tastes good and won't fill you up." The campaign used different ex-jocks, such as Bubba Smith, Billy Martin, and Marv Throneberry to pitch the message in a way that poked fun at each other's weaknesses.

Women's Demographic Changes During the 1970s American women underwent fundamental changes in their aspirations and particularly in their occupational goals. One author called the dramatic rise in the number of working women "the single most outstanding phenomenon of our century."[29] For example, during the decade the number of women engineers increased by 100 percent, the number of female lawyers and judges by 377 percent, and the number of female bank officials by 256 percent.[30]

Table 14–4 summarizes a number of the demographic changes that have affected women over the past forty years. In *education* more women are going to college, and of those, more are studying business. Far more women are going on to get advanced degrees. Concerning *fertility*, women are having children later in life and far fewer of them. The *marital* status of women has also changed, with women marrying later, a smaller proportion of women married at any one time, and a greater proportion getting divorced. Concerning their *occupation*, women are entering the professions, such as law and medicine, at a far greater pace. The number of women who work and also have children under six years old increased over 800 percent between 1950 and 1982. However, the earnings gap between women and men has actually increased.

One consequence of the entry of women into the professional work force is **role conflict.** Role conflict occurs when the demands of different roles

Table 14–4 Some Demographic Changes Affecting Women and Men

Dates	Change
1940–1980	Number of women doctors increases by 500%
1950–1981	Average marital age for women increases from 20.3 years to 22.3 years
1950–1980	Divorce rate doubles
1950–1981	Proportion of married women among all adult women declines from 67% to 59%
1965–1980	Expectations for children by married white women decline from 3.1 to 2.1 children
1950–1980	Fertility rate drops from 3.3 children to 1.8
1950–1981	Percent of women attending college moves from 15% to 41%
1966–1978	Number of women majoring in business increases 300% as compared to 66% for men
1950–1982	Percent of working women with children under 6 increases from 12% to 50%
1982	For the first time in a recession men's unemployment rate surpasses women's
1955 to 1982	Earnings gap between men and women widens from 65% to 76%

Source: Data adapted from Daphine Spain and Suzanne M. Bianchi, "How Women Have Changed," *American Demographics*, May 1983, 19–25.

collide. One important source of role conflict is the difficulty of balancing motherhood with career. For companies, however, such conflict can represent opportunities. For example, one company has been built around selling fashionable maternity clothes. The company, called Lady Madonna, targets women who want to look good in maternity clothes, whether on the job or out on the town. Figure 14–1 shows the cover of a *Lady Madonna* catalog. The cover reveals Jane Seymour modeling an outfit and looking terrific. The message to women is that *you* can in part resolve the conflict of mother and career by looking good in maternity clothes.

Segmenting the Women's Market The women's market is heterogeneous, and researchers have identified a number of different segmentation schemes. One approach to segmenting the women's market is to identify the various roles that women have. Traditionally, women have had such roles as wife, mother, homemaker, hostess, and single girl preparing for marriage and motherhood.[31] Only recently have roles outside of the family, such as professional or career women, taken on importance to marketers.

One author has suggested that the women's movement (feminism) has had a significant impact on women by influencing their economic aspira-

Figure 14–1 A catalog targeting pregnant women who want to look attractive. (*Courtesy of D. F. Corey Enterprises, Inc., and Jane Seymour.*)

tions, household role, and general lifestyle.[32] In one research study the author divided women into three groups—**traditionalists, moderates,** and **feminists.** Table 14–5 presents the demographic characteristics of the three groups. As can be seen, those scoring high on a feminism scale tended to be younger, have higher amounts of education, more often be Jewish, less often describe themselves as housewives, and more often have lower family incomes than the moderates and traditionalists.

In the study the respondents answered a series of questions to assess lifestyle differences among the traditionalists, moderates, and feminists. A number of lifestyle differences were found. In particular, large differences appeared in how the three groups viewed the issue of sex stereotyping. For example, feminists viewed very negatively advertisements that pictured a woman's place as in the home and depicted women as sexual objects. In addition, feminists wanted to see more young girls playing with mechanical toys in ads, whereas traditionalists disapproved of such ads. Other lifestyle differences were that feminists tended to display more self-confidence, were less sympathetic to television, and were more sympathetic to taking risks and trying out new ideas. The questions in Highlight 14–3 can help you gauge the extent to which you identify with feminist ideals.

The magazine readership of the three groups was also investigated. The study revealed that the feminists preferred national news magazines, such as *Newsweek* and *Time*. In contrast, traditionalists and moderates tended to prefer homemaker magazines, such as *Woman's Day* and *Family Circle*. Dramatic differences were found in the appeal of *Ms.* magazine. Practically no traditionalists read the publication, whereas a substantial number of feminists did.

Table 14–5   Demographic Characteristics of Traditionalists, Moderates, and Feminists

	Percent of Group		
Demographic Variable	**Traditionalist**	**Moderate**	**Feminist**
Age (18–30)	46%	64%	74%
Education (college or more)	34	43	61
Full-time workers	34	48	42
Housewife	25	15	7
Religion			
Protestant	40	38	36
Catholic	50	34	26
Jewish	2	4	16
Income (family)			
Lower than $10,000	26	27	39
$25,000 or more	21	22	13

SOURCE: Data adapted from Alladi Venkatesh, "Changing Roles of Women—A Life-Style Analysis," *Journal of Consumer Research*, 7, September 1980, 189–197.

HIGHLIGHT 14–3

How Much Do You Agree with Feminist Thinking?

The series of questions shown below form a five point scale to measure the extent to which someone agrees with feminist ideals. To take the scale indicate whether you "strongly agree," "agree," "neither agree nor disagree," "disagree," or "strongly disagree" with each statement. Your score can range from a minimum of 10 to a maximum of 50. Questions 2, 3, 5, 6, and 8 are reverse scored, so that "strongly agree" counts five points and "strongly disagree" counts one point. The lower your score the more you tend to agree with feminist thinking.

1. The word "obey" should be removed from the marriage service.
2. Girls should be trained for homemaking and boys for an occupation suited to their talents.
3. The initiative in courtship should come from men.
4. A woman should expect just as much freedom of action as a man.
5. Women should subordinate their careers to home duties to a greater extent than men.
6. Motherhood is the ideal "career" for most women.
7. Within their marriage, women should be free to withhold or initiate sexual intimacy as they choose.
8. The husband should be regarded as the legal representative of the family group in matters of law.
9. The decision whether to seek an abortion should rest with the wife.
10. A woman should not be disqualified from any occupation on the basis of her sex alone.

In another segmentation scheme women were divided into three groups based upon the wife's occupation—nonworking wives, low occupational status wives, and high occupational status wives.[33] High occupational status wives were managers, professionals, teachers, nurses, and so forth. Low occupational wives were secretaries, clerical workers, retail workers, and service workers.

The results of the study revealed substantial consumption differences among the families of the three groups. Concerning food consumption, the low occupational status group consumed more convenience foods and beverages such as instant breakfast, TV dinners, canned ravioli, hamburgers, and hot dogs. (Interestingly, these results parallel the food consumption patterns of families in the lower social classes.) Low occupational status women also were the greatest users of mail and newspaper coupons. The usage of makeup was also investigated. The low occupational status women used the most rouge, eye shadow, and facial makeup base. These families also tended to watch the most television and own the largest number of television sets. In automobile ownership the groups were similar, except that the high occupational status group of women tended to have smaller and newer second cars in the family.

The differences in consumption patterns shown by families with working wives who have varying occupational statuses point to the importance of including the wife's occupation in measures of social class. Because the wife's occupational status often differs from that of her husband and because the wife has a major impact on purchase decisions, the inclusion of the wife's occupation in measures of social class seems warranted. (More is said about social class in Chapter 16.)

A number of other classification schemes have been developed to segment women. One approach developed by an advertising agency classified women into four groups. They were career women (22 percent), just-a-job women (37 percent), stay-at-home women (28 percent) and plan-to-work women (13 percent).[34] One area of difference among the groups was in their autonomy of financial decisions. Career women bought their own cars and had their own investments. Just-a-job women had their own checking and saving accounts but did not have investments. The plan-to-work women tended to have young children. They used financial services in a manner similar to career women, but at a lower level. The stay-at-home women were the least involved in financial services.

Portrayal of Women in Advertising A major criticism of advertising over the past decade and a half has been its portrayal of women. The charge is that the pervasive tendency of ads to show women as sex objects, as working in menial jobs, or as housewives leads to a false and misleading stereotype. Over the years a number of studies have been conducted of print advertisements found in magazines to determine the occupations depicted and the sex of the models in the ads.

Table 14–6 gives the results of studies investigating how working men and women were shown in 1958, 1970 and 1978.[35] The results reveal a strong trend for women increasingly to be cast in print advertising in more business and professional positions. In 1958 no women were shown in professional positions. By 1978 almost 22 percent of women shown were professionals. Conversely, the depiction of women in secretarial positions decreased dramatically over the time period, from 74.4 percent in 1958 to 17.4 percent in 1978.

Table 14–6 Occupations of Workers Shown in Print Advertisements (in percentages)

	1958		1970		1978	
	Women	**Men**	**Women**	**Men**	**Women**	**Men**
Professional	0.0%	20.9%	0.0%	19.4%	21.8%	30.9%
Entertainment/sports	11.1	7.2	58.3	20.0	30.4	20.3
Middle-level business	5.6	31.3	8.3	6.8	30.4	13.8
Secretarial/clerical	74.4	0.0	16.6	1.7	17.4	3.3
Blue collar	8.9	40.6	16.7	52.0	0.0	31.7

Source: Data adapted from Marc Weinberger et al., "Twenty Years of Women in Magazine Advertising: An Update." *1979 Educator's Conference Proceedings*, Neil Beckwith, et al. (eds.), Chicago, IL: American Marketing Association, Series 44, 1979, 375.

A second feature of interest found in Table 14–6 is that men are much more frequently shown in blue-collar positions than women. In fact in 1958 no women were cast in a blue-collar role, despite the fact that women are increasingly working in factories and in construction jobs. Clearly, it seems more socially acceptable to show men in blue-collar occupations than women.

The studies of 1958, 1970, and 1978 advertisements also examined portrayals of the roles of nonworking women, as indicated by the material in Table 14–7. Somewhat surprisingly the percentage of occasions in which women were shown in **decorative roles** actually increased over the twenty-year period. A decorative role is one in which a woman merely is placed in an ad as an adornment to look pretty. In particular, the use of females in decorative roles accompanying males increased rather dramatically. In 1958 women were used as male decorations less than 14 percent of the time. In contrast, in 1978 the percentage had risen 44.2 percent. Such "decorative" ads are the very ones that tend to show women as sex objects. Thus, although advertisers began to portray women more favorably in terms of occupations, the exploitation of women as sex objects, if anything, increased over the years. Interestingly, though, when the roles of men were examined, a similar pattern was found. Between 1958 and 1978 the percentage of men used as decoration in print advertisements almost doubled. It seems that men are increasingly being used as sex objects as well.

Another point of interest shown in Table 14–7 is that the percentage of ads in which women were portrayed in recreational settings was essentially static. In the 1980s a clear physical-fitness trend has developed for women, and ads are increasingly showing women exercising. Figure 14–2 shows a print ad for American Express in which a woman is cross-country skiing with an infant in a front pack.

Table 14–7   Roles of Nonworking Women Shown in Print Advertisements (in percentages)

Role	1958 Alone or with Female	1958 With Male	1970 Alone or with Female	1970 With Male	1978 Alone or with Female	1978 With Male
Family	18.0%	32.0%	21.0%	25.0%	13.8%	24.4%
Recreational	7.5	54.7	9.0	64.0	6.2	31.4
Decorative	74.5	13.3	70.0	11.0	80.0	44.2
	100.0%	100.0%	100.0%	100.0%	100.0%	100.0%

SOURCE: Data adapted from Marc Weinberger et al., "Twenty Years of Women in Magazine Advertising: An Update," *1979 Educator's Conference Proceedings*, Neil Beckwith et al. (eds.), Chicago, IL: American Marketing Association, Series 44, 1979, 375.

Figure 14–2 American Express targets the active woman. (*Courtesy of American Express, Inc.*)

Targeting the Male Subculture

Much less has been written on segmenting the male subculture. One researcher noted that many marketers have overlooked changes among males.[36] With over ten percent of all American households headed by men and with women increasingly working, the male role has expanded. Three segments of men were identified by the researcher. Following are brief descriptions of the characteristics of each segment.

1. **Old-fashioned men.** Such males are unaware of social changes. They do not mind being called sexist because they believe women belong in the home. They object to seeing dominant women displayed in advertisements. They are displeased if their wives work and have been known to refuse to mow the lawn in response to their wives' inability to perform all of their traditional chores.
2. **Lip-service liberals.** These men are described as confused about the social changes. They are more relaxed about their masculinity and speak of being sympathetic toward females. However, their actions sometimes belie their sentiments.
3. **Expressive men.** Expressive men were described as more open and expressive of their feelings. They are younger and live outside the South. They will share responsibilities with women and believe that such sharing is enriching.

The image of the "old-fashioned man" is a popular one for advertisers. Marlboro cigarette ads have become famous for showing cowboys herding cattle against a backdrop of mountains. This image has propelled the brand into one of the leading sales positions. More recently Camel cigarettes has developed a theme that updates the Marlboro image. In the Camel ads a raw-boned, well-muscled male is shown in assorted outdoor locations lighting a cigarette. He is the modern cowboy—independent and proud, whether riding a motorcycle, driving a four-wheel drive vehicle, or climbing a mountain. Figure 14–3 shows one of the ads in the campaign.

The author of the segmentation studies of men, however, also noted that product attributes that involve toughness and strength are still important when marketing to men.[37] The reason why many after-shave products "sting" is that men want them that way. But changes in male self-perceptions are occurring. For example, men are becoming more interested in dieting as revealed by Diet Pepsi commercials showing slim men as well as women.

If a marketer, though, wants to target men for a product that has any connection with what is feminine, it is important to use highly masculine men. For this reason the Miller's Lite beer campaign uses ex-jocks. In a similar manner, FTD Florists chose the ex–pro-football player Merlin Olsen to endorse sending flowers to people for whom you care.

In summary, the social roles of men are changing, just as they are changing for women. As a consequence, new segments of male consumers are beginning to appear. However, more research needs to be performed to identify the nature and characteristics of these segments.

Figure 14–3   Advertising directed to the "macho" male. *(Courtesy of R. J. Reynolds Tobacco Company.)*

Managerial Implications

An excellent example of an industry heavily influenced by demographic and subcultural trends over the past twenty years is the toy industry. During the 1960s the toy industry flourished. Members of the baby-boom generation were in their childhood. With their numbers expanding, the total market for toys grew rapidly. The growth of the industry slowed in the 1970s; although, with the shrinking number of children born, sales were surprisingly strong. The reason was that the divorce rate increased and households became smaller. With each adult obligated to supply toys to the few children being born during the baby-bust years, sales of toys stayed strong. When births began to rise in the early 1980s, as the baby boomers began to have children, toy manufacturers again got on the fast track. Companies like Toys Я Us did extremely well.

An important principle to note is that toys are for all ages. A ten-year-old may want a motorcross bike. A forty-year-old's toy could be a sports car. An executive for Milton Bradley—a leading toy manufacturer—noted that more elderly are good for his company. Why? Older people enjoy puzzles, and this age group is growing.[38]

An executive at Coleco, another major toy manufacturer, stated that demographics are used in his company to develop profiles of customers for new product development, for research, and for media planning. The idea is "to know who we are selling to and how to reach them."[39] In other words, the executive was stating that identifying the demographic and subcultural characteristics of populations is useful in following the marketing concept. The marketing mix is designed in part around the needs, wants, and lifestyles that flow from consumers belonging to a particular subculture or demographic group.

Understanding the subcultural and demographic characteristics of groups of people is important in developing the marketing mix. Just as important, however, is the idea that trends can be analyzed in order to identify new product opportunities. By finding subcultures that are expanding in numbers, the marketer may be able to enter a market early and beat the competition. Thus, the expanding numbers of elderly consumers are becoming an important target group for insurance companies, drug manufacturers, and others.

In addition to helping companies identify new marketing opportunities, tracking trends in subcultures also can forestall marketing calamities. For example, as the baby-boom generation has aged, companies failing to change their product lines to match the changing tastes of the group have faltered. Ten years ago the baby-boom group was in large part teenagers. The study of the teenage subculture was extremely important in the mid-1970s. During that time the teenage market was growing three times faster than the general population. Because teenagers are heavy buyers of records and tapes, the industry did well during the early 1970s. In the 1980s, however, record sales have fallen, and the industry is hurting in large part because of the shrinking number of teenagers in the population. Record manufacturers are adapting by turning to video versions of hit songs as a means of increasing interest in records by teenagers and young adults. In fact, in 1983 a cable television channel began playing only video segments.

Different subcultural and demographic groups may have great importance to specific industries. For example, women are extremely important to department stores. These retailers have had to adapt their strategies in response to the changes that have occurred in women's lifestyles. For example, the increase in the number of working women has led department stores to expand their hours into the evening.

In one study the researchers asked whether retailers should adapt their policies concerning the hiring and training of salesclerks because of the changing perceptions, values, and needs of women?[40] Focusing on the different needs of feminists versus moderate and traditional women, the researchers found some important differences. In particular, feminists expected more from retail salesclerks.. The feminists expected the salesclerk to be more professional and to have high standards of appearance, courtesy, and product knowledge. The feminists wanted to be treated in a friendly, but not familiar, manner. From a managerial perspective the results were clear. If feminists make up a substantial portion of a department store's clientele, salesclerks must be trained to meet their higher expectations. Training should focus more on product knowledge than the "closing techniques" commonly emphasized.

In summary, the different subcultures in the United States offer a number of opportunities for marketers. First, the subcultures may be targeted as market segments. In particular, new products may be designed for the needs of specific groups, such as medical insurance to supplement medicare assistance for the elderly. Promotion is also affected by the divergent lifestyles and preferences of subcultures. For example, how a woman is portrayed in an advertisement has profound meaning to a feminist.

In addition to being important for segmenting the market, studying the changing demographic characteristics of subcultures can assist marketers in locating marketing opportunities. Product opportunities can be found in identifying subcultures that are growing rapidly. For example, Chapter 15 focuses on the fastest-growing subculture in the United States—Hispanics. Conversely, marketing debacles can be avoided by leaving markets that are shrinking. The corporate reorganization by Levi Strauss resulting from the decrease in the number of teenagers in the early 1980s exemplifies such a corporate reaction.

SUMMARY

A subculture is a group of people who represent a subdivision of a national culture. One or more unifying features distinguish the group, whose members share patterns of behavior distinct from that found in the national culture. Demographic characteristics are often used to identify subcultures, such as ethnicity, nationality, and religion.

In Chapter 14 two subcultures were selected for attention—age and sex. Age groupings having particular importance for marketers in the late 1980s and 1990s are the baby-boom generation and the elderly. Although not a subculture in the strict sense of the word, the baby-boom generation does have extreme importance to marketers because of its size and buying power. With the baby-boom generation now in their thirties and forties, their influence is increasing rapidly as they move toward their peak earning years. Their taste for products is also maturing. When combined with their high education levels, these factors indicate the importance of marketers to focus on providing high-value products.

The elderly represent a legitimate subculture because of their distinct lifestyles and buying patterns. Of particular interest to marketers are decrements in the perceptual and motor skills of the elderly. Many elderly begin to have deterioration in their ability to see and hear. These problems have implications for advertising and packaging products. In addition, many elderly suffer from some form of arthritis. This can cause problems in opening bottles that have child-proof lids. The unique needs of the elderly influence their buying patterns. For example, as people age their appetites tend to decrease. This results in the need for smaller package sizes. But the vast majority of the elderly do not consider themselves to be old. When asked how old they feel, most respond with an age substantially lower than their chronological age.

Women and men also form distinct subcultures. However, more work has been done on identifying segments of women than of men. A common approach to segmenting women is to base the divisions in some way on whether the woman is working, plans to work, or is not working and has no plans to go into the work force. Another approach involves segmenting women on their views regarding feminism. Researchers have paid less attention to segmenting the male market. In one approach men were divided into three segments—old-fashioned men, lip-service liberals, and expressives. However, it may be that men are most effectively segmented based on such demographic characteristics as income, occupation, and education.

From a managerial perspective the study of subcultures and their demographic components have importance for both marketing opportunity analysis and developing the marketing mix. With changes in the numbers of people making up a subculture, marketing opportunities may emerge. In addition, the particular lifestyle and buying habits of a group of consumers may also have implications for the development of the marketing mix. For example, because many elderly people live on a relatively low, fixed income, they are highly responsive to retailers who give them price breaks. A common pricing tactic among drugstores is to give those people over sixty-five years of age a 10 percent discount on drugs purchased.

Key Terms

Subculture
Nationality
Race
Baby-boom generation
Fertility rate
Baby bust

Mortality rate
Immigration
Mature consumer
Feel-age
Look-age
Do-age

Role conflict
Feminist women
Moderate women
Traditionalist women
Female marketing segments:
  Career
  Just-a-job

Stay-at-home
Plan-to-work
Decorative roles
Expressive men
Lip-service liberals
Old-fashioned men
Adult toys

Review Questions

1. Identify the various segments of elderly consumers that have been discussed.
2. What are five major demographic changes that have occurred to women over the past fifty years?
3. Define the concept of subculture. How do subcultures differ from the demographic variables that are frequently used to label them?
4. Describe the age distribution of the baby-boom group of consumers. Describe the impact of the aging of the baby-boom group on two industries.
5. Table 14–1 presents projected U.S. population trends between 1990 and 2000. Based upon the table, identify the age groups that will increase in size between 1990 and 2000 and those that will decrease in size during the time period.
6. What are the various factors that influence accuracy of age projections of the population?
7. Identify three ways in which the elderly process information differently from the rest of the adult population.
8. In what ways do the consumption patterns of the elderly differ from the rest of the adult population?
9. Discuss how the demographic profiles differ among the traditional, moderate, and feminist segments of female consumers.
10. The portrayal of men and women in advertising has changed over the past thirty years. Based upon Table 14–5, identify how the portrayal of the occupations of men and women in print advertisements changed between 1958 and 1978.
11. Considering the use of women as ''decoration'' in print advertisements, how did this change between 1958 and 1978?
12. Identify three segments of male consumers. How is each of these segments described?

Discussion Questions

1. Subcultures can be found in most large collections of people. Consider the university or college you are now attending. Identify as many subcultures as you can within your school. Describe the norms, values, and behaviors of the subcultures that set them apart.
2. Because of the long lead times required for planning and bringing new products to market, managers must often look five to ten years into the fu-

ture. What marketing opportunities and problems might the baby-boom group present to managers between the years 1995 and 2000? Specifically, consider implications for brokerage firms and the producers of diapers.
3. Suppose that you were the director of marketing for an investment group that decided to develop a shopping center specifically targeted to the elderly market. What types of services, stores, and amenities would you attempt to put in the shopping center to be successful? What problems might be encountered in targeting a shopping center specifically for the elderly?
4. What types of changes would you recommend to the medical community to serve the elderly group more effectively? (Medical community here refers to hospitals, medical offices, and drug companies.)
5. Identify the various types of role conflict that career women may experience. Do these conflicts present any marketing opportunities?
6. Identify the various types of role conflict that career men may experience. Do these conflicts present any marketing opportunities?
7. Go through the print advertisements found in two recent magazines. Categorize the occupations in which women are shown in the ads. How do these compare to those depicted in Figure 14–6 of the text?
8. Take the same two magazines as used in question 7 and categorize the occupations in which men were depicted. To what extent do the occupations shown accurately represent the distribution of occupations found in the United States today?
9. Consider the male students on the campus at your university or college. To what extent can segments of ''old-fashioned men,'' ''lip-service liberals,'' and ''expressive men'' be found? Are there other segments of men that should be included?

References

1. D. O. Arnold, *The Sociology of Subcultures*, Berkeley, Calif.: Glendasary Press, 1970.
2. R. T. Reynolds, B. Robey, and C. Russell, ''Demographics of the 1980s,'' *American Demographics*, 2, January 1980, 11–19.
3. ''Americans Change,'' *Business Week*, February 20, 1978, 64–80.
4. ''Americans Change.''
5. Daniel Machalaba, ''More Magazines Aim for Afflu-

ent Readers," *The Wall Street Journal*, October 14, 1982, 31, 39.

6. Bureau of Labor Statistics, *Survey of Consumer Expenditures*, 1973.

7. Landon Jones, "The Baby-Boom Consumer," *American Demographics*, 3, February 1981, 28–35.

8. Jones, "The Baby-Boom Consumer."

9. Gregory Spencer and John Long, "The Census Bureau Projections," *American Demographics*, 5, April 1983, 24–31.

10. Reynolds, et. al., "Demographics of the 1980s."

11. Bryant Robey, "Age in America," *American Demographics*, 3, July/August 1981, 14–19.

12. Reynolds et al., "Demographics of the 1980s."

13. J. B. Mason and W. O. Bearden, "Satisfaction/ Dissatisfaction with Food Shopping Among Elderly Consumers," *The Journal of Consumer Affairs*, 13, 1979, 359–369.

14. Ivan Ross, "Information Processing and the Older Consumer: Marketing and Public Policy Implications," in *Advances in Consumer Research, IX*, Andrew Mitchell (ed), Ann Arbor, Mich: Association for Consumer Research, 1981, 31–39.

15. L. W. Phillips and B. Sternthal, "Age Differences in Information Processing: A Perspective on the Aged Consumer," *Journal of Marketing Research*, 14, November 1977, 444–457.

16. Ganesan Visvabharathy and David Rink, "Selected Policy Issues Regarding the Elderly," *American Marketing Association Proceedings*, Chicago, Ill.: American Marketing Association, 1983, 396–398.

17. Cheryl Russell, "Who's Having Those Babies," *American Demographics*, 4, January 1982, 36–47.

18. Eugene Carlson, "Parking Violations . . . Changes in Population . . . State Worries," *The Wall Street Journal*, June 14, 1983, 31.

19. Benny Barak and Leon Schiffman, "Cognitive Age: A Nonchronological Age Variable," in *Advances in Consumer Research, VIII*, Kent B. Monroe (ed.), Ann Arbor, Mich.: Association for Consumer Research, 1981, 604.

20. Lois Underhill and Franchellie Cadwell, "What Age Do You Feel?" *The Journal of Consumer Marketing*, 1, Summer 1983, 18–27.

21. Jack Botwinick, *Aging and Behavior: A Comprehensive Integration of Research Findings*, 2d ed., New York: N.Y.: Springer Publishing Co., 1978.

22. L. G. Schiffman, "Perceived Risk in New Product Trial by Elderly Consumers," *Journal of Marketing Research*, 9, February 1972, 106–108.

23. J. G. Towle and C. R. Martin, "The Elderly Consumer: One Segment or Many?" in *The Elderly Consumer*, F. E. Waddell (ed.), Columbia, Md.: Antioch College, 232–242.

24. James Merrill and William Weeks, "Predicting and Identifying Benefit Segments in the Elderly Market," in *American Marketing Association National Educator's Proceedings*, Chicago, Ill.: American Marketing Association, 1983, 399–403.

25. "The Power of the Aging in the Marketplace," *Business Week*, November 20, 1971, 52–58.

26. Aimee Stern, "Ageless Ad Appeal," *Marketing Communications*, May 1983, 21–26.

27. Judith Bardwick and Elizabeth Donvan, "Ambivalence: The Socialization of Women," in *Women in Sexist Society*, V. Gornick and B. Moran (eds.), New York: N.Y.: Basic Books, 1971, 145–149.

28. "Women Aren't the Only Ones Changing: Marketers Should Take Note of Men, Too," *Marketing News*, July 22, 1983, 13.

29. Rena Bartos, "What Every Marketer Should Know About Women," *Harvard Business Review*, May–June 1978, 73.

30. Dorris Walsh, "About Those New Women," *American Demographics*, 4, October 1982, 26–29.

31. Allaadi Venkatesh, "Changing Roles of Women—A Life-Style Analysis," *Journal of Consumer Research*, 7, September 1980, 189–197.

32. Venkatesh, "Changing Roles of Women."

33. Charles Schaninger and Chris Allen, "Wife's Occupational Status as a Consumer Behavior Construct," *Journal of Consumer Research*, 8, September 1981, 189–196.

34. Walsh, "About Those New Women."

35. Marc Weinberger, Susan M. Petroshius, and Stuart Westin, "Twenty Years of Women in Magazine Advertising: An Update," in *1979 Educators' Conference Proceedings*, Neil Beckwith, et al. (eds.), Chicago, Ill.: American Marketing Association, Series 44, 1979, 373–377.

36. "Women Aren't the Only Ones Changing."

37. Ibid.

38. David Finlay, "Demographics for Fun and Games," *American Demographics*, 3, November 1981, 38–39.

39. Finlay, "Demographics for Fun."

40. John Burnett, Robert B. Amason, and Shelby Hunt, "Feminism: Implications for Department Store Strategy and Salesclerk Behavior," *Journal of Retailing*, 57, Winter 1981, 71–85.

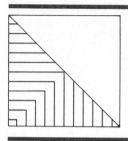

15
Religious, Black, Hispanic, and Geographic Subcultures

Subcultural Food Preferences

One way to identify a subculture is through the group's food preferences. Nowhere is this better exemplified than for Jews, for whom the preparation of food is a part of their religion. For many Jews food must be prepared in accordance with dietary laws to make them kosher. Symbolized by a *U* surrounded by a circle or by the letter *K* on the package, kosher foods are prepared under stringently supervised conditions.

The connotation of wholesomeness associated with kosher foods has broadened their appeal of people concerned about health. For example, 80 percent of Manischewitz wine is sold to non-Jews, in part because it is marked "kosher."

Subcultures can also be regionally based, and not surprisingly food preferences differ across regions. People in the Northeast like their coffee stronger, prefer rolls and rye bread for their sandwiches, and have a taste for hard candies. On the West Coast people are into health foods, dieting, and dry salad dressings.

One market researcher summarized the food preferences of regions, as follows:

Westerners adopt new food preferences quickly.
The East is more ethnically oriented.
Southerners stick to national brands.
The Midwest is still "meat and potatoes." (a)

The mass media of the United States have accelerated the spread of regional foods. Currently, the Mexican food craze is galloping across the country. One reason is that the spicy food increases the intake of liquids. Restau-

457

rants find this fact beneficial because profits on alcoholic beverages are higher than the profits on food. In fact, the Mexican food craze has even spread to Barrow, Alaska—a village above the arctic circle where in the winter the night lasts for three months. The restaurant Pepe's North of the Border thrives because of the popularity of its tacos, cooked by imported Mexican chefs, among its Eskimo customers, who love hot sauce. (b)

Perhaps the best example of regional differences in food preferences was stated by a young woman living in Santa Cruz, California. She said, "In Santa Cruz, it's a more serious crime to eat red meat than to use drugs." Her attitude differs substantially from those in the Midwest, where eating lean red meat is still popular and where using drugs is viewed negatively.

Based on (a) "Grocery Marketing," *Advertising Age,* Special Supplement, October 11, 1982, M9–11, 14, 15; and (b) Ken Wells, "Hot Stuff in the Arctic," *The Wall Street Journal,* February 7, 1984, 1.

INTRODUCTION

Chapter 15 continues the discussion of subcultural and demographic factors important to marketers, and focuses on four distinct topic areas—religion, race, nationality, and region. Within each demographic dimension subcultures may form. For example, various religious subcultures exist within the United States. The Christian religion forms the majority subculture, but even within it a number of deep divisions exist—particularly between its conservative and moderate wings. In addition to the Christian subcultures, a number of other smaller religious groups exist that share similar lifestyle, attitudinal, and consumption patterns. These include Jews, Moslems, and some Far Eastern groups.

Race and nationality are also important demographic dimensions that may be used to describe subcultures. For example, researchers may speak of a black subculture. In so doing they are using a racial classification to describe a group of people who share similar values. (The black subculture will be described in some detail in this chapter.) On the other hand; researchers may refer to the Chinese, Japanese, and Korean subcultures. In this case they are using nationality as a method of describing the subculture, because each group shares the same racial background. (All are said to be Mongoloid as opposed to Negroid or Caucasoid.)

Another term sometimes used to describe subcultures is ethnicity. While the term, ethnicity, is used in a variety of ways, it generally refers to a group bound together by ties of cultural homogeneity. Thus, the group is linked by similar values, customs, dress, religion, and language. Ethnicity is frequently closely linked to nationality. Thus, one may speak of Mexican-Americans as an ethnic group, because they share a common national ancestry along with a similar culture. However, in countries with a heterogeneous culture one may find many ethnic groups, such as in the United States and the Soviet

Union. Because of the growing importance of Hispanics in the United States, the chapter will discuss this subcultural group in some detail.

The various regions of a country may also form the basis around which subcultures may form. The United States is sufficiently large and climatically diverse that a number of differences can be found in the behavioral characteristics and values of people in its various regions. In part, these differences result from the effects of different ethnic, nationality and racial groups congregating in specific regions. Thus, the Southwestern portion of the United States has a strong Hispanic influence with distinct food preferences and lifestyles based in part on the large numbers of Mexican-Americans in the region and in part on the climate peculiar to the area. Regions are the fourth major subcultural classification which will be discussed in the chapter. Highlight 15–1 describes how the populations of various regions differ in preference for one consumer product—pickup trucks.

RELIGIOUS SUBCULTURES

Religion is an important basis around which subcultures may form. A religion's set of beliefs, symbols, norms, and teachings can dramatically influence its members' lifestyles. In the United States the major religions are the Christian and Jewish faiths. Through the 1970s religious affiliation in the United States generally declined. However, the decline seems to have ended by 1980. One reason for the bottoming out of the decline is the aging of the baby-boom generation. People are least likely to belong to a church when they are in the teens and twenties. With the baby-boom generation moving into their thirties, interest in religion is expected to increase.[1]

HIGHLIGHT 15–1

Pickup Truck Popularity Varies by Region

What is the most popular motor vehicle in the Southeast, the Upper Midwest, and the South Central regions of the U.S.? In two of the three instances, the motor vehicle of choice is a truck.

In the states bordering Montana the most popular vehicle on the road is the Ford F150—a half-ton pickup. In the states surrounding Louisiana, the winner is the Chevrolet C10—another half-ton pickup. In the Southeast and states bordering the Great Lakes the Oldsmobile Cutlass is the most frequently purchased car.

Why do these regional differences occur? No one really knows, but some guesses are:

□ In the Southeast the conservative Cutlass image fits the population's lifestyle.

□ In the Upper Midwest the Ford pickups have long represented "brawn" and have appealed to the rugged lifestyle of the region.

□ In Texas and Louisiana people wanted fancy pickups, and Chevy beat the market in offering frills on gussied-up pickups, called "cowboy Cadillacs."

Based on Eugene Carlson, "Personality of Area's Drivers Offers Key to Auto's Success," *The Wall Street Journal*, December 13, 1983, 29.

The Christian population of the United States has been divided into five market segments:

1. *Nominal Christians.* Christians who rarely participate in religious study.
2. *The churched.* Those who express their faith through regular attendance at church.
3. *The Jesus-committed.* Those who are more involved with their church and often contribute to parachurch ministries, such as Billy Graham's crusades.
4. *Born-again Christians.* These individuals view Jesus as their personal savior and regularly read the Bible and Christian literature.
5. *Born-again Evangelicals.* These Christians believe in the "inerrancy" of the bible and in converting the "unsaved."[2]

Most Catholics and Protestants may be placed in the first three categories. Fundamentalist Christians make up the final two categories. In this section of the chapter, we focus on the two religious subcultures that appear to be the most cohesive—the Fundamentalist Christian and the Jewish subcultures. In each group religious beliefs have a major impact on the way the members live and consume products and services.

The Fundamentalist Christian Subculture

Born-again Christians and Born-again **Evangelicals** make up a sizable proportion of the total Christian population in the United States. For example, Born-again Evangelicals appear to represent almost 20 percent of all Americans. They tend to be older, more often female and nonwhite. In addition, they are more often Protestant, less well-to-do, and less well educated than other categories of Christians.[3]

However, Born-again Christians and Evangelicals are the fastest growing segments of the overall Christian subculture. During the 1970s, middle-of-the-road Protestant groups, such as Methodists, lost membership. Some have argued that the decline resulted from their membership being more likely to marry out of the church. More conservative denominations, like the Southern Baptists, grew during the same time period.[4]

The Fundamentalist Christian groups have market power. The Christian publishing business is a $400 million-a-year industry. Thomas Nelson, Inc., the world's largest producer of Bibles, has been a hot growth stock valued for its consistently increasing earnings. Twenty million dollars a year are spent on Christian periodicals.[5]

In addition, conservative Christian groups have learned to use the media. Six hundred seventy radio stations each devote at least fifteen hours a week to religious programming. They also own forty television stations and two cable networks. In 1982 "televangelists," such as Jerry Falwell, raised over $500 million from their followers.[6]

Fundamentalist Christian groups have also discovered marketing. For example, they have begun to hire and use advertising agencies in order to promote their message more adroitly. In addition, they have a commitment to research. The Southern Baptist Convention was instrumental in forming the Census Access for Planning the Church (CAPC). The objective of the organization is to analyze demographic trends in order to identify where to position new churches and where to move old churches. One evangelical group has advocated the idea that to maximize growth a church should mirror in its membership the demographic patterns of the surrounding community.[7]

Religion has been used as a segmentation variable. One discount furniture store owner selects cities to locate his outlets based on the population's religious preferences. The owner targeted his "middle-class taste range" furniture to middle-of-the-road Fundamentalist Protestants.

According to the authors of an article on the furniture store, the midrange fundamentalists view the Bible as God's word, but they do not believe in direct divine revelation as do more conservative fundamentalists. The more liberal groups view the Bible as allegorical and not as a static religious standard.

The executive running the furniture store believed that the middle-of-the-road Protestants were attracted to his line of furniture. A study was conducted to test the executive's "seat-of-the-pants" ideas. The results revealed that slightly more sales than expected by chance were going to the targeted group of middle-range fundamentalists, supporting the executive's contentions.[8]

In summary, Fundamentalist Christian groups are both the users of marketing principles and the targets of marketers. They are increasingly attempting to spread their spiritual beliefs and are doing it with electronic sophistication. Similarly, marketers are recognizing that this segment can be profitable. Book publishers, music producers, and furniture and apparel manufacturers are targeting the group. In fact, Christian symbols are being used as logos on clothing in some areas. People are exchanging their alligators and ponies for fish, crosses, and doves.

The Jewish Subculture

Another subculture based in part on religion is Judaism. According to 1980 census data, Jews make up approximately 2.8 percent of the United States population. They are concentrated in New York City, where about 15 percent of the total U.S. population of Jews live.[9]

As noted in the introductory vignette, food preparation is a particularly important part of the Jewish subculture. Keeping the home **kosher** is a major preoccupation within many Jewish households and represents a marketing opportunity for companies.

When an individual is born a Jew, he or she inherits both a religion and an ethnic origin. The combination of religious and ethnic identification has a strong impact and tends to solidify the subculture, making it more cohesive than many others. Because of informal social interactions, religious training, ethnic heritage, and a long and troubled history, the pressure to conform to Jewish beliefs, symbols, and rituals is high.

The impact of being Jewish on the peoples' consumption behavior may be found in advertising targeted to Jews. Izmira vodka once had a headline which stated, "Finally, you can serve the finest imported vodka without buying Russian." Izmira vodka is manufactured in Turkey, and the distributor sought to turn this fact into an advantage by subtly alluding to the oppression historically experienced by Russian Jews.

One indicator of a cohesive subculture is that its members prefer to affiliate with each other rather than with members of other subcultures. This tendency exists for Jews not only in the business sphere but also in where they vacation. American airlines realized that their Jewish clientele was flocking to Florida rather than the Caribbean. A consulting firm was asked to develop a booklet on Jewish history in the Caribbean, and it quickly sold out. Sanka coffee once put on a sweepstakes in which the top prize was a Pan Am flight to Israel.[10]

Jews are a highly valued market segment in part because of their impressive buying power. They tend to have a high socioeconomic status and consequently possess above-average incomes. Various authors have suggested that such economic success derives from their belief in individual responsibility, in self-education, and in maximally stimulating children. In one study it was found that self-ratings of Jewish ethnicity correlated with childhood information exposure, with adult information seeking, and with consumption innovativeness. Thus, when compared to non-Jews of similar economic status, the Jewish respondents revealed a tendency to seek information prior to buying and to be early adopters.[11] For marketers of new products, the Jewish segment is a particularly important target.

THE BLACK SUBCULTURE

In the last section it was noted that the Jewish subculture is based in part on religious identification and in part on racial heritage. The **black subculture** is a relatively pure example of racial heritage forming the basis around which a subculture is based. Even though the black consumer is relatively easily recognized because of skin color, the subculture is not homogeneous. It has been argued that four **black segments** exist—Negroes, blacks, Afro-Americans, and recent foreign black immigrants.[12] Others have identified three segments—the affluent, mature shoppers; the less affluents; and black youth.[13] In another instance, a black-owned company, Johnson Products, marketed their products to two segments of blacks. The strivers segment seeks to achieve middle-class status. In contrast, the nonstrivers do not have such aspirations and instead seek a separate, "black" identity.[14] Thus, while the following discussion of **black culture** will speak of it as though it were homogeneous, it does reveal distinct segments.

Characteristics of the Black Subculture

A number of factors shape the black subculture, which represents 12 percent of the U.S. population. One major contributor is income deprivation. About 34 percent of all black families have incomes below the poverty level.[15] Other factors influencing the subculture are educational deprivation, a young, highly

Table 15–1   Factors in Blacks' Importance as a Market Segment

1. *Spending power:* $140 billion annually
2. *Increasing size of group:* Population increased 17.3% in 1970s to 6% for whites
3. *Rising socioeconomic status:*
    1970–1980—Black college enrollment increased 93%
    1960–1980—Percentage in white-collar jobs increased 22.6%
4. *Youth:* Median age of 24.9 as compared to 31.3 for whites
5. *Geographically concentrated:* 65% of blacks live in the top 15 U.S. markets
6. *Use certain products heavily:* For example, blacks consume 36% of the hair-condition-ing products and 23% of the chewing gum

Source: Data adapted from David Astor, "Black Spending Power: $140 Billion and Growing," *Marketing Communications*, July 1982, 13–16, 18.

mobile family structure headed by a high proportion of females, and a con-centration of their population in central cities. Discrimination has also had a pervasive impact on the ability to obtain jobs, obtain an education, and move into the neighborhoods of choice. Despite these historical disadvantages, the black subculture is a market segment that is growing in importance. As shown in Table 15–1, it has impressive buying power, it is increasing in size faster than the general population, and it's rising in socioeconomic status.

The black subculture is also marked by the importance of religious and social organizations. Blacks disproportionately belong to Fundamentalist Protestant groups and to political parties—particularly the Democratic party. In order to reach blacks some companies have recognized the need to spon-sor activities for black groups and organizations. In one case Quaker Oats sponsored "The Quaker Gospel Salute." Consumers were asked to send a proof of purchase from the Quaker products they bought along with the name of their favorite gospel choir. For each proof received, Quaker sent ten cents to the church or nonprofit organization of the sender's choice. The four choirs receiving the most recommendations were given a $1,000 contribution from Quaker.[16] A broader consideration of reasons for the importance of blacks as a market segment appears in Table 15–1.

Do You Market Directly to Blacks?

One of the major questions in marketing to blacks is whether companies should market directly to the black subculture or to categories of people who are similar on other demographic characteristics such as income, education, and occupation. In one article discussing this problem an executive stated, "Most of the marketing community remains unconvinced that it makes sense to implement special marketing efforts aimed at blacks."[17] Another executive stated, "We ought to look at people as people . . . things like social class, income, and other similar things play a greater role in forming the person and his attitudes."[18] One study found that the value differences between blacks and whites were accounted for by socioeconomic differences.[19] Some adver-tisers found that education and income differentiated blacks and whites more than did race among middle-class respondents.[20] Another study found that lower-income and higher-income blacks revealed media exposure patterns similar to those of whites with the same income levels.[21] Thus, the same media can generally be used to reach blacks and whites of similar income levels. Based on these ideas, advertisers should not be concerned about using ethnicity as a segmentation variable.

Others, however, believe that under certain conditions appeals should be directed specifically to blacks through black media. In cases where blacks have product needs or preferences that diverge from white preferences or needs, an advertiser can get more for his money by directly targeting blacks. For example, one marketing researcher argued that Procter and Gamble's product Wondra would have done much better had it been targeted directly to blacks. According to the executive, blacks are heavy users of hand and body lotions and would have responded to advertising directed specifically to their needs. However, because Procter and Gamble markets strictly by demographics, the potential advantage was lost.[22]

After interviewing 612 blacks in Atlanta, one researcher concluded that firms that cater primarily to blacks can be more effective by advertising in black publications.[23] It is possible for mass-marketing companies to target blacks directly by using black media. By using magazines such as *Jet* and *Ebony* and radio stations whose audience is predominantly black, a company can utilize themes and symbols that appeal predominantly to the black subculture without fear of "turning off" its white market. Pepsi-Cola has followed this approach. The company has placed advertisements in black media and used the theme "Now It's Pepsi—For Those Who Think Young." The idea has been to appeal to the fact that on average the black population is several years younger than the white population. In addition, Pepsi representatives attend over thirty black national conventions a year and help sponsor numerous black sporting events.[24]

Advertisers have increasingly begun to use blacks to endorse products. Well-known public figures such as Bill Cosby, O. J. Simpson, and Reggie Jackson have crossed the "color barrier" and appeal effectively to all racial groups. Indeed, Bill Cosby has ranked among the most popular and believable spokespersons for years.

That blacks are not targeted more often is surprising when one realizes that in 1982 they had $140 billion worth of buying power. Yet, national advertisers spent less than 1 percent of their budgets trying to reach blacks through black-owned media. Black media draw a large proportion of the 37 percent of blacks with white-collar jobs and the 17 percent of black households with incomes over $25,000.[25] Advertising and promotional strategies that have affected the sales of beauty products for blacks are explored in Highlight 15–2.

Black Consumption Patterns

One of the problems with making generalizations about how the consumption patterns of blacks and whites differ is that much of the published research on black buying habits occurred in the 1960s and early 1970s. To the extent that blacks have progressed economically and to the extent that dis-

HIGHLIGHT 15–2

The Beauty Market and the Black Consumer

In 1982 the market for black beauty products was $1.5 billion. Further, it was growing rapidly at a 25 percent-a-year clip. The problem was that retailers were not giving the beauty products adequate shelf space, proper displays, and enough in-store promotions according to executives of some companies offering the beauty products for blacks.

One product, Black Tie fragrance, was a cologne targeted to the general public by a black-owned firm. Whenever it was given the shelf space, it did fine. The problem was that retailers tended to put it at the ethnic cosmetics counter, where few Anglos would go to buy something.

Another problem was that black-owned compa-

nies were not adept at using specialized marketing techniques, such as couponing and giving out samples on a massive scale. It took companies a while to recognize that the way to reach blacks with such promotional techniques was at group events, such as concerts and churches.

But, as noted by one black executive, a new generation of experienced managers is entering black companies. According to the executive,

All that needs to be done now is to modify general marketing techniques to suit the black market.

Based on an article by Andjela Kessler, "Marketing to Blacks Seek More Visibility," *ADWEEK*, September 20, 1982, 56.

crimination has diminished, the findings of the past may not be relevant to the black consumer of the late 1980s.

The overall findings of the research indicate that among middle-income groups the differences between black and white consumers are minor. It is within the lower-income groups that the differences stand out. Perhaps the major differences occur in the area of recreation. Whites engage in more of the following leisure activities than blacks: jogging, boating, golfing, camping and eating out. Conversely, blacks do more disco dancing, use city parks more, buy more records, and more often do artwork and crafts.[26] Music is important in the black subculture, and advertisers often cast their products in "musical" settings. Figure 15–1 shows an advertisement by Gordon's gin. The company is attempting to connect the product to something viewed positively by both blacks and whites, music and romance.

Another major area of black-white consumption differences is in food preferences. For example, 81 percent of the black families in one study were found to purchase cornmeal versus only 14 percent of white families.[27] One black-owned company has tried to utilize these differences in food preferences to develop a line of food items targeted directly to blacks. Called Soul Chef, the brand consists of frozen soul-food dinners, like stewed pork chitterlings and assorted canned vegetables, such as black-eyed peas, collard greens, mustard greens, and turnip greens. The owners of the company, two black persons with MBAs from the University of Chicago, avoided traditional media vehicles and used product sampling almost entirely during their first year of operation. Tapping into the social networks of blacks, the entrepre-

Figure 15–1 **An appeal to the black market segment.** *(Courtesy of Renfield Imports, Ltd.)*

neurs generated awareness by giving away the product at church groups, senior citizen homes, and community groups. The major problem faced by the company was distribution. It was difficult to persuade the headquarters of grocery chains to stock the products outside of black areas.[28]

THE HISPANIC SUBCULTURE

Hispanics are the fastest growing major subculture and demographic group in the United States. A combination of high fertility rates, high immigration rates, the close proximity of Puerto Rico, from which Hispanics can legally enter the United States, and continued problems of illegal immigration lead to a rapidly expanding population. Some researchers have forecast the possibility that Hispanics will become the largest minority in the United States sometime during the 1990s.[29] Their rapidly expanding population has made Hispanics a target for many consumer goods firms. For example, in 1983 Procter and Gamble began to roll out on a national basis their Citrus Hill brand orange juice. Figure 15–2 shows a coupon sent to Hispanics urging them to try the brand. To encourage the potential customers, P&G included a coupon for a free carton of orange juice.

The Hispanic subculture is based upon a number of factors that bind the group together. A common language unites most Hispanics. In fact, only 1 percent of Hispanics do not speak Spanish at all.[30] A common religion, Catholicism, also imparts a sense of commonality to Hispanics. (Over 85 percent of Hispanics are Catholic.) Hispanics also tend to live in urban areas. Eighty percent live in metropolitan areas as compared to 75 percent of the black population.[31]

The Hispanic subculture is also marked by a constant influx of new members through legal and illegal immigration. An analogy of a recycling water fountain has sometimes been used to describe the inflow and outflow of Latinos. A circular pattern exists such that Latinos enter the U.S., stay for a length of time, and then leave. It has been estimated that 30 percent of Mexican immigrants eventually return to Mexico, and it has been suggested that this is the reason why American products sell so well in our southern neighbor nation.[32]

The fact that many Hispanics come to the United States with plans to return to their homeland helps to explain why the group has been slowly assimilated into the American culture. Although Hispanics have had greater success moving into the neighborhood of their choice than blacks, the group has not had the same success as have other Caucasian minorities such as the Irish or Italians. A second potential reason for the lack of assimilation of Hispanics is that many came after the race riots and the civil rights movement of the 1960s. Since that time, cultural diversity has become more acceptable, and many Hispanics simply have chosen to retain their language and traditional cultural ways.[33]

Concerning their value structure, Hispanics reveal a highly conservative pattern. They are more likely than Anglos to express traditional American values concerning the importance of hard work; they are optimistic regarding their future standard of living; they are materialistic and seek the "good life."[34] Hispanics tend to be more family oriented than Anglos, to live more for the present, and to be somewhat less competitive.[35] Hispanics also tend to be cautious in their buying behavior while simultaneously revealing a tendency to be ecologically minded.[36]

Hispanic Segmentation

An important aspect of the study of Hispanics is that they are not one homogeneous group. Actually, four distinct groups, or **Hispanic segments,** exist—Mexican-Americans, Cubans, Puerto Ricans, and Hispanos. Among these groups Spanish is spoken differently, differences in food preferences exist,

Figure 15–2 **Procter & Gamble targets the Hispanic segment with direct-mail coupons.** *(Courtesy of The Procter & Gamble Company.)*

and differences in political attitudes are present. Perhaps most importantly these groups live in different areas of the country.[37]

Mexican-Americans make up the largest of the four groups, comprising some 8.7 million people in the 1980 census, or 60 percent of the total Hispanic market. Puerto Ricans make up 14 percent of the group and Cubans some 5 percent. Other Hispanics account for the remaining 21 percent of the Hispanic population. Among this group are the Hispanos. This group is composed of people who have long lived in the United States. Hispanos are centered in New Mexico and consider themselves original Americans because their ancestors arrived hundreds of years ago with the Spanish conquistadores.[38]

Each of the Hispanic groups can be reached easily because of their geographic concentration. Los Angeles, where 2.1 million Hispanics live, is considered to be the prime target area for reaching Mexican-Americans. Similarly, Miami contains the largest concentration of Cubans and New York City the greatest number of Puerto Ricans. Among the Hispanic groups, the Cubans have the highest incomes (average annual family income is $21,300), whereas Puerto Ricans have the lowest (average annual family income is $11,400).[39]

In addition to being segmented along lines of national origin, one author suggested that Hispanics can be segmented in terms of how long they have lived in the United States.[40] In the study, Hispanic males in Los Angeles were interviewed, and four **Hispanic strata** were identified. The strata were developed to describe the Mexican-American population in the United States. They were:

1. Recent immigrants and illegal aliens. They are the least acculturated and the poorest, and they speak Spanish exclusively. They comprise 60–65 percent of Mexican-Americans.
2. Radical Chicanos. These individuals are native-born Americans but retain close Mexican ties. They are highly political and feel deprived and discriminated against. They speak English but use occasional Spanish phrases. They comprise 20–25 percent of the population.
3. Conservative Chicanos. Making up 10–15 percent of the Mexican-American population, these individuals are beginning to lose their Mexican ties and identify with the American culture.
4. New Rich. Representing only 5 percent of the Hispanic population, these Mexican-Americans have been acculturated and have achieved middle- and upper-middle-class status.

Hispanic Buying Patterns

The consumption patterns of Hispanics do differ somewhat from those of Anglos; however, whether subculture or income explains the differences has not been adequately researched. Table 15–2 presents a summary of a number of dissimilarities in the shopping and consumption patterns of Hispanics and Anglos.

Table 15–2   **Comparison of Hispanic and Anglo Buying and Activity Patterns**

Activity	Which Group Does More	
	Hispanic	**Anglo**
Buy color TVs	≈	≈
Buy tape recorders	≈	≈
Buy TV video games		√
Buy stereos	√	
Buy soft drinks	√	
Buy beer	√	
Spend on food at home	√	
Spend on fast food	√	
Buy sewing machines		√
Shop at discount stores		√
Shop at small, personal stores	√	
Hold credit cards		√
Be venturesome buyers		√
Be skeptical of advertising		√

≈ = About the same (i.e., within 4 percentage points).

Source: Data adapted from *Spanish USA* (SIN National Spanish Television Network, 1981) 12, 13; and *Sales and Marketing Management*, July 27, 1981, A–33.

Note that Hispanics tend to be upscale luxury buyers. They buy color televisions with about the same frequency as Anglos, and stereos with greater frequency.[41] In contrast, they are skeptical of advertising, are *not* very venturesome in their purchases, do not use credit cards as much, are brand loyal, and less frequently shop at discount stories.[42] Their large families help explain why they spend more on food than Anglos. The fact that Hispanics tend to live in inner-city urban areas or barrios helps to explain their patronage of smaller stores. Shopping centers and large discount stores simply are not readily available in inner-city areas.

In one survey it was found that Hispanics tended to favor new products. They were more likely than non-Hispanics to say that they seek new foods, television programs, supermarkets, department stores, magazines, and cleaning products. Hispanics were also found to be brand loyal, to discount the quality of store brand products, and to believe that national brands are the best.[43]

Another study conducted in the Los Angeles area found that Hispanics were greater users than Anglos of products like canned spaghetti (40 percent versus 16.9 percent), baby food (18.1 percent versus 7.9 percent), white bread (90.6 percent versus 63.7 percent). Hispanics used less decaffeinated coffee, frozen juices, dog food, and diet soft drinks.[44]

The causes of these consumption differences could come from a number of factors. Lower income is certainly one likely factor. Another contributing factor is the larger number of children in most Hispanic families. Children consume more canned food products, white bread, and soft drinks than do adults. The Spanish heritage, however, is also likely to influence the buying patterns of Hispanics, particularly for food and leisure products.

Problems in Marketing to Hispanics

A number of problems exist in trying to market to the Hispanic subculture. Perhaps the major difficulty is that four segments of the subculture exist. Marketing to Puerto Ricans is not the same as marketing to Cubans, to Hispanos, or to Mexican-Americans. In fact, even among Mexican Hispanics differences exist. One advertising executive noted that if the United States and Mexico went to war, the Hispanics in California would probably fight for Mexico whereas those in Texas would fight for America.[45]

A second problem in marketing to Hispanics is the differences in the type of Spanish spoken. One company sold ink for fountain pens which was advertised as "not clogging the pen." The word *embarazo*, was used for the word "clog." The problem was that in some Latin countries *embarazo* also means pregnancy. Many Hispanics interpreted the ad as making claims that the ink was a type of contraceptive device. Similarly, the word for "earring," *pantella*, can mean "television screen" or even "lampshade" to some Hispanics. Some companies have simply had trouble translating their standard messages into Spanish. Coca-Cola's slogan, "It's the real thing," had to be changed when officials learned that the translation had an off-color meaning in Spanish.[46]

The differences in culture and in life experiences of Hispanics have hurt marketing efforts to them. Many Hispanic housewives feel uncomfortable going into the large superstores. The huge variety of unfamiliar products proves to be quite intimidating. Coors found that its theme, "The High Country," used to connote the beer's purity and clear taste, had no impact on Hispanics. Hispanics were simply not familiar with the concepts of mountains and hiking; and the imagery—so effective for Anglos—simply was missed by Hispanics.[47]

Marketing Successes

Hispanics can be reached, though, with effective marketing efforts. Their reachability comes in part because the Spanish media has become quite large. A National Spanish Television Network exists which broadcasts in Spanish. By 1984 the network had almost 200 affiliates. Spanish language newspapers are available, and traditional Anglo papers are now adding Spanish language supplements on Sundays.[48] At least 185 radio stations in the U.S. have Spanish language broadcasts on at least a part-time basis. Importantly, Hispanics tend to be heavy viewers of television and listeners of radio.

Hispanics are also fond of festivals and sporting events and companies can tie in to these events. McDonald's paid $30,000 for an indoor carpet for a soccer league in Chicago. Soccer is *the* Hispanic sport, and the company decided that such a sales promotion would reach more people effectively than would media advertising. The golden arches of McDonald's were placed in the center of 3,000 square yards of green carpet on which thousands of Hispanic youths play soccer every year.[49]

Sears has successfully marketed its wares to Hispanics. Using mostly radio, the company built on its highly positive image in Latin America with the slogan "Sears—Your Old Friend."[50] In south Florida one of the largest liquor stores/lounges is called Big Daddy's. The owner, Big Daddy, is a huge Irishman with a sense of consumer behavior. He recognized that 90 to 95 percent of his customers were Latino. Recognizing the trend, he began changing the names of the stores to Papa Grandes, and his Hispanic customers loved it.[51]

Beer manufacturers have targeted Hispanics because they are heavier-than-average beer drinkers. The Miller Brewing Company has been successful in its efforts partly because the company recognized that Hispanics are a proud people. The national television advertisement produced for Miller's Lite beer that stars a Mexican boxer is a classic illustration. One could almost hear the 8.7 million Mexican-Hispanics cheer when the boxer Carlos Palomina said that the U.S. is a nice place to visit but, "Don't drink the water."

In summary, with a youthful population, a high birth rate, a high immigration rate, and increasing buying power, Hispanics are destined to become an increasingly important market force. Because of the differences in the makeup of the Hispanic population, it is crucial for marketers to stick to the basics in attempting to reach the market. Marketers must identify unfulfilled needs and wants through good market research and then reach the subculture and its segments with fundamentally sound marketing programs.

REGIONAL SUBCULTURES

Another major subcultural variable of interest to marketers concerns how populations arrange themselves in the various regions of the United States. Measuring and predicting regional subcultural and demographic patterns is important to marketers for two reasons. First, different regions have distinct lifestyles resulting from variations in climate, culture, and the ethnic mix of people. Consequently, different product preferences exist. For example, regional preferences exist for foods and beverages. Some coffee manufacturers blend their coffee differently for the various regions—heavier in the East, lighter in the West, and with chicory in Louisiana. Second, regional demographic trends have importance from cost and growth perspectives. For many types of goods it is important to shorten the distribution channel as much as possible. New production facilities should be built in areas experiencing the greatest population growth. In addition, companies looking for new growth opportunities should focus on regions expected to experience population increases.

How has the population shifted in the United States over the years? As a general statement, the population of the United States has been moving to the West and South. For example, a study by a private firm revealed that between 1980 and 1983, the economic areas showing the highest growth were in the South and West. The high-growth areas were Texas, Florida, California, Colorado, Utah, and Wyoming. States having cities in which negative growth occurred were Indiana, Iowa, Ohio, Kentucky, and Michigan.[52] Indeed, in 1983 the U.S. Bureau of the Census predicted that by the year 2000, 60 percent of Americans would live in the South and Southwest.

The variations in growth found between 1980 and 1983 occurred because of migration patterns in the United States. At that time the U.S. economy was in a recession, which particularly hurt the so-called smokestack industries— i.e., autos and steel. These industries are centered in the North Central states— the areas experiencing low or negative growth. In contrast, states in the West were not seriously hit by the recession. Indeed, many were experiencing boom times because of the rapid growth of the petroleum industry. Such states included Texas, Colorado, Wyoming, and Utah. Quite simply, people from the depressed North Central states moved in droves to the West seeking employment. However, in 1986 a plunge in energy prices dramatically changed the economic picture for energy producing states, such as Texas, Oklahoma, and Louisiana. In Oklahoma a net outflow of people occurred in 1986. These trends reveal vividly the interplay between economic forces and demographic trends.

Because of the movement of people and industries from one region of the country to another, one finds significant amounts of regional competition. The ad found in Figure 15–3 illustrates such regional competition. Placed in business magazines by a company that owns a number of newspapers in Michigan, the ad directly compares the audience reached by its newspapers to that reached in various "hot" Sun Belt areas. Directed to potential advertisers, the ad effectively communicates the point that the "Boothbelt" should not be overlooked.

Regional population shifts occur for several reasons. One is people's search for jobs. During the severe recession of 1980–82, many workers moved from the North Central states to the West and Southwest in search of employment. People also move for lifestyle reasons. Florida has grown rapidly because of the huge influx of retirees seeking the sun in their retirement years. Consequently, Florida is the nation's oldest state, with a median age of 34.7 years— nearly five years above the national average.[53] Indeed, the proportion of people over sixty-five in Florida is 17.3 percent according to the 1980 census.

A third reason for regional population shifts is differences in birth rates. Differences in birthrates take longer to manifest themselves, but over a ten- to twenty-year period the variations become meaningful. In general, the West is younger than the Northeast and North Central states. The median age in the Northeast is over thirty years, whereas in the West it falls dramatically. For example, Wyoming's median age is 27.1 years and Alaska's is 26.1 Utah is the youngest state, with a median age of 24.2 years.[54] In Utah's case a confluence of demographic factors accounts for the state's youthfulness. The Mormon population and influence in Utah is large. A central focus of the religion is the importance of the family and of childbearing.

Figure 15–3 **Regional competition for advertising dollars is evident in this ad.** *(Courtesy of Booth Newspapers, Inc.)*

The combination of a net inflow of migration and a youthful population portend future above-average population growth in the Western states. The youthful population will tend to have higher birth rates than the older populations found in the Northeast and North Central states.

The regional distribution of minority groups also varies greatly. In 1980 blacks were centered in the South (53 percent) and Northeast (38 percent). People of Spanish origin were centered in the Southwest; Asian peoples were found predominantly in the West—particularly in California and Hawaii.[55] Highlight 15–3 describes the popularity of Los Angeles as an entry point for immigrants. As noted earlier in the chapter, minority groups can make highly profitable market segments. Recognizing the differences in geographic distribution is crucial in profitably reaching such market segments.

Problems in Defining Regions

One of the problems with the U.S. census has been how it defines the regions of the United States. For example, the western United States is defined as including Alaska, Hawaii, and Arizona—three states possessing completely different subcultures, problems, and demographic patterns. Figure 15–4 shows the Census Bureau's regional division of the United States.

A number of authors have attempted to redefine the regions of the United States in an effort to isolate more accurately those areas sharing common subcultures and problems. Joel Garreau made such an attempt in *The Nine Nations of North America.*[56] In Garreau's view North America is composed of **nine mini-countries,** each having its own economic, social, political, and topographical climates. Table 15–3 presents the nine countries and a brief description of their characteristics. Each mini-country has its own culture and sees things from its own perspective. Thus, one reason for the automakers' delayed reaction to Japan's entry into the auto market in the U.S. in the 1970s was that American auto executives lived in the "Industrial Foundry." Had the executives lived in California, a part of "Ecotopia," their view and understanding of the threat would have been completely different.

HIGHLIGHT 15–3

Los Angeles: The New Melting Pot

Early in the twentieth century, Ellis Island in New York City was where European immigrants entered the United States. Over the past two decades immigrants to the United States have come from the south (Hispanics) and the west (Asians). Los Angeles has become the major entry point for both groups of people.

Los Angeles has become a "third world" city where 90 languages are spoken. Within the city one finds Little Tokyo, Koreatown, Chinatown, and smaller areas reminiscent of Saigon, Bangkok, Manila, San Salvador, and Saudi Arabia. Less than 50 percent of L.A.'s population is Anglo. More than 25 percent of its residents are foreign born.

Because the film and television industries are centered in Los Angeles, the city has come to represent the American lifestyle to the world. Some claim that L.A. now absorbs people into the mainstream more easily than New York. Not only is the weather warmer, but so are the people, claimed one of the city's former officials.

Based on "Los Angeles Becomes 'Ellis Island West,' The New Melting Pot of America," *The Sunday Oklahoman,* July 17, 1983, 6.

Figure 15–4 Nine Census Bureau regions. (Adapted by permission, from *Marketing News*, May 13, 1983, section 2, p. 8.)

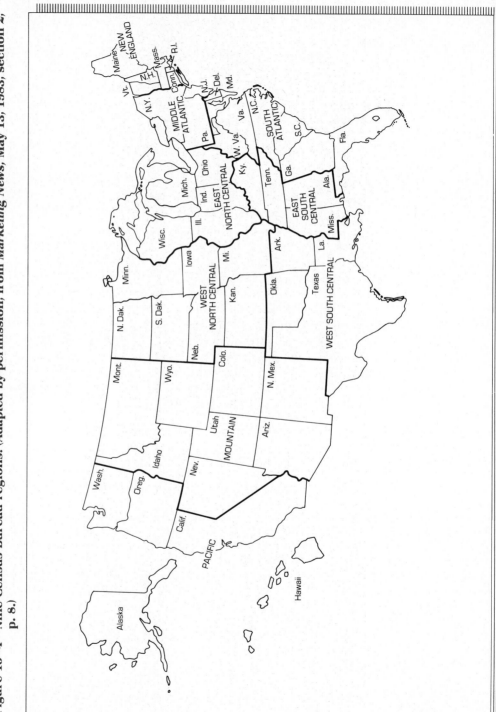

Table 15–3   The Nine Nations of North America

Name	Capital	Description
1. Industrial Foundry	Detroit	Includes Pennsylvania, New Jersey, and the industrial section of New York, Michigan, Ohio, and West Virginia. Is a nation on the decline. But will reemerge in early 21st century. Greatest resource—fresh water.
2. Breadbasket	Kansas City	Includes the farm belt from central Texas north into Canada. Represents mainstream America of conservative, hard-working, religious people. Is stable, peaceful, and productive. Has great political power.
3. Dixie	Atlanta	Includes the Confederate states, except for South Florida. Is undergoing the most rapid changes in North America. People are optimistic about the future, but the progress is all catch-up.
4. New England	Boston	Includes Massachusetts north into Canada. Is the poorest of the nine nations because of the lack of natural resources. However, it may be resurrected because of its intelligent people developing high technology.
5. Ecotopia	San Francisco	Includes Northwest California north into Canada. Is the only part of the West blessed with adequate water. Includes Silicon Valley. Motto is "Leave Me Alone." Oriented to Asia for future.
6. Empty Quarter	Denver	Includes the mountainous states in the western U.S. and Canada. Is the largest nation, with great natural resources, a small population, and little water. Its future will be determined by outsiders who settle and by the government.
7. MexAmerica	Los Angeles	Includes the U.S. Southwest and Mexico. Culture is highly influenced by its Spanish heritage. Number one problem is water. Seen as having unlimited growth opportunities.
8. The Islands	Miami	Includes Southern Florida and the Caribbean Islands. Major industries are illegal drugs, trade with Latin America, and non-Anglo tourism. Garreau calls it the "weirdest and hardest to track" nation.
9. Quebec	Quebec City	Located in the province of Quebec, Canada. Has homogeneous culture and plentiful hydroelectric power. The people are highly independent and feel they can separate from Canada, if they wish.

SOURCE: Data adapted from Joel Garreau, *The Nine Nations of North America*, Boston, Mass.: Houghton Mifflin, 1981.

Other authors have proposed similar divisions of the United States. For example, one marketing research firm has identified fifteen different regions in the United States. The various regions could be classified in terms of how fast they are growing. However, one of the marketing research firm's directors noted that going with growth is not always the best strategy. He identified the following implications for consumer goods firms:

Many "growth" markets in the South and Southwest are overstored and have low average income levels.

Slow-growth markets in the North may be the best opportunity for the 1980s. They are large, understored, and have high income levels.

Several areas in the North are growing in excess of national rates of increase.

Nonmetropolitan areas are growing 50 percent faster than metropolitan areas.

Northern metro areas are losing population to nonmetro areas, but in the South the trend is reversed.[57]

One problem with many of the attempts to define regions is that they have been done "by the seat of the pants." Few attempts have been made to identify empirically areas of the country that have similar characteristics. One exception to this trend exists. The author used a computer program to cluster together the cities that were the most similar on over thirty characteristics.[58] Some of the characteristics that were used to cluster the cities included racial composition, unemployment data, retail sales, automobile numbers, voting percentage, percentage Democratic, and map coordinate. The results indicated that eight clusters were consistently found. A map of the resulting regions is found in Figure 15–5. An interesting exercise is to attempt to name each of the regions.

Gentrification

In the late 1970s and early 1980s a new trend became evident in the movement of people. Previously, professionals moved away from the inner cities to the suburbs. Living inside a large city was expensive, housing was scarce and deteriorating, crime was a problem, and commercial shopping areas were disappearing.[59] However, analysts began to note that in the late 1970s the long-standing trend of movement away from inner cities may have begun to be reversed when young white professionals began returning. Attractions of the inner city were clear. People could be closer to their jobs, public transportation was available, and the architecture of older, city homes was interesting to many.

When researchers began to look at the evidence, however, the trend towards **gentrification** was hard to detect. One study examined the record of ten major cities in the 1970s in which gentrification supposedly occurred. It found that of the ten cities investigated only Washington, D.C, and Philadelphia showed any signs of whites returning to inner cities.[60]

For marketers any changes in the gentrification trend have major impli-

Figure 15–5   An empirically-derived depiction of the regions of the United States. (Adapted by permission of James W. Gentry.)

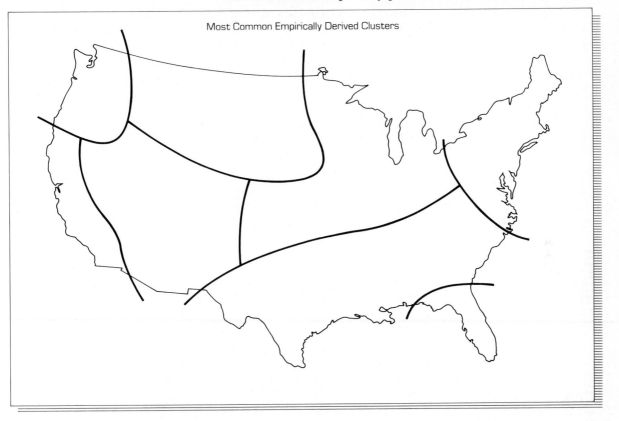

Most Common Empirically Derived Clusters

cations for the location of retail outlets. If the movement of affluent households back to inner cities should increase, it could result in major problems for regional shopping centers. In addition, it would mean new opportunities for those willing to locate outlets back to the core of inner cities. Such a willingness can already be seen in actions by developers. Indeed, in 1983 one of every four new shopping centers was a downtown project.[61] Major projects in cities such as St. Louis, Boston, Atlanta, and Baltimore have helped to revitalize downtown areas.

Managerial Implications

The subcultures identified in this chapter represent some of the most important target markets for marketers over the next decade. The numbers of Hispanics are growing extremely rapidly and represent a marketing opportunity for companies willing to make the investment necessary to understand the subculture. Although not growing as fast as the Hispanic population, black population growth does outpace that of the general populace. The fact that both subcultures are gaining acceptance on a national level is illustrated by their growing influence in the political environment. Blacks have been the mayors of a number of major cities, such as Atlanta and Los Angeles. Similarly, Hispanics have been elected to head such cities as Albuquerque and San Antonio. Jessie Jackson, a black minister, had a major impact on the Democratic platform for the 1984 presidential election.

Region and religion are also factors associated with growth of subcultures. Fundamentalist Christians are an extremely fast growing religious group. Their increasing numbers give them market power, and their conservative religious and political views provide a way for marketers to identify and reach them. The Jewish population, although not growing in numbers, is valued by marketers because of its high income levels. It too is reachable and identifiable and is readily targeted by marketers.

An important question for marketers is whether a subcultural group should be targeted. That is, should a marketer specifically design the marketing mix to reach a group? The answer to this question hinges on the extent to which the group fulfills the requirements for successful segmentation. For a group to be segmented successfully, it must have:

1. Identifiability—Is there some demographic or psychographic characteristic that will allow a company to determine who the people are, where they live, which periodicals they read, which television shows they watch, and which stores they frequent?
2. Reachability—Can the group be reached economically through specialized distribution channels, media, or personal-selling approaches?
3. Discretionary income—Does the group have sufficient income to buy consumer products in sufficient quantities to make segmentation profitable?
4. Size—is the group large enough in size to make it worthwhile for a company to attempt to reach it?
5. Specialized needs—Does the group have needs that differentiate it from other groups of people? If no such specialized needs exist, distinct market offerings to them will not be successful.

Table 15–4 assesses the four subcultures mentioned in this chapter as well as the subcultures identified in Chapter 14 on these five dimensions. (Note that "identifiability" and "reachability" have been combined because in practice they tend to go together.) The table provides an indication of the relative value of the subcultures to marketers. For example, black and Hispanic subcultures make only "fair" segments to target in comparison to many of the others listed. The reason is that their income levels are below average, their size is relatively small, and their reachability is limited.

Table 15–4   Analysis of the Ability to Segment Various Subcultures

| | Dimension | | | | |
Subculture	Identifiability/ Reachability	Income	Size	Specialized Need	Growth Rate
Blacks	Fair	Poor	Fair	Good	High
Hispanics	Fair	Poor	Poor	Good	Very high
Jews	Fair	Good	Very poor	Fair	Static
Fundamental Protestants	Poor	Poor	Fair	Poor	Moderate
Elderly	Good	Fair	Good	Excellent	Moderate
Females	Excellent	Fair	Excellent	Excellent	Moderate
Baby boomers	Very poor	Good	Excellent	Poor	Static
Upper class	Fair	Excellent	Very poor	Good	Low
Upper-middle class	Good	Excellent	Poor	Fair	Low
Lower-middle class	Fair	Fair	Good	Poor	Static
Upper-lower class	Poor	Poor	Good	Poor	Low
Lower class	Very poor	Very poor	Fair	Good	Low
Regions					
Southwest	Excellent	Fair	Fair	Fair	High
New England	Excellent	Fair	Poor	Fair	Low
Northwest	Excellent	Fair	Poor	Poor	Low
Middle Atlantic	Excellent	Fair	Good	Poor	Static
South	Excellent	Fair	Fair	Fair	Low

The ability to segment on each of the dimensions should be interpreted as follows:

Dimension	Interpretation
1. Identifiability	If the subculture is easily identified, an excellent rating is given.
2. Income	If income is high, an excellent rating is given.
3. Size	If the subculture is extremely large, an excellent rating is given.
4. Specialized need	If the subculture has specialized needs, an excellent rating is given.
5. Growth rate	If the growth rate is high, an excellent rating is given.

Income Differences Among the Subcultures

The incomes of the subcultures also vary substantially. In particular, the social classes have extreme income variations because the economic status of people in part determines their social status. The median incomes of blacks and Hispanics are lower than average, somewhat limiting the desirability of targeting the groups. One of the reasons for the importance of Jews as a market segment is the relatively high income levels of this group of people.

Size of the Subcultures

How many people actually belong to a subculture is an important factor for marketers to consider. When size and income of a segment are looked at together, one has a measure of the **market power** of the group. Thus,

$$\text{Market Power} = \text{Size} \times \text{Income}$$

The baby boomers are extremely important to marketers because of their combination of size and income. Baby boomers make up about 32 percent of the population. In addition, they are now nearing their peak earnings years as they begin to reach their forties over the next ten years.

Specialized Need

The element needed by a group to make it a market segment of value is a specialized need. This idea flows from the marketing concept of providing goods and services to fulfill the needs of consumers. The lack of specialized needs among the baby boomers currently limits the group as a target for marketers. However, fifteen years ago, when the group was largely composed of teenagers, it was a more tempting target because more clearly defined needs existed then. Currently the group ranges in age from roughly 25 to 45 years old. During this time span, needs become more hard to define and tend to be governed by the family life cycle. Thus, factors such as whether a person is married, has children, and has a particular type of job are the major factors creating needs for specialized products.

Excellent examples of groups having clearly defined specialized needs are the sexes. Entire industries have been built around fulfilling such needs. The industry that produces feminine hygiene products is now a multibillion dollar industry. The clothing industry is largely separated along sex lines, as are the products for athletics.

Remember Growth

The factor missing from the analysis of the importance of a group as a market segment is growth. With growth come market opportunities, if a company can identify the trend prior to its competitors. Table 15–4 also identifies the relative growth rates of the various groups. Perhaps the major reasons for the importance of the Hispanic market are its incredibly fast growth and the fact that companies had not previously targeted it. Other segments experiencing above-average growth rates are blacks, the region of the Southwest, the elderly, and Fundamentalist Protestants. Groups that are experiencing low or negative growth are Jews, the Middle Atlantic states, the lower-middle class, and teenagers.

SUMMARY

This chapter has discussed a number of the subcultures important to marketers, including subcultures based on region, race, nationality, and religion. Analysis of the growth rates of the subcultures, their geographic concentration, their buying patterns, and their value and belief systems can assist marketers in doing opportunity analysis and market segmentation and in designing the marketing mix. In particular, the changing size of these subcultures can influence the strategic planning of a firm. That is, a firm may decide to move into or leave entire market areas because of a change in their prospects, such as beginning to target the elderly instead of the teenage group in the 1980s.

In Chapter 15 four factors on which subcultures may be based were discussed—religion, nationality, race, and geography. The Fundamentalist Christian subculture is based upon a common, highly conservative view of the Bible's message. The group is one of the fastest-growing religious bodies and has learned to make effective use of mass media to bring in new members and spread the religious and political views of its leadership.

The Jewish subculture is more tightly bound than that of the fundamentalist Christian group. In part this occurs because of the common ethnic background of many Jews and a common language (Hebrew), which many Jews learn to some extent. Although not growing in size, the Jewish subculture can be successfully targeted because of the group's high income levels and specialized needs, particularly in the dietary area.

Much has been written about the black subculture over the past twenty-five years, and marketers have slowly begun to recognize that the group is an important market segment. Factors shaping the black subculture include a common ethnic background, a history of economic and educational deprivation, and a pattern of racial discrimination. A question of concern to marketers is whether or not blacks should be singled out as a specific target group. In most instances blacks are motivated by the same needs and desires as other subcultures. However, in some cases, such as for hair care items, blacks do have specialized needs to which products can be targeted. In addition, companies in their promotional activities can appeal to the ethnic pride felt by many blacks. For example, the use of black endorsers can effectively activate a feeling of pride, which can carry over to a more positive feeling about the product advertised.

The Hispanic subculture is perhaps the fastest growing subculture in the United States. A high birth rate and massive inflows of immigrants contribute to the rapid increase in the number of Hispanics. The subculture is united by a common religion, a common language, and a common nationality of origin. Four important Hispanic groups exist in the United States—Cubans, Puerto Ricans, Mexicans, and Hispanos. Despite differences in when these groups arrived and in where their most recent homeland was, they should be considered as subsegments of the larger Hispanic group.

Hispanics tend to be conservative people who share many of the values of the larger American culture. They believe in upward mobility and in leading a better life. They are conservative in their buying patterns and often in their politics. They show some tendency to buy more-than-average amounts of luxury goods, such as stereos. The appeal of Hispanics to marketers as a market segment results from several factors. Their growing size and increasing incomes are two factors. In addition, their geographical concentration in specific regions of the country also makes the group a lucrative target.

A fourth basis for the development of subcultures is the region of a country. A region may develop a distinct subculture for several reasons. Differences in the religion, ethnicity, and nationality of the people who settle in an area can be extremely important in developing a distinct set of values and behavior patterns. For example, Utah has a distinct subculture in large part because of the influence of the Mormon church, which tends to dominate the state. Mormon doctrine teaches a conservative way of life with a heavy emphasis on the family and on helping others. In the Southwest the Hispanic influence pervades the area.

Another basis for the development of a regional subculture is the climate and terrain of the area. People must learn to adapt to differences in the physical terrain in which they live. Thus, the heat and humidity of the Deep South could be one reason for the slower pace encountered there in comparison to the faster tempo found in the Northeast. Such climatic differences can create quite different needs for clothing—an opportunity for the enterprising marketer.

Key Terms

Race	Black subculture
Nationality	Hispanic segments
Ethnicity	Hispanic strata
Born-again Christians	Nine U.S. "mini-nations"
Evangelicals	Gentrification
Kosher	Market power
Black segments	

Review Questions

1. Identify six different types of subcultures in the United States.
2. How do ethnic and nationality subcultures differ? Give three examples each of ethnicity- and nationality-based subcultures.
3. Compare and contrast the Fundamentalist Christian and the Jewish subcultures.
4. Identify four factors that make the black subculture an important target market.
5. Under which type of circumstances does it make the most sense to target blacks specifically rather than using other variables, such as education and income, which do not specifically use ethnicity as a segmentation variable?

6. Studies performed in the 1960s and 1970s indicated that Black consumption patterns differed from Anglo consumption patterns in two areas in particular. What were these areas, and do you think they persist today?
7. What factors make the Hispanic subculture the fastest-growing group in the United States?
8. Four segments of Hispanics have been identified based upon the specific Spanish country from which they arrived. Identify these four segments and indicate their relative size as well as where they are geographically centered.
9. Identify five buying areas in which Hispanic purchase habits appear to be different from those of Anglos.
10. What are two problems in marketing to Hispanics? What single factor makes the Hispanic market relatively easy to reach?
11. Identify the reasons why regional shifts in population may occur.
12. Identify the nine nations of North America developed by Joel Garreau.
13. What are the five factors necessary for the successful segmentation of a market?
14. Based upon Table 15–4, indicate which subcultures may be viewed as having the easiest reach-

ability, the highest income, the largest size, the most specialized need, and the greatest growth rate.

Discussion Questions

1. Discuss your view of the extent to which nationality or ethnicity makes the better segmentation variable. What are some of the criteria for making such a decision?
2. Because of its size and heterogeneity, the United States clearly has a variety of distinct subcultures within its borders. How subculturally heterogeneous do you perceive the following countries to be: India, Canada, Soviet Union, Germany, and Japan?
3. Religious subcultures often have distinct preferences regarding the consumption of foods. What are some of the distinct food preferences of the following groups: Hindus, Moslems, Jews, and Catholics?
4. Go to the largest grocery store in your geographic vicinity. Attempt to identify any indications of merchandise that is targeted to specific subcultures.
5. Place yourself in the position of the marketing director for Coors, the beer producer in Colorado. During the early and mid-1980s, you had problems reaching the black and Hispanic markets due to allegations that the company was anti-union and generally ultraconservative. What steps would you take in order to increase your market share among black and Hispanic subcultures?
6. Compare and contrast how a company might attempt to market a product such as blue jeans to blacks and Hispanics. Specifically consider the selection of media and the development of advertising themes.
7. Suppose that you were the marketing director for a company that planned to open a chain of new department stores targeted to consumers with income of $80,000 and above. What geographic considerations would influence your decisions as to where to place these stores?
8. Identify five products for which the marketing mix must be varied across the geographic regions of the United States. State the reasons why the marketing mix should be varied for each product.
9. Among the subcultures identified in the last two chapters identify the one(s) which could most easily be targeted for the following products—fur coats, low calorie foods, hair products, and stereos. Please justify your answers.

References

1. Martha Riche, "The Fall and Rise of Religion," *American Demographics*, 4, May 1982, 14–19, 47.
2. George Barna, "Typology Offers Perspectives on Growing Christian Market," *Marketing News*, September 16, 1983, 12.
3. Barna, "Typology Offers Perspectives."
4. Riche, "The Fall and Rise."
5. Barna, "Typology Offers Perspectives."
6. Ibid.
7. Riche, "The Fall and Rise."
8. Howard Thompson and Jesse Raine, "Religious Denomination Preference as a Basis for Store Location," *Journal of Retailing*, 52, Summer 1976, 71–78.
9. Dan Lionel, "How to Reach the Jewish Market," *Editor and Publisher*, December 8, 1979, 30.
10. Lionel, "How to Reach."
11. Elizabeth Hirschman, "American Jewish Ethnicity: Its Relationship to Some Selected Aspects of Consumer Behavior," *Journal of Marketing*, 45, Summer 1981, 102–110.
12. Thomas Barry and Michael Harvey, "Marketing to Heterogeneous Black Consumers," *California Management Review*, 17, Winter 1974, 50–57.
13. Lafayette Jones, "An Uncompromising Challenge," *Advertising Age*, November 29, 1982, M–12, M–14.
14. Raymond Bauer, S. Cunningham, and L. Wortzel, "The Marketing Dilemma of Negroes," *Journal of Marketing*, 29, July 1965, 3.
15. "Persons and Families Below Poverty Level," *Statistical Abstract of the United States: 1986*, Department of Commerce, Bureau of the Census, December 1985, 459.
16. Herbert Allen, "Grass-Roots Involvement Touches the Market's Heart," *Advertising Age*, November 29, 1982, M–10, 11.
17. B. G. Yovovich, "The Debate Rages On," *Advertising Age*, November 29, 1982, M–9, M–10.
18. Yovovich, "The Debate Rages On."

19. Milton Rokeach and S. Parker, "Values as Social Indicators of Poverty and Race Relations in America," *Annals of the American Academy of Political and Social Science, 388*, March 1970, 97–111.

20. Yovovich, "The Debate Rages On."

21. P. E. Choudhurg, E. Connelly and R. Kahlow, "The Effect of Income on Black Media Behavior," in *Marketing 1776–1976 and Beyond*, K. Bernhardt (ed.), Chicago, Ill.: American Marketing Association, 1976, 422–425.

22. Yovovich, "The Debate Rages On."

23. J. V. Petrof, "Reaching the Negro Market: A Segregated Versus a General Newspaper," *Journal of Advertising Research, 8*, June 1968, 40–43.

24. D. Parke Gibson, *$70 Billion in the Black Market*, New York: Macmillan Publishing Co., Inc., 1978.

25. Jody Becman, "Marketing by the Numbers Won't Work Here," *Advertising Age*, November 29, 1982, M–18.

26. Roger Blackwell, H. Mathews, and C. Randolph, *Living in Columbus*, Columbus, Ohio: Nationwide Communications, Inc., 1979.

27. Carl Larson, "Racial Brand Usage and Media Exposure Differentials," in *June Conference Proceedings of the American Marketing Association*, Series 27 Keith Cox and Ben Enis (eds.), Chicago, Ill.: American Marketing Association, 1968, 208–215.

28. Allen, "Grass-Roots Involvement."

29. Maurice Ferre, "Decade of the Hispanic," *Advertising Age*, February 15, 1982, M–14, M–16.

30. Jack Honomichl, "Never Lose Sight of Hispanic Pride," *Advertising Age*, February 15, 1982, M–38, M–39.

31. Cheryl Russell, "The News About Hispanics," *American Demographics, 5*, March 1983, 15–25.

32. B. G. Yovovich, "Cultural Pride Galvanizes Heritages," *Advertising Age*, February 15, 1982, M–9, M–44.

33. Yovovich, "Cultural Pride."

34. B. A. Brusco, "Hispanic Marketing: New Application of Old Methodologies." *Theme*, May–June 1981, 8–9.

35. Danny Bellinger and Humbato Valencia, "Understanding the Hispanic Market," *Business Horizons*, May–June 1982, 49.

36. Cheryl Russell, "The News About Hispanics," *American Demographics, 5*, March 1983, 15–25.

37. "Hispanics: Markets Within a Market," *Sales and Marketing Management*, July 27, 1981, A–33.

38. "Hispanics: Markets."

39. Ibid.

40. Fernando Cervantes, "The Forgotten Consumers: The Mexican-Americans," in *Marketing in the 80's; 1980 Educator's Conference Proceedings*, Richard Bagozzi et al. (eds.), Chicago, Ill.: American Marketing Association, 1980, 180–183.

41. "Hispanics: Markets Within Markets, *Sales and Marketing Management, 127*, July 27, 1981, A–33.

42. Danny Bellinger and Humbato Valencia, "Understanding the Hispanic Market," Spanish USA (SIN National Spanish Television Network), 1981, 12, 13.

43. David Aston, "The Hispanic Market: An In-Depth Profile," *Marketing Communications*, July 1981, 15–19.

44. Russell, "The News About Hispanics."

45. John Sugg, "Miami's Latino Market Spans Two Continents," *Advertising Age*, February 15, 1982, M–9, M–44.

46. Theodore Gage, "Beer Still Tops Wine Spirits," *Advertising Age*, February 15, 1982, M–10, M–11, M–22, M–23.

47. Ed Zotti, "An Idea Whose Time Has Not Quite Arrived," *Advertising Age*, February 15, 1982, M–29, M–32, M–33.

48. Jack McGuire, "Hispanic TV Network Thrives," *Advertising Age*, February 15, 1982, M–34, M–35.

49. "Classy Carpet for the CLASA," *Advertising Age*, February 15, 1982, M–20.

50. Carol Galginaitis, "Luring the Hispanic Dollar; Retailers Boost Ethnic Image," *Advertising Age*, February 15, 1982, M–10, M–11, M–18, M–20.

51. Sugg, "Miami's Latino Market."

52. Eugene Carlson, "Parking Violators . . . Changes in Population . . . State Worries," *The Wall Street Journal*, June 14, 1983, 31.

53. Bryant Robey, "Age in America," *American Demographics, 3*, July/August 1981, 14–19.

54. Robey, "Age in America."

55. *Population Profile of the United States 1981*, Series P–20, No. 374, Section 3, Washington, D.C.: U.S. Bureau of the Census, 1982.

56. Joel Garreau, *The Nine Nations of North America*, Boston, Mass.: Houghton Mifflin, 1981.

57. Bernie Whalen, "Marketing Research Firm Seg-

ments U.S. in 15 Geodemographic Regions,'' *Marketing News*, May 13, 1983, 8.

58. James W. Gentry, ''The Development of the Boundaries of Geographic Subcultures,'' *Advances in Consumer Research, XIII*, Richard Lutz (ed.), Ann Arbor, Mich.: Association for Consumer Research 1986.

59. Jane Newitt, ''Behind the Big-City Blues,'' *American Demographics, 5*, June 1983, 27–29.

60. David Francis, ''Playing the New Demographics,'' *Institutional Investor*, November 1981, 79–86.

61. Claudia Ricci, ''Centers of Some Cities Bloom,'' *The Wall Street Journal*, May 2, 1983, 1, 20.

16
Social Class

Illiteracy: A Major Marketing and Business Research Problem

People rarely move more than one social class away from the class in which they were born. One reason for the failure of people in the lower social classes to move up is the pervasive problem of illiteracy. One research study found that 16 percent of adult whites, 44 percent of adult blacks, and 56 percent of adult Hispanics are functionally illiterate. The Ford Foundation has estimated that up to 28 percent of all Americans may be totally illiterate.

Illiteracy is a major problem for marketers. For marketing researchers illiteracy may influence the refusal or nonresponse rate for interviews and surveys. This rate of nonparticipation ranges from 10 to 70 percent or more of consumers contacted. Marketing researchers are just beginning to recognize the problem, but research firms have not attempted to factor the illiteracy rate into their studies.

The illiteracy problem also affects advertisers. A person unable to read or write cannot use coupons, does not understand print advertising, and ignores the "Yellow Pages." Illiterates must place a great deal of emphasis on the use of pictures. Thus, when viewing television, illiterates will look for pictures or symbols that identify products. These symbols are then used in supermarkets to select products. The result is that illiterates tend to buy highly advertised, brand-name products. They are unable to buy generic products, because the contents of the can are symbolized in writing rather than in pictures.

In one case a supermarket's customers in Detroit suddenly started buying a particular brand of shortening. After some investigation the store managers realized that the manufacturer had changed labels and placed a picture of a chicken on the can. Illiterates began buying the product because they thought the can contained chicken.

Some have suggested that illiteracy affects the sales of product lines that are packaged without the use of pictures on cans or cartons. For example, Campbell's Soup Company packages their soups in red-and-white cans with a written description of the cans' contents. One executive stated that for illiterates the rows and rows of red-and-white Campbell's soup cans are a big blur. Howard Johnson's is said to be popular among illiterates because it prints pictures of all its menu items.

The United States ranks twenty-fourth among nations in literacy. The U.S. has three times the illiteracy rate of the Soviet Union and five times that of Cuba. It can even be argued that our low productivity relative to Japan and Germany occurs in part because of illiteracy. In testimony to Congress, Navy officials stated that 30 percent of all Naval recruits endanger themselves and their expensive equipment because of illiteracy.

Already companies such as Citibank, J.C. Penney, and Xerox have begun funding programs to combat illiteracy. Without increased emphasis on teaching young people to read and write, the chance for upward mobility of lower social classes, in which much of the illiteracy resides, will be low.

Based on Bernie Whalen, "Illiteracy: The Marketing Research Implications," *Marketing News,* May 13, 1983, 1, 18.

INTRODUCTION

Social class is a sociological concept originally developed to account for broad social and political phenomena. As stated by one researcher, the basic question on which work on social class deals is, "Who gets what and why?".[1] The ideas behind the concept of social class flow from the theorizing done on social stratification. Sociologists were and are interested in how differential rankings of people can lead to political and revolutionary activity and in how institutional and stratification arrangements are intertwined.[2]

Social class may be defined as the relatively permanent and homogeneous strata in a society which differ in their status, wealth, education, possessions, and values. All societies possess a hierarchical structure in which the residents are stratified into "classes" of people layered on top of each other. Both actual and perceptual factors distinguish the groups. In real terms the classes differ in their occupations, lifestyles, values, friendships, manner of speaking, and possessions. In perceptual terms the classes recognize that status differences exist among them. Individuals perceive that different classes have diverging amounts of prestige, power, and privilege. Finally, the associations of the classes differ. Behavior is restricted so that members of a class tend to socialize, both formally and informally, with each other rather than with members of other classes. As observed by one theorist, social classes are multidimensional. Three primary factors differentiate the social classes—*eco-*

nomic status (e.g., occupation, wealth, house type and location), *educational credentials*, and *behavioral standards* (e.g., community participation, aspirations, and recreational habits).[3]

As applied to marketing, social class is a narrower concept. Marketers are concerned with how the buying patterns of social classes differ rather than with the political, institutional, and cultural reasons for their existence. For marketers the social classes are more appropriately seen as subcultures with distinct lifestyles, buying patterns, and motivations.[4] Thus, the social classes should be viewed as potential market segments which possess divergent product/service needs, wants, and desires.

The consumer vignette on illiteracy, which introduced the chapter, captures several important points concerning social class. Educational attainment is one important component of social class. Those with greater amounts of education tend to be in higher social classes. Further, the leading method of moving up in social class involves children raising their educational level significantly above that of their parents. However, illiteracy causes severe problems in class mobility. Illiterates tend to become involved in crime more than those who read and write. Fifty percent of prison inmates are illiterate.[5] Further, illiterate parents tend to have illiterate children because their homes contain no books and they cannot read to their kids. Illiteracy not only influences the education level one can achieve (by the way some illiterates do graduate from high school), but also influences other components of social class (i.e., education, occupation, income, and values). Through such pervasive influence illiteracy can lock people into a lower social class status.

What Are the Social Classes?

A variety of different classification schemes have been developed to rank the social classes. Depending on the classification system, the number of categories of social class varies from as few as two to as many as nine. Regardless of the number of categories proposed, they are ordered in a manner that begins with some type of elite upper class and ends with a lower class.

A frequently used social class scheme is Warner's Index of Status Characteristics (ISC).[6] Warner's index uses four variables as indicators of social class. They are: occupation, source of income, house type, and dwelling area. The indicators are weighted, with occupation most heavily emphasized and dwelling area least heavily emphasized in the composite index. Based on the total ISC score, an individual is classified into one of six categories:

1. Upper-upper class.
2. Lower-upper class.
3. Upper-middle class.
4. Lower-middle class.
5. Upper-lower class.
6. Lower-lower class.

A variety of other classification schemes have been developed. The U.S. Bureau of the Census uses three variables to form a socioeconomic status index—income, occupation, and education. The average of these scores results in an index with four classifications:

1. Lower class.
2. Lower-middle class.
3. Upper-middle class.
4. Upper class.

Highlight 16–1 discusses briefly how social class can be measured and identifies four commonly used scales of social class.

HIGHLIGHT 16–1

Measuring Social Class

Several different procedures have been developed to measure social class. In the subjective method consumers rank themselves in a status hierarchy. The reputational method uses a similar approach except that instead of ranking themselves, consumers rank each other in social class.

A more valid approach to measuring social class is through the use of multi-item indices. Below are listed four social class scales and the variables that each uses to rank the social classes.

	Social Class Index			
Variable	Hollingshead	Warner	Census Bureau	Coleman
Occupation	*	*	*	*
Source of income		*		
House type		*		*
Dwelling area		*		
Family income			*	
Education	*		*	*
Neighborhood housing				*
Wife's occupation				*
Wife's education				*
Religious affiliation				*
Associations				*

Name of Indices:
Hollingshead: Index of Social Position (ISP).
Warner: Index of Status Characteristics (ISC).
Census: Census Bureau Index of Socioeconometric Status (SES).
Coleman: Index of Urban Status (IUS).

Note: The indices have various "weighting" schemes for the variables. That is, some variables are more important than others in calculating social status in the four indices. See the text for how the weighting scheme works for Warner's index.

Marketers do employ social class indices in their research. AT&T used the Census Bureau index to develop a profile of the telephone style consciousness of consumers.[7] The results of the study revealed some surprising findings. Most notably, the lower-middle class was found to be very style conscious. For example, they felt that phones should come in patterns and designs as well as colors. Similarly, they agreed more often than other social classes with the statement, "A telephone should improve the decorative style of a room." In contrast the lower social class sought only phones that work and were unconcerned with style. The results of the study suggested that in addition to the obvious target markets of upper-class and upper-middle-class consumers, AT&T should *not* forget the lower-middle-class customer in promoting their decorator telephones.

Table 16–1 provides a recent social status classification scheme and summarizes some of the characteristics of the social classes. The descriptions given in the table have proven quite accurate for at least the last fifty years in the United States. However, recent trends are creating some subtle changes. One trend is a new group of people who might be placed in the lower-upper class. These are upper-middle-class professionals who marry and form high-powered two-income families. Earning from $60,000 to $140,000 a year, these families have substantially greater expendable incomes than traditional upper-middle-class families with a single breadwinner.[8] Because of their high incomes and the need to juggle two careers, these families have become a separate target market.

That social classes are different may be shown by their communication patterns. One study found that people can identify an individual's social class simply by hearing him or her read something.[9] Social classes differ in their speech cadence, voice modulation, and fluency of speech. The choice of words also varies among the social classes.[10] Lower classes describe the world in more concrete terms than do the middle and upper classes. If asked where he or she obtained bubble gum, a lower class child would likely state a person's name. An upper-class child would simply say "from the grocery store."

Problems in Using Social Class in Marketing

Most marketers agree that social class is an important concept. However, examples of its use in marketing are sparse. Much of the published work by marketers on social class was done twenty or more years ago. Relatively few new ideas have been added to the field. Currently, a number of issues remain unresolved in the use of social class as a marketing tool.

What Is Its Definition?   Agreement has not been reached on how to measure the concept. With different studies using divergent indices of social class, their results cannot be compared. As noted earlier, no agreement exists on how many social classes there are.

The Choice-Behavior Fallacy   Some researchers have grown discouraged because social class has not been a good predictor of buying behavior.

Table 16-1 The Social Class Hierarchy

A. Upper Americans

Upper-Upper (0.3%): The world of inherited wealth and old family names. Work occurs as a matter of choice, and members often serve on the boards of directors of major corporations. Serves as a reference for lower classes. Not a major market segment because of small size.

Lower-Upper (1.2%): The newer social elite, drawn from current professionals, corporate leadership. May be extremely wealthy, but the money is relatively new. Is an achieving group and will spend money to show its wealth. Will guard its social class position because of insecurity. Is a major market for specialized, luxury goods, such as Mercedes automobiles.

Upper-Middle (12.5%): The rest of college graduate managers, intellectual elite, and professionals. Lifestyle centers on private clubs, causes, and the arts. Collegiate credentials expected. Housing is extremely important to this group—particularly where the house is located. The quality and appearance of the products are important to this group.

B. Middle Americans

Middle-class (32%): White-collar workers and their blue-collar friends. Live on "the better side of town," try to "do the proper things." Have white-collar friends and acquaintances. Respectability is a key idea to this group. Home ownership, high moral standards, and focus on family are important ideals. They tend to have high school educations or some college but do not reach high levels in their organizations.

Working class (38%): Blue-collar workers; lead "working class lifestyle" whatever the income, school background, and job. Jobs tend to be monotonous, although affluence is possible if they have a "union" job. Tend to stay close to their parents and relatives and live in older parts of town. Do have money for consumer products and with the middle class represent the market for mass consumer goods.

C. Lower Americans

Upper-lower (9%): Working, not on welfare. Living standard is just above poverty. Behavior judged "crude," "trashy." Tend to be unskilled workers.

Lower-lower (7%): On welfare, visibly poverty-stricken, usually out of work (or have the "dirtiest jobs"). Some are bums, common criminals. Have become separated from the upper-lower group because it exists on government transfer payments. With the upper-lower class accounts for only 6 or 7 percent of disposable income.

SOURCE: Data adapted from Richard P. Coleman, "The Continuing Significance of Social Class in Marketing," *Journal of Consumer Research, 10,* December 1983, 265–280.

However, such a result should be expected when only a single indicator like social class is used. Many factors influence product choice behavior in addition to social class.[11]

The Husband-Only Fallacy   Another major problem is the use of the social class position of the husband as the criterion for determining a family's status. Because of the prevalence of working wives and because many pairings of husbands and wives are inconsistent regarding social class, the sexist practice is misleading.[12]

The Present Social Class Fallacy   One cannot assume that a family's current social class is governing their lifestyle and buying behavior. Although it is rare that someone will move more than one ranking up or down in social class, people are mobile in America. An individual's lifestyle, beliefs, and values are based not only on his or her current status, but also on the status of his or her parents. The socialization process will create a tendency to live a certain lifestyle, even though one's social status has moved up or down.[13]

The Single Social Class Fallacy   Measures of social class assume that an individual's social class is an average of his or her position on several dimensions of status. The consistency with which an individual reveals a particular social class across a number of dimensions is called **status crystallization.** Some have argued that those who have low crystallization are more prone to express liberal ideas and advocate changes in the social order.[14] An example of low crystallization would be a Hispanic attorney whose parents were laborers.

The Effects of Aspirations   People differ in their desire to get ahead and move up in social class. In addition, the group from whom an individual obtains his or her values, attitudes, and beliefs (i.e., reference group), may be of a different social class. Such an individual would have low class consciousness and possibly not share the consumption behaviors of members of his or her objectively measured social class.

SOCIAL CLASS AND BUYING BEHAVIOR

Because of the problems of the social class concept, one must interpret the findings of studies investigating its impact on buying behavior with caution. Furthermore, because many of the studies were done more than twenty years ago, additional caution is needed. One cannot be certain that the buying patterns of social classes have remained static over the years.

Shopping Patterns

The reasons for shopping differ among the social classes. The upper classes tend to shop not only out of necessity but also for pleasure.[15] Higher-class women tend to favor stores with a high-fashion image, such as department stores and specialty shops. Lower-class women favor mass merchandisers and price appeal stores.

   The importance of maintaining a certain social image is revealed in the shopping patterns of the upper classes. Products that reflect differences in class, like furniture, are viewed as "socially risky." Upper-class consumers will tend to purchase such products from specialty shops and department stores geared to providing more personal service in an upscale atmosphere. For low-risk products, such as toasters, the upper-class shopper is perfectly willing to buy a brand-name product from a discounter.[16] Similarly, one research study found that for paper towels, soft drinks, and laundry detergents upper-class women placed significantly less importance on brand names than did middle- or lower-class women. In addition, no differences in price consciousness for these products were found among upper-, middle-, and lower-class women.[17]

Social class is a variable on which retailers attempt to segment the market. In particular, Sears Roebuck Company has had difficulties in the past deciding which social class to target. During the mid-1970s, the company attempted to target more upscale shoppers in an effort to upgrade its image. As a result, corporate profits eroded because the company was squeezed between specialty shops, which upscale shoppers tend to favor, and discounters, such as K-Mart and Wal-Mart. A secret document, called the ''Yellow Book,'' was written in order to address the problem. The document warned: ''We are not a fashion store; we are not a store for the whimsical nor the affluent. Sears is a family store for middle-class, homeowning Americans.''

During the 1980s, Sears has more directly targeted the middle-class market. One strategy has been to use celebrities to endorse their clothing lines. Figure 16–1 shows an advertisement with the popular model, Cheryl Tiegs, showing off Sears apparel. The approach has worked, and some analysts estimate that the Tiegs line brought in more than $200 million in sales to Sears in the first fifteen months of its existence.[18] While Sears spokespersons state that the actual figure is considerably lower, the strategy was successful, and the company has expanded the strategy by using other popular spokespersons, such as Stefanie Powers, Arnold Palmer, and Evonne Goolagong.

Sears does appeal to customers in each of the social classes. For example, among millionaires the most frequently held credit card was from Sears. In particular, its power tools are frequently purchased by upper-middle-class and above customers. Again, however, the products the company sells to upper-class consumers are not socially risky items, such as clothing, furniture, and jewelry items. The bulk of Sears sales are to the middle-class consumer, and to a certain extent one can assess the financial health of the middle class by looking at the balance sheet of Sears.

Middle and upper-middle consumers appear to be ideal targets for direct mail marketers, like L. L. Bean. Consumers who purchase via telephone, mail, and catalogs tend to be highly educated, white-collar, upper-income consumers.[19] In addition, the middle and upper classes have been found to be more interested in clothing and fashion than the lower classes.[20] They read more fashion magazines, discuss fashion more often with friends, and tend to use more cosmetics.[21]

The social classes also differ in how much they search for information prior to and during shopping. Middle- and upper-class consumers tend to engage in more information search prior to making a purchase. For example, prior to buying appliances they will read newspapers, brochures, and test reports. In contrast, lower-class consumers are more apt to rely on in-store displays and salespeople.[22] In general, lower-class consumers have less product information. They are less informed about product prices and are no

Figure 16–1   Sears targets the middle class by using Cheryl Tiegs as a model. (*Courtesy of Sears Merchandise Group.*)

more likely to buy products "on sale" than upper-class consumers. Upper-class consumers are also less likely to use price as an indicator of quality. They tend to judge the quality of products on their merits rather than on their price.

Home Decoration

A number of indices use the quality and location of a house as an indicator of social class. Chapin's Social Status scale uses the type of living room furnishings to measure social class standing. Thus, it is not surprising that if one investigates home decoration, social class differences emerge. One study found that the homes of higher social class families tended to contain the following items:[23]

- ☐ Large potted plants.
- ☐ Sculptures.
- ☐ Abstract paintings.
- ☐ Fireplaces.
- ☐ Pianos.
- ☐ Identifiable furniture styles (e.g., French).

In contrast, lower social status homes tended to have in their living rooms:

- ☐ Mixed bulky furniture.
- ☐ Religious paintings.
- ☐ Televisions.
- ☐ General disorder.

Leisure Activities

The leisure activities of social classes differ in predictable ways. A study published in the early 1970s found that the upper-middle and upper classes more often engaged in "prestige" leisure activities, such as ice skating, bicycling, swimming, basketball, and tennis.[24] The authors noted that these sports involved rapid body movements and extensive use of the legs and arms. They suggested that upper-class people may be compensating for the sedentary lifestyle of their prestigious occupations by engaging in vigorous leisure activities. A more recent study confirmed some of these findings. It found that upper-class men are likely to play tennis, golf, jog, ski, attend social activities, read, and do political and community volunteer work. Men in the lower classes are more likely to play football, weight lift, motorcycle, and just do nothing.[25] The research further revealed that the upper classes attend more concerts and college football games. Lower classes watch more television, do more fishing, and go to baseball games and drive-in movies more often.

Concerning exposure to the various media, the upper classes are more frequent readers of magazines and newspapers than lower classes.[26] In addition to watching less television, the upper classes tend to focus on current events, drama programs, and sports. Lower classes watch more soap operas, quiz shows, and situation comedies.[27]

SOCIAL CLASS AND INCOME

An issue concerning social class is its relationship to household income. Some have argued that income is really a better predictor of buying behavior than social class. Early research on the issue was mixed. A study conducted in the mid-1970s found that income was a better predictor of the use or nonuse of entertainment services. However, social class better predicted the frequency of use of the services.[28]

More recently research has shown that the better predictor depends on the type of product or service investigated.[29] Social class was found to be a better predictor of purchases that were not high cost but that symbolically represented lifestyles and values. For example, usage of various food items, such as sweet beverages and wines, were predicted by social class. Income was a superior predictor of purchases of major appliances as well as the frequency of usage of soft drinks, mixers, and distilled alcohol. A combination of social class and income was a good predictor of expensive status products like autos and clothing.

As a summary statement, both income and social class influence buying behavior. As described in Highlight 16–2, family income varies widely within each social class, and great amount of income overlap exists between social classes. Income controls the ability to buy certain high-cost products and to a certain extent how often one can use expensive products, like distilled alcohol or diamonds. Figure 16–2 shows one of the De Beers diamond ads. The appeal is targeted directly to the high-income male. Note that the message is loud and brash—"She married you for richer or poorer. Let her know

HIGHLIGHT 16–2

Middle-Class Income Can Vary Greatly

A "prototype" household of middle-class, or Middle American, status has as its head a man employed in some lower-management office job, earning between $24,000 and $29,000 a year (1983 urban-average dollars), whose wife isn't working. Almost as likely to be middle class is a divorcée with two years of college as an educational credential, who is trying to support two children on a legal secretary's salary of as little as $13,500—and who may be best friend and frequent bridge-playing chum to the wife in the first case. Another middle-class home will contain a working couple, both in office jobs, earning a combined total of $42,000 or even $45,000 a year. A fourth might have as its head the owner of a bowling alley and restaurant, whose wife may or may not be helping to run them. Or the owner could be a widow, divorcée, or never-married women. In any case, the living standard projected by house, car(s), and clothes suggests an income of $60,000 or $70,000 a year, yet the social status is still middle class because, through lack of mobility aspirations and/or social skills, no upper-class connections and acceptance have been established.

Based on Richard P. Coleman, "The Continuing Significance of Social Class to Marketing," *Journal of Consumer Research*, *10*, December 1983, 268.

Figure 16–2 **De Beers seeks to attract the lower-upper-class market.**
(Courtesy of De Beers Consolidated Mines, and N W Ayer.)

how it's going." The ad is clearly *not* directed to an upper-class market segment because it is simply too flashy for upper-class tastes. Social class influences an individual's values, beliefs, and preferences. Thus, products that have an "image" or expressive value, like certain foods and wines, will be controlled more by social class because affordability is not a major issue.

Related to the income–social class debate is the **relative income hypothesis.** Research conducted in the early 1960s revealed that people within the same social class may have different consumption patterns based upon their relative incomes.[30] Individuals with high incomes in a social class were labeled **overprivileged.** Conversely, people with low incomes were labeled **underprivileged.** In their automobile purchases overprivileged consumers were found to purchase higher-prestige autos, such as Buicks and Oldsmobiles. People with average incomes were found to buy Fords and Chevrolets. The underprivileged tended to buy compact cars.

Later research, conducted in the early 1970s, found that the overprivileged owned larger cars than the underprivileged.[31] Whether or not these exact relations hold today is unclear. During the gas crises of the 1970s, it became fashionable for the well-to-do to own small foreign cars. However, it is likely that the distinction between the overprivileged and underprivileged in a social class still holds because of the importance of income in buying behavior. Those with higher incomes in a social class will find ways to reveal their wealth, but the method selected will change with social trends.

What the relative income hypothesis reveals is that income cannot be ignored when one investigates consumers. One must remember, however, that income and social class are correlated. Those with higher incomes will tend to have higher educations, more upscale occupations, nicer homes, better furniture, and so forth.

Just what is the correlation between income and social class? One noted researcher has estimated the correlation to be relatively low (around $r = .40$) in the 1980s.[32] Three reasons were cited for the relatively low correlation. First, historically social class has been based more on occupational differences than on income. Even in the 1980s, blue-collar workers may earn more than white-collar workers in many instances, yet their social status is lower. Second, differences in age can lower the correlation. Young workers traditionally make much less income than older workers. However, a young stockbroker making $20,000 is still in the middle class, and a fifty-year-old cabinet maker earning $40,000 is still in the working class. Finally, family variation in the number of earners has affected the income–social class correlation. With increasing divorce rates it has become common that a woman heads a family. Unfortunately, women traditionally earn less than men. Thus, incomes of families headed by a female tend to be lower. In contrast, in families where both spouses hold jobs, incomes will be relatively higher. However, in most cases neither divorce nor two incomes will influence social class status—only the relative amounts of income available.

How do the classes differ in their attitudes towards spending versus saving their incomes? As a general statement the upper social classes are much more interested in saving than the lower social classes. In one study consumers were asked what they would do if their incomes were doubled for the next ten years.[33] Upper classes indicated that much of the money would be saved. Further, they specified how it would be saved. They frequently mentioned some type of investment vehicles for saving. In contrast, lower-class consumers more often indicated spending goals. When saving was mentioned, the vehicle was usually some type of low-interest-bearing savings account.

PSYCHOLOGICAL DIFFERENCES AMONG THE CLASSES

Many of the differences noted in the consumption behaviors of the social classes can be accounted for by certain differences in the way they psychologically view the world.[34] The middle classes tend to focus on the future. They are generally self-confident, are willing to take risks, believe that they can control their fate, and see their horizons as broad. The middle classes stress rationality, tend to have an urban identification, think abstractly, and see themselves tied to national happenings. In contrast, the lower classes focus on the present and past. They are concerned with security and limited in their horizons. They do not have a well-structured view of the world and are concerned with their family and themselves. Rationality is not emphasized in their buying processes.

Psychological differences in the social classes were demonstrated in a study that investigated how various groups of consumers differed in their perception of the symbolism of products.[35] The results revealed that lower-class individuals tended to believe that those who owned big houses and nice cars obtained them because of "good luck." In contrast, higher social status consumers attributed the ability to purchase status symbols to the self-motivation of the owner. Such results indicate more of a fatalistic view of life among the lower social classes.

These psychological differences account in part for some of the variations found in the buying behavior of the upper and lower classes. The tendency of the lower classes not to save may result partially from their lack of interest and confidence in the future. Their tendency to shop in stores close to their neighborhood reflects in part their more limited horizons, as well as a lack of readily available transportation.

The psychological differences also suggest that promotional themes should be different for the social classes. A focus on achievement, on looking to the future, on abstract product benefits would be more effective with upper-class consumers. Promotions to lower-class consumers should instead focus on showing highly concrete benefits, on eliminating the risk in purchasing the product, and on appealing to home and family needs.

The narrow horizons and lack of tendency to change among the lower classes is demonstrated in their living and buying patterns. One study found that the social classes differed in their choices of how far away from their closest relatives they chose to live.[36] About half of the lower-class and working-class respondents lived within a mile of a close relative. In contrast, only 19 percent of middle-class respondents and 12 percent of the upper-class ones showed such a pattern. Another study, done in the mid-1970s, found that less than 10 percent of the working class owned a foreign car. In contrast, 25 percent of the middle class and 40 percent of the upper-status groups owned some type of foreign car.[37]

These psychological and lifestyle changes are summed up by the following quotation:

> For twenty years researchers have found that ". . . working-class life styles have been almost impervious to change in their basic characteristics—i.e., the limited horizons, the centrality of family and clan. The chauvinistic devotion to nation and neighborhood have been little altered by the automobile, telephone, or television. The modernity—and change—that these people seek is in possessions, not in human relationships or "new ideas." For them, "keeping up with the times" focuses on the mechanical and recreational, and thus ease of labor and leisure is what they continue to pursue."[38]

THE DEMOGRAPHICS OF SOCIAL CLASS

Although a person's actual social class should not be confused with the measures of social class, it is important to investigate the trends in the demographic indicators of social class. A number of demographic variables are highly correlated with social class. In particular, a person's occupation, educational level, and income level are closely related to social class identification. The demographics of these important marketing variables are discussed below.

Occupational and Educational Demographics

Both occupation and education are important components of social class. In fact, varying amounts of prestige are associated with different occupations. Researchers have asked people to rank the prestige of occupations on a variety of occasions. Table 16–2 shows the results of four studies which were conducted in 1925, 1947, 1968, and 1975. An amazing amount of consistency was found across the four studies. For example, the correlation of the rankings between the 1925 and the 1975 studies was .88—very high for social science studies.[39]

The study of **occupational demographics** focuses on the jobs Americans hold and on the past and future changes in these jobs. Several occupational trends occurred during the 1970s. First, the increase in the number of white-collar workers continued. Indeed, by the middle of the 1970s white-collar workers accounted for 50 percent of the labor force. Second, a major force affecting the jobs picture in the 1970s and 1980s is the increasing employment of women. In the 1970s many of the fastest-growing white-collar occupations were ones that traditionally employed women—nursing and

Table 16–2   Occupational Prestige Rankings

Occupation	Dates			
	1925	**1947**	**1968**	**1975**
Banker	1	2.5	4	3
Doctor	2	1	1	1
Lawyer	3	2.5	2	2
School superintendent	4	4	3	5
Civil engineer	5	5	5	4
Army captain	6	6	8	9
Foreign missionary	7	7	7	12
Elementary teacher	8	8	6	7
Farmer	9	12	19	15
Machinist	10	9	12	13
Traveling salesman	11	16	13	16
Grocer	12	13	17	14
Electrician	13	11	9	6
Insurance agent	14	10	10	8
Mail carrier	15	14	18	18
Carpenter	16	15	11	10
Soldier	17	19	15	19
Plumber	18	17	16	11
Bus driver	19	18	20	20.5
Barber	20	20	14	17
Truck driver	21	21.5	21	20.5
Coal miner	22	21.5	23	22
Janitor	23	23	22	23
Ditch digger	24	24	24	24

SOURCE: Data adapted from John Fossum and Michael Moore, "The Stability of Longitudinal and Cross-Sectional Occupational Rankings," *Journal of Vocational Behavior*, 7, 1975, 305–311.

secretarial services. Other fast-growing occupations in the 1970s were accountants, lawyers, engineers, economists, and authors. Occupations showing a net decrease in jobs were farming and private household workers. In general, the number of blue-collar workers grew very slowly in the 1970s.[40]

Although looking at the past is fine, the key issue concerns what will happen to the job market in the future. Certain trends do seem likely to continue. First, the white-collar and service sectors of the economy are likely to continue growing more rapidly than others. Jobs related to providing health services in particular should expand rapidly. Second, the trend towards higher technology should continue. Technical jobs related to computers and medical equipment should expand. Third, women will increasingly find employment, but, hopefully, in higher-status fields, such as medicine, accounting, engineering, and marketing.

Some occupations that grew rapidly in the 1970s may slow markedly in their expansion in the 1980s and 1990s. Currently an oversupply of lawyers and social scientists exists. The ranks of college professors could well decrease in the late 1980s and early 1990s in response to the demographic trend of fewer people reaching college age. Finally, the slow growth rate of blue-collar jobs should continue.

The changing occupational structure of Western countries from blue-collar to white-collar places a strong emphasis on a highly educated adult population. In fact, the number of people with some college education has grown rapidly in the United States. It is estimated that in 1985 over 30 percent of the U.S. population had some college education.[41]

White-collar, college-educated people tend to have a different consumption pattern than blue-collar workers. The college educated tend to consume above-average amounts of furniture, housewares, electronics, men's and women's apparel, and alcohol. The college educated tend to consume less tobacco, appliances, and personal care items.[42] As discussed in Highlight 16–3, completion of a college education affects one's lifetime earnings.

Like the other demographic variables, occupation and education are important factors on which companies segment the market. For example, publishers frequently target magazines specifically to individuals having particular educational backgrounds. The many science-oriented magazines (*Science 86, Discover*, etc.) are aimed specifically at the college educated. Occupation can create an even more homogeneous market segment. Marketers of professional service training, say to accountants, secretaries, or real estate agents, can obtain lists of people engaged in that specific line of work. Direct-mail advertising can then be targeted specifically to such people, increasing dramatically the cost effectiveness of promotional expenditures.

A major change in the occupational structure of the United States is portended by age demographics. It is estimated that by the year 2010, the num-

---

HIGHLIGHT 16–3

A College Education Does Pay

Will getting a college degree make any difference to your financial future? In 1981 males with a college degree earned 37 percent more than those with a high school degree. Female college graduates earned 44 percent more. If you look only at males over 25, their income rises to over 100 percent that of high school graduates. However, the impact of a college degree has the most effect on incomes over $50,000. In 1981, 20.1 percent of households with a college degree holder had incomes of over $50,000. In contrast, only 4.6 percent of the households with a high school degree holder

had incomes over $50,000. That's a 437 percent improvement.

Does having a college degree cause higher incomes? Not necessarily. Other factors could be at work. For example, those who complete college may be more intelligent, harder working, have better connections, and have higher personal goals than those who do not complete college.

Source: "Personal Income: Does an Education Help?," *Sales and Marketing Management*, October 25, 1982, 44.

Figure 16–3   The number of people aged 18–64 for each person 65+.
(*Source:* Middle projection series, U.S. Bureau of the Census.)

The ratio of the working-age population, 18 to 64, to the elderly population, 65 and older,
will decline sharply in the next century—a king-size headache for the Social Security system.

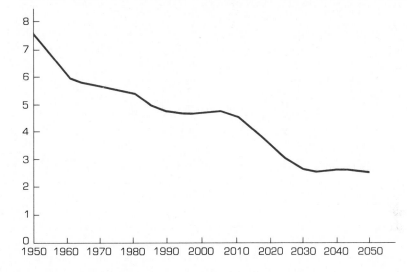

ber of Americans of working age will actually begin to decrease, unless the birth rate increases dramatically.[43] Figure 16–3 reveals the number of workers versus retirees between the years 1950 and 2050. Based on a birthrate of 2.1 children born to each woman, the plot reveals the precipitous fall off in the ratio beginning about the year 2010. The problems for our society of such a dramatic decrease in the number of workers supporting the retired will have major implications for social security and business. For example, where will business get its workers?

**The
Demographics
of Income**

As noted by one researcher:

> income has been underrated as a market criterion. Even in a credit society, one cannot purchase for very long what one cannot pay for. . . . Money does talk back to marketers.[44]

Household income, and in particular its growth, controls the funds that consumers have at their disposal. If income shrinks, the consumer will stop spending. Thus, anticipating changes in income levels of various segments of the population is an important task for the marketer.

Although aggregate household income controls the spending of large masses of consumers, consumers in different income levels can represent distinct market segments. Retailers in particular have been successful in targeting specific income segments. Wal-Mart Stores, a discount chain centered in the

Midwest, has had tremendous success targeting lower-income groups. In contrast, chains such as Nieman Marcus have had success targeting upper-income shoppers.

Regional Minority Group Income Variations In the 1970s the various regions of the United States fared quite differently in income growth. Table 16–3 presents per capita income figures for the various regions in the U.S. between 1969 and 1979. Regions which had the largest percentage growth in income tended to be those starting from the lowest base and having the greatest population growth. Because business opportunities tend to occur where growth is found, it's no wonder that the West South Central states (Texas, Oklahoma, Arkansas, and Louisiana) experienced such positive business conditions in the 1970s, with a per capita income growth of over 32 percent.

Note also that the Pacific region experienced good growth in the 1970s and expanded on its lead in per capita income by $465 over the nearest region—the Middle Atlantic States of New York, New Jersey, and Pennsylvania. Further, despite their high growth rate of 28.8 percent, the East South Central States (Kentucky, Tennessee, Alabama, and Mississippi) still remained the poorest.

The incomes of various subcultural groups also show large differences. For example, median household incomes of blacks and Hispanics were substantially lower than white households. Specifically, in the early 1980s the household income levels of blacks and Hispanics were 58 percent and 73 percent that of whites, respectively. If household wealth (property, savings, investments, and so on) is used, though, the wealth of blacks is only 36 percent that of whites ($24,608 versus $68,891).[45] The disparity in income and wealth of different ethnic groups has profound social implications. Some evidence exists that the gap may be closing, though. For example, between 1967

Table 16–3 Per Capita Income by Region

	1969	1979	Population % Change	Income % Change
New England	$6702	$7401	4.2%	10.7%
Middle Atlantic	6829	7502	−1.1	9.9
East North Central	6494	7484	3.6	15.2
West North Central	5745	7096	5.3	23.5
South Atlantic	5674	7122	20.5	25.5
East South Central	4595	5918	14.6	28.8
West South Central	5202	6883	22.9	32.3
Mountain	5701	7185	37.3	26.0
Pacific	7006	8184	19.9	16.8

Source: Data derived from 1970 and 1980 census information.

Table 16–4   Income Levels for Various Household Groups

	All Households	Family Households	Nonfamily Households	White Households	Black Households	Spanish Households
Median income	$17,710	$21,162	$ 9,456	$18,684	$10,764	$13,651
Mean income	$21,063	$24,118	$12,711	$21,913	$13,970	$16,674

Source: Data from 1980 census information, U.S. Bureau of Census.

and 1983 the ratio of black to white wealth almost doubled. Despite the relative progress, in absolute terms the gap in wealth widened because of the effects of inflation. Table 16–4 presents income levels in 1980 for a number of groups of consumers.

The Two-Income Family Trend   A major trend of the 1970s and early 1980s, which dramatically affects the income profile, is the tendency for families to have two, rather than one, primary wage earners. Between 1968 and 1978 the number of two-earner familes increased some 25 percent to 4.5 million.[46] By the mid 1980s well over 50 percent of all married couples were two-earner families.

Two-income couples tend to be seven years younger, to have higher educational attainment (particularly among the wives), and to have 20 percent higher incomes than traditional couples. Interestingly, the husbands in two-earner families tend to earn less than husbands in traditional families. The difference, though, was more than offset by the wives' earnings.[47]

Two-income families have become an important market segment for some companies. For example, insurance companies quickly recognized that the wife's earnings have become crucial to many families for them to maintain their standard of living. In one memorable television ad, a professional couple moved into a beautiful home in the first scene. In the second scene the wife disappears, taken from her huband by some mysterious, unnamed calamity. The movers then enter the house to remove the furniture and the couple's precious clock from the mantel because the husband could not afford the mortgage payments on his salary alone. The moral—working wives need insurance just as working husbands do.

Two incomes have brought an upward mobility for many couples. Indeed, some marketers claim that the rise in two-income families is the most important change to hit consumer marketing in a decade. Two-income families live differently from one-earner families—even those with the same household income. Dual-income families hire more household help, entertain less at home, and spend more on child care, convenience items, transportation, eating out, and luxury goods.[48] The common thread that separates the be-

HIGHLIGHT 16–4

Predicting Consumption Through Demographics

From a commonsense perspective one must conclude that demographic variables, such as age, sex, and income, influence consumption. Surprisingly, the research evidence on the topic has been mixed. For example, when investigators have tried to predict the consumption of widely advertised grocery items, demographic variables were not particularly helpful. One suggestion as to the cause of the problem is that researchers may be focusing too much on single individuals and not enough on groups of individuals. One study found that when groups of individuals were ex-

amined, it was possible to identify market segments of heavy users of coffee, specifically those forty-five to fifty-five years of age.* No wonder Procter and Gamble hired Lauren Bacall, the well-known middle-aged actress, in 1983 to endorse their new decaffeinated coffee—High Point. The key point—it's difficult to predict the behavior of specific individuals. One must look across large numbers of people to identify underlying trends.

*J. Wheatley, J. Chin and A. Stevens, *Journal of Advertising Research*, 20, December 1980, 31–38.

havior of two-income families from traditional households earning the same total income is *time*. Two-income families have very little free time and buy products and services to increase its availability.

Will the two-income trend continue? A number of factors make it likely. The increased aspirations and education of women point to a continued growth in the employment of women. The birth dearth, which occurred after 1964, will lead to a shortage of new workers entering the work force beginning in the late 1980s. It is likely that the wages of entry-level workers will rise and that more women will step in to reap the benefits of high pay. As more women work, we will see more two-income families. So far nothing indicates a slowdown in the growth of the two-income household.[49] Highlight 16–4 considers some other influences of demographics on consumption patterns.

Managerial Implications

Social class can be an important variable for managers to consider in the marketing planning process. Either alone or in combination with other psychographic and demographic variables, social class can be used to segment the market effectively. In addition, the concept is useful in developing the marketing mix. Finally, trends in the demographic variables frequently used to create social class indices may be important in performing marketing opportunity analyses.

Market Segmentation

Social classes do differ in their buying behavior, thereby allowing companies to target their products to a particular class-based group. For example, one study found that bank card customers used their credit cards in different ways.[50] Upper-class and upper-middle-class customers tended to use their cards for convenience. That is, the cards became a substitute for carrying cash or checkbooks. In contrast, lower classes used the cards for installment purchases. Rather than paying off their charges each month, the lower classes used their bank cards as a way to obtain a loan. Unfortunately, because of the high interest rates charged on outstanding debt on bank cards, such a practice substantially increases the cost of the purchase. From the bank's perspective the lower-class customers can be a valuable target group. The large profit margins that can be obtained from the high interest rates on unpaid credit card balances are quite attractive to banks.

Upper-class customers can be an important market segment to target, particularly during a recessionary economy. The incomes of lower-upper and upper-upper consumers are less affected by economic trends. Figure 16–4 shows a print advertisement for Godiva chocolates. The highly expensive candy was targeted to consumers with higher incomes and used a direct appeal to class consciousness in the copy. From the heading, "Well-bred," to the text, in which such words and phrases as "rare," "belong in a class by themselves," "rich," "noble," "cultured," and "elite" appear, the tone is one of exclusivity.

From a marketing manager's perspective four social class target groups exist:

1. Upper-middle class, lower-upper class, and upper-upper class.
2. Middle class.
3. Working class.
4. Lower class.

The "upper classes" have been combined because of their relatively small numbers and their similar tastes and preferences. The middle and working classes are divided because of their divergent values and ways of viewing the world. The lower classes are combined because of their similarities in outlook and small disposable income.

Developing the Marketing Mix

The targeting of a social class has implications for each component of the marketing mix. For example, if the lower-middle class is identified as a potential market segment, it will be important to establish a national brand. The product will have to be perceived as mainstream with few frills. Its promotion should be done predominantly on national television using traditional American themes—e.g., patriotism, motherhood. Distribution should be to discount stores. The product should be moderately priced. Coupons and sales would prove effective with the lower-middle class segment. Indeed, one can look at the advertising campaigns for Chevrolets and obtain a clear image of the appeals that can be used to reach the lower-middle class.

Developing Marketing Opportunities

Identifying future trends in the key demographic variables making up social class can result in the identification of new marketing opportunities. For example, the increased employment of women has affected the entire child-care industry. National chains of child-care centers have been created to sat-

Figure 16—4 Godiva Chocolatier portrays an upper-class image in its ad. *(Courtesy of Godiva Chocolatier, Inc.)*

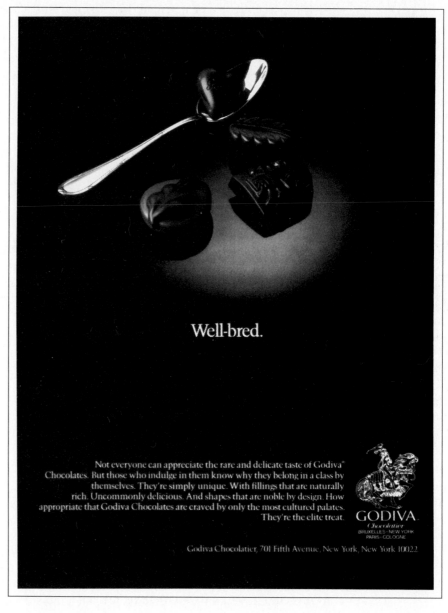

isfy the burgeoning need for high-quality facilities. Increases in the number of college-educated adults means that opportunities lie in developing products that are high in quality and have an investment quality about them. This occurs because those with higher educational attainment tend to move up in class and emphasize the future. Investment firms have capitalized on the focus on the future so important to middle- and upper-class Americans. As John Houseman, the curmudgeonly endorser for the brokerage firm Smith-Barney said, "They make money the old-fashioned way—they *earn* it." The message, that you have to work hard to make it over the long haul, is highly appealing to the middle and upper classes. The increase in the number of educated individuals makes it worthwhile to develop additional investment vehicles for such people. Indeed, in the early 1980s the number of new ways to invest in the stock market and in real estate, oil, and precious metals increased enormously.

SUMMARY

The term *social class* refers to the idea that people divide themselves into hierarchical groups. A variety of factors distinguish these groups, including occupation, wealth, education, possessions, values, and associations. For marketers social class is an important segmentation tool, particularly when used in conjunction with income. A number of social class scales have been developed. For marketers four target groups based on social class exist—a broad upper class, the white-collar middle class, an affluent working class, and a poor lower class.

A number of problems have been identified in using social class in marketing. Some of these include:

1. Too many definitions.
2. The use of the husband to identify a household's class.
3. The reliance on a person's present social class rather than assessing his or her background and aspirations.
4. The assumption that a person has only one social class.

The social classes do display differences in buying behavior. In particular, the purchase of items that have an image or expressive quality is influenced by social class. Because of the wide variations in the amount of income earned by members within a social class, some will be relatively overprivileged and some underprivileged. Thus, when segmenting the market on social class, it is important to assess the effects of income as well.

The social classes do differ in their psychological makeup. In particular, the middle and upper classes tend to focus on the future, whereas the lower classes are caught in the present and past. These differences influence the types of promotional messages that will be attractive to the classes.

Three demographic variables are particularly important to the measurement of social class—occupation, education, and income. Demographic trends in these variables can actually influence the number of people who occupy each social class. Therefore, major changes in the number of blue-collar workers, the number of college-educated people, and in the amount of disposable income available can create market opportunities or liabilities for companies.

In summary, social class influences managerial decision making in three fundamental areas—segmentation, designing the marketing mix, and identifying new marketing opportunities.

Key Terms

Social class
Choice behavior fallacy
Husband-only fallacy
Present social class fallacy
Single social class fallacy
Status crystallization
Relative income hypothesis
Overprivileged/underprivileged
Social class hierarchy

Upper Americans
Middle Americans
Lower Americans
Upper-upper class
Lower-upper class
Upper-middle class
Middle class
Working class
Upper-lower class
Lower-lower class
Occupational demographics

Review Questions

1. Define the concept of social class. How do marketers tend to use the concept in comparison to sociologists?
2. Identify the social classes as defined by Coleman and found in Table 16–1. What is the relative size of each of the social classes?
3. Indicate the four variables most frequently used to assess social class.
4. Delineate four of the six problems identified in the use of the social class concept by marketers.
5. Provide two examples each of how upper and lower social classes differ in shopping patterns and in leisure activities.
6. What is the correlation between social class rank and income? For what types of products may social class be a better predictor of buying patterns than income?
7. Discuss the concept of the relative income hypothesis.
8. Middle and upper social classes seem to differ in the way they view the world and themselves as compared to lower social classes. Identify three psychological differences that separate middle and upper social classes from the lower social classes.
9. Identify the single largest trend you now perceive to be occurring in the demographics of occupations, education, and income.
10. Which of the regions in the United States tended to experience the highest and lowest growth rates in income during the 1970s and early 1980s? Do you believe these trends are still occurring today?
11. It has been said that for the marketing manager four social class groups exist. What are these groups? Why have some of the social class groups been combined in this scheme?

Discussion Questions

1. Consider the types of department stores in your region of the country. Identify the social classes that each of these stores appears to target.
2. In addition to assigning people to social classes, one can also rank institutions of higher education into prestige rankings. Identify two universities or colleges which can be placed into each of the following prestige classifications: highest prestige, moderately high prestige, middle prestige, moderately low prestige, and low prestige. What criteria delineate how the universities are classified?
3. Why is it that people in the United States (including instructors, students, and the author of this text) tend to be uncomfortable discussing the topic of social class?
4. Based upon the knowledge you have of your friends and acquaintances, do you think that social class mobility is increasing or decreasing in the United States? What are the primary means of gaining mobility today in the United States?
5. Draw a map of the city or town about which you are most familiar. Identify by location the areas in

which the various social classes live. What are the implications of this for direct-mail marketers?

6. Go to the magazine section of a good bookstore and thumb through a copy of *Architectural Digest* and of *Better Homes and Gardens*. To which social classes are these publications directed? What are the differences you can identify in the interior decoration of the homes?

7. Do you think that social class or income would be better segmentation tools for targeting heavy users of: opera, college football games, luxury automobiles, expensive jewelry, original art work, luxury vacations? Why?

8. What are some of the reasons why there might be psychological differences among the social classes?

9. The occupational prestige rankings given in Table 16–2 were taken in 1975. To what extent do you think that these rankings might now be different?

References

1. Gerhard Lenski, *Power and Privilege: A Theory of Social Stratification*, New York, N.Y.: McGraw-Hill Book Company, 1966.

2. Leonard Beeghley, *Social Stratification in America*, Santa Monica, Calif.: Goodyear Publishing Co., Inc., 1978.

3. Richard Coleman, "The Continuing Significance of Social Class in Marketing," *Journal of Consumer Research, 10*, December 1983, 265–280.

4. James Carmen, *The Application of Social Class in Market Segmentation*, Berkeley, Calif.: Institute of Business and Economic Research, 1965.

5. Bernie Whalen, "Illiteracy: The Marketing Research Implications," *Marketing News*, May 13, 1983, 1, 18.

6. W. J. Warner, M. Meeker, and K. Eels, *Social Class in America: Manual of Procedure for the Measurement of Social Status*, Chicago, Ill.: Science Research Associates, 1949.

7. Marvin Roscoe, A. Leclaire, and L. Schiffman, "Theory and Management Applications of Demographics in Buying Behavior," in *Foundations of Consumer and Industrial Buying Behavior*, Arch G. Woodside, J. Sheth, and P. Bennett (eds.), New York, N.Y.: American Elsevier Publishing Co., Inc., 1977, 74–75.

8. Joan Throckmorton, "Targeting the Fragmented Middle Class," *Direct Marketing*, August, 1982, 70–71.

9. Dean Ellis, "Speech and Social Status in America," *Social Forces, 45*, March 1967, 431–437.

10. Leonard Schatzman and A. Strauss, "Social Class and Modes of Communication," *American Journal of Sociology, 60*, January 1955, 329–338.

11. Terence Shimp and J. Thomas Yokum, "Extensions of the Basic Social Class Model Employed in Consumer Research," *Advances in Consumer Research, VIII*, William Wilkie (ed.), Ann Arbor, Mich.: Association for Consumer Research, 1981.

12. Shimp and Yokum, "Extension of the Basic Social Class Model."

13. Ibid.

14. Gerhard Lenski, "Status Crystallization: A Non-Vertical Dimension of Social Status," *American Sociological Review, 21*, August 1956, 458–464.

15. Stuart Rich and Subhash Jain, "Social Class and Life Cycle as Predictors of Shopping Behavior," *Journal of Marketing Research, 5*, February 1968, 43–44.

16. V. Kanti Prasad, "Socioeconomic Product Risk and Patronage Preferences of Retail Shoppers," *Journal of Marketing, 39*, July 1975, 42–47.

17. Patrick Murphy, "The Effects of Social Class on Brand and Price Consciousness for Supermarket Prices," *Journal of Retailing, 54*, Summer 1978, 33–38, 89–90.

18. Claire Makin, "Sears' Overdue Retailing Revival," *Fortune*, April 4, 1983, 103–107.

19. Peter L. Gillet, "A Profile of Urban In-Home Shoppers," *Journal of Marketing, 34*, July 1970, 40–45.

20. Rich and Jain, "Social Class and Life Cycle."

21. Gordon R. Foxall, "Social Factors in Consumer Choice, *Journal of Consumer Research, 2*, June 1975, 60–64.

22. Henry Assael, *Consumer Behavior*, Boston, Mass.: Kent Publishing, 1981.

23. F. Stuart Chapin, *Contemporary American Institutions*, New York: Harper & Row, Publishers, 1935, 373–397.

24. Doyle Bishop and Masaru Ikeda, "Status and Role Factors in the Leisure Behavior of Different Occupations," *Sociology and Social Research, 54*, January 1970, 190–208.

25. *The Playboy Report on American Men*, Survey conducted by Louis Harris and Associates, New York, N.Y.: Playboy Enterprises, 1979, 53–54, 57.

26. Leah Rozen, "Coveted Consumers Rate Magazines Over TV: MPA," *Advertising Age*, August 20, 1979, 64.

27. Sidney J. Levy, "Social Class and Consumer Behavior," in *On Knowing the Consumer*, Joseph W. Newman (ed.), New York, N.Y.: John Wiley & Sons, Inc., 1966, 155.

28. R. D. Hisrich and Michael Peters, "Selecting the Superior Segmentation Correlate," *Journal of Marketing*, 38, July 1974, 60–63.

29. Charles M. Schaninger, "Social Class Versus Income Revisited: An Empirical Investigation," *Journal of Marketing Research*, 18, May 1981, 192–208.

30. Richard P. Coleman, "The Significance of Social Stratification in Selling," in *Marketing: A Mature Discipline*, Martin L. Bell (ed.), Chicago, Ill.: American Marketing Association, 1960, 171–184.

31. William H. Peters, "Relative Occupational Class Income: A Significant Variable in the Marketing of Automobiles," *Journal of Marketing*, 34, April 1970, 74–77.

32. Richard P. Coleman, "Continuing Significance of Social Class."

33. Ibid.

34. Pierre Martineau, "Social Classes and Shopping Behavior," *Journal of Marketing*, 23, October 1958, 121–130.

35. Russell Belk, Robert Mayer, and Kenneth Bahn, "The Eye of the Beholder: Individual Differences in Perceptions of Consumption Symbolism," *Advances in Consumer Research*, IX, Andrew Mitchell (ed.), Ann Arbor, Mich.: Association for Consumer Research, 1981, 523–529.

36. Richard Coleman, "Attitudes Towards Neighborhood; How Americans Want to Live," Cambridge, Mass.: Joint Center for Urban Studies of Massachusetts Institute of Technology and Harvard University," Working paper No. 49.

37. Cited in Richard Coleman, "Continuing Significance of Social Class."

38. Ibid.

39. John Fossum and Michael Moore, "The Stability of Longitudinal and Cross-Sectional Occupational Prestige Rankings," *Journal of Vocational Behavior*, 7, December 1975, 305–311.

40. Carol Leon, "Occupational Winners and Losers," *American Demographics*, 3, March 1983, 28–35.

41. James Engel and R. Blackwell, *Consumer Behavior*, 4th ed., Chicago, Ill.: The Dryden Press, 1982.

42. Engel and Blackwell, *Consumer Behavior*.

43. Gregory Spencer and J. F. Long, "The New Census Bureau Projections," *American Demographics*, 5, April 1983, 24–32.

44. Alfred Eisenpreis, "Reaching Undersold Markets," *American Demographics*, 1, January 1980, 20–24.

45. Timothy Schellhardt, "Data on Average Wealth of Blacks Suggest Economic Gap with Whites Is Widening," *The Wall Street Journal*, June 20, 1983, 11.

46. Howard Hayghe, "Two-Income Families," *American Demographics*, 1, September 1981, 35–37.

47. Hayghe, "Two-Income Families."

48. B. G. Yovovich, "Now It's the Baby Boomer's Turn," *Advertising Age*, April 4, 1983, M–11, M–16, M–8.

49. Yovovich, "Now It's the Baby Boomer's Turn."

50. Joseph T. Plummer, "Life Style Patterns and Commercial Bank Credit Card Usage," *Journal of Marketing*, 35, April 1971, 35–41.

17

Cultural and Cross-Cultural Influences

CONSUMER VIGNETTE

Marketing in Japan

One constantly hears of how difficult it is for American companies to compete in the Japanese marketplace. Horror stories abound of unsuccessful efforts. For example, a catsup manufacturer failed in its attempt to entice the Japanese to buy its tomato-based product. Why? The Japanese were quite satisfied with their own condiment—soy sauce. Similarly, the Simmons company sought to sell American-sized beds to the Japanese. The effort was doomed because the Japanese sleep on mats that are put away each morning. Large American beds simply did not fit the lifestyle of the Japanese, who lived in small homes with multipurpose rooms. (a)

Despite such widely publicized failures, some American companies have successfully penetrated the marketplace in the "land of the rising sun." Not surprisingly one such success story involves a quality American corporation—Anheuser-Busch.

The Japanese are Asia's biggest beer consumers, and the country is the fifth largest beer market in the world. Thus, it was a natural market for Anheuser-Busch to enter with its flagship brand—Budweiser. However, succeeding in Japan was difficult. In addition to competing against well-entrenched Japanese beer manufacturers, Budweiser was faced with competition from fifty foreign brands from twenty countries. Despite these obstacles within four years Bud was the leading imported beer, surpassing Heineken in 1982. (b)

Two factors accounted for the success of Budweiser—the Japanese love affair with America and distribution by Japan's largest whiskey manufacturer. The problem of entering the complicated Japanese distribution system is well known. Anheuser-Busch was wise enough to overcome this problem by giving the importing rights to an old and respected Japanese liquor distributor.

Much more interesting were the cultural aspects of Bud's Japanese debut. Prior to its introduction the Budweiser name was already recognized by many Japanese. Tourists often returned from the United States with "Bud" sweatshirts. In addition, Japanese movie directors often used a can of Bud and a pack of Marlboros to evoke an image of America. Thus, when introduced, the brand found a receptive market.

One problem faced by Bud, though, was that many Japanese considered it too watery tasting. The distributor decided to try to turn this liability into a benefit. In Japan the word *American* has a connotation of lightness. For example, "American coffee" in Japan refers to a lightly blended brew. Budweiser was, therefore, specifically identified as an "American styled" beer in order to account for its lighter taste. In effect, the Japanese were given a reason for why it tasted watery: "It's American and supposed to be that way."

The American theme was carried further by showing the distinctive red, white, and blue Budweiser cans against familiar American scenes, like the Grand Canyon. Publicity was gained by sponsoring jazz festivals and by bringing over former and current St. Louis Cardinals baseball players. The baseball-hungry Japanese recognized the connection between baseball, beer, and Budweiser. (Anheuser-Busch owns the Cardinals.)

Few companies have the cultural advantages owned by Budweiser in entering the Japanese marketplace. However, Anheuser-Busch and its Japanese distributor used the advantages exquisitely.

Based on (a) David Ricks, M. Fu, and J. Arpan, *International Business Blunders*, Columbus, Ohio: Grid, Inc., 1974; and (b) Jack Burton, "Japan Agrees: When You Say Bud, You've Said It All," *Advertising Age*, March 28, 1983, M–23.

INTRODUCTION

The importance of understanding culture is well illustrated when marketers unsuccessfully sell their products abroad. By recognizing the differences between their own culture and that of the targeted society, managers can avoid multimillion-dollar mistakes, like that made by Simmons in Japan.

When marketing in one's own country, knowledge of culture is also important. First, each culture has its own set of symbols, rituals, and values to which marketers can tie their products and services. For example, in the United States the eagle is a symbol representative of strength, courage, and patriotism. Companies wanting to create such an image will use the eagle in their advertising or packaging. Whirlpool Corporation has done this in promotions for their household appliances.

Culture is also important to marketers because it can change. Culture is not static; it adapts to changes in economics, politics, technology, demographics, war and peace, and other factors. With changes in culture come changes in values and lifestyles. Such variations can lead to potential corporate catastrophes or marketing opportunities. For example, in the 1980s Americans' emphasis on fitness and slimness has become a major lifestyle trend. As a result, the marketers of running shoes, weight-lifting machines, and related athletic equipment have experienced explosive growth. In contrast, the emerging cultural trend towards health and fitness played havoc with marketers of beef and pork products, because consumers perceived the products as inconsistent with their lifestyles 'because of their high fat and calorie content. Thus, tracking the evolving cultural milieux is an important task for the forward-thinking corporation and should be one component of market opportunity analysis.

WHAT IS CULTURE?

Culture is a set of socially acquired behavior patterns transmitted symbolically through language and other means to the members of a particular society.[1] Culture is a way of life. It includes the material objects of a society, such as footballs, autos, Bibles, forks, and spoons. It also includes ideas and values, such as the concept that people have a right to a choice of products. It even consists of business organizations, which symbolically represent a society—like McDonald's or Anheuser-Busch. The ways we dress, think, eat, and spend our leisure time are parts of our culture.

A number of additional ideas are necessary to round out an understanding of culture. A culture is *learned.* It is *not* present in our genes. Thus, it is transmitted from generation to generation to be shared by future members of the society. The process of learning one's own culture is called **enculturation.** The difficult task of learning a new culture is called **acculturation.**

A culture is also *adaptive.* It changes as a society faces new problems and opportunities. Just as organisms evolve, so do cultures. They take on new traits and discard old useless ones to form a new cultural base. The "sexual revolution" in the United States exemplifies such cultural adaptation. The development of the birth control pill set into motion forces that created an environment conducive to change in the way society views women and sexual relations. With the cultural change a host of marketing opportunities occurred, and entrepreneurs stepped in to form *Playboy* magazine, Fredericks of Hollywood, and a host of other companies and products.

Finally, culture satisfies needs. By providing **norms,** or rules of behavior, a culture gives an orderliness to society. By providing **values** a culture delineates what is right, good, and important. People need to know what is expected of them, what is right and wrong, what they should do in different situations. Culture fulfills such societal requirements.

The task of identifying the elements of one's own culture is difficult. In fact, one author suggested that understanding one's own culture requires knowing something of another culture in order to realize that other people really do things differently.[2] For example, by international standards Americans are fanatics concerning personal hygiene. In most other parts of the world deodorants are rarely used, baths much less frequently taken, and teeth brushed rarely. Indeed, toilet paper is unheard of in some areas of the globe. The American preoccupation with fresh breath appears silly to Mediterranean cultures, whose cuisine is partially built around garlic. However, cultural discomfort is bidirectional. Visitors from mainland China are somewhat revolted when they learn that Americans actually sell food for animals in the same place where food is sold for people.

From a marketing perspective three components of the American culture as they relate to consumer behavior are particularly important: values, rituals, and symbols.

CULTURAL VALUES IN THE UNITED STATES

Cultural values in the United States have a variety of sources. One important source was the European heritage of the early settlers of America. (Although American can be used to describe the people of both North and South America, it will be used in this text to refer to those who reside in the United States). The flight from religious persecution and authoritarian monarchies indelibly etched into the American culture the values of individualism, freedom, and a fear of big government. Some have argued that the American frontier created the values of individualism, informality, equality, and hard work.[3] Certainly, the Judeo-Christian heritage of early Americans also influenced what were to become core American values.

A number of authors have developed lists of core American values.[4] Frequently mentioned values include beliefs in the importance of:

Individualism
Youthfulness
Progress
Materialism
Activity
Achievement
Efficiency
Informality
Equality

Other values sometimes mentioned include: freedom, external conformity, humanitarianism, authority, respect for institutions, mastery of the environment, and religion. The "Protestant Ethic" also flows deeply through the social fabric of the United States. Thus, values relating to hard work and frugality are important to many Americans. Such themes are sometimes used by advertisers. For example, the ad developed by the Peace Corps, shown in Figure 17–1, illustrates an appeal to a work ethic to obtain volunteers. In addition, the ad holds forth the promise of learning about new cultures.

A problem with lists of values is that they are cumbersome. It is difficult to decide when to stop adding new cultural beliefs. To alleviate this problem

Figure 17–1   The Peace Corps employs an appeal to the cultural value of the work ethic. *(Courtesy of Peace Corps.)*

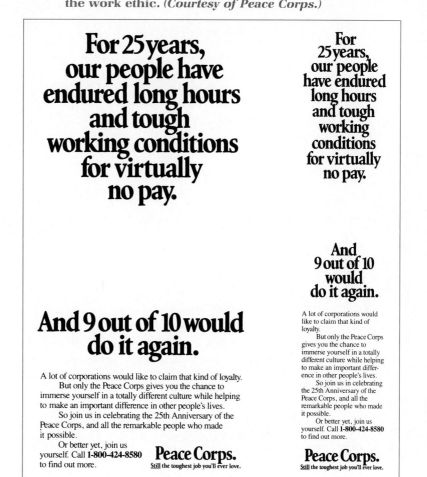

one can organize the various cultural values into dimensions. One organizational structure was suggested by psychologist David McClelland. As discussed in Chapter 3, McClelland argued that three basic motivational factors spur human action—the need for affiliation, the need for power, and the need for achievement.[5] People, and the culture in which they reside, can be evaluated to the extent that they reveal more or less of an emphasis on each of the three motivational dimensions.

Table 17–1 presents the three needs identified by McClelland and some cultural values that exemplify these needs. Somewhat surprisingly the need for affiliation is illustrated by the cultural value of individualism, which may be viewed as a lack of a desire to affiliate with others. Americans place much

Table 17–1 American Cultural Values and the Motivational Needs that they Exemplify

Motivational Needs	American Cultural Values
Need for affiliation	Individualism
	Affiliation
Need for power	Freedom
	Equality
	Informality
	External conformity
	Respect for authority
	Respect for institutions
	Mastery of the environment
Need for achievement	Progress
	Materialism
	Activity
	Efficiency
	Achievement

emphasis on individualism, or the ability to act on one's own without regard for what others think. Although Americans illustrate a strong tendency to affiliate by joining groups, such as churches and civic organizations, an underlying value that emphasizes the importance of the individual exists.

The value of individualism also is reflected in the manner in which the need for power is exhibited by Americans. Americans distrust power when it is wielded by large institutions. Values that illustrate this tendency include the ideas of equality and freedom. However, in instances that do not involve harming individual rights, the need for power is demonstrated. Thus, American values include a tendency to show external conformity, respect for authority, respect for institutions, and a desire for mastery of the environment.

Perhaps the dimension most clearly revealed via McClelland's needs is the need for achievement. Values illustrating the need for achievement include: achievement, progress, materialism, activity, and efficiency.

One must recognize, however, that countercurrents tend to exist regarding cultural values. For example, in the United States the respect for institutions has been steadily falling since the mid-1970s. Similarly, the ecology movement with its emphasis on living in harmony with nature clearly acts as a counterforce against the value of mastering the environment. As noted earlier, culture is adaptive, and one can expect to see movements that are inconsistent with the traditional values of a culture.

Another psychologist who has investigated values extensively is Milton Rokeach. Rokeach identified what he called **terminal** values and **instrumental** values.[6] Terminal values are desired end states—how people would like to experience their lives. Instrumental values are the behaviors and actions

Table 17–2   Rokeach's Terminal and Instrumental Values[a]

Terminal Values	Instrumental Values
World at peace	Honest
Family security	Responsible
Freedom	Ambitious
Equality	Forgiving
Self-respect	Broadminded
Happiness	Courageous
Wisdom	Helpful
National security	Loving
Competence	Capable
Friendship	Clean
Accomplishment	Self-controlled
Inner harmony	Independent
Comfortable life	Cheerful
Mature love	Polite
World of beauty	Intellectual
Pleasure	Obedient
Social recognition	Logical
Exciting life	Imaginative

[a]The values are listed in their order of importance as rated by adults interviewed in 1971.

SOURCE: Adapted from Milton Rokeach, *Understanding Human Values*, New York, N.Y.: The Free Press, 1979.

required to achieve the terminal states. Table 17–2 presents the set of eighteen terminal and instrumental values identified by Rokeach and their order of importance to American adults in 1971.

Consumer Research on Cultural Values

Research linking cultural values directly to the behavior of consumers is scanty. In one research study the authors investigated whether the Rokeach values could differentiate the heavy from light viewers of various media.[7] The results revealed that heavy television viewers tended to have more traditional religious views and to be less concerned with achievement and personal success. Heavy magazine readers revealed a different pattern. They emphasized the importance of competence, were more inner-directed, and were less concerned with interpersonal relations.

Another author investigated whether values were related to the types of automobiles people owned.[8] He found that owners of full-sized cars were more family oriented and felt as though nature or other people controlled their fate. Owners of subcompact cars were more democratically oriented. Owners of sports cars emphasized harmony with the environment and self-fulfillment. The author of the study noted that changing values could lead to shifting consumption patterns. He suggested that a long-term movement towards smaller autos could occur if Americans were to shift to values emphasizing nonmaterialism and harmony with nature.

Other researchers have attempted to show how cultural values influence specific consumption decisions. Figure 17–2 shows the sequence of moving from global values to domain-specific values to evaluations of product attributes.[9] **Global values** consist of peoples' enduring beliefs about desired states of existence and correspond closely to Rokeach's terminal values. **Domain-specific values** are beliefs pertaining to more concrete consumption activities. Examples include beliefs that manufacturers should give prompt service, guarantee their products, help eliminate environmental pollution, be truthful, and so forth. Evaluations of product attributes are highly specific beliefs about individual products. For example, how well does a Corvette handle? Is it easy to repair? (There is much more discussion about product beliefs in Chapter 7.)

The researchers found that people with different global values also exhibited divergent domain-specific values and product evaluations. Indeed, the differences in global values translated to markedly different product preferences. For example, those with global values emphasizing logic, an exciting life, and self-respect preferred compact cars and outdoor recreation. Those with global values emphasizing national security and salvation were more attracted to standard-sized cars and television.

An understanding of cultural values is important to the marketing manager for long-range planning and marketing opportunity analysis. For example, changes in terminal values, such as increased desires for pleasure, excitement, and comfort, could influence how products are named, what their

Figure 17–2 **Organization of the value-attitude system. (Adapted by permission, from Donald E. Vinson, Jerome Scott, and Lawrence Lamont, "The Role of Personal Values in Marketing and Consumer Behavior,"** *Journal of Marketing, 41,* **April 1977, 46.)**

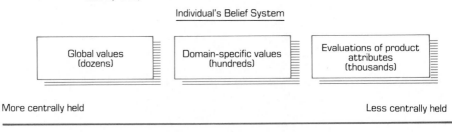

Global values: Enduring beliefs about desired states of existence or modes of behavior.
Domain-specific values: Beliefs relevant to economic, social, religious, and other activities.
Evaluations of product attributes: Evaluative beliefs about product attributes (e.g., sports cars should run very fast and handle very well).

colors are, and how they are designed. In advertising, such global values would influence the underlying tone of the message and the choice of models. Such a trend can be seen in advertising for Coca Cola. Some of the themes have been "Have a Coke and a Smile," "Coke Is It," "I'd Like to Give the World a Coke," and "It's the Real Thing." The theme of giving the world a coke occurred in the 1960s when international tensions were high, and Americans were highly concerned with world peace. The advertisement showed people of different countries in a long line, holding hands, and passing the Coke. The advertisement had dramatic impact and spawned a popular song. Similarly, the theme, "Coke Is It," which began in late 1982, seemed to catch the cultural trend of the times with the emphasis on self and the presence of the so-called me-generation. These themes seemed to catch the changes in cultural values that moved through the United States during the 1960s, 1970s, and 1980s.

CULTURAL RITUALS

Cultural rituals are standardized sequences of actions that are periodically repeated. They have some purpose and generally have a beginning, middle, and end. Rituals can be public or private. They vary from large-scale civic rituals, such as the Super Bowl, to private and personal rituals involving prayer or grooming behavior. The behaviors involved in a ritual are "scripted" so that they are formal and prescribed by convention. The behaviors tend to recur and follow a fixed pattern, and in many cases they involve the consumption and use of products.[10]

The list of consumption-related rituals is long. For example, many of the everyday things we do are rituals. The morning routine of getting up, taking a shower, fixing our hair, eating breakfast, and brushing our teeth is a ritual not shared in many other cultures. Other rituals include rites of passage (e.g., weddings, baby showers, and funerals), religious ceremonies, holiday festivities (e.g., Christmas, Thanksgiving), family activities (e.g., television viewing at prescribed times, the summer vacation, or Sunday dinner), and large-scale public rituals (e.g., singing the national anthem or watching parades and sports events).[11]

The television ritual has become extremely important to our society. As one author noted, "Television provides a series of common, shared experiences and images which have become part of the collective shared traditions of our society."[12] The three-hour "prime-time" entertainment block in fact has a long history in the United States. In the nineteenth century popular theater performances lasted three hours. The three-hour block continued in vaudeville early in the twentieth century and later was used in double-bill movies. Currently, the prime-time ritual begins at seven or eight o'clock in the evening. At about this time millions of Americans begin to wander into their living rooms, plop into easy chairs, and sip and munch their way through three hours of sit-coms, documentaries, movies, and television dramas. The ritual has spawned a huge advertising industry, brought employment opportunities to thousands of people, and generally greased the bearings of American commerce.

Many American rituals take place within specific consumption situations. Christmas is one such consumer situation that is highly ritualized. For most Americans Christmas means gift giving, and an elaborate ritual has built up around the practice. (For Jewish Americans many of the components of Christmas are bound into the celebration of Hanukkah.) The Christmas ritual involves a series of steps. During the summer retailers begin to order merchandise that they saw at "market." Advertising begins in earnest around Thanksgiving. At about this time consumers begin to realize their gift-giving obligations. Children are taken to see the fictional character Santa Claus. Christmas songs are played, and television programming begins to incorporate Christmas into its themes. Consumers begin to shop in earnest, wrap presents, and send Christmas cards. On Christmas Eve and Christmas Day, the religious aspects of the holiday are observed. In addition, the ritual of giving presents, opening them, and exchanging thank-yous occurs. The week after Christmas is filled with returning unwanted gifts to retailers and picking up "bargains" as stores attempt to clear their shelves. The ritual ends with the New Year's Day festivities. These include merriment on New Year's Eve and gross overindulgence in food and football on New Year's Day. The final duty of the Christmas ritual is the making and breaking of New Year's resolutions.

For manufacturers and retailers the key is to recognize the importance of the culturally prescribed **consumer rituals** and to try to tie their products into the ritual. The idea is to identify these ritualistic patterns of behavior and design and promote products that assist the activity. For example, the beauty ritual involves a long series of steps for many women. Some adroit marketers have attempted to lengthen the ritual by adding new steps, such as using an astringent to close facial pores after washing one's face. The Clinique line of products has done this. Similarly, Vidal Sassoon developed a three-step process of cleansing hair—shampoo, remoisturizer, and finishing rinse. The successful and expensive product fit well with the women's hair-washing ritual and promised to provide an important benefit to the consumer—prettier, healthier hair.

CULTURAL SYMBOLS

In addition to values and rituals, cultures have symbols. **Symbols** are entities that represent ideas and concepts.[13] They are important because they communicate complex ideas rapidly with a minimum of effort. For example, if a company wants to communicate the concept of patriotism, a useful symbol is the American flag. A more subtle symbol of patriotism, which also denotes swiftness and strength, is the eagle. By adroitly using these symbols companies and advertisers can tie cultural values to their products or services, thereby, enhancing their attractiveness to consumers.

It can be argued that people "consume" symbols.[14] That is, products may be evaluated, purchased, and consumed based in part on their symbolic value. In order for products to have symbolic value, it must have a shared reality among consumers. Thus, large numbers of consumers must have a common conception of the symbolic meaning of the product. For example, in order for an automobile to have "prestige" value, others in the relevant social group must view it in the same manner as the buyer.[15]

Companies will attempt to symbolize the characteristics of their products via the names chosen for them. For example, auto manufacturers have been highly fond of naming their products after animals. The manufacturers have sought to translate the characteristics of the animal, such as swiftness, agility, and aggressiveness to the automobile. Highlight 17–1 discusses the use of cultural symbols as names for products and one potential pitfall in their use.

Numerous symbols exist in the American culture. The symbol of money—and occasionally power or greed—is the dollar sign ($). The symbol to denote spiritual matters is the cross. To denote contemplation a smoking pipe might be used. Similarly, wearing glasses can indicate intelligence and possibly physical weakness—a la Clark Kent, Superman's alter ego. Planting a tree reveals permanence, and so forth.

Colors also have symbolic value. In the United States black indicates mourning, although it is also worn when formality is indicated. For example, Gloria Vanderbilt brought out a line of black, "formal" jeans for women. Blue indicates coolness—e.g., "Ice Blue Aqua-Velva." White means purity—e.g., wedding dresses and milk products. Pink is feminine, and for babies blue is masculine.

Clothing also has important symbolic meaning for consumers. Table 17–3 identifies a variety of functions that clothing may have for consumers, as well as the potential symbolic value of such clothing. For example, one of the functions of clothing is to act as an emblem of group membership. The popularity of T-shirts and even hats that possess a group emblem well illustrates the symbolic nature of clothing.

CROSS-CULTURAL CONSUMER ANALYSIS

Although a thorough understanding of one's own culture helps, it is not sufficient to do business successfully in a foreign country. The study of the values, language, and customs of the other society is also important when a company engages in international trade. Is international marketing something that a student in Iowa, Texas, or California should be concerned about? *Yes!* Exports accounted for 11.4 percent of the gross national product of the United States in 1982, almost doubling since 1970.[16] In 1985 the high value of the dollar in relation to other currencies severely curtailed exports by making U.S. products more expensive abroad. The result was a depressed manufac-

HIGHLIGHT 17–1

Cultural Symbols Make Good Brand Names

American companies are in love with animals, and one possible reason is that animals make useful symbols. Take the common shirt for example. Embroidered on the front of various brands of shirts have been no less than six different animals—bears, foxes, penguins, ponies, alligators, and dragons.

Without doubt the single product named after animals most frequently is the automobile. I can think of twenty-five or so different animals that have been associated with cars. Cats seem to be the most frequently used animal. There are Jaguars, Cougars, Bobcats, Lynxes, Wildcats, and Pumas. Of course a stable of horses also exists—Mustangs, Pintos, Mavericks, Colts, and Ponies. Flocks of birds are also encountered on highways, like Skylarks, Skyhawks, and Eagles. Actually, though, auto manufacturers prefer naming cars after mythical birds, such as the Phoenix, Thunderbird, Firebird, and Sunbird. Cars have been named after weird creatures, like fish (Barracudas and Stingrays) and insects (Hornets, Honeybees, and Spiders). Finally there are names from species found most frequently in children's zoos, such as Rabbits, Foxes, and Impalas.

After animals, places are the next most popular names for cars. The places may be domestic, like Belair, Malibu, Catalina, Park Avenue, Bonneville, Newport, and New York. Foreign places are also frequently used. Often they are in or near France—the Pari-sienne, Riviera, Versailles, Le Mans and Monte Carlo. But there is also a Spanish influence in cars named Granada, Seville, and Cordoba. Another source of car names is government. Examples include the Monarch, Regal, Regency, Diplomat, and Ambassador. Finally, there are the cars that could have been named after a place *or* a plant. Is the Aspen named after a resort or a tree with white bark? Is the Concord a town in Massachusetts or a grape?

Of course the idea of naming cars after animals, places, and such is to have the concept that the symbol implies carry over to the car. Cars named after racetracks (e.g., Bonneville and Grand Prix) are attempting to capture the image of speed and excitement.

Problems occur, however, when the product concept changes. For example, when the gas crisis struck, Pontiac encountered serious problems with its Grand Prix, Bonneville, Catalina, and Firebird lines. Each of the cars' names seemed to denote a gas-guzzling beast.

Volkswagen had this problem in 1983. The German company attempted to portray the Rabbit as a nimble performance car. As animals, rabbits are nimble indeed, but the name somehow lacked the image of toughness, ferocity, and excitement found in a performance car. The campaign simply failed to arouse the American public.

turing sector, which caused very low growth in the overall U.S. economy. It was not until a dramatic fall in value of the dollar in 1986 that exports began to improve. Furthermore, as the population growth of the United States slows and its markets mature, corporate growth in many instances will come from exports to countries in which markets are expanding more rapidly. As a result **cross cultural analysis,** which refers to the study of foreign cultures and their values, languages, and customs, is becoming increasingly important.

Table 17–4 identifies eight categories of differences in foreign cultures that impact on international business. Of these, perhaps the most important are differences in languages and values. Differences in language can severely impede the communication process. Value differences have a more subtle,

Table 17–3   Clothing: Its Functional Uses and Symbolic Meanings

Function of Apparel	Use of Apparel	Symbolic Meaning	Example of Apparel
Camouflage	Hide the body Cover blemishes or injuries	Sexually conservative	Robes Cosmetics, patches
Display	Reveal body parts	Sexually explicit	Tight or skimpy clothing
Utilitarian	Protect the body	"Down-to-earth," practical	Some jeans, raincoats
Aesthetic	Beautify or enhance the body	Love of beauty	Jewelry
Souvenir	Reminder of past	Love of family or experience	Charm bracelet
Emblematic	Group membership Connotative	Show membership in a group Reveal social class or wealth	Fraternity jacket Expensive jewelry

SOURCE: Adapted in part from a table in Rebecca Holman, "Apparel as Communication," in *Symbolic Consumer Behavior*, Elizabeth Hirschman and Morris Holbrook (eds.), Proceedings of the Conference on Consumer Aesthetics and Symbolic Consumption, Ann Arbor, Mich.: Association for Consumer Research, May 1980, 8.

but equally important, impact on marketing. For example, differences in orientations as to body hair on women across cultures severely limit the ability to market razors. The Austrian marketing director for Gillette once said, "We don't have to advertise women's razors here. I can personally give razors to all four Austrian women who want them."[17]

In other instances languages may differ, but a similarity of values can offer marketing opportunities. Figure 17–3 shows a page from a catalog for Lady Madonna maternity clothes. The advertisement is written in both French and English and features the actress Morgan Brittany. It is possible to target women in the two cultures because they share similar values about how women who are pregnant may look.

The difficulty of entering a new culture can generally be gauged by the

Table 17–4   International Business Cultural Factors

1. *Language:* spoken, written, mass media, linguistic pluralism
2. *Values:* as related to time, achievement, work, wealth, change, risk taking, science
3. *Law:* Common law, antitrust, international regulations
4. *Politics:* nationalism, sovereignty, power, imperialism, ideologies
5. *Technology and material culture:* transportation, energy system, communications, urbanization, science
6. *Social organization:* social mobility, status systems, authority structures, kinship
7. *Education:* literacy, human resource planning, higher education
8. *Religion:* philosophical systems, sacred objects, rituals

SOURCE: Adapted from Vern Terpstra, *The Culture of International Business*, Cincinnati, Ohio: South Western Publishing, 1978.

Figure 17–3 **This catalog targets both English- and French-speaking cultures.** (*Courtesy of D. F. Corey Enterprises, Inc., and Morgan Brittany.*)

Cover page photo:
SA1525–Pants, $72.00

SA4053–Camisole,
$49.00

SA4610–Kimono, $92.00

La page titre:
SA1525–Pantalon,
$72.00

SA4053–Camisole,
$49.00

SA4610–Kimono, $92.00

Below:
3550–B/A floral print
skirt-suit, cotton/rayon,
black, $139.00

Ci-dessous:
3550–Ensemble à jupe
a/a. coton/rayonne, noir,
$139.00

JANE SEYMOUR of numerous Movies/Mini series and MORGAN BRITTANY of Television's DALLAS and GLITTER are featured in LADY MADONNA's FALL WINTER 85' collection. LADY MADONNA fashions capture these beautiful and exciting actresses with a unique blend of sophistication, glamour and sensuality. We invite you to celebrate your pregnancy in flirtatious sportswear, classic business wear and glamourous evening wear.

JANE SEYMOUR grande vedette de cinema et de petit émission et MORGAN BRITTANY de "DALLAS" et "GLITTER" sont presentees dans la collection automne hiver 85 de LADY MADONNA. Les modes de LADY MADONNA captive ces belles, femmes élégants à la mode avec un l'aeir sophistiqué et de sensualité. Nous vous invitons à celebrer votre grossesse avec les ensembles d'affaires classiques, de sport et de soirees.

similarities of languages and values between the culture of origin and the culture of entry. (Here values are defined very broadly to include views on religion, technology, social relations, and politics.) Figure 17–4 shows the language and value dimensions. The four cells indicate the relative difficulty of entering the new culture. Thus, in *cell 1* language and values are similar between the cultures. Therefore, the difficulty of marketing in the country would be relatively low. Examples of such countries include Canada, Britain, and Australia. Conversely, in *cell 4* language and values are highly different, and entry is difficult. Examples of countries include Russia, Iran, and China. Fewer countries fall into *cells 2* and *3*. However, Japan is an example of a country with a very different language but somewhat similar values—such as hard work and the importance of science and achievement. In cell 2 India is an example of a country with differing values and a similar language. (English has become the language of commerce of India.)

Over the past couple of decades America's foreign trade has increasingly been focused on Third World, or developing, countries and countries around the **Pacific Rim.** Our European trade ties have decreased in importance. The Pacific Rim includes North America, South America, Australia, Indonesia, East

Figure 17–4 Difficulty of successfully marketing in a new culture.

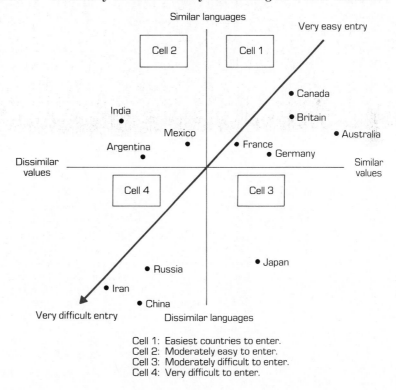

Cell 1: Easiest countries to enter.
Cell 2: Moderately easy to enter.
Cell 3: Moderately difficult to enter.
Cell 4: Very difficult to enter.

Asia, and Siberia. The region has 50 percent of the world's population and five of the world's ten "supercities."[18]

East Asia in particular will become increasingly important to the United States. Composed of Japan, Korea, China, and Southeast Asia, the region in 1983 had 26 percent of the world's population and produced 70 percent of the world's 64K random-access computer memory circuits.[19] The culture, however, has marked dissimilarities to that found in the United States. The countries follow the Confucian ethic. The moral philosophy does not subscribe to a supreme being and emphasizes the virtues of work, frugality, and education.[20]

Within the region Japan will increasingly become a trading partner with and competitor to the United States. Table 17–5 compares and contrasts a number of the values found in the two societies. One of the major cultural differences of the countries is in how the individual is viewed. In the United States the individual is seen as more important than the state. In Japan the group, family, and state are relatively more important. As one international consultant put it, "The Japanese are a consensus-bonded, group-oriented culture . . . Americans are individually motivated and independently oriented."[21]

The differences in the cultures can also be seen in how companies view employees and customers. Japanese companies tend to assume that their customers are correct and honest in all cases. The attitude of American companies tends to go in the other direction. In a similar way Japanese firms motivate their employees with job security and longevity. As stated by one American executive about U.S. firms, "It is not unusual for a management person to have one bad season and return from vacation and find his office locked and his name no longer on the door."[22]

Table 17–5 Comparison of Values in United States and Japan

United States	Japan
Judeo-Christian theism	Confucianism
Individualism	Affiliation
Protestant ethic	Virtues of frugality, work, education
Democracy	Democracy
Liberty	Government over individual
Private property	Close-knit social structure
Merit differentiation	Mutuality of obligations
Equality	Vertical relationships
Self-fulfillment	Family/group orientation
Rationality	Emotion/intuition
Youthfulness	Maturity

SOURCE: Adapted from Robert Bartels "National Culture—Business Relations: United States and Japan Contrasted," in *International Marketing Management*, Erdener Kaynak (ed.), New York, N.Y.: Praeger Publishers, 1984.

The Japanese are also a more conservative people than Americans. For example, *Playboy* magazine has been in Japan only since 1975, and *Penthouse* is finding it difficult to break into the Japanese market. A *Penthouse* executive called Japan the most conservative country in which the magazine publishes.[23] For example, although bare-breasted women can be shown on late-night television, by law no pubic hair is allowed to be shown in the print or television media in Japan. The conservatism is also revealed in the more formal communications style of the Japanese. For example, if a Japanese executive were to state that something is "difficult" to do, what he may mean is, *no* to the request. He is simply being polite.[24] Similarly, a backslapping, joking American executive or salesperson would have difficulty in successfully dealing with the more reserved Japanese.

Cross-Cultural Problem Areas

The potential for trouble when dealing with new cultures is high. The following is a brief discussion of a number of potential pitfalls of which marketers should be aware when dealing with consumers in a different culture.

Translations In addition to having difficulty in dealing with everyday speech in foreign countries, marketers must be aware of the problem of accurately translating their product's brand name into new languages. Examples of mistranslations abound.[25] For example, Colgate-Palmolive introduced its Cue toothpaste into the French market without changing the name. They did not realize that in French, "cue" is a pornographic word. A paper manufacturer had its name translated into Japanese. The name became "He who envelops himself in ten tons of rice paper." General Motors had "body by Fisher" translated into "corpse by Fisher" in Flemish. The list of translation faux pas is long. The method of avoiding such problems is called "back-translation." The process involves successively translating the message back and forth between languages by different translators. In this way, subtle and not so subtle differences in meanings can be located.[26]

Time Perception Time is an important situational factor influencing consumers and is discussed in more detail in Chapter 10. In international settings it can cause problems because different cultures may view time divergently. Time is a commodity in the United States. For example, Americans speak of "spending" and "wasting" time. As a consequence, Americans hate to be kept waiting. In many other cultures, time is much less important. A foreign executive may keep an American client waiting for forty-five minutes or longer and think nothing of it. To the foreign business person forty-five minutes is insignificant and the minimum length of time one should expect to wait.[27] Meanwhile, the American is chewing-out the secretary for the delay.

Symbols What something means in one culture may not mean the same in other cultures. For example, the number 7 is unlucky in Ghana and Kenya but lucky in India and Czechoslovakia. The triangle is negative in Hong Kong and positive in Columbia. In some remote areas of the world people believe that when their picture is taken their "spirit" has been captured. Purple is associated with death in many Latin-American countries. In Mexico yellow flowers are a sign of death, whereas in France they denote infidelity.[28] Similarly, gifts may represent different feelings in different cultures. One does not give cutlery in Russia, West Germany, or Taiwan.[29]

Friendship   Americans tend to make friends easily, but they also drop them rapidly as well. In some countries, friendship replaces the legal or contractual system.[30] Therefore, friends are made very slowly and retained for long lengths of time. As a consequence, the Chinese, Japanese, and others view with skepticism Americans who come on strong; they tend to see the Americans as insincere and superficial.

Etiquette   Matters of etiquette can also create discomfort and misunderstandings. For example, in Japan the exchange of business cards, or Meishi, is a necessary social ritual. With the exchange the individuals know where they stand and their respective status.[31] The exchange of hugs and a kiss on the cheek among males in Eastern Europe strikes many Americans as strange and inappropriate. However, the ritual is a basic part of the manner in which people are greeted in that part of the world. Another matter of etiquette that differs around the world is how food is eaten. For example, many Europeans consider eating food with your fingers (e.g., sandwiches or french fries) disgusting.

Nonverbal Behavior   Nonverbal behaviors are those actions, movements, and utterances that people use to communicate in addition to language. They include movements of the hands, arms, head, and legs as well as body orientation and the space maintained between people. Different cultures have divergent norms concerning such nonverbal behavior. Spatial differences are one example. Americans have four zones surrounding them—intimate, personal, social, and public.[32] The intimate zone is from zero to eighteen inches away. Public zones are from twelve feet or further away. Business tends to be conducted in the social zone of from four to seven feet.

People in other cultures, however, may not space themselves in the same way as Americans. In Middle Eastern and Latin American cultures people tend to interact at a much closer distance. Consequently, the American becomes uncomfortable as the foreign businessman closes in on him. The result has been described as a sort of waltz, with the American backtracking and the foreign client pursuing. The problem is that the American is seen as standoffish and the foreigner as pushy.[33]

Ethnocentricity   A natural tendency of humans is to assume that what they do or what their country does is the right and proper thing to do. When marketing in new cultures, business executives must stifle the tendency to look down on others because they do things differently. Furthermore, they must inhibit the urge to try to change the behavior of foreign peoples because what they do is not as "good" as the American way. One can see this attitude in the actions of Simmons Company in trying to convert the Japanese to sleeping on beds. The problem of ethnocentrity, though, does not exist only in Americans. An American executive working for a Japanese firm noted that his Japanese bosses believed that American consumers should behave like Japanese consumers.[34] With high gas prices and interest rates, the Japanese could not understand why Americans did not use motorbikes as their main transportation mode.

Executives must recognize that consumption patterns can differ substantially across cultures. The problem is difficult, however, because when no evidence exists to refute it, people tend to believe that what they like and dislike, others will also like and dislike. The following are examples of some culturally based differences in consumption found in other countries.

- ☐ Married men in France use more cosmetics and beauty aids than their wives.[35]
- ☐ Dutch women report more interest in high-fashion clothing than American women.[36]
- ☐ In some Middle Eastern countries "hot" and "cold" refer to the heaviness of food rather than to the foods' spiciness or temperature.[37]

Similarly, attitudes towards consumption activities differ markedly across cultures. When given the statement, "A house should be dusted and polished three times a week," 86 percent of the Italians agreed whereas only 25 percent of Americans did. To the statement, "Everyone should use a deodorant," 89 percent of Americans agreed, but only 53 percent of Australians agreed.[38]

When in a foreign country even the most basic liberties that Americans enjoy may be unavailable. For example, the ability to move freely even varies across cultures. In Moslem countries, the activities of women are greatly restricted. A Singer Company manager was jailed when he encouraged Sudanese women to leave their homes to attend demonstration classes for sewing machines. The solution was to have men attend the classes. They became convinced of the value of the machines and ordered their wives to the classes.[39]

Cross-Cultural Marketing Strategy

A major issue in marketing internationally has concerned the **standardization of the marketing plan.** Can the marketing mix be standardized across national boundaries? The debate has focused on two well-known marketers. One is Philip Kotler, who argues against standardization across markets. The second is Theodore Levitt, who argues that a rapid homogenization of the world's wants and wishes is occurring for the "advanced" things that the world makes and sells.[40] Levitt gives as one example the image, which many retain, of the 1979 Iranian hostage crisis. During the worst of the period when the Iranians held the U.S. embassy hostage, one could see on television "inflamed young men in fashionable French-cut trousers and silky body shirts open to the waist, with raised modern weapons, thirsting for blood in the name of Islamic fundamentalism."[41]

No simple answer exists to the question of whether the marketing mix can be standardized. In some countries, like Japan or the Soviet Union, distribution systems will be quite different from those found in the United States. The product may also have to be adapted to the tastes and preferences of different cultures. For example, a U.S. company found that its room deodorizer had to undergo reformulation prior to entering the British market. The fragrance was made stronger, and the packaging was changed in order to appeal to British consumers.[42] The problem of standardization strikes most strongly in the advertising area. Pepsi-Cola in the 1960s saved about $8 million annually by standardizing promotional films.[43] Other companies like Coca-Cola and Levi Strauss and Company have adopted a strategy of attempting to standardize their world image.[44] Impulse, a body spray deodorant, has followed a global advertising strategy by using a "boy meets girl" love story theme across the thirty-one countries in which it was marketed in 1985. To avoid cultural differences the company allowed each of the local agencies to shoot its own version of the basic storyboard. Each of the commercials uses the same copyline: "If a complete stranger suddenly gives you flowers—that's impulse. Men just can't resist acting on Impulse."[45] The romantic fantasy commercials involve a young man acting irrationally when a woman wearing the perfume walks by. Upon smelling the perfume, he searches for a flower seller, grabs a bunch of flowers, and chases after the woman. The successful brand was first developed in 1972 in South Africa, from where it moved to Brazil. It didn't reach the U.S. until 1982. Within two years of its debut in West Germany, it had garnered 36 percent of the country's total deodorant market.[46]

Although standardized marketing efforts across countries are cheaper to run, serious problems occur for many, if not most, products. The goal of a global marketer is to have what Coca-Cola calls, "One sight, one sound, one sell."[47] However, in most cases too many obstacles get in the way of this goal for it to be implemented. Differences in such areas as government regulations, electrical outlets and voltages for electrical products, and cultural mores make standardized marketing impractical in many instances. For example, Philip Morris was not allowed in Britain to have commercials showing the Marlboro cowboy because government authorities felt that children worship cowboys and would take up smoking. The final commercials showed non-cowboys driving around Marlboro country in jeeps.[48]

Examples of the problems of global marketing abound. Kool-Aid sells well in Venezuela but cannot be sold in Europe. Nestle, the huge Swiss company, sells coffee in every country in the free world. However, the advertising and the taste of the coffee varies from country to country. Philip Kotler argues that, "There are only a very few products, if any, that you can safely standardize."[49]

The concept that companies can standardize their marketing plans around the world contradicts the marketing concept. The consumer should be at the center of the marketing plan. Because consumers differ to varying degrees around the world, so too should marketing plans differ. One recent study found some evidence that companies are increasingly tailoring their efforts to the culture.[50] Indeed, in some countries resentment seems to exist concerning the sameness of McDonald's stores and of Coca-Cola campaigns found around the world.[51] These multinational companies have become symbols of the United States. In countries where Americans are viewed less favorably, a marketing mix tailored to the culture is crucial.

Managerial Implications

From a managerial perspective the study of culture has importance for domestic as well as international marketing. On the domestic front a sense of the predominant values, customs, and rituals can assist the marketing manager in developing promotional themes and in the general product-planning process. In international marketing an understanding of culture can prevent dramatic marketing mistakes, as well as assist in the development of the marketing plan.

An excellent example of a failure to attend to culture may be found in the actions of the United States Football League, which was started in 1982 to compete with the powerful National Football League. The component of the marketing plan of its founders was to avoid competing directly with the NFL by playing games in the spring and summer of the year. However, after three years of severe losses the league decided to move the season to the fall and compete directly against the NFL. Although the change of the season may not save the league, it did indicate a recognition of one cultural feature of the United States. Most sports are seasonal games. Baseball is played in the spring and summer, football in the fall, and basketball in the winter and spring. The behavior of an entire culture is based upon these beliefs. To base a marketing plan on the idea of breaking a cultural tradition, as did the USFL, is to court disaster.

In international marketing the study of culture takes on particular importance because the marketer may not have an intuitive feel of the values, customs, rituals, and symbols of the countries to which products and services are being exported. One Hungarian company is finding out the importance of culture firsthand. The company, Novotrade Inc., makes computer games. It has successfully exported the games to Europe but is having a difficult time entering the U.S. market successfully. The problem seems to be that the themes of the games are too peaceful. According to one expert, "Americans want antisocial software where the main character is destroyed or maimed. . . . The games are simply too peaceable, too prosocial." In contrast, the Hungarian games are nonviolent, such as Pet's Clinic, in which the goal is to diagnose the illness of a dog. A spokesman for the company said that "Maybe we won't be the best sellers in the world, . . . but there's a lot of people who want to play peaceful games."[52]

A case of a company gearing its product development and promotional strategy successfully to another country is Coca-Cola. The company is marketing a coffee-flavored soft drink, called Georgia, in Japan. The brand, which is not sold in the U.S., has captured 18 percent of the sales of coffee-flavored soft drinks in Japan.[53] Sold through vending machines that can cool the drink in the summer and heat it in the winter, the drink's popularity is growing rapidly. Interestingly, however, it is unlikely that it would succeed in the United States because of a lack of the proper type of vending machines and because of the cultural preference for and prevalence of freshly brewed coffee. Georgia is an excellent example of a product that was developed and exported specifically for the tastes and preferences of a foreign culture.

Because of the reticence of many American companies to expand into foreign countries, various countries are increasingly advertising themselves and soliciting business through U.S. publications. In Figure 17–5 is found an ad that was placed by Puerto Rico in *Business Week* magazine. Although Puerto Rico is part of the United States, its Hispanic culture is quite different from that of the mainland. The ad effectively communicates the potential financial advantages of moving production facilities there.

SUMMARY

Think back to the vignette at the beginning of the chapter concerning Budweiser beer in Japan. The marketing effort was successful because the product fit the Japanese culture and lifestyle. The values, customs, and beliefs of the Japanese were compatible with the offering of the American beer. But just as managers must carefully consider cultural similarities and differences when marketing in a foreign country, they must also be aware of cultural factors when marketing in their own country. For example, the proper use of symbols and rituals can smooth the promotional effort considerably.

Culture consists of the learned values, rituals, and symbols of a society, which are transmitted through both the language and the symbolic features of the society. Cultural values consist of the shared views of a society concerning the desired state of existence and the appropriate economic, social, religious and other behaviors in which its members engage. Cultural symbols are concrete objects that represent an abstract concept. They can be utilized by managers in naming their products and in designing promotional materials. Cultural rituals are periodically repeated patterns of behavior. Tying products to the rituals can be a successful marketing strategy.

When engaging in international marketing, the problems encountered will vary with the degree of dissimilarity of language and values between the culture of origin and the culture of entry. Other factors to consider in international marketing are differences in laws, politics, technology, education, and religion. Specific problem areas include doing translations as well as ac-

Figure 17–5 **This ad encourages American businesses to locate their operations in Puerto Rico, outside of the mainland United States.** *(Courtesy of Economic Development Corporation, Commonwealth of Puerto Rico.)*

La Fortaleza, the executive office of Governor Rafael Hernández-Colón, San Juan, Puerto Rico.

Puerto Rico. Now the door's open even wider for American business.

Many mid-sized and large U.S. firms have recently expanded or announced expansions in Puerto Rico. Among them, such Fortune 500 and other leading names as Emerson Electric, American Hospital Supply, Playtex, Paradyne, Cooper Vision, and Upjohn.

"This office is committed to the same comprehensive tax-incentive policies and infrastructure buildup that have attracted companies to Puerto Rico for 40 years. And now we're implementing an 'outreach' program linking our highly skilled workforce with the lower-cost labor production of our Caribbean neighbors. It's all part of the expanded promise Puerto Rico offers—and we're delivering."

A secure investment climate where average profits run way above average.

• No U.S. corporate income tax on earnings in Puerto Rico.
• Local tax exemptions start at 90% of industrial development income.

A proud workforce that delivers high skills, loyalty, and an extraordinary return on every payroll dollar.

• Specialized training provided for traditional and high-tech production.
• Lower absenteeism and turnover than U.S. mainland.
• Double the output per dollar of production wages over U.S. average.
• Management at top levels is 94% Puerto Rican.

Also important:

• No quotas, no duties, to $3.8 trillion U.S. market.
• Modern highways, port facilities, international airport, U.S. communications and postal systems.
• 3¼ hours to New York, 2¼ to Miami, 1 hour to Caracas, Venezuela, and about four sailing days to U.S. Atlantic and Gulf coasts from Port of San Juan.

"Find out why so many corporate leaders come to Puerto Rico, to stay. Send in the coupon on this page or call us toll-free at 1-800-223-0699. Then, I invite you to come for a visit. Our doors are always open."

For more information, please complete and send in this coupon. Or call today **1-800-223-0699.**

NAME & TITLE_____
COMPANY_____
ADDRESS_____
CITY_____STATE____ZIP_____
TELEPHONE (   )_____
PRODUCT or SERVICE_____
☐ current expansion project   ☐ future expansion planning

Commonwealth of Puerto Rico
Economic Development Administration
1290 Avenue of the Americas
New York, N.Y. 10104-0092   BW113

Puerto Rico
The climate is right.

counting for differences in time perception, symbols, etiquette and nonverbal behavior between the cultures. Another tendency to avoid is **cultural "ethnocentricity,"** or the tendency to believe that the values, beliefs, and ways of doing things as specified by one's own culture are right and correct. A major debate in international marketing concerns the extent to which the marketing plan can be standardized across cultures. Although such standardization can bring about large economies of scale, in practice the approach is difficult to implement successfully. Although consumers may have similar emotions, such as love, hate, greed, and envy, their expression and symbolism can be dramatically different as one moves from culture to culture. As a result, the marketing plan in most cases must be tailored to some degree to match the consumer preferences of each culture. Because of the economic importance to the United States of exports, international marketing—and with it the study of foreign cultures—is becoming increasingly important.

Key Terms

Culture
Enculturation
Acculturation
Norms
Terminal values
Instrumental values
Global values
Domain-specific values
Consumer ritual

Cultural symbol
Pacific Rim
Standardization of marketing plan across cultures
Cultural ethnocentricity
Values
Cross-cultural analysis

Review Questions

1. Define the concept of culture. What are its basic characteristics?
2. What are seven core American values that have been identified?
3. Identify four examples each of the terminal values and instrumental values defined by Milton Rokeach. How do instrumental and terminal values differ?
4. Consumers may be regarded as having belief systems that include global values, domain-specific values, and evaluations of product attributes. Define these terms and indicate how they are related.
5. What is a consumer ritual? Identify three consumer rituals that influence the purchase patterns of consumers.
6. Define the concept of a consumer symbol. What

are examples of clothing that act as symbols to consumers?
7. Identify five of the eight categories of differences in foreign cultures that may impact on international business.
8. Compare and contrast the cultural values of Japan to those of the United States.
9. Seven cross-cultural problem areas were identified in the text. Identify four of these pitfalls and how they could influence the reactions of consumers to marketing offerings.
10. What is meant by cultural ethnocentricity?
11. What are the factors one must consider prior to attempting to standardize the marketing mix across cultures?

Discussion Questions

1. In 1986 some editorial writers were arguing that movies and television shows produced in the United States were teaching children to be violent. Instances of nine- to twelve-year-olds actually murdering other children were cited as examples. To what extent do you think that the media can influence such cultural values of people?
2. Two highly popular television shows in 1986 were "The Cosby Show" and "Miami Vice." Compare and contrast the cultural values that these two shows portray.
3. Global values, domain-specific values, and evaluations of product attributes are often related. Con-

sider the attributes that you prefer in automobiles. How do these preferred attributes reflect your domain-specific values and global values?

4. Describe a ritual that you go through consistently in your everyday life. It could be a religious ritual, some type of grooming ritual, or even one involving the preparation of food, among other things. To what extent is this ritual shared by others?

5. Go through a magazine and look at the advertisements. Identify as many cultural symbols as you can that are shown in the print ads. In each case what is the advertiser attempting to do by using the symbol?

6. Consider the popular singer Madonna. What is the symbolic function of the clothing she wears?

7. In this chapter the statement was made that "The Japanese are a consensus-bonded, group-oriented culture . . . Americans are individually motivated and independently oriented." What are the advertising implications of this statement? To what extent do you agree with the statement that Americans are individually motivated and independently oriented?

8. Compare how easy it would be to standardize the advertising of a perfume versus the advertising of a soft drink around the world.

9. Suppose that you are the marketing director for the firm that produces California Coolers, the citrus-based alcoholic product that is sold similarly to beer. You wish to sell the product internationally. What types of problems might you have in selling the product in such countries as Mexico, India, Japan, Saudi Arabia, France, and Britain?

References

1. Melanie Wallendorf and M. Reilly, "Distinguishing Culture of Origin from Culture of Residence," in *Advances in Consumer Research, X*, R. Bagozzi and A. Tybout (eds.), Ann Arbor, Mich.: Association for Consumer Research, 1983, 699–701.

2. Henry Fairchild, *Dictionary of Sociology*, Totawa, N.J.: Littlefield, Adams and Co., 1970.

3. Theodore Wallin, "The International Executives' Baggage: Cultural Values of the American Frontier," *MSU Business Topics, 24*, Spring 1976, 49–58.

4. Cora DuBois, "The Dominant Value Profile in American Culture," *American Anthropologist, 57*, December 1955, 1232–1239.

5. David McClelland, J. W. Atkinson, R. A. Clark, and E. L. Lowell, *The Achievement Motive*, New York, N.Y.: Appleton-Century-Crofts, 1953.

6. Milton Rokeach, *Understanding Human Values*, New York, N.Y.: The Free Press, 1979.

7. Borris Becer and P. Connor, "Personal Values of the Heavy User of Mass Media," *Journal of Advertising Research, 21*, October 1981, 37–43.

8. Walter Henry, "Cultural Values Do Correlate with Consumer Behavior," *Journal of Marketing Research, 13*, May 1976, 121–127.

9. D. E. Vinson, J. Scott, and L. Lamont, "The Role of Personal Values in Marketing and Consumer Behavior," *Journal of Marketing, 41*, April 1977, 44–50.

10. Dennis Rook, "Ritual Behavior and Consumer Symbolism," *Advances in Consumer Research, XI*, Thomas Kinnear (ed.), Ann Arbor, Mich.: Association for Consumer Research, 1984, 279–284.

11. Ray Brown, *Rituals and Ceremonies in Popular Culture*, Bowling Green State University, Bowling Green, Ohio: Popular Press, 1980.

12. Michael Marsden, "Television Viewing as Ritual," in *Rituals and Ceremonies in Popular Culture*.

13. Charles Morris, *Signs, Language, and Behavior*, New York, N.Y.: George Braziller, Inc., 1946.

14. Elizabeth Hirschman, "Comprehending Symbolic Consumption: Three Theoretical Issues," in *Symbolic Consumption Behavior*, Elizabeth Hirschman and Morris Holbrook (eds.), Proceedings of the Conference on Consumer Aesthetics and Symbolic Consumption, May 1980, 4–6.

15. Hirschman, "Comprehending Symbolic Consumption."

16. "Survey of Current Business," U.S. Department of Commerce. Extracted from various issues of the publication.

17. Anne B. Fisher, "The Ad Biz Gloms Onto Global," *Fortune*, November 12, 1984, 80.

18. Hank Koehn, "Scenario Calls for Pacific Rim to Flex Its Economic Muscle by the Year 2010," *Marketing News*, July 22, 1983, 16.

19. Koehn, "Scenario Calls for Pacific Rim."

20. Gerson Goodman, "American Samurai," *Sales and Marketing Management*, October 12, 1981, 45–48.

21. Goodman, "American Samurai."

22. Ibid.

23. Jack Burton, "Penthouse Takes on Playboy in Japan," *Advertising Age*, June 27, 1983, 10.

24. Burton, "Penthouse Takes on Playboy."

25. For excellent discussion of the problems of translations see David Ricks, Marilyn Fu, and Jeffrey Arpan, *International Business Blunders*, Columbus, Ohio: Grid, 1974.

26. James Engel and Roger Blackwell, *Consumer Behavior*, New York, N.Y.: The Dryden Press, 1982.

27. E. T. Hall, *The Hidden Dimension*, New York, N.Y.: Doubleday & Co., Inc., 1966.

28. Hall, *The Hidden Dimension*.

29. S. B. Hitchings, "Beware When Bearing Gifts in Foreign Lands," *Business Week*, December 6, 1976, 91–92.

30. M. E. Metcalfe, "Islam, Social Attitudes Heart of Arab Business," *Advertising Age*, August 18, 1980, 5–16.

31. S. Lohr, "Business Cards: A Japanese Ritual," *The New York Times*, September 13, 1981, D1–D2.

32. E. T. Hall, *The Silent Language*, New York, N.Y.: Doubleday & Co., Inc., 1959.

33. H. W. Smith, "Territorial Spacing on a Beach Revisited, A Cross-National Explanation," *Social Psychology Quarterly*, 44 June 1981, 132–137.

34. Goodman, "American Samurai."

35. D. J. Tigert, C. W. King, and L. Ring, "Fashion Involvement: A Cross Cultural Comparative Analysis," in *Advances in Consumer Research*, VII, J. C. Olson (ed.), Chicago, Ill.: Association for Consumer Research, 1980, 17.

36. P. Kotler, *Marketing Management: Analysis, Planning, and Control*, Englewood Cliffs, N.J.: Prentice-Hall, Inc., 1980, 666.

37. A. Mehrabian and J. Russell, *An Approach to Environmental Psychology*, Cambridge, Mass.: MIT Press, 1974, 10.

38. J. T. Plummer, "Consumer Focus in Cross-National Research," *Journal of Advertising*, 6 Spring 1977, 10–11.

39. J. Douglas McConnell, "The Economics of Behavioral Factors on Multi-National Corporations," in *Combined Proceedings of American Marketing Association*, Series No. 33, Fred C. Allvine (ed.), Chicago, Ill.: American Marketing Association, 1971, 261.

40. Theodore Levitt, *The Marketing Imagination*, New York, N.Y.: The Free Press, 1983.

41. Levitt, *The Marketing Imagination*.

42. "Europeans Insist on Pretesting," *Advertising Age*, August 24, 1981, 38.

43. R. Heller, "How Pepsi-Cola Does It in 110 Countries," in *New Ideas for Successful Marketing*, J. S. Wright and J. L. Goldstucker (eds.), Chicago, Illinois: American Marketing Association, 1966, 700.

44. D. Chase and E. Bacot, "Levi Zipping Up World Image," *Advertising Age*, September 14, 1981, 34, 36.

45. Brian Oliver, "A Little Romance Puts Impulse on Global Path," *Advertising Age*, June 24, 1985, 39, 40.

46. Oliver, "A Little Romance."

47. Fisher, "The Ad Biz Gloms."

48. Ibid.

49. Ibid.

50. S. W. Dunn, "Effect of National Identity on Multinational Promotional Strategy in Europe," *Journal of Marketing*, 40 October 1976, 51.

51. Dunn, "Effect of National Identity."

52. Bob Davis, "These Hungarian Computer Games May Be Too Pacific for U.S. Tastes," *The Wall Street Journal*, September 21, 1984, 33.

53. Jack Burton, "Coke in Japan Riding High with Georgia Coffee," *Advertising Age*, March 19, 1984, 48.

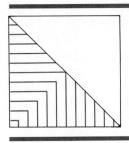

18

The Economics of Consumption

CONSUMER VIGNETTE

What Do All of the Numbers Mean?

It is March of 1983, and you are a vice-president at Harley-Davidson Motor Company. During the early 1980s your company has experienced major problems. Consumers have stopped buying your large motorcycles and switched to less expensive, more technologically advanced Japanese brands. The immediate problem is to set production goals for the next six months.

In setting your production goals, you must carefully consider the behavior of consumers. Will they in general be buying motorcycles over the next year or so? You recognize that this question is largely a function of the economy and other factors beyond your control, such as a renewed oil crisis like those occurring in the 1970s which sent motorcycle sales skyrocketing.

You assume that over the next year Harley-Davidson's market share will stay about the same. If the economy improves, its total sales will increase commensurate to the overall increase in the sales of motorcycles. The question, then, is what in the world is the economy going to do over the next year?

One indicator of future economic activity is an index developed by economists that measures retail sales. This measure assesses how much consumers are spending. Because consumer goods account for two-thirds of the gross national product, the index can be a good indicator of trends in consumer spending.

A problem has arisen, however. While other leading indicators, such as stock prices and money supply growth, have gone up recently, retail spending has decreased. After what has happened to your company over the past three years of recession/depression, you can't afford to make a mistake and raise production quotas only to have the economy fail to expand.

You consult with an economist who works for your company occasionally. She tells you that the high interest rates and large unemployment rates are scaring people out of purchases. That seems reasonable, but you happen to talk to a friend who works for Sears, and he tells you that the sales of all the retailers are increasing. Somehow, all of this doesn't make sense. The numbers are inconsistent.

The next night you are at a cocktail party and happen to meet a sociologist who works in the survey research area. The topic of the economy comes up, and she mentions that the Index of Consumer Sentiment, developed by the University of Michigan Survey Research Center, has suddenly jumped. She is very confident that consumers will soon be buying.

You are now completely puzzled. While you are eating lunch at your desk the next day, you spot an article in *The Wall Street Journal* with the headline "Weak Retail Sales May Be Misleading." The article goes on to point out that the retail sales index may be wrong because consumers have changed their consumption patterns. Consumers are patronizing retailers that are not adequately factored into the index, such as computer stores, factory outlets, and retailers, like flea markets participating in the underground economy. (a)

That afternoon, you raise the production quotas. Did you make the right decision?

Based in part on (a) "Customers Are Back, Most Merchants Say, But Caution Remains," *The Wall Street Journal*, April 8, 1983, pp. 1, 16.

INTRODUCTION

The Harley-Davidson vignette pinpoints a number of issues relevant to a chapter on the economics of consumption. Foremost is the idea that the traditional economic approach to forecasting consumer demand requires supplementation. Because consumers learn from their past experiences with the environment, they will change their responses to economic events. Thus, straightforward econometric forecasting techniques using aggregate data on income levels, interest rates, inflation rates and so forth cannot predict with high accuracy how much consumers will spend. Furthermore, the economic data come from secondhand resources, not directly from consumers. The secondary data are often out-of-date or even misleading, as in the Harley-Davidson case.

A second major point of the case concerns the impact of the economic cycle on consumers and business. If you were to ask the president of General Motors what the most important factor is that influences whether or not someone will buy a car in any given year, he would probably say the economy. Many industries are cyclical. Their sales and profits rise and fall over time. How this economic cycle influences consumers to buy or save is crucial to know. In the author's opinion this is one of the most under researched areas in consumer behavior.

Were you right in raising production quotas in the Harley-Davidson vignette? In reality, the decision turned out to be on target. The economy turned up vigorously in the last half of 1983, and Harley-Davidson's sales improved.

But such decisions based on economic forecasts are always difficult. In particular, other events may occur to influence a company's profit picture. In the above Harley-Davidson instance, not only did the economy improve but the U.S. government also stepped in to levy a 10 percent tariff on the large motorcycles exported by Japan to the United States. The positive impact on Harley-Davidson's sales and profit picture was immediate and direct.

HOW ECONOMISTS VIEW THE CONSUMER

The field of economics is the oldest and most advanced of the social sciences. Consequently, economists have a well-defined view of consumers and the factors that influence their consumption patterns. A trademark of economics is the long set of assumptions on which the field's theories rest. A number of the assumptions deal with the consumption behavior of consumers. Some of these assumptions are:

- □ *Rational behavior.* The average consumer attempts to allocate his or her money so as to achieve the greatest satisfaction from it.
- □ *Preferences.* Consumers have well-defined preferences among products and know how much satisfaction they will obtain from products.
- □ *Information.* Consumers have perfect information about the pricing and availability of products in the marketplace.
- □ *Budget constraints.* Consumers have limited budgets.
- □ *Insatiable desires.* The wants of consumers cannot be completely satisfied.

Are these assumptions realistic? It depends on how they are used. Clearly, not all consumers act rationally, have perfect information, and possess well-defined preferences. However, the assumptions form an excellent base from which certain economic laws have been developed. An important one for our purpose is the "law of demand."[1]

The Law of Demand

The **law of demand** states that an inverse relationship exists between the price of a product and the quantity demanded of the product. This relationship holds for both individual consumers and aggregates of consumers. Thus, as the price of a product falls, more of the product is wanted. The effects of price changes on quantity demanded can be explained in two ways. First, the **income effect** states that when prices are lowered, consumers can afford more of the product without giving up other alternatives. In effect, consumers have more income because of the fall in the price of the product. Second, the **substitution effect** states that when the price of a product falls, it may be substituted for similar goods which are now relatively more costly. An excellent example was the dramatic fall in the price of electronic calculators

Figure 18–1   The law of demand.

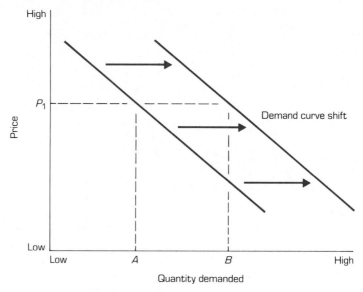

in the 1970s. Not only did they substitute for slide rules, they totally replaced the now-extinct computational instrument.

The relationship between price and quantity demanded results in the familiar downward-sloping demand curve shown in Figure 18–1. The law of demand forms the basis for one of the most common promotional tactics used by marketers—the sale. People will buy more when the price is lower.

Factors Influencing Demand

The demand curve reveals that price directly influences the quantity demanded of a product. In addition, several factors can cause a **demand curve shift** to the right or left, thereby affecting the entire relationship between price and the quantity demanded. Figure 18–1 reveals the effects of a shift to the right of the demand curve. At the same price (P_1) the quantity demanded of a good increases from point A to point B. Just what factors can cause the demand curve to shift to the right or to the left? They are some of the factors that stand at the heart of the study of consumer behavior and include changes in the demographic characteristics of market segments and changes in the tastes and preferences of target groups.

Demographic Trends   Demand may be influenced by two important types of demographic variables—income and population characteristics. Each of these factors is discussed in Chapters 14 and 15 on subcultures and Chapter 16 on social class. Changes in the income levels of target groups will shift the demand curve such that at the same price level they will want more or less of the product than previously. Consider your personal consumption of high-quality gourmet food. Currently, as a student you probably have a limited income. Your consumption of gourmet food is probably quite limited, regardless of your particular preferences. However, after graduation, when you obtain that high-paying job, your income will change dramatically. Gourmet food will be reachable in price for you, and the quantity demanded will therefore increase. Remember, though, that the reverse can occur. The demand for many luxury-type products can shift dramatically to the left, if, for example, your income suddenly decreases by your being laid off in a contracting economy.

A second demographic factor that can shift the demand curve is changes in the numbers of buyers. The changing population characteristics of the United States have enormous impact on the demand for specific products. Changes in the numbers of consumers making up various ethnic groups can cause demand shifts for products targeted to these groups. Similarly, changes in the numbers of consumers in particular age brackets can influence the demand for particular products popular with a specific age group. Earlier in the text, the great impact of the baby-boom generation was discussed. As this huge group of consumers ages, it tends to tire of products it had previously made popular. Thus, when the baby boomers began to have families, their interest in phonograph records waned, and the industry went into a protracted slump.

Through the 1970s companies that sold products for babies and young children were experiencing either little or negative growth. Even outstanding companies, like Gerber Products, were having difficulty showing year-to-year growth in sales. The reason was that the population of babies was decreasing in the 1970s. The companies reacted by trying to broaden the base of consumers who would use the product. Thus, advertisements tried to persuade teenagers and senior citizens that baby food was good and healthful to eat. Fran Tarkenton, the ex–all-pro quarterback, promoted the use of baby shampoo to adults as a mild shampoo which they should try. Such strategies, although effective in some cases, helped minimally. Profits and sales of products targeted to babies did not really begin to rise until the mid-1980s, when the number of babies in the population began to increase.

Changes in Tastes and Preferences   Other factors that act to shift the demand curve are changes in tastes, preferences, and expectations. The study of these three elements makes up what might be described as the core of consumer behavior. The analysis of tastes and preferences brings one into the study of beliefs, attitudes and intentions. Several chapters in this textbook are devoted to providing an explanation of how beliefs and attitudes are formed and just how they influence intentions and behavior.

The way in which changes in tastes and preferences can shift demand for a product is easily demonstrated. During the early 1980s the United States was swept with a fitness craze. This time the trend struck women in particular. Women began to go into bodybuilding. Contests were run to identify the strongest women. Jane Fonda opened fitness salons and coauthored a book titled *Jane Fonda's Workout Book for Pregnancy, Birth, and Recovery.* A movie based around long-distance running, *Chariots of Fire,* won an Academy Award for best picture. The fitness craze dramatically increased the demand for a host of products and services heretofore of little interest to the general public.

Closely related to the concepts of tastes and preferences is that of expectations. All are mental states that influence behavior. Expectations, however, relate to consumer perceptions of the future. In particular, expectations of the future of the economy can dramatically influence current purchase patterns. Consumers can be thought of as miniature economic forecasters trying to identify what the economy will be like a year or two in advance. Importantly, however, consumers in aggregate tend to be more accurate than economists, because the behavior of these consumers will actually influence the economy. Some influences of consumers' perceptions about the supply of goods are discussed in Highlight 18–1.

The fact that consumer expectations influence the purchasing behavior of individuals and that this in turn affects the economy was recognized and researched most thoroughly by George Katona. Katona was part economist and part psychologist. He developed a field of inquiry called **behavioral economics,** which is having increasing influence on the actions of corporations and the federal government.

Opportunity Cost

A particularly important economic principle for consumer behaviorists is that of **opportunity cost.** The core idea of the concept is that when a person buys one product or engages in one task, he or she simultaneously foregoes buying another product or engaging in another task. Each time a consumer takes one action, he or she foregoes another action. Opportunity costs occur because our time and monetary resources are limited. The result is that consumers are constantly making trade-offs.

Opportunity cost has implications for understanding competition. Typically, a firm views other companies in the same industry as its competition. However, the idea of opportunity cost suggests that competitors can be in quite different industries. For example, the opportunity cost of buying a new car could be going on a vacation, enrolling in a university, or making a down payment on a house. In 1983 the Buick division of General Motors recognized that these opportunity costs were competitors just as much as a Ford LTD. According to their general manager, the company made a conscious decision to try to reach consumers early in the decision process, prior to when their reaching a decision about the product category on which to spend their discretionary money. As he said, "It's not just Buick against Oldsmobile or Buick against imports, it's Buick against new furniture." [2]

The concept of opportunity cost can also be used in advertising. The advertisement shown in Figure 18–2 illustrates this idea. With the statement, "For the cost of a morning coffee break, you can break the cycle of poverty

HIGHLIGHT 18-1

Create the Impression of Scarcity to Make People Buy

Here is an important question for all readers of this text who are single. At singles bars do the patrons perceive that members of the opposite sex are better looking early in the evening or later in the evening? A study asked people at singles bars to rate the attractiveness of members of the opposite sex at different times during the evening. As closing time approached, the attractiveness ratings of members of the opposite sex got higher and higher.

The same factor responsible for the changes in the perception of the attractiveness of people at singles bars probably also explains the panic over the Cabbage Patch dolls during the Christmas of 1983. The exploits of shoppers to buy the dolls have become legendary. One person hopped a jet to London, England, in hopes of finding one. In other cases mobs formed outside of shopping centers and then stormed the unlucky retailer who happened to have a supply on hand. Shelves were knocked over and people injured in some instances. One person offered to trade two Rose Bowl tickets for a doll.

How can such behavior be explained? One factor certainly at work is the principle of "scarcity".* Researchers have found that consumers perceive that products in short supply have a higher value than products in abundant supply. The end result is that not only are shoppers willing to pay more for something in short supply, the demand curve actually shifts because the value of the product to the consumer has changed.

One can find numerous instances of companies nearly every day advertising a limited edition of a car, boat, or stamp that can be bought for a premium price. In other cases a sale will be announced with the mention that the product is in short supply. Of course, if it were really in short supply, why have a sale? In each instance, the company is attempting to create the illusion of scarcity and change the demand curve for the product.

*For an excellent discussion of the impact of scarcity see Robert B. Cialdini, *Influence: Science and Practice*, Glenview, Ill.: Scott, Foresman and Company, 1985.

---

for one small child," Foster Parents forces consumers to consider the opportunity cost of a coffee break. The comparison is highly effective and makes the cost of participating seem negligible.

Decreasing Marginal Utility

The idea of **decreasing marginal utility** is that as the consumer buys more of a product, each additional unit brings less utility or satisfaction. In this sense, satiation does occur. After a certain point, the consumer becomes satisfied, bored, full, or overwhelmed with the product.

The collapse of the video game industry in the mid-1980s may be explained in part by the concept of decreasing marginal utility. In 1982 video games were popular in households across the country. Consumers were buying the cartridge games in droves to play on their home computers hooked up to their television sets. The stocks of the makers of the video games skyrocketed. The prices of the stocks of Warner Communications, maker of Atari games, and Coleco doubled or tripled in value.

The success, however, was not long lived. As decreasing marginal utility teaches, the satisfaction with the games began to decrease as each new car-

Figure 18–2 Foster Parents uses the principle of "opportunity cost." (Courtesy of Foster Parents, Inc.)

tridge was bought. Consumers became more reluctant to buy, and manufacturers began to lower the prices in order to increase the quantity demanded. The result: profit margins for the game companies began to deteriorate, and stock prices of the producers of the games plummeted.

Does the idea of decreasing marginal utility conflict with the assumption of economists that consumer desires can never be satiated? The answer is no. Although decreasing marginal utility states that consumers can have too much of any single product, the overall desire remains intact. In the case of video games, consumers grew bored with playing Donkey Kong, Pac-Man, and others. However, the desire for entertainment remained, and consumers moved on to other activities, such as watching MTV. One of the problems of marketers, and particularly marketers of games and fashions, is identifying and catching early new consumer fads and trends.

Price Elasticity

Another economic principle affecting consumers concerns how changes in price influence their purchase patterns—the principle of **price elasticity.** For some products and services, such as electricity, medical care, and bread, large changes in price have relatively little effect on quantity demanded. In such cases the product is said to be *price inelastic.* Conversely, for other products even small changes in price will strongly affect quantity demanded. Examples of such *price elastic* products include restaurant meals, lamb, and automobile tires.

A host of factors influence the price elasticity of a product, including the time horizon over which the quantity demanded is assessed, whether or not the product is a necessity, and the availability of substitutes. Some products and services even have different price elasticities for different target groups. The airline industry prices its service on such a principle. Vacationers are highly price elastic. Thus, the airlines offer reduced fares for those who can make reservations well in advance. Conversely, businesspeople's travel is often spur-of-the-moment. Because they are price inelastic, the airlines tend to charge higher fares to those who make reservations at the last minute and plan to stay only a short time.

Coupons work on a similar principle. Some shoppers are highly price elastic and consequently look for bargains. Such individuals will actively search for coupons in newspapers and on packages in order to obtain lower prices. In effect, companies using coupons are reaching two different target markets with different elasticities of demand and different pricing structures.

THE FIELD OF BEHAVIORAL ECONOMICS

Although economic theories, like the law of demand, can be applied at the individual level, economists are most comfortable talking about aggregates of people. Behavioral economists, or economic psychologists, take another approach. They investigate the behavior of consumer citizens involving economic decisions as well as the behavioral determinants of those economic decisions.[3] For example, one of the early efforts of behavioral economists was to explain changes in the overall economy by analyzing consumers individually. The idea, developed by George Katona, is that the attitudes, motives, and expectancies of individual consumers can be built up to make predictions concerning the economy as a whole. This view is a radical departure from traditional economic thinking.

Behavioral economists have made three major contributions to the understanding of consumer spending patterns. First, they originated and documented the idea that the consumer sector of the economy can strongly influence the course of the aggregate economy. Second, they asked the question, What factors influence the decisions of families to buy or save? Economists tend merely to ask what the results of such decisions are on the economy. Third, the behavioral economists developed a new methodology for making predictions of aggregate economic activities based upon consumer surveys.

The use of the survey research methodology was a major break from the traditional econometric studies of the economy. In the survey approach representative samples of consumers are interviewed to obtain information on consumer attitudes and expectations about their forthcoming buying behavior. Begun in 1946, the surveys of consumer sentiment continue today at the University of Michigan Survey Research Center. In addition, other groups, such as the Conference Board, have developed their own indices of consumer sentiment. Such indices have begun to play an important role in helping private and governmental forecasters estimate the future course of the economy. Table 18–1 gives the questions found in the **Index of Consumer Sentiment.**

Table 18–1   The Index of Consumer Sentiment

The Index of Consumer Sentiment was developed at the Survey Research Center at the University of Michigan. The telephone surveys are run every month and stratify the population by geography and population density. The wording of the five basic questions in the index is as follows:

1. We are interested in how people are getting along financially these days. Would you say that you (and your family living there) are better off or worse off financially than you were a year ago? Why do you say so?
2. Now looking ahead—do you think that a year from now you (and your family living there) will be better off financially, or worse off, or just about the same as now?
3. Now turning to business conditions in the country as a whole—do you think that during the next 12 months we'll have good times financially, or bad times, or what?
4. Looking ahead, which would you say is more likely—that in the country as a whole we'll have continuous good times during the next five years or so, or that we will have periods of widespread unemployment or depression, or what?
5. About the big things people buy for their homes—such as furniture, a refrigerator, a stove, television, and things like that. Generally speaking, do you think now is a good or a bad time for people to buy major household items? Why do you say so?

    In addition, the survey asks respondents about their plans to purchase automobiles over the next year.

Source: Richard T. Curtin, "Indicators of Consumer Behavior: The University of Michigan Surveys of Consumers," *Public Opinion Quarterly*, 46, 1982, 340–352.

Part of the impetus for the development of behavioral economics was the recognition that the United States economy has become consumer driven. Fully two-thirds of our gross national product results from consumer spending. Such has not always been the case. Prior to World War II, consumers simply did not have sufficient income or liquid wealth (e.g., savings, stocks, bonds, and other investments) to offset the influence of business and governmental spending. After World War II, though, a sort of mass affluence struck America. Great numbers of Americans began to experience financial latitude. Discretion existed as to the timing of their spending and saving. Consequently, when consumers began to spend, the economy improved. Conversely, when consumers began to save, the economy contracted.

With disposable income increasing after World War II, the demand for houses, cars and other durable goods rose. The housing and auto industries consequently took on great importance to our economy. The president of General Motors was not joking when he said that "what is good for GM is good for the country."

Because cars and homes are such important purchases to consumers, they represent investments that are done carefully and infrequently. In addition, because money is borrowed to make these purchases, consumers look into the future to try to see if they can afford the purchases. Behavioral economists argue that to the extent that consumers are optimistic about the future, the purchases will be made. If pessimistic, though, consumers will postpone the purchases and save instead. The consumer sentiment surveys were developed to gauge such waves of optimism and pessimism.

A Behavioral Economics Model

A basic idea behind Katona's behavioral economics was that consumer demand depends both on consumers' ability and their willingness to buy.[4] In the short term—a year or less—expenditures may be classified as either necessary or discretionary. The demand for necessary goods, like basic foodstuffs and clothing shows little cyclical variation.

Need tends to govern these purchases, and with unemployment and welfare assistance available the demand for basic foodstuffs and clothing remains. In contrast, **discretionary expenditures** are those that can be postponed or eliminated. In most instances a consumer can delay buying a new car, purchasing a new sofa, or moving to a larger house. Many of these discretionary expenditures are like investments, and consumers tend to make them only when they feel economically confident.

Figure 18–3 diagrams how feelings of **economic optimism-pessimism** may influence the discretionary-spending decisions. When people become pessimistic, their purchase intentions are influenced such that they curtail discretionary expenditures, rebuild financial reserves, and take on less debt. When optimism sets in, their intentions change so that consumers begin to spend, borrow money, and deplete their savings accounts.

The feelings of optimism-pessimism and the consequent development of attitudes, expectations, and intentions all take place within the context of the

Figure 18–3   A model specifying the relation between consumer spending and economic activity.

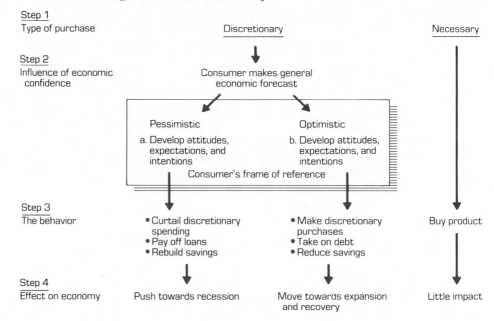

consumer's own frame of reference. The individual consumer's situation will influence his or her reaction to and forecast of the economic environment. If savings are high and the person's job secure, the impact of the economic pessimism will be minimized. Conversely, if the individual's own economic situation is precarious—say he or she works on an auto assembly line—reactions to the pessimism or optimism would be maximized.

Because consumers' frames of reference influence their reactions to their economic forecasts, one finds very different reactions to similar economic events. For example, consumer reactions to expected income increases vary. At times income increases have led to rapid increases in savings. At other times (e.g., the 1982 Reagan tax cut) the savings rate decreased after income rose. If individuals feel secure, they will tend to spend economic windfalls. Conversely, if individuals are worried about their own future, they will act cautiously and save. Responses depend on the consumer's frame of reference, including his own personal economic situation.

Behavioral economists do not adhere to several of the assumptions of traditional economists. First, they recognize that consumers have a "bounded rationality."[5] That is, in most cases consumers merely seek a satisfactory decision, not a perfect decision. The energy and effort required to make perfect, rational decisions are simply not worth it to consumers in most cases. Second, behavioral economists make explicit the recognition that consumers do not have perfect information about products and services. Many, if not most, decisions are made partially in the dark. Third, behavioral economists recognize that multiple motives activate and direct behavior. Motives, in addition to economic desires, direct behavior.[6]

The field of behavioral economics links many of the topics covered in consumer behavior directly to the question of how aggregates of consumers influence the economy. The concept that attitudes and expectations influence buying behavior highlights the importance of studying how attitudes are formed and changed. The idea that consumer motives are numerous underlines the need to study the areas of motivation and personality. Similarly, the idea that the consumer's frame of reference moderates his or her reaction to economic events and forecasts denotes the need to study the areas of culture, demographics, and family influences. Finally, the role of the situation in consumption takes on added importance when one recognizes the impact of the consumer's frame of reference.

THE ECONOMIC CYCLE AND CONSUMER BEHAVIOR

Our society seeks to have stable economic growth, a rising standard of living, high employment, and stable prices. Unfortunately, several of these goals are in conflict. In particular, a trade-off seems to exist between inflation and unemployment. As unemployment rises, inflation decreases; as unemployment decreases, inflation increases. Economists call this relationship the Phillips Curve. Partially because of these conflicting societal goals, the economy, as measured by the gross national product, rises and falls over time in a cyclical fashion. As noted by the behavioral economists, the consumer plays an important role in the **economic cycle.** His behavior influences the cycle, and, in turn, the cycle changes the consumer's actions.

Figure 18–4 shows the phases of the economic cycle. Within a general upward trend of economic activity, the cycle is overlayed. Economists view the cycle as having four phases: peak, recession, trough, and recovery.

At the peak of the cycle employment is at its highest, and the national output of goods is high. However, the seeds of the next recession have already been sown, as evidenced by slipping consumer confidence and a rising price level. With consumer prices rising, interest rates begin to rise. The higher interest rates cause consumers to take on less debt and to begin to save more, resulting in a lower demand for products. Retailers, then, begin to see a lowering of their sales. Their inventories of goods become too large, and they cut back on their orders from manufacturers. Manufacturers then must reduce production levels, lay off workers, and retrench. The economy is now in a full-scale recession.

A recession is a self-feeding process. With layoffs, consumer pessimism deepens. Final demand for products decreases further. Retailers strain to liquidate inventory. Orders to manufacturers decrease further. Manufacturers lay off more workers. A vicious cycle is under way.

Figure 18–4   The business cycle.

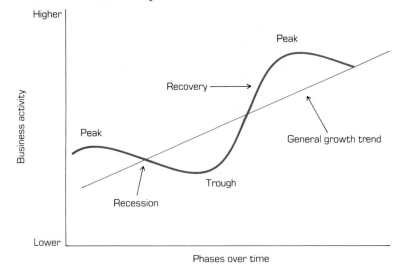

Fortunately, however, retailers eventually work off their inventories, prices begin to decline because of soft consumer demand, and consumers begin to pay off a portion of their debt. At about this point in time the trough of the recession is reached. Here unemployment has almost reached its maximum and output its lowest levels.

During the recovery retailers begin to increase their inventories. Manufacturers receive more orders, and output and employment begin to increase. Consumers become more optimistic, and sales of autos and homes begin rising. Demand increases as the unemployment rate slowly declines, and consumers take on more debt in order to buy products. But the recovery does not last indefinitely. Eventually, a peak is reached, setting the stage for the cycle to repeat itself.

The 1975–82 economic cycle had relatively wide swings of economic activity. The consumer price index nearly doubled. The unemployment rate ranged from less than 6 percent to almost 11 percent. The prime rate ranged from under 6 percent to over 20 percent at one time. Per capita disposable income rose rapidly early in the cycle but barely changed after reaching its peak in 1979. For certain types of expenditures, consumer spending also showed wide swings. Domestic auto sales began the cycle at 6.6 million units sold. At the peak of the recovery, about 9 million units were sold. During the depths of the recession, sales were down to 5.4 million units. Housing starts showed a similar pattern, going from 739,000 starts in 1975 to over 1.5 million in 1978, to below 600,000 during 1981. Figure 18–5 traces this pattern of housing starts.

Figure 18–5   Housing starts during the 1975–82 economic cycle.

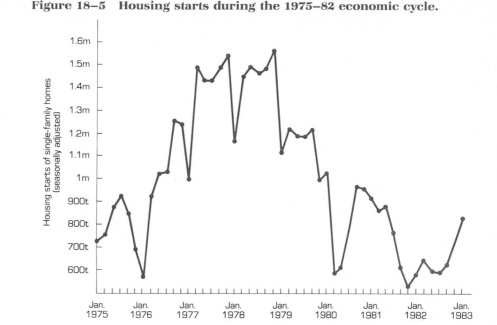

One of the basic concepts of behavioral economists is that consumer discretionary spending varies widely and consequently influences the economic cycle. During the 1975–82 economic cycle consumer discretionary spending in 1972 dollars started at $1,560 per person. It grew 33 percent to over $2,000 per person in 1979. However, three years later it was still at about the same level as in early 1980. This lack of spending by consumers played a large part in causing and maintaining the recession.

Why did consumers not spend their money? Part of the answer can be found in the savings rate figures. At the trough in early 1975 consumers were saving at a 7.2 percent annual rate. As the recovery got going, saving decreased to 5.4 percent and finally reached a low of about 4.3 percent at the peak of the economic cycle. At this point consumers began to become pessimistic. (The consumer sentiment index had dropped 20 percent from a year earlier, and interest rates were going up rapidly.) This resulted in increasing savings, and by the middle of the recession savings were up to 6.3 percent. Savings would eventually peak at about 8.3 percent just before the trough of the recession would be reached. With the increased savings, a lowering of interest rates, and a booming stock market in late 1982 and early 1983, consumer sentiment again began to rise, and the 1983 recovery began in earnest. Although discretionary spending showed the effects of the 1980–82 recession, nondiscretionary spending revealed little of the cyclic variation. Spending on services grew steadily during the cycle with only a slight slowdown during the three-year recession. In a similar manner, food expenditures rose steadily and evenly through the economic cycle.

One problem with the use of aggregated economic indices is that they mask important underlying trends that may run counter to the overall pattern of economic activity. At the trough, which marked the end of the 1975–82 economic cycle, the best-selling types of cars were not the small, inexpensive models. The best-selling cars were the most expensive—the Cadillacs and Mercedes. Other luxury goods were also selling well. Grand pianos, priced at over $10,000, were being bought, but not the less-expensive console pianos. Similarly, department stores found that sales of brand-name and designer apparel were doing well. Consumers were emphasizing luxury and quality during the recession.

Another countertrend could be found underlying the aggregate economic indices. Discount stores showed substantial sales and profit gains during the recession. Stores like Zayre, Wal-Mart, and Dollar General, which offered brand-name goods at discount prices, showed strong earnings gains. Consumers did not stop buying altogether during the recession; they simply changed their buying patterns. As a result, mainline department stores were hurt badly during the 1980–82 recession.

The Wall Street Journal called the pattern in which luxury goods and discount merchandise sell well simultaneously the "**affluent–average guy split.**" During the recession affluent individuals were insulated from layoffs. With cash on hand they didn't have to worry about obtaining loans at high interest rates. Conversely, the average man and woman (including most white-collar workers) were worried about high unemployment and interest rates. Consequently, they shopped frugally for high-quality goods at discount stores.[7]

Innovative products can also sell well during a recession. While appliance sales plummeted, sales of personal computers jumped dramatically. In fact, gatherers of economic statistics for the federal government could not react fast enough to include adequately the huge increase in the sales of personal computers to regular, everyday people. As a result, some of the estimates of consumer spending were thought to be artificially low late in 1983.[8]

Table 18–2 provides an overview of how consumers change their spending patterns during an economic cycle.

It is crucial that businesses understand the impact of the economic cycle on consumer spending patterns. Being prepared for a recession by having inventories and debt trimmed to low levels can save a business. If a company is in a cyclical business, demand for its products can erode dramatically. Because interest rates are normally rising rapidly during the early parts of a recession, a heavy debt load can become backbreaking. With no customers buying the company's products, the end result is often bankruptcy. During the 1980–82 recession record numbers of companies went under.

Table 18–2   Overview of Economic Cycle and Consumer Spending

	Trough	Recovery	Peak	Recession
Savings rate	Very high	Declining	Very low	Begins to build
Consumer debt	Very low	Starts growing	High	Begins to be worked off
Discretionary spending	Very low	Starts growing	High	Begins to slow
Nondiscretionary spending	Moderate to lower	Slight increase	Leveling off	Small drop
Service expenditures	Slightly lower growth	Slight increase	Leveling off	Slight decrease
Consumer confidence	Starting to improve	Rapid increase	Starts falling	Rapid, deep fall
Luxury expenditures	Moderate to high	Slight increase	Stable high level	Slight decrease

CONSUMER SPENDING AND SAVING

Consumer Saving Patterns

The decisions of millions of consumers to spend or save have a major impact on the fortunes of businesses. At the peak of the economic cycle savings are low, leaving little room for consumers to spend more. The recession begins in part because consumers begin to save.[9] A crucial question, then, is, What makes consumers decide to spend or save?

John Maynard Keynes, the famous British economist, was an astute observer of consumers, and he identified a number of reasons why consumers save, rather than spend, their money. Four of these reasons are paraphrased below.[10] Consumers save:

1. As a contingency against unforeseen circumstances.
2. To make a large purchase or go into a business venture.
3. For an anticipated time when one's income will decrease (e.g., old age, going back to school).
4. To enjoy a sense of independence and power.

More recently behavioral economists have noted the great influence that economic pessimism and optimism have on consumer saving behavior. Katona has argued strongly that economic pessimism leads in most cases to increased consumer savings. Other researchers have noted that some people save to reduce feelings of financial uncertainty. In essence they are saving for a "rainy day."[11]

Table 18–3 identifies three major categories of factors that influence the tendency to save. The first category is labeled economic pessimism. Feelings of concern about the general economic situation and of one's own economic fortunes have a number of causes. Clearly, observing others being laid off from their jobs, particularly if they are in a similar line of work as oneself, can result in spending caution. In fact, individuals who experience a cutback in their salaries or wages will sometimes begin to save more because of the pessimism that results.

Table 18–3 Factors Influencing Consumer Tendencies to Save

1. Economic pessimism
    a. Caused by general economic situation
    b. Caused by consumer's own economic situation
    c. Caused by international crises
    d. Caused by high inflation
2. Increase in consumer wealth
    a. Caused by tax cut
    b. Caused by personal windfall (e.g., inheritance)
    c. Caused by sudden improvement in job expectations
3. Personal inclinations and personal situation
    a. Influenced by family wealth
    b. Influenced by consumer's personality
4. Desire to make a large purchase, such as a house

National or international crises can create pessimism. The energy crisis in 1974, resulting from the Arab oil embargo, caused people to postpone purchases of durable goods, to stay closer to home, and to buy smaller cars. All of these behaviors led to more saving.

High inflation has also been shown to be associated consistently with increased saving. Surveys have shown that during periods of inflation people expect to have to spend more on necessities and to have less discretionary money available for nonessential goods and services. In addition, the inflation leads to uncertainty and pessimism, which create a need for more security. Such a need can cause the savings rate to increase.

A second general factor that can increase saving is an increase in wealth. Wealth can increase from a tax cut, a personal windfall (e.g., inheritance, gift, winning a contest or lottery), or a sudden improvement in one's job situation. Generally, people will spend a portion of the increased wealth. Particularly in the short term, however, people will save a substantial portion of the increase in wealth. Consumption habits are not changed easily. As a consequence, an increase in wealth will normally bring an increase in saving along with the purchase of some durable goods (e.g., appliances and stereos) that had previously been postponed.

A third general factor that affects saving tendencies is the individual's personal inclinations and situation. The general wealth of a person influences his saving behavior. Because people save in part to handle that "rainy day," and because a wealthy person has more to lose, people with more wealth will tend to save more. Another personal factor is the consumer's lifestyle. We considered psychographic lifestyles in Chapter 4, and suffice it to say that some individuals by the way they live and work are simply more frugal than others. They buy fewer discretionary goods, go on fewer vacations, live in smaller houses, and drive older cars.

A final factor influencing saving is the desire to make a large purchase.

During the early 1980s many young couples were desperately saving in order to have a downpayment for a house. Unfortunately, many were having little success. In fact, surveys have shown that more than one-third of all consumers are generally dissatisfied with their savings and reserve funds. This is in contrast to the finding that over two-thirds were satisfied with their standard of living. Consumers consider savings to be important but generally have a difficult time accumulating them. Even the allure of owing one's own home or of going overseas on a vacation is insufficient motivation to induce many consumers to increase their savings behavior.

Consumer Spending Decisions

In many respects decisions to spend are the flip side of decisions to save. Consumers spend more when they are optimistic, when economic conditions are perceived as stable, and when inflation is moderate. Expectations of sharp rises in inflation can, however, cause consumers to move up planned purchases. This was noted in 1952, at the start of the Korean War, when consumers thought that the U.S. economy might be placed on a wartime basis. Such behavior, though, is more aptly called hoarding than spending.

A better example of inflation-induced buying occurred during 1978–1979, when consumers were buying houses and automobiles in record numbers while their savings rate plummeted. During this time inflation was running at over 10 percent. Surveys of consumer attitudes done at the University of Michigan clearly revealed that some consumers were consciously buying before prices rose on things they wanted. However, the percentage of people expressing such feelings was relatively low—about 14 percent. The majority of people (79 percent) felt that it was better to avoid debt in times of inflation. When asked if in times of inflation they should buy houses, cars, and furniture before they are needed, only 19 percent said yes, and 71 percent said no.[12]

Other factors can lead large numbers of people to spend. A portion of a tax cut will be spent, particularly on one-time purchase consumer durables. Similarly, a portion of a monetary windfall will be spent. A general lowering of the interest rates is usually accompanied by increased spending. In particular, consumer durables, such as appliances, cars, and furniture, which consumers take on debt to buy, are strongly influenced by the level of interest rates.

During 1985 and 1986 the automobile manufacturers, through their financial subsidiaries, were offering as a sales inducement interest rates on their cars that were in some cases 5 or 6 percentage points below the rates obtainable at banks and credit unions. The idea was to spur lagging auto sales by inducing consumers to buy because of lower interest rates.

Just as personal inclination and habit influence decisions to save, they also influence decisions to spend. Many individuals have a lifestyle that involves spending everything they earn. As it turns out, such a strategy makes a certain amount of sense. In the United States and other Western countries an elaborate social welfare system has been created to protect individuals from misfortune, as well as their own inability to save, through transfer payments in the form of social security, welfare, and unemployment insurance.

Finally, just as people will save to make a large purchase, they will eventually make that purchase. The timing of such spending, though, is likely governed by feelings of economic pessimism and optimism. One cause of economic optimism is a rising stock market. For example, many analysts think the strong recovery that occurred in 1983 after the 1980–82 recession, happened in part because of an exceptionally strong stock market, which put billions of extra dollars in the hands of investors. Indeed, one good predictor of consumer optimism and pessimism is the level of the stock market. Two to four months after a large rise or fall in the stock market, consumer confidence changes to match the direction of the market's advance or fall. Some links between the stock market and consumer spending are discussed in Highlight 18–2.

HIGHLIGHT 18–2

The Stock Market and Consumer Spending

Government planners and businessmen recognize that a tax cut leads to increased consumer spending. Less recognized, though, is the huge impact a booming stock market can have on spending. Why does a bull market increase consumer spending? Because people feel, and perhaps are, wealthier. In fact, a bull market can mean more to consumer spending than a tax cut. In July 1983 consumers received a 10 percent tax cut, which was estimated to add $28 to consumers' pocketbooks. Some of this added cash was saved, and some was spent.

In contrast, the stock market boom of 1982 and 1983 added almost $71 billion to the total value of stocks in the U.S. as of May 1983. The conservative estimate is that 5 percent of this gain was spent, meaning that some $35 billion was used for buying cars, trips, appliances, and other major items.

An amazingly large number of Americans invest in the stock market. Thirty-two million invest directly through mutual funds or their own buying and selling. An additional 100 million invest indirectly through pension funds, retirement programs, and insurance programs.

Some experts argue that the 60 percent increase in the value of stocks between August 1982 and May 1983 was in part responsible for the dramatic rise in consumer confidence in early 1983. It is simply easier to spend money when one realizes that his net worth has increased 50 percent or more.

Anecdotes of the impact of the "paper" stock gains (i.e., the gains are not real until the stocks are sold) abounded. A *Wall Street Journal* article noted that people were spending their money on things like luxury cars, landscaping around expensive homes, and restoration of classic cars. In addition, some argue that even people who own stocks only indirectly, say in their pensions, still feel wealthier and consequently loosen their purse strings.

Unfortunately, the converse is also true. When the stock market goes down, people are poorer. Without doubt, the vagaries of the stock market can influence consumer spending patterns.

Based in part on Douglas K. Pearce, "Stock Prices and the Economy," *Economic Review*, 68, November 1983, 7–22.

ON WHAT DO CONSUMERS SPEND?

A number of factors influence the general question of whether consumers decide to spend or save. Economic pessimism and optimism, the level of interest rates, and the amount of savings on hand all influence whether consumers will start to buy. Another question concerns just how consumers allocate their purchasing resources. During the normal course of allocating their budget, how do consumers spend their hard-earned money?

Table 18–4 provides a listing of eleven categories of consumer spending for the years 1972, 1976, and 1981. The numbers are aggregated across all consumers and are held constant in 1972 dollars so that the effects of inflation will not distort the comparisons. Expenditures on food accounted for the most spending over the ten-year period. Fully 20 percent of expenditures went for food. Furthermore, the percentage changed very little over the ten-year period.

The next most costly item was housing, which rose from 14.5 percent of consumer spending to 16 percent over the period. However, if one adds to the basic cost of housing (i.e., rent and mortgage payments) the cost of utilities and the additional costs of running a house (e.g., repairs), the percentage of expenditures rises to almost 30 percent of the total. The cost of housing takes up a large percentage of a family's budget, and the percentage has been rising steadily.

Auto transportation is the next most costly area, amounting to about 13 percent of total expenditures in each of the three time periods. This figure,

Table 18–4   Consumer Expenditures (in millions of 1972 dollars)

	1972		1976		1981	
	Expenditure	% of Total	Expenditure	% of Total	Expenditure	% of Total
Food	$145,299	20.0%	$169,307	20.6%	$192,351	20.4%
Tobacco	12,593	1.7	12,111	1.5	11,855	1.2
Clothing	68,110	9.4	61,690	7.5	63,302	6.7
Jewelry and watches	4,566	0.6	5,333	0.6	6,620	0.7
Housing	105,517	14.5	126,065	15.3	151,376	16.0
Household operation	75,434	10.4	82,158	10.0	81,972	8.7
Household utilities	29,396	4.0	38,077	4.6	49,475	5.2
Medical care	57,431	7.9	79,881	9.7	99,733	10.6
Auto transportation	93,949	12.9	106,403	12.9	123,260	13.0
Recreation	47,826	6.6	54,495	6.6	60,083	6.4
Foreign travel	5,726	0.8	3,180	0.4	2,530	0.3
Other	80,659	11.1	82,584	10.0	102,181	10.8
Total	$726,506M	100.0%	$821,284M	100.0%	$944,738M	100.0%

SOURCE: Data adapted from the *Survey of Current Business*, U.S. Department of Commerce, selected issues.

however, masks the dramatic effect of rising oil prices on consumer spending. In 1972 gasoline and oil purchases accounted for 31 percent of the money spent on automobiles; by 1981 that figure had increased to 40 percent. In fact, the expenditures on gasoline and oil increased by 60 percent during the ten-year period.

Another area of expenditures showing fairly large increases was medical costs. In 1972, 7.9 percent of the expenditures were to the medical community. By 1981 the percentage had increased to 10.6 percent. This amounted to a 74 percent rise in expenditures on health. This is an amazingly large increase when one realizes that the figures are adjusted for the effects of inflation. Indeed, the rising costs of medical care have become a major social concern in the United States. In early 1983, when the consumer price index actually was going down, the costs of medical care were still rising at about a 10 percent annual rate. How to deal with an industry that takes an ever-increasing percentage of income despite a lowering of prices in general is an important problem now faced by consumers in the United States.

With the percentage spent on housing, gasoline, and medical care going up, some areas of spending had to go down. Amounts spent on tobacco decreased some 29 percent. Similarly, amounts spent on clothing decreased by 29 percent. Interestingly, the amounts spent on household operation decreased by about 16 percent. Whereas mortages, rents, and utilities went up rapidly during the ten-year period, the amount that consumers spent inside their homes on maintenance actually decreased.

Foreign travel also decreased dramatically during the period, declining about 62 percent. One reason for this change in behavior was the decreasing value of the U.S. dollar. Over the ten-year period the dollar lost value relative to most currencies in the world. This made it much more expensive to travel abroad. Consumers respond to economic incentives and disincentives. In this case, the economics of the situation told consumers to stay home, and they did! Between 1982 and 1985 the value of the dollar rose strongly against foreign currencies. Americans began traveling abroad again. In addition, the costs of imported products decreased, resulting in record foreign trade deficits.

Managerial Implications

An interesting question for managers to consider is, What single factor most accounts for the performance of their firm? Is it the managerial ability of those who run the firm, or the high quality work force employed by the brilliant managers? Of course, it is impossible to say with certainty what single factor is most important, but very likely that factor is the state of both the United States and the world economy.

To help understand this point, consider the stock market. One approach is to pick companies that will grow and will multiply your investment several hundred times over. The problem is that this rarely occurs. Similarly, it rarely occurs that a company produces a new product that becomes an overnight success and instantly makes it into another Procter and Gamble. The single factor that most affects the price of stocks is the overall movement of the stock market.[13] Likewise, the thing that most influences the profitability of companies is the health of the economy. Good economic times will hide poor management. Often it takes good management to survive bad times.

Recall the Harley-Davidson case at the beginning of the chapter. Japanese competition certainly hurt Harley-Davidson, but it was the 1980–82 recession that put a choke hold on the company. Of course, Harley-Davidson could not sit back and ignore the Japanese. What it meant was that the poor economy set the stage for the company to feel more strongly the competitive actions of companies like Honda and Kawasaki.

Knowledge of the principles of economics reinforces the importance of the study of demographic factors, such as population trends and income changes, as well as items that influence consumer tastes and preferences. Each factor serves to move the demand curve to the right or left. This means that at a given price, consumers will buy more or less of a product. Imagine how wonderful a manager would feel to experience a sudden surge in demand for the company's principal product without his or her company changing its marketing mix. This occurs when the demand curve shifts. Indeed, this is exactly what happened to bicycle manufacturers in the mid-1970s. When the 1973 energy crisis struck and people had to line up for hours to obtain gasoline, the sales of bicycles surged. Tastes and preferences for transportation changed dramatically.

The problem is how to anticipate these shifts in demand. That is the very reason for studying many of the topics covered earlier in this text, such as demographics, lifestyles, attitudes, personality, motivation, and culture.

The Role of Behavioral Economics

For managers the field of behavioral economics explicitly shows how the actions of consumers influence the economy. In particular, the various measures of consumer sentiment have become important indicators of future consumer buying patterns. Indeed, with the increased publicity given these surveys, it is possible that a self-fulfilling prophecy could occur. That is, if consumer confidence should start to rise, people would read about it, become more confident, and start buying. Simultaneously, corporations read the same information, start rehiring workers and extending working hours. In addition, retailers begin to increase inventories. All this leads to more economic activity, more confidence, etc. Of course, the opposite pattern could also occur, wherein a decline in confidence precipitates a series of pessimistic actions by consumers, retailers, and manufacturers, leading to lowered economic activity.

The key point is that consumer optimism and pessimism influence purchase patterns. Companies must be aware of changes in consumer sentiment in order to adjust production schedules, sales quotas, and inventories. One can even make an argument that large corporations, such as companies like

Sears, General Electric, and IBM should conduct their own sentiment surveys to pinpoint consumer optimism as it applies to their specific target markets.

The Economic Cycle and Managerial Actions

Companies must also be aware of where the economy is in the current cycle and how its product line is affected by economic fluctuations. A key problem to avoid is getting caught with large inventories at the peak of the economic cycle. Because consumer buying tends to fall rapidly as the economy slips into a recession, the excess inventory can become extremely difficult to work off. In addition, because interest rates are normally high and rising at the peak of the cycle, the costs of carrying the inventory become heavy. In order to work off the inventory, companies often must resort to massive price reductions, which can dramatically eat into profits.

The overhead of large inventories occurred to many retailers during the 1980–82 recession. The resulting heavy price cutting accounted in part for the rapid decline in the inflation rate to zero early in 1983. However, the price cutting also accounted for the poor profit picture of many corporations. The auto industry in particular was caught with large inventories of unsold cars, and the major American auto manufacturers' balance sheets dripped with red ink.

Managers should recognize that a number of economic events can have implications for consumer spending. Tax cuts, rising inflation, and a booming stock market can all create the conditions that often lead consumers to increase their spending. Knowledge of these effects can influence the timing and budgeting of television, radio, and print advertising. In addition, it can provide guidance for setting sales quotas for the sales force. Normally, consumers spend in advance of a rise in wealth caused by something they can anticipate, like a tax cut, so advertisements need to be in place well before the actual date of the reduction in taxes.

Economics and Estimating Total Marketing Potential

An important benefit gained by studying the economics of consumption is an ability to estimate the **total market potential** of a product. As Kotler noted, total market potential is the maximum sales in a given period that could be expected from all firms in an industry operating under a given marketing effort and given environmental conditions.[14] The analysis can be implemented in order to determine if a market is of sufficient size to enter with a new product. In addition, it can be used at the territory level to identify markets in which to sell and allocate marketing budgets most efficiently.

SUMMARY

Think back once again to the Harley-Davidson minicase. Take a broad view of the case and ask, How would knowledge of the economics of consumption help you in the decision to set production levels? Actually, you would have quite a bit of knowledge, and perhaps more importantly, you would have sufficient information to ask some of the *right* questions.

One major issue would concern the factors influencing the demand for motorcycles. You would recognize that pricing is important and would try to anticipate what your competitors might do here. You would also be concerned with governmental actions. Indeed, the U.S. government raised tariffs on large imported motorcycles, which gave you a small price advantage. Finally, you would be concerned about factors that might shift the demand curve, such as changes in consumer tastes or changes in the age distribution of your major target market.

Of key importance to you would be consumer optimism and its impact on buying plans. Closely related would be the economy. Where in the economic cycle are you, and what will happen over the next year? In addition, you would be interested in other economic factors that influence consumer expenditures on durables, such as interest rates, tax cuts or hikes, and the state of the stock market. Of particular importance would be the financial status of your target market. Is the disposable income of the target group rising or falling? What is happening to the members' debts? Do they have adequate savings?

Knowledge of the basics of the economics of consumption can directly assist the manager in determining the way of approaching problems related to the marketing mix. Specifically, such knowledge can help the manager to identify the types of information needed to make informed decisions concerning product, price, promotion, and distribution of a product.

Key Terms

Law of demand
Income effect
Substitution effect
Demand curve shift
Behavioral economics
Opportunity cost
Decreasing marginal utility
Price elasticity

Index of Consumer Sentiment
Discretionary expenditures
Economic optimism-pessimism
Economic cycle
Affluent–average guy split
Total market potential

Review Questions

1. What are five basic assumptions that economists make about the behavior of consumers?
2. What is the "law of demand"? How do income effects and substitution effects account for the law of demand?
3. What are the factors that may act to shift the demand curve?
4. What does the opportunity cost of buying a particular product have to do with the nature of that product's competition?
5. How does the principle of scarcity explain why members of the opposite sex look better at closing time in bars?
6. Define the concept of decreasing marginal utility. How does it explain the decline of the video game industry in the early 1980s?
7. Describe what is meant by price elasticity. How does the airline industry utilize price elasticity to segment the market?
8. What are the three contributions that behavioral economists have made to the understanding of consumer spending patterns?
9. How do consumer optimism and pessimism act to influence spending? What types of products are most influenced by consumer sentiment?
10. Draw a diagram of the consumer economic cycle. Indicate how the following variables are related to the economic cycle—consumer savings, consumer economic confidence, consumer debt, and discretionary spending.

11. Identify the factors that influence consumer tendencies to save.
12. Identify the four areas of expenditures on which consumers spend the most. What are the areas in which consumer spending changed the most during the 1970s?

Discussion Questions

1. Consider the state of the economy at the present time. Where in the economic cycle is the economy currently? Based upon the interrelationship between consumer spending and the economic cycle, do you believe that automobile manufacturers should be expanding or reducing inventories?
2. The record industry has had its problems over the past ten years. What factors are acting to shift the demand curve for traditional phonograph record sales?
3. Universities are selling a product (i.e., an education) just as companies sell products. What are some of the opportunity costs of obtaining a college education? What are the opportunity costs of leaving high school and enlisting in the military?
4. Relate an incident in which a company or retailer attempted to create the impression that a product was in short supply, a sale was about to end, or a model of the brand that you liked was about to be sold in order to encourage you to buy. To what extent did this strategy influence you?
5. Go to the library and obtain current information on the consumer savings rate and on the amount of consumer debt. What are the implications of these figures for future purchases of consumer durables?
6. Consider two companies. One sells breakfast cereals and one sells motorcycles. To what extent will each be concerned about how the economic cycle will change in the future? Why?
7. Earlier in the text the family life cycle was discussed. People are viewed as moving through various stages during their lives, including: young single, young married, married with children, empty nest, and sole surviving spouse. How might consumer saving patterns change as a person moves through the stages of the family life cycle?
8. To what extent are people in the United States becoming more or less economically optimistic or pessimistic at the present time? Why do you think this is occurring?
9. Make a list of all the expenditures you normally make each month. What percentage do you spend on food, clothing, jewelry, housing, auto transportation, and recreation? How does this compare to the national percentages?
10. Look in the *Wall Street Journal* and identify the recent pattern of the Dow Jones Industrial stock index. What are the implications of the trend of the index for future consumer spending?

References

1. Campbell R. McConnell, *Economics: Principles, Problems, and Policies*, 8th ed., New York, N.Y.: McGraw-Hill Book Company, 1981.
2. Ralph Gray, "Buick Shifts Its Sights," *Advertising Age*, September 19, 1983, 2.
3. W. Fred van Raaij, "Economic Psychology," *Journal of Economic Psychology*, 1, 1981, 1–24.
4. van Raaij, "Economic Psychology."
5. H. A. Simon and A. Newell, "Human Problem Solving: The State of the Theory in 1970," *American Psychologist*, 26, February 1971, 145–159.
6. Richard T. Curtin, "Curtain on Katona: The Development of Behavioral Economics," in *Contemporary Economists in Perspective*, Greenwich, Conn.: Jai Press, 1984.
7. "Customers Are Back, Most Merchants Say, But Caution Remains," *The Wall Street Journal*, April 8, 1983, 1, 6.
8. "Customers Are Back, Most Merchants Say, But Caution Remains," *The Wall Street Journal*.
9. George Katona, "Consumer Saving Patterns," *Journal of Consumer Research*, 1, June 1974, 1–12.
10. J. M. Keynes, *The Scope and Method of the Political Economy*, New York, N.Y.: Macmillan Publishing Co., Inc., 1930.
11. Alf Lindquist, "A Note on Determinants of Household Saving Behavior," *Journal of Economic Psychology*, 1, March 1981, 39–57.
12. Curtin, "George Katona"
13. Burton G. Malkiel, *A Random Walk Down Wall Street*, New York: W. W. Norton & Co., Inc., 1981.
14. Philip Kotler, *Marketing Management, Analysis, Planning, and Control*, 4th ed., Englewood Cliffs, N.J: Prentice-Hall, Inc., 1980.

PART III

Public Policy and Managerial Implications of Consumer Behavior

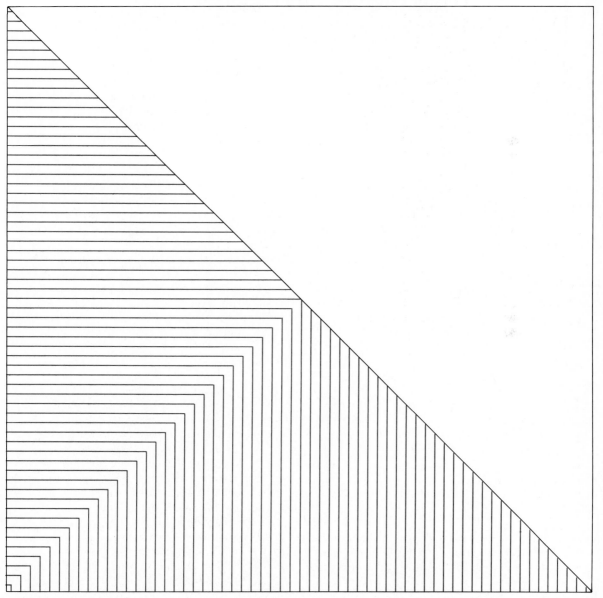

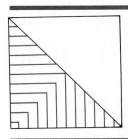

19

Public Policy Issues in Consumer Behavior

CONSUMER VIGNETTE

Marbles In Your Soup?

The Federal Trade Commission reprimanded Campbell's Soup Company in 1969 for advertising in which marbles were added to the bottom of the bowl causing the vegetables and meat to float on top. Their reasoning was that some consumers might be misled about the amount of vegetables and meat in the soup. Today Campbell's Soup Company carefully monitors the portrayal of its products in advertising. For example, the company will randomly select a can of soup off the grocery shelf and examine the can's meat and vegetable proportions. The company is also cautious that the yellow broth doesn't appear golden as a result of the magazine printing process. (a)

Advertising that might mislead children also draws considerable attention from government agencies and consumer protection groups. For example, the Children's Advertising Review Unit of the Federal Trade Commission felt a commercial for two new dolls in the Rainbow Brite collection did not accurately portray the products due to the extensive use of animation instead of actual shots of the dolls. (b) These examples illustrate one aspect of the topic of public policy—the role of the Federal government in monitoring the marketplace.

Based in part on (a) Ronald Alsop, "Ad Directors Fuss Over Foods As Much As Live Models," *The Wall Street Journal,* July 11, 1985, 25: and (b) "Ads Aimed at Kids Get Tough NAD Review," *Advertising Age,* June 17, 1985, 12.

INTRODUCTION

The examples provided in the consumer vignette are just a few of the many instances in which public officials use research generated by consumer researchers to guide their decisions. The idea of applying knowledge gained through the study of consumer behavior to aid in the development of laws and regulations is a relatively new one. This area is called public policy. Public policy involves the creation and enforcement of laws and regulations that are designed to enhance consumer and societal well-being.

This chapter begins with an overview of the development of consumerism, a movement which heightened both government and corporate sensitivity to consumers' needs and dissatisfaction relative to the marketplace. Next, the chapter presents several major public policy issues such as deceptive advertising practices, marketing tactics aimed at children, environmental concerns, and marketing issues related to the elderly. In addition, a new area is introduced—the problem of negligent consumer behavior. Four major forms of negligent behavior—failure to wear seat belts, smoking, drunk driving, and product misuse—are discussed in detail. However, one could include countless other forms of negligent, or even deviant, behavior such as tax evasion or shoplifting. This chapter then discusses contemporary issues in consumer behavior, with particular focus on corporate social responsibility. The chapter concludes with implications for the marketing manager.

CONSUMERISM

In a Lou Harris poll conducted in 1982, more than half of the respondents felt that the deal the consumer gets in the marketplace is worse than ten years ago. More than three-fourths said that the value they get for their money spent on goods and services has declined in the past ten years.[1] Table 19–1 shows just a few of the many concerns consumers have today relating to their participation in the marketplace. The activity of consumerists has slowed from the frenetic pace of the early 1970s, but many feel that "consumerism is most definitely alive."[2]

Historical Background

Consumerism has traditionally been viewed as the "set of activities of government, business, independent organizations, and concerned consumers that are designed to protect the rights of consumers."[3] The development of the consumer movement spans approximately eighty years and can be roughly categorized into four eras.[4] Table 19–2 presents a chronology of the major events that occurred during consumerism's evolution. The four major eras of the consumerism movement are discussed below.

The Muckraking Era (1905–1920) In 1905 Upton Sinclair wrote *The Jungle*, which depicted the atrocious conditions existing in the Chicago meat-

Table 19–1   Problems that Worry Consumers "A Great Deal":
1982 and 1976

Topic	Percentages	
	1982	**1976**
The high prices of many products	67	77
The high rate of interest charged on credit	59	x
The poor quality of many products	51	48
The poor quality of after-sales service and repairs	49	38
Too many products breaking or going wrong soon after you bring them home	46	35
Too many products that are dangerous	40	26
The failure of many companies to live up to claims made in their advertising	39	44
Misleading packaging or labeling	39	34
Failure of companies to handle complaints properly	39	29
Inadequate guarantees or warranties	36	30
Difficulty in obtaining as much credit as you need	18	x
Number of persons in survey	1,252	1,510

x = not asked

SOURCE: Data adapted by permission from D. B. Smith and P. N. Bloom, "Is Consumerism Dead or Alive? Some New Evidence," *Advances in Consumer Research*, XI, Thomas Kinnear (ed.), Ann Arbor, Mich.: Association for Consumer Research, 1984, 370.

packing industry. The public furor that arose from the book's revelations sparked national awareness of the need for consumer protection. Subsequently, Congress passed the Pure Food and Drug Act (1906), the Federal Meat Inspection Act (1907), the Federal Trade Commission Act (1914), the Clayton Act (1914), and the Water Power Act (1920).

The Information Era (1927–1939)   The writings of Stuart Chase and F. J. Schlink in their book, *Your Money's Worth*, once again stimulated interest in the consumer's plight in the marketplace. The primary focus of the book was on advertising and packaging techniques designed to enhance product sales rather than aid the consumer in the correct product selection. *Your Money's Worth* called for objective product-testing agencies who would not be influenced by any one manufacturer but would provide independent product evaluations to consumers. One such agency to arise at this time was the Consumers Union, publisher of *Consumer Reports*. Highlight 19–1 provides insight into the weight this agency carries today.

Probably the most important legal development was the passage of the Wheeler-Lea Act, an amendment to the Federal Trade Commission Act of 1914. This act gave the FTC a more consumer-oriented perspective. Specifically, the Wheeler-Lea amendment gave the FTC additional responsibility concerning deceptive acts and practices. In addition, the FTC was given the

Table 19–2   The Development of the Consumer Movement

Date	Event
	The "Muckraking Era"
1905	Upton Sinclair's *The Jungle*
1906	Pure Food and Drug Act
1907	Federal Meat Inspection Act
1914	Federal Trade Commission Act
1914	Clayton Act
1920	Water Power Act
	The "Information Era"
1927	Stuart Chase and F. J. Schlink's *Your Money's Worth*
1933	Kallet and Schlink's *10,000,000 Guinea Pigs*
1936	Robinson-Patman Act
1938	Food, Drug, and Cosmetics Act
1938	Wheeler-Lea Amendment
1939	Wool Products Labeling Act
	"Continuing Consumer Concern"
1951	Fur Products Labeling Act
1953	Flammable Products Act
1957	Poultry Products Inspection Act
1960	Hazardous Substances Labeling Act
	"Modern Consumer Movement"
1962	Kennedy's Enumeration of Consumer Rights
1965	Ralph Nader's *Unsafe at Any Speed*
1966	Cigarette Labeling and Advertising Act
1966	Fair Packaging and Labeling Act
1966	Child Protection Act
1966	National Traffic and Motor Vehicle Safety Act
1968	Consumer Credit Protection Act
1972	Consumer Product Safety Act
1975	Magnuson-Moss Warranty-Federal Trade Commission Improvement Act

SOURCE: Data adapted from Rogene Buchholz, *Business Environment and Public Policy*, Englewood Cliffs, N.J.: Prentice-Hall, Inc., 1982.

power to issue cease-and-desist orders, fine companies for not complying with such orders, and investigate companies even without a formal complaint against them.[5]

Continuing Consumer Concern (1951–1960)   Interest in the consumer movement waned during the World War II and postwar years. The nation experienced a new prosperity and a hunger for products that had been denied during the war. Public energy was concentrated on rebuilding lives rather

HIGHLIGHT 19-1

Consumers Union: A Force Not To Be Ignored

Did you ever buy a product that didn't quite perform as the advertisements led you to believe? Now the manufacturer probably didn't lie to you. The company may have tested its products under different conditions in which you used them. That's the conclusion drawn by Consumers Union, publisher of *Consumer Reports* magazines.

The specific product under fire in this instance was house paint. According to Consumers Union, paint manufacturers test the coverage of their product by painting a gallon over a 400-square-foot area with special equipment. Stephen E. Taub, who is in charge of testing chemicals and foods for Consumers Union, claims that the average consumer cannot apply paint as thickly as the manufacturers with the basic paint roller.

With a circulation near 3 million and the trust of more individuals than even the Better Business Bureau, the standing of a company's products in *Consumer Reports* can be critical to the company's future. For example, Coleco Industries stock dropped $4.375 a share the day *Consumer Reports* published a critical review of Coleco's Adam home computer system. With respect to the paint testing, Taub said that he had a paint company official "come in here and literally fall on his knees and beg for a review after we lambasted his product. The guy was close to tears." Consumers Union is not a company manufacturers can easily ignore.

Based on "Consumers Union Tests Products in Ways Manufacturers Won't," *The Wall Street Journal*, January 14, 1985, 15.

than fighting for consumer rights. As a consequence, fewer pieces of legislation were passed during the era. Among the regulations passed were: the Fur Product Labeling Act, which provided mandatory specifications relating to labeling and advertising fur products; the Flammable Products Act, which prohibited the making of garments from flammable material; and the Hazardous Substances Labeling Act, which required warning labels on household products that contained toxic, flammable, or irritating substances.

Modern Consumer Movement (1962–1980) The modern consumer movement was inaugurated with the enumeration of the four consumer rights by President John F. Kennedy in 1962. These rights are the right to safety, the right to be informed, the right to redress or to be heard, and the right to choice. Many of the subsequent congressional acts were designed to aid in the protection of these rights.

Another critical event during this time was the publication of Ralph Nader's book *Unsafe at Any Speed*. This book criticized General Motor's attitude toward automobile safety, with particular emphasis on the Corvair. The attention Nader drew from his book incited interest in other consumer areas. Table 19–2 lists just a few of the acts passed since 1965. For example, the Cigarette Labeling and Advertising Act (1966) required the surgeon general's warning with regard to the health hazards of smoking on all cigarette packages. The Child Protection Act (1966) banned the sale of hazardous toys and goods intended for children. The Consumer Credit Protection Act (1968) required that consumers be informed of the full terms and finance charges for consumer loans and installment purchases. In addition, the Consumer Product Safety Act of 1972 established the Consumer Product Safety Commission.

A Reagan Era? With the inauguration of President Reagan in 1980, the vigor of the consumer's movement clearly faded. One former government official described the consumer movement as going ". . . from Nader to nadir after President Reagan took office."[6] A combination of factors appear to be responsible for the decline. Perhaps foremost was the severe reduction in funding for government agencies. For example, the staff of the Environmental Protection Agency was cut by 50 percent.[7] Funding for the Federal Trade Commission and the Consumer Product Safety Commission was also cut substantially. One result of the funding cuts was the reduced ability to track potential problem areas, such as the control of toxic chemicals in the food supply. Similarly, low funding forced the reduction of efforts to identify potential instances in which product recalls should be made. Other areas being hurt included the regulation of pollutants into the environment, the development of nutrition education and disclosure programs, and the regulation of food advertising making health and nutrition claims.

In addition to the funding cuts the basic philosophy of the Reagan Administration certainly set back the consumer's movement. The administration was antagonistic to the government regulation of the marketplace and preferred self-regulation to government regulation. The individuals appointed to head the agencies also shared such a philosophy. The result was a general reluctance to forcefully move against corporations. In addition, the agencies had to justify regulations according to stringent cost-benefit analyses. In contrast, during the Modern Consumer Movement, the burden was on industry to show that they were protecting the consumer.

The question remains as to whether the change of environment found in the Reagan years will continue into the future. In an era of severe international competition the costs of heavy handed regulation can be severe. However, as shown in Table 19–1, consumers remain concerned about such areas as after-the-sale service, product safety, and complaint handling. Hopefully, the correct balance between consumer protection and industry self-regulation will be obtained.

Development of Major Government Agencies

One of the consequences of the consumer legislation was the establishment of government agencies whose purpose entailed guarding consumers against unfair business practices. This section examines some of the major agencies to evolve during the past seventy-five years.

The Federal Trade Commission (FTC) The commission was established in 1914 as a result of the Federal Trade Commission Act for the purpose of curtailing unfair trade practices and limiting monopolies. Some of the options available to the FTC when violations occur include the imposition of fines, the refund of money or return of property, the awarding of damages, and public notification of violations. For example, the FTC ordered ITT-Continental, the makers of Profile Bread, to correct its claim that consumption of the bread would aid in losing weight. In actuality, the bread contained seven fewer calories per slice than most other breads. As a result of FTC intervention, one-fourth of the company's advertising carried the corrective message for one year.[8]

The Food and Drug Administration (FDA)   The FDA traces its roots to the Food and Drug Act of 1906. This act has undergone several amendments to enlarge the FDA's responsibility. The goal of the FDA is to protect consumers from unsafe and impure food, drugs, cosmetics, and therapeutic devices. The dominant activities of this agency include: guarding against the mislabeling of food, drugs, cosmetics, or therapeutic devices; identifying and eliminating improper food preparation or packaging; and establishing quality standards. Criminal prosecution and/or seizure of the production in violation are two remedies available to the FDA.[9] For example, the FDA banned additives such as cyclamates and red dye number two during the early 1970s. The agency nearly banned saccharin in 1978, but public outcry was so intense that the FDA concluded that the cancer-causing properties of the substance needed further research and thus rescinded the ban.[10]

The National Highway Traffic Safety Administration (NHTSA)   This agency was created in 1970 by the Highway Safety Act. Its responsibilities include regulating the safety performance of new and used motor vehicles and their equipment, investigating motor vehicle safety defects, and establishing required average fuel economy standards for new motor vehicles. This agency also has the power to order recalls for safety defects that are not covered by any of their mandatory standards.[11] For example, the NHTSA was the agency responsible for the recall of 14.5 million Firestone "500" radial tires and 1.4 million Ford Pintos and Bobcats during the 1970s.[12]

The Consumer Product Safety Commission (CPSC)   The need for such an agency became apparent after a National Commission study found that product-related accidents resulted in 20 million injuries annually. In addition, 30,000 deaths and 110,000 permanently disabling injuries have been attributed to this type of accident. These product-related incidents cost the economy some $55 billion.[13] Consequently, the Consumer Product Safety Act (1972) established this agency to investigate the causes of product-related accidents and to develop appropriate responses.[14] The commission's primary responsibilities involve:

1. Identifying products that may be unsafe.
2. Establishing labeling and product-safety standards.
3. Recalling defective products.
4. Banning products that pose an unreasonable risk.[15]

The Federal Hazardous Substances Act, the Poison Packaging Prevention Act, the Flammable Fabrics Act, and the Refrigerator Safety Act also fall within the agency's realm. The CPSC has the authority to impose fines ranging from $50,000 to $500,000 with a possible one-year jail sentence; to initiate product recalls; to order refunds; and to disperse public earnings.[16]

Future Directions

What future orientation might consumerism take? From the consumer's point of view, it has been suggested that he or she will be exercising an enlarging role in the marketplace; joining buying clubs, cooperatives, and sharing ownership of expensive goods (e.g., time-sharing of condominiums); and participating in consumer organizations at the local level.[17] From the Federal Trade Commission's perspective, its areas of concern will likely focus on the "marketing" of professional services, the use of comparative disclosures (e.g., energy efficiency ratings on appliances), and the implications of the "new media" such as videodiscs, videotext, and cable television for marketers.[18]

Some authors have suggested that additional areas of research for consumer behaviorists could include: an assessment of the effectiveness of consumer organizations, an investigation concerning the reasons that individuals join and support consumer activist groups, and the development of means by which consumer groups could better aid certain "disadvantaged" groups such as children, minorities, and the elderly.[19]

MAJOR PUBLIC POLICY ISSUES

As discussed in the previous section, the most recent consumerism movement originated during the 1960s, with extensive interest and growth occurring in the 1970s. Some of the major consumer issues to evolve during this time period include deceptive advertising, advertising aimed at children, environmental protection, and marketing practices aimed at the elderly.

Deceptive Advertising

As of 1984, according to the FTC an advertisement may be deemed deceptive if it has the "capacity to deceive a measurable segment of the public."[20] The commission usually considers a deception rate of 20 to 25 percent to be "measurable," although this number could be reduced if consumers stand to lose a large amount of money or could incur physical injury as a result of the deception.[21] Whether or not the advertiser actually intended to deceive consumers is considered irrelevant. Table 19–3 displays the different categories of deceptive claims that may be present in advertising considered misleading by the FTC.

Corrective Advertising   In response to the increased attention given to deceptive advertising tactics in the sixties and early seventies, the FTC began to order corrective measures from some of the guilty parties. The incident that sparked the idea of **corrective advertising** involved Campbell's soup advertisements in which clear marbles were placed in the bottom of the soup

Table 19–3 Categories of Deceptive Claims

Objective Claim—A standard for comparison exists against which the claim may be compared to determine if it is deceptive or not. Example: A Poly-grip commercial that claimed denture wearers could eat foods such as corn on the cob or apples without fear of their dentures loosening. In reality, the front teeth of many dentures are for cosmetic purposes. Polygrip would not be effective for these types of dentures.

Subjective or Opinion Claim—This type of claim is difficult to prove false because trade "puffery" or evaluative claims are allowed. The FTC's position is that advertisements that claim certain products are "the best" are not usually taken seriously by the average consumer.

Implied Claim—This claim involved the overall impression the consumer has concerning a product or service apart from the literal advertising text, or "deception by innuendo." Example: In 1962 a television commercial was shown whose purpose was to display the superiority of Libby plate glass over plain glass. In fact, plate glass does possess many attributes that ordinary glass does not. However, as a means of demonstrating this notion, the commercial showed an outdoor scene filmed from the inside of two car windows—the windows representing each of the two forms of glass. From the inside of the "ordinary glass," viewers saw a distorted scene. The view through the "plate glass" window pictured a perfect view. In actuality, the "ordinary glass" scene had been filmed through a window smeared with Vaseline and the "plate glass" scene had been filmed out of a rolled-down window.

The Claim with Two Meanings—If an advertisement has two meanings, one of which is false, then the entire ad is considered deceptive. Example: In an advertisement from the National Commission on Egg Nutrition that encouraged individuals to eat eggs, the FTC issued a cease-and-desist order which prevented the commercial from containing the statement, "There is no scientific evidence that eating eggs increases the risk of . . . heart disease." The commission decided that research in this area still provided mixed results such that the claim should not be made.

The Unsubstantiated Claim—Affirmative claims for a product that are not reasonably supported. Example: "Miracle" weight-loss products, cosmetics that claim to retard aging or remove wrinkles.

Evaluating the Sufficiency of Information—An advertisement can be deemed deceptive if it fails to disclose relevant facts or conditions. Example: Fresh Horizons, bread which was positioned as having a high fiber content. However, packaging and advertising must disclose that the source of the fiber is tree pulp.

Source: Based on Dorothy Cohen, "Protecting Consumers from Fairness and Deception," in *Consumerism and Beyond: Research Perspectives on the Future Social Environment*, Paul N. Bloom, (ed.), Cambridge, Mass.: Marketing Science Institute, 1982, 68–74.

bowl, causing the vegetables to float on top. The FTC issued a cease-and-desist order which banned this practice because consumers were left with the impression that the soup contained more vegetable pieces than it actually did. A group of law students from George Washington University petitioned the FTC stating that Campbell's should be forced to issue a corrective statement to inform consumers who might not have been aware that they had been deceived. The FTC did not make this requirement of Campbell's but considered the concept of corrective advertising as potentially useful.[22]

Perhaps the most famous of all corrective advertising cases involved War-ner-Lambert's claim that Listerine mouthwash could prevent or lessen the severity of colds and sore throats. The company began manufacturing Listerine in 1879 and advertising the product in 1921. Thus, for more than fifty years Warner-Lambert had been making this claim.

In 1975 the FTC issued its order that Warner-Lambert must attempt to correct misimpressions that their advertisements had created. From September 1978 to February 1980, Warner-Lambert spent more than $10 million on corrective advertising. Nearly 95 percent of this money was devoted to television commercials.[23] Listerine's corrective commercial featured two couples, with each husband finding himself having "onion breath." One husband tried Scope and the other tried Listerine. After sniffing her husband's breath, one wife stated that she hadn't known "clinical tests prove Listerine fights onion breath better than Scope." The other wife replied, "We always knew." The corrective disclosure was placed in the middle of the thirty-second spot and stated, "While Listerine will not help prevent colds or sore throats or lessen their severity, breath tests prove Listerine fights onion breath better than Scope."[24]

Several studies have investigated the impact of Listerine's deceptive claim and the ability of the corrective message to reduce the false impression.[25] One such study found that Listerine's corrective advertising campaign reduced the level of deception by approximately 20 percent.[26] These authors' general conclusion was that long-held personal convictions regarding the efficacy of Listerine were difficult to change. For some individuals, perhaps Listerine did reduce cold symptoms simply because they believed in the product's medicinal power. However, the authors did offer suggestions for enhancing the effectiveness of the corrective campaign:

Listerine's competition could be limited from referring to Listerine as causing "medicine breath."

Given the duration of the misleading advertising claim, the corrective campaign could have been run longer.

More media expenditures could have been devoted to print advertising which would allow the consumer more time to process the information.

Corrective claims could have been available at the point of purchase, such as on the package or label.

Modifications could have been made in the product's apothecary style packaging and medicine taste.

Advertising Substantiation   In 1971 the FTC initiated its advertising substantiation program as a result of the siege of criticism against advertising. The objective of this program was twofold. First, consumers would be provided with information that might help them make rational choices. Second, competition would be encouraged as other companies challenged advertising claims.[27] Thus, the FTC could require companies to provide tests, studies, or other data that supposedly support the advertisements' claims regarding the product's safety, performance, efficacy, quality, or comparative price.[28]

One example involved Bristol-Myers Company. Their advertisements for analgesics used phrases such as "here's proof," "medically proven," or "doctors recommend." In addition, the commercials used visual cues that implied these statements, such as having the spokesperson in a white coat or in a laboratory setting. Such tactics suggested the superiority of their products over those of their competition. The FTC held that in the category of over-the-counter drugs it would be easy for the advertiser to make misleading claims because many consumers are not able to evaluate these claims adequately for themselves. Thus, the commission ordered that Bristol-Myers conduct two well-controlled clinical tests to substantiate their claims of superiority based on scientific evidence. In addition, Bristol-Myers was to stop claiming that any group recommends its products unless the company possessed a reasonable basis for its claim.[29]

The substantiation program was not designed, however, to apply to claims that were merely trade puffery. As a result, this program is often criticized for encouraging marketers to engage in evaluative advertising—vague, subjective claims such as "Our brand tastes the best"—which offers limited relevant information to the consumer.[30] Some researchers suggest that evaluative advertising may delude consumers into believing the brand is somehow unique or superior to those of the competition. However, public policy makers are unlikely to challenge the advertising due to the abstract nature of the claims.[31]

Future Directions   Despite the attempts made during the past fifteen years to monitor deception in advertising, studies show that consumers continue to express concern over potentially misleading advertising. Table 19–4 displays consumers' views of the proportion of advertising that they consider misleading across the various media. Although television advertising has had

Table 19–4   Perceptions of Advertising as Misleading

	All	**Most**	**Some**	**Few**	**None**	**Uncertain**
Telephone	27.0%	40.2%	18.6%	3.7%	3.7%	6.8%
Mail	10.5	50.8	27.5	4.1	3.4	3.7
Television	5.4	33.1	47.8	10.0	1.7	2.0
Home distribution	6.0	27.0	39.3	15.8	4.6	7.4
Magazines	3.8	21.8	50.2	16.3	3.1	4.8
Radio	2.4	17.2	54.1	15.5	3.4	7.2
Classified ads	3.2	17.2	40.0	24.9	3.9	10.9
Newspapers	1.7	16.6	49.7	22.4	5.2	4.5

SOURCE: Adapted with permission from Howard G. Schutz and Marianne Casey, "Consumer Perceptions of Advertising as Misleading," *Journal of Consumer Affairs, 15,* 1981, 340–357.

a greater quantity of misleading advertisements, the respondents in this study viewed telephone advertising as the form with the greatest proportion of misleading advertising. Direct mail placed a close second. These results suggest that greater emphasis might be placed on consumer education material that addresses the issues of mail fraud and telephone misuse.[32]

Children's Advertising

Both marketing managers and public policy makers have reacted to criticisms of advertising, particularly advertising directed at children. The controversy surrounding this issue grew so intense in the late 1970s that the FTC considered banning all advertising aimed at young children.[33] Marketing managers and public policy makers have benefited from consumer behavior research and theory that examines children's responses to advertising.[34] This section analyzes the major areas of criticism in children's advertising and presents their implications for public policy makers.

Can Children Tell the Difference Between Commercials and Programming?   The research that has explored this question has produced mixed results. In an early study, Blatt, Ward, and Spencer found that children ranging in age from five to twelve could all identify the word "commercial," but the younger children (ages five and six) thought the difference between commercials and programs to be based on "affect" (i.e., "commercials are funnier") or "coincidental reasoning" (i.e., "commercials are shorter than programs").[35] The major conclusion is that the child's age is positively correlated with his or her ability to distinguish between programs and commercials.

These results prompted the FTC in 1974 to recommend that television stations take special precautions to delineate the programs from the commercials for young audiences. The Federal Communications Commission (FCC) advised that some form of separator be used before and after each commercial interruption. Under pressure from the FTC in 1978, the National Association of Broadcasters revised its guidelines to provide more detail in the use of separators. Such rules included the use (both audio and video) of "We (or the program's name) will return after these messages" before the commercial and "We now return to (program name) after the commercial."[36] A study that examined the impact of the separator in aiding preschool children to discern between programs and commercials found that the majority correctly identified the programs and commercials as such and that the form of separator (i.e., audiovisual break, audio break only, visual break only, or blank screen) was not significant.[37]

In 1974 the FCC identified another advertising tactic that presented problems for children—the use of program characters to promote products. The commission thought this practice, called **host-selling,** was unfair because of its interweaving of program and commercial and because this technique was taking advantage of the trust children place in their program characters. Therefore, in 1975 both the National Association of Broadcasters and the National Advertising Division (NAD) recommended that host-selling in children's advertising be limited. Specifically, they recommended that no program character, live or animated, be used to deliver a television commercial within or adjacent to any program in which the character regularly appears.[38]

One study that looked at the effect of host-selling on the child's desire for the product compared commercials that either offered a premium (merchandise that is either free or offered at a reduced price to stimulate purchase of the promoted item), used host-selling, or had an announcer. The authors found that children who viewed the host-selling commercial selected the advertised brand significantly more than those who had viewed the announcer commercial. However, the premium commercial was superior to both of these in influencing the children to select the advertised brand.[39]

Another study examined whether the placement of an animated host-selling commercial relative to the cartoon (i.e., before, in the middle of, or following) had any impact on young children's ability to tell the program from the commercial. The study found that the majority of the children recognized that they had seen a commercial regardless of whether or not it involved host-selling, and regardless of its location with respect to the program.[40] The cartoon in Figure 19–1 suggests that not only can children tell commercials from programming, but perhaps that they also enjoy commercials more.

Do Children Understand the Selling Intent of Commercials?   In many cases a child can discriminate between a program and commercial but cannot understand the selling intent behind the commercial.[41] Once again, the child's age has a positive influence on his or her ability to comprehend that the commercial is trying to sell him or her something. In addition, research has shown that when a child attributes persuasive intent to television commercials, the child believes them less, likes them less, and is less likely to desire the advertised product. Conversely, those children who perceive the commercial as informative and helpful trust and like the commercial more and are more likely to want the advertised product.[42]

Do Commercials Make Children Want Products That Are Not Good for Them?   A high proportion of advertising aimed at children is for products that contain large amounts of sugar. As a result of exposure to these types of commercials, children tend to consume more sugared products, have a greater preference for sugared food even if they have not seen the specific product advertised, and are less well informed about proper nutrition.[43] One study found that children who had viewed candy commercials chose candy significantly more than fruit as a snack. In addition, the study found that children who had not seen candy commercials chose fruit as often as children who had viewed fruit commercials or public service announcements (PSAs) that carried a nutrition message.[44]

Figure 19–1   An illustration of the attention-grabbing effects of television commercials on children. (MARVIN *by Tom Armstrong. Copyright © by and permission of News America Syndicate.*)

Given that marketers currently do not fear the FTC banning advertising aimed at children, some researchers have suggested that public policy makers could use a subtler approach in diminishing children's sugar consumption. Both the national networks and local stations could be encouraged to develop public service announcements aimed at the young audience that teach and promote good nutritional habits. In order for such messages to be effective, however, they must be shown on a frequent and continuing basis to combat the multitude of sugared-food advertisements. In addition, the PSAs should contain more of an emotional appeal rather than simply informing the child of the four basic food groups.[45]

Environmental Protection

The energy crisis during the mid-1970s prompted government officials to request that American consumers conserve many natural resources that had been taken for granted many years. One major obstacle appears to hinder effective conservation programs. Most consumers do not personally accept the responsibility to conserve resources, although most individuals would likely state that they favor conservation efforts.[46] Belk and his associates stressed that the attribution of causality for the energy crisis is critical in determining whether or not an individual will conserve. When an individual attributes the cause of the energy shortage to a nonpersonal source (such as the government, foreign powers, or major oil companies), then she or he feels that a nonpersonal solution (such as government intervention) is the answer. However, if the individual perceives the general public as the source of blame, then the person is more likely to engage in conservation behavior.[47]

Conservation behavior can be divided into three basic categories: curtailment behaviors, maintenance behaviors, and efficiency behaviors.[48] Curtailment behavior involves reducing consumption by modifying current behavior. Examples of this form of conservation behavior include adjusting the thermostat, washing clothes in cold water, or driving less. Maintenance behavior involves making sure that energy-consuming equipment and appliances are in good working order. Tuning up the car and getting the furnace cleaned are two examples of maintenance behavior. Efficiency behavior focuses on reduction in energy consumption via structural changes in the home or travel environment. Purchasing a more fuel efficient car, installing solar panels, or insulating the attic are examples of efficiency behavior. The degree of information seeking, financial risk involved, and modification in lifestyle varies with the type of conservation behavior. Therefore, policy makers need to design their conservation programs to complement the form of conservation behavior they are trying to encourage.

Several studies have examined various approaches for motivating consumers to conserve energy. For example, the Department of Energy (DOE) used an incentive to stimulate consumers to conserve. Specifically, the DOE sent out 4.5 million professionally prepared booklets which gave low-cost and no-cost tips for conserving energy. One of the tips suggested installation of a shower-control device to reduce water consumption. A plastic shower-flow-control device was included with the booklet as a form of incentive. Because the correct means to install and use the shower-control device were not immediately obvious, the consumer was motivated to read the booklet. Subsequent follow-up research found that nearly half of the households sampled had installed the shower-control device. In addition, nearly three-fourths of the sample had read the conservation tips booklet. Furthermore, individuals who had installed the shower-control device also reported that they implemented additional conservation tips such as turning down the thermostat, checking for gaps around the fireplace damper, and making adjustments to their furnace.[49] These results suggest promising means of encouraging conservation behavior. However, one researcher noted that consumers would need to be reinforced continually if they are to conserve in the long run.[50]

Another tactic might be to identify "energy responsible individuals" who would act as opinion leaders and role models for others.[51] An additional means of encouraging conservation focuses on consumers' bedtime, which is often determined by prime-time television hours. One author has speculated that a 2 percent savings in residential energy consumption would occur if all four of the Unites States time zones adopted a 7:00 to 10:00 P.M. prime time, as opposed to the 8:00 to 11:00 P.M. prime time that currently exists in the eastern and pacific time zones.[52] Table 19–5 provides an overview of other approaches taken to encourage energy conservation.

The Elderly

An emerging interest of public policy makers involves the role of the elderly consumer in the marketplace. With a current population of 25 million individuals aged sixty-five or older and the movement of the baby-boom segment toward the sixty-five-and-older age group, the sheer population percentage incites concern in the consumer area.[53] Only recently have consumer behavior researchers begun to investigate the ways in which the elderly's buying behavior differs from that of their younger counterparts.[54] These differences not only suggest separate marketing tactics for this age group but also introduce new areas of concern for policy makers.

The Disadvantaged Elderly   Several reasons emerge to suggest why one might consider elderly consumers to be at a disadvantage relative to the rest of the population. First, this segment in general has a lower level of education than younger consumers. Although this group's education level does not necessarily imply inability to make appropriate purchase decisions, one might conjecture that truth-in-lending information, nutritional labels, or unit-pricing may not be used to their fullest extent.[55]

Another area where the elderly may be at a disadvantage concerns information deficiency. As one grows older information exposure decreases rapidly because of retirement, death of a spouse, and children leaving home.[56] In addition, magazines, newspapers, buyers' guides, and television may be out of the reach of some older individuals who are on a fixed, and relatively limited, income.[57] When the elderly perceive a deficiency in the information available to them for product-related decisions, they also experience dissatisfaction with the product category and their shopping experience.[58]

Third, the body experiences physical decline as it ages.[59] Diminished eyesight, motor coordination, and hearing may limit the elderly's mobility and subsequently their access to many services and retail outlets. As a result, this age group may be forced to accept less-than-adequate services and to engage in limited comparison shopping.

Finally, the media is often guilty of portraying the elderly in a negative light.[60] One study found that older characters in advertising are often por-

Table 19–5 Strategies to Promote Conservation and Their Impact

Type	Impact
Information	
Mass advertising	Minimal success in encouraging conservation when used alone; More effective when used in conjunction with other promotional efforts such as direct mail.
Home audits	A potentially effective motivation to conserve in that home audits provide tailored information to the home-owner on how to conserve. However, information may still not stimulate action.
Consumer energy hotlines and energy workshops	Not very effective in changing energy consumption behavior.
Feedback programs	Have produced mixed results in that they make people more aware of how to conserve but do not lead to long-term changes in consumption behavior. Conservation efforts often last only for the duration of the feedback program.
Energy labeling of appliances	Produces little influence on the consumer's purchase decision; However, energy labeling may encourage manufacturers to produce more effective products.
Financial Incentives	
Cash	Reduces energy consumption in the short run, however care must be taken so that the value of the incentive is not greater than the value of the energy conserved.
Price and Taxation	
Increased price	Not very effective because the demand for energy is relatively inelastic. Additionally, consumers typically find out the cost of the energy they consumed *after* it has been consumed, when conservation measures are too late.
Peak-period pricing	Reduces demand while maintaining favorable consumer reaction.
Standards	
Building codes and minimum fuel efficiency	Effective because their impact appears equitable to all. Requires little or no change in consumer lifestyle, and the idea of energy-efficient products generally appeals to the public
Restrictions	
Limiting amount of energy consumed	Viewed negatively by most consumers; however, may be tolerated during "crisis" conditions.

Source: Based on J. R. Brent Ritchie and Gordon H. G. McDougall "Designing and Marketing Consumer Energy Conservation Policies and Programs: Implications from a Decade of Research," *Journal of Marketing and Public Policy,* 4, 1985, 14–32.

trayed as being foolish and eccentric in contrast to younger characters. As a result, both younger and older individuals form unfavorable impressions of the elderly.[61] In other words, "the susceptible elderly individual, faced with role loss and lack of reference groups depends on external labeling" and experiences a negative self-concept when exposed to the media.[62]

Policy Implications   One realization that policy makers and marketers alike must face is the heterogeneity of this age group.[63] Not only do distinctions occur according to age once one gets past sixty-five,[64] but segments also arise due to ability to adjust to retirement[65] and the individual's residence in a rural or urban area.[66] Table 19–6 provides an example of how the sixty-five-and-older age group may be segmented. One potential concern for policy makers might be the "succorance seekers" segment. This group might be more susceptible to medical fraud, for example, given that this segment is characterized by their health concerns and ability to be persuaded by others.

With regard to the urban versus rural segments, one study found that different means of providing information should be used. For example, the urban elderly prefer to gain consumer education and information through their local senior citizens centers. The rural elderly, on the other hand, have less access to such a facility but can be reached through radio and television programming and public service announcements.[67] Some authors have suggested that not only should marketers portray older consumers in a more favorable light in their advertisements, but policy makers should do likewise in PSAs that provide consumer education to this age group.[68]

Table 19–6   Some Segments Within the 65+ Age Group: Their Behaviors and Attitudes

Reorganizers
   Willing to adopt innovations
   Concerned about maintaining appearance
   Enjoy the physical pleasures of life
   Friends are an important factor
   Have a close relationship with their children
   Enjoy going out

Holding On
   Concerned about maintaining appearance

Succorance Seekers
   Easily persuaded by the opinions of others
   Would rather be served themselves than serve others
   Frequently think about their health

Constricted
   Especially cautious about spending money
   Frequently think about their health

Angry
   Especially cautious about spending money
   Would rather be served themselves than serve others
   Frequently think about their health
   Believe they aren't respected

Apathetic
   Would rather be served themselves than serve others
   Frequently think about their health
   Believe they aren't respected

SOURCE: Based on Warren A. French and Richard Fox, "Segmenting the Senior Citizen Market," *Journal of Consumer Marketing, 2,* 1985, 61–74.

NEGLIGENT CONSUMER BEHAVIOR

Most of us would agree with the statements "Seat belts save lives," "Smoking is hazardous to your health," and "Drinking and driving don't mix." Yet many consumers, in some manner or another, exhibit what might be termed negligent behavior. **Negligent behavior** is composed of those actions and inactions that negatively affect the long-term quality of life of individuals and/or society. This type of behavior can occur in two different contexts. The first form of negligent behavior occurs due to the consumption of a product which in and of itself presents a hazard of some sort. The consumption of cigarettes and certain drugs are two examples that fall in this catagory. A second type of negligent behavior occurs when the consumer uses a product in an unsafe manner or fails to use safety features and follow safety instructions. Failure to use seat belts and not following dosage instructions for over-the-counter drugs are examples of this form of negligent behavior.[69]

Two approaches exist to induce people to act in a safer manner. One involves legislation that creates laws forcing consumers to wear seat belts, bans the advertising and sale of cigarettes, and imposes stiffer penalities for drunk driving. An alternative approach involves the use of marketing techniques to encourage more appropriate consumer actions. Consumer behavior research and theory provide insight into how both marketers and public policy makers can influence consumers to behave in a safer manner.

Getting People to Buckle Up

Automobile accidents claim the lives of more than 30,000 individuals a year and result in 500,000 injuries. Seat belts could have prevented more than half of these deaths and injuries, yet only approximately 15 percent of American drivers and passengers wear their seat belts.[70] Beliefs that they would never be in an accident, that seat belts do not provide much benefit even if you do wear them, and that seat belts are uncomfortable are just a few excuses offered by consumers.

Early attempts to persuade consumers to wear their seat belts were dominated by a fear appeal approach depicting the grisly results of nonuse. A National Safety Council campaign in 1969 involving more than $50 million worth of public service media space and air time resulted in no change in the claimed use of seat belts. A subsequent strategy in Michigan used the more emotionally charged theme of "Somebody needs you." At a cost of some $2.1 million, the observed increase in seat belt usage was 4.4 percent, about 270,000 persons. In addition to the expense of such projects, the results have been found to be short lived. If the reminder to buckle up is not present, many individuals do not make the effort simply because it is not engrained in their routine or because they are not devoting their attention to the situation.

The theory of operant conditioning provides an additional perspective. As noted in Chapter 6, the positive reinforcement of a behavior increases the likelihood of that behavior being repeated. The application is clear. To increase the likelihood that people will wear seat belts, they need to be rewarded when they buckle up. Some studies have found that rewarding individuals when they are wearing their seat belts can more than double usage.[71] Rewards need not be elaborate—perhaps discount coupons or bingo chips—and they can easily be administered through any drive-through location. Highlight 19–2 gives an example of one way to reinforce seat belt use. However, one author has stated that "there seems to be no form of educational campaign or message that will persuade more than a small percentage of American motorists to voluntarily wear seat belts."[72] The author suggested that legislating seat belt usage would most likely be the only effective means of getting consumers to buckle up.

To Puff or Not to Puff

Until the late 1960s consumers were exposed to nearly 3,000 cigarette commercials per week representing thirty-eight different brands. Concern over the health hazards that cigarette smoking presents had gained attention in the 1950's. However, it was not until the issuance of the surgeon general's report in 1964 that public policy makers began to exert considerable efforts to alter the public's smoking behavior.

The Department of Health and Human Services (D.H.H.S.) spent more than $2 million in 1967 in an effort to inform consumers of the health hazards of smoking. D.H.H.S. used such tactics as bumper stickers that read "Smoke, Choke, Croak" and endorsements of athletic stars such as Peggy Flemming and Bart Starr claiming, "I don't smoke." In general, the approach was to

---

HIGHLIGHT 19–2

"Flash for Life"

Approximately half of all traffic fatalities and injuries could be prevented if the occupants would only wear their seat belts. Public safety campaigns that use emotional or fear appeal messages have met with limited success. E. Scott Geller, professor of psychology at Virginia Polytechnic Institute and State University, suggests a different approach to encouraging people to buckle up: flash cards. Drivers or passengers who themselves are buckled up display a flash card that reads "Please buckle up—I care" to occupants of other vehicles. After the other individuals have buckled up, the "flasher" then shows a card that says "Thank you for buckling up." Geller states that his method achieved a 22 percent compliance rate.

This strategy incorporates a number of psychological principles. For example, from social learning theory there is the modeling of the "flasher" wearing his or her seat belt. In addition, the flash-card holders themselves become more committed safety belt wearers through self-perception processes. Also, the request to buckle up is presented at a time when the driver can easily respond and is reinforced when displaying the desired behavior with the "thank you" card—a direct application of operant conditioning.

Based on E. Scott Geller, "Seat Belt Psychology," *Psychology Today*, May 1985, 12–13.

depict smokers as distraught coughers, whereas nonsmokers were portrayed as happy and healthy.[73] These promotional efforts possibly had a limited impact. Between 1967 and 1968 cigarette sales fell by 1.3 billion cigarettes, and the number of smokers dropped by 1.5 million to 70 million. However, rather than seeing a steady decline in cigarette sales or the number of smokers, the major behavioral trend has been toward the purchase of low-tar and low-nicotine brands.

Despite a ban on television commercials promoting the product, the cigarette industry continues to survive. Some researchers state that poor communications strategies by anti-smoking groups are in part to blame, but the root causes are the strong social reward for smoking in some circles, such as among teenagers, and certain "deeply held cognitive positions." In other words, many smokers simply tune out or develop counterarguments for antismoking messages.

One study has examined the impact a specific message and an altered format would have on attention and comprehension.[74] The authors tested various combinations of three different message formats and two warning statements (see Figure 19–2). The three format styles included the current rectangular box, an elongated retangular box which represented a mild change

Figure 19–2   **Format changes for a cigarette warning message. (Based on a discussion in Gaurav Bhalla and John L. Lastovicka, "The Impact of Changing Cigarette Warning Message Content and Format," in *Advances in Consumer Research, XI*, Thomas C. Kinnear (ed.), Provo, Utah: Association for Consumer Research, 1984, 305–310.)**

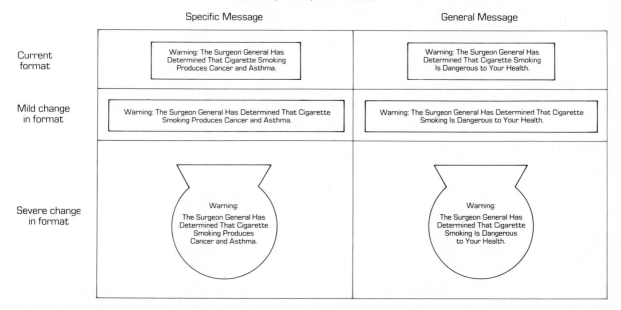

in format, and the severe change in format involving a circular shape. The message within the format was either the current warning, which relates the hazards of smoking in general terms, or a specific warning that details the health risks of smoking. The authors found that unless the *format* of the message (i.e. a format that differed sharply from the current rectangular shape) changed, the change in *content* of the warning message was ineffective. In other words, a strong pictorial variation was needed to attract attention to the message content.

Drinking and Driving	Each year nearly 25,000 people are killed and 900,000 are injured as a result of drunk driving.[75] The 1980s have seen increasing attention given to the issue of drinking and driving, in part because of the efforts of the national organization Mothers Against Drunk Driving (MADD). Public policy makers could make greater use of consumer behavior research concerning this area. Following are some of the methods currently used, along with their strengths and weaknesses.[76]

Informing and Educating   This approach assumes that individuals act rationally in an effort to further their self-interest. Thus, the public should be presented with objective information about the hazards of drunk driving. The major deficit of this method, however, centers around the way consumers perceive the world. The notion of selective attention suggests that the individual most likely to drink and drive will ignore or distort this type of information.

Social Controls   The majority of liquor advertisements portray the beverage as a drink consumed in the presence of others and as a means of heightening one's acceptability. The social controls strategy plays on the understanding that individuals are influenced by the actions and attitudes of those around them. The dominant theme employed in this tactic is to have social influences disapproving of drunk driving. Examples of this strategy include campus meetings of the SADD (Students Against Drunk Driving) organization or commercials showing family and friends disapproving of the undesired behavior.

Economic Incentives   Using concepts derived from behavior modification theory, the object is to reward individuals for demonstrating the desired behavior. Insurance companies currently use this approach by providing reduced rates to individuals who agree not to drink and drive. Some restaurants give a free meal to the person who agrees not to drink so he or she can drive his or her friends who are drinking home. The limitation of this approach is that individuals will not drink and drive only if they perceive the benefits as outweighing the costs.

Economic Disincentives   Rather than rewarding individuals for not drinking and driving, this strategy punishes individuals who do commit the offense. This punishment could occur directly through fines, car repair costs, and high insurance premiums or indirectly through an excise tax on alcohol resulting in higher liquor prices. However, consumers may continue to drink and drive if the benefits of this behavior outweigh the costs.

Product Misuse

Many of us would never think of using a blow dryer in the shower or a lawn mower to trim the hedges. Yet consumers' misuse of products in just such a fashion has prompted marketers and public policy makers alike to exert special precautions in the design and testing of products. In fact, the majority of product-related injuries result not from a flaw in the product itself but through misuse of an otherwise safe product.[77] As one individual put it, "The most dangerous component is the consumer, and there's no way to recall him."[78]

Given that even the most meticulously designed and packaged product is potentially hazardous through consumer misuse, what steps can marketers and public policy makers take to insure maximum safety for consumers? Two primary means exist for resolving this dilemma. The first approach involves setting government safety standards for almost every type of industry. If a company's products fail to meet such standards, then the products are subject to recall. However, it has been estimated that "no more than 20 percent of all consumer product related injuries can be addressed by feasible regulation of the production and distribution of consumer products."[79]

The other alternative lies in consumer education. The rationale behind a consumer education program is that "increased knowledge leads to safer behavior, since the consumer has a better understanding of how products work and is able to assess more accurately the hazards associated with these products."[80] One study examined the impact of a consumer education course on high school students' safety-related knowledge and resulting behavior. The author found that although the students were more aware of the hazards of certain products' misuse, that knowledge did not lead to proper use of the products. In other words, individuals do not always behave the way they know they should with respect to product safety.

Once again, the often-mysterious relationship of beliefs, attitudes, and behavior presents itself. Consumers apparently can know and understand the correct way to use a product and can believe that using the product in a safe manner is beneficial; yet when it comes to letting the knowledge, beliefs, and attitudes influence their behavior—consumers just do not make the leap. This occurrence presents a major area of future study for consumer researchers. Specifically, researchers could focus on which instances would benefit from marketing techniques to push individuals to act upon their knowledge and attitudes and which circumstances require legislation to ensure responsible, safe behavior.

CONTEMPORARY ISSUES IN CONSUMER BEHAVIOR

As noted in the first chapter of this text, consumer behavior concerns itself with the acquisition, consumption, and disposition of goods, services, experiences, and ideas by decision-making units. Although the realm of consumer behavior theory and research presented in this text offers insight to marketing managers and public policy makers, some authors have contended that the present scope of consumer behavior and consumerism is limited.[81] Specifically, the current consumer behavior paradigm concerns itself with *buying* behavior, rather than focusing on *having* behavior, and with how possessing goods and services relates to an individual's sense of well-being.[82]

Consumer Well-Being and the Good Life

Consumer well-being is defined as the extent to which an individual's wants are satisfied.[83] In this context "wants" encompasses not only material goods and satisfaction of physical needs but emotional and social factors as well. However, the government has typically assessed well-being by some form of poverty index. Traditionally, poverty has been defined as the cost of "a food plan judged to be necessary to sustain an adequate nutritional level."[84] This definition of poverty does not mesh well with the notion of consumer well-being previously described. Hauver and his associates state that "the development of a social concept of poverty is a major challenge for consumer research."[85]

In a similar vein, other authors have claimed that "it is time we began to address macro issues and ask how marketing affects consumption values, and thereby, consumer well-being."[86] The issue these authors specifically addressed was the relationship between advertising and American values associated with "the good life." In their study, these authors examined more than 400 advertisements from the top ten magazines spanning the 1900s to the 1970s. They found that the advertisements' themes became increasingly hedonistic. In other words, rather than focusing on the functional or practical aspects of the product, the advertising appeal stressed the luxury of owning the product for its own sake. As further evidence of this trend, the authors found that fewer extraneous models and/or props were used in the advertisement. Instead, the product alone was becoming the focal point.

Marketers often claim that their products, and to some extent their promotional themes, are directly influenced by consumer needs, wants, and values. Some authors have suggested, however, that marketing in general, and advertising in particular, may be viewed as responsible for America's changing values. Rather than responding to consumer's values, advertising may be the source of consumer values. However, some debate exists as to whether advertising actually influences societal values or merely reflects them. Because the decision of the advertising appeal to use in promoting particular products typically requires a value judgment, both marketers and public policy makers need to consider "What image does advertising present of the good, desirable, and worthwhile in life?"[87]

Corporate Social Responsibility

Prior to the 1960s most individuals generally accepted the idea that business's primary objective was to obtain economic profit. This thinking began to change, however, as America's social values changed. Today many companies exert much energy, time, and money to portray themselves as good corporate citizens who act in a socially responsible manner. **Corporate social responsibility** refers to the idea that business has an obligation to help society with its problems by offering some of business's resources.[88] In other words, apart from the traditional goal of making a profit, corporations should also be concerned with such needs as the environment, education, and consumer safety.[89]

Several arguments exist to support the notion that having a positive corporate social responsibility image is important for companies.

Succeeding in the Long Run   One argument for being socially responsible involves a long-term rather than short-term time perspective. A business's self-interest could be advanced if rather than focusing on short-run profits, which would discourage certain expenditures devoted to societal problems, the business instead embraced a long-run view. This position would allow for the necessary expenditures to engage in socially responsible activities, yet would provide future benefits in the form of consumer approval and loyalty.[90] For example, the Adolph Coors Company, which has a reputation of being anti-union, was struck by the Brewery Workers on April 5, 1977. One week later the AFL-CIO approved a boycott of the company's beer. The AFL-CIO later claimed that this action resulted in a 70 percent decline in first-quarter profits that year. Although increased competition could also account for the decline, the negative publicity undoubtedly harmed the image of the Coors brand.[91]

Another example of business focusing on short-term rather than long-term goals involves the hiring of minorities. In many instances companies can get by with paying substandard wages to minorities and thus cut costs in the short run. What companies fail to realize is that substandard wages result in less discretionary income for their minority employees, who might otherwise purchase their companies' products.[92]

Acquiring a Positive Public Image   Another argument centers on the positive public image the company will gain by acting socially responsible.[93] One example of a responsible behavior is product recalls. Some researchers have suggested that a product recall could be seen as an opportunity in that the situation allows the company to show its ability to act professionally in a consumer-oriented fashion.[94] A series of studies by the author of this text examined the impact product recalls could have on consumer impressions of a company. These studies found that consumers perceived a familiar company as significantly less responsible for a product defect than an unfamiliar company;[95] consumers viewed companies who reacted to product defects prior to intervention by the Consumer Product Safety Commission as less responsible for the defects;[96] and consumer impressions of the company were influenced by the speed with which they initiated a product recall.[97] Table 19–7 gives an overview of the implications of these findings. One well-known, recent case of a corporate response to a tragedy is discussed in Highlight 19–3.

Table 19–7 Overview of Product Recall Implications

- Companies should strive to maintain a highly visible, positive corporate image. Such a company is less subject to negative consumer response when a recall is initiated.
- Companies should establish a recall plan that can be quickly implemented should disaster strike. Consumers have a more favorable impression of companies who react quickly in a product-safety situation.
- When a problem is first discovered, it may be best to overstate the problem to the public. Consumers will subsequently develop more favorable impressions of the company when they hear that the problem is not as severe as first expected. If the company displays the reverse behavior—that is, minimizes the problem only to later discover that the difficulty is worse than first announced—the result can be negative consumer impressions.
- Companies should endeavor to manufacture the safest products possible. The safer the products, the less likelihood of severe injuries, negative consumer opinions, and product liability awards.
- Companies should not shy away from press coverage of product recalls. Information from independent sources such as the media, especially when the company is described as behaving in a socially responsible manner, can generate favorable consumer impressions.

SOURCE: Adapted from Joshua Wiener and John C. Mowen, "Product Recalls: Avoid Beheading the Messenger of Bad News," *Mobius*, 4, 1985, 18–21.

HIGHLIGHT 19–3

The Tylenol Tragedy: An Example of Corporate Social Responsibility

In early October 1982 seven persons in the Chicago area died as a result of cyanide-laced Extra-Strength Tylenol capsules. Within twenty-four hours Johnson and Johnson, the makers of Tylenol, initiated a nationwide recall of the 93,400 bottles of Lot MC2880, the first batch from which the poisoned capsules came. Subsequently, additional batches were recalled, bringing the total to 264,400 bottles. Johnson and Johnson also issued half a million mailgrams to physicians, hospitals, and wholesalers warning them of the danger. In addition, McNeil Consumer Products, the subsidiary of Johnson and Johnson that manufactures Tylenol, offered a $100,000 reward for information leading to a conviction in the case. The company also offered cash refunds or tablet exchanges for the 22 million bottles of capsule-form Tylenol.(a)

According to the recommendations given in Table 19–7, the makers of Tylenol conducted a "by-the-book" recall. But did such action actually minimize the adverse effects as the research suggested it would? In what was termed "a marketing miracle," Tylenol had regained most of its number-one market share by the end of December—just three short months after the tragedy occurred.(b) Much of this success is attributed to Johnson and Johnson's "courageous" marketing efforts (millions of coupons for a free bottle of Tylenol were distributed) and the company's direct-action approach. In addition, many industry analysts credited Johnson and Johnson's reputation of concern for public health and well-being for tiding the company over during the first critical days and encouraging loyal customers to return to the product.

Unfortunately, the Tylenol tragedy was replayed in early 1986 when another poisoning occurred. Again, Johnson and Johnson acted responsibly by recalling the product. However, in this case the company went further and permanently withdrew Tylenol Capsules from the market.

Based on (a) "The Tylenol Scare," *Newsweek*, October 11, 1982, 32–36; and (b) Michael Waldholz, "Tylenol Regains Most of No. 1 Market Share, Amazing Doomsayers," *The Wall Street Journal*, December 24, 1982, 1, 6.

Avoiding Government Regulation   A final reason that may be offered for corporate social responsibility is that this behavior may be one means of avoiding government regulation.[98] Given the values society holds today, if business does not respond to societal demands on its own, consumer groups may exert pressure on government to intervene.

All business functions concern themselves to some degree with social responsibility. However, the burden falls mostly to the marketer. Indeed, when a company is perceived as acting unethically or in an irresponsible fashion, marketing is the function most likely to be blamed.[99] Marketers can best avoid this label by following the strategies suggested previously—namely, by maintaining a positive initial corporate image and by responding quickly when difficulties arise. In addition, companies can stress the benefits of their products. For example, in Figure 19–3 an advertisement for Dow Chemical is presented. In the ad the company shows a student graduating from college who is anxious to start work for a company that attempts to find ways to improve the food supply for starving kids. The ad nicely positions Dow as being concerned with social responsibility.

Managerial Implications

The main thrust of the material presented in this chapter has focused on the application of consumer behavior theory and research to public policy. However, the direction that public policy takes also impacts the marketing manager. The discussion of corporate social responsibility suggested a number of considerations for the marketing manager who is faced with a product recall. This section provides additional managerial implications related to some of the topics covered in this chapter.

Children's Advertising

"The criticism of children's advertising can be interpreted as a sign that marketers are failing to satisfy parents' needs."[100] Now that the FTC has withdrawn its proposal of banning advertising aimed at young children, marketers must respond to perhaps an even greater critic and judge of their tactics— the parent. In most cases, the parent is the one responsible for purchasing the advertised product for the child or advising the child on how to spend an allowance. Several studies have examined the amount of parent-child conflict that results when the child does not get an advertised product and the parental attitude toward advertising. The results of these studies suggest that it is well worth marketers' efforts to appeal to the adult as much as, if not more than, they appeal to the child. Table 19–8 provides some suggestions as to how this strategy could be accomplished.

Energy Conservation

Table 19–5 noted that the imposition of standards would be one of the most promising methods of encouraging energy conservation. This approach is effective because the impact of the standard appears equitable for the entire public. In addition, products that are made to meet government standards

Figure 19–3   Dow emphasizes its commitment to social responsibility in this ad. (*Courtesy of Dow Chemical U.S.A.*)

do not require a personal change in lifestyle for the consumer. Also, most individuals agree that energy conservation is a good idea. For the farsighted marketing manager, self-imposition of energy efficiency standards on products may bolster public opinion of the company. In other words, the company may be better off to introduce conservation measures before the government mandates them. As a result, the public may perceive the company as socially responsible if it acts without external pressure from the government.

On a related note, if the public blames a company or industry for a serious energy situation, the public is more likely to desire government interven-

Table 19–8   Suggestions for Making Children's Advertising More Acceptable to Parents

- Increase media expenditures to parental audiences.
- Provide financial support for nutrition education programs in the schools.
- Use nutrition and health themes in promotional contests and premium offers.
- Avoid ambiguities in children's advertising that are likely to be challenged by nutritionally oriented parents.
- Use nutrition content as one criterion for allocating marketing resources (e.g., modify product line to provide a nutritional balance of alternatives).
- Make direct appeals to children to be more nutrition-conscious and responsible consumers.
- Develop advertising messages that provide indications of respect for parental authority.
- Maintain continual monitoring of parental views toward company advertising aimed at children.
- Obtain more parental input in the development of advertising campaigns.

SOURCE: Based on Sanford L. Grossbart and Lawrence A. Crosby, "Understanding the Bases of Parental Concern and Reaction to Children's Food Advertising," *Journal of Marketing, 48*, Summer 1984, 79–92.

tion.[101] To prevent government actions, therefore, business will want to shift blame away from itself. This strategy might be accomplished via corporate advertising by informing the public of the aggregate effects of energy consumption. Additionally, business will want to stress the collective impact of individual conservation efforts and the personal benefit to the consumer.

A final means by which companies can encourage their customers to conserve is through distribution of incentives. As previously mentioned, one of the criticisms of using incentives is that the consumer would need to be continually reinforced if he or she is to continue conservation behavior. However, as the example of the shower-control device demonstrated, incentives that are cost efficient may stimulate consumers to at least consider certain types of energy-saving behavior. One example might include a magnet that encourages the use of cold water for washing machines and dishwashers. This "premium" could be distributed either free at the point of purchase or included in the detergent box.

Enhancing Consumer Well-Being

The traditional conception of poverty focuses on the bare minimum necessary to sustain physical existence. Many companies currently cater to low-income families by providing generic or house brands, which are less expensive. In addition, many supermarkets accept food stamps. However, a reasonable existence is also determined by the social and emotional experiences one encounters.

Besides producing low-cost products, companies could also attempt to meet these psychological needs. For example, theaters could offer films at a minimal price for low-income families, perhaps a few months after they have been released to the general public. Museums, zoos, and concerts could also offer special admission prices. Another approach would be for an outside company to sponsor a cultural event. Not only would such actions meet the needs of poverty-level individuals, but the company would gain in its reputation as a socially responsible corporate citizen. One should note that many companies already engage in some of the actions previously described.

SUMMARY

Consumer behavior research and theory provide insight into areas outside the marketing realm. This chapter demonstrated the role such research and theory play in the development of public policy. The consumer movement that evolved during this century prompted the creation of a number of regulations and agencies whose primary purpose is to protect consumer rights. The Federal Trade Commission, the Consumer Product Safety Commission, the Food and Drug Administration, and National Highway Traffic Safety Administration are just a few examples of such agencies.

This movement also drew attention to a number of marketing tactics, which developed into major public policy issues. During the early 1970s consumers expressed concern over the misleading nature of some advertising. As a result, some companies have been forced to provide corrective advertising in which they state that a previous claim was errant. In addition, the FTC may require substantiation for the claims made in some advertisements.

Another major issue to surface was advertising aimed at young children. Specifically, policy makers have been concerned that young children cannot tell the difference between programming and commercials, that they do not understand the selling intent of commercials, and that advertising makes children want products that may not be good for them or that their parents do not want them to have. Current research suggests that the manufacturers of products consumed by children should target their advertising as much toward the parent as toward the child.

Environmental protection was another issue to emerge during the 1970s, especially when consumers felt the impact of the energy crisis during the mid-1970s. Some studies suggest that consumers would be more likely to engage in conservation behavior if they were persuaded that they would personally benefit. This chapter also provided an overview of various forms of motivations to conserve and their potential effectiveness.

Two relatively new areas in which consumer behavior research is applied to public policy involve issues related to the elderly and negligent consumer behavior. The elderly differ from younger adults in a number of consumption-related areas. These differences suggest that separate strategies are needed in order to help this age group in their decision-making in the market place. Negligent consumer behavior refers to those actions and inactions that negatively affect the long-term quality of life of individuals and/or society. Failure to wear seat belts, smoking, drunk driving, and product misuse are a few examples of negligent behavior.

The chapter also discussed several contemporary issues in consumer behavior. The notions of consumer well-being and the role advertising plays in fostering American values were addressed. Corporate social responsibility, which involves business's obligation to help with society's problems by offering some of its resources, was also included as a contemporary issue. Benefits of acting socially responsible include succeeding in the long run, acquiring a positive public image, and avoiding government regulation. The issue of product recalls was also discussed, along with recommendations of how companies should conduct recalls in order to maintain favorable consumer impressions.

The chapter concluded with an overview of managerial implications that arose from the topics presented. Attention was given to the impact public policy and societal attitudes could have on advertising aimed at children, energy conservation, and enhancing consumer well-being.

Key Terms

Consumerism

Federal Trade Commission (FTC)

Food and Drug Administration (FDA)

National Highway Traffic Safety Administration (NHTSA)

Consumer Product Safety Commission (CPSC)

Deceptive advertising

Corrective advertising

Advertising substantiation

Host selling

Conservation behavior

Negligent consumer behavior

Consumer well-being

Corporate social responsibility

Review Questions

1. Identify the four phases of the consumer movement presented in the text.
2. What is the current status of the consumer movement?
3. In 1982 what were the three most important consumer concerns? What do you think are the three primary consumer concerns today?
4. What are the consumer regulation roles of the FTC, the FDA, and the NHTSA?
5. What are the categories of deceptive advertising that the FTC has considered in the past?
6. To what extent can children tell the difference between commercials and programming?
7. To what extent do commercials tend to make children desire products that are not necessarily good for them?

8. What are the three basic types of conservation behaviors?
9. Why are many elderly consumers disadvantaged?
10. What is the definition of negligent consumer behavior?
11. Identify four examples of consumer negligent behavior.
12. What are the primary methods now being used to attack the problem of drunk driving?
13. What is meant by the idea of corporate social responsibility? Give four examples of how business can act in a socially responsible manner.
14. Identify the reasons for and against businesses actively attempting to portray themselves as socially responsible.
15. According to the text, what are the factors that influence consumer reactions to companies that make product recalls?
16. What are three ways that companies might be able to make children's advertising more acceptable to parents?

Discussion Questions

1. Go through the consumerism issues identified in Table 19–1. To what extent do these issues concern you personally? Do you believe that corporate treatment of consumers has improved or gotten worse over the past five years?
2. Some have argued that the modern consumer's movement ended with the beginning of the Rea-

gan presidency in 1980. To what extent do you agree or disagree with this statement?

3. In 1986 the Federal Trade Commission began to consider whether or not it should take some action to force the large car rental corporations (such as Hertz and Avis) to comply more quickly with manufacturer requests to recall automobiles to fix mechanical problems. In your view, to what extent should government agencies intervene to force such companies (or for that matter individuals) to comply with manufacturer requests to bring cars in when product recalls occur? What kinds of actions could or should a government agency take?

4. From an attributional perspective what may have been the effect of Listerine's corrective ad, which read, "While Listerine will not help prevent colds or sore throats or lessen their severity, breath tests prove Listerine fights onion breath better than Scope." (Note: attribution theory was discussed in Chapter 3 on Motivation.)

5. Political commercials have been called the most deceptive in advertising. Discuss the types of deception that may occur in political advertisements. Try to give specific examples of each type of deception you have seen or heard.

6. Watch Saturday morning cartoons and observe the advertising directed toward children. What are the types of advertising appeals that are being used? To what extent are cartoon characters being used in the advertising? What are your views on what guidelines should be given to companies that advertise to children?

7. During the mid-1980s the emphasis on conservation of resources waned from levels found in the 1970s. What are some of the reasons for these changes? What types of programs do you feel are most effective in promoting the conservation of various natural resources?

8. A variety of approaches exist to controlling consumer negligent behavior. Within the context of controlling drunk driving, discuss the alternative means through which public policy makers can attempt to reduce this consumer problem behavior. Which approaches do you consider to be the most effective?

9. Authors have argued that society in the United States has become increasingly materialistic. What would be your definition of materialism? Write down the themes of five television commercials. To what extent do these themes emphasize owning the product because of its practical benefits versus its materialistic benefits?

10. Two different viewpoints exist concerning the social responsibility of corporations. One states that the only responsibility of a company is to make a profit for its stockholders. The other viewpoint states that businesses have a responsibility to help improve society. Defend your viewpoint on this issue.

References

1. Louis Harris et al., *Consumerism in The Eighties*, Study No. 822047: Louis Harris and Associates, Inc., 1983, 12. Referenced in D. S. Smith and P. N. Bloom, "Is Consumerism Dead or Alive? Some New Evidence," *Advances in Consumer Research*, XI, T. C. Kinnear, (ed.), Ann Arbor, Mich.: Association for Consumer Research, 1984, 369–373.

2. Darlene Brannigan Smith and Paul N. Bloom, "Is Consumerism Dead or Alive? Some New Evidence," *Advances in Consumer Research*, XI. Thomas C. Kinnear (ed.), Ann Arbor, Mich.: Association for Consumer Research, 1984, 369–373.

3. David A. Aaker and George S. Day, *Consumerism: Search for the Consumer Interest*, New York, N.Y.: The Free Press, 1974.

4. Rogene A. Buchholz, *Business Environment and Public Policy*, Englewood Cliffs, N.J.: Prentice-Hall, Inc., 1982.

5. Joe L. Welch, *Marketing Law*, Tulsa, Okla.: Petroleum Publishing Co., 1980.

6. *The New York Times*, January 21, 1983, A-16.

7. "U.S. Environmental Agency Making Deep Staffing Cuts," *The New York Times*, January 3, 1982, 20.

8. William L. Wilkie, Dennis L. McNeill, and Michael B. Mazis, "Marketing's 'Scarlet Letter': The Theory and Practice of Corrective Advertising," *Journal of Marketing*, 48, Spring, 1984, 11–31.

9. Welch, *Marketing Law*.

10. Buchholz, *Business Environment*.

11. Ibid.

12. Walter Guzzardi, "The Mindless Pursuit of Safety," *Fortune*, April 9, 1979, 54–64.

13. Buchholz, *Business Environment*.

14. Rachel Dardis, "Economic Analysis of Current Is-

sues in Consumer Product Safety: Fabric Flammability," *Journal of Consumer Affairs*, *14*, Summer 1980, 109–123.

15. Welch, *Marketing Law.*

16. Buchholz, *Business Environment.*

17. Edward J. Metzen, "Consumerism in the Evolving Future," in *Consumerism and Beyond*, Paul N. Bloom (ed.), Cambridge, Mass.: Marketing Science Institute, 1982, 16–20.

18. Kenneth L. Bernhardt and Ronald Stiff, "Public Policy Update: Perspectives on the Federal Trade Commission," *Advances in Consumer Research, Vol. VIII*, Kent B. Monroe (ed.), Ann Arbor, Mich.: Association for Consumer Research, 1981, 452–454.

19. Smith and Bloom, "Is Consumerism Dead?."

20. Lee D. Dahringer and Denise R. Johnson, "The Federal Trade Commission Redefinition of Deception and Public Policy Implications: Let The Buyer Beware," *Journal of Consumer Affairs*, *18*, 1984, 326–342.

21. "Legal Developments in Marketing," *Journal of Marketing*, *49*, Winter 1985, 155.

22. Wilkie et al., "Marketing's 'Scarlet Letter'."

23. Gary Armstrong, Metin N. Gurol, and Frederick A. Russ, "A Longitudinal Evaluation of the Listerine Corrective Advertising Campaign," *Journal of Public Policy and Marketing*, *2*, 1983, 16–28.

24. Wilkie et al., "Marketing's 'Scarlet Letter'."

25. See Gary M. Armstrong, Metin N. Gurol, and Frederick A. Russ, "Detecting and Correcting Deceptive Advertising," *Journal of Consumer Research*, *6*, December 1979, 237–246; and Richard W. Mizerski, Neil K. Allison, and Stephen Calvert, "A Controlled Field Study of Corrective Advertising Using Multiple Exposures and a Commercial Medium," *Journal of Marketing Research*, *17*, August 1979, 341–348.

26. Armstrong et al., "A Longitudinal Evaluation."

27. John S. Healey and Harold H. Kassarjian, "Advertising Substantiation and Advertiser Response: A Content Analysis of Magazine Advertisements," *Journal of Marketing*, *47*, Winter 1983, 107–117.

28. Dorothy Cohen, "The FTC's Advertising Substantiation Program," *Journal of Marketing*, *44*, Winter 1980, 26–35.

29. "Legal Developments in Marketing," *Journal of Marketing*, *49*, Spring 1985, 149.

30. Terence A. Shimp and Ivan I. Preston, "Deceptive and Nondeceptive Consequences of Evaluative Advertising," *Journal of Marketing*, *45*, Winter 1981, 22–32.

31. Shimp and Preston, "Deceptive and Nondeceptive Consequences."

32. Howard G. Schutz and Marianne Casey, "Consumer Perceptions of Advertising as Misleading," *Journal of Consumer Affairs*, *15*, Winter 1981, 340–357.

33. *FTC Staff Report on Television Advertising to Children*, Washington, D.C.: Government Printing Office, 1978.

34. Scott Ward, "Consumer Socialization," *Journal of Consumer Research*, *1*, September 1974, 1–13.

35. Joan Blatt, Lyle Spencer, and Scott Ward, "A Cognitive-Developmental Study of Children's Reaction to Television Advertising," in *Television and Social Behavior*, Vol. 4, E. A. Rubinstein, G. A. Comstock, and J. P. Murray (eds.), Washington, D.C.: Government Printing Office, 1972, 452–467.

36. Laurene Krasny Meringoff and Gerald S. Lesser, "Children's Ability to Distinguish Television Commercials from Program Material," in *The Effect of Television Advertising on Children*, R. P. Adler (ed.) Lexington, Mass.: Lexington Books, 29–42.

37. Eliot G. Butter, P. Popovich, R. H. Stackhouse and R. Gardner "Discrimination of Television Commercials by Preschool Children," *Journal of Advertising Research*, *21*, April, 1981, 53–56.

38. Meringoff and Lesser, "Children's Ability to Distinguish."

39. Joseph R. Miller, and Paul Busch, "Host-Selling vs. Premium TV Commercials: An Experimental Evaluation of Their Influence on Children," *Journal of Marketing Research*, *16*, August 1979, 323–332.

40. Mariea Grubbs Hoy, Clifford Young, and John C. Mowen, "Animated Host-Selling Advertisements: Their Impact on Young Children's Recognition, Attitudes, and Behavior," *Journal of Public Policy and Marketing*, forthcoming.

41. Blatt, Spencer, and Ward, "A Cognitive-Developmental Study," and Butter et al., "Discrimination of Television Comercials."

42. Thomas S. Robertson and John R. Rossiter, "Children and Commercial Persuasion: An Attribution Theory Analysis," *Journal of Consumer Research*, *1*, June 1974, 12–20.

43. Debra L. Scammon and Carole L. Christopher,

"Nutrition Education with Children via Television: A Review," *Journal of Advertising, 10,* 1981, 26–36.

44. Gerald J. Gorn and Marvin E. Goldberg, "Behavioral Evidence of the Effects of Televised Food Messages on Children," *Journal of Consumer Research, 9,* September 1982, 200–205.

45. Gorn and Goldberg, "Behavioral Evidence."

46. Theo M. M. Verhallen and W. Fred van Raaij, "Household Behavior and the Use of Natural Gas for Home Heating," *Journal of Consumer Research, 8,* December 1981, 253–257.

47. Russell Belk, John Painter, and Richard Semenik, "Preferred Solutions to the Energy Crisis as a Function of Causal Attributions," *Journal of Consumer Research, 8,* December 1981, 306–312.

48. J. R. Brent Ritchie and Gordon H. G. McDougall, "Designing and Marketing Consumer Energy Conservation Policies and Programs: Implications from a Decade of Research," *Journal of Public Policy and Marketing, 4,* 1985, 14–32.

49. R. Bruce Hutton and Dennis L. McNeill, "The Value of Incentives in Stimulating Energy Conservation," *Journal of Consumer Research, 8,* December 1981, 291–298.

50. Michael L. Rothschild, "Providing Reinforcers for Environmentally Unconcerned Consumers," *Advances in Consumer Research, Vol. VIII,* Kent B. Monroe (ed.), Ann Arbor, Mich.: Association for Consumer Research, 1981, 642–643.

51. Phillip E. Downs and Jon B. Freiden, "Investigating Potential Market Segments for Energy Conservation Strategies," *Journal of Public Policy and Marketing, 2,* 1983, 136–152.

52. Donald W. Hendon, "Prime-Time Television, Sleeping Habits, and Energy Conservation," *Journal of Public Policy and Marketing, 1,* 1982, 157–168.

53. "Marketing: The New Priority," *Business Week,* November 21, 1983, 96–106.

54. Ganesan Visvabharathy and David R. Rink, "The Elderly: Neglected Business Opportunities," *Journal of Consumer Marketing, 1,* (4), 1984, 35–46.

55. Ganesan Visvabharathy, "Product Specificity in Public Policy Toward the Elderly," *Advances in Consumer Research, Vol. IX,* Andrew Mitchell (ed.), Ann Arbor, Mich.: Association for Consumer Research, 1982, 23–26.

56. Lynn W. Phillips and Brian Sternthal, "Age Differences in Information Processing: A Perspective on the Aged Consumer," *Journal of Marketing Research, 14,* November 1977, 444–457.

57. Visvabharathy, "Product Specificity."

58. Rohit Deshpande and S. Krishnan, "Correlates of Deficient Consumer Information Environments: The Case of the Elderly," *Advances in Consumer Research, Vol. IX,* Andrew Mitchell (ed.) Ann Arbor, Mich.: Association for Consumer Research, 1982, 515–519.

59. Jack Botwinick, *Aging and Behavior,* New York, N.Y.: Springer Publishing Company, 1973.

60. Ruth B. Smith, George P. Moschis, and Roy L. Moore, "Effects of Advertising on the Elderly Consumer," in *1984 Educators' Proceedings,* Russell W. Belk, Robert Peterson, Gerald S. Albaum, Morris B. Holbrook, Roger A. Kerin, Naresh K. Malhotra, and Peter Wright (eds.), Chicago, Ill.: American Marketing Association, 1984, 1–5.

61. G. Gerbner, N. Signarielli, and M. Morgan, "Aging with Television: Images on Television Drama and Conceptions of Social Reality," *Journal of Communication, 30,* 1980, 37–47.

62. Smith et al., "Effects of Advertising."

63. Visvabharathy, "Product Specificity."

64. Botwinick, *Aging and Behavior.*

65. Warren A. French and Richard Fox, "Segmenting the Senior Citizen Market," *Journal of Consumer Marketing, 2,* Winter 1985, 61–74.

66. John R. Burton and Charles B. Hennon, "Consumer Concerns of Senior Citizen Center Participants," *Journal of Consumer Affairs, 14,* Winter 1980, 366–382.

67. Burton and Hennon, "Consumer Concerns."

68. Smith et al., "Effects of Advertising."

69. Thomas C. Kinnear and Cynthia J. Frey, "Demarketing of Potentially Hazardous Products: General Framework and Case Studies," *Journal of Contemporary Business, 7,* 1978, 57–68.

70. E. Scott Geller, "Seat Belt Psychology," *Psychology Today,* May 1985, 12–13.

71. Geller, "Seat Belt Psychology."

72. Paul Slovic, "Only New Laws Will Spur Seat Belt Use," *The Wall Street Journal,* January 30, 1985, 26.

73. Kinnear and Frey, "Demarketing of Potentially Hazardous Products."

74. Gaurav Bhalla and John L. Lastovicka, "The Impact of Changing Cigarette Warning Message Content

and Format," *Advances in Consumer Research, Vol. XI*, Thomas C. Kinnear (ed.), Provo, Utah: Association for Consumer Research, 1984, 305–310.

75. *National Accident Sampling System*, Washington, D.C.: Government Printing Office, (1982) 14.

76. Laurel Hudson and Paul N. Bloom, "Potential Consumer Research Contributions to Combating Drinking and Driving Problems," *Advances in Consumer Research, Vol. XI*, Thomas C. Kinnear (ed.), Provo, Utah: Association for Consumer Research, 1984, 676–681.

77. Richard Staelin, "The Effects of Consumer Education on Consumer Product Safety Behavior," *Journal of Consumer Research*, 5, June 1978, 30–40.

78. Guzzardi, "The Mindless Pursuit."

79. Staelin, "The Effects of Consumer Education."

80. Ibid.

81. Theodore Suranyi-Unger, Jr., "Consumer Behavior and Consumer Well-Being: An Economist's Digest," *Journal of Consumer Research*, 8, September 1981, 119–131.; Russell Belk, "Acquiring, Possessing, and Collecting: Fundamental Processes in Consumer Behavior," in *Marketing Theory: Philosophy of Science Perspectives*, Chicago, Ill.: American Marketing Association, 1982; Russell Belk and Richard W. Pollay, "Images of Ourselves: The Good Life in Twentieth Century Advertising," *Journal of Consumer Research*, 11, March 1985, 887–897.

82. Belk, "Acquiring, Possessing, and Collecting."

83. Suranyi-Unger, "Consumer Behavior."

84. James H. Hauver, John A. Goodman, and Marc A. Grainer, "The Federal Poverty Thresholds: Appearance and Reality," *Journal of Consumer Research*, 8, June 1981, 1–10.

85. Hauver et al., "The Federal Poverty Thresholds."

86. Belk and Pollay, "Images of Ourselves."

87. Ibid.

88. Buchholz, *Business Environment*.

89. Kenneth E. Miller and Frederick D. Sturdivant, "Consumer Responses to Socially Questionable Corporate Behavior: An Empirical Test," *Journal of Consumer Research*, 4, June 1977, 1–7.

90. Buchholz, *Business Environment*.

91. "Coors Undercuts Its Last Big Union," *Business Week*, July 24, 1978, 47–48.

92. Elizabeth C. Hirschman, "Marketing, Minorities, and Consumption: Traditional and Neo-Marxist Perspectives," *Journal of Public Policy and Marketing*, 4, 1985, 179–193.

93. Buchholz, *Business Environment*.

94. G. Fisk and R. Chandran, "How to Trace and Recall Products," *Harvard Business Review*, November–December 1975, 90–96.

95. John C. Mowen, "Further Information on Consumer Perceptions of Product Recalls," *Advances in Consumer Research, Vol. VII*, Jerry Olson (ed.), Ann Arbor, Mich.: Association for Consumer Research, 1980, 519–523.

96. Mowen, "Further Information."

97. John C. Mowen, David Jolly, and G. S. Nickell, "Factors Influencing Consumer Responses to Product Recalls: A Regression Analysis Approach," *Advances in Consumer Research, Vol. VIII*, Kent Monroe (ed.), Ann Arbor, Mich.: Association for Consumer Research, 1981, 405–407.

98. Buchholz, *Business Environment*.

99. Patrick Murphy and Gene Laczniak, "Marketing Ethics: a Review with Implications for Managers, Educators, and Researchers," in *Review of Marketing, 1981*, Ben M. Enis and Kenneth J. Roering (eds.), Chicago, Ill.: American Marketing Association, 1981, 251–266.

100. Sanford L. Grossbart and Lawrence A. Crosby, "Understanding the Bases of Parental Concern and Reaction to Children's Food Advertising," *Journal of Marketing*, 48, Summer 1984, 79–92.

101. Belk et al., "Preferred Solutions."

20

Consumer Behavior and the Marketing Manager

The Consumer Is the Focus of Successful Marketing Managers

In 1982 the book *In Search of Excellence* was published. Rapidly achieving best-seller status, it concerned the question of why some corporations succeed while others flounder. After doing numerous interviews with executives in successful and unsuccessful companies, the authors identified eight practices that they felt characterized outstanding, innovative companies:

1. A bias for action.
2. Close to the *consumer*.
3. Autonomy and entrepreneurship.
4. Productivity through people.
5. Hands-on management.
6. Stay with known businesses.
7. Simple form, lean staff.
8. Firm central direction, maximum individual autonomy.

Here is the question. Where is *marketing* in the list? Is anything mentioned about the marketing mix of product, price, promotion, and distribution? The answer is *NO!*

What is mentioned is the *consumer*. This focus on the consumer results in a number of corporate obsessions, according to the authors. Some of these obsessions are:

1. Providing outstanding service.
2. Giving the highest-quality products.
3. Locating favorable "niches" where the company serves specialized markets better than others.
4. Listening to users.

Having an understanding of consumer behavior principles is not simply a "nice to have" set of knowledge. Rather, it is fundamental to the survival of companies in a competitive economic environment. The purpose of the last chapter is to review how the consumer behavior concepts identified in the book can be utilized by marketing managers in their decision-making areas of environmental analysis, product positioning, segmentation, and marketing-mix development.

Based in part on Thomas Peters and Robert Waterman, *In Search of Excellence*, New York, N.Y.: Harper & Row, Publishers, 1982.

INTRODUCTION

As the introductory vignette to the chapter shows, the consumer should be the focus of a firm's marketing efforts. The importance of a consumer focus in developing marketing strategy has been emphasized by marketing scholars. For example, in a recent article the authors discussed the problem of how companies should go about developing strategies to obtain a competitive advantage. They stated that "In order to be successful, the strategy—whether driven by cost, technology, distribution, service or other competitive advantages of the firm—has to be *consistent with consumer needs, perceptions, and preferences.*"[1] Of course, it is through the study of consumer behavior that a manager can obtain information on consumer needs, perceptions, and preferences.

An excellent example of a company that listens to users is Thermos, the maker of outdoor coolers. In 1983 marketing research told the company that they were having trouble with retailers accepting their products. Realizing that the retailers who sell their products are customers, just like the consumers who finally use them, Thermos set out to correct the two problems that had been identified. The first problem was that the Thermos products were bulky and could not be stacked on shelves. The second was that product information was placed only on one side of the product, which caused further problems in displaying the product on shelves.

The solution was elegant and simple. Thermos began placing their coolers in boxes, and product information was placed on all four sides of the box. The result was a product that could easily be stacked and that gave greater flexibility in displaying it.

The consumer research done by Thermos also revealed another problem. In its dome-top coolers frost would accumulate on the tray of the cooler. When taken out of the cooler and placed on the ground, the tray would then pick up dirt. The cooler was redesigned so that the tray fit into the top of the cooler, rather than the bottom, eliminating the frost problem completely.[2]

Chapters 1–18 of the text focus on providing the reader with information on the personal, situational, and environmental factors that influence consumers in the marketplace. Chapter 19 applies these findings to the area of public policy. The present chapter concludes the textbook with a review of how consumer behavior principles can be used by marketing managers to increase their effectiveness. Of course, applications of consumer behavior knowledge to marketing management have been provided throughout the text. However, a final summary is useful in order to delineate how the various areas of consumer behavior apply to managerial decision making.

Consumer behavior principles and ideas can be used to assist managerial decision making in four different areas:

1. Environmental analysis.
2. Product positioning.
3. Segmentation.
4. Marketing-mix development.

This chapter briefly reviews the characteristics of each of these important managerial decision areas and indicates how consumer behavior contributes to their implementation by the manager. In addition, the chapter addresses two other managerial issues. One issue concerns whether the same consumer behavior principles can be applied to industrial buying behavior as to consumer buying behavior. A second related issue concerns whether the same consumer behavior principles apply to the marketing of services as to the marketing of products.

CONSUMER BEHAVIOR AND ENVIRONMENTAL ANALYSIS

As defined by Kotler, "The **marketing environment** is that totality of forces and institutions that are external and potentially relevant to the firm."[3] This external environment can pose either threats or opportunities to the firm. Kotler identified a number of different environments that a firm should monitor. These include the demographic, economic, natural, technological, political, and cultural environments. Table 20–1 lists the environments and the consumer behavior areas that are applicable to their understanding and forecast.

Of course, a number of these environments quite obviously relate to consumer behavior. For example, entire chapters were devoted to the relation between economics and consumer behavior and between culture and consumer behavior. Similarly, the close relationship between demographics and subcultures was described in two separate chapters. The goal of the consumer researcher should be to attempt to predict future changes in these environments and how these changes will influence consumers. For example, the publisher of this textbook, Macmillan Publishing Company, has the important problem of predicting changes in the number of consumers who are likely to read its various types of books. An analysis of population trends suggests that beginning in the mid-1980s an area of emphasis should be elementary school textbooks. Between 1984 and 1990 the number of elementary

Table 20–1   Marketing Environments and Their Consumer Behavior Connections

Environment	Consumer Behavior Connection
Demographic	Study of population changes and subcultural values of various demographic groups based on such factors as age, sex, income, education, ethnicity, and geography.
Economic	Study factors influencing consumer economic sentiment and patterns of savings and spending.
Natural	Study of how consumers react to changing weather patterns and to natural disasters, such as earthquakes.
Technological	Study of the diffusion of and consumers' reactions to technological innovations. Study of the user-friendly characteristics of machines and computers.
Political	Study of the impact of laws, rules, and regulations on consumers.
Cultural	Study of rituals, values, and norms of a culture and how they influence consumption behavior.

school children will increase by over 12 percent as the baby-boom generation's children reach school age.[4] (Figure 20–1 portrays the changing number of students in elementary school.) In addition, a possible cultural change is taking place in the United States regarding the role of education. An educational reform movement appears to be under way in which more money is being spent on our schools in an effort to increase the educational competency of the population. The cultural and demographic changes portend a marketing opportunity for a company that can position itself properly with the appropriate textbooks.

This text has focused on how the economic, cultural, and demographic environments can lead to marketing opportunities or liabilities, with less attention being paid to how the natural and technological environments are related to consumer behavior. These are discussed briefly in the following subsections.

The Natural Environment and Consumer Behavior

A number of different features of the natural environment have been identified as important to the marketer. These include potential shortages in various types of raw materials, increased levels of pollution, the fear of contracting deadly diseases, the expansion of desert regions around the globe, the effects of acid rain, and the variations in weather patterns. Each of these changes can influence consumption behavior.

Shortages of raw materials, such as oil, can dramatically influence prices of products and cause consumers to change their buying patterns. Pollution

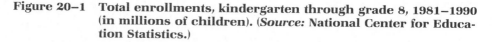

Figure 20–1 **Total enrollments, kindergarten through grade 8, 1981–1990 (in millions of children).** (*Source:* **National Center for Education Statistics.**)

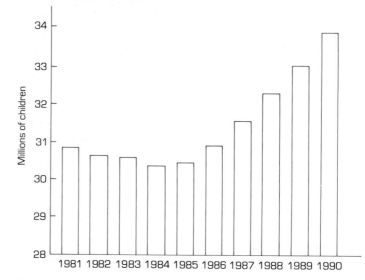

can wipe out or degrade important waterways and ruin industries. For example, the oyster industry in the Chesapeake Bay in Virginia has been severely harmed by the effects of pollution. The effects of disease on consumer behavior are illustrated by the recent fear of contracting AIDS. Fear of the deadly disease is causing changes in the sexual behavior of homosexuals as well as of individuals seeking prostitutes. Even changes in weather patterns are beginning to be linked to short-term changes in consumer behavior. Obviously, short-term cold snaps or rainy spells influence the purchase of clothing. In addition, however, some evidence is beginning to emerge that weather may influence the mood of consumers and, thereby, influence their buying behavior.

The Technological Environment and Consumer Behavior

As noted earlier in the text, technological changes can dramatically influence the lifestyle of consumers. The birth control pill, television, radio, computer, automobile, and airplane have all dramatically influenced the way people live. An overlooked area of research relating technology to consumer behavior is that of investigating the man-machine interface. The problem is one of how to produce machines and products that are easy to use. As applied to consumers, the problem has been identified as one of how to make machines "user friendly."

The goal of making machines user friendly is a crucial one for the computer industry. Indeed, Apple Computer staked much of its future on the user-friendly concept when it came out with the MacIntosh computer. As noted by one writer on the topic, the user-friendly computer should convey its presence by not only having simple, logical software, but also by adding a personal touch of using names, having reactions, and adding humor. In other words, the computer should have a personality.[5]

One of the problems that can occur when a high technology company introduces a new product is that the focus is on the product rather than on the consumer. The product emphasis results in a design that is simple for the engineer to use but difficult for the consumer. In addition, a product emphasis can leave out the important idea of creating a product that produces positive feelings in the user. As noted in the chapters on motivation and attitudes, marketers cannot forget about the feelings of consumers. Whether or not a person buys a product, and certainly whether or not he or she rebuys it, depends to a major extent on whether it is liked—on whether it produces positive feelings.

For the consumer researcher the goal should be to anticipate what changes in the technological environment will occur and how these will influence the consumption patterns of consumers. In addition, the product manager should analyze the extent to which a product is easy to use for consumers and the extent to which it provides positive affective experiences.

The Reciprocity of Consumer and Environment

An important concept that all people should recognize is that consumers can influence the environment, just as the environment can influence consumers. Some of these reciprocal relationships have already been touched on in the book. For example, changes in consumer spending and saving patterns can influence the economy. Similarly, the behavior of millions of consumers acting together can influence the natural environment. Many researchers believe that one of the primary causes of the widening of the deserts in Africa is the actions of people who allow cattle to overgraze and who cut down trees for firewood. Another example is the burning of fossil fuels throughout the world, which may be part of the cause of acid rains as well as a major ''nonnatural'' source of carbon dioxide in the atmosphere. The presence of higher levels of carbon dioxide could lead to changes in the temperature of the earth with potentially devastating results. Other reciprocal relationships include the effects of changing consumer lifestyles and rituals on culture and the effects of consumption on scarce natural resources, such as whales, assorted other sea and land life, and various minerals.

The concepts of social traps and fences, introduced in Chapter 12 on group processes, are excellent tools for the analysis of the process through which millions of consumers acting as individuals can influence the environment. Each individual, acting for his or her own benefit, may engage in a behavior, such as using wood stoves. Individually, the actions of the consumers would have minimal effects on the environment. It is the combined effects of hundreds of families using wood stoves in mountain valleys that can and have led to major smog problems in areas in Colorado and New England.

PRODUCT POSITIONING

Product positioning involves the attempt by the marketer to influence demand by creating a specific product image in order to differentiate it from competitors. Products are positioned based upon the attributes they possess, and two types of positioning strategies may be followed. In **specific positioning,** the company seeks to create strong linkages in consumers' minds among the product, certain key attributes, and benefits. In particular, market leaders will attempt to establish attribute-need linkages in order to create a strong product image. In this approach, other brands are not specifically mentioned; however, the goal is still to differentiate the brand's qualities from the competition's. Crest toothpaste did this effectively by creating the image of a strong tooth-decay fighter. Brands that are not market leaders will often attempt to position themselves in relation to the market leader. Called **competitive positioning,** the goal is to emphasize the attributes possessed by the product in relation to the leading brands. In this approach the company will often use some type of comparative advertising.[6]

A good illustration of positioning is the promotional strategy used by the 7-Up Company. During the 1970s and 1980s, 7-Up had only about a 5 percent share of the soft-drink market, and it was constantly besieged by other lemon-lime flavored drinks—Sprite and Slice. Traditionally, the company used a competitive positioning strategy by promoting itself as an alternative to the colas. In early 1985 the company brought back its highly effective slogan—"the uncola"—as a method of vividly differentiating the brand from colas. However, the company also used other repositioning strategies. For example, in 1982 the company developed a campaign emphasizing 7-Up's lack of caffeine as a way of distinguishing it from colas. Then, in the mid-1980s Sprite and Slice began to threaten its market share. As a result, the company sought a way to position its product as different from these brands. The company began to advertise 7-Up as having no preservatives as the point of difference from Sprite and Slice.[7]

Perceptual Maps

For marketers one of the problems has been that of identifying ways of assessing a brand's position. Perhaps the most frequently used approach involves the creation of **perceptual maps.** Perceptual maps seek to show how consumers position various brands relative to each other on graphs whose axes are formed by product attributes.

Figure 20–2 presents a perceptual map created to assess consumer perceptions of various types of meat products.[8] It was developed by asking consumers to rate the meat products on a series of attributes, such as taste, cost, calories, quality, and time to prepare. A computer program developed at Bell Laboratories, called Multidimensional Preference Scaling, was used to create the perceptual map. What this program does is create a map of how consumers perceive the various products in relation to each other and to various attributes that describe them. For example, in the upper right-hand quadrant one finds a number of attributes that are clustered together—healthy, low

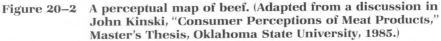

Figure 20–2   A perceptual map of beef. (Adapted from a discussion in John Kinski, "Consumer Perceptions of Meat Products," Master's Thesis, Oklahoma State University, 1985.)

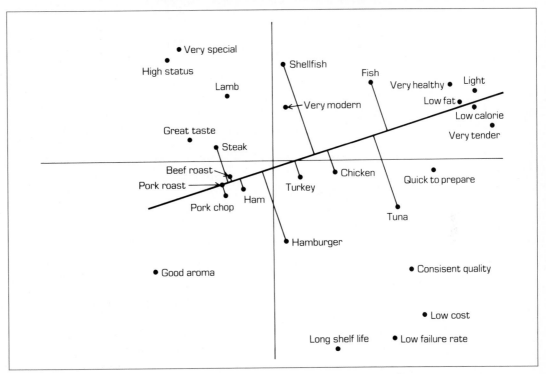

cholesterol, low calorie, and tender. The products positioned closest to these attributes are fish, chicken, and tuna fish. In contrast, the meat products of beef roast, pork roast, pork chop, and ham are clustered together. The attributes closest to them are great taste and good aroma.

The perceptual map shown in Figure 20–2 helps to identify some of the reasons why the consumption of beef has fallen quite dramatically over the past ten years. Consumers have become highly concerned about the value of their time and about the importance of eating in a healthy manner. Beef roast and pork are both positioned far away from the locations of these attributes on the perceptual map. In contrast, food products that are coming on strong, such as fish, chicken, and turkey, are positioned much closer to the clusters of adjectives relating to health and ease of cooking.

From a managerial perspective, the beef and pork industries are facing major problems. Their problem is one of how to change the perception of consumers that their products are less healthy and more time consuming to prepare. The trade association for beef has chosen a strategy of focusing on promotion. In the mid-1980s they developed an advertising campaign that attempted to reposition beef as a lighter, nutritious product. However, the arguments of the ad campaign were counteracted by information coming from various health organizations that linked high cholesterol levels to health problems. Because consumers recognized that beef contains relatively high cholesterol levels, the impact of the ad campaign was lessened. Indeed, the National Beef Council was charged with false advertising by some consumer groups. Instead of focusing on advertising, the beef industry would have been better off to have focused on the product. What the beef industry needs is the development of new beef products that have lower cholesterol levels and are quick and easy to prepare.

Product Differentiation

One of the benefits of doing perceptual maps is the ability to identify whether or not consumers differentiate one product from another. As the perceptual map shows in Figure 20–2, consumers perceived beef roast, pork roast, pork chops, and ham to be very close together. In other words, these products are *not* differentiated well by consumers.

A number of benefits are gained when consumers can differentiate a particular brand from others. Some authors have argued that product differentiation adds "perceived value" to the product. The increase in perceived value helps to increase the "leverage" of the various components of the marketing mix.[9] Thus, in the pricing area brand differentiation can allow the company to command premium prices for a product. In the promotion area, **product differentiation** assists creative personnel in developing messages that promote only the brand advertised and not competitors as well. An example of a clearly differentiated brand using a claim effectively was Mercedes with its unique selling proposition, "Engineered like no other car in the world." Mercedes stands out in its engineering, and the claim is highly believable. Because of its ability to differentiate itself from other brands in the United States, Mercedes can price its cars in the U.S. at twice the levels it sells them for in Germany.

Product differentiation can give a company leverage in other areas as well. A clearly differentiated brand is more likely to gain shelf space in retail stores. In addition, the sales force may be more motivated to sell the brand if it can be clearly distinguished from competitive offerings.

Repositioning

Sometimes companies find it necessary to reposition a brand. Perhaps the classic example of **repositioning** was done by Philip Morris. Originally developed as a product for women, the Marlboro brand featured a special filter and a feminine package. When sales failed to meet expectations, a decision was made to reposition it as a highly masculine product. Using the imagery of cowboys and the West, the brand was established as the number-one selling cigarette.

One problem with trying to reposition products, however, is that it is more difficult to change a preexisting attitude than one that has yet to be formed. For example, for years Miller's High Life beer was advertised as the "champagne of bottled beers." Unfortunately, the unique selling proposition did not appeal to the heavy beer drinkers—blue-collar workers. When Philip Morris bought the brand in the early 1970s, a decision was made to reposition it. The goal was to take the brand from the "champagne bucket and put it . . . into the lunch bucket."[10] The result was a rapid rise in market share during the 1970s for the flagship beer of Philip Morris. However, the effort took five years, millions of dollars, and a major commitment by the company to make it succeed. In contrast, the same company introduced a new beer, Meister Brau in the mid-1980s. Positioning it as tasting as good as Bud, but cheaper, the brand gained market share quickly. The positioning task was much easier with the new brand than with the established brand. Several other examples of repositioning of products are discussed in Highlight 20–1.

THE SEGMENTATION OF THE MARKETPLACE

As defined by Kotler, "**Market segmentation** is the subdividing of a market into distinct subsets of customers, where any subset may conceivably be se-

---

HIGHLIGHT 20–1

The Repositioning of Spam, Velveeta and Snickers

Velveeta, the sixty-year-old cheese product, began to have problems in the 1980s. Long used as a cooking cheese, Velveeta over the past decade began to be replaced by natural cheddars for use in sauces and over hamburgers. The users had forgotten the brand, and the nonusers believed its ingredients to be artificial, according to its product manager.

Rather than dropping the line and attempting to formulate a new cheese, its producer, Kraft, decided to attempt to reposition the product. The goal was to change how consumers view the product from an artificial cheese to a good-tasting product that has all natural, nutritious ingredients. The advertising was labeled "skeptic conversion" by the advertising agency, J. Walter Thompson USA. In the ads a skeptical consumer is shown being slowly convinced that the product is indeed good tasting and natural.

Another "old standby" product, Spam, is undergoing a similar repositioning strategy. Its sales had fallen because it had the image of being made of all kinds of "weird" types of meats. The goal of the repositioning strategy was to convince consumers that it contains only wholesome pork cuts. The advertising involved having consumers taste the product and then guess what it is. The skeptical consumers are slowly convinced that Spam tastes good and is made only of wholesome cuts of pork.

A completely different type of repositioning strategy was used for Snickers, the top-selling candy bar. Mars, the maker of the product, recognized in the late 1970s that consumer preferences were shifting towards wholesome, nutritious foods. The company saw this as an opportunity to reposition the brand from a candy to a snack food. The move made sense because the snack food market is over twice the size of the candy market ($22+ billion to about $10 billion). Using the 1984 Olympic games as the springboard for the effort, Snickers used ex-Olympic athletes to talk about eating Snickers for a snack. A key line in the thirty-second ad spots is, "Packed with peanuts, Snickers really satisfies."

Based in part on Bess Gallanis, "Positioning Old Products in New Niches," *Advertising Age*, May 3, 1984, M50.

lected as a target market to be reached with a distinct marketing mix."[11] For segments to be useful, they should possess the characteristics of *measurability, accessibility,* and *substantiality.* In other words, for a manager to attempt to identify and reach a segment, he or she must be able to assess its characteristics via various demographic, psychographic, or personality measures. In addition, the manager must be able to reach the segments via the marketing mix. Finally, the segment must be large enough to generate sufficient sales for it to be managerially useful.

The advantage of segmentation to the company is that the marketing mix for products and services can be tailored to meet the needs and wants of homogeneous subsets of customers. Because these subsets of consumers may have unique needs and wants not shared by larger groupings of consumers, the total market potential for a general class of product may be expanded. For example, the overall market potential for watches was increased when companies identified specialized needs and wants of consumers for diving watches, running watches, pocket watches, dress watches, and so forth. If only one type of all-purpose watch were offered, total watch sales would be much lower than they currently are. By developing watches for particular segments, the overall number of watches sold increases.

Bases for Segmenting Consumer Markets

Segments are identified by finding groupings of consumers with similar needs and wants. For consumer goods, they are composed of thousands or millions of people. For industrial goods, a segment is normally composed of hundreds or thousands of companies. The problem for the manager is in identifying the *bases for segmentation.* In other words, on what variables can distinct groupings of people or companies be identified? A number of factors have been identified on which people and companies can be grouped. Because the bases of segmenting consumer and industrial markets are somewhat different, they are discussed separately. For consumer markets, three classifications of segmentation variables have been identified. These grouping variables include: (1) various characteristics of the person, (2) the situation in which the product or service may be purchased, and (3) geography. Table 20–2 summarizes these variables, and a brief discussion follows in the next subsections.

Characteristics of the Person   Each individual within a population has a unique set of needs, wants, and aspirations. Fortunately, for marketers particular needs and wants are often shared by large enough numbers of people for the manager to develop a particular product or service to fulfill these needs and wants. It is the sum of large numbers of consumers who share certain needs and wants that creates a market. The characteristics of people on which markets can be formed may be classified into four categories—demographic, behavioral, psychographic, and personality characteristics.

Table 20–2   Bases for Segmenting the Consumer Market

I. Characteristics of the Person

    A. Demographics

1. Age	6. Nationality
2. Sex	7. Education
3. Income	8. Family size
4. Religion	9. Occupation
5. Marital status	10. Ethnicity

    B. Consumption Behavior
       1. Benefits sought
       2. Demand elasticity
       3. Brand loyalty
       4. Usage rate
       5. Other—purchase occasion, media usage, marketing factor sensitivity

    C. Personality characteristics

    D. Psychographic category

II. Situation
    A. Task definition
    B. Antecedent states
    C. Time
    D. Physical surroundings
    E. Social surroundings

III. Geographic

DEMOGRAPHIC CHARACTERISTICS. In the chapters on subcultures, a number of demographic characteristics were discussed that described the characteristics of various groups of people. These demographic characteristics consisted of such variables as: age, sex, income, religion, marital status, nationality, education, family size, occupation, and ethnicity. Such demographic measures of consumers have two important uses in the segmentation process. First, either singly or in combination they can be used to describe various subcultures, whose members share certain values, needs, rituals, and behaviors. Thus, by using a combination of education, occupation, and income, a measure of social class can be developed. By using a combination of age, marital status, and number of children, a measure of the stage of the family life cycle can be obtained. Thus, demographic variables help to identify subcultures that the marketing manager can target with the marketing mix.

The second use of demographic variables is to delineate consumers who are classified into segments via other means. Thus, a manager may want to determine the demographic characteristics of the heavy, medium, and light users of a service, such as automatic tellers (ATMs) at banks. By contacting a large number of consumers, asking them about their frequency of usage of ATMs, and also obtaining demographic information, the manager can develop a profile of the heavy and light users.

Demographic data are perhaps the single most important type of information a marketing manager can gather for the purpose of segmentation. The major reason for this strong statement is that demographic information is the most readily available type of information on individual consumers. The federal government collects a wealth of demographic data through the census. Magazines, newspapers, and television and radio stations collect demographic information on their audiences. Private companies have been developed to provide demographic information on various groups of people. With the wealth of demographic data available, a manager can identify the demographic characteristics of his or her target market. With such information, the manager can then make rational choices concerning the type of media to use to reach the target market as well as to make pricing and distribution decisions.

A good example of the importance of demographic information to assess the characteristics of target markets involves smoking behavior. Recent evidence indicates that heavy smokers are increasingly found among blue-collar workers and those with high school or less education. For example, only 26 percent of men in professional groups were found to smoke, whereas over half of blue-collar men did. Similarly, 40 percent of the women who dropped out of high school were found to smoke, whereas only 15 percent of professional women smoked.[12] Two reasons were offered for why smoking seems increasingly to be a lower-class habit. First, the upper classes may more clearly recognize the link between smoking and various health problems. Second, among upper-class subcultures norms against smoking are developing. One woman described the social pressure as intense, saying, "I never was afraid of lung cancer . . . It's social pressure. People give me dirty looks when I light up in restaurants, or they wave their hands around."[13]

Two implications of the demographics of smoking are clear. First, the cigarette companies are likely to target increasingly less-educated and blue-collar persons with their marketing mix. One sign of such targeting is that the companies have begun to offer cigarettes in more price ranges to appeal to the lower incomes of the less educated and of the blue collar.[14] A public policy implication also exists. Because of their increased tendency to smoke, the less educated and blue collar are likely to have greater health problems in the future. Would it be in the public interest to raise taxes on cigarettes substantially in order to lower the demand for cigarettes among people who have lower incomes? A recent study supports such an argument. The study revealed that low-income consumers and teenagers have a different elasticity of demand for cigarettes than higher-income consumers. The lower-income groups are likely to have a high elasticity of demand, which means that raising the cost of smoking is likely to decrease their demand for cigarettes substantially.[15]

BEHAVIOR AS A BASIS FOR SEGMENTATION.   A complementary approach to using demographic variables to segment the market involves dividing consumers into homogeneous groups based upon various aspects of their buying behavior. A number of different types of **behavioral segmentation** can be identified, including price elasticity, benefits sought, and usage rate. Indeed, each of these bases of segmentation has been discussed previously in the text.

The concept of segmenting on price elasticity was discussed in Chapter 18—"The Economics of Consumption." The idea is that different groups of consumers may react in varying ways to changes in the price of a product or service. As suggested in Chapter 18, the airline industry uses such a segmentation scheme. Fares are set up so that travelers who cannot make reservations in advance pay more. Typically, vacationers can make reservations early and will substitute airline travel for other means of transportation, such as autos, if the price is lower. In contrast, business people and others traveling because of emergencies cannot make reservations early and will fly despite higher fares. In effect, the elasticities of demand for the two groups are different, and the airlines capitalize on it.

Other examples of segmentation via **demand elasticities** exist. The distribution of coupons in part takes advantage of different demand elasticities. One can view coupon users as a distinct segment in comparison to "non-coupon users." Those who choose not to use coupons are relatively more demand inelastic, because they are willing to pay a higher price for a product than those who do cut coupons. Individuals who take the time and effort to clip coupons may be viewed as more demand elastic. That is, they are unwilling to pay a higher price for a product and are willing to invest the time to collect coupons in order to lower the price.

The strategy of conducting an annual or semiannual sale by many furniture manufacturers is based in part on the recognition that different consumer segments have divergent demand elasticities. The demand inelastic segment is composed of consumers who are not particularly price conscious. Such consumers may be sufficiently wealthy that they are not particularly concerned with price. A second reason for their inelastic demand curve is that they may have an immediate need for furniture and cannot wait for the sale to occur. The other group of consumers is relatively more demand elastic, and they are willing to wait until the sale is announced to buy the furniture. Thus, they will buy the product only if it is at a sufficiently low price.

The development of strategies to take advantage of segments possessing different demand elasticities has a number of advantages for managers. Foremost, such practices allow companies to increase their total sales and possibly increase the overall efficiency of their operation. For the airlines, seats that would not have been filled have occupants. Because the marginal cost of filling empty seats in a plane is minimal, the fares from such passengers go almost directly to the bottom line. When done correctly, segmenting via demand elasticity will not influence the image of the product. Thus, by discreetly advertising an annual sale for furniture, jewelry, automobiles or whatever, marketers can help ensure that consumers will not lower the impression of the products because they are priced lower. In other words, less likelihood exists that customers will infer that the product has lower quality because it is lower priced.

In addition to segmenting by demand elasticity, firms may divide the market based on the benefits sought by consumers. Called benefit segmentation, the concept is to develop products and services that possess specific qualities desired by homogeneous groups of consumers. Oftentimes, benefit segmentation results in companies creating products that fit into small, but profitable, "market niches." Among automobile companies, Porsche and Rolls Royce have found exclusive market niches for their products. Each company sells less than 50,000 autos a year—a number too small for larger manufacturers, like General Motors, to care about. Yet, by offering cars that are incredibly luxurious and expensive (i.e., Rolls Royce) or extremely fast and expensive (i.e., Porsche), the companies offer autos that provide benefits a small group of consumers desire.

Perhaps the type of behavior that companies most often segment is usage behavior. Through market research, a company will attempt to identify the light, moderate, and heavy users of their products or services. The company will then attempt to identify the demographic and psychographic characteristics of these groupings of users. Strategies can then be developed to target one or more of the groups by manipulating the marketing mix.

As noted above, usage behavior is often employed in conjunction with other approaches to segment the market. For example, the Beef Industry Council found that the heavy users of beef could be classified via the VALs (Value and Lifestyles) psychographic inventory developed by the Stanford Research Institute. Heavy users were found to belong to groups labeled belongers and emulators. The Beef Industry Council in consultation with their advertising agency decided to target for their advertising moderate and light users of beef, who would act as opinion leaders for other groups. In the VALs inventory, these opinion leader groups were identified as the "achievers," the "experientials," and the "societally conscious."[16] Figure 20–3 gives one of the radio advertisements directed to these groups.

In addition to segmenting via usage rate, the manager can also segment by user status. Thus, from marketing research the manager may be able to obtain profiles of consumers who are nonusers, ex-users, potential users, first-time users, or regular users. In a similar manner, the manager may decide to segment based upon the amount of brand loyalty shown by various user groups. Consumers who are brand loyal to the product or service may be separated from other user groups for special promotional messages. Managers may want to attempt to reach and influence users who show a ten-

Figure 20–3 Radio copy targeted to specific psychographic segments.
(Courtesy of Beef Industry Council.)

**Ketchum
Communications.** ——————————————————— *Radio Copy*

Client:	BEEF INDUSTRY COUNCIL	*Date:*	9-4-85
Product:	Beef	*Length:*	55/5
Title:	''Deb's Beef''	*Job #:*	083-13040
Revision:	3	*Code #:*	083-5617

SFX:	RESTAURANT SOUNDS IN BACKGROUND
MAN 1:	Uh, what do you think? The pea pod piroshki or the wilted spinach salad?
WOMAN 1:	The fettucine with wild mushrooms is good here. What are you having, Debra?
DEB:	The beef.
MAN 2:	Ah the beef. Where's that?
DEB:	There. It says ''le boeuf de bercy.'' It means beef.
CHORUS:	Oh. Ah.
MAN 2:	Are you making a statement, Deb?
DEB:	The statement is, I feel like beef.
MAN 1:	So much for the body beautiful.
DEB:	Check your handy pocket calorie guide, Bozo.
MAN 1:	Bozo.
DEB:	The beef has fewer calories than your pea pod whatever it is.
MAN 1:	Deb, take it easy on the piroshki.
WOMAN 1:	Look at this. Three ounces of beef has fewer calories than my fettucine.
MAN 2:	Fewer calories than my garbanzo quiche.
MAN 1:	More than twice the iron of my breast of pheasant.
WOMAN 1:	More flavor than a bale of wilted spinach.
AVO:	Beef—under 200 calories in a trimmed three ounce serving. So lighten up.
MAN 1:	Look, we're worldly, sophisticated professionals in a trendy, urban restaurant. We can't all order beef.
MAN 2:	Right. I'll order fajitas.
WOMAN 1:	Oh, that's flank steak.
MAN 2:	I know, but it sounds so . . . ethnic.
AVO:	Beef. Good news for people who eat.
LIVE TAG:	

dency to switch between brands through sales promotion devices, such as coupons or contests.

PSYCHOGRAPHIC AND PERSONALITY CHARACTERISTICS. As discussed in Chapter 4, markets may be segmented on the psychographic and personality characteristics of consumers. The use of the VALs lifestyle survey by the National Beef Council is a classic example of how a psychographic inventory can be used for segmentation purposes. In this approach the population is divided into the psychographic categories, such as achievers, belongers, experientials, and so forth, and various consumption habits are identified. The market mix is then geared to appeal to one or more of the psychographically developed segments.

In most instances, psychographic or personality segmentation is combined with behavioral segmentation. That is, the market may be divided first into heavy, moderate, and light users. One or more of these segments is then further analyzed via psychographic inventories. For example, Merrill Lynch wanted to identify the psychographic characteristics of heavy users of brokerage services. The firm found that the "achievers" category of the VALs inventory described the heavy-user segment quite well. Based upon a knowledge of the characteristics of the achiever, the advertising was changed from a theme of herds of bulls thundering across the plains to a single bull making intelligent choices about what directions in which to move.[17] The VALs inventory had shown that achievers are not followers but leaders, who make their decisions independently.

Personality scales also tend to be used with other means of segmentation rather than in isolation. For example, a natural use of sex-role scales would be to identify segments of heavy users of disposable diapers. Completely different promotional campaigns could be necessary to appeal to "androgynous" mothers as compared to "feminine" mothers.

The Situation as a Segmentation Basis Chapter 10 discussed the situation within which a product or service is purchased as an important factor influencing consumption behavior. As noted in the chapter, consumer situations may be classified into five categories—the physical surroundings, social surroundings, temporal surroundings, task definition, and antecedent states. For many types of products, segmentation by situation is the rule. For example, clothing and footwear have to be designed specifically for the physical surroundings (i.e., warm or cold weather, sun or rain) as well as for the task definition (i.e., party, sleep, casual). Research has shown the large impact of situations on the choice of snack food, meat products, and fast-food chains.[18]

The situation may also interact with personal characteristics to form a basis for segmentation. For example, psychographic inventories can be combined with information on usage situations to gain a more detailed view of consumption behavior. For example, it is possible to profile heavy beer drinkers through psychographics. However, additional information is provided if the researcher also learns that the heavy drinking occurs in certain situations, such as at parties or after playing basketball or softball. Indeed, some researchers argue that one of the advantages of psychographic inventories is that they typically obtain information on the situations in which products are bought or consumed.[19]

Geographic Segmentation For many products and services an important basis for segmentation is geography. As noted in Chapter 15, geography can form the basis of distinct subcultures, which possess different values and lifestyles. For example, Ford Motor Company began to segment the United States in 1985 when it began introducing its new car line, the Merkur. Imported from Europe, the Merkur line was developed to challenge BMW and Mercedes. As a part of the strategy, Ford decided to focus on selling the cars on the East and West coasts. The company felt that consumers who lived on the coasts would be more receptive to a new European-styled car than those living in the interior of the country.

In addition to segmenting on region, marketers can also segment on the size of cities, counties, or SMSAs. Other means of geographic segmentation include density of population and climate. Companies are increasingly turning to geographers to assist them in segmenting the marketplace, because of geographers' expertise in recognizing the effects of geographics on consumers. For example, the corporation owned by the golfing great, Jack Nicklaus, has hired a sports geographer to assist the company in identifying new locations to build golf courses.

Bases for Segmenting Industrial Markets

Although overlap exists in how industrial and consumer marketers segment the marketplace, differences do exist. Perhaps the most important difference is the variation in types of information that exist on industrial firms and on consumers. For example, the federal government has developed a system for categorizing all businesses into homogeneous groups. Called the **Standard Industrial Classification System** (SIC), the data base classifies and identifies groups of business firms that produce the same type of product. The SIC system can assist the industrial marketer in identifying potential new customers, in estimating market potential, and in delineating groups of companies that are likely to have similar product or service needs.

One suggestion for segmenting industrial markets involves the identification of macrobases and microbases for segmentation.[20] **Macrosegmentation** involves identifying groups of companies having similar buying organizations and facing similar buying situations. Table 20–3 identifies a number of these macrobases for segmentation. Examples of segmentation categories based upon the characteristics of the organization include size of the company, its geographical location, its usage rate, and whether the company is centralized or decentralized. An example of a segmentation category based on a characteristic of the purchasing situation is whether the purchase is a new task, a modified rebuy, or a straight rebuy.

Table 20–3 Some Macrobases of Segmentation

Segmentation Basis	Example
1. Characteristics of buying organization	
a. Size	Small, medium, large; can be based on overall sales.
b. Geographic location	New England versus Southwest
c. Usage rate	Light, moderate, heavy user
d. Buying structure	Centralized versus decentralized
2. Product application	
a. SIC code	Varies by product
b. End market served	Varies by product
3. Characteristics of purchasing situation	
a. Type of buying situation	New task, modified rebuy, straight rebuy
b. Stage in decision process	Early versus late stage

SOURCE: Based on Michael D. Hutt and Thomas Speh, *Industrial Marketing Management*, New York, N.Y.: The Dryden Press, 1981, 112.

Microsegmentation in industrial marketing focuses on identifying the characteristics of the decision-making units within each of the various macrosegments. As such, microsegmentation requires more in-depth knowledge of buying organizations. One example of a basis for microsegmentation is the key criteria used by the buying organization. Analogous to benefit segmentation in consumer marketing, the approach involves identifying the product and producer attributes sought by buyers. These could include quality of product, delivery reliability and speed, and supplier reputation. Another microsegmentation variable involves identifying the purchasing strategy of buyers. For example, in some situations it may be important to identify whether purchasers use an optimizing or a satisficing buying strategy. If an optimizing buying strategy is used, sellers are likely to be forced to comply with large numbers of product specifications. Although often criticized, military procurement procedures sometimes involve attempts to optimize the performance of equipment. The result is very high technical standards, which can lead sellers to charge extremely high prices for their products in order to pay for the added costs of meeting the specifications. Other microsegmentation bases include the importance of the purchase, the purchaser's attitude towards vendors, and the personal characteristics of buying agents, such as age, education, risk-taking tendencies, confidence, and cultural background.

MARKETING-MIX DEVELOPMENT

Consumer behavior principles are extremely important in the development of the marketing mix. From new product development to the planning of the strategy for distribution, pricing, and promotion, the facts, theories, and concepts of consumer behavior can have bottom-line results. Some of these ap-

Table 20–4   Consumer Behavior Applications to New Product Development

Managerial Application	Consumer Behavior Concept
New product idea generation	*Attitude formation:* Identify benefits consumers want and the product attributes that offer such benefits. *Lifestyle:* Identify lifestyle changes and the needs and wants generated. *Situation analysis:* Identify situations in which product needs are not being met.
Concept testing	*Product positioning:* Identify whether product concept is perceived by consumer to be positioned as desired. *Attitude formation:* Do consumers perceive the product to have the attributes desired?
Product development	*Information processing:* Is the product user friendly? Does the package gain attention? Can consumers remember the name? *Attitude formation:* How do consumers react to the name and packaging? Do consumers like the prototype product?
Market testing	*Attitude formation:* Do consumers have the anticipated beliefs, affective reactions, and intentions? *Postpurchase satisfaction:* Are consumers rebuying it? Are they developing brand loyalty? *Situation:* Are consumers using the product in the expected situations?

plications are discussed briefly in the following subsections. Table 20–4 lists a number of the applications.

New Product Development

In this section the term *product* is used very broadly to include physical objects, services, places, organizations and so forth.[21] As such, the question addressed concerns how consumer behavior principles can assist the firm in creating new products. These principles can be applied to four separate areas of the new product development process—idea generation, concept testing, product development, and market testing.

Idea Generation   Within the area of new product development, consumer behavior concepts perhaps have the greatest impact on **idea generation.** No less than five major areas of consumer behavior can be used to help managers develop ideas for new products. These include the analysis of consumer attitudes, lifestyle changes, situational factors, other cultures, and subcultures. For example, the study of consumer attitudes regarding existing products can be used to identify consumer desires for particular product attributes. If consumers believe that existing products fail to possess attributes that are desired, a new product opportunity may exist. Colgate-Palmolive recognized that consumers wanted to have toothpaste that was easier to dispense. The company developed a pump that was economical and easy to use. The result was that Colgate toothpaste rapidly increased its market share and threatened to replace Crest as the number-one-selling toothpaste.

Another approach to identify new product ideas is to investigate the changing lifestyles of consumers. By using psychographic analysis, a company may be able to identify new consumer trends and the new product ideas to meet the wants and needs created by the trends. The physical fitness and health trends that have swept the United States in the 1980s have offered companies numerous opportunities for new product ideas.

Situation analysis can also help to identify new product ideas. By investigating the effects of time, task definition, social surroundings, physical surroundings, and antecedent states of consumers, marketers may develop new product ideas. For example, the situation of traveling has led companies to develop a wide variety of products to make the experience more comfortable and profitable for consumers. The huge cellular phone market has developed in response to the needs of executives traveling in cars to have telephone contact with their offices and clients.

Cross-cultural and subcultural analysis can bring similar benefits. By investigating how consumers use products, either in other cultures or in subcultures, a company may identify new product ideas that can be applied to the U.S. marketplace. For example, the idea to market the bowl-shaped, quick-cooking frying pan called the wok was borrowed from Oriental cooking practices. Many day-care centers use sleeping mats like those found in Japan for children to take naps on. The centers simply do not have the space to place and store dozens of cots.

Concept Testing   Another aspect of the new product development process is the pretesting of the product concept, known as **concept testing.** A product concept is the particular "consumer meaning that the company tries to build into a product idea."[22] The product concept for a new personal computer may be to build a computer that consumers perceive to be user friendly, portable, IBM-compatible, powerful, and midpriced. In order to check out whether consumers have such a product concept, the firm can do product positioning analysis as well as surveys to determine the attitudes consumers may possess towards such a concept.

Product Development   After determining if consumers perceive the product concept as management intends, the company can begin the **product development** process. Here, prototypes are developed, tested, named, and packaged. A variety of consumer behavior concepts are important in this phase. For example, researchers should be concerned with how consumers process information about the product. Is the product user friendly (i.e., easy to use, not too complex, and so forth)? Does the packaging of the product gain attention? Can consumers remember the name of the product?

The researchers must also be concerned about the attitude formation process when testing the product and packaging. Do consumers like the prototype product? Do they believe the claims made about it? Do consumers like the packaging?

Market Testing After the product development phase is concluded satisfactorily, a product is moved into **market testing.** Although not always done, market testing involves placing the product into limited distribution to consumers in order to identify any potential problems and to test the entire marketing mix. In this phase, additional attitudinal measures are taken to determine if consumers are forming the expected beliefs, affective reactions, and buying intentions. In addition, postpurchase satisfaction is examined. Are consumers happy with the product after purchase? Are they rebuying it? Are they showing signs of developing brand loyalty? The manager will also want to know if consumers are using the product in the expected situations. In general, the goal of the market test is to determine if the marketing strategy seems to be working. Therefore, all the consumer behavior areas previously mentioned will apply.

The Effects of Competition Throughout the new product development process, managers must be concerned with the products and actions of competitors. Consumers will not perceive a brand in isolation of competitors. Thus, assessment of how the product compares to competitive offerings is crucial. A decision to move into full-scale production would be a gross mistake if it were based on the finding that consumers rate your product as "good" on various attributes but rate competitors as "excellent" on the same attributes. Furthermore, managers cannot assume that the competitive environment will remain constant while product development occurs. When engaging in product development, managers are constantly trying to hit a moving target. Changes occurring in the cultural, economic, and natural environments make the process exceptionally risky.

Promotional Strategy Implications

For the marketing manager, consumer behavior has its greatest application in the promotional strategy area. From advertising to personal selling to sales promotion to public relations, consumer behavior concepts and principles form a basis for much of the manager's strategy. The strategic and practical implications of consumer behavior on promotional activities of the firm are discussed further in the following subsections.

Advertising Applications At minimum, ten of the major topic areas discussed in the text have application to advertising. Table 20–5 identifies these areas along with a brief identification of how they may be applied.

One application to which a number of the areas apply is that of developing advertising themes. When developing advertising materials, it is useful to think in terms of what kinds of ideas, images, and feelings the creative people

Table 20–5   Advertising Implications of Consumer Behavior

Consumer Behavior Concept	Application
Cultural/subcultural values	Development of advertising themes
Opinion leader analysis	How to reach and influence opinion leaders
Analysis of decision maker	How to reach and influence decision makers
Personal influence	Effects of sources, influence techniques
Motivation	Development of advertising themes, how to reduce risk and reactance, how to encourage consumers to make appropriate attributions
Information processing	Gaining attention, increasing recall and recognition, how consumers organize perceptions, factors influencing the reception of information
Learning	Creating affective responses through classical conditioning, encouraging modeling behavior, analyzing the contingencies of the environment
Attitudes	How to create beliefs, identifying important attributes to emphasize, how to change attitudes, effects of various types of messages on consumers
Psychographics/personality	Develop profiles of target audience in order to reach and appeal to them more effectively
Decision process	How to engage problem-solving activities, how to assist search behavior, providing information for evaluation activities, providing information to influence postpurchase evaluations

should attempt to evoke in consumers. One approach to developing concepts for the advertising theme is to analyze three related areas of consumer behavior. They are the cultural/subcultural values of the target market, the motivations of the target market, and the psychographic/personality characteristics of the target market. Particularly for products such as beer, perfume, and cigarettes, developing a theme for the product, and with it an image, is crucial.

The Budweiser campaign based around the theme "This Bud's for You" is a nice example of the development of an advertising campaign based upon knowledge of the psychographic/personality characteristics of a target market. Each different ad in the campaign focuses on a different type of occupation and the people who work in it. Because Budweiser targets heavy-drinking, blue-collar workers, the ads have avoided depicting white-collar jobs, honoring instead such people as firemen, soldiers, airline baggage handlers, and mechanics. Clearly, marketers at Anheuser-Busch have developed a psychographic profile of their target market. The company knows the values of the group and the images that motivate them. The successful campaign well illustrates how such concepts can be used to develop an advertising theme that can be successfully used for many years.

Advertisers must also be extremely familiar with the basic communications model of source, message, channel, and receiver. For example, having an understanding of the basic factors that make a source a good spokesperson for a product can result in highly effective advertising campaigns. For example, if one merely looks at how audiences rate John McEnroe, the hot-tempered tennis star, the tendency would be to avoid using him at all costs. However, Bic has been extremely successful using McEnroe as a spokesperson for their disposable shavers. Two reasons probably account for the success. First, McEnroe is extremely memorable. Placing him in the ads may cause consumers to pay more attention to the ads and to remember them. Second, the ads cleverly make use of McEnroe's legendary hot temper by tying it to the message of the commercial. Although McEnroe may not be known as likable, he is probably viewed as quite trustworthy because of his outspokenness, and the ads make nice use of this characteristic of the tennis star. Figure 20–4 shows one of the ads and how the link is made.

The investigation of consumer attitudes is another particularly important area for advertisers. The goal of many advertisements is to create certain beliefs in consumers about the attributes of a product. In order to know the beliefs on which to focus, market researchers must identify the attributes that the target market views as most important. In addition, the advertiser must have information on the type of message to use to influence the beliefs. Should fear appeals be used? Would a celebrity endorser be the most effective source of information? Should comparative advertising be used? These are the types of questions that the knowledge of attitude formation and change can assist the manager in answering.

In addition to forming beliefs, advertisers are also interested in creating feelings. Feelings can result from changes in beliefs, but this process is slow and uncertain because of the impact of outside information received by the consumer. The direct influence of feelings through the use of classical conditioning processes is frequently attempted by advertisers. Of course, to use classical conditioning principles effectively, marketers need a knowledge of learning processes.

Advertisers must also be aware of the decision process used by consumers to buy their product. The advertiser may have to "assist" consumers in recognizing that a problem exists which his product might eliminate. Advertising should assist the consumer in the search process by bringing the product to the attention of consumers. Appropriate information should be provided to assist the consumer in evaluating the product in comparison to other brands. Even the rudimentary knowledge that can be gained on the type of choice process used by consumers (i.e., whether compensatory or noncompensatory) can provide information on which product features to emphasize. Such is true even with a "product" like one's speech pattern, as discussed in Highlight 20–2.

Personal Selling   Many of the areas of importance to advertisers will also be of relevance to those engaged in personal selling. Knowledge of attitude formation and change processes can assist marketers in developing specific

Figure 20–4 **Bic's ads using John McEnroe as their spokesperson have been very successful.** *(Courtesy of Bic Corporation.)*

messages for their sales force. Similarly, the analysis of cultural/subcultural differences between the sales force and clients can help the company avoid various problems that can arise through inappropriate statements or actions. For example, when dealing with Japanese business personnel, a manager

HIGHLIGHT 20–2

How to Change Your Accent and Become a Star

How does a beautiful movie star with a Southern accent play a British aristocrat? One possibility is to have someone else's voice dubbed in. The problem is that when the star goes on talk shows, everyone snickers behind her back that she is the "stunning beauty fit to be seen, not heard."

Another possibility is to hire a New Yorker named Sam Chwat, who owns a company that can train even native Oklahomans to sound like they were born in London, Paris, or Tel Aviv.

Indeed, a humiliating experience such as the one described occurred to the actress Andie MacDowell. In *Greystoke* she played the British heiress who fell in love with Tarzan. The problem was that to correct her Southern accent, the voice of another actress was dubbed. Because of the resulting quips, she turned to Mr. Chwat. As a result of the training, she has played roles requiring a mid-American accent and a French accent.

Mr. Chwat's company performs their miracles by using a technique they call "coding." In each dialect letters are pronounced differently. So the company trains their students to mentally code the letters the way they sound in the "foreign" dialect. Take the following sentences—"We need help with the housework. Every time we try to hire someone, they would say, 'I don't do windows.'"

The coding for saying the sentence with a Yiddish accent is—"Ve need help vit da housewoik. Efery time ve try to hire someone, they'd say, 'I don't do vindoce.'"

Is it worth all the effort to change an accent? Accents are just one of the many characteristics of a source that may influence people. Because consumers have stereotypes of the characteristics of people with various accents, it may be difficult for a source to have the desired impact. For example, could someone with a German accent be taken seriously as a jock from the country? In contrast, could someone with a Southern drawl be believable as an urbane psychiatrist?

Accents matter. With managers having to spend more and more time speaking in front of the public, taking lessons to improve less acceptable speech patterns can make a difference.

Based on Lenore Skenazy, "The Rising Wizard of Speechmasters," *Advertising Age*, September 19, 1985, 3, 61.

does not want his or her sales force to come on too quickly and to act too informal with the more reserved and polite Japanese.

A consumer behavior area of particular importance to personal selling is that of personal influence. Particularly when engaging in personal selling to consumers, as opposed to industrial selling, managers find knowledge of various influence techniques important. For example, information on self-perception processes suggests that salespeople should do everything they can to get the consumer to touch the product, use it, drive it, imagine that they own it, and so forth. The more actions a salesman can get a consumer to engage in regarding the product, the more likely it is that the consumer will picture himself or herself as owning the product.

Sales Promotion Applications   Sales promotion has been defined as all of the supplementary promotional activities done in addition to advertising and personal selling.[23] It includes such items as providing product literature, using direct mail, providing dealer incentives, using point-of-purchase (POP) materials, and providing consumer incentives.

Consumer behavior principles can influence planning in each of the areas, but in the areas of direct mail, POPs, and consumer incentives the applications are quite strong. Direct-mail marketers attempt to identify highly specific segments of consumers to whom they can direct advertising materials or catalogs. The goal of these attempts is to pinpoint precisely a segment of consumers that is likely to be influenced by the materials received and then reach the group directly through the mail. Accordingly, sophisticated direct-mail marketers will develop precise demographic and psychographic profiles of the segment that they plan to reach. By combining the demographic information that can be obtained from ZIP codes and census information with information obtained from lists of magazine readers and catalog readers, marketers can pinpoint segments quite precisely.

Another important sales promotion area involves the use of POP materials in retail stores. Like packaging, POP displays seek to catch the consumer's attention and interest. Knowledge of consumer perceptual processes is an important base from which to design the displays. In particular, the Gestalt principles of perceptual organization are relevant. Principles such as contrast, movement, and closure can be incorporated into designs that catch attention and convey a message instantaneously.

Consumer behavior principles also have application in the creation of effective sales incentives. Sales incentives include such devices as price-off deals, sampling, contests, and the use of premiums, coupons, and trading stamps. A number of these sales incentives deal with techniques to change the price of the product. Such devices as rebates, coupons, trading stamps, and price-off deals effectively change the price the consumer pays for the product. Therefore, principles from economics must be considered, such as the elasticity of demand. These sales promotion devices are effective only as long as they are directed at segments of consumers who possess different elasticities of demand from those who do not use the incentives. Thus, if every customer were given a price-off deal, the company has effectively lowered the price of the product. Instead, the company wants to direct sales incentives to segments that possess different elasticities of demand in order to maximize sales. For example, the car manufacturers begin to lower the price of autos to car dealers only towards the end of the "car year." Dealers can pass on these incentives to consumers, if they choose. The point is that the people who buy cars late in the year are likely to have different price elasticities than those who buy cars early in the year. In effect, a two-tier pricing system exists which maximizes total car sales and profits.

Public Relations   Public relations is a broad area that focuses on the interface between the corporation and consumers. Areas of concern include managing the publicity that emerges from the firm and handling consumer questions and complaints. The areas of consumer behavior that apply most directly to public relations are those of attitude formation and change. In particular, the manager of public relations must be concerned with the effects of negative publicity on the firm and its products. Earlier in the text it was noted that negative information has a disproportionate impact on consumer attitudes. Individuals involved in the public relations effort therefore must monitor news media and consumers constantly in order to identify quickly any negative information about the company that is seeping into the marketplace. Types of negative information a manager may have to deal with include: rumors, product recalls, product disasters (e.g., an airplane crash), corporate financial problems, illegal activities of senior corporate officials, and complaints of consumer groups about advertising.

In planning public relations activities the manager must be concerned with how the public will perceive the source of information and the message that is given. In many instances, corporate officials will act as spokespersons for the company. Providing training to these individuals in how to present themselves is an important task for companies that have a high public profile.

Similarly, determining what types of messages to provide to the public in response to negative information is crucial for managers. One study performed by the author of the textbook found that in circumstances in which early information on the extent of the problem is ambiguous, the type of message can be particularly important. In the study, a company was described as discovering that it had a product problem, but the extent of the problem was not immediately known. Subjects in the study then received a series of messages from the company which were described as given to the public at one-month intervals. Three different sets of the messages were created. In one set, the first message described the problem as extremely severe, the second message described the problem as not as severe as first thought. The final message described the problem as less severe than either of the first two messages. In another set, the first message described the problem as extremely minor, the second message described the problem as more serious than first thought, and the final message described the problem as even more serious than thought. Importantly, the final outcome in the two conditions was exactly the same. That is, the messages mirrored what could happen if a company takes a denial strategy versus a "let's-bring-it-into-the-open strategy." Consumer perceptions of the company were dramatically different in the two conditions. The company that first overestimated the seriousness of the problem was perceived much more positively than the company using the denial strategy.[24]

Pricing and Distribution Applications

Although the applications of consumer behavior principles are not as numerous in the areas of pricing and distribution, they are still important. The fewer points of application result in part from the fact that many managerial decisions regarding pricing and distribution are made relatively inflexible. For example, in the pricing area many companies use fixed rules for pricing, such as cost plus 10 percent. However, when companies adopt greater flexibility in their pricing policies, the importance of recognizing consumer behavior ideas increases. Some of these ideas are discussed below.

Pricing Applications   One of the major areas of application of consumer behavior principles to pricing is in predicting the likely impact of price changes on consumers. That is, how will consumers react when companies raise or lower the price of a product? An economic analysis would predict that such price changes would result in either an increase or decrease in quantity purchased because of the effects of the law of demand. However, certain consumer behavior ideas suggest that in some instances the law of demand may not hold. In particular, Weber's Law suggests that the price change must be greater than some threshold level before the change is recognized. If the price is being lowered, it should be lowered enough so that consumers will perceive that a change has occurred. In contrast, if the price is being raised, in most instances the company would prefer that the price increase not be enough for consumers to perceive a difference.

In addition to studying how consumers process information on price changes, researchers are also interested in the effects of price changes on consumer attitudes. One relationship that has been discussed is the price-quality relationship. Under some circumstances consumers will estimate the quality of a product based in part upon its price. Companies will frequently attempt to use the price-quality relationship in order to distinguish their products from the competition. For example, the advertisements by Curtis-Mathes for their televisions use the tag line, "Curtis-Mathes TV sets are expensive, but they're darn well worth it." If a company wishes to develop an image of exclusivity, setting the price at a high level is one means of accomplishing such a goal.

In some instances the price-quality relationship can work against companies. For example, part of the marketing strategy developed by MCI in competing against AT&T is to price its services at a lower level. The result is the possible perception that the services are of lower quality. AT&T sought to further such a reaction in its advertising.

Of course, managers cannot forget to consider the various economic principles relevant to setting prices. Having an understanding of the law of demand, of demand elasticities, of opportunity cost, and of the principles of scarcity can influence pricing decisions. Noteworthy is the fact that many of these ideas are particularly relevant to the use of sales promotion devices that rely on various methods of changing the price of a product, such as sales, coupons, and rebates.

Distribution   Perhaps the area of consumer behavior most relevant to the distribution component of the marketing mix is the study of the consumer's decision process. In particular, the extent to which consumers engage in search behavior should influence the intensity of distribution. If a product is bought under low-involvement conditions, it is unlikely that consumers will engage in much search behavior prior to buying it. Therefore, for companies that sell low-involvement products, a diverse distribution system is usually needed. In other words, the company should seek to place the product in as many retail outlets as possible in order to have the product available whenever a need arises that it could fulfill. To identify such low-involvement products in extensive distribution, one has merely to look in most convenience stores. These stores focus on supplying such products to the public as toothpaste, soft drinks, bread, and laundry detergent. (In some instances, products such as soft drinks, toothpaste, and toilet paper can be highly involving. Thus, one finds the emotional reactions of some consumers to the reformulation of Coca-Cola in 1985. Similarly, shortages of toilet paper can result in massive hoarding of the product. In general, however, such products are relatively low in involvement.)

Another consumer behavior area of application is that of demographics. Companies must be concerned about where to place new retail outlets and where to place distribution centers. Analyzing population shifts among regions of the country can pay dividends in keeping costs down and in matching the distribution of the product to growth areas. Similarly, companies must be concerned with the placement of retail stores in cities and towns. Questions involving where to place shopping centers should be answered in part by analyzing population patterns and by assessing the demographic characteristics of the possible sites.

Even the placement of convenience stores should be made in part on the basis of the analysis of consumer behavior. For example, one fast-growing chain of convenience stores in the Rocky Mountain region has found that they can place two identical stores on opposite sides of a busy street in Denver and reach completely different segments of the population. The wide and busy street acts as a barrier so that customers are picked up only from cars going in one direction.

The study of consumer attitudes is also relevant to product or service distribution. Companies that sell products through networks of wholesalers and/or retailers must ensure that the image of the retailer matches the image of the product. If the product is being advertised as upscale and expensive, the company would not want it distributed through discount stores. In a similar manner, companies that operate through franchises want to ensure a consistency of image across the franchises. For example, McDonald's Corporation has created a highly detailed contract which its franchisees must sign. The contract sets out specific guidelines which the franchisee must follow in maintaining the property and in serving the customers. Through these means, McDonald's can create a uniform product that consumers appreciate as they go from store to store across the country.

CONSUMER VERSUS INDUSTRIAL PURCHASE BEHAVIOR

The thrust of this text has been on marketing products, services, and ideas to consumers. Earlier in the book it was argued, however, that the concepts that apply to consumer marketing can also be used in industrial marketing.

It is somewhat controversial to state that the same principles apply to both consumer and industrial marketing. Traditionally, these areas have been separated, and it has been argued that a dichotomy exists between the fields. More recently, however, researchers have begun to believe that many more similarities than differences exist between industrial and consumer marketing.

Table 20–6 describes a series of proposed differences between consumer and **industrial/organizational purchase behavior.** The differences are classified as to whether they originate from market characteristics, product differences, organizational set-ups, or other factors. For example, in the area of market differences, it has been argued that industrial markets tend to be driven by derived demand. That is, the demand for industrial products is created by demand for other products in which the industrial products are used. Other supposed market differences involve the belief that industrial buyers are more rational, more knowledgeable, more geographically concentrated, and so forth.

Differences between industrial and consumer buying have also been argued to exist in the types of products bought. Industrial products have been described as more technically complex, as less frequently bought, as having higher service requirements, and as involving greater amounts of negotiation. Another area of difference involves the organizational setup in which industrial buyers are viewed as having greater reciprocity with sellers, as more concerned with the adequacy of supply, and as having a shorter channel length. Finally, authors have argued that message appeals, delivery importance, sales force compensation, and leasing arrangements are different for industrial and consumer buyers.

In most instances, however, the proposed differences between industrial and consumer buying have been shown to be illusory. Counterexamples can be given for most cases in which a difference is purported to exist. For ex-

Table 20–6   Dimensions of Differences Between Industrial and Consumer Marketing

Market	Product	Organization of Operational Set-up	Others
Derived vs. primary demand	Technical complexity	Channel length	Message appeal
Elasticity of demand	Purchase frequency	Promotion mix	Delivery importance
Demand fluctuation	Classification	Reciprocity	Sales force compensation
Number of suppliers	Service requirement	Adequacy of supply	Sales force training
Number of buyers	Amount of information search	Degree of integration	Leasing
Number of influencers	Negotiated prices		
Geographic concentration	Dollar volume		
Knowledgeability	Riskiness		
Rationality			

SOURCE: Based on Table 1 in Edward Fern and James Brown, "The Industrial/Consumer Marketing Dichotomy," *Journal of Marketing, 48,* Spring 1984, 68–77.

ample, in many cases consumer demand is derived. The purchase of flour, sugar, gifts, lumber, and many other items is made so that these products can be used to make something else. Furthermore, industry buys many products for primary demand purposes, such as typewriters and light bulbs.[25] One can find instances in which consumers engage in group decision making (e.g., a family decision) and instances in which a single person controls an industrial purchase. While the number of buyers of industrial products is often smaller, in some instances the numbers do run into the hundreds of thousands for materials such as racks, heavy duty carpeting, and so forth. Similarly, one can find instances in which consumers act highly rationally, and industrial purchasers act irrationally. One can find circumstances in which consumers engage in a great deal of negotiation for prices, such as when buying a car or stereo. Consumers not only engage in the leasing of products, such as automobiles, but also buy extremely technical products, such as computers. In sum, the differences between industrial and consumer purchasing are a matter of degree. It is not a dichotomy.

In one discussion of industrial versus consumer buying, one research team suggested that a good way of examining the question involves asking whether more differences exist *between* industrial and consumer marketing than *within* industrial or consumer marketing. That is, if a greater number of ways exist to market products to industrial markets than there are distinctions between industrial and consumer markets, no reason for the dichotomy exists.[26]

To test this idea, the researchers developed three general propositions and examined whether they applied to both industrial and consumer purchasing. When industrial and consumer buying were compared, the authors found that the propositions applied equally well to the two areas. For example, Proposition 2 stated that the more frequently buyers purchase a product, the more continuous the availability of the offering and the communication associated with the offering should be. The authors argued that the proposition applied not only to such consumer products as beer, bread, milk, cigarettes, and candy bars, but also to such industrial products as office supplies and janitorial supplies in industrial markets. Based upon such reasoning, the authors concluded that more differences exist in marketing within a consumer or industrial market than exist when moving from a consumer to an industrial market.

In summary, the same consumer behavior principles that apply to consumer marketing apply to industrial marketing. This statement should not be surprising when one recognizes that people make the decisions in both instances. Thus, the same sociological, economic, anthropological, psychological, and consumer behavior principles are working. When differences are found in the buying behavior of organizations and consumers, it will be because of the different demands of the tasks and different organizational setups, not because the principles change. Thus, firms may market their products/services differently in some instances to industries and consumers. However, the differences in marketing result from variations in the type of product bought rather than differences in the principles which guide buying behavior.

An excellent visual depiction of this point is found in Figure 20–5. The figure shows the number of products bought by industrial buyers and consumer buyers on the vertical axis and the type of products bought on the horizontal axis. Two curves are drawn—one for consumer buying and one for industrial buying. What the curves suggest is that the actual marketing mix is similar for many products, such as housing, tools, autos, and electrical motors. Where differences are found, they are at the extremes. The marketing mix for a consumer product, such as toothpaste, will not precisely find an industrial counterpart. On the other hand, the marketing mix for selling an industrial product, such as a nuclear power plant, will not have a consumer counterpart. All in all, however, more similarities than differences exist between consumer and industrial marketing. Furthermore, the differences result from variations in the type of product sold and in organizational structures rather than from differences in buying behavior principles.

Figure 20–5   **Industrial versus consumer goods marketing. (Based on a discussion in Jagdish Sheth, "The Specificity of Industrial Marketing,"** *P.U. Management Review,* **2, January–December 1979, 53–56.)**

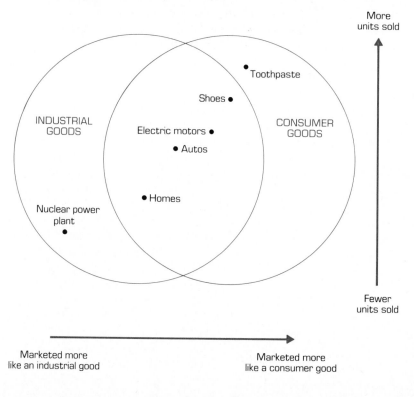
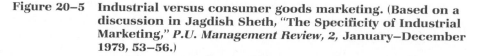

THE BUYING OF GOODS AND SERVICES: IS THERE A DIFFERENCE?

Throughout the textbook the point has been made that principles of consumer behavior can be applied to the marketing of services as well as the marketing of goods. Thus, the environmental, situational, and individual factors that influence consumers in the buying process for goods will also influence them in the buying process for services.

During the 1980s a growing literature developed on services marketing. The general thrust of the literature is that in a number of ways the marketing of services is different from the marketing of goods. Table 20–7 identifies the areas in which services marketing is said to be different from product marketing. The four major areas of difference are: (1) **intangibility** (services are more intangible than products), (2) **inseparability** (production and consumption are inseparable for services), (3) **heterogeneity** (greater chances exist for variations in performance of services than in the production of products), and (4) **perishability** (services cannot be saved but are consumed when performed).[27]

Authors may disagree over the importance of these differences, but they can agree that a product is more concrete than a service. One can see, hold, and feel a product. A product can be retained after its production. However, the key point in the view of a consumer researcher is whether the processes used in the purchase of products and services are different.

One author has argued that consumer decision processes differ between goods and services.[28] After reviewing the work on services, the author developed several hypotheses concerning how the decision process may differ when a consumer buys a product or a service. Several of these hypotheses follow:

Table 20–7   Unique Features and Problems of Services Marketing

Unique Feature	Resulting Problem
Intangibility	Services cannot be stored
	Cannot protect services through patents
	Cannot readily display or communicate services
	Prices are difficult to set
Inseparability	Consumer involved in production
	Other consumers involved in production
	Centralized mass production of services difficult
Heterogeneity	Standardization and quality control difficult
Perishability	Services cannot be inventoried

SOURCE: Adapted from Valarie Zeithaml, A. Parasuraman, and Leonard L. Berry, "Problems and Strategies in Services Marketing," *Journal of Marketing*, 49, Spring 1985, 33–46.

H1. Consumers seek and rely more on information from personal sources than from nonpersonal sources when evaluating services prior to purchase.

H2. Consumers engage in greater postpurchase evaluation and information seeking with services than with products.

H3. Consumers use price and physical facilities as the major cues to service quality.

H4. The consumer's evoked set of alternatives is smaller with services than with products.

H5. Consumers adopt innovations in services more slowly than they adopt innovations in goods.

H6. Consumers perceive greater risks when buying services than when buying products.

A couple of points should be made about this set of hypothesized differences between buying services and products. First, they are merely hypotheses. They have not been tested via research. Second, each of the hypotheses states only that a particular consumer behavior process occurs to a greater or lesser degree when buying a service than when buying a product. For example, hypothesis 6 states only that *more* perceived risk exists when a consumer buys a service as opposed to a product. Nothing is said to indicate that somehow the process of risk perception is fundamentally different when buying services than when buying products. The same point also holds true for each of the other hypotheses.

In many respects the efforts to study services marketing parallel those of industrial marketing. When researchers first began to differentiate industrial from consumer marketing, they attempted to argue that somehow the fundamental processes were different in the two fields. Similarly, at this early stage of investigating services marketing, some are making the same argument—i.e., that services marketing is fundamentally different from product marketing.

What this author believes is that within a few years researchers will reach conclusions parallel to those found with industrial marketing. In extreme examples, consumers may act somewhat differently when purchasing services as compared to products. However, the basic psychological, economic, sociological, and anthropological processes will operate in each instance. Furthermore, upon careful examination researchers will find that more differences exist in the way consumers purchase various types of services than exist in the way consumers purchase products versus services.

SOME CONCLUDING COMMENTS

The textbook you have just completed has a number of themes and goals. The purpose of this last section is to review briefly these themes and goals and to identify some future directions of the field. The themes of the text include developing an understanding of the consumer environment, of the processes influencing the individual consumer, and of the managerial and public policy implications of these themes. These are reviewed briefly in the following subsections.

The Consumer Environment

In the culture of the United States consumers have a myriad of products, services, and ideas that they may acquire, consume, and dispose. As the model of consumer behavior in Chapter 1 denotes, these consumption activities are influenced by a variety of environmental forces that affect the consumer's "lifespace." The lifespace is composed of the totality of factors impacting upon the consumer at any given point in time. These environmental forces are analyzed in the nine chapters making up Part II of the text and include:

1. The economic environment.
2. The various cultural and subcultural environments.
3. The effects of groups, such as the family.
4. The effects of other people.
5. The effects of various consumer situations.

The Study of the Individual Consumer

Each of the environmental forces acts to push the consumer towards particular consumption activities. However, in studying how these factors influence consumers, one must also investigate the factors that influence how individual consumers react to the various environmental factors. The elements of the person are discussed in the eight chapters found in Part I of the text. These topics of discussion include:

1. Consumer buying: the decision-making process.
2. Motivation.
3. Personality and psychographics.
4. Information processing.
5. Learning.
6. Attitudes.
7. Persuasion.
8. Postpurchase processes.

The Managerial and Public Policy Implications

One of the major goals of the book is to show how the investigation of the consumer environment and of the individual consumer could improve the decision making of marketing managers and public policy makers. Each chapter contains specific illustrations of the application of the consumer behavior principles that are identified. In addition, Chapters 19 and 20 discuss respectively the public policy and managerial implications of consumer behavior concepts.

One of the major teaching points of the model of consumer behavior presented in Chapter 1 is that to understand the consumption process one must take a holistic view. That is, the various forces operating on the consumer do not act individually and separately to influence consumption. Instead, they combine to create pressures to propel the consumer towards various actions. Their effects are moderated by the learning history of the consumer, by his or her particular motivational structure, personality, and attitudes, and by his or her individual way of processing information. One must look at the consumer and his or her environment as a whole in order to achieve even a rudimentary understanding of the consumption process.

The Leadership Role of the Consumer Researcher

Although consumer researchers obtain many of their ideas from observing the actions of managers and public policy makers, they also have a leadership role to play. Because the consumer researcher does not have the everyday requirements of making profits or of creating and enforcing laws and regulations, he or she can take a broader view of the consumption process and its relation to our society. The consumer researcher is in a unique position to identify long-term trends and possibly spot new ones that may or may not be of benefit to the society.

An example of the ability of consumer researchers to take such a broad view of society is the work being done on materialism. **Materialism** may be defined as the importance a consumer attaches to worldly possessions, where at the highest levels possessions assume a central place in life and provide the greatest sources of satisfaction and dissatisfaction.[29] The general view is that although materialism has existed since ancient times, it has only been within the last few hundred years that the masses have had the discretionary income to seek psychological well-being through the ownership of goods.[30] As stated by one well-known consumer researcher:

> The rationale for studying differences in materialism is that the resulting knowledge and measurement may be useful for examining the human and social impact of a much-neglected aspect of consumer behavior.[31]

Arguments can be made that at either extreme (i.e., the total absence of or the complete domination of materialism) materialism can be harmful. One role of the researcher, then, who studies materialism is to identify from a historical perspective the extent to which materialism influences the functioning of a society, from the establishment of interpersonal relationships to the making of laws to the extent of the happiness of its members.[32]

In addition to assisting marketing managers and public policy makers, consumer researchers should, in the view of this author, attempt to perform the research necessary to improve society. Consumer researchers can help to improve society through their more traditional role of investigating the environmental and personal determinants of consumption. In addition, however, it is through the study of topics such as materialism, consumer perceptions of corporate ethical behavior, and cross-cultural consumption patterns that consumer researchers can take the broad, macroview which is also required for playing a leadership role in improving society. The investigation of materialism, ethics, and cross-cultural consumption are at the leading edge of consumer behavior thought at the present time. One can anticipate an enlargement of their discussion in future editions of the text.

Key Terms

Marketing environment
Specific positioning
Competitive positioning
Perceptual maps
Repositioning
Behavioral segmentation
Demand elasticities
Industrial Classification
   System
Industrial macrosegmen-
   tation
Industrial microsegmen-
   tation

Concept testing
Product development
Market testing
Industrial/organizational
   purchase behavior
Intangibility
Inseparability
Heterogeneity
Perishability
Materialism

Review Questions

1. Identify the four key managerial strategy areas in which consumer behavior may be of assistance.
2. Identify five of the six environmental areas in which consumer behavior information may be of assistance to managers. In addition, give two specific examples of the consumer behavior information that would be of assistance in each area.
3. What is meant by the idea of a reciprocity between consumers and the environment?
4. Identify and give examples of two different types of positioning.
5. What is a perceptual map? How can perceptual maps be used to help position products?
6. How have managers attempted to reposition Spam, Velveeta, and Snickers?
7. What are the three factors that should be present for a segment to be managerially useful?
8. Identify the bases for segmenting the consumer market.
9. What is the single most important type of information that marketers should gather for purposes for segmentation? Why?
10. What is meant by behavioral segmentation? What are three types of behavioral segmentation?
11. How does the segmentation of industrial markets differ from the segmentation of consumer markets?
12. What are the four areas of product development in which consumer behavior principles may assist managers?
13. List eight of the ten consumer behavior concepts

that can be used to assist promotion. Give an example of an application for each of the concepts.
14. Identify one example each of how a consumer behavior principle can assist the manager in: sales promotion, public relations, pricing, and distribution.
15. What are the four areas in which industrial and consumer markets may differ? Give specific examples of each of these areas.
16. What is meant by the statement that more differences exist *within* industrial or consumer markets than *between* industrial and consumer markets?
17. To what extent do the consumer processes that influence the purchase of goods differ from the processes affecting services?

Discussion Questions

1. You are in the planning department at the corporate headquarters of General Motors. You have just been assigned the task of identifying the likely environmental factors that will be influencing consumer tastes and preferences for automobiles over the next ten years. Outline the various factors you would consider in making such an analysis.
2. A reciprocal relationship exists between consumers and the environment. Thinking in terms of both individual and industrial consumers, what are three different areas of consumer-environmental reciprocity? What are the public policy and managerial implications of these reciprocal relationships?
3. Identify two current examples of specific and competitive positioning of products or services. How effective do you consider each of these marketing strategies to be?
4. Perceptual maps can be used to identify a brand's position relative to competitors. Based upon your personal knowledge and understanding of the universities that high school students in your region consider, develop a perceptual map that the "typical" student might have of these universities.
5. Consider the automobile industry or other major industry with which you are familiar, such as cosmetics. Among the brands of autos with which you are familiar, which are highly differentiated from other brands? Which are poorly differentiated? How could the poorly differentiated brands be better distinguished from their competitors?
6. Again consider the automobile industry or other

major industry with which you are familiar, such as cosmetics. Identify as many variables as you can on which the industry appears to segment the marketplace. Furthermore, identify specific brands that target the various segments. Are there segments of the marketplace that have not been adequately reached?

7. Suppose that universities and colleges decided to engage in benefit segmentation and specifically mentioned their benefits provided in their promotional activities. First, identify the various benefits that colleges and universities provide students. Second, sketch out a print advertisement for your college or university which promotes the benefits it offers.

8. You work in the planning department for a company that has developed a prototype of a new processed beef product. The product tastes and looks just like a high-quality piece of steak. However, it is made of beef chuck and costs about half as much as steak. Furthermore, it contains about half the calories and cholesterol of steak. Outline the consumer behavior considerations that you would have in developing the marketing mix for the product.

9. Compare and contrast the various differences you think might exist in marketing the IBM Personal Computer to individual consumers versus industry.

10. Compare and contrast the marketing of fast food (a service industry) to the marketing of clothing (a product industry). To what extent do consumer behavior principles apply equally well to each industry? Please cite specific instances in which the examples do or do not apply equally to each industry.

References

1. Yoram Wind and Thomas Robertson, "Marketing Strategy: New Directions for Theory and Research," *Journal of Marketing*, 47, Spring 1983, 12.

2. "Thermos Hopes to Cool Competition with Revamped Marketing Strategy," *Advertising Age*, December 23, 1983, 1, 12.

3. Philip Kotler, *Marketing Management: Analysis, Planning, and Control*, 4th ed., Englewood Cliffs, N.J.: Prentice-Hall, Inc., 1980, 23–24.

4. Macmillan Publishing Company, *1984 Annual Report*, 25.

5. Neil Frude, "The Affectionate Machine," *Psychology Today*, December 1983, 23–24.

6. Kotler, *Marketing Management*.

7. Scott Hume, "An Un-happy Seven-Up Returns to an Old Theme," *Advertising Age*, March 11, 1985, 10.

8. John Kinski, "Consumer Perceptions of Meat Products," Master's thesis, Oklahoma State University, 1985.

9. Thomas Robertson, Joan Zielinski, and Scott Ward, *Consumer Behavior*, Glenview, Ill.: Scott, Foresman and Company, 1984.

10. "These Days It's Miller Time Less Often, Worrying Brewer," *The Wall Street Journal*, February 10, 1983, 33.

11. Kotler, *Marketing Management*, 195.

12. Trish Hall, "Smoking of Cigarettes Seems to be Becoming a Lower-Class Habit," *The Wall Street Journal*, June 25, 1985, 1, 16.

13. Hall, "Smoking of Cigarettes."

14. Ibid.

15. *Associated Press*, "High Tax May Help Cut Smoking," *The Daily Oklahoman*, September 9, 1985, 3.

16. "1985 Oklahoma Beef Commission Marketing Plan," *Oklahoma Beef Commission*, Oklahoma City, Okla. 1985.

17. Joseph Plummer, "Emotions Important for Successful Advertising," *Marketing News*, April 12, 1985, 18.

18. Russell, W. Belk, "Situational Variables and Consumer Behavior," *Journal of Consumer Research*, 2, December 1975, 157–164.

19. Peter Dickson, "Person-Situation: Segmentation's Missing Link," *Journal of Marketing*, 46, Fall 1982, 56–64.

20. Michael D. Hutt, and Thomas Speh, *Industrial Marketing Management*, New York, N.Y.: The Dryden Press, 1981.

21. Kotler, *Marketing Management*.

22. Ibid., p. 321.

23. Edmund Faison, *Advertising: A Behavioral Approach for Managers*, New York, N.Y.: John Wiley & Sons, Inc., 1980.

24. John C. Mowen and S. B. Pollman, "An Exploratory Study Investigating Order Effects in Reporting Negative Corporate Communications," *Advances in Consumer Research*, IX, Andrew Mitchell (ed.), Ann

Arbor, Mich.: Association for Consumer Research, 1982, 215–220.

25. For an excellent discussion of the industrial/consumer dichotomy, see Edward J. Fern and James R. Brown, "The Industrial/Consumer Marketing Dichotomy: A Case of Insufficient Evidence," *Journal of Marketing, 48,* Spring 1985, 68–77.

26. Fern and Brown, "The Industrial/Consumer."

27. Valarie Zeithaml, A. Parasuraman, and Leonard Berry, "Problems and Strategies in Services Marketing," *Journal of Marketing, 49,* Spring 1985, 33–46.

28. Valarie Zeithaml, "How Consumer Evaluation Processes Differ Between Goods and Services," *Marketing of Services,* James Donnelly and W. R. George (eds.), Chicago, Ill.: American Marketing Association, 1981. 186–190. The numbering of the hypotheses found in the text differs from that found in the article.

29. Russell W. Belk, "Three Scales to Measure Constructs Related to Materialism: Reliability, Validity, and Relationships to Measures of Happiness," *Advances in Consumer Research, XI,* Thomas Kinnear (ed.), Provo, Utah: Association for Consumer Research, 1984, 291–297.

30. Robert S. Mason, *Conspicuous Consumption: A Study of Exceptional Consumer Behavior,* Westmead, England: Gower, 1981.

31. Russell W. Belk, "Materialism: Trait Aspects of Living in the Material World," *Journal of Consumer Research, 12,* December 1985, 265–280.

32. Belk, "Materialism: Trait Aspects."

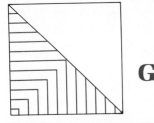

Glossary

Absolute threshold: The lowest level at which a stimulus can be detected.

Acceptable risk: The level of risk that a consumer will tolerate when purchasing a product or service.

Acculturation: The difficult task of learning a new culture.

Achievement motivation: The motivation identified by David McClelland to strive for success and to perform up to one's capabilities.

Actual product performance: A consumer's perception of the level of performance displayed by a product. Actual performance is compared to expected performance in order to determine product satisfaction.

Actual state: The state of being that is experienced by a consumer at any particular point in time. When the actual diverges sufficiently from the desired state, need recognition is said to occur.

Adaptation level: The level of intensity of a stimulus to which a consumer has become accustomed or adapted.

Adult toy: Products targeted to adults that may be used as toys, such as sports cars.

Advertising substantiation: The concept developed by the Federal Trade Commission that companies have to provide evidence for the truth of their advertising claims.

Advertising wear-out: The concept that with too many exposures to an advertisement consumer's responses to it may become more negative.

Affect referral heuristic: A rule of thumb in which a consumer chooses a product based upon an overall recollection of his or her evaluation of an alternative.

Affluent–average guy split: The idea that during recessions the affluent are frequently less harmed by the economy than the less affluent.

AIO statements: Used in psychographic inventories, AIO statements obtain information on consumers' activities, interests, and opinions.

Androgyny: A social psychological personality characteristic denoting an individual who can react to a given situation with appropriate masculine or feminine characteristics.

Antecedent states: The temporary physiological and mood states that a consumer brings to a consumption situation.

Aspirational group: A group to whom an individual would like to belong. If it is impossible for the individual to belong to the group, it becomes a symbolic group for the person.

Assimilation effects: The idea that a communication may be viewed as more congruent with the position of the receiver than it really is, because it falls within the latitude of acceptance.

Associationists: A group of cognitive psychologists who during the first half of the twentieth century investigated the processes through which people form associations between stimuli.

Atmospherics: The process through which consumer reactions may be influenced by the design of buildings and spaces, including their interior space, the layout of the aisles, the texture of the carpets and walls, and their scents, colors, shapes, and sounds as experienced by the customers.

Attitude: The amount of affect or feeling for or against a stimulus.

Attribute-benefit beliefs: The consumer's perception of the extent to which a particular attribute will result in or provide a particular benefit.

Attribute importance: The relative importance of a product or service characteristic to a consumer in relation to other characteristics.

Attribute-object beliefs: The consumer's perception of the extent to which a particular object possesses a particular attribute.

Attitude-toward-the object models: Models of consumer choice that are based upon how consumers combine their beliefs about product attributes to form attitudes about various brand alternatives.

Attributes: The characteristics or features that an object has.

Attribution theory: A set of theories that specify the various means through which people identify the causes of action of themselves, others, and objects.

Audience erosion: The idea that with the proliferation of remote-control television devices consumers can "zap" out commercials, resulting in an erosion of the audience watching advertisements.

Augmenting principle: A principle from one of the attribution theory models which states that the role of a given cause in producing a given effect is discounted if other plausible causes are also present.

Autonomic decision: Decisions of lesser importance that either the husband or wife may make independently of the other.

Awareness set: A subset of the total universe of potential brands and products available of which a consumer is aware.

Baby-boom generation: The large post–World War II group of people generally viewed as born between 1946 and 1964.

Baby bust: A period after 1964 when fertility rates plunged far below replacement level, resulting in a fewer children being born in the United States.

Background factors: The environmental influencers such as the consumer's socioeconomic status, sex, age, social class, and religious background.

Balance theory: A type of cognitive consistency approach in which people are viewed as maintaining a logical and consistent set of interconnected beliefs.

Behavioral bases for segmentation: Bases for segmentation based upon the behavior of consumers. Such behavioral bases include segmenting based upon price elasticity, benefits sought, and usage rate.

Behavioral economics: An approach to economics based upon the investigation of the behavior of individual consumers. An example is the use of survey research methods to assess the economic confidence of consumers.

Behavioral influence perspective: Behavioral influence occurs when strong environmental forces create circumstances in which the consumer is propelled to perform some action without developing strong feelings or beliefs about the action.

Behavioral intention model: A consumer choice model which states that behavior results from the formation of specific intentions to behave.

Beliefs: The cognitive knowledge people have of the relations among attributes, benefits, and objects.

Benefit segmentation: The division of the market into relatively homogeneous groups of consumers based upon a similarity of needs.

Benefits: The outcomes that product or service attributes may provide.

Black leisure activities: The specific pattern of leisure activities associated with the black subculture.

Black segments: Four segments of blacks have been identified—Negroes, blacks, Afro-Americans, and foreign black immigrants.

Bogies: Fear rumors that may spook the marketplace.

Boomerang effect: When messages fall into the latitude of rejection, the receiver of the communication may view the message as more extreme than it really is.

Born-Again Christians: Persons belonging to the fundamentalist subculture who view Jesus as their personal savior and regularly read the Bible and Christian literature.

Brand expectation: The expectations that a consumer forms regarding the performance of a brand.

Brand loyalty: The biased behavioral response, expressed over time by some decision-making unit with respect to one or more alternative brands out of a set of such brands which results from a psychological (decision-making) process.

Buyer's regret: A postpurchase phenomenon in which the preference for a chosen alternative actually falls below that of a rejected alternative.

CAD: A personality scale developed to measure the interpersonal orientation of consumers. CAD stands for "compliance, aggression, detachment."

Categories of adopters: Groupings that describe how quickly consumers adopt new products, including: innovators, early adopters, early majority, late majority, and laggards.

Central route to persuasion: Persuasion that occurs under high involvement circumstances. It is marked by the creation of cognitive responses.

Choice: The process in which consumers make a choice between two or more brand alternatives.

Choice behavior fallacy: The error of using only one measure or social indicator, such as social class, to predict consumption behavior.

Classical conditioning: A type of learning in which a conditioned stimulus is paired with an unconditioned stimulus. Through repetition the conditioned stimulus will eventually elicit a conditioned response.

Closure: A principle of perceptual organization which describes the tendency of people to fill in missing information in order to create a holistic image.

Clutter: The problem of consumers being exposed to so many ads that confusion results.

Coding: A process in which a person draws associations between information to be learned and that already in memory in order to transfer more readily the information from short-term to long-term memory.

Cognitive differentiation: The complexity with which a consumer views a stimulus, such as a product. As the complexity of the schema with which consumers hold information increases, their cognitive differentiation increases.

Cognitive elements: Those people, objects, and qualities of objects about which a person may think and cognitively examine.

Cognitive era: The period from 1975–1981 when consumer research was dominated by an emphasis on the study of information processing and attitudes.

Cognitive learning: Learning processes that are not considered to require reinforcement and that involve such mental activities as thinking, remembering, problem solving, developing insight, forming concepts, and learning ideas.

Cognitive personality theory: A group of personality theories that focus on identifying individual differences in how consumers process and react to information.

Cognitive responses: The thoughts consumers may develop in response to messages.

Communications situation: The type of situation in which a consumer is positioned when a communication is received.

Comparative appraisal: A process in which a person evaluates his or her attitudes and abilities by comparing them with the attitudes and abilities of others.

Comparative message: A type of message in which the communicator compares the positive and negative aspects of his position to the positive and negative aspects of a competitor's position.

Compensatory models: A class of choice models in which consumers are viewed as analyzing each alternative in a broad evaluative fashion. A choice is said to be compensatory when high ratings on some attributes may compensate for low ratings on other attributes.

Competitive positioning: A strategy of positioning a product or service by relating its attributes to those possessed by the leading brands. Thus, the brand is positioned in relation to the attributes of competing brands.

Complaint behavior: The overt actions taken by consumers to bring their product or service dissatisfaction to the attention of others.

Compliance: The act of conforming to the wishes of another person or group. Compliance involves the conformity to the wishes of the group without necessarily accepting the group's dictates.

Concept testing: The pretesting of the product concept among consumers.

Conditioned response: The response elicited by the conditioned stimulus when classical conditioning occurs.

Conditioned stimulus: A previously neutral stimulus which when paired with an unconditioned stimulus may elicit a conditioned response.

Conformity: A change in behavior or belief as a result of real or imagined group or individual pressure.

Conjunctive heuristic: A type of choice heuristic in which the consumer sets minimum cutoffs on each product attribute. If the product rating falls below the minimum cutoff level on any attribute, the product is rejected from further consideration.

Conservation behaviors: Actions taken by consumers to conserve resources, including curtailment behaviors, maintenance behaviors, and efficiency behaviors.

Constant-sum scales: In such a scale respondents are asked to divide a certain number of points among attributes proportionate to the importance of each attribute.

Consumer behaviors: Everything that people do that is related to acquiring, disposing, and using products and services.

Consumer involvement: The level of perceived personal importance and/or interest evoked by a stimulus (or stimuli) within a specific situation.

Consumer primacy: The concept that the consumer should be at the center of the marketing effort.

Consumer Product Safety Commission: This agency investigates the causes of consumer product accidents and develops appropriate regulatory responses to consumer safety issues.

Consumer ritual: Standardized sequences of actions that are periodically repeated.

Consumer situation: Those temporary environmental and personal factors that involve the time and place of a consumer activity, influence buying behavior, and do not include the consumer's long-term characteristics or the product's features.

Consumer socialization: Processes by which young people acquire skills, knowledge, and attitudes relevant to their functioning as consumers in the marketplace.

Consumer well-being: The extent to which an individual's wants are satisfied.

Consumerism: The set of activities of government, business, independent organizations, and concerned consumers that are designed to protect the rights of consumers.

Consumption situation: The type of consumer situation that exists during the act of consumption of a product or service.

Context effects: The concept that the background or context in which stimuli are embedded will influence the perception of the stimuli. Thus, the background programming in which an advertisement is placed may influence the interpretation of the advertisement.

Continuous innovations: A modification of an existing product to improve performance, taste, reliability, and so forth. Continuous innovations result in few, if any, consumer lifestyle changes.

Contrast effect: Occurs when the attitude statement falls into the latitude of rejection so that it is perceived as more opposed to the receiver's position than perhaps it really is.

Corrective advertising: Advertising mandated by a federal agency to be employed to correct consumer impressions that were formed by previous misleading advertising.

Corporate social responsibility: The idea that business has an obligation to help society with its problems by offering some of its resources.

Counterarguments: A type of cognitive response which occurs when the consumer begins to think of arguments which refute the claims of the message.

Covert consumer behavior: The intentions which consumers form to behave in a particular way with regard to the acquisition, disposition, and use of products and services.

Cross-cultural analysis: The study of foreign cultures, and their values, languages, and customs.

Crowding: A psychological state which occurs when a person perceives that his or her movements are restricted because of limited space.

Cultural ethnocentricity: The feeling among some consumers that the values, beliefs, and ways of doing things as specified by one's own culture are "right" and "correct," and generally better than those of other cultures.

Cultural symbol: Entities which represent the shared ideas and concepts of a culture.

Culture: A set of socially acquired behavior patterns transmitted symbolically through language and other means to the members of a particular society. It is a way of life.

Deceptive advertising: An advertisement may be deemed deceptive if it has the "capacity to deceive a measurable segment of the public."

Decision-making perspective: Occurs when consumers move through a series of rational steps when making a purchase. These steps include: problem recognition, search, alternative evaluation, choice, and post purchase evaluation.

Decision process: The steps through which consumers move when purchasing a product or service, including problem recognition, search, alternative evaluation, choice, and post purchase evaluation.

Decorative roles: The use of women in advertisements as adornments to products in order to merely make the product look prettier.

Decreasing marginal utility: The concept that as a consumer obtains more of something, each additional unit brings less utility or satisfaction.

Defense mechanisms: Psychological adjustments made by people to keep themselves from recognizing personality qualities or motives which might lower self-esteem or heighten anxiety.

Demand curve shift: The shift of the demand curve to the right or left resulting from such factors as changes in population size or tastes and preferences.

Demand elasticities: The ratio of the percentage change in quantity demanded to the percentage change in the price of a good.

Demographics: Characteristics of various groups of people as assessed by such factors as age, sex, income, religion, marital status, nationality, education, family size, occupation, and ethnicity.

Depth interview: Long, probing one-on-one interviews to identify hidden reasons for purchasing products and services.

Desired state: The preferred state that a consumer would like to achieve. When differences between the desired state and the actual state are sufficiently large, a need state is said to exist.

Detached nuclear family: Pattern in which middle-class children strike off on their own to form families away from their parents.

Developmental phase: One of the consumer behavior eras that make up the history of the field. It lasted from about 1964 through 1974.

Difference threshold: The amount of difference in the level of two stimuli required for a person to detect a difference 50 percent of the time.

Diffusion: The idea that substances or even ideas can gradually spread through a medium of some type and reach a state of equilibrium.

Discretionary expenditure: Expenditures that can be postponed or eliminated.

Discriminative stimulus: A stimulus that occurs in the presence of a reinforcer and does not occur in its absence.

Discontinuous innovation: An innovation that produces a major change in the lifestyle of consumers.

Discounting principle: The idea from attribution theory that people will examine the environmental pressures that impede or propel a particular action. When a person moves with the environmental pressures, little understanding of the person's true motivations can be gained, and, therefore, the information is discounted.

Dissociative group: A reference group with whom the person does not wish to be associated.

Dissonance: An imbalanced state that results when a logical inconsistency exists among cognitive elements.

Do age: The age represented by what an elderly person is capable of doing.

Domain-specific values: Beliefs relevant to economic, social, religious, and other activities.

Door-in-the-face: A compliance technique that involves the requester first making a very large request, which is usually refused by the target. This request is then followed by a moderate request, which is more often complied with than if no large request had been made.

Drawing conclusions: A message strategy in which the presenter draws the conclusions of the message for the audience.

Drive: The physiological arousal that occurs when a need is felt.

Dynamic continuous innovations: Innovations that involve a major change in an existing product and result in minor changes in consumer lifestyles.

Economic cycle: The cycle that traces the flow of an economy. It has four phases—peak, recession, trough, and recovery.

Economic optimism-pessimism: The reactions of consumers to various economic and personal events that result in variations in feelings of economic confidence.

Ego: The component of the personality defined in psychoanalytic theory as standing for reason and good sense and as following the reality principle.

Emotional dissatisfaction: A postpurchase state that occurs when actual performance is perceived to be lower than expected performance.

Emotional satisfaction: A postpurchase state that occurs when the actual performance exceeds expected performance.

Enculturation: The process of learning one's own culture.

Enduring involvement: Occurs when a product relates to a consumer's needs, values, or self-concept.

Environmental analysis: The assessment of the forces and institutions external to the firm and of how these may impact upon the marketing effort.

Equity: Occurs when the ratio of the outcomes and inputs are perceived by one party of an exchange to equal the ratio of the outcomes and inputs of the other party to the exchange.

Ethnicity: A description of group bound together by ties of cultural homogeneity. Ethnic groups are frequently based around national origins.

Evangelicals: Fundamentalist Christians who believe in the "inerrancy" of the Bible and in converting the "unsaved."

Even-a-penny-will-help technique: A compliance technique based on the universal tendency for people to want to make themselves "look good."

Evoked set: Consists of those brands and products recalled from long-term memory that are acceptable for further consideration.

Exchange process: A process in which two parties transfer something of value between each other.

Expectancy confirmation: Results when the performance of a product is perceived to meet a consumer's expectations.

Expectations: A person's prior beliefs about what should happen in a given situation.

Expected product performance: The expectations that consumers form about the performance of a product. If such expectations are violated product dissatisfaction may result.

Experiential perspective: Occurs when consumers make purchases principally because of strong positive feelings rather than because of a decision process or strong environmental pressures.

Expressive men: A segment of the male market that is considered to be more open and expressive of feelings.

Expressive role: A role found in many groups that involves a person helping to maintain the group and provide emotional support for its members.

Extended family: Consists of the nuclear family plus the husband and/or wife's mother, father, and/or other kinfolk.

External attribution: An attribution of the cause of action to some factor outside of an individual, such as attributing the reason for an endorsement to the money paid to the endorser.

External roles: Involve communications and involvement with people outside of the family.

External search: The consumer soliciting information from outside sources rather than from his or her memory.

Extinction: A gradual reduction in the frequency of occurrence of an operant behavior resulting from a lack of reinforcement of the response.

Fads: Temporary fashion or other trends followed by a group.

Family decision stages: The steps in the decision process used by a family to purchase products or services.

Family life cycle: The idea that families may move through a series of stages in a developmental fashion.

Fear appeals: A type of message in which the communication is designed to create some level of fear in the target audience.

Federal Trade Commission: A federal agency charged with the responsibility of curtailing unfair trade practices and limiting monopolies.

Feel-age: A way of describing the age of an elderly consumer based upon the age that the person describes himself or herself as feeling.

Feminist market segment: A female market segment that tends to espouse feminist ideas. Tend to be younger, have more education, and more often be Jewish.

Fertility rate: The number of births per 1,000 women of childbearing age.

Field theory: An approach to the study of human behavior that takes as one of its basic tenets the principle that the analysis should begin with the study of the situation as a whole.

Figure and ground: A figure is the action object observed moving against the ground. The ground is the context or background within which the figure is observed.

Focus group: Long sessions in which five to ten consumers are encouraged to talk freely about their feelings and thoughts concerning a product or service.

Food and Drug Administration: A federal agency charged with the responsibility of protecting consumers from unsafe and impure foods, drugs, cosmetics, and therapeutic devices.

Foot-in-the-door technique: A compliance technique that operates through the influencer making two requests—the first, a small request, is followed by a moderately sized second request.

Forgetting: The inability to recall from memory some desired piece of information. It occurs when either the retrieval or the response-generation process breaks down.

Formal group: A group whose organization and structure are defined in writing.

Frame of reference: Represents an individual's prior experience, feelings, and interests on the issue in question.

Gatekeeper: Individuals who have the ability to control information to a decision maker.

General inventories: A means of classifying situations in which all situations are identified based upon a series of simple categories, such as pleasure, arousal, and dominance.

Gentrification: The process in which urban professionals begin to move back into the inner-city neighborhoods, displacing lower-income residents.

Gestalt psychologists: An influential group of psychologists prominent during the early twentieth century who believed that biological and psychological events do not influence behavior in isolation of each other.

Global values: Enduring beliefs about desired states of existence or modes of behavior.

Gravitational model: The concept that the size of a retail trading area can act like a magnet to exert pressure to attract shoppers.

Group: A set of individuals who interact with one another over some period of time and who share some common need or goal.

Group shifts: The tendency of groups of individuals to reach decisions that systematically differ from those that individuals reach.

Habit: A behavior that displays a repetitive quality, persists through time, has positive feelings attached to it, and is difficult to alter.

Habitual purchases: Purchases that occur as a result of a habit.

Hedonic consumption: The consumption of products and services based primarily on the desire to experience pleasure and happiness.

Hedonic relevance: The concept that a person reacts more strongly to stimuli that bring pleasure or pain.

Heuristic models: Choice models in which a consumer uses simplified rules of thumb to assist in choosing among brands.

Heuristics: Simplified "rules-of-thumb" used to make decision making less complex.

Hierarchies of effects: Various models that explain the order in which beliefs, feelings, and behavior occur.

High-involvement decision making: The decision process that occurs when consumers attach high personal importance to a decision. It is marked by extended decision making and high levels of information processing.

Higher-order conditioning: Occurs when a conditioned stimulus acts to classically condition another previously neutral stimulus.

Hispanic strata: A description of the Mexican-American population in the United States in which four groups are identified—recent immigrants and illegal aliens, radical Chicanos, conservative Chicanos, and the new rich.

Host-selling: The use of a program character to promote products.

Household: A group of people living under one roof.

Humorous messages: A type of message based on use of humor.

Husband-only fallacy: The use of social class position of the husband as the criterion for determining a family's status.

Ideal self: How a person would ideally like to perceive himself.

Identification: The normal process through which children acquire appropriate social roles through the conscious and unconscious copying of the behavior of significant others.

Immigration: To come into a country of which one is not a native for permanent residence.

Impersonal threats: Threats to behavioral freedom that come from impersonal sources.

Impulse buying: Buying action undertaken without a problem previously having been consciously recognized or a buying intention formed prior to entering the store.

Incentives: The products, services, and people that are perceived as satisfying needs.

Income effect: An economic principle stating that when prices are lowered, consumers can afford more of the product without giving up other alternatives.

Index of Consumer Sentiment: An index of consumer economic confidence developed at the University of Michigan Center for Survey Research.

Industrial classification system: Identifies groups of business firms that produce the same types of products.

Industrial microlevel and macrolevel segmentation: Segmenting industrial markets based on macro- (e.g., groups of companies having similar buying organizations) and micro- (e.g., identifying product and producer attributes sought by buyers) bases.

Inert set: Those brands to which a consumer is essentially indifferent.

Inept set: Those brands that a consumer considers unacceptable.

Informal group: A group that has no written organizational structure.

Informational influence: The influence of an individual by a group via the information the group transmits.

Informational overload: An uncomfortable state experienced by a consumer resulting from receiving more information than can be comfortably processed during a period of time.

Information processing: The process through which consumers receive stimulation, transform it into meaningful information, store the information in memory for later use, and retrieve the information for decision making.

Information search: The acquisition of information about products and services in order to solve a problem identified in the problem-recognition stage of the decision process.

Ingratiation: Self-serving tactics engaged in by one person to make himself or herself more attractive to another.

Ingratiator's dilemma: The problem of what can occur if the ingratiator is caught manipulating the target person, with the result being a loss rather than a gain of power.

Inner-directeds: A category within the VALS psychographic inventory that describes people who seek intense involvement in whatever they do.

Inoculation: Presentation and then refutation of arguments that the "other side" may present in order to immunize the audience against the message of the "other side."

Inputs: According to equity theory, inputs are the contributions to an exchange made by each of the parties to the exchange.

Inseparability: A factor that differentiates services from products, based upon the concept that production and consumption cannot be separated.

Instrumental responses: The behaviors (operants) of an organism that can be operantly conditioned.

Instrumental role: Within a group the instrumental role is taken by the person who deals with the problem of getting the group to achieve certain goals and complete certain tasks.

Instrumental values: Behaviors and actions required to achieve various terminal states.

Intangibility: The idea that services may be difficult to feel, touch and taste.

Integrateds: A category within the VALS psychographic inventory that describes consumers who are mature and balanced and who have managed to "put together" the best characteristics of the inner and outer personalities.

Intention: The determination of a consumer to engage in some act, such as purchasing a product or service.

Internal attribution: An attribution that the cause for an action was internal to the person or thing in question rather than to some external factor.

Internal search: The first phase of the search process in which the consumer attempts to retrieve from long-term memory information on products or services that will help to solve a problem.

Intrinsic satisfaction: Satisfaction that results from one's own interest in doing something rather than from the external benefits of doing it.

Involuntary attention: An innate response that occurs when a consumer is exposed to something surprising, novel, threatening, or unexpected.

Involvement—medium match: The concept that products and services should be advertised on media that match the consumers' level of involvement with the product or service.

JND: A principle of perception that stands for "just noticeable difference."

Kosher: A strict method of food preparation identified with the Jewish subculture.

Latitudes of acceptance: The area surrounding a person's attitude about an issue. When messages fall within this area, they are assimilated so that they are viewed as consistent with the attitude of the person.

Law of contiguity: States that the things which are experienced together become associated.

Law of demand: States that there is an inverse relationship between the price of the product and the quantity of the product demanded.

Learning: A process in which experience leads to a relatively permanent change in behavior or potential for a change in behavior.

Learning mechanisms: Processes through which a person retains information from the environment.

Lexicographic heuristic: A type of choice model in which the consumer first ranks the attributes and then selects the brand rated highest on the highest-ranked attribute.

Libido: A term found in psychoanalytic theory that refers to sexual energy.

Lifespace: The totality of factors that impinge upon and may influence a consumer at any given point in time.

Lifestyle: "How one lives."

Lip-service liberal: A psychographic segment of men who are described as confused about current social changes. They are somewhat concerned about their masculinity, but speak of being sympathetic towards women; however, their actions sometimes are inconsistent with these sentiments.

Likert scale: A type of attitude scale that involves asking a consumer to indicate the amount of his or her agreement or disagreement with a statement.

Look age: The age represented by how old an elderly person looks.

Long-term memory: The type of memory that has unlimited capacity and permanently stores information.

Low-involvement decision making: A shortened decision process resulting from the consumer perceiving little importance in a purchase.

Low-involvement hierarchy: The hierarchy of effects that occurs in low-involvement decision making in which beliefs are formed first, followed by behavior, and finally by attitude formation.

Lower social class Americans: A description of social class that refers to the combination of the upper-lower and lower-lower social classes.

Lower-lower class: The lowest of the social classes, whose members are typically out of work (or have the "dirtiest jobs"); includes bums and common criminals.

Lower-upper class: The next-to-the-highest social class, composed of the newer social elite, drawn from current professional, corporate leadership.

Main effects: A concept taken from the analysis of variance that refers to the investigation of individual variables without considering their possible interactions with other variables.

Market power: A measure of the potential importance of a subculture based upon its size and income levels.

Market segmentation: The subdividing of a market into distinct subsets of customers, where any subset may conceivably be selected as a target market to be reached with a distinct marketing mix.

Market testing: Placing the product into limited distribution to consumers in order to identify any potential problems and to test the entire marketing mix.

Masculinity-femininity scale: A scale designed to assess the extent to which individuals possess characteristics associated with the masculine and feminine dimensions of personality.

Materialism: The importance a consumer attaches to worldly possessions, where at the highest levels possessions assume a central place in life and provide the greatest sources of satisfaction and dissatisfaction.

Mature consumer: A person aged sixty-five years or older. Mature consumers differ from younger people in information processing and consumption patterns.

Marketing concept: Marketing activities directed at satisfying needs and wants through human exchange processes.

Marketing environment: The totality of forces and institutions that are external and potentially relevant to the firm.

Marketing mix: The components of marketing that can be used to develop strategy, including product, price, promotion, and distribution.

Marketing opportunity analysis: The process of attempting to identify potential marketing opportunities within the business environment.

Media-message match: The process of attempting to match the type of media with the type of message in order to maximize advertising effectiveness.

Memory control processes: Methods of handling information that people use to get information into and out of memory.

Mere exposure: A psychological process in which positive feelings and evaluations towards a stimulus may be formed simply through repeated exposures to the stimulus.

Message complexity: The amount and difficulty of information that a message contains.

Message construction: The strategies a communicator may use regarding where and how much information should be placed in a message.

Message content: The general strategies of message development that a communicator may use to communicate an idea to an audience. Examples of types of message content include fear appeals, humor, and message complexity.

Method of loci: A technique to aid the memory of lists by creating a mental image of a house that has locations on which the items of the list may be placed. To recall the list, the person takes a mental stroll back through the house picking up the items.

Middle Americans: A description of a combination of the social classes including the middle class, lower-middle class, and working class.

Middle class: Average pay white-collar and blue-collar workers who live on "the better side of town" and try to "do the proper things."

Moderates: A female market segment that tends to be younger, have more education, and to be full-time workers.

Mood state: A temporary state characterized by positive or negative feelings.

Mortality rate: The number of people per 1,000 who die per year.

Motivation: An activated state within a person that leads to goal-directed behavior.

Motivation research: Research popular during the 1950s that used a psychoanalytic approach to identify the underlying reasons that consumers made purchases.

Multiattribute choice models: Those models identify how consumers combine their beliefs about product attributes to form attitudes and make choices among various brand alternatives.

Multistep flow model: A model of personal influence which states that information is transmitted from the mass media to three distinct sets of people—gatekeepers, opinion leaders, and followers.

National Highway Traffic Safety Administration: Federal agency that regulates the safety performance of new and used motor vehicles and their equipment, investigates motor vehicle safety defects, and establishes required average fuel economy standards for new motor vehicles.

Nationality: A group's national heritage.

Need driven: A psychographic category identified in the VALS inventory that is characterized by persons striving simply to meet basic food and housing needs.

Need for affiliation: A basic social need identified by McClelland which is similar in nature to Maslow's belongingness need.

Need for power: A basic social need identified by McClelland that refers to the need of people to gain and exercise control over others.

Need recognition: Occurs when a discrepancy develops between an actual and a desired state of being.

Needs: Result from a discrepancy between an actual and a desired state of being.

Negativity bias: The tendency of consumers to give more weight to negative information than positive information when they make decisions to buy a product or service.

Negligent consumer behavior: The actions and inactions of consumers that negatively affect their own long-term quality of life and/or that of society. Examples include drunk driving, product misuse, and failing to use seat belts.

Networking: A strategy of entering into a group of individuals for the purpose of sharing information in order to move ahead in one's career.

New product idea generation: A process of generating new product ideas, as well as identifying benefits, consumer wants, and the product attributes that offer such benefits.

Nine North American "mini-nations": The assertion that North America can be divided into nine culturally distinct nations.

Noncompensatory models: Models of choice that emphasize that high ratings on some attributes will not compensate for low ratings on other attributes.

Norm of reciprocity: A societal norm stating that if a person does something for you, you should do something in return for that person.

Normative influence: Occurs when norms act to influence behavior.

Norms: Rules of behavior.

Nuclear family: Consists of a husband, wife, and offspring.

Object-attribute belief: A belief that a product has certain attributes.

Objects: The products, people, companies, and things about which people hold beliefs and attitudes.

Observational learning: A process in which people learn by observing the actions of others.

Occupational demographics: The study of the jobs held by people and the past and future changes in these jobs.

Old-fashioned men: A psychographic segment of males consisting of men who are unaware of social change.

One- versus two-sided message: Messages in which both sides of an issue are mentioned.

Operant conditioning: A process in which the frequency of the occurrence of a bit of behavior is modified by the consequences of the behavior.

Operants: The naturally occurring actions of an organism in the environment.

Opinion leader: Those people who influence the purchase decisions and opinions of others.

Opponent-process theory: The physiological process in which a person receives a stimulus that elicits an immediate positive or negative reaction. The immediate positive or negative emotional reaction is followed by a second emotional reaction that is opposite in valence to the feeling initially experienced.

Opportunity cost: The concept that when a person buys a product or engages in one task, he or she simultaneously foregoes buying another product or engaging in another task.

Optimum stimulation level: A person's preferred amount of physiological activation or arousal.

Orientation reflex: The physiological response of a person to a novel or unexpected stimulus which involves an increase in arousal and the orientation of the person to the stimulus.

Outcome: The results of an exchange, which a person assesses in relation to the inputs to determine if the exchange was equitable.

Outer directeds: A psychographic group identified by the VALS inventory that tends to focus on what people think of them and gears their lives to the "visible, tangible, and materialistic."

Ovarian symbol: Symbol for the female in psychoanalytic theory.

Overprivileged: Individuals with high incomes within a particular social class.

Overt consumer behaviors: These include various consumer actions, such as: buying a product or service, providing word-of-mouth information about a product or service to another person, disposing of a product, and collecting information for a purchase.

Pacific Rim: The countries that are situated on the Pacific Ocean.

Paired associate learning: The learning of pairs of words or concepts by attempting to associate them with each other.

Perceived freedom: A motivational need experienced by people to maintain their behavioral freedom.

Perceived risk: A consumer's perception of the overall favorability of a course of action based upon an assessment of the possible outcomes and on the likelihood that those outcomes will occur.

Perception: The ways in which people organize and interpret information received so that it has meaning.

Perceptual contrast: The perceptual phenomenon in which a stimulus acts as an anchor and causes other stimuli to be viewed as more extreme than they really are.

Perceptual maps: Graphs that show how consumers position various brands relative to each by way of axes that are formed by product attributes.

Perceptual organization: The means through which people organize and make sense out of the disjointed stimuli that they receive through their senses.

Peripheral cues: Information that is not related to the "substance" of messages and that tends to be used by consumers in low-involvement circumstances. Peripheral cues include the use of such information as the likability or physical attractiveness of a source as a means to make inferences.

Peripheral route to persuasion: Persuasion that occurs under low involvement circumstances. It is marked by a lack of cognitive responses and of diligent consideration of the pros and cons of an issue.

Perishability: A characteristic of services referring to the idea that they cannot be saved and must be consumed as they are performed.

Personal influence: Refers to the idea that one individual may intentionally or unintentionally influence another in his or her beliefs and attitudes about or actions toward something.

Person-by-situation-by-product interaction: The concept that the characteristics of the person may interact with the different situations and different products to form unique marketing opportunities.

Personality: The distinctive patterns of behavior, including thoughts and emotions, that characterize each individual's adaptation to the situations of his or her life.

Persuasion: A process in which a communication is delivered in order to change beliefs and/or attitudes in a desired manner.

Phallic symbol: A symbolic representation of masculinity according to psychoanalytic theory.

Phased strategy: A strategy of combining various decision heuristics in order to make a product or service choice (e.g., using a conjunctive model followed by a lexicographic model).

Psychological reactance: The motivational state resulting from a threat to a person's behavioral freedom.

Physical surroundings: The concrete physical and spatial aspects of the environment encompassing a consumer activity.

Physiological states: Refers to temporary personal feelings, such as tiredness or drunkenness, which may influence buying behavior. Physiological states are a subcategory of antecedent states—one of the types of situational factors that can influence consumers.

Pipe dreams: Wishful thinking or hopes concerning something that is going to happen.

Pleasure principle: A psychoanalytic concept upon which the id operates.

Positive reinforcer: A stimulus whose presence as a consequence of a behavior increases the probability of the behavior recurring.

POSSLQs: The federal government acronym for unmarried couples who cohabit.

Postpurchase attitudes: Attitudes of satisfaction/dissatisfaction towards a product developed by a consumer after he or she buys and uses a product.

Postpurchase evaluations: The evaluations of a product after it is purchased and used.

Postpurchase satisfaction/dissatisfaction: Emotional feelings of satisfaction or dissatisfaction with the performance of the product.

Power sources: Factors that can increase the personal power of a person in a relationship, such as economic resources, cultural and subcultural values, and the degree of dependence in a relationship.

Predisciplinary phase: The earliest phase in the history of consumer behavior, in which the first individuals to make the consumer a focus of study were economists attempting to explain factors influencing the demand for products.

Present social class fallacy: The assumption that a family's current class is governing their lifestyle and buying behavior.

Price elasticity: Refers to the extent that changes in price influence consumer buying. A price inelastic product would reveal little change in purchase patterns as a result of changes in price.

Price quality relationship: The concept that consumers infer higher quality with higher prices and vice versa.

Primacy versus recency effect: The relative impact of information placed either at the beginning or the end of the message. Primacy refers to earlier information having greater impact. Recency refers to the most recent information having the greater impact.

Primary group: A group of which a person is a member and with whom that person interacts on a face-to-face basis.

Priming: Occurs when a small amount of exposure to a stimulus leads to an increased drive to be in the presence of the stimulus.

Primitive consumer behavior: Purchases and activities that exhibit personal spirituality, ancestral traditions, and communal methods of resource distribution.

Private acceptance: Occurs when a person actually changes his or her beliefs in the direction of the group.

Proactive interference: The type of forgetting that occurs when earlier information that has been received interferes with the recall of information received later.

Product acquisition: The process of searching, evaluating, and choosing among alternative brands.

Product-attribute association: The relationship between the brands held in a consumer's memory and the qualities or attributes of the brands.

Product development: The process in which prototypes are developed, tested, named, and packaged.

Product differentiation: The process of developing the marketing mix so that consumers can distinguish one brand from other brands.

Product disposition: What consumers do with a product after they have completed their use of it.

Product innovators: The small set of consumers who are the first to buy new products.

Product positioning: The use of the marketing mix in order to cause consumers to perceive a product in a certain way relative to other brands. A brand's position is usually described in terms of its characteristics in relation to the characteristics of other brands.

Product-specific inventories: Situational inventories that are developed to be product specific.

Product symbolism: The use of products as symbols—frequently done in order to project one's self-concept.

Psychoanalytic approach: An approach to personality based upon the work of Sigmund Freud and his followers.

Psychographics: A general approach to measuring lifestyles that frequently makes use of questions assessing activities, interests, and opinions.

Psychophysical judgment: A judgment by a person about the physical properties of a stimulus, such as its weight.

Public policy: The investigation of the laws and regulations that impact upon consumers.

Punisher: Any stimulus whose presence after a behavior decreases the likelihood of the behavior recurring.

Purchase roles: Includes the various roles in the buying and using of products by family members or industrial buying groups.

Purchase situation: Relatively temporary environmental and personal factors that are present during the actual purchase of a product or service.

Race: The biological heritage of a person or group. Three basic races have been identified—Mongoloid, Negroid, and Caucasoid.

Rating scale: General scales in which the consumer is asked to rate his or her favorability, attitude, or other reaction towards something.

Reactance: A motivational state that results when a person believes his or her behavioral freedom to be threatened.

Reality principle: In psychoanalytic theory the principle that controls the functioning of the ego.

Recognition versus recall task: Two different means of assessing memory. A recognition task involves the person in identifying whether or not something has been seen previously. A recall task requires the person to recall information from long-term memory.

Reference group: A group whose values, norms, attitudes, or beliefs are used as a guide for behavior by an individual.

Reflected appraisal: A process in which a person evaluates his or her attitudes and behaviors by assessing how other people react in social interactions.

Regional birthrate differences: Varying birthrate levels associated with regional subcultural differences.

Rehearsal: The process in which an individual may maintain information in short-term memory and/or transfer information to long-term memory by silent verbal repetition of the information.

Reinforcement: Any stimulus that occurs after a behavior and changes the likelihood that the behavior occur again.

Relative income hypothesis: The concept that within a social class differences in income levels may exist leading to underprivileged and overprivileged groups that show differential spending patterns.

Repeat purchase behavior: Purchase behavior in which the consumer is merely buying a product repeatedly without actually having brand loyalty towards it.

Repositioning: The process of changing consumer perceptions of the nature of a brand in relation to other brands.

Response generation: The concept that the recall of a memory results from the person actively constructing a response rather than simply pulling from a memory an accurate representation of the stored information.

Respondent conditioning: The process of classically conditioning an organism.

Retrieval: The process in which the individual searches through long-term memory in order to identify within it the information to be recalled.

Retroactive interference: The concept that recently learned material interferes with the recollection of older material in memory.

Role conflict: The idea that individuals may simultaneously occupy two roles with conflicting demands, such as being both a mother and an executive.

Role-related product cluster: The set of products necessary for the playing of a particular role.

Roles: The specific behaviors expected of a person in a position.

Rumors: Information or stories in general circulation without certainty about facts.

Sales promotion: Various promotional tools with short-term managerial goals. Examples include contests, premiums, and coupons.

Satisficing: The concept that consumers will frequently attempt to make only satisfactory decisions rather than perfect decisions because of limitations in time, information-processing ability, or appropriate facts.

Schedule of reinforcement: The frequency and timing of reinforcers form a schedule of reinforcement that can dramatically influence the pattern of operant responses.

Schema: The total package of associations that are brought to mind when a memory node is activated.

Secondary reinforcer: A previously neutral stimulus that acquires reinforcing properties through its association with a primary reinforcer.

Segmentation: The subdivision of the marketplace into relatively homogeneous subsets of consumers who can be reached with a distinct marketing mix.

Selective attention: The concept that consumers will select and pay attention to some stimuli and not others.

Selective exposure: The concept that consumers will select and expose themselves to some stimuli and not others.

Self-concept: The totality of the individual's thoughts, perceptions, and feelings having reference to himself or herself as an object.

Self-perception: The concept that an individual may observe his own actions in order to infer his attitudes and beliefs.

Semantic concepts: The meanings attached to words, events, objects and symbols.

Semantic differential: A type of measurement scale in which subjects are asked to describe something by rating it on various scales anchored by opposite-meaning adjectives or statements.

Sequential segmentation: A process of segmenting the market in which lifestyle segments are first identified and then analyzed for personality differences.

Serial learning effect: Items in the beginning of a list and items at the end of the list are mostly readily learned, whereas items in the middle of the list are learned much less rapidly.

Sensations: The immediate impressions left by firing of nerve fibers in response to the physical stimulation of the senses.

Sensory memory: The highly brief memories resulting from the firing of nerve fibers in a person's brain.

Sentiment connection: A term used in balance theory to denote an affective connection between two cognitive elements.

Shaping: A process through which a new operant behavior is created by reinforcing successive approximations of the desired behavior.

Short-term memory: Describes the process in which a person temporarily stores information while it is being processed. Short-term memory is noted for its limited capacity.

Sign tracking: The concept that organisms have a tendency to orient themselves towards and attend to unconditioned stimuli.

Situational inventories: Inventories of either a general or a product-specific nature designed to describe the characteristics of consumer situations.

Social class: The relatively permanent and homogeneous strata in a society that tend to differ in their status, occupations, education, possessions, and values.

Social comparison: The process through which people evaluate the "correctness" of their opinions, the extent of their abilities, and the appropriateness of their possessions.

Social facilitation: The concept that when performing a task in front of other people a person will become aroused. The arousal will tend to enhance performance on easy tasks and hinder performance on difficult tasks.

Social class hierarchy: The description of the social classes in terms of a hierarchy of lower classes to higher classes.

Social judgment theory: A psychological theory that describes how an individual reacts to attitudinal statements depending upon the relationship of the statement to the person's own attitudes.

Social surroundings: The effects of other people on a consumer in a consumption situation.

Social threats: External pressure by other people to induce a consumer to do something.

Social traps and fences: The psychological phenomenon based upon the finding that individuals will respond to short-term reinforcers which can lead to long-term negative outcomes for a group.

Socialization agents: Individuals directly involved with a consumer who have influence because of their frequency of contact with the consumer, importance to the consumer, or control over rewards and punishments given to the consumer.

Source credibility: A construct used to describe sources of information composed of the dimensions of expertise and trustworthiness.

Source derogation: A type of cognitive response that involves negative thoughts about a source of information.

Source expertise: The extent of knowledge that the source is perceived to have about the subject on which he or she is speaking.

Source likability: The degree to which a source elicits positive or negative feelings among consumers.

Source trustworthiness: The extent to which the source is perceived to provide information in an unbiased, honest manner.

Specific positioning: A strategy designed to create strong linkages in consumers' minds among the product, certain key attributes, and benefits.

Spontaneous brand switching: The consumer tendency of periodically buying a new brand, even when nothing indicates that consumers are unhappy with the brand previously used.

Standard learning hierarchy: A high-involvement hierarchy of effects in which beliefs occur first, followed by the development of feelings or affect, followed by the occurrence of a behavior.

Standardization of marketing plan: The proposal that marketing plans can be standardized in international marketing.

State anxiety: A temporary or transitory emotional state resulting from a specific situation.

Status crystallization: The consistency with which an individual displays a single social class. A person with low status crystallization would be placed in different social classes based on different measures.

Stimulus discrimination: Occurs when an organism behaves differently when in the presence of one stimulus versus another stimulus.

Stimulus generalization: Occurs when an organism's behavior in the presence of one stimulus generalizes so that it appears in the presence of another similar stimulus.

Store layout: The physical organization of a store which creates specific traffic patterns, assists in the presentation of merchandise, and helps to create a particular atmosphere.

Subculture: A subdivision of national culture, based around some unifying characteristics such as social status or religion, whose members share similar patterns of behavior distinct from those of the national culture.

Subliminal stimulation: The concept that stimuli presented below the level of conscious awareness may influence behavior and feelings.

Substitution effect: The economic principle that when the price of a product falls, the product may be substituted for similar goods that are relatively more costly.

Superego: Discussed within psychoanalytic theory, the superego is the conscience, or "voice within" a person, which echos the morals and values of parents and society.

Support argument: A type of cognitive response in which the person develops thoughts supportive of a persuasive communication.

Syncratic decision: Important decisions in which the husband and wife participate jointly.

Target market: A consumer segment that a company focuses on reaching with its marketing mix.

Task definition: The occasion that spurs a purchase, such as a gift-giving occasion, a party, or even a type of meal.

Terminal values: Desired end states—how people would like to experience their lives.

Theory: A set of interrelated statements defining the causal relationships among a group of ideas.

Time as a consumer situation: The concept that the amount of time available forms a situational context which acts to influence the acquisition, consumption, and disposition of products and services.

Time compression: Through electronic means radio and television commercials may be compressed so that they last a shorter length of time.

Tolerance for ambiguity: A personality construct that assesses how a person reacts to situations that have varying degrees of ambiguity or inconsistency.

Total market potential: The total amount of consumer dollars estimated to be available for expenditure on a particular product or service.

Traditionalists: A female market segment that tends to be older, less educated, and less frequently working than other female market segments.

Trait: Any characteristic on which one person may differ from another in a relatively permanent and consistent way.

Trait anxiety: The predisposition of a consumer to react with more or less anxiety to various situations.

Trickle-down theory: A model of mass communications which holds that information moves from upper classes to the lower classes.

Two-factor theory: A theory that may explain advertising wear-out by proposing that message repetition results in two consumer responses: in one instance repetition causes an increase in learning; in the other it causes an increase in boredom.

Two-step flow model: A model of mass communications which holds that mass communications first influence opinion leaders, who in turn influence followers.

Types of risk: Various risk factors that may influence consumers including financial risk, performance risk, physical risk, psychological risk, social risk, time risk, and opportunity-loss risk.

Unawareness set: The group of brands which are unknown to a consumer.

Unconditioned response: The response elicited by an unconditioned stimulus.

Unconditioned stimulus: Any stimulus capable of eliciting autonomically an unconditioned response.

Unique selling proportion: A quick, hard-hitting phrase that captures a major feature of a product or service.

Unit relation: Defined in balance theory, a unit relation occurs when an observer perceives that two cognitive elements are somehow connected to each other.

Upper Americans: A description of a group of social classes including the upper-upper, lower-upper, and upper-middle class.

Upper-lower class: A social class whose members are employed rather than being on welfare, have a living standard just above poverty level, and tend to be unskilled workers.

Upper-middle class: A social class described as composed of college graduate managers, intellectual elite, and professionals.

Urban legends: A type of folklore that describes fictitious occurrences in urban life.

Use situation: A type of situation based upon the task definition. The situation in which a product or service is expected to be used.

VALS: A psychographic approach in which consumers are divided into four broad groups of individuals—the need-driven group, the inner-directeds, the outer-directeds, and the integrateds.

Value-expressive influence: The concept that the values and attitudes of a reference group will influence a person who wishes to be part of and be liked by the group.

Vicarious learning: A type of learning that occurs when a person observes the reinforcements received by others as being contingent on their actions.

Vivid versus abstract information: A well-established finding in psychology which states that messages using vivid, concrete words tend to have greater impact on receivers than messages containing more abstract information.

Von Restorff effect: The concept that a unique item placed in a series of homogeneous items will tend to be recalled more easily.

Voluntary attention: A process in which the consumer actively searches out information in order to achieve some type of goal.

Working class: Average pay blue-collar workers who tend to have monotonous jobs, and live close to parents and relatives.

Zeigarnik effect: The tendency of people to continue cognitively processing information about a task while it is going on or after it is interrupted.

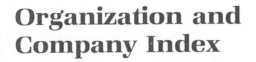

Organization and Company Index

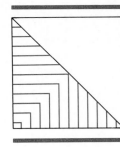

Name Index

Aaker, D. A., 600*n*
Abelson, R., 273*n*, 302*n*
Abrams, B., 71*h*, 236*h*, 296*h*
Ackof, R., 128*n*
Adams, J. S., 301*n*
Adler, R. P., 601*n*
Ajzen, I., 233*n*
Albaum, G. S., 602*n*
Alessio, J. C., 301*n*
Allen, C. T., 195*n*, 456*n*
Allen, H., 485*n*
Allison, N. K., 127*n*, 601*n*
Allport, G. W., 397*n*
Allvine, F. C., 128*n*, 362*n*
Alput, L., 114*t*
Alreck, P., 321*t*, 334*n*
Alsop, R., 2*h*, 60*h*, 89*n*, 363*n*, 569*h*
Alwitt, L., 335*n*
Amason, R. B., 456*n*
Anderson, J., 333*n*
Anderson, W. T., 128*n*
Andreason, A., 302*n*
Antil, J. H., 33*t*, 58*n*, 234*n*
Apple, W., 335*n*
Arenson, S. J., 302*n*
Aristotle, 348
Armstrong, G. M., 601*n*
Arndt, J., 362*n*, 408*t*, 429*n*
Arnold, D. O., 455*n*
Arnould, E., 13*h*
Aronson, E., 233*n*, 302*n*
Arpan, J., 516*h*, 540*n*
Asch, S. E., 334*n*, 373, 397*n*
Assael, H., 233*n*, 362*n*, 363*n*, 513*n*

Assmus, G., 274*n*
Aston, D., 486*n*
Astor, D., 463*t*
Atkin, C. K., 430*n*
Atkinson, J. W., 89*n*, 334*n*, 539*n*
Atkinson, R., 89*n*, 127*n*, 195*n*
Atkinson, R. C., 89*n*, 127*n*, 160*n*, 195*n*

Bacot, E., 540*n*
Bagozzi, R., 206*h*, 273*n*, 486*n*, 539*n*
Bahn, K. D., 128*n*, 514*n*
Baker, M., 363*n*
Bandura, A., 195*n*
Banks, S., 334*n*
Barak, B., 456*n*
Bardwick, J., 456*n*
Barna, G., 485*n*
Barry, T., 485*n*
Bartels, R., 530*t*
Bartos, R., 456*n*
Bass, F. M., 234*n*, 397*n*
Bauer, R., 90*n*, 485*n*
Baumann, D., 363*n*
Bearden, W. O., 302*n*, 329*t*, 334*n*, 335*n*, 456*n*
Becer, B., 539*n*
Beckwith, N., 447*t*, 448*t*, 456*n*
Becman, J., 486*n*
Beeghley, L., 513*n*
Belch, G., 206*h*, 274*n*
Belk, R. W., 128*n*, 333*n*, 334*n*, 335*n*, 362*n*, 514*n*, 583, 602*n*, 603*n*, 642*n*, 643*n*
Bell, M. L., 514*n*
Bellinger, D., 334*n*, 486*n*

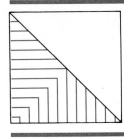

Subject Index